A Thousand Judgements
Festschrift for Maria Macuch

A Thousand Judgements

Festschrift for Maria Macuch

Edited by
Almut Hintze, Desmond Durkin-Meisterernst
and Claudius Naumann

2019

Harrassowitz Verlag · Wiesbaden

Published with the financial support of the Corpus Inscriptionum Iranicarum, the Societas Iranologica Europaea and the Ancient India and Iran Trust, Cambridge. Moreover, results incorporated in this standard have received funding from the European Research Council (ERC) under the European Union's Horizon 2020 research and innovation programme (The Multimedia Yasna, grant agreement No 694612).

Bibliografische Information der Deutschen Nationalbibliothek
Die Deutsche Nationalbibliothek verzeichnet diese Publikation in der Deutschen Nationalbibliografie; detaillierte bibliografische Daten sind im Internet über http://dnb.dnb.de abrufbar.

Bibliographic information published by the Deutsche Nationalbibliothek
The Deutsche Nationalbibliothek lists this publication in the Deutsche Nationalbibliografie; detailed bibliographic data are available in the internet at http://dnb.dnb.de.

For further information about our publishing program consult our website http://www.harrassowitz-verlag.de

Printed on permanent/durable paper.
Satz und Layout: Claudius Naumann
Printing and binding: Hubert & Co., Göttingen
Printed in Germany

ISBN 978-3-447-11094-5

Contents

Preface

This volume in honour of MARIA MACUCH brings together twenty-six articles by friends and colleagues to celebrate the academic work of the foremost living expert of Sasanian law. While the title *A Thousand Judgements* is obviously inspired by MARIA MACUCH's seminal edition of the text of the same name, it also alludes to the familiar situation in which scholars in the humanities find themselves all too often, namely that they have to make reasoned judgements on the basis of limited evidence. The subjects covered here include Iranian linguistics and philology, Judeo-Persian, Zoroastrian law and religion, Manichaeism, and the Babylonian Talmud.

It is a cause of great sadness that a contributor to this book, YAKOOV ELMAN, did not live to see the publication of this volume: he died on 30 July 2018 after a long illness and will be sorely missed. YAKOOV ELMAN was a great bridge-builder between Babylonian Rabbinic and Zoroastrian cultures. Always open for new perspectives, he strove to understand the Babylonian Talmud in its historical setting of Iranian Zoroastrian civilisation. He and MARIA MACUCH met for the first time in 2003 at the Irano-Judaica conference in Piliscsaba, Hungary, and a friendship characterized by mutual esteem grew between the two scholars over the years.

The publication of this volume was supported with generous subsidies by the *Societas Iranologica Europaea*, as whose President MARIA MACUCH served from 2003 to 2007, by the *Corpus Inscriptionum Iranicarum*, of which she has been a member since 2007, by the *Ancient India and Iran Trust*, Cambridge, which elected her an Honorary Fellow in 2013, and by the *European Research Council*. The editors express their profound thanks to these four organisations. Special thanks are due to the publisher, Harrassowitz, particularly to Frau BARBARA KRAUSS, for the competent production of this book.

London and Berlin, July 2018 — The Editors

Publications by Maria Macuch

Books

1) *Das sasanidische Rechtsbuch Mātakdān i Hazār Dātistān (Teil II).* Wiesbaden 1981 (AKM XLV, 1). xii, 268 pp.
2) (Ed. with C. MÜLLER-KESSLER and B. FRAGNER) *Studia Semitica necnon Iranica: Rudolpho Macuch septuagenario ab amicis et discipulis dedicata.* Wiesbaden 1989. xliv, 418 pp.
3) *Rechtskasuistik und Gerichtspraxis zu Beginn des siebenten Jahrhunderts in Iran: Die Rechtssammlung des Farroḫmard i Wahrāmān.* Wiesbaden 1993 (Iranica 1). xiv, 807 pp.
4) (Ed. with M. MAGGI and W. SUNDERMANN) *Iranian Languages and Texts from Iran and Turan: Ronald E. Emmerick Memorial Volume.* Wiesbaden 2007 (Iranica 13). xxvii, 490 pp.
5) (Ed. with R. E. EMMERICK) *Pre-Islamic Iranian Literature. Companion Volume I to A History of Persian Literature.* London 2009 (A History of Persian Literature XVII). xxii, 526 pp.
6) (Ed. with D. WEBER and D. DURKIN-MEISTERERNST) *Ancient and Middle Iranian Studies. Proceedings of the 6th European Conference of Iranian Studies, held in Vienna, 18–22 September 2007.* Wiesbaden 2010 (Iranica 19). X, 278 pp.
7) (Ed. with I. COLDITZ and B. JOKISCH) *Transferprozesse in spätantiken Rechtssystemen. Rezeption, Transformation und Rekontextualisierung von Rechtsbegriffen.* Wiesbaden 2017 (Episteme in Bewegung 10). vi, 122 pp.

Articles

8) "Die Zeitehe im sasanidischen Recht – ein Vorläufer der šī^{c}itischen *mut*^{c}*a* Ehe in Iran?" In: *AMI* 18 (1985), pp. 187–203.
9) "Sasanidische Institutionen in frühislamischer Zeit (Zusammenfassung)." In: *Transition Periods in Iranian History: Actes du symposium de Fribourg-en-Brisgau (22–24 Mai 1985).* Leuven 1987 (StIr, Cahier 5), pp. 177–179.
10) "Die Erwähnung der Ordalzeremonie des Ādurbād i Māraspandān im Ardā Wīrāz Nāmag." In: *AMI* 20 (1987), pp. 319–322.
11) "Barda and Bardadārīh. ii. In the Sasanian Period." In: *EIr.* Vol. III, Fasc. 7. London 1988, pp. 763–766.
12) "Der *dastwar,* ‚auctor', im sasanidischen Zivilprozeß." In: *AMI* 21 (1988), pp. 181–192.

13) "Ein mittelpersischer *terminus technicus* im syrischen Rechtskodex des Īšōʿbōḫt und im sasanidischen Rechtsbuch." In: *Studia Semitica necnon Iranica Rudolpho Macuch septuagenario ab amicis et discipulis dedicata.* Wiesbaden 1989, pp. 149–160.
14) "Eine alte Bemessungsgrundlage für die ‚Tagesration' in den Pahlavi-Schriften." In: *Salaires, prix, poids et mesures.* Ed. by R. Gyselen. Paris 1990 (Res orientales 2), pp. 139–142.
15) "Charitable Foundations in the Sasanian Period." In: *EIr.* Vol. V, Fasc. 4. Costa Mesa, California 1991, pp. 380–382.
16) "Inzest im vorislamischen Iran." In: *AMI* 24 (1991), pp. 141–154.
17) "Die sasanidische Stiftung ‚für die Seele' – Vorbild für den islamischen *waqf*?" In: *Iranian and Indo-European Studies: Memorial Volume of Otakar Klíma.* Ed. by P. Vavroušek. Praha 1994, pp. 163–180.
18) "Herrschaftskonsolidierung und sasanidisches Familienrecht: zum Verhältnis von Kirche und Staat unter den Sasaniden." In: *Iran und Turfan: Beiträge Berliner Wissenschaftler, Werner Sundermann zum 60. Geburtstag gewidmet.* Ed. by Chr. Reck and P. Zieme. Wiesbaden 1995 (Iranica 2), pp. 149–167.
19) "Die Konstruktion der Wirklichkeit im sasanidischen Recht." In: *Proceedings of the Second European Conference of Iranian Studies held in Bamberg, 30th September to 4th October 1991, by the Societas Iranologica Europaea.* Ed. by B. G. Fragner [et al.]. Rom 1995 (Serie orientale Roma 73), pp. 415–424.
20) "The Use of Seals in Sasanian Jurisprudence." In: *Sceaux d'orient et leur emploi.* Textes réunis par R. Gyselen. Bures-sur-Yvette 1997 (Res orientales 10), pp. 79–87.
21) "Dämonen. IV. Iran in vorislamischer Zeit." In: *Der Neue Pauly: Enzyklopädie der Antike.* Bd. III. Stuttgart 1997, pp. 260–261.
22) "Zur Bildersprache der persischen mystischen Dichtung." In: *Religiöse Sprache und ihre Bilder: Von der Bibel bis zur modernen Lyrik.* Ed. by A. Hölscher and R. Kampling. Berlin 1998 (Schriften der Diözesanakademie Berlin 14), pp. 175–199.
23) "Familie. III. Iran, Sāsānidenperiode." In: *Der Neue Pauly: Enzyklopädie der Antike.* Bd. IV. Stuttgart 1998, pp. 407–408.
24) "Frau. E. Iran, Sāsānidenperiode." In: *Der Neue Pauly: Enzyklopädie der Antike.* Bd. IV. Stuttgart 1998, pp. 633–634.
25) "Iranian Legal Terminology in the Babylonian Talmud in the Light of Sasanian Jurisprudence." In: *Irano-Judaica IV: Studies Relating to Jewish Contacts with Persian Culture Throughout the Ages.* Ed. by Sh. Shaked and A. Netzer. Jerusalem 1999, pp. 91–101.
26) "Gottes-Suche und Gottes-Erfahrung in der persischen Sufi-Dichtung." In: *Gottes-Krise und Gott-Trunkenheit: Was die Mystik der Weltreligionen der Gegenwart zu sagen hat.* Ed. by M. Delgado and A. P. Kustermann. Würzburg 2000, pp. 134–158.
27) "A Zoroastrian Legal Term in the Dēnkard: *pahikār-rad.*" In: *Iran: Questions et connaissances.* Vol. I: *La période ancienne.* Ed. by Ph. Huyse. Paris 2002 (StIr, Cahier 25), pp. 77–90.
28) "The Talmudic Expression 'Servant of the Fire' in the Light of Pahlavi Legal Sources." In: *JSAI* 26 (2002) [= *Volume in Honour of Shaul Shaked*], pp. 109–129.
29) "On the Treatment of Animals in Zoroastrian Law." In: *Iranica Selecta: Studies in honour of Professor Wojciech Skalmowski on the occasion of his seventieth*

birthday. Ed. by A. van Tongerloo. Turnhout 2003 (Silk Road Studies 8), pp. 167–190.

30) "Zoroastrian Principles and the Structure of Kinship in Sasanian Iran." In: *Religious Themes and Texts of pre-Islamic Iran and Central Asia: Studies in honour of Professor Gherardo Gnoli on the occasion of his 65th birthday on 6 December 2002*. Ed. by C. G. Cereti, M. Maggi and E. Provasi. Wiesbaden 2003 (Beiträge zur Iranistik 24), pp. 231–246.

31) "Pious Foundations in Byzantine and Sasanian Law." In: *La Persia e Bisanzio. Convegno internazionale, Roma, 14–18 ottobre 2002*. Ed. by Gh. Gnoli. Roma 2004 (Atti dei convegni Lincei 201), pp. 181–196.

32) "On Middle Persian Legal Terminology." In: *Middle Iranian Lexicography: Proceedings of the Conference held in Rome, 9–11 April 2001*. Ed. by C. G. Cereti and M. Maggi. Roma (Orientalia Romana 8) 2005, pp. 375–386.

33) "Inheritance. i. Sasanian Period." In: *EIr.* Vol. XIII. New York 2005, pp. 125–131.

34) "Language and Law: Linguistic Pecularities in Sasanian Jurisprudence." In: *Languages of Iran: Past and Present. Iranian Studies in Memoriam David N. MacKenzie*. Ed. by D. Weber. Wiesbaden 2005 (Iranica 8), pp. 95–108.

35) "The Function of Temporary Marriage in the Context of Sasanian Family Law." In: *Proceedings of the Fifth Conference of the Societas Iranologica Europaea held in Ravenna, October 6–11, 2003*. Vol. I: *Ancient and Middle Iranian Studies*. Ed. by A. Panaino and A. Piras. Milano 2006, pp. 585–597.

36) "On the Legal Nasks of the Dēnkard." In: *Religious Texts in Iranian Languages: Symposium held in Copenhagen May 2002*. Ed. by F. Vahman and C. Pedersen. Copenhagen 2007, pp. 151–164.

37) "The Pahlavi Marriage Contract in the Light of Sasanian Family Law." In: *Iranian Languages and Texts from Iran and Turan. Ronald E. Emmerick Memorial Volume*. Ed. by M. Macuch, M. Maggi and W. Sundermann. Wiesbaden 2007 (Iranica 13), pp. 183–204.

38) "Sasaniden." In: *Handwörterbuch der antiken Sklaverei*. Ed. by H. Heinen [et al.]. Stuttgart 2008 (Forschungen zur antiken Sklaverei, Beiheft 5).

39) "Der ‚iranisierte' Islam: Zur Entstehung einer eigenwilligen Synthese." In: *Iran und iranisch geprägte Kulturen: Studien zum 65. Geburtstag von Bert G. Fragner*. Ed. by B. Hoffmann, R. Kauz and M. Ritter. Wiesbaden 2008 (Beiträge zur Iranistik 27), pp. 315–335.

40) "An Iranian Legal Term in the Babylonian Talmud and in Sasanian Jurisprudence: *dastwar*." In: *Irano-Judaica VI: Studies Relating to Jewish Contacts with Persian Culture Throughout the Ages*. Ed. by Sh. Shaked and A. Netzer. Jerusalem 2008, pp. 126–138.

41) "Zur juristischen Terminologie der Berliner Pahlavi-Dokumete." In: D. Weber: *Berliner Pahlavi-Dokumente. Zeugnisse spätsassanidischer Brief- und Rechtskultur aus frühislamischer Zeit*. Wiesbaden 2008 (Iranica 15), pp. 249–266.

42) "Pahlavi Literature." In: *The Literature of Pre-Islamic Iran. Companion Volume I to A History of Persian Literature*. Ed. by R. E. Emmerick and M. Macuch. London 2009 (History of Persian Literature XVII), pp. 116–190.

43) "Gelehrte Frauen: ein ungewöhnliches Motiv in der Pahlavi-Literatur." In: *Literarische Stoffe und ihre Gestaltung in mitteliranischer Zeit. Colloquium anlässlich*

des 70. Geburtstags von Werner Sundermann. Ed. by D. Durkin-Meisterernst, Chr. Reck and D. Weber. Wiesbaden 2009 (Beiträge zur Iranistik 31), pp. 135–151.

44) "Disseminating the Mazdayasnian Religion: An Edition of the Pahlavi Hērbedestān Chapter 5." In: *Exegisti monumenta. Festschrift in Honour of Nicholas Sims-Williams.* Ed. by W. Sundermann, A. Hintze and F. de Blois. Wiesbaden 2009 (Iranica 17), pp. 251–277.

45) "Die sasanidische fromme Stiftung und der islamische *waqf*: Eine Gegenüberstellung." In: *Islamische Stiftungen zwischen juristischer Norm und sozialer Praxis.* Ed. by A. Meier, J. Pahlitzsch and L. Reinfandt. Berlin 2009, pp. 19–38.

46) "Judicial and Legal System. iii. Sasanian Legal System." In: *EIr* XV. New York 2009, pp. 181–196.

47) "The Hērbedestān as a Legal Source: A Section on the Inheritance of a Convert to Zoroastrianism." In: *BAI* 19 (2009), pp. 91–102 [= *Iranian and Zoroastrian Studies in Honor of Prods Oktor Skjærvø*].

48) "Legal Constructions of Identity in the Sasanian Period." In: *Iranian Identity in the Course of History. Proceedings of the Conference Held in Rome, 21–24 September 2005.* Ed. by C.G. Cereti. Roma 2010 (Orientalia Romana 9), pp. 193–212.

49) "Allusions to Sasanian Law in the Babylonian Talmud." In: *The Talmud in its Iranian Context.* Ed. by C. Bakhos and M. Rahim Shayegan. Tübingen 2010, pp. 100–111.

50) "Incestuous Marriage in the Context of Sasanian Family Law." In: *Ancient and Middle Iranian Studies. Proceedings of the 6th European Conference of Iranian Studies, held in Vienna, 18–22 September 2007.* Ed. by M. Macuch, D. Weber and D. Durkin-Meisterernst. Wiesbaden 2010, pp. 133–148.

51) "Die vorislamischen Wurzeln des Schāhnāme von Ferdausi." In: *Heroische Zeiten. Tausend Jahre persisches Buch der Könige.* Ed. by J. Gonnella and Ch. Rauch, Berlin 2011, pp. 22–27.

52) "The *adwadād* Offence in Zoroastrian Law." In: *Shoshannat Yaakov. Jewish and Iranian Studies in Honor of Yaakov Elman.* Ed. by Sh. Secunda and St. Fine. Leiden/Boston 2012 (The Brill Reference Library of Judaism 35), pp. 247–269.

53) "The Pre-Islamic Roots of Firdausi's *Shahnama.*" In: *Heroic Times. A Thousand Years of the Persian Book of Kings.* Ed. by J. Gonnella and Ch. Rauch. Berlin 2012, pp. 22–27.

54) "Editing Pahlavi Legal Texts: Difficulties and Future Tasks." In: *The Transmission of the Avesta.* Ed. by A. Cantera. Wiesbaden 2012 (Iranica 20), pp. 519–540.

55) "Vorislamisches iranisches Recht." In: *Handbuch der Iranistik.* Ed. by L. Paul. Wiesbaden 2013, pp. 123–132.

56) "Iranische Literaturen in vorislamischer Zeit." In: *Handbuch der Iranistik.* Ed. by L. Paul. Wiesbaden 2013, pp. 281–311.

57) "Ardashir's Genealogy Revisited." In: *Iran Nameh. A Special Issue Honoring Jaleh Amouzgar.* Ed. by P. Pourshariati and M. Tavakoli. Vol. 29 (2014), pp. 80–94.

58) "Mādayān ī hazār dādestān, 'Book of a Thousand Judgements'. Pahlavi Law-Book from the Late Sasanian Period (first half of the seventh century)." In: *EIr* (Online publication: http://www.iranicaonline.org/articles/madayan-i-hazar-dadestan).

59) "Jewish Jurisdiction within the Framework of the Sasanian Legal System". In: *Encounters by the Rivers of Babylon: Scholarly Conversations between Jews, Iranians and Babylonians in Antiquity.* Ed. by U. Gabbay and Sh. Secunda. Tübingen 2014, pp. 147–160.

60) "The Case against Mār Abā, the Catholicos, in the Light of Sasanian Law." In: *ARAM. Zoroastrianism in the Levant and the Amorites.* Vol. 26.1&2. Oxford 2014, pp. 47–58.

61) "Law in Pre-modern Zoroastrianism." In: *The Wiley Blackwell Companion to Zoroastrianism.* Ed. by M. Stausberg and Y. Sohrab-Dinshaw Vevaina. Oxford 2015, pp. 289–298.

62) "Legal Implications of Mazdakite Teaching According to the Dēnkard." In: *Husraw Ier Reconstructions d'un Règne. Sources et Documents.* Ed. by Chr. Jullien. Paris 2015 (StIr. Cahier 53), pp. 155–174.

63) "Precision Orientated Legal Terminology in the Sasanian Law of Inheritance." In: *From Aṣl to Zā'id: Essays in Honour of Éva M. Jeremiás.* Ed. by Iv'an Szántó. Piliscsaba 2015, pp. 129–146.

64) "Substance and Fruit in the Sasanian Law of Property and the Babylonian Talmud." In: *The Archaeology and Material Culture of the Babylonian Talmud.* Ed. by M.J. Geller. Leiden/Boston 2015, pp. 245–259.

65) "Türken in der zoroastrischen Literatur." In: *Eine hundertblättrige Tulpe – Bir ṣadbarg lāla. Festgabe für Claus Schönig.* Ed. by I. Hauenschild, M. Kappler and B. Kellner-Heinkele. Berlin 2016, pp. 308–331.

66) "The Legal Context of the Tabarestan Court Records (Tab. 1–8,10)." In: *Words and Symbols: Sasanian Objects and the Tabarestān Archive.* Ed. by R. Gyselen. Bures-sur-Yvette 2016 (Res Orientales XXIV), pp. 145–169.

67) " 'This is the Law of the Persians'—An Allusion to the Sasanian Law of Surety in the Babylonian Talmud." In: *Iran-Nameh.* New Series. Vol. 1, No. 2, 2016 [= *Memorial Volume in Honour of Professor Amnon Netzer (1934–2008)*], pp. XVIII–XXVIII.

68) "A Legal Controversy from the Sasanian Period in a Late Pahlavi Rivāyat Text." In: *Studia Philologica Iranica. Gherardo Gnoli Memorial Volume.* Ed. by E. Morano, E. Provasi and A.V. Rossi. Roma 2017, pp. 257–272.

69) "A Case of Loan and Mortgage in a Late Pahlavi Text." In: *Zur Lichten Heimat. Studien zu Manichäismus, Iranistik und Zentralasienkunde im Gedenken an Werner Sundermann.* Ed. by a Team "Turfanforschung". Wiesbaden 2017 (Iranica 25), pp. 355–370.

70) "Descent and Inheritance in Zoroastrian and Shiite Law: a Preliminary Study." In: *Der Islam* 94 (2), 2017, pp. 322–335.

71) "Pahlavi Legal Documents from Tabarestān on Lease, Loan and Compensation: the Juristic Context (Tab. 13,14, 15, 17, 18, 23)." In: R. Gyselen (ed.): *Sasanian Coins, Middle-Persian Etymology and the Tabarestān Archive. Res Orientales XXVI.* Bures-sur-Yvette 2017, pp. 165–195.

72) "Einleitung." In: I. Colditz, B. Jokisch and M. Macuch (eds.): *Transferprozesse in spätantiken Rechssystemen. Rezeption, Transformation und Rekontextualisierung von Rechtsbegriffen.* Wiesbaden 2017 (Episteme in Bewegung 10), pp. 1–7.

In the press:

73) "A Pahlavi Legal Term in Jesuboxt's Corpus Iuris: *wehdādestān(īh).*" In: *Irano-Judaica VII: Studies Relating to Jewish Contacts with Persian Culture Throughout the Ages.*

74) "Mazdakite Heresy and Esotericism in the late Zoroastrian Tradition." In: *Knowledge to die for: Transmission of Prohibited and Esoteric Knowledge in Space and Time, Proceedings of the Topoi Excellence Cluster, FU Berlin, May 2–4, 2011.*

75) "Descent in Faridun's Line: An Epic Narrative in the Light of Zoroastrian Law." In: *Festschrift for Philip G. Kreyenbroek.* Ed. by Sh. Farridnejad.

Articles on the history of scholarship

76) "Rudolf Macuch." In: *Und das Leben ist siegreich! / And Life is Victorious. Mandäische und samaritanische Literatur / Mandean and Samaritan Literature. Im Gedenken an Rudolf Macuch / In Memory of Rudolf Macuch (1919–1993).* Ed. by R. Voigt. Wiesbaden 2008 (Mandäistische Forschungen 1), pp. 9–16.

77) "Geschichte der Iranistik an der Freien Universität Berlin." In: *Kleine Wissenschaftsgeschichte der FUB.* [im Druck]

78) "'Behalte den Flug in Erinnerung ...' – Leben und Werk von Rudolf Macuch." Conference in Liptovský Mikuláš (Slovakia), Sept. 19–20 2014.

79) "Rudolf Macuch." In: *Christlicher Orient im Porträt – Wissenschaftsgeschichte des Christlichen Orients."* II. Ed. by P. Bukovec. Hamburg 2014, pp. 1035–1054.

Reviews

80) D. Monchi-Zadeh: *Die Geschichte Zarers. Ausführlich kommentiert.* Uppsala 1981 (Studia Indoeuropaea Upsaliensia 4). In: *ZDMG* 133 (1983), pp. 454–455.

81) F. M. Kotwal/J. W. Boyd (eds.): *Ērbadistān ud Nīrangistān. Facsimile Edition of the Manuscript TD.* Cambridge/London 1980 (Harvard Iranian Series 3). In: *OLZ* 79 (1984), Nr. 6, pp. 581–583.

82) K. Mosig-Walburg: *Die frühen sasanidischen Könige als Vertreter und Förderer der zarathustrischen Religion. Eine Untersuchung der zeitgenössischen Quellen.* Frankfurt a. M. 1982 (Europäische Hochschulschriften, Reihe 3; Geschichte und ihre Hilfswissenschaften 166). In: *ZDMG* 135 (1985), pp. 134–135.

83) Ph. Gignoux: *Le livre d'Ardā Vīrāz. Translittération, transcription et traduction du texte pehlevi.* Paris 1984 (Recherche sur les Civilisations, Cahier 14). In: *ZDMG* 139 (1989), pp. 252–253.

84) E. Pataq Simon: *Narsai. Cinq homélies sur les paraboles évangéliques. Introduction et traduction.* Paris 1984. In: *ZDMG* 140 (1990), pp. 158–159.

85) S. Berengian: *Azeri and Persian Literary Works in Twentieth Century Iranian Azerbaijan.* Berlin 1988 (Islamkundliche Untersuchungen 124). In: *Der Islam* 69 (1992), pp. 352–353.

86) M. Boyce: *A Persian Stronghold of Zoroastrianism. Based on the Ratanbai Katrak lectures, 1975.* Oxford 1977 (Persian Studies Series 12) [repr. Lanham/New York/London 1989]. In: *Der Islam* 69 (1992), pp. 171–173.

87) A.V. Williams: *The Pahlavi Rivāyat Accompanying the Dādestān ī Dēnīg.* Part I: *Transliteration, Transcription and Glossary.* Part II: *Translation, Commentary and Pahlavi Text.* Kopenhagen 1990 (Historisk-filosofiske Meddelelser 60, 1–2). In: *ZDMG* 142 (1992), pp. 386–388.

88) D. Weber: *Ostraca, Papyri und Pergamente. Textband.* London 1992 (Corpus Inscriptionum Iranicarum, part III: *Pahlavi Inscriptions*, vol. IV: *Ostraca* and vol. V: *Papyri*). In: *OLZ* 89 (1994), Nr. 5/6, pp. 576–581; *ZDMG* 145 (1995), pp. 182–184.

89) K.M. JamaspAsa: *The Avesta Codex F 1 (Niyāyišns and Yašts). Facsimile Edition with an Introduction.* Wiesbaden 1991. In: *ZDMG* 145 (1995), p. 222.

90) F.M. Kotwal/Ph.G. Kreyenbroek: *The Hērbedestān and Nērangestān.* Vol. I: *Hērbedestān.* Paris 1992 (StIr, Cahier 10). In: *BSOAS* 58 (1995), pp. 372–375.

91) M. Kunke: *Nomadenstämme in Persien im 18. und 19. Jahrhundert.* Berlin 1991 (Islamkundliche Untersuchungen 151). In: *Der Islam* 73 (1996), pp. 26–28.

92) Sh. Shaked: *Dualism in Transformation. Varieties of Religion in Sasanian Iran.* London 1994 (Jordan Lectures 1991). In: *ZDMG* 146 (1996), pp. 653–656.

93) Ph. Gignoux/A. Tafazzoli: *Anthologie de Zādspram. Édition critique du texte Pehlevi traduit et commenté.* Paris 1993 (StIr, Cahier 13). In: *ZDMG* 149 (1999), pp. 425–430.

94) D. Yeroushalmi: *The Judeo-Persian Poet ʿEmrani and his "Book of Treasure".* Edited, Translated & Annotated Together with a Critical Study. Leiden 1995 (Etudes sur le judaisme médiéval 15). In: *ZDMG* 152 (2002), pp. 425–427.

95) C.G. Cereti: *The Zand ī Wahman Yasn. A Zoroastrian Apocalypse.* Rom 1995 (Serie orientale Roma 75). In: *ZDMG* 153 (2003), pp. 230–235.

96) D.M. Friedenberg: *Sasanian Jewry and its Culture. A Lexicon of Jewish and Related Seals.* Introduction by N. Golb. Urbana/Chicago 2009.

Editor of *Iranica*

Maria Macuch has been editor of the *Iranica* series (Harrassowitz Verlag, Wiesbaden) since 1993. The following volumes have been published so far:

97) Vol. 1, 1993: M. Macuch: *Rechtskasuistik und Gerichtspraxis zu Beginn des siebenten Jahrhunderts in Iran. Die Rechtssammlung des Farroḫmard i Wahrāmān.* XIV, 807 pp.

98) Vol. 2, 1995: *Iran und Turfan. Beiträge Berliner Wissenschaftler, Werner Sundermann zum 60. Geburtstag gewidmet.* Ed by Chr. Reck and P. Zieme. VIII, 296 pp.

99) Vol. 3, 1996: P. Sohn: *Die Medizin des Zādsparam. Anatomie, Physiologie und Psychologie in den Wizīdagīhā ī Zādsparam, einer zoroastrisch-mittelpersischen Anthologie aus dem frühislamischen Iran des neunten Jahrhunderts.* XVI, 250 pp.
100) Vol. 4, 1999: F. Schirazi-Mahmoudian: *Literarische Verwendung persischer Termini und Redewendungen im Werke Ṣādeq Hedāyats. Ein Kompendium.* XIX, 982 pp.
101) Vol. 5, 2000: I. Colditz: *Zur Sozialterminologie der iranischen Manichäer. Eine semantische Analyse im Vergleich zu den nichtmanichäischen iranischen Quellen.* XIII, 454 pp.
102) Vol. 6, 2003: *Persian Origins—Early Judaeo-Persian and the Emergence of New Persian. Collected Papers of the Symposium, Göttingen 1999.* Ed. by L. Paul. VIII, 283 pp.
103) Vol. 7, 2004: A. Cantera: *Studien zur Pahlavi-Übersetzung des Avesta.* X, 379 pp.
104) Vol. 8, 2005: *Languages of Iran: Past and Present. Iranian Studies in Memoriam David Neil MacKenzie.* Ed. by D. Weber. XXVII, 307 pp.
105) Vol. 9, 2005: Ph.G. Kreyenbroek/Kh.J. Rashow: *God and Sheikh Adi are Perfect. Sacred Poems and Religious Narratives from the Yezidi Tradition.* XVII, 435 pp.
106) Vol. 10, 2006: B. Reinhold: *Neue Entwicklungen in der Wakhi-Sprache von Gojal (Nordpakistan): Bildung, Migration und Mehrsprachigkeit.* x, 370 pp.
107) Vol. 11, 2006: I. Schneider: *The Petitioning Systems in Iran: State, Society and Power Relations in the Late 19th Century.* XII, 226 pp., 18 Tafeln.
108) Vol. 12, 2007: A. Hintze: *A Zoroastrian Liturgy: The Worship in Seven Chapters (Yasna 35–41).* XIV, 607 pp.
109) Vol. 13, 2007: *Iranian Languages and Texts from Iran and Turan: Ronald E. Emmerick Memorial Volume.* Ed. by M. Macuch, M. Maggi and W. Sundermann. XXVII, 490 pp.
110) Vol. 14, 2008: G. König: *Die Erzählung von Ṭahmuraṣ und Ǧamšid: Edition des neupersischen Textes in Pahlavi-Schrift (MU 29) nebst zweier Parallelfassungen.* VIII, 172 pp.
111) Vol. 15, 2008: D. Weber: *Berliner Pahlavi-Dokumente: Zeugnisse spätsassanidischer Brief- und Rechtskultur aus frühislamischer Zeit.* XXXII, 288 pp., 46 Farbtafeln.
112) Vol. 16, 2008: F.M. Kotwal/A. Hintze: *The Khorda Avesta and Yašt Codex E1. Facsimile Edition.* X, 607 pp.
113) Vol. 17, 2009: *Exegisti monumenta. Festschrift in Honour of Nicholas Sims-Williams.* Ed. by W. Sundermann, A. Hintze and F. De Blois. XXXVIII, 596 pp.
114) Vol. 18, 2010: G. König: *Geschlechtsmoral und Gleichgeschlechtlichkeit im Zoroastrismus.* XI, 517 pp.
115) Vol. 19, 2010: *Ancient and Middle Iranian Studies. Proceedings of the 6th European Conference of Iranian Studies, held in Vienna, 18–22 September 2007.* Ed. by M. Macuch, D. Weber and D. Desmond-Meistererernst. X, 278 pp.
116) Vol. 20, 2012: *The Transmission of the Avesta.* Ed. by A. Cantera. XVIII, 552 pp.
117) Vol. 21, 2015: Th. Jügel: *Die Entwicklung der Ergativkonstruktion im Alt- und Mitteliranischen. Eine korpusbasierte Untersuchung zu Kasus, Kongruenz und Satzbau.* XXXIV, 968 pp.

118) Vol. 22, 2016: D. Buyaner: *Penitential Sections of the* Xorde Avesta (patits). *Critical Edition with Commentary and Glossary.* X, 519 pp.

119) Vol. 23, 2016: M. Á. Andrés-Toledo: *The Zoroastrian Law to Expel the Demons: Wīdēwdād 10–15 Critical Edition, Translation and Glossary of the Avestan and Pahlavi Texts.* X, 394 pp.

120) Vol. 24, 2017: *Holy Wealth: Accounting for This World and The Next in Religious Belief and Practice. Festschrift for John R. Hinnells.* Ed. by A. Hintze and A. Williams. XXVIII, 294 pp.

121) Vol. 25, 2017: *Zur lichten Heimat. Studien zu Manichäismus, Iranistik und Zentralasienkunde im Gedenken an Werner Sundermann.* Ed. by a Team "Turfanforschung". XII, 754 pp.

122) Vol. 26, 2018: Götz König: *Studien zur Rationalitätsgeschichte im älteren Iran. Ein Beitrag zur Achsenzeitdiskussion.* VIII, 244 pp.

Conferences and papers delivered

123) "XXI. Deutscher Orientalistentag", Congress of the *Deutsche Morgenländische Gesellschaft,* March 24–29, 1980, Berlin. Paper: "Zur Ḫwasrāyūn/ēn-Ehe im sasanidischen Recht".

124) "Transition Periods in Iranian History", Symposium of the *Societas Iranologica Europaea,* May 22–24, 1985, Freiburg i. Br. Paper: "Sasanidische Institutionen in frühislamischer Zeit".

125) "Second European Conference of Iranian Studies", held by the *Societas Iranologica Europaea,* September 30–October 1, 1991, Bamberg. Paper: "Die Konstruktion der Wirklichkeit im sasanidischen Recht".

126) "Third Irano-Judaica International Conference", under the auspices of the *Ben-Zvi Institut,* July 3–6, 1994, Jerusalem. Paper: "Iranian Legal Terminology in the Babylonian Talmud in the Light of Sasanian Jurisprudence".

127) "Frauen und Transformationsprozesse in außereuropäischen Gesellschaften", Lecture Series of the *Freie Universität Berlin,* winter term 1996. Paper: "Fremd- und Selbstwahrnehmungen: zwei Reiseberichte englischer Frauen über Persien".

128) "Religiöse Sprache und ihre Bilder", Lecture Series of the *Freie Universität Berlin* and *Diözesanakademie Berlin,* summer term 1996. Paper: "Zur Bildersprache der persischen mystischen Dichtung".

129) "Islam ist nicht gleich Islam: Annäherungen an eine Weltkultur", Lecture Series of the *Freie Universität Berlin,* winter term 1997. Paper: "Iran und Islam: Aspekte einer eigenwilligen Synthese".

130) "‚Gott allein genügt' – die Gottes-Krise der Gegenwart und die Gott-Trunkenheit in der jüdischen, christlichen und islamischen Mystik", Conference of the *Akademie der Diözese Rottenburg-Stuttgart,* May 12–14, 1999, Stuttgart. Paper: "Gottes-Suche und Gottes-Erfahrung in der persischen Sufi-Dichtung".

131) "Fourth European Conference of Iranian Studies", held by the *Societas Iranologica Europaea*, September 6–10, 1999, Paris. Paper: "A Zoroastrian Legal Term in the Dēnkard: *pahikār-rad*".
132) "New and Current Trends in Iranian Studies", Colloquium of the Board of the *Societas Iranologica Europaea,* March 25, 2000, Ravenna. Paper: "The Legal Background of an Iranian Expression in the Babylonian Talmud".
133) "Middle Iranian Lexicography", Conference of the *University of Rome "La Sapienza"* and the *Istituto Italiano per l'Africa e l'Oriente*, April 9–11, 2001, Rome. Paper: "On Middle Persian Legal Terminology".
134) "Religious Texts in Iranian Languages", Mid-term Conference of the *Societas Iranologica Europaea* and the *University of Copenhagen,* May 18–22, 2002, Copenhagen. Paper: "On the Legal Nasks of the Dēnkard".
135) "La Persia e Bisanzio", Conference of the *Accademia Nazionale dei Lincei* and the *Istituto Italiano per l'Africa e l'Oriente,* October 14–18, 2002, Rome. Paper: "Pious Foundations in Byzantine and Sasanian Law".
136) Lecture at the *School of African and Oriental Studies,* May 1, 2003, London. Paper: "On the Treatment of Animals in Zoroastrian Law".
137) "Fifth Irano-Judaica International Conference", under the auspices of the *Ben-Zvi Institute,* September 14–17, 2003, Piliscsaba (Hungary). Paper: "An Iranian Legal Term in the Babylonian Talmud and in Sasanian Jurisprudence: *dastwar*".
138) "Fifth European Conference of Iranian Studies", held by the *Societas Iranologica Europaea,* October 6–11, 2003, Ravenna. Paper: "The Function of Temporary Marriage in the Context of Sasanian Family Law".
139) "And Life is Victorious!", Conference on Mandaean and Samaritan Literature—in Memory of Rudolf Macuch (1919–1993), Freie Universität Berlin, October 1–2, 2003. Paper: "Rudolf Macuch, Life and Work".
140) Colloquium of the Board of the *Societas Iranologica Europaea,* March 28–29, 2004, Kraków (Poland). Paper: "Language and Law: Linguistic Peculiarities in Sasanian Jurisprudence".
141) "XXIX. Deutscher Orientalistentag: Barrieren – Passagen", Congress of the *Deutsche Morgenländische Gesellschaft,* October 20–24, 2004, Halle (Germany). Paper: "Pious Foundations and their Legal Status in Sasanian Iran".
142) "Islamische Stiftungen *(waqf)* und ihre sozialen Funktionen im Spannungsfeld von Stiftungsrecht und Stiftungspraxis", workshop of the *Freie Universität Berlin,* December 3–4, 2004. Paper: "Die sasanidische fromme Stiftung und das islamische *waqf*: Eine Gegenüberstellung".
143) "Iranian Identity in the Course of History", Mid-term Conference of the *Societas Iranologica Europaea,* September 21–24, 2005, Rome. Paper: "Legal Constructions of Identity in the Sasanian Period".
144) "Literarische Stoffe und ihre Gestaltung in mitteliranischer Zeit", Colloquium in honour of the 70th birthday of Professor Werner Sundermann at the *Berlin-Brandenburgische Akademie der Wissenschaften,* March 30–31, 2006, Berlin. Paper: "Gelehrte Frauen: ein ungewöhnliches Motiv in der Pahlavi-Literatur".
145) "Recent Research in Iranian Studies", Colloquium of the Board of the *Societas Iranologica Europaea,* April 28, 2006, Berlin. Paper: "Legal Terminology in the Pahlavi Model Marriage Contract".

146) "Sixth Irano-Judaica International Conference", under the auspices of the *Ben-Zvi Institute,* September 10–12, 2006, Hamburg. Paper: "A Pahlavi Legal Term in Jesuboxt's Corpus Iuris: *wehdādestān(īh)*".
147) "The Talmud in its Iranian Context", Conference at the *University of California in Los Angeles,* May 6–7, 2007. Paper: "Allusions to Sasanian Law in the Babylonian Talmud".
148) "Orient und Okzident: Konflikte und Koexistenz von Rechtskulturen", Conference of the *International Max Planck Research Institute for Comparative Legal History,* June 27–29, 2007, Schloss Ringberg, Tegernsee (Germany). Paper: "Zoroastrisches Recht im islamischen Gewand: zur Fortwirkung vorislamischer Institutionen in islamischer Zeit".
149) "Sixth European Conference of Iranian Studies", held by the *Societas Iranologica Europaea,* September 18–22, 2007, Vienna. Paper: "Incestuous Marriage in the Context of Sasanian Family Law".
150) "Kulturwissenschaftliche Iranforschung", series of lectures at the *Institut für Iranistik, Österreichische Akademie der Wissenschaften,* January 10, 2008, Vienna. Paper: "Die iranische Zeitehe: eine vorislamische Institution im schiitischen Gewand".
151) "Zoroastrians Past and Present", International Conference held at the *Ancient India and Iran Trust,* June 7–8, 2008, Cambridge. Paper: "The Clause on Property in the Model Pahlavi Marriage Contract".
152) "Iranian Jewry: From Past to Present", International Conference at the *University of Maryland, College Park,* November 1–3, 2008. Paper: "The Sasanian Legal System and the Babylonian Talmud".
153) "Talmudic Archeology", International Conference held at *University College London,* June 22–24, 2009. Paper: "Substance and Fruit in the Sasanian Law of Property and the Babylonian Talmud".
154) "Poets, priests, scribes and (e-) librarians. The transmission of holy wisdom in Zoroastrianism", International Mid-term Conference of the *Societas Iranologica Europaea* at the *University of Salamanca,* September 2–5, 2009. Paper: "Editing Pahlavi Legal Texts: Difficulties and Future Tasks".
155) "New Trends in Late Antique Iran", Panel of the *Association for the Study of Persianate Societies,* International Conference of the *Middle Eastern Studies Association* (MESA), November 21–24, 2009, Boston. Paper: "The Clause on Property in the Pahlavi Marriage Contract".
156) "The Family as a Social Unit in the Legal Systems of the Near and Middle East (3rd–13th Centuries)" ("Die Familie als Sozialverband in den orientalischen Rechtssystemen [3.–13. Jh.]"), Interdisciplinary Workshop at the *Institut für Iranistik* of the *Freie Universität Berlin,* March 27, 2010. Paper: "Heiratsmuster und Erbschaftsstrategien im zoroastrisch-sasanidischen Familienrecht".
157) "Zoroastrianism in the Levant", ARAM Society for Syro-Mesopotamian Studies, 05–07 July 2010. The Oriental Institute, Oxford University. Paper: "The Case against Mār Abā, the Catholicos, in the Light of Sasanian Law".
158) "Knowledge to die for: Transmission of Prohibited and Esoteric Knowledge in Space and Time", Topoi Excellence Cluster, FU Berlin, May 2–4, 2011. Paper: "Heresy and Esotericism in the Zoroastrian Tradition".

159) "Encounters by the Rivers of Babylon: Scholarly Conversations between Jews, Iranians and Babylonians" Jerusalem, May 23–25, 2011. Paper: "Jewish Jurisdiction within the Framework of the Sasanian Legal System".
160) "Seventh European Conference of the SIE (ECIS 7)", held in Cracow, Sept. 7–10, 2011. Paper: "A Legal Controversy from the Sasanian Period in a Late Pahlavi Rivāyat Text".
161) Bailey Memorial Lecture; *Department of Near Eastern Studies,* University of Cambridge, December 13, 2013. Paper: "Kinship Ties and Fictive Alliances in Sasanian Law".
162) "De Byzance á Samarkand: Sources et Documents sur le règne de Husraw Ier", Conference in Paris, *École Normale Supérieure,* Oct. 17, 2014. Paper: "Legal Implications of Mazdakite Teaching According to the Dēnkard".
163) "Wissensbewegungen – Bewegliches Wissen", Ringvorlesung des SFB 980 ("Episteme in Bewegung"), Freie Universität Berlin, Institut für Philosophie, January 22, 2014. Paper: "Zum Transfer normativen Wissens am Beispiel des zoroastrischen und islamischen Rechts".
164) "Sláva Šláchetným (Glory for the Noble) 2014". Liptovský Mikuláš (Slovak Rep.), Sept. 19–20, 2014. Paper: ",Behalte den Flug in Erinnerung …' – Leben und Werk von Rudolf Macuch".
165) "Iran and Islam: Early Encounters. Formation of Islam and Transformation of Iranian Religious Traditions", CERES, Ruhr-University of Bochum, Germany, March 12–13, 2015. Paper: "Descent and Inheritance in Zoroastrian and Shiite Law".
166) "Ehsan Yarshater Lectures". *University of California Los Angeles* (UCLA), USA, November 6–22, 2015. Five lectures: *Sasanian Law in its Social Context*: (1) Legal Sources and Instruments of Law; (2) Kinship Ties and Fictive Alliances; (3) Property and Inheritance; (4) Civil and Criminal Proceedings; (5) Sasanian Law and Other Legal Systems.
167) Lecture *University of Chicago,* USA, May 13, 2016: "Constructing Descent: Legal Strategies of Succession and Inheritance in Sasanian Iran".
168) Lecture *World Zoroastrian Organisation,* London, June 5, 2016: "The Zoroastrian Background of Sasanian Law".
169) "Minorities and Majorities in the Middle East and Asia". *Comenius University* Bratislava, Slovakia, September 14th–15th, 2016. Paper: "Rudolf Macuch—A Life Dedicated to the Study of Minorities".
170) Lecture *University of St. Andrews,* Scotland, October 17, 2016: "Middle Persian Court Records from Tabarestān: Recent Evidence on Legal Proceedings in Eighth-Century Iran".
171) Workshop *University of St. Andrews,* Scotland, October 18, 2016. Paper: "Legal Constructions of Consanguinity: Succession in Sasanian Iran".
172) Lecture *Freie Universität Berlin,* January 11, 2018. Paper: "Middle Persian Records from Tabarestān: Evidence on Legal Proceedings in Eighth Century Iran".

Abbreviations

AcIr	Acta Iranica
AKM	Abhandlungen für die Kunde des Morgenlandes
AMI	Archäologische Mitteilungen aus Iran
AoF	Altorientalische Forschungen
APAW	Abhandlungen der Preußischen Akademie der Wissenschaften
ArOr	Archiv orientální
AWN	*Ardā Wirāz nāmag*
BAI	Bulletin of the Asia Institute
BSOAS	Bulletin of the School of Oriental and African Studies
BSOS	Bulletin of the School of Oriental Studies
BTT	Berliner Turfantexte
CFM	Corpus Fontium Manichaeorum
ČHP	*Čidag handarz ī pōryōtkēšān*
CRAI	Comptes rendus des séances de l'Académie des Inscriptions et Belles-Lettres
Dd	*Dadēstān ī dēnīg*
Dk	*Dēnkard*
DkM	*Dēnkard*, ed Madan 1911
EIr	Encyclopaedia Iranica
Fīō	*Frahang ī ōīm*
H	*Hāδōxt Nask*
HdO	Handbuch der Orientalistik
HuR	*Husraw ud rēdag*
IIJ	Indo-Iranian Journal
IPNB	Iranisches Personennamenbuch
JA	Journal Asiatique
JAOS	Journal of the American Oriental Society
J̌F	*J̌ōšt ī Friyān*
JQR	Jewish Quarterly Review
JSAI	Jerusalem Studies in Arabic and Islam
KAP	*Kārnamag ī Ardaxšīr ī Pābagān*
KNRm	Inschrift des Kerdīr in Naqš-e Rustam
KSM	Inschrift des Kerdīr in Sar Mašhad
LIV	M. Kümmel / Th. Zehnder / R. Lipp / B. Schirmer / H. Rix (eds.): *Lexikon der indogermanischen Verben. Die Wurzeln und ihre Primärstammbildungen.* Wiesbaden ²2001.
MHD	*(Mādayān) ī Hazār dādestān. Teil I*
MHDA	*(Mādayān) ī Hazār dādestān. Teil II*
MSS	Münchener Studien zur Sprachwissenschaft

NTS	Norsk Tidskrift for Sprogvidenskap
OLA	Orientalia lovaniensia analecta
Pass.A	*Passage A*
PRDd	*Pahlawī Riwāyats* zum *Dādestān ī dēnīg*
REA	*Riwāyat ī Ēmēd ī Ašawahištān*
SBE	Sacred Books of the East
SHAW	Sitzungsberichte der Heidelberger Akademie der Wissenschaften, Philosophisch-historische Klasse. Heidelberg.
SI	Studia Islamica
SÖAW	Sitzungsberichte der Österreichischen Akademie der Wissenschaften
SOR	Serie Orientale Roma
SPAW	Sitzungsberichte der Preußischen Akademie der Wissenschaften
StIr	Studia Iranica
TPhS	Transactions of the Philological Society. London.
Vd.	*Vīdēvdād*
VOHD	Verzeichnis der Orientalischen Handschriften in Deutschland
WZ	*Wizīdagīhā ī Zāspram*
WZKM	Wiener Zeitschrift für die Kunde des Morgenlandes
Y.	*Yasna*
Yt.	*Yašt*
ZDMG	Zeitschrift der Deutschen Morgenländischen Gesellschaft
ZWY	*Zand ī Wahman Yasn*

Ritual Competence and Liability of Minors in Ancient Zoroastrianism

On Avestan *dahmō.kərəta-* and *śiiaoϑnāuuarəz-*

Miguel Ángel Andrés-Toledo*

The technical meaning of the Av. compounds *dahmō.kərəta-* and *śiiaoϑnāuuarəz-*, accompanying *apərənāiiūka-* "minor, underage", confronts us with the problem of the legal status of minors in ancient Zoroastrian sources. In this contribution to the *Festschrift* to Prof. Dr. Maria Macuch, one of the experts in Zoroastrian legal texts to whom it is most appropriate to address such a discussion and who I had the pleasure of working with during some years at the Institut für Iranistik in Berlin, I will try to highlight the ritual and juridical implications of those compounds, until now not rightly understood, referring to minors.

Av. *dahma-* "instructed" (Bartholomae 1898, pp. 224–225, n. 1), the first element of the Avestan compound *dahmō.kərəta-*, stems from the PIr. verbal root **danh-* "to teach, to instruct" (Cheung 2007, pp. 56–57), represented in Old Avestan by *dąh-* "to learn" (Y 43.11, 49.9; Bartholomae 1904, p. 746) and related to Ved. *daṁs-* "to be able", both going back to IE. **dens-* "to be expert, to be able" (Mayrhofer 1992–2001, vol. 1, pp. 688–689).[1] It usually refers to persons instructed in religious matters and acquainted with the rituals.[2] The second element of the compound, Av. *kərəta-*, is the PPP. of the verb *kar-* "to do, to make" (Cheung 2007, pp. 236–238). As a simple word, Av. *dahma-* is

* Universidad de Salamanca. This article has been written thanks to the funding of the State Research Bureau and the European Social Fund under the Ramón y Cajal 2016 action (RYC-2016-19510).

1 Other Avestan words related to the same verbal root are *dąstuua-* "instruction" (Y 46.7), *daŋra-* "skillful" (Y 46.17, Yt 13.134, 15.40, F 3e, f, Vr 2), *daŋhah-* "skillfulness" (Ny 1.16) and *dąhišta-* "most instructed" (Y 13.3, Vr 3.1, 3.5, A 3.4, Vyt 42, N 62.4; Bartholomae 1904, pp. 681, 745, 746). Within the Zoroastrian vocabulary, other well-known cognates derived from the same root are Phl. *dastwar* and NP. *dastūr* "religious authority, high priest" (Nyberg 1974, p. 59).

2 Cf. also the epithet Av. *aršuuacastəma-* "knowing the right utterances most" (Bartholomae 1904, p. 206), accompanying Av. *dąhišta-* "most instructed" in Y 13.3, Vr 3.1, 3.5, A 3.4 and N 62.4.

widely attested in the Avestan literature;[3] its antonym *adahma-*, on the contrary, is only found in V 18.62 and Yt 10.138. In compounds we find Av. *dahma-* in Av. *dahmāiiuš.harəϑri-* (Y 62.2 [= Ny 5.8, Any 3]), Av. *dahmō.pairi.aŋharšta-* (Y 68.10 [= Ny 1.18], V 14.4, 18.72), Av. *dahmō.pairišta-* (Y 65.10), Av. *dahmō.yaoždāta-* (V 14.4, 18.72) and Av. *dahmō.kərəta-*.

The compound *dahmō.kərəta-*, only applied to *apərənāiiūka-* "minor, underage" in the extant Avestan corpus, is attested in the following passages:

Y 26.9 (= 59.26)

Av. |a| *vīspanąm. apərənāiiūkanąm. dahmō.kərətanąm. ašaonąm. frauuašaiiō. yazamaide.* |b| *ādaxiiunąmca. ašaonąm. frauuašaiiō. yazamaide.* |c| *uzdaxiiunąmca. ašaonąm. frauuašaiiō. yazamaide.*

|a| We worship the *frauuaṣ̌i-* of all the minors, *dahmō.kərəta-*, righteous. |b| And we worship the *frauuaṣ̌i-* of the righteous of the land. |c| And we worship the *frauuaṣ̌i-* of the righteous out(side) of the land.

Phl. |a| *harwispīn aburnāyagān ī dahmān-kardān ī ahlawān frawahr yazēm* |b| *ādehīgān ī ahlawān frawahr yazēm* |c| *uzdehīgān-iz ī ahlawān frawahr yazēm*

|a| We worship the *frawahr* of all the minors, *dahmān-kardān*, righteous. |b| We worship the *frawahr* of the righteous of the land. |c| And we worship the *frawahr* of the righteous out(side) of the land.

V 13.23

Av. |a| *dātarə. gaēϑanąm. astuuaitinąm. ašāum. yō. spānəm. tarō.piϑβəm. dasti. yim. taurunəm. cuuat̰. aētaēšąm. šiiaoϑnanąm. āstāraiieiti.* |b| *āat̰. mraot̰. ahurō. mazdå. yaϑa. aētahmi. aŋhuuō. yat̰. astuuaiṇti. apərənāiiūkəm. dahmō.kərətəm. šiiaoϑnāuuarəzəm. [vərəziiāt̰. šiiaoϑnəm.] paiti. tarō.piϑβəm. daiϑiiāt̰. aϑa. āstriieiti.*

|a| Maker of the material creatures, Righteous, whoever gives scarce food to a dog that (is) a young dog, how many of these actions make him a sinner? |b| And Ahura Mazdā said: "as if in this material life he would give scarce food to a minor, *dahmō.kərəta-*, actionable [he may do an action], so he sins."

Phl. |a| *dādār kē sag tar-pihīh dahēd ī tarunag cand pad awēšān kunišnān āstārēd* |b| *u-š guft ohrmazd kū cīyōn ka-š andar axw ī astōmand aburnāyag ī dahmān-kard [kū az wehān zād ēstēd] ī kunišn-warz [kū kunad ā-š ō bun] ka warzēd*

3 In Y 1.15, 2.15, 3.17, 4.20, 6.14, 7.17, 17.15, 22.17, 23.3 [= 67.3], 24.25, 32.16, 59.15, 61.1, 66.14, 68.15, 71.19, 72.1, Vr 1.7, 2.9, 11.16, V 7.71, 12.1, 12.3, 12.5, 12.7, 12.9, 12.11, 12.13, 12.15, 12.17, 12.19, 13.35 [= Vyt 6.44], 13.55, 18.62, P 31.2, 56.2, Yt 5.92, 10.16, 10.137, Vyt 1.1 [= AZ 1], H 11.2, 14.1, N 1.1, 7.3, 9.2, 26.2, 27.2, 86.1–3, 87.1, 87.8; accompanying *āfriti-*, in Y 1.15, 2.15, 3.17, 4.20, 6.14, 7.17, 7.26, 8.1, 17.15, 22.17, 24.25, 59.15, 61.1, 66.14, 70.3, 71.19, 72.1, Vr 1.7, 2.9, 9.2, 11.16, V 7.41, 9.37, 22.5, 22.11, 22.18, P 31.2, 32.2, A 1.1, 1.13, S 1.30, 2.30. It is noteworthy that its Pahlavi equivalent, Phl. *dahm*, is restricted to the technical language of the Pahlavi translations of Avestan texts. Indeed, we find Phl. *dahm* in Dk 3.84.6, 8.4.2, 8.45.3, 9.12.26–27, 9.22.2, 9.29.13, P 31.2, 56.2, RAF 143.4, ZFJ 474, 620, 666; + *āfrīn*, in GrBd 3.16, 26.94, Dk 3.195.8, 3.196.8, 7.9.3, 9.22.1, PRDd 10g1, 46.4–5, 65.14, P 31.2, 32.1–2; Phl. *dahmīh* in Dk 8.54.6, 8.54.8, ZFJ 474; and Phl. *adahm* in Dk 9.12.27, ZFJ 620.

kunišn [ka margarzān-ē bē kunēd ā-š yāt-ē ō bun <ī> gyān] abar tar-pihīh dād hē ēdōn āstārēd

|a| Maker, whoever gives scarce food to a dog that (is) a young dog, how much does he sin by those actions? |b| And Ohrmazd said: "as if in this material life he would have given scarce food to a minor, *dahmān-kard* [that is, he is born of good (people)], actionable [that is, (what) he does, it (goes) to his account], when he does an action [if he commits a (sin) worthy of death, then it (goes) to the account of his soul as a *yāt* (sin)], so he sins."

Av. *dahmō.kərəta-* has been translated in very different ways by scholars. SPIEGEL's (1852, p. 194) translation "rein" is actually much closer to the second element of the Avestan compound *dahmō.yaoždāta-* "ritually purified" (V 14.4, 18.72) than to Av. *dahmō.kərəta-*. HOVELACQUE (1876, p. 34) hesitated about translating Av. *dahmō.kərəta-* by "de bonne origine". DARMESTETER/MILLS' (1880, p. 158) translation "born of pious parents", DARMESTETER's (1892, p. 200) "né de parents virtueux", BARTHOLOMAE's (1904, p. 706) "von einem *D.* (gemacht, d. i.) gezeugt" and WOLFF's (1910, p. 399) "von einem Gemeinder gezeugtes" are motivated by the Pahlavi gloss *kū az wehān zād ēstēd* "that is, he is born of good (people)" to the Pahlavi translation *dahmān-kard* of the Avestan compound in V 13.23, without noticing, however, that Av. *kar-* "to do, to make", from which its second element *kərəta-* comes, never means "to give birth to a child" in Avestan. DUCHESNE-GUILLEMIN (1936, p. 118) literally translated Av. *dahmō.kərəta-* by "id. (= fait) par le D.", that is, "done by the *dahma-*". More recently, KELLENS (2010, p. 109) translated it in Y 26.9 by "(dejà) reconnus religieusement-habilités".

As far as I know, none of these scholars noticed that Av. *dahmo.kərəta-* is the heir of an Indo-Iranian formula **dasmá- kar-* "to perform competently (a ritual)", belonging to the Indo-Iranian religious technical terminology, as the parallel RV 1.74.4 *dasmát kr̥ṇóṣy adhvarám* "you perform the ritual competently" clearly demonstrates. Accordingly, Av. *dahmō.kərəta-* is to be understood as "able to perform competently (a ritual)". Apart from this technical religious meaning, we must take into account the juridical consequences of being religiously instructed among the ancient Zoroastrians. Indeed, when someone was instructed (Av. *dahma-*), he or she was already supposed to know what is right, as Yt 10.16 (GERSHEVITCH 1959, pp. 80–81), where Av. *dahma* is glossed by *vīduš.aṣ̌a* "who know what is right", suggests:

ẏōi. dim. dahma. [vīduš.aṣ̌a.] zaōϑrābiiō. frāiiazənte

the instructed ones [who know what is right], who worship him with libations

If one is religiously instructed and knows what is right, he or she may automatically become legally responsible. This explains not only why Av. *dahma* is glossed by *vīduš.aṣ̌a* in Yt 10.16, but also why Av. *dahmō.kərəta-* is followed in V 13.23b by Av. *šiiaoϑnāuuarəz-*, which has the clear juridical meaning "liable". This latter compound, attested in V 13.23b, 38b, 15.1c, 2e, 4e, 6d, 7c, 8e and VN 4, was interpreted by Spiegel (1852, p. 194) as "Sünder." Darmesteter/Mills' (1880, p. 158) and Darmesteter (1892, p. 200) translated it by "who can answer for himself" and "dejà responsible pour ses actes" respectively. Bartholomae (1904, p. 1713) read *š́iiaoϑnəm.vərəz-* in V 13.23b and distinguished it from *š́iiaoϑnāuuarəza-* (V 13.38b, 15.1c, 2e, 4e, 6d, 7c, 8e), wrongly understood by him as a thematic extension of the former; he translated the former by "eine Tat tuend sva. ein Geschäft, einen Dienst verrichtend" and the latter by "der die Tat begeht, Täter." Duchesne-Guillemin (1936, p. 64) also distinguished between *š́iiaoϑnəm.vərəz-* and *š́iiaoϑnāuuarəz-*, which he rendered by "qui fait un acte" and "qui commet l'acte" respectively. Humbach/Jamaspasa (1969, pp. 18–19) interpreted it as *š́iiaoϑnāuuarəza-* in VN 4 and translated it as "performer." Kellens (1974, p. 69) read *š́iiaoϑnəm.vərəz-* in V 13.23b and, following Bartholomae, translated it by "qui accomplit un travail". Av. *š́iiaoϑnəm.vərəz-* is based on the reading of the Pahlavi Vīdēvdād manuscripts, but the variant *š́iiaoϑnāuuarəza* of the Iranian Vīdēvdād Sāde manuscripts is to be preferred on the basis of the parallels with *°uuarəz-* as a second element of compound in other Avestan passages. As regards the possibility of a thematic *š́iiaoϑnāuuarəza-*, equivalent to *š́iiaoϑnāuuarəz-*, the fact that all these parallels attest a root noun *°uuarəz-* as a second element makes unlikely and unnecessary the existence of a thematic form *š́iiaoϑnāuuarəza-* only in V 13. In my opinion, there is only one compound Av. *š́iiaoϑnāuuarəz-*, which means "liable (in a process)" in V 13.38b, 15.1c, 2e, 4e, 6d, 7c and 8e. On the contrary, in VN 4, where it is preceded by Av. *huuaršta*, it must be understood as "doing well-done actions". This twofold semantic character might be present in V 13.23b, but it is clear that the Pahlavi commentators understood it in a juridical sense, insofar as they added the gloss *ka margarzān-ē bē kunēd ā-š yāt-ē ō bun <ī> gyān* "if he commits a (sin) worthy of death, then it (goes) to the account of his soul as a *yāt* (sin)".

It seems that V 13.23b refers to a minor, able to perform a ritual and liable, but if so, two questions arise: when exactly were Zoroastrian minors allowed to engage in ritual performances and considered legally responsible? Was this fact linked with the age at which they were invested with the sacred girdle?

References to minors engaging in rituals or in activities related to them are found in the Avestan and Pahlavi texts of the Nērangestān. Thus, according to N 22.1–2 and 22.5 (Kotwal/Kreyenbroek 1995, pp. 120–121), a minor can perform the office of *zaotar-* priest:

N 22.1

Av. *⁺kahiiācīṯ. nā. dahmanąm. zaoϑrāδā. ratufriš.*

Any instructed man in (the office of) *zaotar-* satisfies the *ratu-*;

Phl. *mard kadār-iz-ē az dahm zōtīh radīhā*

Any man among the instructed one(s) in the office of *zōt* (acts) according to the *rad*;

N 22.2
Av. *nāirikåscīt̰. apərənāiiūkahecīt̰.*

even a woman, even a minor.

Phl. *nārīg-iz [pad ān ī xwēš] aburnāyag-iz [pad ān ī kasān]*

even a woman [privately], even a minor [publically].

N 22.5. Pahlavi commentary
ā-z aburnāyag ka zīrak u-š yašt warm ud abēgumān pad kār ī yazišn ā pad har kār-ē šāyēd (...)

And a minor, if he/she (is) wise and (has learnt) the Yašt by heart and has no doubt about the performance of the Yasna, then he is allowed for every ritual performance. (...)

According to Dk 8.22.21 (M 724.18–20; West 1892, p. 80), which belongs to the lost Avestan legal book Duzd-sar-ōzad, a woman and a minor can be better acquainted with the law than an adult man:

abar dānāgīh ī nārīg ud aburnāyag ī āgāh-dād pad dādwarīh abar az purnāy mard ī anāgāh-dād

About the wisdom of a woman and a minor who know the law in a judgment above an adult man who does not know the law.

In N 30.8 (Kotwal/Kreyenbroek 2003, pp. 130–131), a special bowl and a *parāhōm* for minors (Phl. *tašt ī aburnāyagān ud parāhōm ī aburnāyagān*) are mentioned in the context of the *āb-zōhr* ceremony:

(...) *zōhr ēn and ciš nē stānišn* haomiiąn *ud wars du tašt ī aburnāyagān ud parāhōm ī aburnāyagān cē az any yazišn-ē and juttar bawēd kū zōhr pad šab stadan ā šāyēd*

For the *(āb-)zōhr* the following things are not to be taken: the *haomiiąn*, the bull's hair sieve, the bowl for the minors and the *parāhōm* for the minors, because it is different from any other Yasna, so that it is allowed to take the *(āb-)zōhr* at night.

According to N 87.1–3 (Kotwal/Kreyenbroek 2009, pp. 92–93), minors who have been instructed (Av. *dahmanąm. apərənāiiūnąm*) are allowed to bring firewood and *barsom* twigs:

N 87.1
Av. *yō. kəmcit. dahmanąm. apərənāiiūnąm. aštəm. dasti.*

Whoever gives the message to any of the instructed minors:

Phl. *kē kadār-iz-ē az* ⁺*dahmān* ⁺*aburnāyān* ⁺*aštagīh dahēd [kū-š abar dastwar bawēd]*

Whoever gives the message to any of the instructed minors [that is, he is a religious authority over him/her]:

N 87.2
Av. *hā.mē. bara.* ⁺*aēsmąsca. barəsmaca.*

"you, bring me firewood and *barəsman-* (twigs)"

Phl. *kū ān man bar ēzm ud barsom*

"bring me that, firewood and *barsom* (twigs)"

N 87.3
Av. *yezi.šē. +dāitīm. daδāiti. +ratufriš.*

if he/she gives it to him according to the prescriptions, he/she satisfies the *ratu-*.

Phl. *agar [rad] ān-iz drūnišn dahēd [kū nē* nōiṯ. ϑriiąm. upamanąm. +frauuaxšanąm. *gōwēd] +ā radīhā*

if he/she gives [to the *rad*] that reaping too [that is, he does not say: "(let him) not (cut) three of the upper twigs"], then (he/she acts) according to the *rad*.

Nothing is said in the Avestan text of the Nērangestān or in its Pahlavi translation about the age from which minors were allowed to engage in ritual activities, but some information about this has been transmitted in PRDd 17a1 and VīD 18. According to PRDd 17a1 (Williams 1990, vol. 1, pp. 88–89), only a child older than seven years might perform the Yašt: *dar ēn kū aburnāyag ī haft-sālag yašt nē abāyēd kardan ān ī hašt-sālag ōh abāyēd kardan* "This chapter (says): 'a seven year old minor must not perform the Yašt; an eight year old one might perform it'."[4]

In VīD 18 (Sanjana 1848, pp. 160–161; West 1892, p. 471; Bartholomae 1901, p. 100), referring to the age when a minor was invested with the sacred girdle, the commentaries of Rōšn and Abarag about the age from which a minor can perform certain religious services are included:

Av. *yaṯ. +aēte. yō. mazdaiiasnō. apərənāiiūkō. auui. hē. hapta. sarəδa. frajasāiti. stəhrpaēsaŋhō. aiβiiā̊ŋhānō. paitiš. maiδiiāi. +būjiiamnō. auui. hē. nara. pascaiti. nəmaŋhəṇti.*

When this one who (is) a Mazdean minor exceeds seven years, after being invested in the middle/at the waist with the girdle adorned with stars, men greet him.

Phl. *kē az awēšān māzdēsnān +aburnāyag abar ān ō pad dād ī haft-sālag frāz rasēd +ēbyānghan pad ān mayān bandēd abar ān mard pas niyāyišnōmand ast [kū frēzwānīg <ī> dēn ī weh] [rōšn guft <kū> frēzwānīg ī dēn pas az haft sāl padīriftan pādixšāy cīyōn frēzwānīg ruwānān ud abārīg hamāg kār ī dēn] [abarag guft <kū> frēz <ī> wuzurg cīyōn nō-šabag ud nōgzōd ud +wisparad ud rapihwin <ud> abārīg kār ī dēn pas <az> pānzdah-sālag framūd ēstēd]*

Whoever (being a) minor among those Mazdeans exceeds the age of seven years will tie the girdle in the middle/at the waist; then this man is worthy of praise [that is, it is mandatory for the Good Religion] [Rōšn said: "it is a rule to accept the mandatory religious (services) after seven years, like the mandatory ones for the souls and all the other religious services."] [Abarag said: "great mandatory (services) such as the nine-nights (ritual), the *nōgzōd*, the Wisparad, the Rapihwin and other religious services are prescribed (for) those older than fifteen."]

4 Williams (1990, vol. 2, p. 32) translated: "This chapter: a seven year old boy should not perform worship; an eight year old should do so."

It is evident that Rōšn's exegetical school differed from that of Abarag regarding the minimal age for performing some mandatory rituals: according to the former, children after the age of seven years might engage in some rituals, but according to the latter only those older than fifteen years were allowed to perform major religious services. Notwithstanding, it is unclear whether children were invested with the sacred girdle for the first time at the age of seven, as stated in VīD 18, or at the age of fifteen, as in Yt 8.13–14 and V 18.54–59. Nevertheless, from V 15.45c and some references to lost Avestan legal books in the Dēnkard it can be inferred that children older than seven years acquired a status in ancient Zoroastrian law according to which they were considered to be more independent from their parents and, after being religiously instructed, became legally responsible. Thus, according to the Avestan text of V 15.45c and its Pahlavi translation, a child had to be protected until he or she was seven years old:

> Av. *xšuuaš. mā̊ŋhō. sūnō. θrāθrəm. hapta. sarəδa. apərənāiiūkahe.*
>
> during six months (one has to take) care of a dog, during seven years of a minor.
>
> Phl. *šaš māh sag srāyišn [kū-š pānagīh juttar abāyēd kardan] haft sāl aburnāyag*
>
> during six months one has to take care of a dog [that is, one must protect it separately], during seven years (one has to take care) of a minor.[5]

Until the age of seven, the children's father may atone for them, according to the Pahlavi commentary of V 7.72A–B, which means that from the age of eight on they had to atone for their own acts:

> |A| *ka nē atuwānīgīh ziyānag rāy hād ā paydāg hē kū kē kasān rāy pad patit bawēd ā-š patītīh kār* |B| *aburnāyag haft-sālag rāy az abestāg paydāg ka-š pid pad patit bawēd ā šāyēd* yezi. ⁺aēšąm. ptarō. ⁺išarə.štāitiia.
>
> |A| If because of incapacity it were not (possible) for the woman (to pay for it), then it would be manifest that whoever undergoes penitence for other people, his penitence (is) of use. |B| As regards a seven year old minor, it is manifest from the Avesta: "when his/her father undergoes penitence for him/her, then it is allowed (according the following Avestan text) 'if their parents on the spot'."

In later Pahlavi sources, or perhaps in diverging old sources transmitted in later texts, the vicarious atonement was extended to children between the ages of eight and fifteen, as we read in PRDd 53.1 (Asmussen 1965, p. 48; Williams 1990, vol. 1, p. 195; vol. 2, pp. 91 and 354):

> *patitīgīh ka zan a-tuwānīg ud ka šōy pādixšāy mard rāy šāyēd pid aburnāyag ī hašt-sālag tā pānzdah-sālag ka bē kunēd šāyēd* (…)
>
> As regards penitence, if a woman (is) unable and if her husband is *pādixšāy*, it is allowed for the man (to undergo penitence on her behalf). As regards an eight

5 Cf. PRDd 29.1 (Williams 1990, vol. 1, pp. 132–133; vol. 2, p. 55): Phl. *az-iz ēn wāzag kū pus tā pānzdah-sālag parwarišn* "and according to this saying, until a son is fifteen years old one has to nourish him".

year old to fifteen year old minor, if his/her father undergoes it (on his/her behalf), it is allowed. (...)

According to Dk 8.17.10 (M 696.20–697.2; WEST 1892, p. 41), which belongs to the Zaxmestān ("code of the wounds") section of the lost Avestan legal book Nigādom, and as rightly interpreted by MACUCH (1993, p. 32), if a minor under eight years of age, or an eight year old child not yet instructed, killed someone, the parents are given the responsibility for it:

> *abar kuštan ī haft-sālag aburnāyag ī a-hammōxt hašt-sālag-iz pad wēnišn ī pidarān wināhgārīh ī pidarān pad-iš ka-šān abāz dāštan tuwān abāz nē darēnd ud ān ī ka-šān abāz dāštan nē tuwān*
>
> About a killing by a seven year old minor (or) a non-instructed eight year old too in custody of his/her parents; the guiltiness of the parents therefore when they can avert it (but) do not avert it and that when they cannot avert it.

Religious instruction and liability of minors is clearly linked in the passage mentioned before, which recalls the connection between *dahmō.kərəta-* and *śiiaoϑnāuuarəz-* in V 13.23b. The age of seven years marked the boundary for judging punishable acts committed by minors and it made a difference that they were instructed or not.

The limit on the age from which a minor might be liable was also discussed in some lost Avestan books, as indicated by the references in Dk 8.19.21 (M 700.1–3; WEST 1892, p. 46) and 8.19.28 (M 700.14; WEST 1892, p. 47), which belonged to the Hamēmālestān ("code of the opponents") section of the Nigādom; 8.20.83 (M 714.1–2; WEST 1892, p. 65), which belonged to another section of the Nigādom; and 8.22.2 (M 722.21–723.4; WEST 1892, p. 77; MACUCH 1993, p. 32), which belonged to the Duzd-sar-ōzad:

> Dk 8.19.21
> *abar zanišn ī pad snah ī uspurrīg ud anuspurrīg ka purnāyān aburnāyagān ud aburnāyagān ka hamayārīhā kunēnd*
>
> About smiting by a complete or an incomplete blow, when adults do it to minors or when minors do it in collaboration (with adults).
>
> Dk 8.19.28
> *abar sāmān ī pādifrāh ī aburnāyag pad wināh kunēd*
>
> About the limit on the punishment of a minor for a sin he/she commits.
>
> Dk 20.83
> *abar šāyistan ī margarzān aburnāyag pad jādūg-gōwīh ka-šān sālār abāg*
>
> About the possibility that minors (are) worthy of death by sorcery, when the guardian is with them.
>
> Dk 8.22.2
> *ud abar gāh rasišn ō aburnāyagān hammōzišn az sālār <ud> pid ud ēwēnag ī-š hammōzišn ud gāh ī ō bun būd ī aburnāyag wināh ud paymānag ī wināh*

ī aburnāyīhā ud tōzišn andar aburnāyīh ud ān-iz ī andar purnāyīh wināh az a-hammōzišn ī aburnāyag ī hammōzišn cē andar ham dar

And about the arrival of the time for the instruction of minors by a guardian and father and the mode of his instruction; the time when the minor's sin goes to his/her account; the extent of the sin during childhood; the atonement during childhood and that too during adulthood; the sin because of not instructing a minor (due for) instruction, which is in the same chapter.

The issue about the liability of minors, with the aggravating factor of committing a sin or crime after having been instructed, was continued in some works of the Pahlavi literature that probably quoted parts of the Pahlavi translations and commentaries of the lost Avestan books mentioned before. Thus, we know from Šnš 5.1–2 (Tavadia 1930, pp. 91–92) that the sin of chattering while eating was in force for children from the age of eight years on:

Šnš 5.1
drāyān-jōyišnīh ī ān ī aburnāyagān ī panj-sālag ō bun nēst ud az panj-sālag tā haft-sālag ka-š pid pad hammōxtārīh a-wināh ā-š ō bun nēst ud ka wināhgār ō bun ī pidar

The (sin of) chattering while eating in case of five year old minors is not for their account. From five year olds to seven year olds, if their father (is) innocent regarding their instruction, then (the sin) is not for his account, but if (he is) guilty, (it is) for the account of the father.

Šnš 5.2.
ud az hašt-sālag tā pānzdah-sālag mard ud zan agar-iz pad yašt kardan a-wināh bē-š iθā. *ud* aṣ̌əm. vohū. *tuwān guftan ud nē gōwēd ā-š drāyān-jōyišnīh ō bun ud ka-š yašt warm tuwān kardan ud* iθā *<ud>* aṣ̌əm. vohū. *gōwēd būd kē guft kū ēdōn bawēd cīyōn ka-š yašt nē kard ēstēd ud gētō-xrīd nē bawēd ud būd kē guft kū drāyān-jōyišnīh nē bawēd*

And from eight year olds to fifteen year olds, for (both) man and woman, even if they (are) innocent as regards the performance of the Yašt, but they can recite *iθā* and *aṣ̌əm. vohū* and they do not recite it, then the (sin of) chattering while eating (goes) to their account. And if one is able to memorize the Yašt and does not recite *iθā* and *aṣ̌əm. vohū*, there was (a commentator) who said: "it is so as if he/she does not perform the Yašt and there is no *gētō-xrīd*"; and there was (a commentator) who said: "there is no (sin of) chattering while eating".

From the age of seven on, a minor was guilty of having anal sex with an adult, although the degree of sin was higher for the adult, according to ZFJ 598 (Jamasp-Asa / Mahyar Nawabi / Tavousi 1979):

ka dō kōdag ī weh-dēn kūnmarz kunēnd ayāb ēk purnāy ud ēk aburnāyag ā-šān wināh cīyōn

If two children of the Good Religion, or one adult and one minor, have anal sex, what (is) their sin?

purnāyag margarzān aburnāyag ān ī narīh ud ān ī mādagīh ka haft-sālagīh rasēnd ⁺ō purnāy rawišnīh ēg-išān harw ēk-ēw tanāpuhl-ēw ō bun

As for the adult, he (is) worthy of death; as for the minors, the one being of the masculine sex and the other being of the feminine sex, if they have turned into seven year olds at the time of the sexual encounter with the adult, then a *tanāpuhl* sin (goes) to the account of each of them.

A reduction of the sentence was foreseen, however, for eight year old children, as indicated in RAF 59.1–2 (ANKLESARIA 1969, vol. 1, pp. 31 and 117–118, vol. 2, pp. 73–74):

RAF 59.1
kōdak-ēw ī hašt-sālag kē zaxm ayāb rēš-ēw ayāb zyān-ēw pad mard ayāb pad kōdak-ēw ī hašt-sālag kunēd ēg-iš wināh ud tāwān cē

(There is) an eight year old child who inflicts a wound, harm or damage to a man or to another eight year old child; then what is the sin and compensation for him/her?

RAF 59.2
cīyōn man dānēm ka zaxm kunēd yāt-ēw ka wēš zanēd kū yāt-ēw pas-iz yāt-ēw tōzišn ud ka wināh ī cīyōn margarzān kunēd frāy az yāt-ēw ō bun nē bawēd ud tōzišn kunēd sāl-ēw bē tōzišn aburnāyag wināh ēn and ō bun bōdōzadīh ud kādyōzadīh ud ēw-mōg-dwārišnīh ud drāyān-jōyišnīh ud drō-cāšišnīh u-š tanāpuhl ud margarzān ō bun nē bawēd

As far as I know, if he/she inflicts a wound, (it is) one *yāt* (sin); if he/she beats more than (the extent of) one *yāt* (sin), then too it is to be atoned as one *yāt* (sin). And if he/she commits a sin equivalent to a (sin) worthy of death, it is for his/her account no more than one *yāt* (sin) and he/she undergoes the atonement; it is to be atoned during one year. These sins (go) to his/her account: willful offence, injury by negligence, running bare-footed, chattering while eating and false teaching; and a *tanāpuhl* and a (sin) worthy of death (do) not (go) to his/her account.

According to PRDd 34a1–2 (WILLIAMS 1990, vol. 1, pp. 140–141, vol. 2, pp. 60–61 and 325), children under seven years of age were considered innocent, but those between eight and fifteen added their sins to their own account to a lesser degree than adults:

PRDd 34a1
ēn-iz paydāg kū aburnāyag ī haft sāl bowandag bawēd ka-š pid pad frahang kard a-wināh harw wināh ī ōy kunēd pādifrāh ud rēš pad dēwān kunēd

This is also manifest: "A minor who completes seven years, when he/she has been educated by his/her father, he/she is innocent; every sin he/she commits causes punishment and harm to the demons.

PRDd 34a2
az hašt sāl tā pānzdah sāl ka margarzān kunēd ā-š yāt-ēw ō bun bawēd ka jādūgīh xwāhēd ā-š tanāpuhl-ēw wināh ud abārīg wināh ī ōh kunēd ā-š tā yāt-ēw ⁺ō bun

From eight years to fifteen years, if he/she commits a sin worthy of death, then it is one *yāt* (sin) to his/her account; if he/she seeks a sorcerer, then (it is) a *tanāpuhl* sin, and the other sins he/she may commit (go) as one *yāt* to his/her account."

The fact that children between eight and fifteen years were already legally responsible also determined that the destiny of their souls after death was different from that of children up to the age of seven, as we read in PRDd 65.12 (WILLIAMS 1990, vol. 1, pp. 234–235, vol. 2, pp. 114–115 and 325):

> *ud ruwān ī aburnāyagān kē-š dād haft-sālag ān-iz kē-š haft sāl kam tā pid ud mād widard dādestān ī pid ud mād bē-š ka-š drahm-ēw ī purr pad ruwān bē dahēnd* <az> *ahlawān judāg bē* ⁺*bawēnd ān ī hašt-sālag*[6] *ān-iz ī tā pānzdah-sālag āmār ī xwēš cīyōn pad dēn paydāg ōh bawēd*
>
> And regarding the souls of minors who are seven years old and also those who are less than seven years old, until their father and mother pass away, their judgment (is that) of their father and mother; unless they give one full drachm for their souls, they are separate from the righteous. As regards those eight years old and also those until fifteen years old, their own reckoning would be as it is manifest in the religion.[7]

Summing up, knowledge of the religious prescriptions subsequently meant legal responsibility for their acts and therefore liability according to ancient Zoroastrian law. From the sources adduced above we can conclude that instructed children older than seven were considered to be able to perform certain rituals as well as actionable. If, with DARMESTETER (1892–1893, p. 1.200, n. 32), we link the age of ritual and legal responsibility to the moment when minors were invested with the sacred girdle, we will have to accept that VīD 18, according to which minors were invested with the sacred girdle after the age of seven, preserves a tradition different to that attested in Yt 8.13–14 and V 18.54–59, according to which minors wore it for the first time when they reached fifteen years of age. The former seems to have been predominant in ancient Zoroastrian law, but we cannot exclude that Yt 8.13–14 and V 18.54–59 reflect a coexistent tradition,

6 WILLIAMS (1990, vol. 1, pp. 234–235; vol. 2, pp. 114–115 and 325) wrongly edited Phl. <7> *haft*. Taking into account that minors from the age of eight on were liable according to the parallels mentioned before, I prefer the variant <8> *hast* of the J manuscript.

7 See also PRDd 8d7 and 8d9 (WILLIAMS 1990, vol. 1, pp. 52–53; vol. 2, pp. 12–13 and 278–279), where the children's souls share the destiny of those of their parents after death: PRD 8d7: *ruwān-iz ī aburnāyagān kē tā haft sāl bē mīrēd ā-š ruwān pad xwaršēd pāyag ēstēd ud ka pid ahlaw abāg pid bē ō wahišt ud ka pid druwand ka mād ahlaw abāg mād bē wahišt šawēd ka-š pid ud mād harw dō druwand abāg pid ud mād bē ō dušox šawēd* "And as regards the soul of the minors, when one dies until seven years (of age), his/her soul stands at the sun station, and if his/her father (is) righteous, (he/she goes) with his/her father to Paradise; and if his/her father (is) unrighteous, if his/her mother (is) righteous, he/she goes with his/her mother to Paradise. If his/her father and mother (are) both unrighteous, he/she goes with his/her father and mother to Hell." PRD 8d9: *būd dastwar kē-š guft kū ōy kār ud kirbag ī xwēš rāy bawēd cē az abastāg paydāg kū ohrmazd ān dōšāram ka pid frazand parwarēd ā-š ēdōn dād kū-š tā haft sāl ruwān abāg pid ud mād ruwān-iz ī aburnāyag zahāg bawēd* "There was a religious authority who said: 'It is because of his/her own pious deeds and merits, because it is manifest from the Avesta that Ohrmazd loves it; when the father nourishes his child, then the law (is) so: the soul (of a child) until seven years (of age) (remains) with his/her father and mother; the soul of the minor is their child.'"

in which children only after fifteen years of age became ritually competent and therefore liable in other ancient Zoroastrian communities.

Bibliography

Anklesaria, B.T. 1969: *The Pahlavi Rivāyat of Ādurfarnbag and Farnbag-Srōš*. Bombay.
Asmussen, J.P. 1965: *Xuāstvānīft. Studies in Manichaeism*. Copenhagen.
Bartholomae, Ch. 1898: "Arica VIII." In: IF 7, pp. 223–233.
— 1901: "Arica XIV." In: IF 12, pp. 92–150.
— 1904: *Altiranisches Wörterbuch*. Straßburg.
Cheung, J. 2007: *Etymological Dictionary of the Iranian verb*. Leiden.
Darmesteter, J. 1892–1893: *Le Zend-Avesta*. Paris.
Darmesteter, J./L.H. Mills 1880: *The Zend-Avesta. Part I: Vendîdâd*. Oxford.
Duchesne-Guillemin, J. 1936: *Les composés dans l'Avesta*. Paris/Liège.
Geldner, K.F. 1886–1896: *Avesta. The Sacred Books of the Parsis*. Stuttgart.
Gershevitch, I. 1959: *The Avestan Hymn to Mithra*. Cambridge.
Hovelacque, A. 1876: *Le chien dans l'Avesta*. Paris.
Humbach, H./K.M. Jamasp Asa 1969: *Vaeϑā Nask. An Apocryphal Text on Zoroastrian Problems*. Wiesbaden.
JamaspAsa, K.M./Y. Mahyar Nawabi/M. Tavousi 1979: *Ms. TD2. Iranian Bundahišn*. Vols. 54–55. Shiraz.
Kellens, J. 1974: *Les noms-racines de l'Avesta*. Wiesbaden.
— 2010: *Études avestiques et mazdéennes*. III: *Le long préambule du sacrifice (Yasna 16 à 27.12, avec les intercalations de Visprad 7 à 12*. Paris.
Kotwal. F.M./Ph.G. Kreyenbroek 1995: *The Hērbedestān and Nērangestān*. Vol. II: *Nērangestān, Fragard 1*. Paris.
— 2003: *The Hērbedestān and Nērangestān*. Vol. III: *Nērangestān, Fragard 2*. Paris.
— 2009: *The Hērbedestān and Nērangestān*. Vol. IV: *Nērangestān, Fragard 3*. Paris.
Macuch, M. 1993: *Rechtskasuistik und Gerichtspraxis zu Beginn des siebenten Jahrhunderts in Iran. Die Rechtssammlung des Farroḫmard i Wahrāmān*. Wiesbaden.
Madan, Dh.B. 1911: *The Complete Text of the Pahlavi Dinkard*. Vols. I–II. Bombay.
Mayrhofer, M. 1992–2001: *Etymologisches Wörterbuch des Altindoarischen*. Heidelberg.
Nyberg, H.S. 1974: *A manual of Pahlavi. Part II: Glossary*. Wiesbaden.
Sanjana, P.D. 1848: *Vijarkard Dīnī*. Bombay.
v. Spiegel, F. 1852–1863: *Avesta, die heiligen Schriften der Parsen, aus dem Grundtexte übersetzt, mit steter Rücksicht auf die Tradition*. Leipzig.
Tavadia, J.C. 1930: *Šāyast-nē-šāyast. A Pahlavi text on Religious Customs*. Hamburg.
West, E.W. 1892: *Pahlavi texts. Part 4: Contents of the Nasks*. Oxford.
Williams, A.V. 1990: *The Pahlavi Rivāyat accompanying the Dādestān ī Dēnīg*. Part I: *Transliteration, trancription and glossary*. Part II: *Translation, Commentary and Pahlavi Text*. Copenhagen.
Wolff, F. 1910: *Avesta. Die heiligen Bücher der Parsen übersetzt auf der Grundlage von Chr. Bartholomae's Altiranischem Wörterbuch*. Straßburg.

Les fonctions religieuses et la loi zoroastrienne : le cas du *hērbed*

SAMRA AZARNOUCHE

Étant fondé sur la loi zoroastrienne, le système juridique de l'Iran préislamique est nécessairement lié au corps ecclésiastique et à ses institutions. Parmi les acteurs de la loi qui nous sont connus pour l'ère sassanide, un nombre considérable représente des fonctions religieuses du zoroastrisme : des prêtres, tels que le *mowbed* « prêtre », le *rad* « chef spirituel » ou le *mowbedān mowbed*, figure suprême du clergé, aussi considérée comme la plus haute autorité légale, exerçaient une activité juridique de concert avec les fonctionnaires *(kārdār)* et les juges *(dādwar)*[1]. L'une des figures notoires du clergé zoroastrien, le *hērbed*, semble avoir joué, dès la fin de l'ère sassanide, un rôle non négligeable au sein du système juridique. Bien que cet aspect des activités du *hērbed* ne soit jamais explicitement décrit dans les textes relevant de cette période ou de l'ère post-sassanide, plusieurs témoignages textuels en moyen-perse nous invitent à reconsidérer la nature de cette fonction dans le contexte des pratiques législatives et à tenter d'éclaircir les conditions dans lesquelles ce dignitaire religieux a pu intervenir dans la procédure juridique ou lors de l'élaboration des décrets légaux.

C'est un honneur d'offrir au Professeur MARIA MACUCH le fruit de ces réflexions, basées à l'origine sur nos recherches doctorales[2], et de saluer son inlassable effort pour rendre intelligibles et accessibles la littérature et le vocabulaire juridique de l'Iran ancien.

Le « *Hērbed* », polyvalence ou polysémie ?

Au sein de la classe sacerdotale des *āsrōn*, le *hērbed* détient théoriquement la fonction d'instructeur religieux[3]. Son nom continue le terme avestique *aēϑra-paiti-*, dont le membre *aēϑra-* n'a jamais reçu d'étymologie convaincante, et qui

1 MACUCH 1981, pp. 188–208.

2 *Éducation religieuse et profane sous l'ère sassanide, avec une édition commentée du texte moyen-perse* Husraw ī Kawādān ud Rēdag-ē « *Khosrow fils de Kawād et un page* », thèse de doctorat sous la direction du Prof. PH. HUYSE, École Pratique des Hautes Études, PSL, Paris 2012, partiellement éditée dans AZARNOUCHE 2013.

3 MACKENZIE 1971, p. 43 : « teacher-priest ».

désigne conjecturalement le maître des *aēϑriia-* et des *hāuuišta-*, les « disciples » et « novices », auxquels il est chargé de communiquer oralement la connaissance des textes sacrés. Dans les écrits à connotations doctrinales, on remarque qu'il est investi de la mission de « gardien du *mąϑra* » ou de défenseur de l'intégrité du texte liturgique face à l'« hérétique » ou l'« apostat » (av. *aṣ̌əmaoγa-*, mp. *ahlamōγ*) qui déforme et profane la parole divine. Le thème avestique de l'adversité entre l'*aēϑrapaiti* et l'*aṣ̌əmaoγa-* exposé par exemple au Yašt 13.105, se retrouve avec une forte résonance dans le Dēnkard (7.8.11–15) : dans un temps apocalyptique apparaîtront des ennemis de la religion accompagnés de puissants *ahlamōγ* qui s'opposeront aux *hērbed* et transgresseront leur enseignement[4]. Le rôle théologique du *hērbed*-maître consiste avant tout à garantir le salut de ses disciples (mp. *hāwišt*), en leur transmettant l'Avesta et son *zand*, ce qui lui confère le statut de « nourricier de l'âme » *(parwardār ī ruwān)*[5]. La fonction de maître n'est toutefois ni la seule qui soit assignée au *hērbed*, ni même la plus fréquemment attestée dans l'ensemble de la documentation post-sassanide. Selon les contextes, ses compétences spécifiques sont tantôt de l'ordre de l'enseignement, tantôt du culte et du rite, tantôt – comme nous allons le voir en détails – de l'expertise juridique. On s'est donc à juste titre interrogé sur le véritable rang que le *hērbed* occupait au sein du clergé. Parmi les études consacrées à la prêtrise en Iran ancien[6], un article de Marie-Louise Chaumont, paru en 1960, se concentre exclusivement sur ce titre, à travers les sources préislamiques (Chaumont 1960, pp. 55–80) et les sources en langues arabe et persane (id., pp. 161–179) dont il est dressé un inventaire assez complet. L'approche chronologique laisse cependant sans réponse la question de savoir si le terme *hērbed* avait acquis des significations diverses au cours du temps, ou bien si, dès l'origine, la personne du *hērbed* pouvait endosser plusieurs fonctions religieuses.

Face à ce désordre sémantique aggravé par l'assimilation accidentelle de ce terme à la fonction plus élevée de *mowbed*, Chaumont est amenée à conclure que le *hērbed* équivaut dans les livres pehlevis au sens générique de « prêtre type » (id., p. 172), en relevant entre autres un passage du Kārnāmag ī Artaxšēr ī Pābagān (X.9)[7] où Ardashīr – désirant connaître le châtiment réservé au régicide – s'adresse au *mowbedān mowbed* en l'appelant « *hērbed* ». Le même cas de figure se présente dans la version pehlevie du Vīdēvdād 4.45 où le terme *hērbedān* est glosé par le nom d'Ādurbād Mahraspandān, *mowbedān mowbed* de Shāpuhr II, ou encore dans la célèbre anecdote du Dēnkard 6 D10 où deux *mowbed* nommés Ādurfarrbay et Ādurbōzēd interrogent un *hērbed* nommé Wehdād :

4 Molé 1967, pp. 82–83.
5 Pahlavi Rivāyat 29.4 (Williams 1990, I, pp. 132–133; II, pp. 55–56).
6 Citons quelques-unes d'entre elles : Wikander 1946 ; Gignoux 1983a, 1983b, 1986 ; Kreyenbroek 1987a, 1987b, 1994, 2003.
7 Grenet 2003, p. 98.

> *amā-iz abestāg ud zand warm ud mowbedān mowbed hēm tō čē rāy pad hērbedīh nām wēš barēnd ku amā* [8]? « Alors que nous aussi connaissons de mémoire l'Avesta et le *zand* et sommes des *mowbedān mowbed*, comment se fait-il qu'en ta qualité de *hērbed*, ton nom soit plus souvent cité que le nôtre ? »

Chaumont conteste efficacement l'hypothèse de Wikander (1946) qui accordait une primauté ancienne à la fonction des *hērbed* par rapport à celle des « *mowbed* du Fārs », notamment sur la base du supposé nom du feu contenu dans leur titre[9]. La thèse du renversement des dignités pendant l'ère sassanide avait d'ailleurs convaincu de Menasce, qui remarquait toutefois que la charge de *hērbed* avait survécu en tant qu'une fonction propre, cumulable avec celle du *mowbed*[10].

Cela est en effet le cas du mage Kerdīr, qui arbore ce titre au début de sa carrière alors qu'il occupe déjà une haute dignité à la cour de Shāpuhr I *(Kerdīr ēhrbed)*[11], d'où l'on déduit qu'au 3ème siècle de notre ère, *hērbed* (*ēhrbed* dans la graphie archaïque des inscriptions) désignait déjà une fonction plus large que le « maître d'école » chargé de faire réciter les textes et que ses prérogatives n'étaient plus exclusives à l'enseignement sacerdotal.

Au rapport direct de cette dignité avec l'acquisition du savoir des textes sacrés, les sources arabes font une allusion unique décrivant les méthodes de mémorisation de l'Avesta :

> Les Mazdéens ne sont jamais parvenus à retenir par cœur leur livre révélé ; aussi leurs savants et leurs prêtres *(hirbaḏ)* en font apprendre des fragments, par exemple un septième, un quart ou un tiers, à beaucoup [de fidèles] ; l'un d'eux commence par réciter le fragment qu'il a retenu, un second reprend à son tour, puis un troisième et ainsi de suite jusqu'à ce qu'à eux tous ils aient achevé la récitation de tout le livre, car il est impossible à un seul de l'apprendre en entier ; on cite cependant un Mazdéen du Sīstān qui, postérieurement à l'année 300 [912], le savait intégralement par cœur[12].

Pourtant, dans la majorité des sources arabes, c'est en tant qu'officiant ou spécialiste des rites que le *hērbed* nous apparaît, comme dans cet extrait – inconnu de Chaumont – tiré d'*al-Majmūʿ fī al-muḥīṭ bi-l-taklīf* de ʿAbd al-Jabbār, maître des muʿtazilites sous les Bouyides :

> [...] Le *hērbed* est chargé de cette opération (= la purification de l'accouchée) après avoir déshabillé et mis à nu la femme. Il le fait de sa propre main, en voyant de ses propres yeux [...] Il prend pour cela des honoraires selon les possibilités de la femme. Il commence, en la déshabillant pour la purification, par prendre sa robe. Le moins qu'il prenne au plus pauvre des pauvres c'est quatre miṯqāl d'argent (env.

8 Shaked 1979, pp. 184–185.
9 Wikander tentait d'établir un lien étymologique entre **aēϑra-* et *ātar-* (Wikander 1946, p. 17).
10 de Menasce 1946, pp. 174–175.
11 Gignoux 1983a, pp. 254–255.
12 al-Masʿūdī, *Les prairies d'or*, I, p. 204, §549.

2 grammes). Selon les Perses et les mages, au temps de leur royaume, le *mowbedān mowbed* recevait ainsi quatre millions de dinars, qu'il dépensait pour les *hērbed*[13].

Le rôle de purificateur *(yōjdahrgar)* est encore attesté dans la Rivāyat ī Ēmēd ī Ašawahištān[14], tandis que celui du gardien du feu ou maître du pyrée apparaît sporadiquement dans les textes arabo-persans tardifs[15]. Au 9ème siècle de notre ère, le statut du *hērbed*, tel que le dépeint le chef de la communauté, Manuščihr, présente une situation intermédiaire entre le maître et l'officiant[16]. Il est intéressant de noter qu'à cette époque de trouble pour les Zoroastriens d'Iran l'unique supériorité des *hērbed* sur les *hāwišt* était dans la connaissance du *zand*. Ainsi, le *hērbed* qui a étudié et mémorisé des textes légaux et leurs exégèses, tels que le Vīdēvdād et le Nērangestān, serait en droit de réclamer un salaire supérieur pour accomplir (ou superviser) le même rite que le *hāwišt* – connaissant seul le texte avestique – accomplirait pour un prix inférieur[17].

Croyant devoir répartir les compétences juridiques et ritualistes respectivement entre les dignités des *mowbed* et des *hērbed*, Chaumont s'étonne de trouver plusieurs auteurs musulmans pour attribuer au second des fonctions du premier en matière de loi alors que les ouvrages pehlevis « ne prêtent nulle compétence de cet ordre aux hērbads » (Chaumont 1960, p. 166). Cette dernière assertion mérite d'être réévaluée à la lumière de lectures récentes ou de documents nouvellement apparus, car, bien que la tâche dévolue à ces prêtres n'y soit guère expliquée dans le détail, il existe plusieurs témoignages démontrant l'utilité de leur présence au sein de l'institution judiciaire.

Le pouvoir décisionnel du *hērbed* en matière de loi est évoqué à de multiples reprises, notamment dans le code de loi sassanide, Mādayān ī Hazār Dādestān 5.13 : ... *dādestān bē rāyēnīdan čiyōn hērbedān gōwēnd* « ... la procédure doit être conforme à ce que les *hērbed* ont dit »[18], mais aussi dans des textes non légaux comme ce passage dédié au calendrier religieux dans le Bundahišn 25.8 : *hērbedān wizīr ī nasā ud abārīg tis pad hāmīn ud zamestān az ēn ōšmārag kunēnd*[19] « c'est selon ces considérations que les *hērbed* émettent leur verdict sur les (cas de pollution par des) cadavres etc., en été et en hiver ». On imagine sans peine que c'est à l'occasion de concertations collégiales que des points juridiques étaient débattus *(uskārd)*, non sans quelques controverse[20] : *hērbedān ud mow-*

13 Monnot 1974, p. 288.

14 Par ex. Rivāyat ī Ēmēd ī Ašawahištān 9, 10, 11, 12 (Safa-Isfehani 1980, pp. 56–77) ; Rivāyat ī Ēmēd ī Ašawahištān 14 montre explicitement que la qualité de *yōjdahrgar* s'additionne aux compétences originelles du *hērbed* (id., pp. 82–83).

15 Voir également Frahang ī Pahlavīg XIII.5 : MRŠY' « master of fires » (Nyberg 1988, p. 82).

16 Kreyenbroek 1987a.

17 Id., pp. 196, 201.

18 Macuch 1993, pp. 87, 97.

19 Pakzad 2005, p. 286.

20 Sur les controverses exégétiques et les différentes écoles de commentateurs voir Gignoux 1995 et Secunda 2012.

mardān ī ōšmurd-mānsar ī dranjēnīd-zand ī uskārd-dādestān « les *hērbed* et les *mowmard*[21] qui ont énuméré le *mantra* (avestique), récité le *zand* et discuté de la loi »[22] ; « il [= Ardashīr] établit l'ordre des Mobedhs et des Hirbedhs, chargés de rendre la justice *(al-aḥkām)* et de décider ce que la loi permettait et ce qu'elle défendait *(al-ḥalāl wa'l-ḥarām)* »[23].

En tant que spécialiste des textes et des exégèses, et sans doute aussi à titre de rhéteur, le *hērbed* entre également sur la scène des controverse interconfessionnelles[24] : c'est l'homme qui apporte les réponses aux détracteurs du zoroastrisme. La Rivāyat d'Ādurfarrbay ī Farroxzādān porte comme intitulé : *pursišnīhā ēw čand az hērbed Ādurfarrbay ī Farroxzādān, hudēnān pēšōbāy* « quelques questions (à l'intention) du *hērbed Ādurfarrbay ī Farroxzādān,* guide des fidèles de la Bonne Religion »[25]. Que la figure emblématique de l'orthodoxie mazdéenne, premier auteur du Dēnkard et champion des controverses religieuses soit qualifié si simplement de *hērbed* (et non de *mowbed*, par exemple) nous rappelle le cas de Kerdīr au début de sa carrière. Ce terme semble quitter ici le domaine de l'objectivité pour revêtir une signification plus symbolique, celle de « savant », de « maître spirituel » ou d' « autorité intellectuelle ». Il n'en reste pas moins que, dans le corps du texte, la fonction de *hērbed* est mise en relation avec le domaine juridique et le fondement sacré des décrets légaux :

La réponse à une question sur les lois matrimoniales est introduite par la phrase : *čiyōn man dānom ud az hērbedān ōwōn āšnūd* « à ce que je sais et ce que j'ai entendu des *hērbed…* »[26], de même sur le problème de la pureté de l'eau, le conseil des *hērbed* dicte la loi : … *čiyōn hērbedān pad uskār guft…* « tel que les *hērbed* ont dit après délibération … »[27].

Au chapitre 73 de ce même texte, il est fait état d'un conflit entre deux écoles de juristes connus de la littérature juridique sassanide, Abarag d'une part, et Dādfarrox et Wehšābhur de l'autre. L'auteur du traité conclut par :

> *hērbedān kam wardēnīdan ān ī abāyēd kardan ka meh-dādestānīh-ē nē paydag ō wēš gugāyīh čāštag im-iz čāštag ō ān kē abestāg gugāyīh ayyārtar ud abērtar hangāštan* « Les *hērbed* doivent modifier le moins possible ce qui doit être fait. Si une ‹ application excessive de la loi › n'est pas manifeste, (qu'ils adoptent) le commentaire théorique[28] qui s'appuie sur une majorité de témoignages. Aussi, qu'ils

21 Sur ce titre, voir Gignoux 1983a, p. 263.
22 Dādestān ī Dēnīg Int.8 (Jaafari-Dehaghi 1998, pp. 32–33, avec quelques modifications dans la traduction).
23 al-Tha'ālibī, *Histoire des rois des Perses*, p. 485.
24 Par ex. Dēnkard 3.80, où un *hērbed* est interrogé par un Juif sur le *xwēdōdah* (de Menasce 1973, p. 85).
25 Rezai Baghbidi 1384/2005, p. 1.
26 Rivāyat ī Ādurfarrbay ī Farroxzādān 28 (id., p. 24).
27 Rivāyat ī Ādurfarrbay ī Farroxzādān 39 (id., p. 31).
28 Sur *čāštag* (litt. « enseignement, doctrine ») « commentaire théorique » de la loi canonique par opposition à *kardag* « pratique légale », voir Macuch 1993, pp. 717–188, 2009b, pp. 182–183.

tiennent compte du commentaire théorique auquel les témoignages de l'Avesta sont le plus favorables et plus nombreux (à le confirmer) »[29].

Il faut en conclure que les *hērbed* étaient chargés de produire les *čāštag* « commentaires théoriques » (litt. « enseignements ») à l'appui de références tirées de l'Avesta et d'adapter à la procédure juridique la prescription légale supposée leur être fidèle. Ces *hērbed* n'étaient sans doute pas à distinguer des théologiens et juristes de la cour, mais ils sont nommés ici seulement en qualité d'experts en exégèses, et surtout en faisant appel à leur savoir mnémonique de l'Avesta et leur habilité à repérer et à réciter la formule avestique qui étaiera la sentence pénale.

Dans l'acception de « maître », le verbe le plus fréquemment associé à l'activité du *hērbed* est *čāštan* ou *čāšīdan* « enseigner »[30] (*hammōxtan* est également attesté mais dans un sens moins précis), et le contenu de cet enseignement religieux est désigné par le terme *hērbedestān*. C'est par le syntagme *hērbedestān kardan* « litt. faire le *hērbedestān* », récemment discuté par Maria Macuch[31], que s'exprime la notion de suivre le cursus de l'éducation religieuse par les laïcs et les membres de la classe sacerdotale destinés à la prêtrise. Ce cursus incluait en théorie l'apprentissage de la loi et des commentaires *(dād ud zand)*[32], bien qu'une tradition conservatrice remontant probablement à l'époque de Khosrow Ier ait eu tendance à restreindre l'apprentissage des commentaires aux cercles des prêtres[33]. Le fait d'aller assister aux cours des *hērbed* s'exprime par *(ō) hērbedestān kardan šudan* (ou *āmadan*) « aller faire (ou « venir faire ») le *hērbedestān* »[34]. Une troisième expression se rapportant à cette institution est métaphorique : *tan bē ō hērbedestān dādan* « s'adonner à (l'étude) du *hērbedestān* », attestée avec des variantes : *tan bē ō hērbedestān abespārdan* « confier son corps au *hērbedestān* »[35] ou *tan bē ō hērbedestān rādēnīdan* « se dévouer (litt. faire don de son corps) au *hērbedestān* »[36], ou encore dans la forme reprise dans le Dēnkard 9 *tan pad hāwištīh bē ō hērbedān rādēnīdan*[37] « se livrer aux *hērbed* en tant que disciple », en admettant que *rādēnīdan* soit un causatif formé sur *rād* « généreux ». En réalité, les verbes *dādan* et *rādēnīdan* qui apparaissent dans ces gloses ne sont pas employés de manière aléatoire, mais répondent précisément à deux manières d'exprimer la notion d'« offrande » dans la traduction pehlevie qui elle-même décalque ou reproduit par paronomase ce qui en aves-

29 Rezai Baghbidi 1384/2005, p. 58.
30 Par exemple, Hērbedestān 8.5 (Kotwal/Kreyenbroek 1992, p. 50), 14.2 (p. 68), 15.1 (p. 70), 18.3–4 (p. 78).
31 Macuch 2009a, pp. 264–266.
32 Hērbedestān 2.5 (Kotwal/Kreyenbroek 1992, p. 30), 12.6 (p. 64).
33 Shaked 1994, pp. 77–80.
34 Hērbedestān 1.1 (Kotwal/Kreyenbroek 1992, p. 26 *et passim*).
35 Šāyest nē Šāyest 17.8 (Kotwal 1969, p. 73).
36 Yasna 19.16, Yasna 46.17.
37 Madan 1911, p. 924.6–7.

tique pourrait s'en rapprocher, c'est-à-dire les syllabes */dă/* et */răd/.* Ce tableau permet de mieux illustrer ces correspondances :

	dādan		*rādēnīdan*	
	Y 19.12	Y 51.5	Y 19.16	Y 46.17
av.	*dim ahūmca ratūmca* ***ādadaṯ***	*yə̄* ***dāϑaēibiiō*** *ərəš ratūm, xšaiiąs*	⁺***rāiti****. hankərəϑəm*	*hadā vəstā, vahmə̄ṇg səraošā* ***rādaŋhō***
trad.	*ka-iz ō ōy ahū ud <u>rad</u>* ***dahēd***	*kē* ***dahišn*** *ō ōy rāst <u>rad</u> pad pādaxšāyīh*	*u-š pad* ***rādīh*** *hangerdīgīh bowandag*	*pad ast-dahišnīh ō ān ī ašmā niyāyišn rawēd pad srōš* ***rād-dahišnīh***
glose	*[kū tan bē ō hērbedestān* ***dahēd****]*	*[kū pad pādaxšāyīh ī-š ast tan bē ō hērbedān* ***dahēd****]*	*[ēdōn ō xwēš šāyēd kardan ka tan bē ō hērbedān* ***rādēnēnd****]*	*[ay ast-dahišnīh ēd dēn ī ašmāh gōwēd ud tan-iz* ***rādēnēd*** *ō hērbedestān]*

Tout porte à croire que l'exégète du *Yasna* a tenté de cristalliser les notions de don et de charité dans l'image de l'apprentissage religieux, c'est-à-dire le don de soi ou le sacrifice de son existence à l'étude. Les traductions pehlevies des deux exemples basés sur *dādan* montrent que cette action converge vers le *rad* et peut donc s'interpréter comme « s'en référer à l'autorité juridique ». Cela renvoie à l'attestation du Šāyest nē Šāyest 17.8 selon laquelle « se livrer au *hērbedestān* » équivaut à se fier à l'autorité qui possède les textes (*hamāg abestāg ud zand warm* « qui a mémorisé tout l'Avesta et le *zand* »), c'est-à-dire au *rad* selon cet autre extrait du même texte :

> Šāyest nē Šāyest 8.2 :
> *ōy ī margarzān wināh andar radān garzišn ud tan bē abespārdan ǰud az radān tan bē abespārdan nē bawēd* « [For] him who is a *margarzān* [sinner], the sin is to be expiated unto the spiritual leaders, and the body is to be submitted; [the expiation] does not take place except by submitting the body [to] the spiritual leaders »[38].

En d'autres termes, la soumission inconditionnelle à l'enseignement des *hērbed* équivaut à s'en remettre à la loi.

38 Tavadia 1930, p. 104.

Le *hērbed* dans l'archive du Tabaristān

Une implication autrement plus concrète du *hērbed* dans le système légal peut être confirmée par des documents de nature juridique connus depuis peu. Il s'agit d'une archive post-sassanide datée du 8ème siècle de notre ère, conservée dans une collection privée et composée d'une trentaine de lettres et documents écrits en pehlevi cursif sur tissu ou sur peau. Cette archive provient de la province du Tabaristān, plus précisément d'un seul village dont le nom, inconnu par ailleurs, peut être lu « Askēnrad ». Près de la moitié de cette archive qui représente les seuls témoins authentiques des pratiques juridiques du zoroastrisme a été déchiffrée et présentée récemment par Philippe Gignoux[39]. Le style elliptique, l'usage du jargon administratif et les difficultés liées à l'écriture du pehlevi cursif sont autant d'entraves à la compréhension de cette source primaire. Sa nature juridique ne fait toutefois aucun doute : il y est question de plainte *(garzišn)*, de jugement *(dādestān)*, de conflit *(pahikār)*, de verdict *(wizīr)* etc.[40]. L'une des particularités de cette collection est dans la récurrence d'un nom : un homme appelé Farroxabzūd, qualifié du titre de *hērbed*, apparaît sur presque la moitié des documents dont certains lui sont directement adressés – comme l'indique la formule d'adresse conventionnelle *ō hērbed ī xwadāy Farroxabzūd namāz* « au *hērbed*, Monsieur Farrox-abzūd, salut ! »[41] – et d'autres sont émis par lui. Il aurait, selon Gignoux, une fonction de juge ou de médiateur, voire de témoin[42]. Dans le document 1A, Farroxabzūd signale à son correspondant qu'il a bien reçu le document relatif à une plainte[43], et dans la réponse à ce document avec lequel elle est scellée, il est dit que le jugement doit de préférence avoir lieu en présence du *hērbed* : *dādestān [...] ō pēš hērbed weh kardan* (1B)[44]. D'autres documents de cette archive attestent de la nécessité de la présence de Farroxabzūd pour le dépôt de la plainte *(sāxt ī pēšēmār)*[45] et le double document 7A–B semble correspondre à une attestation de présence du plaignant auprès de Farroxabzūd les 11ème et 21ème jours du mois de Farwardīn de l'an 87.

À ce stade du déchiffrement de cette précieuse documentation, nous pouvons provisoirement déduire que Farroxabzūd – qui n'a apparemment pas de sceau personnel – ne tient pas le rôle de juge[46], ni celui de témoin au sens juridique du terme, mais qu'il doit assister aux séances de jugement en tant que médiateur

39 Gignoux 2012.
40 Id., p. 34.
41 Document 1B (id., p. 36), 8B (p. 58). *Hērbed (ī) xwādāy* est la formule de politesse réservée au *hērbed*, voir Ēwēnag Nāmag Nibēsišnīh 41 (Jamasp-Asana 1913, p. 139) et Pahlavi Rivāyat 62.28 (Williams 1990, I, pp. 226–227, II, pp. 109, 263).
42 Gignoux 2012, p. 32.
43 Id., pp. 36–38.
44 Id., pp. 36, 40.
45 3B (id., p. 44), 5B (p. 48), 6A–B (p. 50).
46 C'est toutefois la traduction choisie dans le glossaire de ces textes (Gignoux 2012, p. 92).

et être informé en personne du motif du conflit. Sa tâche est également d'ordre administratif puisqu'il reçoit directement la correspondance traitant de l'action judicaire et doit y répondre.

Conclusion

La diversité des rôles assignés au *hērbed*, en particulier ceux témoignant de la dégradation de sa condition, serait l'indice de la déchéance progressive du titre due à l'éclatement de l'église zoroastrienne après la chute de l'Empire sassanide[47]. Cette disparité ne permet sans doute pas de se représenter avec précision ce qu'était la vocation du *hērbed* à l'époque sassanide, mais il semble que la dignité originelle de « spécialiste des textes sacrés » soit implicite dans l'ensemble des attestations. Cette constante doit être prise en compte comme le fil conducteur entre les différentes sources et époques où le *hērbed* est cité. À ce titre, « *hērbedīh* » nous apparaît dès lors non pas comme la désignation exclusive d'une fonction ou d'une profession ecclésiastique, mais plutôt comme celle de la qualité intellectuelle et des compétences d'un membre de la classe des *āsrōn* en mesure d'agir comme un « livre vivant » et de réciter en toutes circonstances les textes liturgiques et/ou juridiques appropriés. L'aptitude du *hērbed* à fournir des témoignages textuels *(abestāg gugāyīh)* à la demande des juristes et des jurisconsultes, ou encore à vérifier la conformité des décrets avec les textes, faisait de lui l'incontournable référence au sein du système juridique.

C'est certainement à cette aptitude que fait allusion Kārnāmag ī Artaxšēr ī Pābagān (X.9) : ce sont seules ses compétences juridiques que le roi invoque quand il s'adresse le chef du clergé en le nommant « *hērbed* ».

Bibliographie

Azarnouche, S. 2013: Husraw ī Kawādān ud Rēdag-ē « *Khosrow, fils de Kawād, et un page », texte pehlevi édité et traduit.* Paris (Cahiers de Studia Iranica 49).

Chaumont, M.-L. 1960: « Recherches sur le clergé zoroastrien : le hērbed. » In : *Revue de l'histoire des religions* 15, pp. 55–80, 161–179.

Gignoux, Ph. 1983a: « Die religiöse Administration in sasanidischer Zeit: ein Überblick. » In : H. Koch/D.N. MacKenzie (éds.): *Kunst, Kultur und Geschichte der Achämenidenzeit und ihr Fortleben.* Berlin (Archäologische Mitteilungen aus Iran, Ergänzungsband 10), pp. 253–266.

— 1983b: « Titres et fonctions religieuses sasanides d'après les sources syriaques hagiographiques. » In : *Acta Antiqua Academiae Scientiarum Hungaricae* 28, pp. 191–203.

47 Kreyenbroek 1987b.

— 1986: « Pour une esquisse des fonctions religieuses sous les Sasanides. » In : *Jerusalem Studies in Arabic and Islam* 7, pp. 93–108.

— 1995: « La controverse dans le mazdéisme tardif. » In : A. LE BOULLUEC (éd.): *La controverse religieuse et ses formes*. Paris, pp. 127–146.

— 2012: « Une archive post-sassanide du Tabaristān (I). » In : R. GYSELEN (éd.): *Objets et documents inscrits en* pārsīg. Bures-sur-Yvette (Res Orientales 21), pp. 29–96.

GRENET, F. 2003: *La geste d'Ardashir fils de Pâbag. Kārnāmag ī Ardaxšēr ī Pābagān*. Die.

JAAFARI-DEHAGHI, M. 1998: *Dādestān ī Dēnīg*. Part I: *Transcription, Translation and Commentary*. Paris (Cahiers de Studia Iranica 20).

JAMASP-ASANA, J.M. 1913: *The Pahlavi Texts. Contained in the Codex MK*. Vol. II. Bombay.

KOTWAL, F.M. 1969: *The Supplementary Texts to the Šāyest nē Šāyest*. Copenhaguen (Det Kongelige Danske Videnskabernes Selskab, Historisk-filosofiske Meddelelser 44, 2).

KOTWAL, F.M./PH.G. KREYENBROEK 1992: *The Hērbedestān and Nērangestān*. Vol. I: *Hērbedestān*. Paris (Cahiers de Studia Iranica 10).

KREYENBROEK, PH.G. 1987a: « The *Dādestān ī Dēnīg* on Priests. » In : *IIJ* 30, pp. 185–208.

— 1987b: « The Zoroastrian Priesthood after the Fall of the Sasanian Empire. » In : PH. GIGNOUX (éd.): *Transition Periods in Iranian History*. Paris (Cahiers de Studia Iranica 5), pp. 151–166.

— 1994: « On the Concept of Spiritual Authority in Zoroastrianism. » In : *Jerusalem Studies in Arabic and Islam* 17, pp. 1–15.

— 2003: « Hērbed. » In : *EIr* XII, Fasc. 3, pp. 226–227.

MACKENZIE, D.N. 1971: *A Concise Pahlavi Dictionary*. London (repr.1986, 1990).

MACUCH, M. 1981: *Das sasanidische Rechtbuch ‚Mātakān I hazār Dātistān' (Teil II)*. Wiesbaden (AKM 45.1).

— 1993: *Rechtskasuistik und Gerichtspraxis zu Beginn des siebenten Jahrhunderts in Iran. Die Rechtssammlung des Farroḫmard i Wahrāmān*. Wiesbaden (Iranica 1).

— 2002: « A Zoroastrian Legal Term in the *Dēnkard* : *Pahikār-rad*. » In : PH. HUYSE (éd.): *Iran : questions et connaissances. Actes du IVᵉ Congrès européen des études iraniennes, organisé par la Societas Iranologica Europæa, Paris 6–10 septembre 2000*, Vol. I : *La période ancienne*. Paris (Cahiers de Studia Iranica 25), pp. 77–90.

— 2009a: « Disseminating the Mazdayasnian Religion. An Edition of the Pahlavi Hērbedestān Chapter 5. » In : W. SUNDERMANN/A. HINTZE/F. de BLOIS (éds.): *Exegisti monumenta. Festschrift in Honour of Nicholas Sims-Williams*. Wiesbaden (Iranica 17), pp. 251–277.

— 2009b: « Judicial and Legal Systems iii. Sasanian Legal System. » In : EIr. XV, Fasc. 2, pp. 181–196.

MADAN, D.M. 1911: *The Complete Text of the Pahlavi Dinkard*. 2 Vols. Bombay.

al-Masʿūdī, Abū 'l-Ḥasan ʿAlī b. al-Ḥusayn b. ʿAlī: *Les prairies d'or* (Murūǧ al-ḏahab wa-maʿādin al-ǧawhar). 4 Vols. BARBIER DE MEYNARD/PAVET DE COURTEILLE (trad.), nouvelle édition revue par Ch. PELLAT. Paris 1962–1997 (Société asiatique, Ouvrages orientaux).

Menasce, J. de 1946: compte-rendu de: Stig Wikander: *Feuerpriester in Kleinasien und Iran*. Lund 1946. In : *Revue de l'histoire des religions* 132, pp. 170–175.

— 1973: *Le troisième livre du Dēnkart*. Paris (Travaux de l'Institut d'Études Iraniennes de l'Université de Paris III, 5).

Molé, M. 1967: *La légende de Zoroastre selon les textes pehlevis*. Paris (Travaux de l'Institut d'Études Iraniennes de l'Université de Paris III, 3).

Monnot, G. 1974: *Penseurs musulmans et religions iraniennes. ʿAbd al-Jabbār et ses devanciers*. Paris / Le Caire / Beyrouth (Études musulmanes 16).

Nyberg, H.S. 1988: *Frahang i Pahlavīk. Edited with Transliteration, Transcription and Commentary from the Posthumous Papers of Henrik Samuel Nyberg*. Éd. par B. Utas et C. Toll. Wiesbaden.

Pakzad, F. 2005: *Bundahišn. Zoroastrische Kosmogonie und Kosmologie*. Band I: *Kritische Edition*. Tehran (Ancient Iranian Studies Series 2).

Rezai Baghbidi, H. 1384/2005: *The Revāyat of Ādur-Farrōbay ī Farroxzādān*. Tehran (Ancient Iranian Studies Series 1).

Safa-Isfehani, N. 1980: *Rivāyat-i Hēmīt-i Ašawahištān. Edition, Transcription and Translation. A Study in Zoroastrian Law*. Harvard (Harvard Iranian Series 2).

Secunda, Sh. 2012: « On the Age of the Zoroastrian Sages of the Zand. » In : *Iranica Antiqua* 47, p. 317–349.

Shaked, Sh. 1979: *The Wisdom of the Sasanian Sages. An Edition with Translation and Notes of* Dēnkard, *Book Six, by Āturpāt-I Ēmētān*. Boulder, Colorado (Persian Heritage Series 34).

— 1994: *Dualism in Transformation. Varieties of Religion in Sasanian Iran*. London (Jordan Lectures in Comparative Religion 16).

Tavadia, J.C. 1930: *Šāyest-nē-šāyast. A Pahlavi Text on Religious Customs*. Hamburg (Alt- und Neu-Indische Studien 3).

al-Thaʿālibī, Abū Manṣūr: *Histoire des Rois des Perses (Ghurar akhbār mulūk al-furs wa siyarihim)*. Texte arabe publié et traduit par H. Zotenberg. Paris 1900.

Wikander, S. 1946: *Feuerpriester in Kleinasien und Iran*. Lund (Skrifter utgivna av Kungl. Humanistiska vetenskapssamfundet i Lund 40).

Williams, A.V. 1990: *The Pahlavi Rivāyat Accompanying the Dādestān ī Dēnīg*. 2 Vols. Copenhagen (Historisk-filosofiske Meddelelser 60).

Zur Haar- und Nagelpflege im Zoroastrismus

Beiträge zur Erklärung mittelpersischer Rechts- und Religionsterminologie. III.

David B. Buyaner

Meine geringe Gabe zur Festschrift für Maria Macuch verbinde ich mit dem aufrichtigsten Dank der Jubilarin gegenüber, einem um so innigeren, da die dem nachfolgenden Beitrag zugrunde liegenden Beobachtungen ihr Entstehen im höchsten Maße der so wirksamen wie herzlichen Unterstützung verdanken, die ich seitens Professor Macuchs für meine Arbeit im von ihr geleiteten Institut für Iranistik genossen habe. Ich hoffe, daß die folgende Miszelle, die eine merkwürdige Parallele zwischen einem von den Pahlavi-Quellen wie dem Talmud beschriebenen Brauch zum Gegenstand hat, auf ihr Interesse stößt.

Unter den zahlreichen Variationen des Themas der rituellen Reinheit im Zoroastrismus hat der Gegenstand der rechten Haar- und Nagelpflege eine besondere Stelle inne: Der ganze siebzehnte Fragard des Vīdēvdāds behandelt diesen Gegenstand getrennt von der größeren Problematik der durch den Kontakt mit dem Leichnam sowie der mit den intravitalen Ausflüssen verursachten Unreinheit. Trotz der ausgeprägt zoroastrischen Färbung der Stellen, in denen dieses besondere Thema behandelt wird, sind manche mit Haar und Nägeln verbundenen Motive mit jenen in den anderen indogermanischen Traditionen vergleichbar. So erinnert das Gebet für das Wachsen der Pflanzen des sein Haar ordnungsgemäß vergrabenden Mannes (V 17.5) an die Stelle bei Aulus Gellius, an der die vorgeschriebene Pflege der Haar- und Nägelabschnitte des Flamen Dialis behandelt worden ist:

V 17.5:[1]

Avesta	PÜ
āaṯ. aϑra. maγəm.[a] *auua.kanōiš.*[b] *+dištīm.*[c] *+xrūždisme.*[d] *+vītastīm.*[e] *varədusme.*[f]	*ēg anōh [ōh*[g]*] <maγ> be kanāh*[h] *[+ēw*[i]*] dišt*[j] *[+ka*[k]*] saxt zamīg*[l] *[+ēw*[m]*] widast [ka] narm*

1 Siehe Hss. L^{4}, ff. 239r, ll. 15–239v, l. 9; K^{1}, f. 283r, ll. 2–13.

Avesta	PÜ
Dann sollst du da ein Loch graben – eine kleine Spanne[2] (tief) im Hartboden, eine grosse Spanne (tief) im Weichboden;	Dann sollst du da <ein Loch> [so] graben – [eine] kleine Spanne (tief), [wenn] der Boden hart (ist), [eine] grosse Spanne (tief), [wenn] (er) weich (ist);
paiti.[n] *dim.*[o] *ābarōiš.*[p] du sollst (die Haarabschnitte) einbringen,	*abar* +*ōy*[q] *[anōh ān*[r]*] barāh* darauf [dahin] sollst du [es] einbringen,
aϑa.[s] +*imą.*[t] *vacō.*[u] *framruiiå.*[v] *vārəϑraγnīš.*[w] *zaraϑuštra.*[x] dann sollst du diese sieghaften Worte rezitieren, O Zaraϑuštra:	*ēg*[y] *ēn gōwišn frāz gōw*[z] *ī*[aa] *pērōzgar* +*zarϑuxšt*[ab] dann rezitiere diesen Spruch, den sieghaften, O Zarϑuxšt:
at̰. axíiāi.[ac] *ašā.* +*mazδå.*[ad] *uruuarå.*[ae] *vaxšat̰.*[af] „So mag Mazdā die Pflanzen für sie durch die Wahrheit züchten".[3]	*ēdōn pad*[ag] *ān ī*[ah] *[ōy] tarsagāhīh*[ai] *[ka gāw*[aj] *<ī> ēk-dād*[ak] *tan be dād*[al]*] ohrmazd urwar*[am] *waxšēnēd [kū-š*[an] *be abzāyēnēd*[ao]*]* „So züchtet Ohrmazd die Pflanzen [d. h., mehrt sie] durch [seinen] Gehorsam [als der alleingeschaffene Bulle seinen Körper dahingab]".

a K^1: *m[....]* b K^1: *(auu)a[......]* c L^4: *[..]štəm.*; K^1: *[.....](m)* d L^4: *xruždisme.*; K^1: *xraō(ž)dism[.]* e L^4: *vītastəm.*; K^1: *vīta[....]* f K^1: lac. g K^1: ʾw' h L^4: HPLWNʾh; K^1: H(PL)WN i Mss.: HNA j K^1: dyšt... sht lac. k L^4: AYK l K1: [..]yk m L^4: HNA; K^1: H(NA) n K^1: *p[....]* o K^1: lac. p K^1: [......](š) q L^4: KN; K^1: ʾ(w') r L^4: s. l. ZK scr. s K^1: *aϑa. imą.* lac. t L^4: *imąm.* u K^1: *(v)acō.* v L^4: *framruiiå.* u. s. l. *-m-* scr.; K^1: *framru(iiå).* w K^1: *vār(əϑ)[.](a)γ[...]* x K^1: *[......](š)tra.* y K^1: lac. z K^1: *YM[...]* aa K^1: Y pylwckl lac. ab L^4: zltwhštl; K^1: [....](h)št' ac K^1: *axí(ii)āi.* u. s. l. *-i* scr. ad L^4: *mazδā.*; K^1: lac. ae K^1: *[.....]rå.* af K^1: *(va)[.]št̰.* ag K^1: lac. ah L^4: W praescr. ai K^1: t[..]kʾyy h aj K^1: TWR(A) ak K^1: (ʾyw)k(dʾ)t al K^1: d[.]t' am K^1: (ʾ)wlwl an L^4: AYK ao L^4: ʾpzʾyynyt s. l. -yt scr.; K^1: ʾpzʾ[....]

2 Av. *dišti-* ‚kleine Spanne' (phl. d(y)št/*dišt* ‚id') ist der Breite von zehn Fingern gleich; Av. *vītasti-* (phl. wtst(')/*widast*) ist der Breite von zwölf Fingern gleich (s. FĪŌ 732–733, KLINGENSCHMITT 1968, S. 238–239).

3 Diese Phrase ist ein Zitat aus Y 48.6. Das Wort *axíiāi.* ‚für sie' bezieht sich auf die Kuh, welche Y 48.5 erwähnt. So ist der Pahlavi Kommentar über den alleingeschaffenen Bullen zusammen mit der Übersetzung zitiert worden. Angesichts der Übertragung des Zitats zusammen mit der ursprünglichen Erläuterung leuchtet es ohne weiteres ein, daß der Hintergrund nicht nur dem Verfasser der vorliegenden Vīdēvdādstelle, sondern auch den späteren Pahlavi Kommentatoren ganz klar war. So entbehrt der Versuch LINCOLNS (1977, S. 356f., Anm. 21), av. *axíiāi.* infolge des angeblichen Mißverständnisses des Gāϑā-Dialekts seitens der Vīdēvdādverfasser in diesem Zusammenhang als sich auf den Beter beziehend zu interpretieren („for this one [standing here], that is, for me"), jeder Grundlage. Vgl. Anm. 12.

Aulus Gellius, *Noctes Atticae* 10.15.15:[4]

> *Unguium Dialis et capilli segmina subter arborem felicem terra operiuntur.* „Die abgeschnittenen Haare und Nägel des Dialis sind in die Erde unter einem früchtereichen Baum einzugraben."

Die Ähnlichkeit zwischen dem avestischen und dem römischen Gebrauch wurde schon vor langer Zeit bemerkt.[5] Man kann noch weitere Beispiele zum Vergleich heranziehen. So pflegte man nach der in verschiedenen Ländern Deutschlands üblichen Sitte, das abgeschnittene Haar unter einem Holunderbusche zu begraben usw.[6] Erläutert wurden all diese Parallelen nach der die Köpfe der Forscher jeweils beherrschenden Theorie der Entstehung der Landesgebräuche. In einem Aufsatz, der den indogermanischen Hintergrund des im oben angeführten Abschnitt des Vīdēvdāds geschilderten Brauches behandelt, lehnt LINCOLN die vormals aufgestellten Hypothesen bezüglich dessen Natur ab, beginnend bei FRAZER und endend bei MARY DOUGLAS, und schlägt eine Erklärung vor, der zufolge die Vergrabung des Haares unter einem Baum sowie dessen Gleichstellung mit dem erstrebten Pflanzenwuchs als die den Schöpfungsakt mit der Urmenschenzergliederung nachbildende und der Aufrechterhaltung des Weltbaus dienende Quasi-Opfergabe anzusehen ist.[7] Meines Erachtens fällt hier das das angemessene Maß mißachtende Streben auf, die gesamte Vielfalt der religiösen Phänomene zur Blaupause im Sinne der ELIADEschen Theorie zu machen, was, wie es mit den allbeliebten Theorien häufig geschieht, eher den Nachfolgern denn deren Stifter selber eigen ist. Noch wesenhafter ist die undifferenzierte Hintansetzung der ehemals unangefochtene Autorität genießenden, heutzutage aber als überholt geltenden Ansichten – wie z.B. die Theorie von FRAZER in deren Neigung, alles durch das Apotropäische zu erklären.

Im vorliegenden Falle liegt aber die Erklärung im FRAZERschen Sinne nahe, und im Grunde genommen läuft sie auch dem Herangehen von ELIADE nicht entgegen: Nimmt man als Maßstab die offensichtliche Tatsache an, daß die Gebräuche verschiedener Völker, Haarabschnitte unter einem Baum zu vergraben, auf der Analogie zwischen Haar und Pflanzen beruhen – unabhängig davon, ob diese aus jeweiligem Schöpfungsmythos oder einer primitiven Gedankenverknüpfung stammt – so kommt man letztendlich zum Schluß, es sei unmöglich, die sympathetische Magie ohne Tatsachenzwang aus der Reihe der Erklärungsbegriffe herauszunehmen. Das Haar tritt hier als potentieller Kraftträger im ELIADEschen Sinne auf.[8] Das Wesentlichste in diesem Begriffe ist dessen

4 Siehe ROLFE 1927–1952, II, S. 250–251.

5 Siehe z.B. DARMESTETER 1880, S. 186, n. 3, S. 187, n. 2; DARMESTETER 1895, S. 190, n. 1; REICHELT 1911, S. 154.

6 Siehe WUTTKE 1869, S. 294–295, §464.

7 Siehe LINCOLN 1977, S. 361.

8 Gemeint sind die eine Schüsselrolle im ELIADEschen Ansatz spielenden Begriffe der ‚Kraft' *(force)* und der Kratophanie (s. ELIADE 1949, S. 26–27 et passim).

Doppelgerichtetheit, die auf dem dualistischen Grunde des hochentwickelten Zoroastrismus nicht umhinkonnte, betont zu werden. Noch deutlicher als im Bezug auf die Haarabschnitte tritt sie im Falle der Nägel hervor, wobei das Motiv der zu Dämonenwaffen werdenden Nägel eine spezifischere Parallele im eschatologischen nordischen Mythos findet, und zwar in dem aus den unbeschnittenen Nägeln der Toten gezimmerten Schiffe Naglfar, das in der Zeit der Götterdämmerung die aus der Hölle durchbrechenden Ungeheuer zur Schlacht mit den Göttern und Einherjern fahren soll. Es seien die einschlägigen Stellen des Vīdēvdāds (V 17.7–10) und der Snorra-Edda (Gylfaginning 51) angeführt:

V 17.7–10:[9]

Avesta	PÜ
sruuābiia.[a] *mayəm. auua.kanōiš. ništara.*[b]*naēmāṯ. nmānahe.*[c] Für die Nägel sollst du ein Loch von der Außenseite des Hauses graben,	*sruw rāy may be*[d] *kanišn*[e] *az*[f] *kustag-tar nēmag ī*[g] *mān* Für die Nägel (ist) ein Loch von der Außenseite des Hauses zu graben,
auuaṯ. aipi. yaϑa. kasištahe.[h] *ərəzuuō. fratəməm. +ṯbaṣ̌iš.*[i] geradeso (tief), wie (lang) die Endphalange des kleinen Fingers (ist);	*[ān ī] and abar cand [ān ī] +kahist*[j] *angust frāzdom bazag* über [ein] solches mehr wie [das] vorderste Glied[10] des kleinen Fingers (beträgt);
paiti dim. ābarōiš. Du sollst (die Nägel dahin) einbringen,	*abar +ōy*[k] *[anōh*[l]*] barāh*[m] Darauf [dahin] sollst du (die Nägel) einbringen,
aϑa +imą.[n] *vacō. framruiiå.*[o] *vārəϑraγnīš.*[p] *zaraϑuštra.* dann sollst du diese sieghaften Worte rezitieren, O Zaraϑuštra:	*ēg*[q] *ēn*[r] *gōwišn*[s] *frāz gōwāh*[t] *<ī> pērōzgar zarϑuxšt*[u] dann sollst du diesen Spruch rezitieren, <den>[11] sieghaften, O Zarϑuxšt:

a K^1: *[.](r)auuābiia.* b K^1: *[....](ra).* c Mss.: *nəmānahe.* d K^1: BR[.] e K^1: lac. f K^1: (MN) g K^1: om. h K^1: *(ka)sištahe.* i L^4: *ṯbiṣ̌iš.*; K^1: *ṯbišiš.* Die Lesung *+ṯbašiš.* ist hier laut der in den ältesten indischen Vīdēvdād-Sāde Hss. (wie z. B. L^1, f. 195r, l. 3; B^2, f. 282v, l. 14; M^2, f. 213v, ll. 5–6 usw.) gefundenen Angaben wiederhergestellt. Die vorgeschlagene Emendation wird auch von der Entsprechung *+ṯbašiš.* (V 6.10, 12, 14; 17.7; 18.44) ~ *baši.* (N 90.4, FīŌ 579) bestärkt (s. Appendix 1). j Mss.: kyyšst k L^4: KN; K^1: ʾw' l K^1: TE m L^4: YḆLWNʾh; K^1: [..]LWNʾh n Mss.: *imąm.* o K^1: *fram[.....]* p K^1: *[.......]γnīš.* q L^4: ADYN; K^1: AD[.](N) r L^4: ẔNE; K^1: ẔN[.] s K^1: lac. t L^4: YMRWNʾh u. W praescr.; K1: [.....]ʾh u L4: zltwhšt; K1: zltwšt'

9 Siehe Hss. L^4, ff. 240r, l. 9 – 241v, l. 7; K^1, ff. 283v, l. 13 – 285r, l. 10.

10 Über av. *+ṯbaṣ̌iš-* ‚Glied, Phalange' und dessen Pahlavi Übersetzung bck/*bazag* s. Appendix 1.

11 Das Izāfe, die die Pahlavi Übersetzung mit der avestischen Vorlage in Einklang bringt, ist hier nach der parallelen Stelle V 17.5 ergänzt (s. o.).

Avesta	PÜ
aṣ̌ā.[v] *+vohū.*[w] *manaŋhā.*[x] *yā.*[y] *sruiiē.*[z] *parō.*[aa] *magaonō.*[ab] „Mit Aša und Vohu Manah, durch die ich mich unter den Glaubigen hören lasse“;	*aśwahišt*[ac] *wahman*[ad] *kē srūd ēstēd pad ān*[ae] *ī*[af] *frōddom*[ag] *mayīh*[ah] *[pad ān ī frōddom abēzag wehīh]* „Aświahišt (und) Wahman, die im tiefsten Loche [in der tiefsten heiligen Güte][12] verkündet worden sind“;
xšaϑrāi.[ai] *vairiiāi.*[aj] *<pairi.karəm. pairi.kāraiiōiš.> tišrō.*[ak] *yaṯ. vā. xṣ̌uuaš.*[al] *yaṯ.*[am] *vā. nauua.* Mit einer Metallschneide sollst du <Furchung (um das Loch)> drei(mal) oder sechs(mal) oder neun(mal) <herumziehen>	*pad +xšahrewar*[an] *[pad] pērāmōn*[ao] *kārišnīh*[ap] *pērāmōn [ēd] kārēh se ayāb šaš ayāb*[aq] *nō* Mit einer Metallschneide sollst du [das] (Loch) [durch] Umfurchung drei(mal) oder sechs(mal) oder neun(mal) herumziehen[13]

v K^1:*aṣ̌(ā).* w L^4:*vōhū.*;K^1:*(vō)[..]* x K^1:*[....]ŋhā.* y L^4:*yāsruiiē.* z K^1:*sruiie.* aa L^4: *parāmagaonō.* ab K^1: *ma[.....]* ac K^1: lac. ad L^4: s. l. whwmn scr. ae K^1: lac. af K^1: (Y) ag L^4: plwtwm; K^1: p[.....] ah K^1: mγyh PWN ZK lac. ai K^1: *x(š)[.....]* aj K^1: *[......]āi.* ak L^4: *tiṣ̌arō.* al K^1: *x[.....]* am K^1: *[.](a)ṯ.* an Mss.: xštl ao K^1: [....] mwn ap L^4: k'lšnyh u. s. l. -'- scr.; K^1: k'[...]yh aq K^1: 'd[..] ar K^1: *frasrāuuai[.](ō) iš.* as K^1: *[...]rō.* at K^1: lac. au K^1: 'dwp 6 lac. av K^1: 'šm aw L^4: YHSNNyt; K^1: d'lyt' ax K^1: M[.] ay K^1: 'y[..] az K^1: lac. ba K^1: (B)RA bb L^4: *mrəγa.* bc K^1: ywdt... AYT lac.

12 Der Spruch *aṣ̌ā. vohū. manaŋhā. yā. sruiiē. parō. magaonō.* stellt ein Zitat aus Y 33.7 dar, genauso wie in V 17.5 das Gebet füt Wachstum (Y 48.5) zitiert worden ist (s. Anm. 3). Wie es schon von DARMESTETER (1880, S. 188, Anm. 1; 1895, S. 191, Anm. 3) und REICHELT (1911, S. 154) erkannt wurde, ist im Satz ein Wortspiel benutzt, denn die Form *sruiiē.* kann entweder als 1° Pers. Sgl. Pass. des *sru-* ‚hören‘ oder als Akk. Dual. des *sruuā-* ‚Nagel‘ verstanden werden. REICHELT weist auch auf die dahinterstehende Umdeutung des av. *magaonō.* hin: „‚O *A.*, O *VM.*, the nails of the pure are for you‘ “ (REICHELT 1911, S. 154f.). Meines Erachtens zeigt die kontextbedingte Änderung der Pahlavi-Übersetzung des zitierten Satzes und zwar die Ersetzung des sich auf phl. mγyh/*mayīh* ‚(Gemeinde der) Reine‘ beziehenden Epithets pl'lwn'/*frārōn* ‚gerecht, fromm‘ (J^2, f. 209v, l. 3) oder Adverb plwn'/*parrōn* ‚weg, aus‘ (K^5, f. 166v, l. 13) durch plwtwm/*frōddom* ‚tiefste, niedrigste‘, daß das Wort *mayīh* hier auch umgedeutet und dem vorgehenden mγ/*maγ* ‚Loch‘ gleichgesetzt worden ist. Trotz des üblichen Ansatzes, alle derartigen Abweichungen durch die vermutete Ignoranz der Vīdēvdāds- bzw. PÜ-Verfasser zu erklären, glaube ich, daß es eher an einem zielbewußten Wortspiel liegt. Vgl. Anm. 3.

13 Das Auftauchen der Übersetzung der in den beiden ältesten Handschriften des Pahlavi-Vīdēvdāds ausgelassenen Wörter *pairi.karəm. pairi.kāraiiōiš.* besagt bestimmte Unabhängigkeit der PÜ-Überlieferung von der des avestischen Vīdēvdāds (s. HUMBACH 1973, S. 112f.; CANTERA 2004, S. 28f.). Außerhalb der iranischen Tradition ist das Motiv des vor den Dämonen und dem bösen Geist schützenden magischen Kreises u.a. im slavischen Aberglauben gut bezeugt (s. LEVKIEVSKAJA 2002, S. 37ff.). Dies kann in der Form der um das zu schützende Objekt mit einem Messer, Kohle, Feuerhaken usw. herumzuziehenden Linie, der um ein Dorf oder eine einzelne Hofanlage auszuziehenden Furche usw. auftreten. Einen besonderen Fall des magischen Kreises stellt bei den Slaven der

Avesta	PÜ
ahunəmca. vairīm. frasrāuuaiiōiš.[ar] *tišrō.*[as] *yat̰. vā. xšuuaš. yat̰.*[at] *vā. nauua.* und das Ahuna Vairiia drei(mal) oder sechs(mal) oder neun(mal) rezitieren	*ahunawar-ez frāz srāyēh se ayāb*[au] *šaš ayāb nō [ēn kū fradom aṣ̌əm.*[av] *vohū. se frauuarāne. cē gāh dārēd*[aw] *šnūman <ī> srōš u-š wāz frāz girišn dōlag bālā ēdōn ciyōn az*[ax] *abestāg gōwēd u-š pahnā ēdōn kunišn ī-š ēk*[ay]*-ēk*[az] *andar be*[ba] *ēstēd paiti. tē. mərəγa.*[bb] *jud*[bc]*-dādestān hēnd hast kē pēš gōwēd hast kē pas]* und das Ahunwar drei(mal) oder sechs(mal) oder neun(mal) rezitieren [d.h. zuerst (rezitiere) Aṣ̌əm Vohū, (danach) drei Frauuarāne, denn dies bewahrt den Platz; (daraufhin ist) das Šnūman von Srōš (auszuführen) und sein Wāz (ist) zu nehmen. Die Tiefe des Behälters (muß) so (sein), wie es im Avesta angeordnet (worden ist), und die Breite (ist) so zu machen, daß (die Nägel) dahin im Einzelnen hineinkommen. Die Urteile (im Bezug auf das Gebet) „*Dir, O Vogel…*" sind unterschiedlich: es gibt eine (Autorität), die sagt, (man müsse dies) zuvor (rezitieren), es gibt eine andere, die sagt, (möge es) danach (gemacht werden)].
paiti. tē. ⁺mərəγa.[bd] *aṣ̌ō.zušta.*[be] *imā̊.*[bf] *sruuā̊.*[bg] *vaēδaiiemi.*[bh] „Dir, O Vogel Aṣ̌ōzušta, weise ich diese Nägel zu,	*abar ō*[bi] *tō murw ī*[bj] *ašōzušt [agar] ēn sruw*[bk] *niwēyēnom [kū ēn sruw be ō*[bl] *tō niwēyēnom*[bm]*]* „[Wenn] ich auf dich, O Vogel Ašōzušt, diese Nägel weise [d.h. ich weise dir diese Nägel zu],
imā̊.[bn] *sruuā̊.*[bo] *āuuaēδaiiemi.*[bp] diese Nägel überweise ich;	*[u-t*[bq] *ō] ēn sruw*[br] *niwēyēnom [kū tō be ō*[bs] *ēn sruw niwēyēnom*[bt]*]* [und dich] weise ich zu diesen Nägeln [d.h. ich weise dich diesen Nägeln zu],

bd L^4: *mrəγa.*; K^1: [...]*ə(γ)a.* be K^1: *aṣ̌(ō).zušta.* bf K^1: *im(ā̊).* bg K^1: lac. bh K^1: *vaēδaiieimi.* bi L^4: OL; K^1: ʾw' bj K^1: Y... Z̲NE lac. bk K^1: [.]lw(b)' bl L^4: KN; K^1: ʾw' bm K^1: lac. bn K^1: lac. bo K^1: *s[...]ā̊.* bp K^1: *āuuaēδaiie[..]* bq K^1: APt OL Z̲NE lac. br K^1: [.]lw(b)' bs L^4: s. l. OL scr.; K^1: ʾw' bt K^1: n[......]

Gürtel dar (s. LEVKIEVSKAJA 2002, S. 31–35), was offensichtlich dem Umbinden des sakralen Gürtels (av. *aiβiiåŋhana-*; phl. ʾypyʾ(ng)hn/*ayβyā(ng)han* oder kwstyk(')/*kustīg*) bei den Zoroastriern entspricht.

Avesta	PÜ
imå̄sə.tē.[bu] *sruuå̄.*[bv] *mərəγa.*[bw] *+aṣ̌ō. zušta.*[bx] *hiiārə.*[by] *arštaiiasca. karətaiiasca.* [bz] *ϑanuuarəca.*[ca] *iṣ̌auuasca.*[cb] *ərəzifiiō.* [cc]*parəna.*[cd] *+asanasca.*[ce] *fradaxṣ̌aniia.*[cf] *paiti. daēuuō. māzaniiąn.*[cg] mögen diese Nägel dir, O Vogel Aṣ̌ōzušta, zu Lanzen, Messern, Bogen, mit Adlerfedern befiederte Pfeilen und Schleudersteinen gegen die māzanischen Dämonen werden.“	*awēšān*[ch] *sruw*[ci] *tō murw*[cj] *ī ašōzušt*[ck] *[agar] bawād aštar*[cl] *kārd*[cm] *ud sanwar ud*[cn] *tigr-ez ī +āluh-parr*[co] *ud sag-ez ī kōbēn abar ō dēwān*[cp] *<ī> māzanīgān*[cq] [Wenn] diese Nägel dein werden, O Vogel Aṣ̌ōzušta, (werden sie) zu Lanzen, Messern, Bogen, mit Adlerfedern befiederten Pfeilen und Schleudersteinen gegen die māzanischen Dämonen.“
yezi. nōiṯ. paiti.+vaēδaiieiṇti.[cr] *tå̄. sruuå̄.*[cs] *pascaēta.*[ct] *bun. +māzainiianąm.*[cu] *daēuuanąm.*[cv] *arštaiiasca.*[cw] *karətaiiasca.*[cx] *+ϑanuuarəca.*[cy] *+iṣ̌auuasca. +ərəzifiiō.*[cz] *parəna. +asanasca.*[da] *+fradaxṣ̌aniia.*[db] *paiti. daēuuō. māzaniiąn.*[dc] Wenn sie (d. h. die Māzdayasnier) diese Nägel (dem Vogel Aṣ̌ōzušta) nicht zuweisen, sollen sie (d. h. die Nägel) dann zu Lanzen, Messern, Bogen, mit Adlerfedern befiederten Pfeilen und Schleudersteinen der māzanischen Dämonen werden (…)[14]	*agar*[dd] *nē abar niwēyēnd*[de] *[kū paiti.*[df] *tē.*[dg] *mərəγa. nē gōwēnd] awēšān*[dh] *srū pas*[di] *bawēnd*[dj] *māzanīgān*[dk] *dēwān*[dl] *aštar ud*[dm] *kārd ud sanwar ud*[dn] *tigr-ez ī āluh-parr*[do] *ud*[dp] *sag-ez ī kōbēn ī dēwān ī*[dq] *māzanīgān* Wenn sie (die Nägel dem Vogel Ašōzušt) nicht weisen [d. h. „*Dir, O Vogel…*“ nicht sagen], werden diese Nägel daraufhin zu Lanzen, Messern, Bogen, mit Adlerfedern befiederten Pfeilen und Schleudersteinen der māzanischen Dämonen (…)[15]

bu L^4: *imå̄.sətē.*; K^1: *[..](å̄).se.te.* bv K^1: *srauuå̄.* bw L^4: *marγa.* bx L^4: *aṣ̌aozušta.*; K^1: *a[.]ō.zu[..](a).* by L^4: *hiiarə.* bz K^1: *ka(r)ətai(ia)sca.* ca K^1: *ϑnauuarəca.* cb K^1: *ašauu[…](a).* cc K^1: *ə[….]fiiō.* cd K^1: *paəna.* ce L^4: *asnaca.*; K^1: *asanaca.* cf L^4: *fradaxṣ̌aēniia.* u. *-ē-* del.; K^1: *fradax[.....]a.* cg K^1: *māzaēniiąn.* u. *-ē-* del. ch K^1: OLE(š) […] ci K^1: […](b)[.] cj K^1: m(w)l(w') ck L^4: ʾšwzwšt'; K^1: ʾšwkzwšt' cl Hss.: ʾlštl cm Hss.: SKYNA u. K^1 k praescr. cn K^1: W om. co Hss.: ʾlypl cp K^1: ŠDYAʾn' om. cq K^1: mʾzdy<u>sn</u>ykʾn' u. ŠDYAʾn' add. cr L^4: *vaēδaiianti.*; K^1: *vaēδiianti.* cs K^1: *s(ra)uuå̄.* ct K^1:*pascaeta.* cu L^4:*māzdaiiasnanąm.* u. i. l. *-m* scr.; K^1:*mazaini[.](a)nąm.* cv K^1:*da[…]anąm.* cw L^4: *arštakiiasca.* u. *-k-* del. cx L^4: *karəštaiiasca.*; K^1: *ka[.........]* cy Mss.: *ϑanuuarəca. iṣ̌auuasca.* om. u. ŌḌ add. cz L^4: *ərəzīfiiō.*; K^1: *ərəzīfiō.* da L^4: *asnaca.*; K^1: *asna[..]* db L^4: *fradaxṣ̌niia.*; K^1: *[…](d)axṣ̌aēniia.* dc K^1: lac. dd L^4: HT; K^1: [.]T de K^1: W praescr. df K^1: *pait[.]* dg K^1: *tē. mərəγa. nē* lac. dh K^1: [.]LEšʾn di K^1: AH(L) dj K^1: YHW(W)[..] dk K^1: lac. dl L^4: ŠDYAʾn; K^1: [..](Y)Aʾn dm K^1: om. dn K^1: om. do L^4: ʾlwhpl; K^1: ʾlwh[..] dp K^1: W… kwpyn Y lac. dq K^1: om.

14 Die Wörter *paiti. daēuuō. māzaniiąn.*, sowie ihre Pahlavi Übersetzung *ī dēwān ī māzanīgān*, sind hier unübersetzt gelassen, denn sie stellen eine mechanische Wiederholung derselben Wortfügung („gegen die māzanischen Dämonen“) dar, die den vorgehenden Paragraph (V 17.9) logisch abschließt, aber im vorliegenden Zusammenhang fehl am Platze ist.

15 Die oben zitierte Stelle des Vīdēvdāds ist in der späteren, d. h. Pahlavi und neupersisch-zoroastrischen Literatur mehrmals angedeutet worden, z. B. Großer Bundahišn

Cf. Gylfaginning 51:

> *Þá verðr ok þat, at Naglfar losnar, skip þat, er svá heitir. Þat er gert af nöglum dauðra manna, ok er þat fyrir því varnanar vert, ef maðr deyr með óskornum nöglum, at sá maðr eykr mikit efni til skipsins Naglfars, er goðin ok menn vildi seint, at gert yrði.*
>
> „Dann geschieht es auch, daß das Naglfar gelöst wird, das Schiff, das so heißt. Dies ist aus den Nägeln der toten Männer gemacht worden. Und deswegen wird gewarnt: wenn ein Mann mit unabgeschnittenen Nägeln sterbe, setzt dieser Mann viel Baustoff dem Schiffe Naglfar zu, von dem die Götter und die Menschen kaum wünschen, daß es hergestellt werde."

Es lassen sich weitere Beispiele des Glaubens heranziehen, daß die Nägel als Lebenskraftsträger angesehen werden, und daß darum Vorsichtsmaßnahmen dagegen zu treffen sind, einem fremden bzw. feindlichen Wesen Zugang zu ihnen zu ermöglichen. Nach dem norwegischen Aberglauben muß man die abgeschnittenen Nägel begraben oder verbrennen, damit sie nicht in die Hände der dämonischen Wesen (Huldrevolks oder Elben) bzw. der Finnen[16] geraten, andernfalls machen jene die Kugel davon, um damit das Vieh zu schießen.[17] In der slawischen Tradition stellen Nägel sowie Zähne die Stätte der Lebenskraft dar. Das ist der Grund dafür, daß kein Hexenmeister seine Nägel abschneidet und so nach diesem Merkmal erkannt werden kann.[18] Hervorzuheben ist in diesem Zusammenhang, daß weder das Avesta noch die verwandten indogermanischen Traditionen die Haar- und Nägelabschnitte mit Unreinheit assoziieren. Diese Kategorie hat zwar mit der im Eliadeschen Sinne aufgefaßten sakralen Kraft viel zu tun, dennoch sind die beiden Begriffe reinlich auseinanderzuhalten. Im Laufe der Entwicklung der zoroastrischen Orthopraxie wurde der Fall der Haare und Nägel gerade im Sinne der Behandlung des Unreinen umgedeutet, und die einschlägigen Objekte sind in die umfassende Kategorie der intravitalen Abfälle (phl. *hixr* bzw. *hixr-nasā*)[19] geraten. So erwähnen die eng mit

24.29–30 (Hs. TD^2, S. 154.15–155.4), Šāyast nē Šāyast 12.6 (s. Kotwal 1969, S. 28–29), Ṣad dar Naṣr 14 (Dhabhar 1909, S. 13–14), Rivāyat-e Kāmah Bohrah (s. Unvala 1922, Bd. I, S. 246.13–247.11, Dhabhar 1932, S. 250), Rivāyat-e Kāmdīn Šāpūr (s. Unvala 1922, Bd. I, S. 247.13–19, Dhabhar 1932, S. 250–251).

16 Vgl. die avestischen „mazānischen Dämonen", die die beiden Eigenschaften, d.h. die Dämonität und die fremde Herkunft, vereinen.

17 Siehe Meyer 1883, S. 523.

18 Siehe Levkievskaja 2000, S. 383.

19 Die Beziehung zwischen den Begriffen *hixr* und *nasā* wurde ausführlich von König (2010, S. 341–345) betrachtet. Wie er gezeigt hat, ist das Verhältnis ambig, und die Definitionen von Quelle zu Quelle variieren. So ist die kennzeichnende Eigenschaft des *hixr* dem *nasā* gegenüber nach Dādestān ī dēnīg, sowie nach Pahlavi Rivāyat zum Dādestān ī dēnīg seine Trockenheit (Dd 16.9, PRDd 55.3, s. König 2010, S. 344–345). Dementgegen bestimmt der Pahlavi Kommentar zum V 5.4, der ‚Leichnam' *(nasā)* werde ‚Exkrement' *(hixr)* nachdem dieser von einem Geier gegessen (und gekotet) worden sei (s. König 2010, S. 341). Damit scheint der primäre Unterschied jener zwischen dem ‚Leichnam'und dem ‚Exkrement' zu sein, was auch immer sein physischer Zustand sein mag. Dieselbe Idee

der PÜ des Vīdēvdāds verbundenen, doch zur späteren Stufe der zoroastrischen Exegetik gehörenden, Bußgebete Patit ī pašēmānīh und Patit ī murdagān[20] Haar und Nägel zusammen mit Zahnstocher[21] und den nach dem Schlafe für unrein geltenden Händen[22]:

---

wird in Dēnkard 5.12.2 (DkM 444.22–445.4, s. AMOUZGAR/TAFAZZOLI 2000, S. 48–49, KÖNIG 2010, S. 342) erläutert, wo *nasā* und *hixr* als „zwei Arten Leichnam" *(dō ēwēnag murdag)* genannt worden sind. Da die Bedeutung des *nasā* als selbstverständlich gilt, wird dies ohne weiteres erwähnt, während das *hixr* als „abgestorbene Körperteile eines lebendigen Wesens" bestimmt wird: *ud abar pahikaftagīh <ī> harw dō ēwēnag murdag ēk nasā ēk abārīg hixr ciyōn daštān <ud> šuδr ud xōn ud mēšag ud +xāyūg ud abārīg ī az mardōm ud sag <ud> abārīg gyānwar ī rēman-pid andar zīndagīh bahrīhā mīrēd* „Und über das Berühren der beiden Arten Leichnam, (derer) eine *nasā* (ist) und (derer andere) die übrigen (Arten) *hixr* (bestehen), wie z.B. Menstrual(blut), Samen, Blut, Harn, Schleim und die anderen (Exkrete) des Menschen, des Hunds und der anderen Lebewesen unreinen Fleisches, (welche Exkrete) im (Laufe) des Lebens teilweise absterben." So leuchtet es ein, daß das *nasā* in diesem Zusammenhang als Sonderfall des *hixr* zu betrachten ist. Wahrscheinlich wurde die Bedeutung des letzten Begriffs späterhin zu dem, was hier als *abārīg hixr* d.h. „alle Arten *hixr*, die nicht *nasā* sind" bestimmt worden ist, beschränkt. Insofern das *nasā* die allerhöchste besudelnde Kraft aufweist, ist zu vermuten, daß die Haltung des Dādestān ī dēnīg sowie des Pahlavi Rivāyat (Dd 16.9, PRDd 55.3, s. oben) sich dadurch erklärt. Die semantische Verwandtschaft der beiden Begriffe hat das asyndetische Syntagma bzw. Hendiadys *hixr-nasā* hervorgerufen, das entweder *hixr* und *nasā* umfaßt oder dem *hixr* synonym ist.

20 Die Pahlavi-Bußgebete Patit ī pašēmānīh und Patit ī murdagān haben einen gemeinsamen Kern. Der einzige Unterschied zwischen den beiden Texten besteht im Refrain, der sich in Patit ī pašēmānīh auf die Buße der eigenen Sünden des Pönitents und in Patit ī murdagān auf jene für die Sünden seiner verstorbenen Verwandten bezieht. Da die vorliegende Stelle zum gemeinsamen Hauptteile der beiden Texte gehört, ist sie hier aufgrund aller einschlägigen Handschriften, zu denen ich mir Zugang verschaffen konnte, dargestellt worden. Der Pahlavi Patit ī pašēmānīh befindet sich in den Hss. TD[23] und Parsi 3/4, während der Pahlavi Patit ī murdagān in einer einzigen Hs., K[27], enthalten ist. Aus dem Vergleich mit den vom berühmten Pahlavi Schreiber Pešōtan Rām Kāmdīn umgeschriebenen Handschriften, z.B. M[51a], M[51b], Parsi 3/4 usw., wird deutlich, daß die Hs. K[27] von derselben Hand stammt und somit zu den ältesten Pahlavi-Sprachdenkmälern zählt. Obwohl sie nicht nur dank diesem Umstand, sondern auch inhaltlich in mehrfacher Hinsicht einzigartig ist (vgl. oben über Patit ī murdagān), wurde deren Edition durch HAMPEL (1974) einer strengen Kritik unterzogen, die wohl teilweise gerechtfertigt war, aber die die wertvolle Handschrift für lange Zeit dem wissenschaftlichen Gebrauch zu Unrecht entzog. Die gegenwärtig vorbereitete Edition der Bußabschnitte des Xorde Avesta verfolgt den Zweck, diesen Irrtum richtigzustellen.

21 Über die Etymologie von phl. KKA-pl(y)š(n') / *dandān-parišn* ‚Zahnstocher' s. Appendix 2.

22 Im Falle der Entsprechung phl. špyk/*šabīg* ~ pāz. *šavīn.* (vgl. die Pāzand-Versionen: ANTIÂ 1909, S. 121, l. 6: *dasta.šavī*; oder E[1], f. 48v, sin. marg.: *dast.šavī*) befassen wir uns wahrscheinlich mit einer Kontamination zweier sinnverwandten, dennoch differenzierten Begriffe: phl. *dast <ī> šabīg* ‚Nachthände' (s. DHABHAR 1963, S. 109, Anm. 5 (5)), d.h. die Hände, die nach dem Schlafe schmutzig (d.h. mit dem Ochsenharn ungewaschen) geblieben sind, und np. *dast-šūy* , Händewaschen, Ochsenharn; Pottasche' (DHABHAR 1932, S. 633; STEINGASS 1892, S. 523). Die Authentizität des seltenen technischen Terminus im Pahlavi YDE Y špyk / *dast ī šabīg* ist unter anderem aus der folgenden Stelle des Ardā Wirāz Nāmag ersichtlich (AWN 58.3): *ēn ruwān ī ōy druwand mard kē-š pad*

Patit ī pašēmānīh / Patit ī murdagān 6.1–4[23]
pad patit hēm[a] *az wināh*[b] *<ī>... mōy*[c] *nāxun*[d] *dandān*[e]*-parišn*[f] *dast <ī> šabīg*
„Ich büße die Sünde <der>... (Vernachlässigung der Pflicht im Bezug auf) Haar, Nägel, Zahnstocher (und) die ‚Nachthände' "

a TD^{23}: HWEm om. b K^{27}: 's c K^{27}: m praescr. d Parsi 3/4: W praescr. e TD^{23}, K^{27}: KKA; Parsi 3/4: dnd'n' f TD^{23}: plšn›; Parsi 3/4: plyš; K^{27}: plynš

Wie unten gezeigt wird, bewahren die späteren zoroastrischen Gebräuche sowie ihre Arealparallelen trotz der obigen Systemumsetzung Spuren der früheren Vorstellungen, nämlich die Zuschreibung von übernatürlichen Kräften an Nägel, sowie die mit ihnen sekundär assoziierten Gegenstände (wie z.B. Zahnstocher).[24] So wird die aus der Fahrlässigkeit dem Zahnstocher gegenüber stammende Gefahr in Šāyast nē šāyast 10.20 und 12.13 betrachtet:

---

gētīg sar ud rōy ī xwēš <ud> ***dast ī šabīg*** *ud abārīg rēmanīh ī handam ī xwēš pad āb ī ēstādag <ī> wuzurg ud xānīg <ī> rawān was šust ud hōrdat amahraspand āzard* „Das ist die Seele jenes sündhaften Mannes der, (während des Lebens) in der körperlichen Welt, Kopf, Gesicht, **Nachthände**, und die übrige Unreinheit seiner Glieder im grossen stehenden Wasser und (in den) Quellen des fließenden (Wassers) häufig wusch und Hōrdat Amahraspand peinigte." Die Notwendigkeit, die schmutzigen Hände (phl. *dast ī šabīg*) beim Aufstehen zuerst mit dem Ochsenharn (phl. *gōmēz*, *āb ī zarr*, np. *gūmīz*, *āb-e zarr*, *dast-šūy*) zu waschen, ist in *Ṣad dar Bundeheš* 78.7 erwähnt worden (s. Dhabhar 1909, S. 149; vgl. Übersetzung Dhabhar 1932, S. 558): *bāmdād naxost dast ba āb-e zarr bebāyad šostan va pas ba āb-e pāk va har cīz-ī palīdī bar andām bāšad tā zang mānde bavad va pāk na šavad be-bāyad brīdan be parhīxtan* „Im Morgenrot muß man die Hände zuerst mit dem ‚goldenen Wasser' (d.h. dem Ochsenharn, D.B.) und daraufhin mit dem reinen Wasser waschen. Sollte eine Unreinheit auf einem Körperteil sein, folglich (irgendein) Rost (darauf) geblieben sein und (trotz des Waschens) nicht sauber werden, ist es durch Schneiden zu entfernen."

23 Siehe Hss. TD^{23}, f. 108r, ll. 5, 7; Parsi 3/4, S. 4, l. 11; 5, ll. 4–5; K^{27}, S. 61, ll. 14–15; 62, l. 5.

24 Daß die späteren Substitute der Nägel die mit den letzten assoziierten Vorstellungen (nämlich ihre Fähigkeit, unter Umständen zu Waffen der Dämonen zu werden) ererbt haben, ergibt sich u. a. aus der folgenden Stelle des Andarz ī Dastwarān ō Weh-dēnān (s. Jamasp-Asana 1913, S. 123–124; ADWd 18–19): 18 *pursīd kū *abargīr ud dandān-parišn sar ō zamīg abāyēd mālīdan ayāb nē* 19 *guft hād abāyēd ēd rāy cē myazd ī wehān ka pad nērōg <ī> yazdān kunēnd tā mardōmān pēš az freh-būd-xwarišnīh *abargīr ud dandān-parišn dārēnd ahreman ud dēwān <ud> wišūdagān pad garānōmandīh anāgīh ēstēnd ud ka *abargīr ud dandān-parišn sar ō zamīg nē mālēnd ō zēn-abzār ī ahreman ud dēwān rasēd hast-ešān pad ān nērōg drust tuwān kardan* „18 (Man) fragte: ‚Muß (man) den Wischer (?) und die Zahnstocherspitze an der Erde abstreichen oder nicht?' 19 Sei gesagt: ‚(Man) muß deshalb, weil während des Mahls, das die Gerechten durch Gottes Kraft machen, solang die Menschen sich vor dem übermäßigen Essen an den Wischer (?) und den Zahnstocher machen, bleiben Ahreman, die Dämonen und die Ausgeburten (der Hölle) in Schwere und Unheil, aber wenn sie den Wischer (?) und die Zahnstocherspitze an der Erde nicht abstreichen, wird (dies) zu Waffen Ahremans und der Dämonen; (So verhalten) heißt sie dadurch kräftig, gesund und mächtig machen.' " Das Wort <'plgyl> ist hier aufgrund des np. *bar-gereftan* (Präsensstamm *bar-gir-*) ‚wegnehmen, abwischen' als *abargīr* transkribiert und als ‚Wischer' übersetzt worden. Wahrscheinlich wird darunter ein Gegenstand verstanden, mit dem man die Lippen abwischen kann.

ŠnŠ 10.20[25]
ēk ēn kū dandān-⁺parišn[a] *pōst*[b] *pāk be tāšišn cē dastwarān cāšt kū ka-š*[c] *dandān-parišn pad pōst ō*[d] *dahan kard be ōftēd ud zan ī*[e] *ābustan ka-š pāy abar nīhēd pad nasā būdan bīmōmand*[f]
„Eins ist das, daß die Basthaut des Zahnstochers rein abzulösen ist, denn die (religiösen) Authoritäten belehrten: Wenn (jemand, nachdem) er den Zahnstocher mit der Basthaut in den Mund gesteckt hat, (diesen) fallenläßt, und wenn eine schwangere Frau sich (diesen) unter die Füße tritt, ängstigt sie sich vor dem Leichnam-Werden (des Nasciturus)."

a Hss.: plš b K[20]: KN PWME add. et del. c K[20]: AMT d K[20]: KN e K[20]: Y om. f Hss.: bym ʾwmnd

ŠnŠ 12.13[26]
ēk ēn kū dandān-parišn[a] *tōf xūb az-eš bē tāšišn*[b] *cē pōryōtkēšān hast kē guft kū kē-š tōf abar ō dandān kunēnd ud bē abganēnd zan ī*[c] *ābustan kē-š*[d] *pāy abar nīhēd pad nasā būdan gumān*
„Eins ist das, daß die (Ober)schicht des Zahnstochers gut abzulösen ist, denn es gibt (einen der) Urlehrer, der sagte, daß diejenigen, die dessen (Ober)schicht auf die Zähne legen und (diesen) wegwerfen, die schwangere Frau, die sich (diesen) unter die Füße tritt, das Leichnam-Werden (des Nasciturus) argwöhnen (lassen)."

a Hss.: plšnʾ b K[20]: tʾššnʾ om. c K[20]: Y om. d K[20]: s. l. MNW pʾd QDM HNHTWNyt scr.

Dieselbe Idee ist im neupersischen Traktat Ṣad dar Naṣr 17 (Dhabhar 1909, S. 15) ausgedrückt worden:

1. *inke cun xelāl tarāšand yā cub-i dar bon-e dandān xᵛāhand kardan bāyad ke pust na-dārad*
2. *ke agar pust andak māye bar-ān bavad cun dar dandān konand va beyafganand agar zan-e ābestan pāy bar ān nehad bim ān bavad ke kudak ba-ziyān āyad*

„1. Wenn man den (Interdental)raum putzt oder die Zahnwurzeln mit einem Stikken bearbeiten will, darf man die Basthaut nicht beibehalten;
2. Denn wenn eine Kleinmenge Basthaut darauf bleibt, wenn man (den) bei den Zähnen anwendet und wegwirft, (so) wenn eine schwangere Frau (diesen) unter die Füße tritt, entsteht die Befürchtung, daß dem Kind Schaden zugefügt werden."

Erstaunlicherweise zeigt diese Glaube einen merkwürdigen Anklang an eine im Babylonischen Talmud (Moʿed Kaṭan 18a) enthaltene Vorstellung:

šlšh dbrym nʾmrw bṣprnym hqwbrn ṣdyq śwrpn ḥsyd zwrqn ršʿ ṭʿmʾ mʾy šmʾ tʿbwr ʿlyhn ʾšh ʿwbrh wtpyl
„Drei Dinge wurden über die Nägel ausgesagt: ‚Derjenige, der sie vergräbt, ist gerecht; derjenige, der sie verbrennt, ist tugendhaft, und derjenige, der sie wegwirft,

25 Siehe Hss. K[20], f. 72r, ll. 14–18; M[51a]: ff. 107r, l. 17 – 107v, l. 5; Tavadia 1930, S. 136.
26 Siehe Hss. K[20], f. 168v, ll. 11–14; M[51a], f. 133v, ll. 6–11; Kotwal 1969, S. 30–31.

ist ein Bösewicht!‘ Was ist der Sinn? Damit eine schwangere Frau sie sich unter die Füße tritt und abortiert.“

Obwohl die Pahlavi-Texte die mit dem Zahnstocher verbundenen Regeln behandeln, während im Talmud die Nägel betrachtet werden, ist mit Sicherheit zu vermuten, daß die Ansätze beider Traditionen im vorliegenden Falle aus derselben Wurzel stammen, zumal, wie wir gesehen haben, der Zahnstocher und die Nägel im späten Zoroastrianismus zusammenhängen. Wahrscheinlich ist es gerade die talmudische Tradition, die im vorliegenden Falle die archaische Verbindung widerspiegelt. Die nichttriviale Analogie zwischen den zwei oben angeführten Aberglauben erklärt sich vermutlich durch den großzügigen gegenseitigen Ideenaustausch zwischen dem iranischen und dem semitischen Kulturgebiet in Spätantike und Frühmittelalter. Ob die Quelle der Entlehnung der iranischen oder der semitischen bzw. hebräischen Tradition zugehört, bedarf aber weiterer Forschung.

Appendix 1: av. +*t̰baṣ̌iš-* ‚Glied, Phalange‘ ~ *baši.* ‚ein Längenmaß' ~ phl. bck/*bazag* ‚id.‘

Die PÜ des av. +*t̰baṣ̌iš-*[27] ‚Glied, Phalange‘, d. h. bck/*bazag* ist der von av. *baši.* ‚ein Längenmaß‘ gleich: av. +*baṣ̌i.drājaŋhō.*[28] ~ PÜ bck dlʾhnʾy / *bazag-drahnā* (N 90.4); av. *baši.* ~ PÜ bcynk/**bazēnag* (FīŌ 579), s. Kotwal/Kreyenbroek 2009, S. 98f.; Klingenschmitt 1968, S. 173f.[29] Die dadurch bewiesene semantische Identität, sowie die naheliegende phonetische Vergleichbarkeit zweier avestischen Bezeichnungen des der Fingergliedsbreite entsprechenden Längenmaßes veranlaßte Henning, deren ursprüngliche Gleichheit zu vermuten (Henning 1942, S. 235, Anm. 6). Später wies Klingenschmitt auf die damit verbundenen, jedoch seiner eigenen Annahme nach überbrückbaren, formalen Schwierigkeiten hin (Klingenschmitt, ibid.). Bei beiden Forschern kam es jedoch nicht zum naheliegenden Versuch, die etymologische Erklärung der avestischen Formen im Zusammenhang mit denen der Pahlavi-Übersetzung zu geben. Die Vermutung Horns (1893, S. 43), phl. <bck> ‚Phalange, Fingerglied‘ sei eine Nebenform des wck/*waccag* (> np. *bacce* ‚Jungtier, Kind, Bursche‘ usw.), ist angesichts des Anlauts der avestischen Formen aufzugeben. Noch angreifbarer

27 Siehe oben.

28 Hs. HJ: *baṣ̌idrajaŋhō.*, f. 191 v, l. 10.

29 Jenseits der Pahlavi-Übersetzung des Vīdēvdāds kommt diese Längenmaßbezeichnung in einer wahrscheinlich auch vom Avesta abstammenden Stelle des Dēnkards vor: … *dahrag ī cand angust ī kahist frāzdom bazag* „… eine Sichel (lang wie) ein paar vorderste Glieder des kleinen Fingers“ (DkM 718.21–22). Vgl. PV 17.7 *cand [ān ī]* +*kahist angust frāzdom bazag*, wo phl. *cand* ‚wieviel, soviel, ein Paar‘ irrtümlicherweise dem av. *yaϑa.* ‚(in dem Maße) wie‘ entspricht.

ist der Versuch Klingenschmitts, das angeblich aus dem ai. **buzaina-* stammende Pahlavi-Geistwort **būcīnā*, sowie die statt <bck> stellenweise vorkommende Nebenform <bwck>[30] zur Erklärung des Pahlavi-Worts heranzuziehen (Klingenschmitt 1968, S. 173f.). Das entscheidende Argument dagegen stellt die Tatsache dar, daß aram. *bwṣynʾ* ‚eine Pflanze, Lampendocht', das auch in den Pahlavi-Heterogrammen BWṢYNA/*xiyār* ‚Gurke' und HLBWṢYNA/*harbūzag* ‚Wassermelone' erscheint (Nyberg 1988, S. 4, 43, 67), zweifellos aus dem gleichbedeutenden Akkadischen *buṣīnu(m)* bzw. *buṣinnu(m)* entlehnt worden ist. Da der akkadische Pflanzenname seit der altakkadischen Periode bezeugt ist (Oppenheim et al. 1965, S. 348), ist die Hypothese von dessen iranischer Etymologie ohne weiteres indiskutabel.

Indessen liefern die obigen Formen alles, dessen die etymologische Beurteilung der Sippe bedarf. Der bivariante Anlaut der avestischen Formen setzt urar. **du̯-* voraus (vgl. einerseits gav. *dvaēšah-* vs. jav. *t̲baēšah-* ‚Feindschaft', andererseits av. *dva-* ‚zwei' vs. *biš* ‚zweimal'). Phl. bck/*bazag* und bcynk/**bazēnag* weisen somit die nordwestiranische Entwicklung **du̯-* > *b-* auf. Die Entsprechung av. *-š-* ~ phl. *-z-* (< **-c-*) kann in derselben Weise erklärt werden, wie av. *apaši.* (Nom. Sing. Fem.) ‚rückwärts' (Yt 10.20) vs. phl. *abāz* ‚id.' (Adv.), d. h. durch den analogen Ausgleich des Deklinationsparadigmas oder, einfach ausgedrückt, den Wandel des ursprünglichen **-ci* zu *-ši* in Analogie zu den unbelegten obliquen Kasus, wo **-ci̯-* > *-š-* regelmäßig ist (vgl. Bartholomae 1893, S. 266f. im Bezug auf das av. *apaši.* vs. aind. *ápācī*). So ist die hinter dem av. *baši.* (< **bacī-*) stehende urarische Form wie ein Kompositum mit dem zweiten Glied *-Hn̥c-*: *-Hanc-* (~ aind. *-n̥c-*: *-añc-*), stammend aus dem idg. **h₂enk-* ‚biegen' (LIV, S. 268), d. h. **du̯-Hn̥c-ī-* < idg. **du̯-h₂n̥k-ih₂-* ‚Gelenk' (lit. ‚die Doppeltbiegende') wiederherzustellen. Semantisch ist diese Etymologie ganz trivial, und formal ist sie wiederum mit m. *apą̇š.*/f. *apaši.* (~ aind. m. *ápāṅ*/f. *ápācī*), sowie mit *fraš* (Nom. Sing. Mask.) ‚vorwärts' (~ aind. *prāṅ* ‚id.') usw. vergleichbar. So muß die aktuelle Stammform mit dem langen *-ī-*, d. h. *bašī-* (und nicht **baši-*, wie bei Bartholomae 1904, S. 952) wiederhergestellt werden. Dies stimmt auch mit der in Frahang ī ōīm vorkommenden Form *baši.* (K^{20}: *baṣ̌i.*, f. 83v, l. 8; M^{51a}: *baši.*, f. 123v, l. 17) überein (für den von Bartholomae angenommenen Stamm **baši-* würde man Nom. Sing. Fem. **bašiš.* erwarten). Da das kurze *-i* im ἅπαξ λεγόμενον *⁺baṣ̌i.drājaŋhō.* (N 90.4; Hs. HJ: *baṣ̌idrajaŋhō.*, s. o.) geradeso gut dem ursprünglichen *-ī* wie dem *-i* entsprechen kann, so gibt es keinen Anhalt dafür, die vermutete Stammform *bašī-* (< **bacī-*) auszuschließen. Was den Stamm *⁺t̲baṣ̌iš-* betrifft, ist dieser wahrscheinlich als ein sekundäres Derivat mit dem aus dem *bašī-* übertragenen *-š-* anzusehen.

30 Siehe V 6.10, Hs. K^1, f. 116r, l. 7.

Appendix 2: phl. KKA-pl(y)š(n')/ *dandān-parišn* ‚Zahnstocher'

Die Etymologie der Bezeichnung des Zahnstochers im Persischen ist von großem Interesse nicht nur schlechthin, sondern auch als Fallstudie für das gegenseitige Verhältnis zwischen dem Pahlavi und dem neuersischen Lautsystem. JUNKER (1912, S. 19, Anm. 2) verglich phl. pl(y)š(n') mit <plš> (*Ayādgār ī Zarērān* 100, 103–105), welches üblicherweise als ‚Lanze' übersetzt und von BARTHOLOMAE (1906, S. 144) mit dem zweiten Bestandteil des avestischen Kompositums *ərəzatō.frašna-* (Yt 10.112) identifiziert wird.[31] Was auch immer das tatsächliche Verhältnis zwischen phl. <plš> und av. **frašna-* oder **frašan-* (s. BARTHOLOMAE, ibid.) sein mag – keines der beiden Wörter ist mit der Pahlavi-Bezeichnung des Zahnstochers vergleichbar, nicht nur aus dem semantischen Grunde, auf den TAVADIA (1930: 136, n. 20[1]) zurecht hinwies,[32] sondern auch angesichts np. *dandān-āfrīz*, *-āprīz*, *-farīz*, *-parīz*, *-āfrīš*, *-ăprīš*, *-farīš* und *-parīš* ‚Zahnstocher' (STEINGASS 1892, S. 538). Das Vorgehen mancher das vorliegende Problem behandelnden Forscher, die Formen, die aus dem Rahmen des vorgefaßten Schemas des Verhältnisses zwischen dem Mittel- und dem Neupersischen fallen, aus der Betrachtung auszuschließen, ist methodologisch unannehmbar. So behauptet TAVADIA (ibid.) daß „...since *ăprīš* is not possible (sic! D. B.), we may not trust *parīš*, whereas *afrīš* and *farīš* speak for (Pahlavi, D. B.) *frēš*". Die neupersischen Formen mit dem auslautenden -z sind von ihm überhaupt unerwähnt geblieben. Mit Rücksicht darauf, daß a) manche Pahlavi Formen das *-y-* enthalten, die anderen aber nicht; b) dasselbe auch für das auslautende *-n* gilt; c) es Varianten der neupersischen Fortsetzung des phl. pl(y)š(n') mit den anlautenden *p-* und *ăp-* gibt und d) die neupersischen Formen zwischen *-š* und *-z* schwanken, gelangen wir zur Etymologie phl. *parišn* < air. **pari-riź-na-* (vgl. av. *raēz-*, np. *lištan* ‚lekken') mit einer Haplologie und der regelmäßigen Entwicklung air. **-źn-* > pers. *-šn-*. Die einzige „echte" neupersische Form ist *parīz*, die aus der Etymonsvariante **pari-raiź-* (< idg. **lei̯ǵ^h-* ‚lecken', s. LIV, S. 404) stammt. Np. *āfrīz*, *-farīz*, *-āfrīš*, *-farīš*, d.h. all die Formen mit dem anlautenden oder dem inlautenden /f/, sind durch den arabischen Einfluß (vgl. np. *fārsī* ~ phl. *pārsīg*, np. *fīrūz* ~ phl. *pērōz*, np. *tanāfūr* ~ phl. *tanāpuhl* usw.) ohne weiteres erklärbar, während die umgekehrte Entsprechung, d.h. phl. /f/ ~ np. /p/ kaum wahrscheinlich ist. Die neupersischen Formen mit dem auslautenden *-īš* sind als aus demselben Etymon

31 Diese Identifizierung wurde auch von GERSHEVITCH (1959, S. 261) und MALANDRA (1973, S. 276), meines Glaubens zu eilfertig, angenommen. Die alternative Gleichsetzung des phl. pl(y)š(n') mit av. *parša-* ‚Getreideähre' von JUNKER (ibid.) überzeugt auch nicht, denn sie läßt die neupersischen Formen mit dem auslautenden -z unberücksichtig (s. unten).

32 BAILEY (1953, S. 31) lehnt Einwendungen TAVADIAS ohne ausreichenden Grund ab. SHAKED (1992, S. 149, Anm. 35) nimmt die Identität des phl. pl(y)š(n') ‚Zahnstocher' mit plš/**fraš* ‚Lanze' ohne weiteres an.

wie phl. pl(y)š(n')/*parišn* stammend, mit dem zweiten Vokal unter dem Einfluß des np. *parīz* usw. ausgedehnt, oder als Darstellungen des alternativen Etymons **pari-raiš-* < urar. **pari-raįj*^{h}*ž-* (< idg. **leįǵ*^{h}*-s-*) mit Auslautsverhärtung zu erklären.[33] Ein Einfluß anderer Natur tritt in den neupersischen Formen mit dem anlautenden *ā-* auf, die wahrscheinlich durch den Einfluß des in der Wendung *dandān āfrīn kardan* „1. dentes polire 2. dentiscalpium facere" (VULLERS 1855, S. 910) vorkommenden np. *āfrīn* zu erklären sind.

Bibliographie

Handschriften

B^2 *The Avestan manuscript B2 (Vīdēvdād Sāde) of the Bombay University Library.* Avestan Digital Archive Series 3. Hrsg. von J.J. FERRER. Salamanca 2008.

E^1 *The Khorda Avesta and Yašt Codex E1. Facsimile Edition.* Hrsg. von F.M. KOTWAL und A. HINTZE. Wiesbaden 2008 (Iranica 16).

HJ *Nirangistan. A Photozincographed Faximile of a MS. Belonging to Shams-ul-Ulama Dastur Dr. Hoshangjee Jamaspjee of Poona.* Hrsg. von D.P. SANJANA. Bombay 1894.

J^2 1. *The Ancient Manuscript of the Yasna with its Pahlavi Translation (A.D. 1323) Generally Quoted as* J_2 *and now in the Possession of the Bodleian Library. Reproduced in Facsimile and Edited, with an Introductory Note by L.H. MILLS, D.D., Translator of the Zend-Avesta, Part III ('Sacred Books of the East', Vol. XXXI).* Oxford 1893.
2. *The Avestan manuscript J2_500 (Yasna Indian Pahlavi) of the Bodleian Library (University of Oxford).* Avestan Digital Archive Series 28. Hrsg. von J.J. FERRER. Salamanca 2012.

K^1 *The Avesta Codices K3a, K3b and K1. Codices Avestici et Pahlavici Bibliothecae Universitatis Hafniensis.* Hrsg. von K. BARR und H. IBSCHER. Copenhagen 1941.

K^5 *The Avesta Codex K 5. Codices Avestici et Pahlavici Bibliothecae Universitatis Hafniensis.* 3 Teile, Bd. VII–IX. Hrsg. von K. BARR. Copenhagen 1937–1939.

K^{20} *The Avesta Codices K 20 and K 20b. Codices Avestici et Pahlavici Bibliothecae Universitatis Hafniensis.* Bd. I. Hrsg. von A. CHRISTENSEN. Copenhagen 1931.

33 Vgl. av. ^{1}*naēza-* ‚Spitze', phl. *nēzag* ‚Speer' (< ai. **naiź-*, idg. **neįǵh-* ‚durchstoßen') ~ np. *nīš* ‚Stachel', *nīštar* ‚Lanze'. Das armenische Lehnwort *patnēš* ‚χάραξ, Palisadenwall' (< mwi. **patnēš* < ai. **pati-naiš-*, vgl. georg. *p̣aṭnez-* ‚Dammschüttung, Pfahl, Pfahlzaun, Nagel' < mwi. **patnēz* < ai. **pati-naiź-*) stammt letzendlich aus dem urar. **pati-naįjhž-* < idg. **neįǵh-s-* mit Auslautsverhärtung, s. BELARDI 1962, S. 153, 157f.; GIPPERT 1993, Bd. I, S. 202–203.

K[27]	Königliche Bibliothek zu Kopenhagen, ungefähr das 14. Jh. AD.
L[1]	*The Avestan manuscript L1_4200 (Indian Vīdēvdād Sāde) of the British Library*. Avestan Digital Archive Series 38. C. REDARD (Hrsg.). Salamanca 2012.
L[4]	*The Avestan manuscript L4 (Pahlavi Vīdēvdād) of the British Library*. Avestan Digital Archive Series 5. A. CANTERA (Hrsg.). Salamanca 2008.
M[2]	*The Avestan manuscript M2 (Vīdēvdād Sāde) of the Bayerische Staatsbibliothek in Munich*. Avestan Digital Archive Series 12. M. Á. ANDRÉS-TOLEDO (Hrsg.). Salamanca 2009.
M[51a]	Cod. Zend. 51a, Bayerische Staatsbibliothek, München (s. BARTHOLOMAE 1915, S. 38–56).
Parsi MS 3/4	ein Teil der Komposithandschrift Parsi MS 4 (Wilson no. 12), John Rylands University Library, Manchester, ungefähr Ende des 14 Jh. A. D., sechs vereinzelte Folios.
TD[23]	*Khorde Avesta & an Incomplete Pahlavi Text of the Mēnōy i Xrat*. KH. M. JAMASP ASA, M. NAWABI und M. TAVOUSI (Hrsg.). Shiraz, 1976 (The Pahlavi Codices and Iranian Researches 4).

Sekundärliteratur

AMOUZGAR, J. / A. TAFAZZOLI 2000: *Le cinquième livre du Dēnkart. Transcription, traduction et commentaire*. Paris (Studia Iranica. Cahier 23.).

ANTIÂ, E. K. 1909: *Pâzend Texts*. Trustees of the Parsee Punchâyet (Hrsg.). Bombay.

BAILEY, H. W. 1953: „Indo-Iranian Studies". In: *TPhS*, S. 21–42.

BARTHOLOMAE, CH. 1899: „Arica III". In: IF 2, S. 260–284.

— 1904: *Altiranisches Wörterbuch*. Strassburg.

— 1906: *Zum altiranischen Wörterbuch*. Strassburg.

— 1915: *Die Zendhandschriften der K[öniglichen] Hof- und Staatsbibliothek in München*. München (Catalogus Codicum Manu Scriptorum Bibliothecae Regiae Monacensis. Tom I, Pars VII, Codices Zendicos Complectens).

BELARDI, W. 1962: „Sull' origine delle voci armene antiche composte con *pat**." In: *Ricerche Linguistiche* 5, S. 149–169.

CANTERA, A. 2004: *Studien zur Pahlavi-Übersetzung des Avesta*. Wiesbaden (Iranica 7).

DARMESTETER, J. 1880: *The Zend-Avesta*. Teil I: *The Vendîdâd*. Oxford.

— ²1895: *The Zend-Avesta*. Teil I: *The Vendîdâd*. Oxford (Sacred Books of the East 4).

DHABHAR, B. N. 1909: *Ṣaddar Naṣr and Ṣaddar Bundehesh*. Bombay.

— 1932: *Persian Rivāyats of Hormazyār Framarz and Others. Their Version with Introduction and Notes*. Bombay.

— 1963: *Translation of Zand-i Khūrtak Avistāk*. Bombay.

ELIADE, M. 1949: *Traité d'histoire des religions*. Paris.

GERSHEVITCH, I. 1959: *The Avestan Hymn to Mithra*. Cambridge.

GIPPERT, J. 1993: *Iranica Armeno-Iberica. Studien zu den iranischen Lehnwörtern im Armenischen und Georgischen*. 2 Bde. Wien (Veröffentlichungen der Kommission für Iranistik 26).

Hampel, J. 1974: *Die Kopenhagener Handschrift Cod. 27: eine Sammlung von zoroastrischen Gebeten, Beschwörungsformeln, Vorschriften und wissenschaftlichen Überlieferungen.* Wiesbaden (Göttinger Orientforschungen III/2).

Henning, W.B. 1942: „An Astronomical Chapter of the Bundahishn". In: JRAS 74/3–4, S. 229–248. [Reprint: *W.B. Henning Selected Papers.* II. Leiden 1977 (Acta Iranica 15), S. 95–114].

Horn, P. 1893: *Grundriss der neupersischen Etymologie.* Strassburg.

Humbach, H. 1973: „Beobachtungen zur Überlieferungsgeschichte des Awesta." In: *MSS* 31, S. 109–122.

Jamasp-Asana, J.M. 1913: *The Pahlavi Texts contained in the Codex MK copied in 1322 A.C. by the Scribe Mehr-Âwân Kaî-Khôsrô.* Bd. 2. Bombay.

Junker, H.F. 1912: „Ein mittelpersisches Schulgespräch. Pazandtext mit Übersetzung und Erläuterungen." In: SHAW 15.

Klingenschmitt, G. 1968: *Farhang ī ōīm: Edition und Kommentar.* Inaugural-Dissertation der Philosophischen Fakultät der Friedrich-Alexander-Universität zu Erlangen-Nürnberg (nicht veröffentlicht).

König, G. 2010: *Geschlechtsmoral und Gleichgeschlechtlichkeit im Zoroastrismus.* Wiesbaden (Iranica 18).

Kotwal, F.M. 1969: *The Supplemantary Texts to the Šāyest nē-šāyest.* Kopenhagen.

Kotwal, F.M./Ph.G. Kreyenbroeck 2009: *The Hērbedestān and Nērangestān.* Bd. IV: *Nērangestān, Fragard 3.* Paris (Studia Iranica, Cahier 38).

Levkievskaja, E.E. 2000: *Mify russkogo naroda.* Moskva.

— 2002: *Slavjanskij obereg. Semantika i struktura.* Moskva.

Lincoln, B. 1977: „Treatment of Hair and Fingernails among the Indo-Europeans." In: *History of Religions.* Bd. 16/4. Chicago, S. 351–362.

Malandra, W.W. 1973: „A Glossary of Terms for Weapons and Armor in Old Iranian." In: *IIJ* 15, S. 264–289.

Meyer, E.H. 1883: *Indogermanische Mythen.* I. *Gandharven-Kentauren.* Berlin.

Nyberg, H.S. 1988: *Frahang i Pahlavīk.* Edited with transliteration, transcription and commentary from the posthumous papers of Henrik Samuel Nyberg by Bo Utas with the collaboration of Christopher Toll. Wiesbaden.

Oppenheim, A.L. et al. 1965: *The Assyrian Dictionary of the Oriental Institute of the University of Chicago.* Bd. 2. Chicago.

Reichelt, H. 1911: *Avesta Reader.* Strassburg.

Rolfe, J.C. 1927–1952: *The Attic nights of Aulus Gellius.* 3 Bde. London/Cambridge (Mass.).

Shaked, Sh. 1992: „Some Iranian themes in Islamic literature." In: *Recurrent Patterns in Iranian Religions: From Mazdaism to Sufism. Proceedings of the Round Table Held in Bamberg (30 September–4 October 1991).* Paris (Studia Iranica 11), S. 143–158. [Reprint: *From Zoroastrian Iram to Islam. Studies in Religious History and Intercultural Contacts.* Aldershot-Brookfield 1995].

Steingass, F.J. 1892: *A Comprehensive Persian-English dictionary, including the Arabic words and phrases to be met with in Persian literature.* London.

Tavadia, J.C. 1930: *Šāyast-nē-šāyast. A Pahlavi Text on Religious Customs.* Hamburg.

Unvala, M.R. 1922: *Dârâb Hormazyâr Rivâyat.* With an introduction by J.J. Modi. 2 Bde. Bombay.

VULLERS, I. A. 1855: *Lexicon persico-latinum etymologicum cum linguis maxime cognatis Sanscrita et Zendica et Pehlevica comparatum, e lexicis persice scriptis Borhâni Qâtiu, Haft Qulzum et Bahâri aġam et persico-turcico Farhangi-Shuûri confectum, adhibitis etiam Castelli, Meninski, Richardson et aliorum operibus et auctoritate scriptorium Persicorum adauctum.* 2 Bde. Bonn.
WUTTKE, A. 1869: *Der deutsche Volksaberglaube der Gegenwart.* Berlin.

About the Epithet *paurauuaniia-* of the Zoroastrian Sacred Girdle (Y 9.26)

Alberto Cantera

In Y 9.26 Zaraθuštra addresses the god Haōma, who came to him during his performance of a sacrifice[1], with the following words:

> *frā.tē mazdā̊ barat̰*
> *paurauuanīm aiβiiā̊ŋhanəm*
> *stəhrpaēsaŋhəm mainiiu.tāštəm*
> *vaŋᵘhīm daēnąm māzdaiiasnīm*
> *āat̰ aŋhe ahi aiβiiāstō*
> *baršnuš paiti gairinąm ...*
> "Mazdā brought to you the ... *(paurauuanīm)* girdle adorned with stars and fashioned in the world of thought, the good Vision obtained in the sacrifice to Mazdā. You have tied it in the heights of the mountains."

The text is clear but for the epithet *paurauuanīm*, which unfortunately is attested only in this passage. Mazdā brought the girdle *(aiβiiā̊ŋhana-)* to Haōma, who has tied it in the heights of the mountains. The whole action is set in a celestial scenario, as shown by the adjectives *stəhrpaēsaŋhəm mainiiu.tāštəm.*[2] Haōma probably ties his girdle to the highest point of the earth, the entry to the sky, the Harā Bərəzaitī.

1 Identifying the concrete ritual action performed by Zaraθuštra when Haōma approaches is difficult, but the joint mention of the fire and the recitation of the Gāθās brings to mind the long liturgy. The expression *atrəm pairi.yaōždaθəṇtəm* could be read in connection with the ritual action described in the Nērangestān (N 55 and 56), when the functions of the *ātrauuaxš* and of the *frabərətar* are being defined: the first should kindle *(aiβı.vaxšaiiāt̰)* the fire and then purify *(yaōždaθat̰)* the three corners of the fire, whereas the purification of the fourth corner is left to the *frabərətar.* Unfortunately, the ritual moment for this action in the Sassanian liturgy is not indicated. There are also some differences with respect to Y 9.26, since there Zaraθuštra is reciting the Gāθās (that is, acting as *zaotar*) and purifying the fire (acting as *ātrauuaxš*) as well. The ritual instructions of the manuscripts mention only one action similar to the one depicted in the Nērangestān. It happens in the paragṇa, during the recitation of Y 0.3.

2 Cf. also Y 10.143 for the chariot of Miθra; Y 13.42 for the sky. In connection with *haōma* these adjectives appear in Yt 10.90 for the pestle and mortar with which Miθra pressed *haōma* on the Harā Bərəzaitī.

This celestial girdle offered to Haōma by Mazdā is equated with the good Vision *(daēnā-)* obtained in the sacrifice to Mazdā. The identification of the Vision with the girdle appears in the Wīdēwdād (V 18.1) too:

> *paiti.dānəm ainīm baraiti anaiβiiāstō*
> *daēnąm diβžaṯ haca āϑrauua saŋhaite*
> "Who wears a mouth-mask *(paiti.dāna-)* different (from the prescribed one) and has not girded the Vision, calls himself *āθrauuan* with lies."

The same identification is to be found in Pahlavi literature (WZ 4.6).

This image of the Vision as a celestial sacred girdle adorned with stars and fashioned in the world of thought probably implies the conception of the Vision *(daēnā-)* as the Milky Way.[3] The night view of the galaxy is equated with a girdle tied by *haōma* to the Harā Bərəzaitī. This picture has been very successful in Pahlavi literature.[4] In fact, Y 9.26 (or another passage containing exactly the same expression) is quoted in the Dādestān ī Dēnīg (Dd 38.15):

> *ān wazurg xwarrah ī gumān-wizār ī abēzag dēn ēdōn hučihr ud dūr-brāzišn būd čiyōn gōwīhēd andar mānsar kū +ēbyānghan ī star-pēsīd ī mēnōyan-tāšīd weh dēn ī mazdēsnān*
> "That great Glory of the doubt-dispelling, holy Vision was so beautiful and resplendent from afar, as it is said in the Mąθra: 'The girdle adorned with stars and fashioned in the world of thought is the good Vision of the Mazdā-worshippers.' "[5]

What does *pauruuanīm* mean as an epithet of the celestial girdle? The word is attested only in this passage, so that we can figure out its meaning solely with the assistance of etymological enquiries and the help of the Pahlavi translation. My first readings of the Pahlavi translation were in the beginning of the 1990s in the courses given by MARIA MACUCH. Much of my later work has been determined by these early classes with her and the many that followed during a decade. Unfortunately, in this case the Pahlavi translation does not help us as much as we could wish; but an analysis is, nevertheless, necessary.

The Pahlavi translation (PT) has <plwnd>. BAILEY (1943, p. 145 n. 1), however, under the influence of DHABHAR's edition (1949), reads it as <plwny> which he interprets as a transliteration of the Avestan word. This transliteration would have been understood as *parwand* "enclosure" so that the Vision was put in connection with the enclosure of the sky. BAILEY's interpretation combines several mistakes. First, despite DHABHAR's edition <plwny>, the manuscripts unanimously show <plwnd>, so that the interpretation of the spelling as

3 This identification explains why the Vision and the river Arəduuī share the same epithet *pərəθū.frākā-* (PIRART 2012, p. 173). Another image in which the *haōma* on the Harā Bərəzaitī appears together with the Milky Way is the mortar adorned with stars and fashioned in the world of thought again on the Harā Bərəzaitī (Yt 10.90).

4 Other passages of Pahlavi literature in which the same image appears are GrBd 6J.1, GrBd 28.8. For further passages vid. KÖNIG 2010, p. 335ff.

5 Cf. JAAFARI-DEHAGHI 1998, p. 159.

a transliteration is not very likely. Secondly, the subsequent interpretation as the "enclosure" of the sky is doubtful in itself. BAILEY edits the Pahlavi translation as follows (BAILEY 1943, p. 145):

> *frāč tō ān ī ohrmazd burt* plwny *star-pēsīt ī mēnōkān-tāšīt vēh dēn I māzdēsnān ut-aš aiβyāhanīh ēt kūčēgōn kustīk aak mart ēv-kartak dēn-ič ī apāk hōm ēv-kartak ut-aš ēv-kartakīh ē ku tāk hōm nē x^{v}arēd pad dēn āstavān nē bawēt hōm x^{v}art kār andar yazišn*
>
> "To thee Ōhrmazd gave the *parwany* (*parwand* 'enclosure'), star-adorned, fashioned in the mēnōk, the good Dēn of the Mazdayasnians. Its being a girdle is this that a girdle is united with a man, so the Dēn, too, is united with the Hōm. Its being united is this that till he drink hōm he is not an initiate of the Dēn[6]; after hōm has been drunk, he is occupied in worship."

BAILEY has omitted the central word *aibyāhan*. Although it is omitted in ms. 500 (J 2) and ms. 510 (K 5) as well, the combined Yasna manuscripts such as ms. 400 (Pt 4) show it clearly at the expected position (after *parwand*). The gloss beginning with *aibyāhnanīh ēd kū...* is a clear indication that *aibyāhan* was in the original and that ms. 500 (J 2) and ms. 510 (K 5) share an omission already present in their common original. If *aibyāhan* is not omitted, however, then the interpretation of *parwand* as a substantive "enclosure" becomes difficult.

It would rather seem that the Pahlavi exegetes have connected Av. *pauruuanīm* with Phl. *parwand*. Although MACKENZIE records only the meaning "enclosure" for it, it is sometimes almost used as a synonym of *aibyāhan*, a meaning that fits well the etymology of the word (*pari-band-* "to tie around"), cf. Dd 38.14:

> *u-šān dīd wasān rōšnān ān-iz ī dēn xwarrah kē band ud drubuštīh ud parwand ī wispān kāmagān kirbagān kē brāzīhēd rōšn kustīg homanag u-ṡ +parwandēd pad parwand ī wispān rōšnān čiyōn parwand ān ī harwisp-āgāh xrad +parwandēd wispān-āgāh yazdān*
>
> "And they saw a multitude of luminaries and the Glory of the Vision, which is the belt, the fortification and the girdle of all those who love virtues, and which shines like a brilliant *kustīg*. It encircles them with the girdle of all lights, as the girdle of omniscient wisdom encloses the all-knowing gods.[7]"

The synonymy of *parwand* and *kustīg* is obvious in Dd 30 which deals with *pērāhan* and *kustīg*. After discussing the requirements of the *pērāhan*, it proceeds to those of the girdle (Dd 39.2):

> *parwandīh ī dēn ī dō-tāg ī dō-tōf ī čīyōn ān-iz ī dō-tōf ī dēnīg <ī> parwandīhēd āgāhīhān kārān xwad ast dō bāzišn ī xwānīhēd āsnīg ud gōšōrū<d>īg*

6 In fact, this is clearly a reference to the sacrificial course of the long liturgy. The consumption of the *haōma* is the step preceding the *āstuiti*, the sacerdotal consecration. As the commentary states, only after the consumption of the *hōm* (and the *āstuiti-*) does the priest take up his function.

7 Translation inspired by the translation of JAAFARI-DEHAGHI (1998, p. 157), but with some changes.

> "The wearing of the Vision as a belt which is of two folds and double-layered. It is like the double layer of the wisdom of the Vision which encloses the works of those who have knowledge. There are two parts which are called 'innate' and 'acquired' (wisdom)."[8]

Therefore, it seems that the Pahlavi exegetes have mistakenly connected *paurunaniia-* with Phl. *parwand*, a word almost synonymous with *aibyāhan*, the translation of *aiβiiåŋhana-*. Unfortunately, the Pahlavi translation offers no help towards the interpretation of the *hapax legomenon paurunanīm*.

Thus we can only try to guess its meaning on the basis of an etymological hypothesis producing a likely meaning for the context of Y 9.26. The result will obviously be quite speculative, which is why Bartholomae (1904, p. 873) gave up proposing translations altogether. The first[9] interpretation based on an etymological connection was proposed by Geldner (1877, p. 140), who related it to Ved. *párur(/páruṣ)-, párvan-*. This etymological reference continues to be the most likely and the most widely accepted to this day. However, the meaning he proposed has been less successful. He suggested a meaning "gegliedert", which does not seem very likely for a girdle.[10] On the basis of the same etymological connection, Kellens (2007, p. 65) translates "solennelle" starting from a meaning "articulation (rituelle)" of the Vedic word. Pirart (2004, p. 302) also accepts Geldner's etymological interpretation, but proposes a purely contextual meaning: "que l'on se met autour des reins".

More interesting is the translation recently offered by Skjærvø (2011, p. 191) "with knots", which is still based on the same etymological connection. Accordingly, this epithet would refer to a feature of the action of "tying" the sacred girdle. The tying of the girdle follows a well-established pattern. It is fastened three times around the waist. After the second fastening, two knots are tied at the front while reciting one Ahuna Vairiia at each knot. Then, after the third fastening, the girdle is tied with two knots at the back, while reciting the Aṣ̌əm Vohu twice (Modi 1922, p. 178). The Pahlavi literature insists on the importance and symbolism of the four knots of the girdle:

> GrBd6J.1
> *čiyōn gōwēd kū xwarrah ī wehdēn ī māzdēsnān pad *aybyāhan homānāg ī ast kustīg homānāg ī star-pēsīd ī mēnōyān tāšīt 3 tāg pad 4 grih pērāmōn āsmān bē dāšt*

8 Cf. Jaafari-Dehaghi 1998, p. 165, Skjærvø 2011, p. 209.

9 Previously, Haug (Haug/West et al. 1884, p. 182) had proposed an astrological interpretation. Av. *paurunanīm* would be related to Persian *parû, parvah* "Pleiades" and the girdle would be the belt of Orion. König (2010, p. 334) accepts, though with some doubts, Haug's interpretation.

10 Later (Geldner 1903, p. 422), he seems to have given up this interpretation and to have preferred the connection with *paurnua-* "first, prior to, anterior to". Schwyzer (1929) translates "uralt" but gives "gegliedert" as an alternative.

"As it says: The Glory of the good Vision of the Mazdeans was held around the sky like the Girdle, that is, the *kustīg*, adorned with stars and fashioned in the world of thought, with three folds and four knots."[11]

VD 161
dō grih pēš ud dō grih pas handāzag āxšīgān ud sē bann ī kustīg ō abar mayān menišn ud gōwišn ud kunišn
"Two knots at the front and two knots at the back is the measure of .... The three folds of the *kustīg* around the waist are the thoughts, the words and the actions."

Actually, Skjærvø's translation of *paurunaniia-* is confronted by an important problem. The meaning "with knots" is based on the meaning "knot" of Vedic *páruṣ, párvan-* recorded in the Vedic and Sanskrit dictionaries. Nevertheless, although dictionaries give "knot" as the first meaning, Vedic *páruṣ, párvan-* is never used as "knot" in the sense of a fastening formed by looping and tying a piece of rope or cord. The usual word for "knot" with a cord is Ved. *granthí*.

The formation and semantics of Vedic *páruṣ, párvan-* have been analysed by Hoffmann (1974). It is a heteroclite from the root *par-* "to pierce, to go through". The basic meaning is "joint" of an animal. It belongs to sacrificial vocabulary. The "joint" is the point through which the knife goes when cutting the sacrificial victim:

RV10.89.8b–c
asír ná párva vr̥jinā́ śr̥ṇāsi prá yé mitrásya váruṇasya dhā́ma yújaṃ ná jánā minánti mitrám
"Wie das Schlachtbeil die Gelenke, so zerhaust du die Falschheiten derer, die wider des Mitra und Varuṇa Gesetz fehlen wie Leute gegen einen verbündeten Freund."[12]

From this basic meaning derives the frequent sense "knot (of plants)". The "knot" is the "joint" of the plants and it is at this point, too, that the sacrificial knife should cut plants: AV 12.3.31 *áhiṁsanta 'oṣadhīr dāntu párvan* "they should cut the plants at the knot without hurting them". Finally, *páruṣ, párvan-* can also be used for the union, the "joint" between two time periods, the exact moment for carrying out the sacrifice or another ritual action: RV 10.53.1: *yajñásya vidvā́n páruṣaś cikitvā́n* "who knows the sacrifice; who has recognised the right moment (for the sacrifice)"; hence, Kellens' translation "solennelle" for Av. *paurunaniia-*.

There is, however, an additional meaning of *páruṣ-, párvan-* attested in the R̥g-Veda, but not listed by Hoffmann. As already recognised by Grassmann (1873, p. 792) and Geldner (1951, 1, p. 448), in RV 4.22.2 *páruṣ-, párvan-* seems to be used in the sense of "tuft (of wool)":

11 Cf. Skjærvø 2011, p. 101.
12 Geldner 1951, 3, p. 285.

> *vṛ́ṣā vṛ́ṣandhiṃ cáturaśrim ásyann*
> *ugró bāhúbhyāṃ nṛ́tamaḥ śácīvān*
> *śriyé páruṣṇīm uṣámāṇa ū́rṇāṃ*
> *yásyāḥ párvāṇi sakhyā́ya vivyé*
> "Der Bullenhafte, der die einen Bullen enthaltende (?) vierkantige (Keule) mit den Armen schleudert, der Gewaltige, Mannhafteste, Mächtige, der zum Prunk sich in graue Wolle kleidet, deren Flocken er zur Freundschaft umgelegt hat."[13]

In this image, Indra is described as wearing tufts of wool. He is not wearing a garment of woven wool, but simply tufts of wool attached here and there so that he has the appearance of a cloud (cf. the Maruts wearing *paruṣṇī urṇā* "grey wool" in RV 5.52.9). A tuft can, indeed, be conceived as similar to the "knot" of a plant: it is the point from which the thread is spun, just like the "knot" is the point from which a new branch arises; furthermore, the thread is cut from the tuft like the branch from the knot.

If we take this meaning as the basis for *paruuaniia-*, then the meaning of the epithet of the girdle would be "made from tufts of wool", which would, indeed, be very suitable for the Zoroastrian girdle. When speaking about the sacred girdle, Pahlavi literature insists on three topics: its symbolism, how it has to be tied and how it should be made. Up to this day, the production of the sacred girdle follows a very special procedure with specific weaving tools. I reproduce here MODI's description (1922, p. 174)[14]:

> The *kusti* is made up of lamb's wool. The wool is at first combed and then spun into fine threads on a hand-spindle called *châtri*. Two such long threads are prepared on two spindles or *châtris*, and are then twisted into one. This thread is then woven into the *kusti* on a hand-loom called *jantar* [...], the ends of which are movable, so that it can be adjusted to the length required. The twisted thread is passed round the loom 72 times; so, the *kusti* consists of 72 threads, divided into six strands, each of twelve threads. A continuous thread is made to pass, in the process of weaving, through each of the six strands. When the weaving is almost finished, and when about a foot of the threads remains to be woven, the whole thread is removed from the loom and handed to a priest to be cut and consecrated. It is the privilege of the women of the priestly class to weave and prepare a sacred thread, and it is the privilege of a priest to cut and consecrate it.

The very beginning of the process is the spinning of two threads from two different tufts of wool which are then combined into a single one. Pahlavi literature pays special attention to the materials allowed for the production of the girdle, wool being the main one. It is stated clearly already in the Nērangestān that the main feature of the material is that it has to be spun on the spindle:

13 After GELDNER 1951, 1, p. 448.
14 See also WEST (1882, p. 122) quoted in SCHWYZER (1929, p. 23).

N 67.6
kustīg az ēn and tis ē šāyēd pašm buz pašm uštar pašm ud mōy sōšans guft kū pambagēn-z šāyēd pad kaz ud abrēšum ǰuddadestān būd hēnd dōk-rištag šāyēd
"The sacred cord may be made of the following materials: wool of the goat and the camel, wool mixed with hair. Sōšans said: 'That made of cotton is also permissible.' They disagreed as regards coarse silk and (ordinary) silk. That which is spun on the spindle is permissible."[15]

Similar information is found in the Šāyest-nē-šāyest:

Šnš 4.1
kustīg ka az piring kard estēd nē šāyēd buz pašmēn ud pašmēn uštar pašm šāyēd ud az mōyēn pad naxēzīg šāyēd
"A *kustīg*, when it is made of damask, is not allowed. (When) it is of goat's wool, of wool or of camel's wool, it is allowed. Of hair it is allowed for the lowly."[16]

The close connection between "wool" and sacred girdle is emphasised in the Draxt ī asurīg. The goat speaking about itself affirms:

kustīg az man karēnd ān-um spēd pašm
"They make the *kustīg* of me. I am the white wool."

In this context, the meaning "made of tufts of wool" seems a likely epithet for the girdle. The meaning "tuft of wool" is, indeed, attested for Vedic *páruṣ-*, *párvan-* in RV 4.22.2 and the semantic shift from "joint (of animals)" and "knot (of plants)" to "tuft (of wool)" seems likely. Observe that the cutting of the thread when the *kustīg* is ready is a task exclusively performed by priests.

Bibliography

Bailey, H.W. 1943: *Zoroastrian Problems in the Ninth-Century Books.* Oxford.
Bartholomae, C. 1904: *Altiranisches Wörterbuch.* Straßburg.
Dhabhar, B.N. 1949: *Pahlavi Yasna and Visperad.* Bombay.
Geldner, K.F. 1877: *Über die Metrik des jüngeren Avesta, nebst Übersetzung ausgewählter Abschnitte.* Tübingen.
— 1903: „Das achtzehnte Kapitel des Vendidād." In: *Sitzungsberichte der königlich preussischen Akademie der Wissenschaften*, pp. 420–431.
— 1951: *Der Rig-veda aus dem Sanskrit ins Deutsche übersetzt und mit einem laufendem Kommentar versehen.* Cambridge, Massachussetts.
Grassmann, H. 1873: *Wörterbuch zum Rig-Veda.* Leipzig.
Haug, M./E.W. West et al. 1884: *Essays on the sacred language, writings, and religion of the Parsis.* London.
Hoffmann, K. 1974: „Ved. dhánuṣ- und páruṣ-." In: *Sprache* 20, pp. 15–25.
Jaafari-Dehaghi, M. 1998: *Dādestān ī Dēnīg. Part I.* Paris.

15 Kotwal/Kreyenbroek 2009, p. 29.
16 Cf. Tavadia 1930, p. 85.

König, G. 2010: *Geschlechtsmoral und Gleichgeschlechtlichkeit im Zoroastrismus.* Wiesbaden (Iranica 18).

Kellens, J. 2007: *Études avestiques et mazdéennes.* Vol. 2. *Le Hōm Stōm et la zone des déclarations (Y7.24–Y15.4 avec les intercalations de Vr3 à 6).* Paris.

Kotwal, F.M./P.G. Kreyenbroek 2009: *The Hērbedestān and Nērangestān.* Vol. IV: *Nērangestān, Fragard 3.* Paris.

Modi, J.M. 1922: *The religious ceremonies and customs of the Parsees.* Bombay.

Pirart, E. 2004: *L'éloge mazdéen de l'ivresse. Édition, traduction et commentaire du Hōm Stōd.* Paris.

— 2012: *Corps et âmes du mazdéen : le lexique zoroastrien de l'eschatologie individuelle.* Paris.

Schwyzer, E. 1929: "Profaner und heiliger Gürtel im alten Iran. Mit Exkurs über die idg. Terminologie für ‚Gürtel' und ‚gürten'." In: *Wörter und Sachen. Kulturhistorische Zeitschrift für Sprach- und Sachforschung* 12, pp. 20–37.

Skjærvø, P.O. 2011: *The spirit of Zoroastrianism.* New Haven.

Tavadia, J.C. 1930: *Šāyast-nē-šāyast. A Pahlavi Text on Religious Customs edited, translitered and translated with Introduction and Notes.* Hamburg.

West, E.W. 1882: *Pahlavi Texts.* Part II. Oxford.

Eine vergessene zoroastrische Märtyrerin?

Iris Colditz

1. Das *Mādayān ī J̌ōšt ī Friyān*

Der Pahlavi-Text *Mādayān ī J̌ōšt ī Friyān* „Buch von J̌ōšt dem Friyānischen" (ǰF),[1] ein Beispiel für die ehemals reiche mittelpersische Weisheitsliteratur, enthält einen Rätselwettstreit zwischen J̌ōšt aus dem tūrānischen Geschlecht der Friyān und dem Zauberer Axt auf Leben und Tod.[2] Seine Entstehungszeit ist unklar, in seiner erhaltenen Form wird er aufgrund linguistischer Kriterien in das 9.–11. Jahrhundert datiert.[3] Der legendenhafte Kern ist wesentlich älter, die Namen der beiden Protagonisten werden bereits im Avesta genannt (Yt.5.81–83), wo auch auf den Rätselstreit angespielt wird.[4] Kłagisz (2014) untersucht das *Mādayān ī J̌ōšt ī Friyān* als vermutlich ursprünglich magischen Text. Auf eine lange mündliche Tradition verweisen auch einige Stilmittel wie das der Wiederholung.[5] Das ǰF ist in den Handschriften zusammen mit dem *Ardā Wīrāz nāmag* und dem *Hādōxt Nask* überliefert.[6] Diese Texte behandeln gemeinsame Themen: das Schicksal der Individualseele nach dem Tod und die Auswirkung

1 Ed. Jamaspji-Asa/Haug/West 1872; Berthélemy 1889; Ja'fari 1986; Weinreich 1992; Cantera/Andrés Toledo 2006. Vgl. auch Macuch 2009b, S. 170.

2 Ein in der indoeuropäischen Literatur weit verbreitetes Thema (Cantera/Andrés Toledo 2006, S. 69). Vgl. auch die Rätselfragen des Aŋra Mainiiu an Zarathustra in Vd.19.4–10. Zu den Parallelen in der Märchensammlung „1001 Nacht" vgl. Cantera/Andrés Toledo 2006, S. 84 Anm. 58, S. 87 Anm. 74. Kłagisz (2014, S. 111) sieht in den Gegen-Rätselfragen des J̌ōšt an den Axt eine Art Weiße Magie, mit dem er den Zauberer mit dessen eigenen Waffen (d.i. Schwarze Magie) schlägt, sowie in den Rätseln ursprünglich Zaubersprüche („spells").

3 Vgl. Weinreich 1992, S. 44 Anm. 4–5; Cantera/Andrés Toledo 2006, S. 69f.; Weinreich 2011, S. 4.

4 Vgl. Cantera/Andrés Toledo 2006, S. 70–72. Die Zahl von 33 (in ǰF) bzw. 99 Rätselfragen (in Yt.5) ist wohl als symbolisch aufzufassen.

5 Vgl. die Verfluchung des Axt durch J̌ōšt (Weinreich 1992, S. 54 Anm. zu Z. 51); J̌ōšt kann sich wegen der Unreinheit der Lagerstatt des Axt erst beim dritten Mal setzen; 33 (d.h. zehn mal drei + drei) Fragen stellt Axt, drei Fragen J̌ōšt.

6 Die Handschriften M51b (= H6), K20 und K26 gehen vermutlich auf eine Vorlage des Mihrpanāhag ī Srōšayār ī Nēšāpūr zurück, daneben gibt es die Parsi-Version M52 (= H7) und die späte Handschrift L15 (Jamaspji-Asa/Haug/West 1872, S. 226; Weinreich 1992, S. 45–47; Cantera/Andrés Toledo 2006, S. 69). Der Text wird hier (mit kleineren Abweichungen) nach der Edition von Weinreich zitiert.

des irdischen Verhaltens darauf gemäß eines frommen (*ahlaw* „gerechten“) Lebens im Gegensatz zum sündigen (*druwand* „trughaften“). In der Begegnung mit der Reflexion des eigenen himmlischen Selbst (av. *Daēna*, mp. *Dēn*) wird die Seele mit ihren eigenen guten bzw. schlechten Gedanken, Worten und Taten zu Lebzeiten konfrontiert. Nachdem die Götter Mihr und Srōš über sie Gericht gehalten haben, gelangt die Seele des Frommen in das Paradies, die des Trughaften in die Hölle. Auch das J̌F greift diese Thematik auf.

Die beiden Hauptfiguren des Textes sind in der Forschung bereits ausführlicher untersucht worden. J̌ōšt[7], av. Yōišta, ist wohl zu *av. yōišta-* „jüngster“ als Superl. zu *yuuan-* zu stellen und könnte die prototypische narrative Figur des „Klugen Jüngsten“ reflektieren. Außer in Yt.5 wird er auch in Yt.13.120 erwähnt, wo sein *frauuaṣ̌i* verehrt wird. Er gehört dem mit der Spitāma-Familie Zarathustras verbundenen Clan der *Friyān* an, av. *Friiāna* als Patronym zu **Friya-*, vgl. elam. *Pir-ri-ya-na*, sarmato-skyth. Φλιανος (Gignoux 1986, Nr. 381; Zgusta 1955, S. 164; Mayrhofer 1979, Nr. 147; Tavernier 2007, S. 184), soghd. pryʾnʾk *Friyānē* (Lurje 2010, Nr. 927, als *Friyāne(?)*). Sein Widersacher Axt[8] wird ebenfalls in Yt.5.82 genannt als av. *Axtiia-*, vielleicht eine Kurzform zu einem (Abwehr-?)Namen mit av. *axti-* „Leid, Schmerz“. Seine Epitheta av. *duždāh-* „des Einsicht/Absicht schlecht ist, unverständig, arglistig“ bzw. „geizig, mit schlechten Gaben“ und *təmaŋᵛhaṇt-* „finster“ weisen ihn als zu Aŋra Mainiiu und den Daēuuas gehörig aus. Erst in der Pahlavi-Literatur wird Axt als „Zauberer“ *(jādūg)* bezeichnet. In einigen Texten wird er als direkter Gegenspieler Zarathustras aufgefaßt[9] und mit dem feindlichen Kay Wēp, av. *Kauui Vaēipiiō*, gleichgesetzt, der Zarathustra im Winter kein Obdach gab.[10]

Dagegen haben die Nebenfiguren der Geschichte bisher kaum Aufmerksamkeit gefunden. Mit den folgenden Ausführungen zu der Protagonistin des Textes soll ein Beitrag zur Analyse von Weiblichkeitsmustern in der Pahlavi-Literatur geleistet werden. Gerade die Weisheitsliteratur mit ihren Dichotomien und Metaphern vermittelt Grundzüge normgerechten Verhaltens im sasanidischen Iran (3.–7. Jh.) und thematisiert die Rolle der Frau in der zoroastrischen Gemeinde und der Familie. Da dieses Thema in der Forschung immer noch unterrepräsentiert ist,[11] soll hiermit insbesondere eine Würdigung der Jubilarin,

7 Vgl. zum folgenden Cantera/Andrés Toledo 2006, S. 72–75. Zum Namen vgl. Bartholomae 1904, Sp. 1299; Mayrhofer 1979, Nr. 407; Cantera/Andrés Toledo 2006, S. 72 mit Anm. 11; vielleicht noch in soghd. wyštkk *Wēštak* (Lurje 2010, S. 1387) und baktr. ιηστο *Yet* bzw. ιηστο *Yest* (Sims-Williams 2010, Nr. 183) erhalten.

8 Vgl. dazu Kanga 1989; Cantera/Andrés Toledo 2006, S. 75f. Zum Namen vgl. Bartholomae 1904, Sp. 51; Mayrhofer 1979, Nr. 63; Cantera/Andrés Toledo 2006, S. 75 mit Anm. 19; vielleicht auch in elam. *Mar-šá-ak-ti-iš* = **Marša-axti-* (Mayrhofer 1973, Nr. 8.997; Tavernier 2007, S. 484).

9 Vgl. Dk 3.195–196 (DkM 209.1–212.7) (Menasce 1973, S. 202–205). Vgl. auch König 2005, S. 177 Anm. 58.

10 Zu *Vēp/Vaēipiiō-* vgl. König 2007; 2010, S. 206–221.

11 Vgl. u. a. Bürgel 1979; Hutter 1997; Choksy 2002; Baum 2003.

Maria Macuch, verbunden werden, die in ihren zahlreichen Arbeiten zur Rekonstruktion des vorislamischen Rechtswesens in Iran unschätzbare Beiträge zur Untersuchung der Stellung der Frau im sasanidischen Ehe-, Familien- und Erbrechts geleistet hat.[12] Darüber hinaus gilt ihr Interesse der Frage nach einer „Konstruktion von Weiblichkeit“. So widmet sie sich in ihrem Aufsatz „Gelehrte Frauen: ein ungewöhnliches Motiv in der Pahlavi-Literatur“ (2009a) dem aus der zoroastrischen Moraldogmatik resultierenden Frauenbild.[13] Ich hoffe, daß der vorliegende Beitrag das Interesse Maria Macuchs findet, und verbinde damit meinen herzlichsten Dank für die kollegiale und freundschaftliche Unterstützung und fruchtbare Zusammenarbeit, die noch viele Jahre andauern möge. *drōd ud āfrīn ud harw farroxīh ud rāmišn.*

2. Die Figur der Hufrih

Die Protagonistin des ǰF spielt nur in zwei Rätselfragen eine Rolle und wird erst spät im Text eingeführt. Bis zu diesem Punkt hat ǰōšt bereits 26 Rätsel des Zauberers Axt erfolgreich gelöst. Die 27. Frage lautet:

> *pāy kadām nēktar ud nēkōgtar čē was pāy ī man dīd ēg-iš pāy ān nēkōgtar ud nēktar ī man dīd ī Hufrih ī tō xwah ī man zan.*
>
> „Welche Füße (sind) am besten und wohlgefälligsten? Denn von den vielen Füßen, die ich sah, sind alsdann die Füße am wohlgefälligsten und am besten, die ich bei Hufrih, deiner Schwester und meinem Weibe, sah.“ (Weinreich 1992, S. 97–99; Jamaspji-Asa/Haug/West 1872, S. 228, 259; Cantera/Andrés Toledo 2006, S. 96f.)

Diese Fragestellung enthält eine Reihe wichtiger Informationen. Der Zauberer nennt seine Ehefrau Hufrih, die zugleich die Schwester des ǰōšt ist.[14] Lesung und Deutung des Personennamens werfen Probleme auf. Die Pahlavi-Schreibung  ist nicht eindeutig. Jamaspji-Asa/Haug/West (1872, S. 228 Anm.) lesen hwplš *Hupārš* mit Hinweis auf die Parsi-Form هوورش, هورش *Huwarš* in M 52; dem schließen sich mit einigen Zweifeln auch Jaʿfari (1986, S. 72 Anm. 3) und Cantera/Andrés Toledo (2006, S. 97 Anm. 163) an. Bereits Justi (1895, S. 131) vermutete in der Parsi-Form eine Verlesung der Vorlage. Eine Form *Huwarš* könnte die jüngere Aussprache einer Lesung hwplš *Hubarš* aus älter *Huparš* darstellen, was „mit guten Flecken; die sehr Gefleckte“ bedeuten kann, aus Präfix *hu-* „gut“ und *parš*, < av. *parša-* „gefleckt, gescheckt“, vgl. dazu Namen wie av. *Paršaṯ.gu-*, *Paršiṇta-* (Mayrhofer 1979, Nr. 248, 249), akkad. *Par-šú-ú* = **Paršava-(?)* (Tavernier 2007, S. 265), oder „mit guten Ohren“ mit

12 Vgl. die Bibliographie Maria Macuchs im vorliegenden Band.
13 Zu diesem Problem vgl. auch Panaino 1997; König 2010, S. 98–133.
14 In Yt.13.120 wird die *frauuaṣ̌i* des Yōišta verehrt, um Anfeindungen aus eigener Familie zu widerstehen. Weinreich (1992, S. 69) verweist auf den vorliegenden Text, wo Axt als Schwager des ǰōšt gewissermaßen zur Familie gehört.

av. *parša-* „Spitze, Ohr“, vgl. elam. *Pír-šá-mar-da* = **Paršavarda-* (Tavernier 2007, S. 265). Ein solcher Name erscheint jedoch für eine Frau, deren Schönheit gerühmt wird, eher ungewöhnlich. Bei gleicher Transliteration könnte auch *Hufraš* „die sehr Taugliche, die außerordentlich Exzellente“ gelesen werden, aus *hu-* und *fraš*, < av. *fraša-* „tauglich, exzellent, ausgezeichnet“ (Bartholomae 1904, Sp. 1006f.), vgl. dazu av. *Frašaoštra-*, *Frašō.kara-*, *Frašauuaxša-* (Mayrhofer 1979, Nr. 126–129), elam. *Da-a-hu-pír-ra-šá* =**Dahyu-fraša-* (Tavernier 2007, S. 163), mp. *Dād-Fraš-Gušnasp* (Gignoux 2003, Nr. 95). Hier soll, Weinreich folgend, der Lesung von 𐫆𐫇𐫛𐫓𐫏𐫆 als hwplyh *Hufrih* „die sehr Liebe“ bzw. „die sehr Liebende“, aus *hu-* und *frih* „lieb, wert“, < av. *friia-* (Bartholomae 1904, Sp. 1026), mp. *frih-*, *frī-*, auch in der Bedeutung „gut“, der Vorzug gegeben werden.[15] Der Name ist bereits altiranisch belegt: elam. *Ma-u-pír-ia-* = ap. **Vaufrya-*, elam. *Ma-par-ri-ia* = ap. **(H)uvāfrya-* (Tavernier 2007, S. 212, 343), vgl. auch av. *huuāfrita-* „sehr beliebt, hochbeliebt“ (Bartholomae 1904, Sp. 1854). Desweiteren könnte der Name auch auf die Zugehörigkeit der Namensträgerin zur Friyān-Familie anspielen. Daneben könnte auch die Möglichkeit einer altertümlicheren Lesung als hwplyʾ *Hufriyā* erwogen werden (Justi 1895, S. 131; Jaʿfari 1986, S. 72 Anm. 3), vgl. ähnliche Bildungen wie mp. *Wispān-friyā* (Justi 1895, S. 371), elam. *Am-pi-ri-ia* = **Ham-frya-* (Tavernier 2007, S. 195). Mit *Hu-* gebildetete Frauennamen sind schon im Avesta belegt: *Hučiθrā-*, *Humāiiā-*, *Hutaosā-* (Mayrhofer 1979, Nr. 172, 177, 179), vielleicht auch *Huuarəδī-* (ebd. Nr. 182).

Hufrih wird vorgestellt als Schönheitssymbol. Insbesondere die Wohlgestalt ihrer Füße soll nicht ihresgleichen haben. Aussagen zum weiblichen Schönheitsideal im vorislamischen Iran finden wir zum einen in der Beschreibung der Göttin Arəduuī Sūrā Anāhitā in Yt.5, die sich möglicherweise an Kultstatuen orientiert.[16] Gepriesen werden ihre Statur, ihr Hals, ihre Brüste, jedoch nur ihre goldenen Schuhe, nicht ihre Füße.[17] In eschatologischen Texten begegnet darüber hinaus die ähnliche Beschreibung der Dēn, av. Daēna, die der Seele am dritten Tag nach dem Tod gegenübertritt. Die Daēna des Gerechten, des Aša-Ausübers (av. *aṣ̌auuan*, Phl. *ahlaw*) gleicht einer schönen jungen Frau.[18]

15 Nach Sundermann (1992b, S. 147; 1994, S. 258, 262; 2001, S. 512 Anm.) sind mp. Personennamen mit *Frih-* als Vorderglied als „lieb dem …“, „Freund/Geliebte(r) des …“, bei Verwendung als Hinterglied als „liebend“ zu übersetzen. Weinreich (1992, S. 69 Anm. zu Z. 239) übersetzt den Namens mit „die Liebreiche“.

16 Vgl. Yt.5.64, 78, 126–129 (Wolff 1910, S. 174f., 181; Darmesteter 1883, S. 69, 72, 82f.; Kellens 1984, S. 334). Zur Göttin Arəduuī vgl. Boyce/Chaumont/Bier 1985; Boyce 1985; Pirart 2003. Eine identische Beschreibung der Göttin Aṣ̌ī findet sich in Yt.13.107. König (2010, S. 113–121) verweist auf die Ähnlichkeit zur Beschreibung der „Geliebten“ (av. *vaṇta-*) mit erotischer Konnotation für irdische Frauen.

17 Vgl. Y.5.64, 78 (Darmesteter 1883, S. 69, 72; Bartholomae 1904, Sp. 42, 1679; Wolff 1910, S. 174f.).

18 Vgl. H 2.9 (Jamaspji-Asa/Haug/West 1872, S. 284f., 311; vgl. auch Darmesteter 1883, S. 652f.; Kellens 1995, S. 55; Piras 2000, S. 52f., 70, 88–95); AWN 4.18–19 (Jamaspji-

Doch auch hier werden die Füße nicht erwähnt. In den Pahlavi-Texten finden sich auch Beschreibungen der Schönheit irdischer Frauen, z. B. im Text *Husraw ud rēdag* „Husraw und der Page“, der auch die Füße in das weibliche Schönheitsideal einbezieht. Danach ist der ideale Fuß kurz *(pāy kōtāh)*, schneeweiß *(wafrēn)* und mit gewölbten Sohlen *(azēr pāy wišādag)*.[19]

Wie der Text weiter mitteilt, ist Hufrih die Schwester des J̌ōšt. Ihr Ehemann Axt wird am Beginn der Geschichte als Zauberer *(ǰādūg)* und Anführer einer Armee fremder Eindringlinge vorgestellt, der in die Heimat des J̌ōšt, das „Land der Rätselfragenlöser“ *(šahr ī frašnwizārān)*[20], einfällt, es verwüstet und alle Menschen tötet, die seine Fragen nicht beantworten können. Er ruft J̌ōšt als den besten Rätselfragenlöser an seinen Hof und erscheint wie ein Herrscher über ein eigenes Reich. Hufrih ist die Verbindung mit Axt kaum freiwillig eingegangen. Sie bezeichnet ihren Ehemann genau wie ihr Bruder als „Schuft, Druggenossen, Tyrann“ *(mar ī druwand ī sāstār)* und ergreift im Rätselstreit Partei für ihren Bruder. Aus Sicht der zoroastrischen Moral- und Rechtsvorstellungen ist ein solches Verhalten für eine Ehefrau unangebracht. In der Munt-Ehe *(pādixšāy)*[21], der regulären Form der arrangierten Ehe in der Sasanidenzeit, gelangt die Frau in die Abstammungslinie und unter die Vormundschaft *(sālārīh)* ihres Mannes und schuldet ihm Botmäßigkeit *(framān-burdārīh, tarsāgāhīh)*.[22] Die Unbotmäßigkeit der Ehefrau wird in Texten juristischen Inhalts als Straftat

---

Asa/Haug/West 1872, S. 18, 154f.; vgl. auch Gignoux 1984, S. 49, 156f., als 4.9); PRDd 23.7 (Dhabhar 1913, S. 82f.; Williams 1990, I, S. 118f.; II, S. 48). Vgl. auch Vd.19.30 (Darmesteter 1883, S. 269f.; Wolff 1910, S. 430); KSM 35 = KNRm 59–60 (Back 1978, S. 452; Skjærvø 1983, S. 281 §13; MacKenzie 1989, S. 48, 56, 60, §26; Gignoux 1991, S. 43, 51, 83, 90, 94, §22).

19 HuR 96 (Unvala 1921, S. 35; Monchi-Zadeh 1982, S. 59, 82; König 2010, S. 110f.).

20 Phl. *frašn* ist entlehnt von av. *frašna-* „Frage; Befragung; Besprechung, Unterredung“ (Bartholomae 1904, Sp. 1009f.), das bereits in dem av. Verweis auf die Geschichte in Yt.5.82 verwendet wird. Der Terminus bezeichnet weiter eine Literaturgattung didaktischen Inhalts im Avesta (vor allem im *Vīdēvdād*), in der Zarathustra durch Ahura Mazdā in einem Dialog (*āhūiriš frašnō* „ahurische Frage“, *āhūiriš tkaēšō* „ahurische Belehrung“) belehrt wird (Hintze 2009, S. 39–40; Colditz 2009). Die Übersetzung von *frašn* mit „Rätsel, Rätselfrage“ ist daher interpretierend. Daneben wird das echt-mp. Wort *pursišn* „Frage, Befragung“ als participium necessitatis (Gerundivum) zu *purs* „fragen“ verwendet (MacKenzie 1971, S. 69; Durkin-Meisterernst 2004, S. 287). Die syntaktische Verknüpfung von *frašn* mit *wizārdan* „unterscheiden, trennen; entscheiden; interpretieren, erklären“ (MacKenzie 1971, S. 92; Nyberg 1974, II, S. 210) in der Bedeutung „Rätsel lösen“ ist im Avestischen noch nicht bezeugt. Zu *frašn-wizārān* „Rätsellöser“, wörtl. „Fragenerklärer“, vgl. auch Phl. *xwamn-wizārān* „Traumdeuter“ (KAP 1.12, 13, s. Sanjana 1896, 3f. [Übersetzung], 3f. [Pahlavi-Text]).

21 Vgl. Macuch 1981, S. 73–77, Anm. 4; 1995b; 2003; 2005; 2007, S. 192f.

22 Vgl. das Eheversprechen der Braut in dem auf das Jahr 1278 n. Chr. datierten, aber auf sasanidische Vorlagen zurückgehenden Formular eines Heiratsvertrages *Abar paymānag ī kadag-xwadāyīh* (§5, s. Jamasp-Asana 1897–1913, S. 141f.; Macuch 2007, S. 186, 190f.). Das Thema wird wiederholt in der Weisheitsliteratur behandelt (vgl. z. B. Pass. A.11, s. Jamasp-Asana 1897–1913, S. 78).

angesehen.[23] Die Ehe der Hufrih mit dem Zauberer Axt entspricht also in keiner Weise dem zoroastrischen Ideal. Es handelt sich nicht um eine als besonders religiös verdienstvoll propagierte Kerninzest-Ehe *(xwēdōdah)*[24], aber auch um keine der anderen bekannten Eheformen.[25] Schon die Bezeichnung des Axt als Zauberer *(ǰādūg)* schließt ihn aus der zoroastrischen Gemeinschaft aus, da Zauberei den sasanidischen Rechtstexten zufolge als Verbrechen gilt.[26] Somit handelt es sich um eine unerwünschte Eheverbindung zwischen einer Zoroastrierin und einem Nicht-Zoroastrier. Man könnte deshalb eine frühere Entführung der Hufrih durch Axt annehmen. Diese Praxis wird im Avesta thematisiert, vgl. die Entführung von Saŋhauuāčī und Arənauuāčī, der zwei Schwestern des Θraētaona, durch den Drachen *(aži-)* Dahāka[27] und die Klage der Göttin Aṣ̌i über Frauenraub.[28] Allerdings ist J̌ōšt nicht ausgezogen, seine Schwester zu retten, sondern sein Land und dessen Bewohner. Und so beantwortet er die 27. Frage des Zauberers richtig, daß die Füße (das Fließen?) des Wassers *(pāy ī āb)* wegen ihrer belebenden Wirkung auf die Vegetation am schönsten und besten sind, während der menschliche Fuß (hier: der Hufrih) deren Vertrocknen (= Zerstörung) bedeutet.[29]

Das Verhältnis der Ehefrau zu ihrem Mann ist auch Thema der 28. Frage des Axt an J̌ōšt, woran die Ehefrauen große Freude hätten *(zanān wuzurg rāmišn az čē)*. In seiner Antwort geht J̌ōšt zunächst auf die vom Zauberer intendierte Lö-

23 Das sasanidische Rechtsbuch *Hazār dādestān* widmet der Unbotmäßigkeit ein eigenes Kapitel (MHDA 4.13–8.2: *dar ī a-tarsāgāyīh*, s. Macuch 1981, S. 96–120, vgl. auch ebd. S. 88f. Anm. 26). Bei dreimaliger Wiederholung gilt sie sogar als „todeswürdig" *(margarzān)* (PRDd 34c4, ed. Dhabhar 1913, S. 108.8–11; Williams 1990, I, S. 142f., II, S. 61; Macuch 1981, S. 115 Anm. 7).

24 Zur *xwēdōdah* vgl. REA 22, 24, 27–30 (Anklesaria 1962, S. 84–86, 96–98, 104–110; Menasce 1962, S. 138–144; Safa-Isfehani 1980, S. 155–158, 175–178, 189–206); PRDd 8 (Dhabhar 1913, S. 9–21; Williams 1990, I, S. 48–61, II, S. 10–17, 126–137). Vgl. auch Macuch 1991; 1995a, S. 157–163; 2010.

25 Bei der Hilfsehe *(čagar)* verbleibt die Frau in der Abstammungslinie ihrer Familie und untersteht deren Gewalthaber. Dies gilt auch für die Konsens-Ehe *(gādār, xwasrāyūn/-ēn)*, zudem hat Hufrih bei ihrer Abneigung gegen Axt diesen kaum selbst gewählt. Zu den Eheformen vgl. Macuch 1981, S. 73–77 Anm. 4, S. 89–95 Anm. 31, S. 100–113, Anm. 2; 1985, S. 197–200, 1995a; 2003; 2005; 2007, S. 192–194).

26 Zauberei gilt wie Ketzerei, als Strafe wird dem Zauberer ein Halsband und ein schweres Gewicht auf die Schultern gelegt und sein Vermögen konfisziert (MHDA 15.11–12, 15–17; 38.12–39.1, s. Macuch 1981, S. 37f., 65, 145, 222), oder sie gilt sogar als todeswürdiges *(margarzān)* Verbrechen (Dk 5.10.3 = DkM 443.23–444.5, s. Amouzgar/Tafazzoli 2000, S. 46f.). Vgl. dazu die Strafen für Apostaten und Ketzer, darunter auch Mani (Colditz 1998).

27 In Yt. 5.33–34 bittet Θraētaona die Göttin Anāhitā um Hilfe, um seine Schwestern zurückzuführen.

28 Vgl. Yt.17.59 (König 2010, S. 56, 124f.; vgl. auch Wolff 1910, S. 283).

29 Die Antwort des J̌ōšt könnte sich auch auf Anāhitā als Gottheit der Gewässer beziehen (Jamaspji Asa/Haug/West 1872, S. 258 Anm. 6; Cantera/Andrés Toledo 2006, S. 9 Anm. 167).

sung des Rätsels ein, die Ehefrauen hätten Freude „an mannigfachen Gewändern und der geziemenden Stellung einer Hausherrin, wenn sie so etwas ihr eigen nennen“ *(az paymōzan ī gōnag gōnag ud kad-bānūgīh ī sazāgwār ka-šān dārēnd).* Die richtige Antwort des J̌ōšt lautet dagegen: „Die Ehefrauen (haben) große Freude am Zusammensein mit ihren Ehemännern“ *(zanān wuzurg rāmišn az būdan ī abāg šōy ī xwēš).* Doch Axt akzeptiert diese Antwort nicht und schlägt stattdessen vor, seine Frau Hufrih zu befragen, da „sie noch nie die Unwahrheit gesprochen hat und (sie) nie sprechen wird“ *(u-š hagriz drō nē guft ud nē gōwēd).* Deshalb muß auch der Zauberer zugestehen: „An ihre Worte werden wir uns halten“ *(ud pad gōwišn ī ōy bē ēstēm).* Die beiden Kontrahenten stellen Hufrih das Rätsel, nicht ohne sie aufzufordern: „Löse diese Rätselfrage der Wahrheit entsprechend!“ *(ēn frašn rāstīhā bē wizār).* Hier wird nun Hufrih nicht nur nach ihrer Meinung befragt, sondern fungiert als Schiedsrichterin über zwei Meinungen, man könnte sagen, als Richterin im juristischen Sinn. Ihre Wahrheitsliebe qualifiziert sie dafür. Hufrih ist damit in eine dramatische Situation gestellt, die sie erst überdenken muß, denn ihre Antwort entscheidet sowohl über ihr eigenes Schicksal als auch über das ihres Bruders und damit ihrer Heimat[30]:

> *škoft-iz ō man mad kē čiš-iz mar ī*[31] *druwand ī sāstār ī jādūg ka-m*[32] *bē nē hilēd tā bē ōzanēd čē agar drō gōwam ēg-am brādar rāy bē ōzanēd ud man druwand bē bawam*
>
> „Bedrängnis ereilte mich, denn dieser Schuft, Druggenosse, Tyrann und Zauberer läßt doch nicht von mir ab, bis er mich tötet. Denn wenn ich die Unwahrheit sage, dann tötet er meinen Bruder und ich werde trügerisch.“ (Weinreich 1992, S. 70f.; Jamaspji Asa/Haug/West 1872, S. 231, 259; Cantera/Andrés Toledo 2006, S. 98)

Hufrih entscheidet sich für die Wahrheit:

> *ud bē ēdōn weh kū*[33] *rāst gōwam ud čē agar drō gōwam xwad druwand bē bawam ud dād ud dēn ud ēwēn bē wišōbēd bē ka man pad rāstīh ōzanēd ahlawtar bē bawam*
>
> „So ist (es) allein besser, wenn ich (es) wahrheitsgetreu sage. Denn wenn ich die Unwahrheit sage, dann werde ich selbst trügerisch, und (der Zauberer Axt) vernichtet Gesetz, Religion und Brauch. Aber wenn er mich um der Wahrheit willen tötet, werde ich (noch) wahrhaftiger.“ (Weinreich 1992, S. 70f.; Jamaspji Asa/Haug/West 1872, S. 231f., 259; Cantera/Andrés Toledo 2006, S. 98)

Deshalb bestätigt sie die Antwort ihres Bruders auf die Rätselfrage:

> *zanān wuzurg rāmišn az paymōzan ī gōnag gōnag ud kadag-bānūgīh ī sazāgwār bē ka-šān gādan abāg nēst pad dard ud dušrāmīh ud čiš-iz rāmišn ī ān nēst bē dard ud dušxwārīh ud ka-šān gādan abāg ast ēg-išān pad rāmišnīgtar bawēnd*

30 Vgl. auch Cantera/Andrés Toledo 2006, S. 99 Anm. 178.

31 Weinreich: *ō man mad *ēstēd *kē ēn mar ī*

32 Weinreich: **kē-m*

33 Weinreich: **ka*

„Die Ehefrauen (haben) große Freude an mannigfaltigen Gewändern und der geziemenden Stellung einer Hausherrin, aber wenn sie keinen Beischlaf haben, (verfallen sie) in Schwermut und Trübsinn, und (sie haben) keinerlei Freude an jenen (Dingen), sondern nur Schwermut und Überdruß. Wenn sie jedoch Beischlaf haben, dann sind (sie auch) über diese Dinge noch froher." (Weinreich 1992, S. 70–72, 74; Jamaspji Asa/Haug/West 1872, S. 231f., 259; Cantera/Andrés Toledo 2006, S. 98)

Daraufhin tötet Axt seine Frau für diese Antwort, die J̌ōšt Recht und ihm selbst Unrecht gibt. Damit wäre die Episode mit Hufrih eigentlich beendet, die nächste Rätselfrage könnte sich direkt anschließen. Statt dessen findet sich an dieser Stelle ein Einschub eschatologischen Inhalts:

ud ruwān ī Hufrih pad hamzamān ō garōdmān šud u-š wāng kard kū nēk man tā nūn ahlaw būd hēm ud nūn-iz ahlawtar hom anāg tō Axt ī ǰādūg tā nūn druwand būd hē ud nūn-iz druwandtar šud (hē)
„Die Seele der Hufrih begab sich im selben Augenblick zum Garōdmān und rief: ‚Wohl mir! Bis jetzt war ich[34] wahrhaftig, aber jetzt bin ich sogar (noch) wahrhaftiger! Übel dir, Zauberer Axt. Bis jetzt warst du trügerisch, aber jetzt bist du sogar (noch) trügerischer geworden!'" (Weinreich 1992, 72, 74; Jamaspji Asa/Haug/West 1872, 232, 260; Cantera/Andrés Toledo 2006, 99)

Dieser kurze Abschnitt enthält interessante Aussagen:

1. Die Seele Hufrihs steigt direkt zum höchsten Paradies Garōdmān (aav. *garō. dəmāna-*, jav. *garō.nmāna-* „Haus des Loblieds", s. Bartholomae 1904, Sp. 512f.) auf, dem Aufenthaltsort Ohrmazds und der Amahraspandān, an den nur die Seelen der wahrhaft Gerechten gelangen. Dies charakterisiert Hufrih als religiös Gerechte.[35] Garōdmān wird bereits in Frage 11 im ǰF angesprochen: „Was (ist das für eine) Sache, die in der materiellen Welt Ohrmazd und den Amahraspandān gleich ist?" *(čē ān čiš ī pad gētīg ō Ohrmezd ud amahraspandān homānāg ast)*. Die Antwort des J̌ōšt greift die Hierar-

34 Die Seele der Hufrih spricht in der 1. Sg., so wie die Seele des gerechten Wīrāz während der Jenseitsreise im *Ardā Wīrāz nāmag*. Dagegen wird die Vision des Priesters Kerdīr (KSM, KNRm) von lysyk **rēsīg* genannten Personen (Gignoux 1991, S. 74; MacKenzie 1989, S. 68: Sterbliche, bzw. die Seelen gerade verstorbener Gerechter; Skjærvø 1983, S. 300f.: als Medium für die Vision dienende Personen) in der 1. Pl. erzählt; als Akteur der Erlebnisse fungiert dort ein „Mann von der gleichen Gestalt wie Kerdīr" *(ān mard ka ān ōwōn čiyōn Kerdīr)* (seine Seele?), von der in der 3. Sg. berichtet wird.

35 Vgl. Malandra 2001. Die eschatologischen Texte H 2.15 (Jamaspji-Asa/Haug/West 1872, S. 289f., 313f.; Darmesteter 1883, S. 651–655; Kellens 1995, S. 55f.; Piras 2000, 54, 62, 66, 71, 105 Kommentar), AWN 7–15 (Jamaspji-Asa/Haug/West 1872, S. 24–42, 157–165; Gignoux 1984, S. 52–67, 161–170), PRDd 23.13–14 (Dhabhar 1913, S. 84; Williams 1990, I, S. 118f.; II, S. 48) beschreiben eine hierarchische Gliederung des Paradieses entsprechend dem Grad der Frömmigkeit des Verstorbenen zu Lebzeiten: Ort der Sterne *(star pāyag)* = Ort der guten Gedanken *(humat)*, Ort des Mondes *(māh pāyag)* = Ort der guten Worte *(hūxt)*, Ort der Sonne *(xwaršēd pāyag)* = Ort der guten Taten *(huwaršt)*, Garōdmān bzw. der Ort des endlosen Lichts *(anagr rōšn)*.

chisierung des Paradieses auf und vergleicht die Amahraspandān im lichten Paradies *(rōšn garōdmān)* und die „anderen Menschen, wenn sie den religiösen Pflichten nachkommen und fest im Glauben sind“ *(abārīg mardōm ka xwēškār ud awestwār ast)* mit einem Landesherren *(dahibed)*, umgeben von den Gefolgsleuten *(*pasānīgān)*, die den Plejaden gleichen, und den kleinen Sternen (Weinreich 1992, S. 61–63; Jamaspji-Asa/Haug/West 1872, S. 220f., 254f.; Cantera/Andrés Toledo 2006, S. 91). Die Antwort auf die Frage 26, die der Hufrih-Episode unmittelbar vorhergeht, hebt die Gerechtigkeit des Gottes Rašn(?)[36] hervor, der über die Seelen aller Menschen richtet, unabhängig von Reichtum (*pārag nē stānēd* „Geschenke nimmt er nicht an“) und gesellschaftlicher Stellung (*xwadāy ud bandag* „Herr und Diener“) (Weinreich 1992, S. 67–69; Jamaspji-Asa/Haug/West 1872, S. 228, 258; Cantera/Andrés Toledo 2006, S. 96).

2. Nach Hufrihs Tod wird ihre Seele noch gerechter *(ahlawtar)*. Dies entspricht den zoroastrischen Vorstellungen, wonach das irdische Verhalten das künftige Seelenschicksal bestimmt, da die Taten dem Jenseitskonto hinzugerechnet werden. Hierzu finden sich deutliche Parallelen zur Beschreibung der Dēn des religiös Gerechten in der eschatologischen Literatur, deren positive Eigenschaften durch die guten Gedanken, Worte und Werke des Verstorbenen zu seinen Lebzeiten noch verstärkt werden.[37]

Dieser Abschnitt hat eine wichtige Funktion für das folgende Geschehen, denn er leitet ein retardierendes Moment ein. J̌ōšt kann die folgende 29. Rätselfrage[38] des Zauberers nicht lösen und nimmt eine Auszeit, um Wasser zu lassen. Verzweifelt sieht er keinen Ausweg und klagt:

36 Die Lesung der Zeichen ist unsicher. Weinreich emendiert zu *Rašn*. Dagegen lesen Jamaspji-Asa/Haug/West und Cantera/Andrés Toledo die Zeichen als *Wāy*.

37 Vgl. H 2.14: „I was lovely *(friθąm)* and thou madest me still lovelier *(friθōtarąm)*; I was fair *(srīrąm)* and thou madest me still fairer *(srīrōtarąm)*; I was desirable *(bəraxδąm)* and thou madest me still more desirable *(bəraxδōtarąm)* … “ (Jamaspji-Asa/Haug/West 1872, S. 288f., 312f.; Darmesteter 1883, S. 654; Kellens 1995, S. 55f.; Piras 2000, S. 54, 61, 66, 70, 102–104 Kommentar); AWN 4.28–33: „Though I have been stout *(frabīh)*, I am made stouter *(frabīhtar)* through thee; and though I have been virtuous *(nēk)*, I am made more virtuous *(nēktar)* through thee; and though I have been worthy *(arzānīg)*, I am made more worthy *(arzānīgtar)* through thee; … and though I have been exalted *(burzišnīg)*, I am made more exalted *(burzišnīgtar)* through thee …“ (Jamaspji Asa/Haug/West 1872, S. 19f., 155; Gignoux 1984, S. 48–51, 157f., als 4.14); PRDd 23.12: „And I was lovely *(nēkōg)*, and by you I was made lovelier *(nēktar)*, I was comely *(abāyišnīg)* and by you I was made more comely *(abāyišnīgtar)* …“ (Dhabhar 1913, S. 83f.; Williams 1990, I, S. 118f.; II, S. 48). Auch die Daēna/Dēn spricht in der 1. Sg.

38 Die Frage zielt auf die Landwirtschaft ab, im Zoroastrismus die Grundlage von „Gedeihen und Erhaltung der ganzen Erde“ *(hamāg gēhān zīwišn ud dārišn az ōy)*. Die richtige Antwort lautet: „ein Paar Zugrinder mit einem Mann, der das Feld bestellt“ *(gāw-ēw (ē) ǰuxt ast ī abāg mard-ēw kē kār ī warz kunēd)*. Cantera/Andrés Toledo (2006, S. 99 Anm. 184) verweisen auf das alte indoeuropäische Rätselmotiv der Vielzahl von Körperteilen, in das die Frage des Zauberers gekleidet ist.

> *škoft-iz ō man mad ĕstēd kē ēn mar ī druwand ī sāstār (ud) kē nē hilēd tā bē ōzanēd čē agar (ān ī zīndag ud) čē ān kē murdag abāz zīndag bawēd ēn frašn wizārdan nē tuwān hād*
> „Bedrängnis hat mich ereilt, denn dieser Schuft, Druggenosse und Tyrann läßt doch nicht ab, bis (er mich) tötet.[39] Denn wenn auch die, die tot sind, wieder lebendig werden, so kann diese Rätselfrage (doch) nicht gelöst werden." (WEINREICH 1992, S. 73f.; JAMASPJI-ASA/HAUG/WEST 1872, S. 234f., 261; CANTERA/ANDRÉS TOLEDO 2006, S. 100)

In dieser Situation erscheint ihm Gott Nēryōsang als Bote von Gott Ohrmazd mit der richtigen Antwort, sodaß er das Rätsel lösen kann. Es ist nicht zu übersehen, daß zwischen dem Tod der Hufrih und der Lösung des Rätsels durch göttlichen Beistand ein direkter Zusammenhang bestehen muß. Dies wird dadurch unterstrichen, daß es sich bei der 29. Frage möglicherweise um die ursprünglich letzte Frage des Textes handelt.[40] Nēryōsang ist im zoroastrischen Mythos nicht nur der Bote Ohrmazds, sondern ein Mittler zwischen der geistigen *(mēnōgīg)* und der stofflichen *(gētīg)* Welt, zwischen Leben und Tod.[41] Durch ihren Tod, der als Selbstopferung aufgefaßt werden kann, stellt Hufrih eine Beziehung zwischen beiden Welten her. Sie nimmt ihren Tod bewußt auf sich, um ihren Bruder zu retten. Ihr Name könnte dann als ein sprechender aufgefaßt werden: „die sehr Liebende" wegen der Liebe zu ihrem Bruder. Zugleich wählt sie den Tod, um so ihre eigene Seele *ahlaw* zu erhalten, d. h. im kosmisch-eschatologischen Kampf die Seite des *aṣ̌a* nicht zu verlassen. CANTERA/ANDRÉS TOLEDO (2006, 99 Anm. 183) sehen hier ein Wortspiel zwischen *ahlaw* „fromm" und *ahlaw* in der Bedeutung „selig (nach dem Tod)". Hufrihs Rolle wäre dann die einer Märtyrerin für den Glauben. Zwei weitere Fragen im ǰF lassen sich mit diesem Aspekt in Verbindung bringen. So erwähnt Frage 8 die fromme Gabe *(ahlaw-dād)* an Arme, Priester und Laien der eigenen Gemeinschaft als eine der nicht obligatorischen religiösen Pflichten, die aber bei ihrer Einhaltung zu

39 Bis hierher stimmt diese Klage fast wörtlich mit der der Hufrih überein.

40 CANTERA/ANDRÉS TOLEDO (2006, S. 77–81) verweisen auf die Parallelen in der Reaktion des Axt auf die jeweils richtige Antwort in Fragen 1 und 29 (Axt erkennt selbst seine Niederlage und den eigentlichen Triumph Ohrmazds an) und sehen darin die literarische Struktur einer Ringkomposition. Die folgenden Fragen 30–33 wurden möglicherweise künstlich angefügt. Des weiteren verweist WEINREICH (2011, S. 5) auf die besondere Bedeutung des Terminus *arz* „Wert" als spiritueller Wert (hier von Land und Saatgut, Ochsen und Pflügen sowie Inzestehe) in den Fragen des ǰōšt an den Zauberer Axt. Natürlich kann nur ein frommer Zoroastrier deren spirituellen Wert im Rahmen der gesamtkosmischen Eschatologie ermessen, nicht aber der Zauberer.

41 Er führt zusammen mit Yima vor Zarathustras Geburt dessen *frauuaṣ̌i*, die bei den Unsterblichen weilt, zur Erde damit Zarathustra geboren werden kann. Er sorgt für die Bewahrung des Samens Zarathustras in der Obhut der Göttin Anāhitā bzw. im See Kayānsīh (av. Kąsaoiia), damit seine späteren Söhne (als Erlöserfiguren) geboren werden können, sowie eines Teils des Samens Gayōmards (av. Gaiiō.marətan), woraus das erste Menschenpaar entsteht. Vgl. BOYCE 1975, S. 60f., 94, 140, 277, 290; 1982, S. 18, 140f., 250, 252; STAUSBERG 2002, S. 65.

einer höherer Position im Paradies verhilft.[42] Hufrih wählt die höchste Form der Gabe, indem sie sich selbst darbringt. Frage 10 thematisiert den Menschen, der furchtlos *(abēbīm)* vor dem Tod ist, d.h. er fürchtet nicht das Gericht über die eigenen Werke nach dem Tod.[43] Dies ist der religiös Gerechte *(ahlaw)*, dessen Seele ihren Platz in Garōdmān findet. Hufrih ist demnach furchtlos gestorben, und die Rede ihrer Seele bestätigt ihren Status als Gerechte. Hufrihs Tod kann somit als religiöser Akt aufgefaßt werden. Vor ihrer Antwort, die über ihr Leben oder Tod entscheidet, bedeckt sie sich mit einem Umhang[44] *(u-š čādur abar *sar nihuft)*. Die Bedeckung des Kopfes während religiöser Zeremonien ist heute bei Zoroastrierinnen in Iran und Indien üblich und setzt vermutlich eine sehr alte Tradition fort.[45]

Die Rechtschaffenheit und das Selbstopfer der Hufrih stehen in Opposition zu den schlechten Taten, die der Zauberer Axt begangen hat. Er hat nicht nur Hufrih erschlagen, sondern jeden, der seine Rätsel nicht lösen konnte, darunter 900 Magier *(moγ-mard)* und 9 Töchter aus dem Spitāmān-Geschlecht (d.h. des Zarathustra). Axt tötet sogar seinen eigenen Bruder, um die Richtigkeit der Beantwortung der Frage 23 „Was ist am kältesten?" *(čē sardtar)* zu beweisen: es ist das Gift im Herzen *(zahr pad dil)* des trughaften Bruders, das in der Hand des J̌ōšt schmilzt. Dieser Dualismus zwischen der wahrhaftigen *(ahlaw)* Hufrih und dem trügerischen *(druwand)* Zauberer wird auf deren beider Seelenschicksale projeziert: während die Seele der Hufrih noch wahrhaftiger *(ahlawtar)* wird, wird die des Axt durch seine Taten (und vor allem durch die Tötung der Hufrih) noch trughafter *(druwandtar)*. Das gegenteilige Seelenschicksal des Gerechten und des Trughaften wird bereits in Frage 6 behandelt: Während der mächtige Wohlhabende *(hangad ī tuwānīg)* und der fromme Arme von schlechtem Leben *(škōh ī driyōš ī wad-zīwišn)* nach dem Tod eine gerechte Seele *(ruwān-ahlaw)* haben, ist die Seele des Armen von schlechtem Leben *(škōh ī wad-zīwišn)* nach seinem Tod trughaft *(ruwān-druwand)*.[46]

42 Weinreich 1992, S. 60f. Anm. zu Z. 128; Cantera/Andrés Toledo 2006, S. 89 Anm. 90.

43 Weinreich 1992, S. 61 Anm. zu Z. 145.

44 Die Frauenkleidung im vorislamischen Iran ist wenig dokumentiert. Beschrieben wird seit der medisch-achämenidischen Zeit u.a. ein als Übergewand/Mantel/Schleier über dem Hauptgewand getragenes Stück Stoff, das im Mittelpersischen als *čādur* bezeichnet wird. Es konnte den hinteren Kopf und Nacken bedecken, oder es wurde über der Schulter (bei Tänzerinnen auch um die Hüften) drapiert. Ein Einfluß des griech. *himation*, später des röm. *pallium*, wird vermutet. Vgl. Gheiby 1990; Shahbazi 1992; Kawami 1992; Peck 1992.

45 Russel (1990) verweist auf die Abbildung von Frauen mit bedecktem Kopf vor einem Räuchergefäß auf einem Stück Stoff aus Pazyryk aus achämenidischer Zeit. Dagegen vergleicht Weinreich (1992, S. 72 Anm. zu Z. 279) das Tragen des Čādor bei Hufrih mit einer ähnlichen Sitte bei Selbstmörderinnen im Pamir, aber die Hintergründe dieser Sitte werden nicht näher erläutert. Als religiöser Akt kann sie vermutlich nicht aufgefaßt werden.

46 Zur Opposition von *driyōš* und *škōh* vgl. Sundermann 1976, S. 184; Weinreich 1992, S. 58 Anm. zu Z. 106; Colditz 2000, S. 189f., 204f.

3. Hufrihs Funktion in der Erzählung

Es wird offensichtlich, daß die Geschichte der Hufrih sich nicht nur gut in die Thematik des gesamten Textes einpaßt, sondern der Figur der Hufrih sogar ein deutlicher Symbolcharakter zukommt. Der Vergleich mit anderen weiblichen literarischen Gestalten zeigt Parallelen zur indoeuropäischen Figur der „Schicksalsfrau“[47] als Mittlerin zwischen der stofflichen und der geistigen Welt. Diese treten oft auch in Gruppen auf und verkünden einer anderen Person an einem Wendepunkt des Lebens ihr künftiges Schicksal, was auch als ein unabänderlicher Richterspruch aufgefaßt werden kann. Vgl. dazu die zwei (oder drei?) Frauen am Wegesrand im KAP 3.18–19 (SANJANA 1896, S. 13f. [Übersetzung], S. 16f. [Pahlavi-Text], als 2.17–18), die Ardaxšīrs zukünftige Herrschaft voraussagen. Desweiteren überbringt im selben Text (3.1) die anonym bleibende Lieblingsdienerin (*kanīzag-ēw abāyišnīg* „ein geziemendes Mädchen“) des Ardawān dem Ardaxšīr die Prophezeihung in den Träumen Ardawāns über seine künftige Herrschaft und verhilft ihm zur Flucht. Auch die drei rechtskundigen Frauen am Wege im MHD 57.2–12 (MACUCH 1993, S. 388, 393, 400f. Anm. 10), die dem Juristen Ādurfraz komplizierte Rechtsfragen stellen, spiegeln in gewisser Weise solche „Schicksalsfrauen“ wider, indem sie „die rätselhafte, enigmatische und ungebändigte Seite dieser Disziplin aufzeigen“ (MACUCH 2009a, S. 149). In abgewandelter Form findet sich das Motiv der „Schicksalsverkünderinnen an den ‚Einbruchstellen des Jenseits‘“ auch in der Gestalt der Daēna/Dēn, deren dichotomische Ausbildung als schöne oder abstoßende Frau die Personifizierung des eschatologischen Schicksals der Seele darstellt (ebd. 147f.; vgl. auch SUNDERMANN 1992a, S. 162). Auch die Gestalt der Hufrih weist einige Bezüge zur Beschreibung der Daēna/Dēn auf, ohne daß sie mit dieser identifizierbar ist.

Darüber hinaus läßt sich Hufrih als „gelehrte Frau“ auffassen, da sie über das notwendige religiöse Wissen verfügt, um sich über die Konsequenzen ihres Handelns bewußt zu sein.[48] Der zoroastrische Katechismus *Čīdag handarz ī pōryōtkēšān* „Ausgewählte Weisheitssprüche der religiösen Führer“ (auch *Pandnāmag ī Zarduxšt* „Buch der Ratschläge Zarduxšts“) listet die religiösen und ethischen Prinzipien und täglichen Pflichten des volljährigen Zoroastriers auf.[49] Eine Reihe von Aussagen dieses Textes lassen sich direkt mit der Hufrih-Episode

47 Vgl. zum folgenden MACUCH 2009a, S. 145–149. Zum Motiv der Schicksalsfrau in den indoeuropäischen volkstümlichen Narrativen vgl. BREDNICH 1964.

48 Zur religiösen Erziehung und Bildung von Frauen vgl. Macuch 2009a, S. 137–141.

49 Ed. JAMASP-ASANA 1897–1913, S. 41–50; KANGA 1960. Vgl. auch HUTTER 2009. Der Text ist an Männer und Frauen gerichtet, da der Ausdruck in ČHP 1 *harw mardōm* als „alle Menschen“ und nicht nur als „alle Männer“ aufgefaßt werden muß. So heißt es in ČHP 33–44, wo die Pflicht von Vater und Mutter für die religiöse Erziehung der Kinder thematisiert wird, auch *harw kē andar gētīg …* „jeder der in der Welt …“ und verweist auf die Ausbildung im Hērbedestān. Der Text *Hērbedestān* schließt in seiner av. Version Frauen *(nāirika)* ausdrücklich ein, während seine mp. Version die religiöse Ausbildung von Frauen einschränkt. Vgl. MACUCH 2009a, S. 138–141. Zur eschatologischen

und ihrer Funktion in Beziehung setzen. So wird darin ein Zusammenhang zwischen den irdischen Aufgaben *(xwēškārīh)* und dem daraus resultierenden jenseitigen Verdienst *(mizd)* hergestellt.[50] Zu diesen weltlichen Pflichten gehört auch, unbeirrbar *(a-wardāg)* in Glauben und Religionspraxis zu sein und Gut von Böse zu unterscheiden.[51] Rechtschaffenheit *(menišn ī frārōnīh)* und wahre Rede *(uzwān rāstīhā)* gehören zu den zu wahrenden Regeln, so wie auch Falschheit mit Wahrhaftigkeit *(druzīh pad rāstīh)* bekämpft werden soll.[52] Durch diese Rechtschaffenheit *(ahlāyīh)*, das sind die guten Gedanken, Worte und Taten *(humat, hūxt, huwaršt)*, gelangt der Gläubige zum Paradies *(wahišt)*, zu Garōdman.[53] Der Text schließt mit der Aufforderung, die Ehrfucht vor der Seele *(āzarm ī ruwān)* nicht um des Körpers willen *(tan rāy)* aufzugeben und zu vergessen.[54]

Hufrih erweist sich als eine Frau, die über das in ČHP geforderte religiöse Wissen verfügt und konsequent danach handelt. Durch ihr klares Bekenntnis zum Glauben und durch ihre Wahrhaftigkeit erscheint sie geradezu als Ideal bzw. Modell für *die* fromme Zoroastrierin. Dies ist ungewöhnlich, da das Frauenbild in den Pahlavi-Texten meist eine Dichotomie zwischen der „guten Frau“ (= Ehefrau) und der „schlechten Frau“ (= Hure) konstruiert.[55] Hufrih ist im Kontext des zoroastrischen Wahrheitsgebots die weibliche Variante des „Wahrhaftigen Menschen“ *(mard ī ahlaw)*.[56] Darunter sind zum einen als „Prototyp der Menschen“ Gayōmard, Zarathustra und Sōšāns zu verstehen, zum anderen aber die „Figur eines idealen moralisch-religiösen menschlichen Daseins ... wer ein bestimmtes an jener Idealität orientiertes Verhalten zeigt und über bestimmte Fähigkeiten verfügt“, d.i. der „Mensch der ohrmazdischen Schöpfung“ (König 2005, S. 162–165), worunter einige Texte (z.B. *Mēnōg ī xrad*, *Wizīdagīhā ī Zādspram*) explizit Männer *und* Frauen verstehen (ebd. S. 165f. Anm. 23). Eine solche geschlechtsunspezifische Auffassung ist sonst im Avesta zu beobachten, wo Frauen wie Männer als gleichwertige Mitglieder der Gemeinde (auch in exponierter Stellung) als Rezipienten religiöser Bildung und Akteure religiöser Rituale beschrieben werden.[57] Dieses Frauenbild scheint sich in Hufrih noch

Bedeutung des religiösen Wissens, inbesondere als Vorbedingung für das Zustandekommen von *frašegerd*, vgl. Weinreich 2011, S. 12–18.

50 ČHP 1 (Jamasp-Asana 1897–1913, S. 41; Kanga 1960, S. 1, 13, 20).

51 ČHP 4 (Jamasp-Asana 1897–1913, S. 42f.; Kanga 1960, S. 2f., 13f., 21).

52 ČHP 17, 38 (Jamasp-Asana 1897–1913, S. 44, 46f.; Kanga 1960, S. 4f., 8, 15f., 23, 26).

53 ČHP 10, 17, 54 (Jamasp-Asana 1897–1913, S. 43f., 49f.; Kanga 1960, S. 3f., 11, 14f., 18, 22f., 29).

54 ČHP 56 (Jamasp-Asana 1897–1913, S. 50; Kanga 1960, S. 12, 18, 29).

55 Vgl. Panaino 1994; 1997; Choksy 2002. König 2010 (S. 98–150), bestimmt mindestens drei Frauenbilder: 1. ein ästhetisch-moralisches Idealbild in der säkularen Literatur, 2. die Verbindung dieses Ideals (auch = Daēna) mit der Vorstellung einer damit einhergehenden moralischen Schlechtigkeit, 3. eine Tradition, welche die Frau als notwendiges Übel betrachtet.

56 Vgl. zum folgenden König 2005.

57 Vgl. dazu König 2010, S. 112–134; Goldman 2012.

widerzuspiegeln. Die Gestalt der Hufrih könnte vielleicht ein Überrest einer älteren Version der Geschichte darstellen, auch wenn sie im Avesta nicht erwähnt wird. Der enge thematische Zusammenhang des *Mādayān ī Jōšt ī Friyān* mit dem *Hāδōxt Nask* und dem *Ardā Wīrāz nāmag*, die ausdrücklich auch die Seelen der weiblichen Gerechten des guten Denkens, Redens und Handelns in Garōdmān erwähnen,[58] könnte dafür sprechen.

Desweiteren verweisen Cantera/Andrés Toledo (2006, S. 74–81) auf den eschatologischen Kontext des J̌F. J̌ōšt wird in einer Reihe von Texten[59] zu den Unsterblichen (*ahōš*) gerechnet, die eine wichtige Rolle im letzten Weltalter, den 3000 Jahren von der Offenbarung der Religion an Zarathustra bis zur Erneuerung der Welt *(frašegerd)*, spielen. J̌ōšt ist somit ein Vertreter des Guten im Kampf gegen die Kräfte der Lüge. Hier gibt es Parallelen zum uranfänglichem Kampf zwischen Ohrmazd und Ahreman bzw. zum Kampf zwischen Zarathustra und den Dēws. Der Wettkampf der Rätsel ist somit eine Episode im eschatologischen Prozeß, der erst zur Besinnungslosigkeit und dann zur Vernichtung der Lüge führt. Die Niederlage des Axt ist zugleich die Niederlage Ahremans und der Dēws. Der Sieg des J̌ōšt ist demnach in gesamtkosmischer Hinsicht eschatologisch notwendig. Dieser eschatologische Aspekt bezieht auch Hufrih ein. Ihre Tötung durch Axt als Vertreter der Lüge läßt an das Motiv der „Tötung des Wahren Menschen" denken, die einen Schöpfungs- bzw. Erlösungsakt zur Folge hat.[60] So wird Gayōmard durch Ahreman getötet, was zur Entstehung der verschiedenen Arten von Lebewesen einschließlich des Menschen führt. Zarathustras wird von Tūr ī Brādrōrēš (auch Brātarwaxš, av. *Braθrō.raēṣa-) ermordet, der auch als „Zauberer" *(ǰādūg)* bezeichnet wird, wodurch das Heilsgeschehens *(frašegerd)* eingeleitet wird. Als Feind des Zarathustra gilt auch Kay Wēp (av. Vaēpiia-), der wiederum mit dem Zauberer Axt identifiziert wird.[61] In der Geschichte von J̌ōšt ist der Tod der Hufrih zugleich Vorbedingung für den Sieg der Wahrheit über die Lüge.

58 Vgl. H 2.18 (Jamaspji-Asa/Haug/West 1872, S. 292f., 310f.; Darmesteter 1883, S. 655; Piras 2000, S. 55, 67, 71, 110–114 Kommentar); AWN 13.1 (Jamaspji-Asa/Haug/West 1872, S. 35, 162; Gignoux 1984, S. 63, 165f.).

59 Vgl. Dk 3.389 (DkM 367.3) (Menasce 1973, S. 346); Dd 89.2 (Anklesaria 1970, S. 8f., 12); WZ 35.4 (Anklesaria 1964, S. cxxiii, 150f.; Gignoux/Tafazzoli 1993, S. 123); ZWY 3.2 (Anklesaria 1957, S. 6, 103; Cereti 1995, S. 81, 134, 150); PRDd 54.1 (Dhabhar 1913, S. 164f.; Williams 1990, I, S. 196f., II, S. 91, 244f. Anm.). Zu einem Vergleich der Listen vgl. Cereti 1995, S. 176–179.

60 Vgl. zum folgenden König 2005, S. 172–184.

61 Vgl. König 2005, S. 177 Anm. 58.

4. Fazit

Es wird deutlich, daß Hufrih nicht auf eine Nebenfigur reduziert werden kann. Vielmehr bündeln sich in ihr symbolhaft die verschiedenen inhaltlichen Aspekte des Textes. Sie ist keine Repräsentantin einer der üblichen Weiblichkeitsmuster der Pahlavi-Literatur,[62] sondern verweist als Ideal der frommen Zoroastrierin vermutlich auf ältere, aus dem Avesta bekannte Auffassungen. Als literarische Figur weist Hufrih Bezüge zum Motiv der oft anonym bleibenden hilfreichen Mittlerin auf, die Nachrichten überbringt, den Hauptfiguren durch Tricks hilft usw. Hufrih dagegen leitet die entscheidende Wende der Handlung ein. Am ehesten ist sie mit dem Motiv der „gelehrten Frau" bzw. der „Schicksalsfrau(en)" vergleichbar, deren Reden und Handeln eine Auswirkung auf das Schicksal des Helden hat und die auch eine Beziehung zwischen dem irdischen Leben und der jenseitigen Welt herstellt. Dabei ist Hufrih keine singuläre Frauengestalt, sondern hat eine literarische „Schwester" im *Kārnāmag ī Ardaxšīr ī Pābagān* in der Frau des Ardaxšīr, Tochter des letzten Arsakidenkönigs Ardawān. Aufgefordert von ihren Brüdern unternimmt diese einen Mordanschlag auf den König.[63] Die Brüder appellieren an die Verpflichtung der Schwester gegenüber der eigenen (arsakidischen) Familie *(xwēšān, xwēšāwandān, *ham-tōhmagān)*, gegen den Sünder *(wināhgār)*, Feind Gottes *(yazadān dušman)* und Vertragsbrecher *(mihr-drōz)* Ardaxšīr vorzugehen. Dadurch werde ihre Seele des Paradieses wert *(tō ruwān wahištīg)*, ihr werde ewiger Ruhm zuteil *(nām ī ǰāwēdānag ō xwēš kard *bawēd)*, sie werde wegen ihrer guten Tat von den anderen Frauen geehrt und geachtet *(nāmīgdar ud grāmīgdar)*. Auch hier setzt sich eine Schwester unter Gefahr ihres Lebens für das Schicksal ihrer Brüder ein, indem sie zur Vernichtung eines Feindes (aus Sicht der Arsakiden) beiträgt. Die Episode ist allerdings in einen höfischen Kontext gekleidet. Die höhere Symbolhaftigkeit der Hufrih erschließt sich aus dem eschatologischen Kontext des ǰF. Die Parallelen ihrer Person sowohl zur Dēn/Daēna als auch zum „Wahrhaftigen Menschen" verweisen auf den Beitrag ihres Handeln für den Sieg des Guten im gesamtkosmischen Kampf gegen die Lüge. Auch der Tod der Hufrih ordnet sich darin ein. Letztlich kann Hufrih auch als Personifikation jenes legitimen Opfers verstanden werden, mit dem Yōišta in Yt.5.81–83 die Göttin Arəduuī Sūrā Anāhitā um den Sieg über den bösen Axtiia im Rätselwettstreit bittet. Axt dagegen tötet im ǰF seinen Bruder – ein illegitimes Opfer, das die Göttin nicht erhort.

62 Die Frau als Schönheitssymbol, gute Ehefrau (mit der Hufrih jedoch die moralischen Werte Wahrhaftigkeit und Frömmigkeit teilt), Sünderin bzw. Verführerin, Hure.

63 KAP 9 (Sanjana 1896, S. 43–50 [Pahlavi-Text], 38–42 [Übersetzung]). Der Anschlag mißlingt, und sie wird trotz ihrer Schwangerschaft zum Tode verurteilt, jedoch vom Oberpriester versteckt. Sie gebiert den Thronfolger Šābuhr, und beide werden später von Ardaxšīr wieder glücklich empfangen.

Allgemeine Abkürzungen

akkad.	akkadisch	Phl.	Pahlawī
ap.	altpersisch	Pl.	Plural
av.	avestisch	röm.	römisch
baktr.	baktrisch	sarmat.-skyth.	sarmato-skythisch
elam.	elamisch	Sg.	Singular
griech.	griechisch	soghd.	soghdisch
mp.	mittelpersisch	Superl.	Superlativ

Bibliographie

Amouzgar, J./A. Tafazzoli 2000: *Le cinquième livre du Dēnkard.* Paris (StIr. Cahier 23).

Anklesaria, B.T. 1957: *Zand-ī Vohūman Yasn and two Pahlavi Fragments.* Bombay.

— 1962: *Rivāyat-ī hēmīt-ī asavahistān.* Bombay (K.R. Cama Oriental Institute Publication).

— 1964: *Vichitakiha-i Zatsparam, with text and introd.* Bombay.

Anklesaria, P.K. 1970: „Dādestān ī Dīnīk 89." In: M. Boyce/I. Gershevitch: *W.B. Henning Memorial Volume.* London, S. 8–13.

Back, M. 1978: *Die sassanidischen Staatsinschriften.* Téhéran/Liège (AcIr 18, Trois. sér., Textes et Mémoires 8).

Bartholomae, Ch. 1904: *Altiranisches Wörterbuch.* Straßburg (Nachdruck Berlin 1961).

Baum, W. 2003: *Schirin: Christin – Königin – Liebesmythos. Eine spätantike Frauengestalt – Historische Realität und literarische Wirkung.* Klagenfurt.

Berthélemy, A. 1889: *Une légende iranienne.* Paris.

Boyce, M. 1975: *A History of Zoroastrianism. I: The Early Period.* Leiden/Köln (HdO 1/8/1/2/2A).

— 1982: *A history of Zoroastrianism.* II: *Under the Achaemenians.* Leiden/Köln (HdO 1/8/1/2/2A/2).

— 1985: „Ābān Yašt." In: *EIr* I, S. 60–61.

Boyce, M./M.L. Chaumont/C. Bier 1985: „Anāhīd." In: *EIr* I, S. 1003–1011.

Brednich, R.W. 1964: *Volkserzählungen und Volksglaube von den Schicksalsfrauen.* Helsinki.

Bürgel, J.Ch. 1979: „Die Liebesvorstellungen im persischen Epos Wis und Ramin." In: *Asiatische Studien* 23, S. 65–98.

Cantera, A./M.A. Andrés Toledo 2006: „Los acertijos indoiranios: cuestiones de vida o muerte (II). El Madayan i Yošt i Friyan." In: *Aula Orientalis. Supplementa* 22, S. 69–108 *(Studies Presented to Joaquín Sanmartín).*

Cereti, C. 1995: *The Zand ī Wahman Yasn. A Zoroastrian Apocalypse.* Rom (SOR 75).

Choksy, J. 2002: *Evil, Good and Gender. Facets of the Feminine in Zoroastrian Religious History.* New York [u.a.] (Toronto studies in religion 28).

Colditz, I. 1998: „Notes on the problem of punishment and conversion in Manichaeism.“ In: N. Sims-Williams (Hrsg.): *Proceedings of the Third European Conference of Iranian Studies, Part 1.* Wiesbaden, S. 27–37 (Beiträge zur Iranistik 17).

— 2000: *Zur Sozialterminologie der iranischen Manichäer. Eine semantische Analyse im Vergleich zu den nichtmanichäischen iranischen Quellen.* Wiesbaden (Iranica 5).

— 2009: „‚Autorthema‘, Selbstproklamation und Ich-Form in der alt- und mitteliranischen Literatur.“ In: Durkin-Meisterernst/Reck/Weber 2009, S. 27–64.

Darmesteter, J. 1883: *The Zend-Avesta.* Part II: *The Sīrōzahs, Yasts and Nyāyis.* Oxford (SBE 23 [reprint Delhi-Varanasi-Patna 1969]).

Dhabhar, E.B.N. 1913: *The Pahlavi Rivāyat accompanying the Dādistān-ī Dīnīk.* Bombay (Pahlavi Text Series 2).

Durkin-Meisterernst, D. 2004: *Dictionary of Manichaean Texts III: Texts from Central Asia and China.* Part 1: *Dictionary of Manichaean Middle Persian and Parthian.* Turnhout (CFM. Subsidia).

Durkin-Meisterernst, D. / Ch. Reck / D. Weber (Hrsg.) 2009: *Literarische Stoffe und ihre Gestaltung in mitteliranischer Zeit. Colloquium anlässlich des 70. Geburtstags von Werner Sundermann.* Wiesbaden (Beiträge zur Iranistik 31).

Gheiby, B. 1990: „Čādor (2) i. In Early Literary Sources.“ In: *EIr* IV, S. 609–611.

Gignoux, Ph. 1984: *Le livre d'Ardā Vīrāz. Translittération, transcription et traduction du texte pehlevi.* Paris.

— 1986: *Noms propres sassanides en moyen-perse épigraphique.* Wien (IPNB/II/2/).

— 1991: *Les quatre inscriptions du Mage Kirdīr.* Paris (StIr 9).

— 2003: *Noms propres sassanides en moyen-perse épigraphique. Supplément [1986–2001].* Wien (IPNB/II/3/).

Gignoux, Ph. / A. Tafazzoli 1993: *Anthologie de Zādspram: édition critique du texte Pehlevi.* Paris (StIr. Cahier 13).

Goldman, L. 2012: „Women ii. In the Avesta.“ In: *EIr* (online version).

Hintze, A. 2009: „Avestan Literature.“ In: Macuch/Emmerick 2009, S. 46–62.

Hutter, M. 1997: „Shirin und Khosrau: Realität und Idealisierung von Liebe im späten Sasanidenreich.“ In: *Eros, Liebe und Zuneigung in der Indogermania. Akten des Symposiums zur indogermanischen Kultur- und Altertumskunde in Graz, 29.–30. September 1994.* Graz, S. 15–30.

— 2009: „Das so genannte Pandnāmag ī Zardušt: Eine zoroastrische Auseinandersetzung mit gnostisch-manichäischem Traditionsgut?“ In: Durkin-Meisterernst/Reck/Weber 2009, S. 123–133.

Jaʿfari, M. 1986: *Mātikān-e yūšt-e fryān. Matn-e Pahlavi, āvā-nevisi, tarjome, vāže-nāme [Book of Yušt Son of Fryān. Pahlavi Text, Transcription, Translation, Glossary].* Teheran.

Jamasp-Asana, J. M. 1897–1913: *Pahlavi Texts. Contained in the Codex MK., Copied in 1322 A. D. by the Scribe Mehr-Âwân Kai-khûsrû.* Bombay [Repr. Teheran 1969].

Jamaspji-Asa, H. / M. Haug / E.W. West 1872: *The Book of Arda Viraf. The Pahlavi text prepared by Dastur H. Jamaspji Asa, revised and collated with further MSS., with an English translation and introduction, and an appendix containing the texts and translations of the Gosht-i Fryano and Hadokht-Nask by M. Haug, assisted by E. W. West.* Bombay, S. 205–266.

Justi, F. 1895: *Iranisches Namenbuch.* Marburg (Nachdruck Hildesheim 1963).

Kanga, M. F. 1960: *Čītak Handarž ī Pōryōtkēšān. A Pahlavi text edited, transcribed and translated into English with introduction and a critical glossary and with a foreword by Professor H. W. Bailey*. Bombay.

— 1989: „Axt." In: *EIr* III, S. 123.

Kawami, T. 1992: „Clothing iii. In the Arsacid period." In: *EIr* V, S. 337–339.

Kellens, J. 1984: *Le verbe avestique*. Wiesbaden.

— 1995: „L'âme entre le cadavre et le paradis." In: *JA* 283, S. 19–56.

Kłagisz, M. 2014: „Middle Persian Mādīgān ī Yōšt ī Fr(i)yān as a Magical Text?" In: *The Polish Journal of the Arts and Culture* 9/1, S. 107–126.

König, G. 2005: „Zur Figur des ‚Wahrhaftigen Menschen' *(mard ī ahlaw)* in der zoroastrischen Literatur." In: *ZDMG* 155, S. 161–188.

— 2007: „Wer ist der *vīpta-/vaēpaiia(ṇt)* des Vīdēvdād?" In: *AoF* 34/2, S. 370–387.

— 2010: *Geschlechtsmoral und Gleichgeschlechtlichkeit im Zoroastrismus*. Wiesbaden (Iranica 18).

Lurje, P. B. 2010: *Personal Names in Sogdian Texts*. Wien (SÖAW 808. Iranische Onomastik 8. IPNB/II/8/).

MacKenzie, D. N. 1971: *A concise Pahlavi dictionary*. London.

— 1989: „Kerdir's Inscription. Synoptic Text in Transliteration, Transription and Commentary." In: G. Hermann / D. N. MacKenzie (Hrsg.): *The Sasanian Rock reliefs at Naqsh-i Rustam. Naqsh-i Rustam 6*. Berlin (Iranische Denkmäler 13. Reihe II: Iranische Felsreliefs I).

Macuch, M. 1981: *Das sasanidische Rechtsbuch „Mātakdān i Hazār dātistān" (Teil II)*. Wiesbaden (AKM 45.1).

— 1985: „Die Zeitehe im sasanidischen Recht – ein Vorläufer der šīʿitischen *mutʿa*-Ehe in Iran?" In: *AMI* 18, S. 187–203.

— 1991: „Inzest im vorislamischen Iran." In: *AMI* 24, S. 141–154.

— 1993: *Rechtskasuistik und Gerichtspraxis zu Beginn des siebenten Jahrhunderts in Iran: Die Rechtssammlung des Farroḫmard i Wahrāmān*. Wiesbaden (Iranica 1).

— 1995a: „Herrschaftskonsolidierung und sasanidisches Familienrecht: zum Verhältnis von Kirche und Staat unter den Sasaniden." In: Ch. Reck / P. Zieme (Hrsg.): *Iran und Turfan: Beiträge Berliner Wissenschaftler, Werner Sundermann zum 60. Geburtstag gewidmet*. Wiesbaden, S. 149–167 (Iranica 2).

— 1995b: „Die Konstruktion der Wirklichkeit im sasanidischen Recht." In: B. G. Fragner et al. (Hrsg.): *Proceedings of the Second European Conference of Iranian Studies held in Bamberg, 30th September to 4th October 1991*. Rom (SOR 73).

— 2003: „Zoroastrian Principles and the Structure of Kinship in Sasanian Iran." In: C. G. Cereti / M. Maggi / E. Provasi (Hrsg.): *Religious Themes and Texts of pre-Islamic Iran and Central Asia: Studies in honour of Professor Gherardo Gnoli on the occasion of his 65th birthday on 6 December 2002*. Wiesbaden, S. 231–246 (Beiträge zur Iranistik 24).

— 2005: „Inheritance. i. Sasanian Period." In: *EIr* XIII, S. 125–131.

— 2007: „The Pahlavi Marriage Contract in the Light of Sasanian Family Law." In: M. Macuch / M. Maggi / W. Sundermann: *Iranian Languages and Texts from Iran and Turan. Ronald E. Emmerick Memorial Volume*. Wiesbaden, S. 183–204 (Iranica 13).

– 2009a: „Gelehrte Frauen: ein ungewöhnliches Motiv in der Pahlavi-Literatur." In: DURKIN-MEISTERERNST/RECK/WEBER 2009, S. 135–151.

– 2009b: „Pahlavi Literature." In: MACUCH/EMMERICK 2009, S. 116–190.

– 2010: „Incestuous Marriage in the Context of Sasanian Family Law." In: M. MACUCH / D. WEBER / D. DURKIN-MEISTERERNST (Hrsg.): *Ancient and Middle Iranian Studies. Proceedings of the 6th European Conference of Iranian Studies, held in Vienna, 18–22 September 2007.* Wiesbaden, S. 133–148 (Iranica 19).

MACUCH, M. / R.E. EMMERICK (Hrsg.) 2009: *Pre-Islamic Iranian Literature. Companion Volume I to A History of Persian Literature.* London (A History of Persian Literature XVII).

MADAN, D.M. 1911: *The Complete Text of the Pahlavi Dinkard. Part I (books III–V), part II (books VI–IX).* Bombay.

MALANDRA, W. 2001: „Garōdmān." In: *EIr* X, S. 317f.

MAYRHOFER, M. 1973: *Onomastica Persepolitana. Das altiranische Namengut der Persepolis-Täfelchen.* Unter Mitarbeit von J. HARMATTA, W. HINZ, R. SCHMITT und J. SEIFERT. Wien (SÖAW 286).

– 1979: *Die altiranischen Namen.* Wien (IPNB/I/).

MENASCE, J. de 1973: *Le troisième livre de Dēnkart.* Paris (Travaux de l'Institut d'études iraniennes de l'Université de Paris 5. Bibliothèque des œuvres classiques persanes 4).

MONCHI-ZADEH, D. 1982: „Xusrōw Kavātān ut Rētak." In: J. DUCHESNE-GUILLEMIN / P. LECOQ (Hrsg.): *Monumentum Georg Morgenstierne.* II. Leiden, S. 47–91 (AcIr 22. Hommages et Opera Minora 3).

NYBERG, H.S. 1974: *A Manual of Pahlavi.* I, II. Wiesbaden.

PANAINO, A. 1994: „Figure femminili divine e demoniache." In: G.L. PRATO: *Miti di origine, miti di caduta e presenza del femminino nella loro tradizione interpretativa. XXXII Settimana Biblica Nazionale (Roma, 14–18 settembre 1992).* Bologna (Ricerche storico bibliche 6), S. 47–70.

– 1997: „Nāirikā- e jahikā- nell'aldilà zoroastriano." In: *Bandhu. Scritti in onore di Carlo della Casa.* Vol. II, Torino, S. 831–843.

PECK, E.H. 1992: „Clothing iv. In the Sasanian period." In: *EIr* V, S. 739–752.

PIRART, É. 2003: „Les parties étiologiques de l'Ardvīsūr Bānūg Yašt et les noms de la grande déesse iranienne." In: *IIJ* 46, S. 199–222.

PIRAS, A. 2000: *Hādōxt Nask 2. Il Racconto zoroastriano della sorte dell'anima. Edizione critica del testo avestico e pahlavi, traduzione e commento.* Roma (SOR 88).

RUSSEL, J.R. 1990: „Čādor (2) ii. Among Zoroastrians." In: *EIr* IV, S. 610.

SAFA ISFEHANI, N. 1980. *Rivāyat-i Hēmit-i Ašawahištān. A Study in Zoroastrian Law.* Harvard.

SANJANA, D.P. 1896: *The Kârnâmê î Artakhshîr î Pâpakân: being the oldest surviving records of the Zoroastrian emperor Ardashîr Bâbakân, the founder of the Sâsânian dynasty in Irân.* Bombay (Repr. Ann Arbor, Mich., Univ.Microfilms 1978).

SHAHBAZI, SH. 1992: „Clothing ii. In the Median and Achaemenid periods." In: *EIr* V, S. 723–737.

SIMS-WILLIAMS, N. 2010: *Bactrian Personal Names.* Wien (Iranische Onomastik 7. IPNB/II/7/).

SKJÆRVØ, P. O. 1983: „Kirdir's Vision: Translation and Analysis." In: *AMI* 16 (1983 [1985]), S. 269–306.
STAUSBERG, M. 2002: *Die Religion Zarathushtras. I. Geschichte.* Stuttgart.
SUNDERMANN, W. 1976: „Commendatio pauperum. Eine Angabe der sassanidischen politisch-didaktischen Literatur zur gesellschaftlichen Struktur Irans." In: *AoF* 4, S. 167–194.
— 1992a: „Die Jungfrau der guten Taten." In: PH. GIGNOUX (Hrsg.): *Recurrent Patterns in Iranian Religions. From Mazdaism to Sufism. Proceedings of the Round Table held in Bamberg (30th September–4th October 1991).* Paris, S. 159–174 (StIr. Cahier 11).
— 1992b: *Der Sermon vom Licht-Nous. Eine Lehrschrift des östlichen Manichäismus. Edition der parthischen und soghdischen Version.* Berlin (BTT XVII).
— 1994: „Iranische Personennamen der Manichäer." In: *Die Sprache* 35/2, S. 244–270 (= W. SUNDERMANN/CH. RECK/D. WEBER/C. LEURINI/A. PANAINO [Hrsg.]: *Manichaica Iranica. Ausgewählte Schriften von Werner Sundermann.* I. Roma 2001, S. 485–513 [SOR 89,1]).
TAVERNIER, J. 2007: *Iranica in the Achaemenid period (ca. 550–330 B. C.). Lexicon of Old Iranian proper names and loanwords, attested in Non-iranian texts.* Leuven [u. a.] (OLA 158).
UNVALA, J. M. 1921: *The Pahlavi Text 'King Husrav and his boy'.* Paris.
WEINREICH, M. 1992: „Die Geschichte von Jōišt ī Friyān." In: *AoF* 19/1, S. 44–101.
— 2011: „No Help for Evil Axt. Ahriman's Image and the Advent of Frašagird in the Story of Jōišt ī Friyān." In: *Orientalia. Proceedings of the Department of Iranian Studies, Yerevan State University* 13, S. 4–21.
WOLFF, F. 1910: *Avesta. Die heiligen Bücher der Parsen.* Strassburg.
ZGUSTA, L. 1955: *Die Personennamen griechischer Städte der nördlichen Schwarzmeerküste.* Prag.

Manichaean Book Quires

DESMOND DURKIN-MEISTERERNST

Whilst the form and physical structure of Manichaean books from Egypt—consisting of large format Coptic codices written on papyrus and a small format Greek codex on parchment—are quite clear, the same cannot be said for the remnants of Manichaean books found in Turfan on the Silk Road and held in the German Turfan Collection in Berlin. The Berlin Turfan Collection contains a great variety of book formats from small to large, roughly in the same range as the books found in Egypt but with many intermediary models, yet many details about Manichaean books from Turfan remain unclear because not a single book has survived as such, just bifolia, single pages and fragments of pages. The aim of this article, based on a lecture given on the 3rd of March 2011 at La Sapienza in Rome at the kind invitation of Arianna d'Ottone, is to supply some details not on Manichaean books from Turfan but on the quire in such books, because for that, at least, there is evidence. It is a pleasure to dedicate this to MARIA MACUCH.

IBSCHER (in POLOTSKY/BÖHLIG 1940, pp. xii–xiv) established that the Coptic Manichaean book with the title Kephalaia consists of quires of six bifolia each, yielding 24 pages front and back. The pages are 31,5 cm high and 18 cm wide. IBSCHER discovered that the quires are marked with letters (used as numbers) in the upper margin near the inner fold. IBSCHER (in Allberry 1938, pp. xii–xiii) deals with the ratio between bifolia and codex and concludes that no more than fifty bifolia were used to make a codex, in this case the Coptic Manichaean Psalm-Book with a page size of 27 × 17,5 cm. This suggests a maximum of eight quires (= 48 bifolia) in the codex, but while this is attested in Egypt there is no reason to think that so many quires should always have been bound together to make codices. This uncertainty about the interrelationship between quires and book size means that for the damaged remains of Manichaean books found in Turfan no reliable statements about the extent of books can be made. The Cologne Mani Codex, a Greek codex, was described by HENRICHS/KOENEN (1970) as being composed of quires of six bifolia each; the surviving 192 pages are in eight quires, a number that agrees with that of the Coptic Manichaean Psalm-Book. In contrast to the Coptic codices the Greek Cologne Mani Codex has a tiny page size of 4,5 × 3,5 cm and HENRICHS/KOENEN (1970, p. 101) established that this is the smallest codex yet to become known. Some book fragments from Turfan are also quite small, though not quite as small as this. The Turfan fragments provide ample evidence for page sizes similar to the largest and smallest sizes represented by the Egyptian Manichaean books and additionally present the whole range of page sizes between the two, from large pages written in undivided long lines but also in columns to a whole series of medium sized and small sized pages written in proportionally large or small script. Therefore, while the Egyptian material might suggest standard sizes for the Coptic codices at the upper and lower ends of the range, the Turfan material shows that a whole range of book sizes was being produced and used for widely different purposes, from private prayer books to lectionary type public books possibly put on display or placed so that others apart from the person reading the text out loud could follow it.

In the Berlin Turfan Collection only one Manichaean book shows a remnant of an original binding. This is the item with the signatures M801a and MIK III 53 kept in the Museum for Asiatic Art, Berlin. It was edited by HENNING (1936), who discovered that the order of pages which the binder gave the 'booklet' was wrong. HENNING concluded that the book had fallen apart and that part of what survived was sown together by someone without any regard for the contents. This remarkable object has quite a small page size, 9 × 3,2 cm. The size allows us to presume that the book was kept on someone's person, comparable to the Cologne Mani Codex, though the two books are entirely different in content. On the basis of the contents of the surviving pages HENNING (1936, p. 5) established that, of the surviving bifolia, nine belonged to one quire, which he suggested originally contained fourteen or even more bifolia; of the other quire (quire I) three bifolia survive; this quire is written in a slightly smaller script than the better preserved quire (quire II). He lists the headlines on each page, including the various colours, blue, olive, violet, red, used for the headlines to give an idea of the effort put into making this book. These proved useful in his reconstruction of the correct sequence of the pages. On the basis of HENNING's work, GULÁCSI (2005, pp. 61–64) presents the two surviving quires of M801a = MIK III 53 (she identifies the faded red of the headlines as orange). She suggests (but without reference to the contents of the booklet) that the larger quire (quire II) had fifteen bifolia and, following Henning 1936, 5, states that the headlines confirm the order of the pages within the quire 'since they not only read continuously across the two facing pages, but also are written in the same color of ink' (GULÁCSI 2005, p. 61). This refers to the design of open pages in a quire, to which we will return later. The real surprise here is the very large size of the quire, which may (or may not) have applied to both of the more or less preserved quires of the small book. The book therefore consisted of at least two quite unwieldly wads of paper that must have caused the book binder difficulties. In a table on p. 64 GULÁCSI accordingly compares the Coptic and Greek texts with 4 & 6 and 6 each bifolia in a quire with the 'Iranian texts' (sic) with a 'minimum' (!) of 15 bifolia in a quire. She is aware that the number of bifolia in the quire of M801a is very high 'two to three times the number of bifolia seen in the gatherings of East Mediterranean Manichaean codices' (p. 61) but does not pursue the matter.

In order to obtain some clarity on this it is necessary to look for more information on quires in the Iranian Manichaean fragments. In her painstaking reconstruction of the two Parthian hymn cycles from scattered fragments, Boyce (1954) also comes to some conclusions about the size of the quire in some of the many manuscripts. On p. 25 she suggests on the basis of the extent of text present on fragments belonging together that in one manuscript 'there appear to have been twelve double sheets in the quire'. This is not as high as the fourteen or fifteen in M801a but is still double the number in the large Coptic codices. The page format is considerably larger than M801a so the large size of the quire will not have made it unwieldly. A further source of information on quire size can be found in the manuscript of the Šābuhragān. The title of this Middle Persian work indicates that Mani dedicated and presumably also gave a copy of the original text to the Sasanian king Šābuhr in an attempt to win the king over to the new syncretistic religion. In his re-edition of this text MacKenzie established that the manuscript had quires of eight bifolia each (MacKenzie 1980, p. 288), two of which have survived. There in his footnote 2, MacKenzie points out that 'the Šābuhragān MS comes closer to the form of the Coptic Kephalaia codex ...'. The Manichaean collection from Turfan shows not only a great range of page sizes but apparently also a similar flexibility in quire sizes. The fact that M801a with its small page size puts more bifolia into the quire than the Šābuhragān manuscript with its larger page size (15 × 10 cm) suggests the possibility that there might be some inverse relationship between quire size and page size which in turn might imply standard paper sizes at least to some extent. The size of a bifolio in M801a is 9 × 6,4 cm = 57,6 cm^2; the size of a bifolio of the Šābuhragān is 15 × 20 cm = 300 cm^2. Clearly, the smaller size could not have been cut from a sheet with the dimensions of the larger bifolio without wastage. Rather, it is clear that papermakers produced a range of paper sizes, from which the smaller bifolia would be made by folding and cutting. The fourteen bifolia of M801a require 806 cm^2 and the eight bifolia of the Šābuhragān require 2400 cm^2 of paper, three times as much as the small book. The lack of a good range of properly attested quires makes it impossible to test this relationship any further. In any case, it seems unlikely that the numbers and proportions are relevant. Rather the quire will have been made using more than one sheet of paper, as necessary. There is even evidence for pages made by glueing sheets together.

The surviving well designed pages of the Šābuhragān allow us to make some observations about the overall design of quires and therefore to develop on what has already been observed about the use of colour in the headlines across open pages in M801a. Here the individual pages of the quire, physically linked each to another page in the bifolia of the quire, can form new units with the following page, sharing features between successive bifolia. The overall design of an open double page (which is identical with a physical bifolio only in the centre page of a quire) is an issue for the scribes and craftsmen who produced these manuscripts.

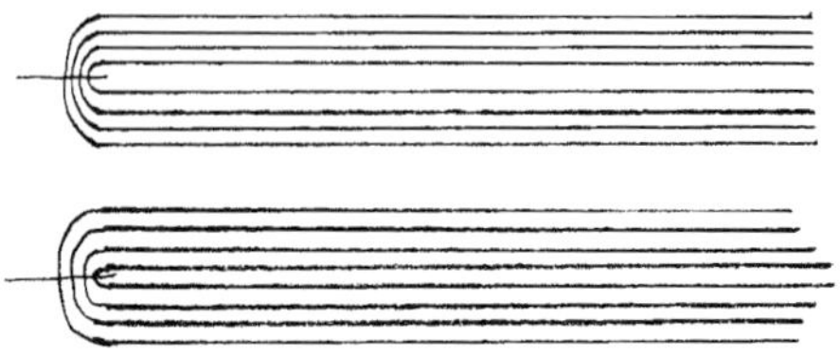

Fig. 1

One factor that greatly influences the handling of a book is whether the pages are cut at the outer margins to give a smooth surface, thus allowing the user to pick a place in the book easily to open it or if the slight rounding that results from having pages of equal size in the quire is left unchanged. If the centre-page and the outer bifolio of the quire have exactly the same size the centre-page can be expected to jut out slightly while the other pages successively fall back as they have to warp around the increasingly thick bundle of previous pages. Compare the schemes in Fig. 1.

However, the measurements of the pages in the first quire of the Šābuhragān are the following:

M542b II	J	|	H	M542b+ I	10.1 cm
(lost)		|	G	M470a+	10.1 cm
(lost)		|	F	M535+	10.0 cm
M472 II	M	|	E	M472 I	9.9 cm
(lost)		|	D	M482 I	9.8 cm
M477 II	O	|	C	M477 I	9.9 cm
M475a II	P	|	B	M475a I	9.7 cm
M519 II	Q	|	A	M519 I	? >7.3 cm

Here, pages H and J are the centre pages; pages A and Q are the first and last pages of the quire, the outer wrap. The reader starts the quire at A recto and finishes it at Q verso. The damage to A/Q is such that the precise size of the bifolio cannot be determined but there seems to be a steady increase in the size of the page from B to H, which indicates that neither of the above schemes seems to have been followed because for the upper of the two schemes given above the page size should decrease from A to H and for the lower one the values would have to be constant. There is some uncertainty about this because not enough of page A has survived to yield a measurement and page C seems to contradict the trend and, in any case, the surviving page sizes may be a result of wearing down the edges of some pages through use. There is also the possibility that the differences in the values are too slight to be significant or depend on how flat the individual pages are within the sheets of glass used to protect them.

The Manichaean fragments in the Turfan collection, dating from the 9th and 10th centuries and belonging to the Uigur Manichaean community, are almost exclusively written on paper. Yet these are in the main carefully made copies of manuscripts made during the Sasanian period and on the territory of the Sasanian empire centuries earlier and most likely to have been written on parchment. Since the hair and flesh sides of parchment have slightly different textures it is

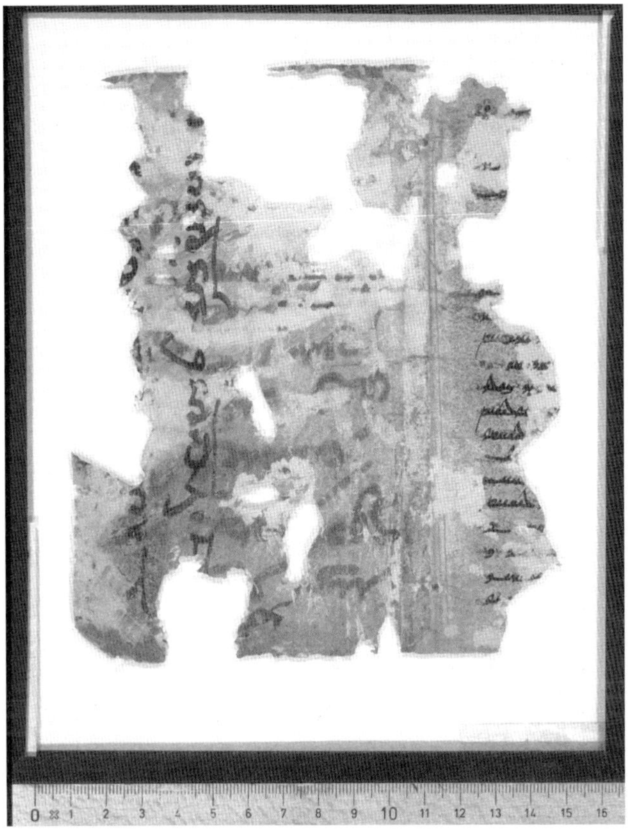

Fig. 2: So 14470 I recto (on the left) and II verso (on the right)

possible that there were certain rules for where to put the smoother side. Possibly there was, for example, a preference for placing miniatures on one of the two sides. If this were the case we could expect at least some of these features to be continued in the design of books despite the change to paper with its greater surface uniformity.

There is some evidence that the first page could be left empty. In So 14470, though there is some (clearly subsequent) writing on the recto, we can be sure that the recto was first left empty because the text on the following verso is the beginning of this text (see Fig. 2). It is possible that the recto was not just the first page of its quire but, in turn, actually the first page of the whole book. This might be the reason for leaving this page blank, or perhaps the page was intended to be an illustrated first page. However, while it is tempting to suggest that illustrated pages might have been first pages in quires this is clearly not so, since illustrations are also attested on verso pages, see below.

The scripts used by the Manichaeans are all right-to-left scripts; accordingly the books are also read from right-to-left. The right-hand page of this bifolio is the last page in the quire, showing the normal script size for this manuscript. The vertical writing in large script and other writings on the left-hand side are clearly secondary and confirm that the page was initially left blank.

The first recto pages of a quire share features that apply generally to recto pages. These include marginal letters such as a p to indicate a refrain or other letters indicating the initial letters of hymns which are always placed upside-down on recto pages but the right way up on verso pages. This is discussed in DURKIN-MEISTERERNST 2013. It seems to be related to the orientation of illumination on recto pages, which also contrasts with their orientation on verso pages, and which can be explained by a common principle underlying both sides, i. e. that the image is oriented towards the inner margin. Since the text is read horizontally but the picture has to be viewed vertically, the image and the text are never in the same orientation because the image is turned whereas the orientation of the text is constant (Fig. 3):

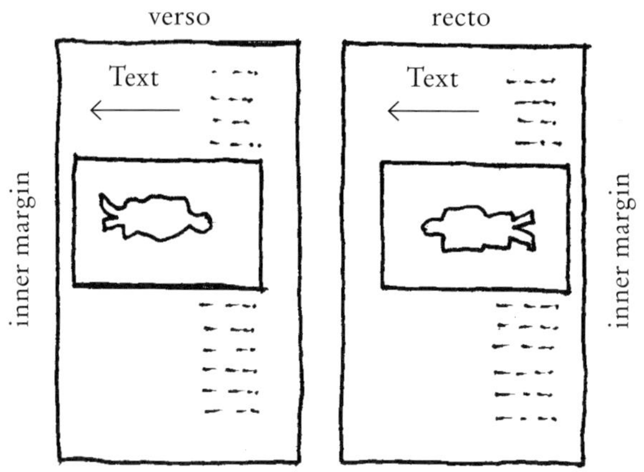

Fig. 3

The orientation of the images is due to the adoption of a feature of an album (Fig. 4)

Fig. 4

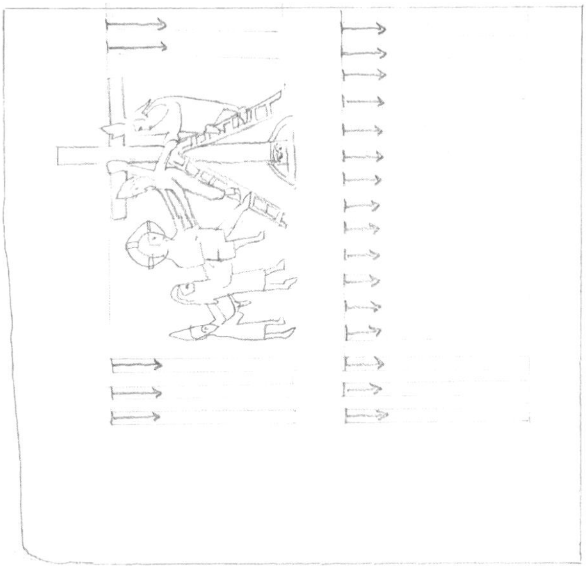

Fig. 5: Drawing of the lower part of a page from an Armenian manuscript, with an illustration in the second column oriented towards the central margin and therefore agreeing with the orientation in Manichaean books

For the person showing the image to his audience this had the advantage, in the case of a heavy book at least, that he did not have to lift the book up from the table or rostrum, he only needed to turn it towards the audience.

Interestingly, the same occurs in some illustrated Armenian manuscripts (s. plates 15 [10th c.], 16 [11th c.], 18 [11th c.], 20ff [10th and 11th c.] in *Armenian Miniatures from the Matenadaran Collection*. Yerevan 2009). There, even when the image is small enough to have fitted in either orientation into the space available, the orientation to the central margin is chosen (s. plates 9–13 [10th–11th c.] in the same book). See Fig. 5 (lower half of plate 13 on p. 77).

Other features of recto pages are attested on the fragment M6 (Fig. 6) There, each strophe of the abecedarian hymn begins with an introductory *ʾwn* 'O' on the recto only even though the hymn continues on the verso. The scribe is anxious to present the hymn in a more elaborate form on the recto than on the verso page. M6 recto also illustrates the use of initial or decorative letters in the first line.

In this image the first line of the column on the right contains šwbʾn ° ʾwn which consists of the last word of a verse followed by a punctuation mark and ʾwn before the first word of this verse bzmg, which is in the next line. In all the scribe writes ʾwn thirteen times on this page, always after a punctuation mark, and before the initial word of the verse. Even though the text continues on the verso the scribe never once uses ʾwn there.

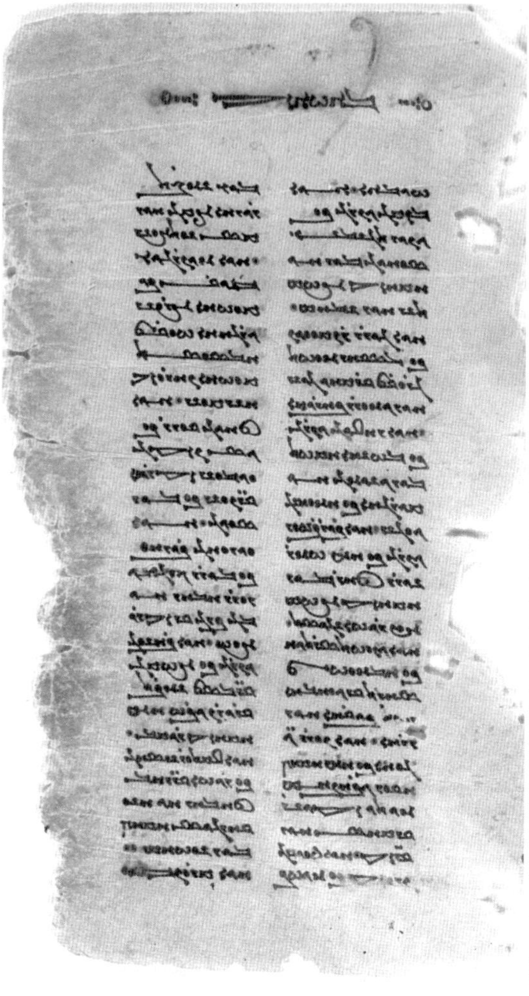

Fig. 6: M6 recto

In the first line of the column on the left the scribe writes bwd nhxt and uses for the final d in bwd a special form of the letter with a extension to the left. This form contrasts with the simple form of the same letter in the middle of rwd'n, the first word in the second line immediately below bwd. This extended, decorative form of the letter d is used by the scribe once again in the third line of the column on the right in tgnbnd. There it is combined with an extended joining line to ensure that the word extends to the end of the line, a device employed by Manichaean scribes either on its own or with extendable letters to present the text neatly on the page and which is visible on this page a number of times, e.g. in the fourth line of the column on the left. On the verso of this same page M6 the scribe uses d and r (the latter is distinguished from d by a dot but is otherwise identical with d) three times in this way, with the extended form of d/r at the end of the line. In bwd however, the extended, decorative d is not at the end of the line and is clearly not being used just to extend the spelling but rather because the first line on the recto receives special treatment. Note that this is not the beginning of the text which began just prior to this page. The feature is linked not to the text but to the page itself.

An important feature of double pages in the open book is the opportunity it provides to combine the headline of the verso of the first page with that on the recto of the second page to yield a continuous text, as I showed in Durkin-Meisterernst 2008, pp. 3–5. Care is taken to design double pages parallel to each other, as Henning established for the distribution of the colours of the headlines in M801a (quoted above) and as the following scheme for the quire of the Šābuhragān shows:

J	red	H
red		red
K		G
(lost)		red
L		F
(lost)		black
M		E
(lost)		red
N		D
black		red
O		C
black		red
P		B
black		black
Q		A
black		black

The reader starts the quire at A recto with a black header. From then on, through the quire, the colour of the header is common to both pages of the open book, i.e. A verso and B recto both have a header in black; B verso switches to red which is taken up on C recto, and so on. However, the scheme seems to be limited to double pages, there seems to be no overall pattern that characterises the quire as a whole. This shows clearly that the scribe, working on a prepared quire rather than on loose pages, was anxious to produce pleasing and symmetrical double pages as he came to them. However, he was not following an overall design pattern for the quire apart from general consistency in the distribution of the written text on the page using the same script, letter size etc. Judging by this quire the centre pages are not marked or decorated in any way that goes beyond the treatment of double pages elsewhere in the quire.

On the last verso page of a quire a quire mark can be expected and one such is probably preserved on M76 verso in the lower margin (see DURKIN-MEISTERERNST 2008, p. 7). In similar book cultures such as Syriac, the quire mark consists of a letter used for its numerical value. The book binder uses these letters to place the quires in the correct order in the book. In some cases, the first recto page of the following quire is marked with its own number; sometimes the number of the following quire is written on the last verso of the preceding quire to yield a consistent pattern that the book binder simply has to match to obtain the correct sequence. There was therefore at least the possibility of consistent patterning between the last verso of one quire and the first recto of the next quire on what would, in the bound book, yield a double page. Whether this was always uppermost in the mind of the scribe as he moved from the end of the one quire to the beginning of the next one, is impossible to judge.

An interesting question concerns the presence of illuminated pages in a quire. Lack of evidence for an overall design of the quire makes this question very difficult to tackle, namely, whether every book had (at least) one illuminated page and whether this miniature had a particular place in the book or in the quire. Not many illuminated pages have survived. Importantly, all of them are on single pages; none are on double pages. It seems that centre pages were not used for illuminations, despite the larger surface these double pages offer and even the comparatively flat surface centre pages provide. In fact, given the orientation of the attested miniatures shown above, the use of the large surface provided by double pages is not to be expected. The images are always oriented towards the central margin as a base line. Even though this base runs through the centre of an open double page it is not crossed. This is a confirmation of the use of the book as an album and the need to display the page with the miniature by placing it vertically. This allows only one page to be shown because the other page is not visible to the viewer.

If the hair/skin side of parchment books were relevant for the illuminator we could expect the illumination to be always placed only on recto or only on verso sides. But some illuminations are certainly on verso sides, as GULÁCSI 2005, pp. 147 (MIK III 4979), 150 (Or.8212–1692), 152 (MIK III 36) and 164 (MIK III 4959) shows. Of course, this also shows that the relative position of miniatures within the book was not necessarily fixed, even though, on the other hand, the miniatures generally do not directly illustrate or refer to the text present on the same page as the miniature. Note that the Šābuhragān quire presented here has no pictorial decoration and no miniature. Unfortunately, this does not allow the conclusion that the whole book had no miniatures. Perhaps there was no miniature in this quire because this quire was not the first quire in the book?

One reason for suggesting that most or all books had at least one illuminated page is that the presence of such an illumination might have been the cause of the deliberate destruction of the Manichaean books all of which were ripped apart, possibly in order to dislodge the illuminated page and destroy that. The non-illuminated pages were allowed to fall to the ground where some of them survived. The desire to destroy the illuminated pages may not have been simply Islamic iconoclasm as the German excavators of a hundred years' ago often suggested. It may have been a more general superstitious fear of strange images of beings that might have been identified as demonic and also in part be due to simple vandalism.

References

ALLBERRY, C.R.C. 1938: *A Manichaean Psalm-Book, Part II.* Stuttgart (Manichean Manuscripts in the Chester Beatty Collection 2).

BOYCE, M. 1954: *The Manichaean Hymn-Cycles in Parthian.* London/New York/Toronto.

DURKIN-MEISTERERNST, D. 2008: "Aspects of the organization of Manichaean books in Central Asia." In: *Gazette du livre médiéval* 52–53, pp. 1–15.

— 2013: "Die Orientierung der Bilder in manichäischen Bücherfragmenten in der Turfansammlung." In: C. MARKSCHIES/J. VAN OORT (eds.): *Zugänge zur Gnosis. Akten zur Tagung der Patristischen Arbeitsgemeinschaft von 02.–05.01.2011 in Berlin-Spandau.* Leuven, pp. 277–284 and 336–346 (Abb. 5–15).

GULÁCSI, ZS. 2005: *Mediaeval Manichaean Book Art. A Codicological Study of Iranian and Turkic Illuminated Book Fragments from 8th–11th Century East Central Asia.* Leiden/Boston (Nag Hammadi & Manichaean Studies 57).

HENNING, W.B. 1937: *Ein manichäisches Bet- und Beichtbuch.* Berlin (APAW 1936, Nr. 10) [= W.B. HENNING: *Selected Papers I*, pp. 417–558].

HENRICHS, A./L. KOENEN 1970: "Ein griechischer Mani-Codex." In: *Zeitschrift für Papyrologie und Epigraphik* 5, pp. 97–216.

POLOTSKY, H. J./A. BÖHLIG 1940: *Kephalaia. 1. Hälfte.* Stuttgart (Manichäische Handschriften der Staatlichen Museen Berlin 1).

The Torah of Temporary Marriage

A Study in Cultural History

Yaakov Elman †

I have more than once recounted to Maria the "awe and trembling" with which I reached out to take hold of the *Rechtskasuistik des siebzehnten Jahrhunderts* volume of her superb edition of the "Sasanian lawbook" (MHD) in NYU's Bobst Library some 15 years ago. I might add that part of that awe was the intense attraction of Rechtskasuistik in her title to a talmudist. It has thus been my constant companion since, as Maria has become a valued and faithful friend as well, and one of the Iranists who made my entrance into the field both pain-free and immensely enjoyable. The following study depends not only on her edition of MHD, but also her thoughtful article on the institution of temporary marriage in its Sasanian context, and I offer it happily in her honor. As usual, since the paper is addressed to a dual audience, that of Iranists and talmudists, I apologize for some notes that are unnecessary for one group or the other.

"Appearances can be deceiving", the old adage goes, and this is nowhere more appropriate than at the frontiers of intercultural contact. A custom borrowed from another culture can acquire a new meaning and rationale in the host culture, even one sharply at odds with its origins, and, if my supposition is correct, the following study illustrates this process.

One of the most enduring institutions of Iranian culture, and one which survived the transition to Islam, is that of "temporary marriage". However, though it survived, it lost some of its legal valence, and instead took on the exclusive motive of "marriage for pleasure" in its translation from one cultural context—Zoroastrianism—to another—Islam. In this paper I would like to examine its translation into yet another cultural context already in ancient times, that of Sasanian rabbinic culture.

In a series of papers published in the last decade I have pointed to many indications of Babylonian Jewish acculturation to Middle Persian customs and mores, and I have also, from time to time, noted the differing valences of such borrowings.[1] That is, in the last decade it has become clear that the Babylonian

1 For a summary view, see Y. Elman: "Middle Persian Culture and Babylonian Sages: Accomodation and Resistance in the Shaping of Rabbinic Legal Tradition." In: C.E. Fonrobert/M.S. Jaffe (eds.): *Cambridge Companion to Rabbinic Literature.* New York 2007, pp 165–197.

Jewish community of late antiquity—"talmudic times"—was acculturated to the Iranian environment in which it had existed for more than seven centuries, and its rabbis were not less acculturated than their non-rabbinic brethren. In the urban areas, at least, many if not most Jews spoke Persian in its Middle Persian form, were familiar with Iranian culture and mores, and to varying extents had internatized Iranian values and adopted Iranian customs. There is hardly a more convincing proof of this than the fact that two prominent rabbis are reported as having contracted temporary marriages when away from home.

In this paper I wish to concentrate on the way that that custom gained an entirely new meaning in its Jewish locale. I will do so by examining pertinent statements by R. Nahman, who is reported to have customarily contracted such marriages when visiting Shekhunziv. ISAIAH GAFNI, followed by DANIEL BOYARIN, have noted the similarity of the rabbinically-problematic Iranian custom of "temporary marriage" that the Babylonian Talmud (hereafter: the Bavli) reports was practiced by two prominent talmudic sages, Rav and R. Nahman.[2] Luckily, we have a good deal of information about both of them, but it happens that the data on R. Nahman's view of sin and sexuality can serve us to understand how a pious, sin-fearing rabbi could adopt such a seemingly un-rabbinic custom. In the end, it was a complex mixture of Zoroastrian and rabbinic values that made temporary marriage an acceptable option as a solution to a rabbinic problem.

Temporary marriage, which is enshrined in Sasanian legal sources, allows a woman to be married for a set time, and then return to her former status—even that of a woman married to someone else. Of course, this form of temporary marriage is forbidden by the biblical prohibition of Deuteronomy 24:1–4, since a married woman who is divorced from her husband cannot return to him after being married to someone else. Presumably the above rabbis married women who were otherwise unattached, but the fact that they married them for "a day" or "days" is sufficiently unsettling to warrant further examination.

Unfortunately, the name given to this institution in Arabic is *mutʿah*, "enjoyment", which, while interculturally interesting, is misleading for our period. To understand the cultural metamorphosis the institution underwent in traversing the space from Iranian to rabbinic culture, we must first examine its meaning in the former. Fortunately, the custom has been the subject of a careful study by the *doyenne* of Pahlavi legal scholars, MARIA MACUCH. After an exhaustive analysis of the relevant Sasanian legal sources, she concluded as follows:

> Summarizing the details we were able to gather on temporary marriage, it seems evident that this form of matrimony was an integral part of Sasanian family law, since it gave flexibility to a marriage system, built on the most important

2 For Gafni, see ISAIAH M. GAFNI: *The Jews of Babylonia in the Talmudic Era: A Social and Cultural History* [Hebrew]. Jerusalem 1990, p. 272. For Boyarin, see DANIEL BOYARIN: *Carnal Israel. Reading Sex in Talmudic Culture.* Berkeley 1993, pp. 144–145.

> principle that no Zoroastrian man should die without leaving offspring! Since a woman—according to the unwritten rule in every patrilineal society—could only be married to one man at a time, this form of time-limited marriage opened additional options. A woman could conclude a *pādixšāy* marriage ["marriage with full matrimonial rights"—YE] on a temporary basis and enter the lineage of her husband for this period with all the legal consequences of this type of wedlock and the rights of a *pādixšāy* wife. After the marriage expired, she could re-enter her original lineage and put her reproductive capacities at the disposal of her native family (as an *ayōgēn*[3] or *stūr*[4]) by concluding a *čagar* marriage.[5] The reversed sequence was also possible: she could remain in her own lineage by concluding a *xwēdōdah*-wedlock with her father or brother for a certain period, then, after the expiry of the marriage contract, enter an exogamous marriage. In short: temporary marriage was one of the important means of using the fertility of a female to the fullest degree without having to give up the patrilineal line of descent. In the context of Sasanian family law temporary marriage has an important function, and, consequently, its logical place in the underlying pattern of kinship and marriage. Moreover, this type of marriage was by no means restricted to women of an inferior economic or social standing, as is the case in the post-Sasanian period up to this day. On the contrary, every Zoroastrian woman of standing was obliged to act as *ayōgēn* or *stūr*[6] if necessary and to enter a time limited marriage in order to procure offspring for a deceased father, brother or husband. In the context of Shīʿī family law, on the other hand, it remains a strange fossil, alien to the concept of Muslim marriage and highly controversial. We have, therefore, good reasons to assume that temporary marriage is in fact one of the age-old institutions of Iranian law that survived the Muslim invasion of Iran and was therefore only adapted to Muslim law in those regions where this ancient custom had been practiced for many centuries.[7]

Thus, in its original context, temporary marriage had little to do with "enjoyment". However, it hardly functioned as an aid to reproduction in rabbinic society, and the talmudic passages that deal with it point up the problems that would result if there were offspring. Moreover, the two rabbis who are reported to have contracted such marriages are known to have had offspring from their permanent wives, and no offspring are recorded from these temporary marriages.

3 "Intermediary successor"; see M. Macuch: "The Function of Temporary Marriage in the Context of Sasanian Family Law." In: *Proceedings of the Fifth Conference of the Societas Iranologica Europaea held in Ravenna, October 6–11, 2003*. Vol. I: *Ancient and Middle Iranian Studies*. Ed. by A. Panaino / A. Piras. Milano 2006, pp. 585–597, here p. 590, n. 36 and the literature noted there.

4 "Substitute successor or proxy"; see *ibid.*, p. 592.

5 For this form of auxiliary marriage, see M. Macuch: *Das sasanidische Rechtsbuch Mātakdān i hazār Dātistān (Teil II)*. Wiesbaden 1981 (AKM XLV, 1), p. 7f.

6 An Iranian form of "levirate marriage", except that the male partner need not be a levir, but anyone within or without the family designated by the *paterfamilias* or the court.

7 Macuch 2006, pp. 595–597. The interested reader is referred to an earlier paper of hers: "Die Zeitehe im sasanidischen Recht – ein Vorläufer der šīʿitischen mutʿa-Ehe in Iran?" In: *AMI* 18 (1985), pp. 187–203.

Again, as noted, because of the biblical prohibition of remarrying one's former wife if she had been married in the meantime would have made it impossible situation for the temporary wife's former husband to reunite with her. If this institution was employed by some rabbis, and, we must assume, non-rabbis as well, it must have had another meaning within its new cultural context. Moreover, rabbinic strictures on non-marital expressions of sexuality make the Muslim understanding of this custom untenable within the rabbinic system of family law and ethics. What then could have been its meaning/rationale within that system? As we shall see, the ultimate rationale seems to be due to a tight amalgam of both rabbinic and Zoroastrian values, one that might also have served as its justification within the Zoroastrian ethical system as well.

Rav and R. Nahman were considered major rabbinic authorities both in their own time and later on; indeed, their views are still determinative in several areas of Jewish law, R. Nahman in matters of civil law, and Rav in matters of ritual law. It should however not be thought that their authority insured them against criticism; R. Nahman, in particular, is criticized for his upper-class speech and lifestyle, and the licentiousness of his daughters.[8] It is thus significant that he is *not* criticized for contracting temporary marriages. The practice was not considered deviant or subject to criticism, even though even when his very choice of "upper-class" ("preppy"?) words in a conversation with another rabbi is criticized severely.

Fortunately, the rabbis who are reported to have contracted such marriages were well-known, and a good deal of information exists about them. Moreover, such an investigation does not depend on the reliability of our data, since we will be dealing with images and their meaning to the community that preserved them. Images can be instructive even on a personal or historical level; in this case, such an investigation may give us important insights into how the rabbis themselves construed such a problematic borrowing. In the decades since WILLIAM S. GREEN and JACOB NEUSNER raised doubts about the historical reliability of attributions, scholars have shied away from even considering the possibility of "rabbinic biography". While I am on record as opposing this hypercritical point of view,[9] the following essay is not an excursion into rabbinic biography *per se*, nor even an attempt to build an intellectual profile of a particular rabbi, although we will be concentrating on one in particular, R. Nahman. Rather, I hope to understand why the Bavli would preserve—with seeming equanimity—reports of two prominent rabbis (Rav and R. Nahman) acting so "unrabbin-

8 See "Middle Persian Culture and Babylonian Sages", p. 171; for criticism of R. Nahman, see *ibid.*, pp. 173–175.

9 See my „Review Essay: Argument for the Sake of Heaven: *The Mind of the Talmud: An Intellectual History of the Babylonian Talmud.*" In: *JQR* 84/2–3 (Oct 1993–Jan 1994), pp. 261–282, and, more recently: "Hercules Within the Halakhic Tradition: A Response to Ronald Dworkin." In: *Dinei Yisrael* 25 (2008), pp. 7*–42*; and "The Socioeconomics of Babylonian Heresy." In: *Jewish Law Association Studies* XVII (2007), pp. 80–126.

ically" as to contract temporary marriages in the Iranian style, and how they might have understood such an action within their own moral universe. In order to strengthen my case, however, I have drawn all the justificatory statements from those attributed to R. Nahman. As far as I can see at present, a similar reconstruction cannot be attempted in the case of Rav, although there are some indications that he held views similar to those of R. Nahman in this matter, as we shall see.

Such an attempt is all the more urgent since both sages, Rav and R. Nahman, are also reported as acting against fornication. Thus, the report of their contracting temporary marriage presents us with what we may call a cultural *lectio difficilior*, since the indices of his acculturation to Middle Persian culture and Sasanian mores are precisely those that we might expect to be the subject of criticism. In fact, though R. Nahman is criticized in the Bavli for employing Iranian words when words used by the rabbis or common people would have sufficed (Qiddushin 70a–b), or for allowing the women of his household minimal contact with men outside the family circle (ibid.), and was accused of a Iranian-like arrogance (*ibid.* and compare Shabbat 94a and Avoadah Zarah 71a), as noted above, he is not criticized for adopting this most striking instance of Iranian culture. It may be that the reports of Rav's contracting such marriages shielded R. Nahman from such criticism; Rav seems to have been immune to the criticism that was leveled against R. Nahman. Alternatively, it may be that the narrator of Qiddushin 70a–b did not see anything wrong in the practice himself, even though one of the redactors of the report of R. Nahman's marriages was uncomfortable with the practice and suggested that the marriage was in name only and was not consummated (Yoma 18b, Yevamot 37b).

This is all the more remarkable in light of one aspect of this story which I did not touch upon in my earlier analysis of it, one which relates to the Bavli's views of acculturation. Earlier I noted that in the story of the confrontation between R. Nahman and R. Yehudah of Pumbedita noted above, which is narrated from an anti-Mahozan point of view, R. Nahman is severely criticized for his use of words that are neither typical of rabbinic usage nor of that of the people.[10] In particular, in regard to two of them (*etrunga* and *anbag*), he is criticized for the Iranian pronunciation. It would seem that the narrator's view of the proper conduct of a rabbi also involved the purely *cultural*, rather than strictly *religious*, aspects of Jewish life. In our own terms, we might refer to R. Nahman's "preppy accent," which the narrator saw as due to arrogance *(ramut ruha)*, and which in his eyes was as serious as allowing the women of his household to have some contact, minimal as it was, with males from the outside. The fact the some Hasidic groups consider it to be a mark of piety to speak English with a Yiddish accent would indicate that that view is still prevalent. This may have less to do with maintaining a Judeo-Persian dialect than guarding the Jewish character of

10 See "Middle Persian Culture and Babylonian Sages", pp. 173–175.

Babylonian Jewish Aramaic. Another factor relates to the socioeconomic aspects of this "preppy accent", which is clearly part of the narrator's accusation against R. Nahman for being arrogant, both in terms of the negative value given to that character trait in rabbinic sources, but also because it was considered a hallmark of the Iranian national character, as I noted above. But it is note-worthy that one of the favorable alternatives, *itztaba*, is of Greek origin!

The immensity of the influence of Rav and R. Nahman's on the final shape of the Bavli—whatever the historicity of our information about them—constitutes an important cultural datum that enables us to understand the role that acculturation plays in the formation of that redactional artifact that we call "the Bavli." It is also worthy of note that R. Nahman's disciple, Rava, also a citizen of the cosmopolitan community of Mahoza, while permitting polygyny, did not himself engage in it, nor, as far as we know, of temporary marriage. Indeed, even though he is on record as approving polygyny—as is Rav[11]—it is important to note that neither of them, nor their colleagues, as far as we know, engaged in the practice. We will go into this further below.

It is clear from various reports regarding these sages that both were members of the aristocratic rabbinic elite; Rav's grandsons married into the exilarch's family (Hulin 92a), and R. Nahman seems to have been the son-in-law of another exilarch (Hulin 124a). As I have demonstrated elsewhere, though Rav voiced the opinion that anyone who learns anything from a magus is worthy of death (Shabbat 75a), he himself dispenses such information, presumably because he considered such information to be "common knowledge" and not particularly Zoroastrian in origin.[12]

Rav died in 247 CE, R. Nahman died around 320 CE, while Rava died in 351/352.[13] Since R. Nahman quotes Samuel, who died in 254, some 60 times, and notes that his father was a scribe in Samuel's court (Bava Metzia 16b), his lifetime then overlaps the reigns of some eight Sasanian kings—from Shapur I to Shapur II. The period of these reports—and Rava's possible reaction to them, spans over a century of early Sasanian rule—what we may term the "Golden Age" of Sasanian-Jewish relations. While there seems to have been a breakdown in relations with the regime after 468, it should be noted that the Bavli's redactors were still concerned with close Jewish social interactions with their non-Jewish neighbors well into the fifth century. I described the situation in another paper:

> Mahoza was part of a huge *entrepôt*, *the* metropolis of the entire Sasanian Empire, with a heterogeneous population, where Iranian soldiers were common and some were billeted with Jewish families (Shabbat 47b, Pesahim 5b, Taanit 20b, 21a),

11 For Rav, see Pesahim 113a, for Rava, see Yevamot 65a, and see below.

12 *Ibid.*, pp. 193–194.

13 For the first, see AARON HYMAN: *Toledot Tannaim va-Amoraim*. Jerusalem 1964, vol. III, p. 943b, for his discussion, he gives the date as 631 of the Seleucid Era. For Rava, see *ibid.*, p. 1057a, where he gives 663 S.E. I make no great claim for these dates, but cite them for convenience.

> with a large population of proselytes (Qiddushin 73a) and Christians, as there certainly were in Ctesiphon, some of whom were originally Jews. In the same West Tigris conglomerate, was the *catholicos*, bishop of Ctesiphon and eventual head of the Persian Christian Church; both he and the exilarch, the political head of the Jewish community, were kept within call of Shapur II's great audience hall and palace across the river (Eruvin 57b).
>
> Mahoza's Jews were wealthy, cosmopolitan, canny (Berakhot 59b), skeptical of rabbinic authority (Sanhedrin 99b–100a, Makkot 22b); Mahozans had the reputation of being perspicacious (Berakhot 59b) and delicate (Shabbat 109a); the women were pampered (Pesahim 50b) and idle (Shabbat 23b), and the men pursued still more wealth (Berakhot 59b).[14]

Since Mahoza was part of the larger metropolis of Ctesiphon, which as one of the termini of the Silk Route from China, it was a center of international trade, and, given R. Nahman's position as a judge in the exilarch's court, it is hardly surprising that his word is almost always authoritative in matters of civil law. He reports of himself that his "colleague Huna"—that is, R. Huna, the premier disciple of Rav—said of him that he and "King Shapur are brothers as regards civil law" (Bava Qamma 96b). It should be noted that R. Nahman's master Samuel, an acknowledged authority in civil law, also resided in a trading center, Neharde'a, at the junction of Nehar Malka and the Euphrates.

In our context, this is particularly revealing of the cultural situation, for it is clear that R. Nahman was the most "Persianized" of the prominent Babylonian rabbis, as I have demonstrated in a number of studies. Most striking is the fact that this Iranization, including his practice of "temporary marriage" when away from home while visiting Shkhuntziv, and Rav doing so when visiting Mahoza-Weh Ardaxšir (Yoma 18b, Yevamot 39b), did not diminish their standing in the eyes of the rabbinic community (though, as I have shown, that was not true of at least one representative of less acculturated Pumbeditan rabbinic community). Indeed, his authority was such that, as in a case set forth in Bava Qamma 96b he also exercised super-judicial authority, as he is reported to have commented to Rava:

> Did I not say to you that when I am sitting in judgment you should not make any suggestions to me, for Huna our colleague said with reference to me that I and 'King' Shapur[15] are [like] brothers in respect of civil law? That person [who misappropriated the pair of oxen] is a notorious robber, and I want to penalize him.[16]

14 See "Socioeconomics", pp. 81–82.

15 Although Shapur II reigned from 309–370, and R. Nahman died in 320, it is likely that the reference is to Shapur I, since in all probability Shapur II, who was crowned *in utero*, did not assume active rule until 325. See Soncino *ad loc.*, SOLOMON FUNK: *Die Juden in Babylonien*. Berlin 1902, I, p. 73. The plural may then refer to both R. Nahman and his teacher Samuel, who was close to Shapur I (see Sanh 94a).

16 For a discussion of this passage, and the legal background of which it is part, see HANINA BEN-MENAHEM: *Judicial Deviation in Talmudic Law: Governed by Men, Not By Rules*, London 1991, pp. 14–115.

Likewise, in an exchange between R. Huna and R. Nahman, the former admits that the law is decided in accordance with the Mahozans' view, because "you (pl.) are close to the gate of the exilarch, and civil cases[17] are frequent there" (Bava Batra 65a). It should be noted that the same had been said of his master Samuel (Bava Batra 115b).

This Mahozan authority in matters of civil law continued in the next generation with his disciple Rava, also a member of the cosmopolitan Mahozan society, and also eventually a member of the exilarch's circle. Although this degree of high-handed authority is not reported of Rava, he too seems to have been regarded as the supreme authority in the next generation.[18] Indeed, the Mahozan school displays a marked preference for the law as practiced; typical of Rava is the praise of professional judges: "he is a judge and descends to the profundities of the Halakha" (Bava Qamma 39a, 53a, Bava Metzia 117b (read: Rava); a similar attitude may be discerned in R. Nahman (Ketubot 10a [in the name of Samuel], Gittin 34a–b, Qiddushin 42a–b, and see Bava Batra 65a, where R. Huna concedes R. Nahman's point). Nevertheless, none of these scholars noted for their authority in commercial law and torts restricted their teaching to these areas, and Samuel, R. Nahman and Rava are all mainstays of the Babylonian Talmud's discussions on other matters as well.

I

The balance of this paper will be devoted to R, Nahman's adoption or use of the Iranian custom of "temporary marriage." I have elsewhere pointed out that the Bavli's redactors—with perhaps one exception—seem to have had no particular *moral* qualms about this practice; the Bavli's discussions deal only with technical points, and any problems are ironed out.[19]

Rabbinic Judaism had come to terms with other institutions that seemed to skirt the edges of rabbinic norms, such as the biblical institution of *yefat toar* (Deuteronomy 21:10–14), where a woman taken in battle could be taken but would eventually have to opportunity to be married to the soldier who took her captive. As the rabbis put it, "the Torah recognized *(dibberah kenegged)*

17 See Rashbam on Bava Batra 65a s.v. *de-meqarvitu*, second interpretation, following Rabbenu Hananel. Alternately, "judges are frequently [in session there]", following his first interpretation.

18 Rava seems to have adjudicated at least one case in Pumbedita (Bava Qamma 27b). He also, like his master, reversed other judges' rulings (Bava Qamma. 117a), and levied fines (Hulin 132b).

19 See "Middle Persian Culture and Babylonian Sages", p. 171.

a man's evil inclination" (Qiddushin 21b); but in good rabbinic fashion they placed sharp limits on the practice.[20]

But how are we to understand the practice of Rav and R. Nahman? The reports of their temporary marriages are analyzed from a halakhic point of view, with two technical objections that are dealt with in technical fashion. The morality of the practice is not addressed; indeed, there is no indication that there was a moral issue for Babylonian rabbis, except very indirectly, by a redactional alternate suggestion. In the discussion referenced above, I took this moral indifference as an indication of the high degree of acculturation to Iranian norms and customs the late antique Babylonian Jewry had attained. But, while sociologically this approach can be justified, that question still remains: how did these venerable and venerated rabbis justify the practice in their own minds? How was it reconciled with rabbinic notions of proper behavior? It should be remembered that while polygyny was practiced by the Sasanian upper classes, and either countenanced or even recommended by some rabbis, as noted above, we do not hear of it in rabbinic circles. More to the point, perhaps, the Bavli has no report of either Rav or R. Nahman as taking a second wife in the lifetime of their first.[21] And yet these short-term liaisons were apparently perfectly acceptable. Indeed, R. Nahman himself, in his role as a judge in Mahoza, had sentenced a young newly-wed husband to be whipped because he had brought a charge of unchastity against his new wife, since he detected a lack of virginity in her. Since he had been a young bachelor prior to the wedding, R. Nahman admonished him with: "How would you know? Have you visited [the red-light district of] Mabrakta?" (Ketubbot 10a). And Rav had a couple whipped for contracting their marriage by the (rabbinically legal) mode of marital intercourse (Yevamot 52a); indeed, he disapproved of contracting marriage without the usual familiar agreements *(shiddukh)*, as reported in Qiddushin 12b.

The puzzle deepens when we compare other reports of R. Nahman's views. As we shall see, he thought of himself as a paragon of a sin-fearing person, to be compared to the saintly Rabbi Judah the Patriarch. To a modern mind this is difficult to swallow.

Let me first present the report as it appears in Yoma 18b, since it seems to have been the earlier one:

20 See in general Moshe Halbertal: *Interpretive Revolutions in the Making: Values as Interpretive Considerations in the Midreshei Halakhah* [Hebrew]. Jerusalem 1997, esp. pp. 13–41.

21 A. Schremer has suggested that some polygyny existed among Jews in Roman Palestine; see his "How Much Polygyny in Roman Palestine?" In: *Proceedings of the American Academy for Jewish Research* 63 (1997–2001), pp. 182–223. This does not seem to have been very common among rabbis either there or in Babylonia, but see n. 27 and the text below.

Yoma 18b

Whenever Rav came to Darshis [that is, Weh Ardaxšir, known to the Jews as Mahoza], he would announce: Who would be mine for a day? Whenever R. Nahman would come to Shekhunzib [on the eastern bank of the Tigris] he would have it announced: Who will be mine for a day?

But has it not been taught: No man should marry a woman in one country and then go and marry a woman in another country lest they [their children] might marry one another with the result that a brother would marry his sister or a father his daughter, and one fill all the world with *mamzerut* [bastardy[22]] to which the scriptural passage refers: "And the land become full of lewdness?" (Leviticus 19:29)—

I will tell you: [The affairs of] the rabbis are well-known [and either the wife or the children will proudly proclaim their connection to the rabbi].

But did not Rava say: If one has proposed marriage to a woman and she has consented then she must await seven clean days [because she sees blood; how then could they wed on the spot]?—

The rabbis informed them before by sending their messengers earlier. Or, if you like, say: They only arranged for private meetings with them, because 'You cannot compare one who has bread in his basket with one who has no bread in his basket'. [That is, having a wife at least theoretically available may mitigate his desire.]

In Yev 37b the reports are embedded in a much more elaborate discussion on doubt and certainty; here in Yoma 18b, the possibility of illegitimate births when a man has intercourse with many women is raised.

At any rate, the above passage deals with two problems connected to the practice, both of them technical rather than moral or ethical, and proposes two technical answers. First, there is the problem of lewdness, not, as we might expect (from our point of view) of the practice itself, but rather of its possible effects: the offspring of such marriages might marry one another and engender *mamzerim*. The answer is pragmatic: rabbis' travels and doings are well-known (and, we might add) the offspring of such marriages were presumably proud of their heritage and presumably no stigma attached to it, and so there was no danger of such *mamzerut*.

The second problem is that (according to Rava, R. Nahman's disciple), women who become engaged to be married experience a flow of "blood of desire," and so, according to a custom initiated byBabylonian women themselves, must wait till that flow ceases and for seven "clean days" thereafter; this blood is thus equivalent to menstrual blood, which causes ritual impurity. How then can the rabbis marry these women soon after their arrival in town?

The Talmudic passage—that is, the redactor(s)—then proposes another answer to this problem, one that is not only pragmatic, but has a cultural valence.

22 The rabbinic *mamzerut* is not strictly equivalent to the English "bastardy", but the rendering will do for our purposes. Generally, we retain the Hebrew.

This alternate answer is that the couple *did not actually have sexual intercourse*, and so there was no need to wait seven days after the engagement. However, if this is true, then there was no problem of possible *mamzerut* either! This answer seems to reflect redactional discomfort over this practice. In other words, in the century and a half that separated R. Nahman from the redactors of the Talmud, the attitude to temporary marriage had changed, at least in some rabbinic circles.

But there are more serious problems with this response. The rabbis—and Rav and R. Nahman among them—were well aware of the power of sexuality. What is the point of bread in one's basket if one never eats it (to use the redactional metaphor), and, indeed, is forbidden to eat, since there is the problem of an issue of blood or *memzerut*? Furthermore, according to rabbinic law, newlyweds may not remain alone when the bride has had her period before the marriage has been consummated. A *baraita* in Ketubot 4a requires that the couple part; the groom "sleeps with the men" and the bride with the women. In light of Abaye's remark in Sukkah 53a that man's desires are in proportion to his greatness in Torah, it is unlikely that even rabbis would be allowed to remain in private with their new brides in such circumstances! Nor, we may add, it is no more likely even without Abaye's observation, for if these rabbis could restrain themselves, why go through the charade of contracting a marriage in the first place? Of course, the point of the use of the "bread in one's basket" observation is precisely this: that having the right to eventually satisfy one's desires, one can wait. But according to this alternate response, one waits in vain, since the temporary bride is never available for intercourse!

Again, the phrase, as introduced in Ketubbot 4a, refers to a case in which one of the parents of the couple died during the festivities: in that case, the marriage is first consummated, and then the couple separates for the seven days of mourning. But, the *baraita* emphasizes, this is not the case if the bride's menses come, for then they separate immediately! Thus, the scenario suggested by the alternate answer does not really respond to the query regarding "engagement blood", which is equivalent to menstrual blood, though it might be used to answer the question regarding the possibility of *mamzerut*. If the woman has become a menstruant, they must separate, and what then is the point of the temporary marriage altogether?

Moreover, it is clear that this alternate does not read well with the earlier part of the Talmudic passage either, since that earlier part supposes that there is indeed a danger of *mamzerut*, since intercourse *does* take place. Without intercourse, there can be no offspring, and no problem.

The considerations noted above sharpen the difficulty that this report raises. Just how difficult this practice is to justify in rabbinic terms may be seen by the ways that the translators of the Soncino Talmud explain the matter. Here are the explanations proffered in the two volumes of the Soncino Talmud that deal with the two passages that contain this report, the first in Yoma 18b, the second in Yevamot 37b.

> This strange statement, completely contradicted by the saintly character of both Rab (v. 'Er. 100a, Hag. 5a, Keth. 48b, Sanh. 76a) and R. Nahman, has been explained through an account in Babli [Avodah Zarah] 76b. King Shapur entertained two guests, Bati b. Toba and Mar Judah. In accordance with Iranian custom, he "honoured" them by sending to each a concubine. This gift was rejected by Mar Judah, but accepted by Bar Toba. Rab and R. Nahman, as leaders of their people would find themselves similarly embarrassed by such attention, on the occasion of their official visits to Iranian cities. Some princes are known to have taken the refusal of their "gift" as a serious affront. In order to avoid complications, these Rabbis hit upon the device of declaring themselves married, i.e., provided with a wife in the city they visited, going to the length of marrying "for a day" the local wife, thus helping them to escape the royal "gift".' For another explanation v. Yeb., Sonc. ed., p. 235 n. 7.
>
> That alternate explanation is as follows:
>
> Yoma l.c. [Rashi: 'for the days' (plur.). He was anxious to establish a home in Shekunzib which he often visited on business affairs and consequently wished to secure a wife to bless his home whenever he would stay there, v. Obermeyer[23], p. 191].

Unfortunately, there is no indication that R. Nahman was the king's guest in Shekhunziv, or that he would have been offered sexual hospitality. Indeed, from King Shapur's admonition to Tuvi b. Batni in Avodah Zarah 76b—that he was not certain that Tuvi was Jewish since he had not refused the slave-girl, it is clear that Tovi *could have refused, as the king's rabbinic guests had indeed done.* Indeed, if anything, their refusal raised their status in the king's eyes, quite to the contrary of Soncino's explanation. As to the second explanation, why would either of them "establish a home" for a day, or perhaps, "a few days", following Rashi's variant, when, of course, the standard version is the cultural *lectio difficilior* and to be preferred? Needless to say, the impulse for these explanations is apologetic, but we, as historians, must understand this report in its historical and cultural context.

Of course, the real problem with these explanations is precisely historical and cultural: they assume that this custom must be explained *away* rather than explained *on its own terms.* In this collision with Iranian and Jewish/rabbinic culture, we must understand how the rabbis, and perhaps more particularly Rav, who, as noted above, asserts that one who learns anything from a Zoroastrian priest is worthy of death (Shabbat 75a) understood (or justified or rationalized) his actions?

SONCINO's explanations are cases of special pleading, all the more so when we see that the Bavli's discussion manifests no particular moral problem with the practice. However, this is not to say that that there were no problems at all, even after the two technical objections were dealt with. However, this report

23 Referring to JACOB OBERMEYER: *Die Landschaft Babylonien im Zeitalter des Talmuds und des Gaonats. Geographie und Geschichte nach talmudischen, arabischen und andern Quellen.* Frankfurt a.M. 1929.

highlights a cultural gap which offers us an opportunity to explore and understand that gap between those two cultures, that is, of bridging that gap to help us better understand the society that brought forth the Bavli, and the culture it shared with its Iranian overlords.

SONCINO's explanations reflect its writers' and editors' unease with the institution of temporary marriage even within the rabbinic system. That is to say, even if all the requirements were fulfilled—a wedding ceremony and a divorce afterwards—we will have to understand how Rav and R. Nahman themselves justified the practice in their own minds. Indeed, immediately after the Bavli's reports of these temporary marriages it cites a *baraita* which disapproves of marrying a woman with the intent of divorcing her!

Indeed, even the alternate answer seems to assume that though temporary, the marriage was contracted in the usual halakhic manner, with *huppah* and *qiddushin*, that is, with the usual customs that mark passage into the marital state. But if so, why refrain from intercourse? Again, since the marriage is for "a day" or "days", what of the marriage's end? Was there a divorce? By suggesting that the rabbis refrained from intercourse, the redactor implicitly admits that this marriage was irregular. And if it was intended only to respond to the problem of "engagement blood", the first answer was more to the point: the "marriage" took place only after seven clean days had elapsed.

It should also be noted that while it is the *third*-generation amora R. ZEIRA who reports on the stringency of "seven clean days" (Berakhot 31a) the redactors posit it of Rav in the *first* amoraic generation. Of course, it is possible that the stringency had been accepted before R. Zeira's time, and SHAI SECUNDA in his as yet unpublished dissertation has suggested that the practice had its roots in Palestine in Rabbi's time, that is, in the generation *before* Rav.[24] Still, R. ZEIRA takes it as an example of a stringency adopted by the "daughters of Israel", and *not* one enacted by the rabbis, a fact stressed by Rava in a conversation with his disciple R. Papa (Niddah 66a). Elsewhere I have suggested that its stringency arose as a Babylonian Jewish women's response to a Zoroastrian "holier than thou" attitude to Jewish menstrual practices, which were more lenient than Zoroastrian ones.[25] If so, the Palestinian parallels are irrelevant, and the redactional supposition is just that: a supposition. For our purposes, however, it is important, because it highlights the redactional discomfort with the practice of temporary marriage.

However, before dealing with the discomfort, we must first investigate the possible ways that these temporary marriages were contracted within the

24 For a full discussion of the issue, see his as yet unpublished dissertation: "*Dashtana—Ki Derekh Nashim Li": A Study of the Babylonian Rabbinic Laws of Menstruation in Relation to Corresponding Zoroastrian Texts*. Yeshiva University 2007, pp. 144–189.

25 „Acculturation to Elite Persian Norms in the Babylonian Jewish Community of Late Antiquity." In: E. HALIVNI/Z.A. STEINFELD Y. ELMAN (eds.): *Neti'ot David*. Jerusalem 2004 [appeared in 2005], pp. 31–56; see p. 34.

system of rabbinic law. Given these rabbis' positions in the community, it is inconceivable that they were done totally *à la Perse*, without *huppah* and *qiddushin*. Indeed, if we assume that they were not carried out in the usual way, how did Rav and R. Nahman draw the line between temporary marriage and fornication *(zenut)*, an issue that was of concern to both of them, as noted above.

There are a number of R. Nahman's statements that bear on the issue; his policy seems to have been that marriages and divorces should not be made too onerous, and that the law should take cognizance of human intention. Thus, Rava reports the following views of R. Nahman in Qiddushin 9a, 19a–b, 43a–b, and 22b–23a, respectively. In the first R. Nahman permits betrothal even when effectuated by a declaration written on material worth less than the statutory *perutah*, and with only the consent of either the father or the woman herself. In the second, Rava says in R. Nahman's name that a father may appoint his daughter as his agent in receiving the betrothal money or gift, even if that gift is transference of a debt even though there is no actual monetary consideration, and in the third, Rava says in R. Nahman's name that a man can appoint two agents who will serve both as agents and witnesses to the betrothal, while in Gittin 22b–23b R. Nahman validates a divorce document written by a non-Jew, and defends his ruling against multiple objections by Rava.

In other words, it would have been relatively easy—according to his own view on these matters—for R. Nahman to have taken care of the mechanics of a regular marriage and divorce, even within a few days, or perhaps even less if arrangements had been made in advance.

And, indeed, the very fact that it is attributed to only these two prominent rabbis, Rav and R. Nahman—both connected to the exilarch's circle—suggests that it conformed to the first response that limited such a practice only to rabbis whose doings were well-known, and that the report may have originated as a critique against those very circles. In its present form, however, the critique is muted, if, indeed, it was intended as a critique at all.

There is another source (Qiddushin 6a) that touches on temporary marriage that should be mentioned, a disquisition on returnable gifts made by R. Nahman's disciple, Rava. In it Rava questions the very applicability of his teacher's innovation (on the model of Sasanian law) of returnable gifts to betrothal, though it is not clear that he was rejecting the institution of temporary marriage.

In Sasanian law, temporary marriage can scarcely be separated from the Sasanian practice of conditional (and returnable) gifts, and it is R. Nahman who first applied this Sasanian principle to a problem that arose within a rabbinic framework, as I have documented elsewhere.[26] However, Rava, R. Nahman's disciple, in his review of the circumstances under which his master's principle that "gifts given on condition that they be returned are nevertheless [valid] fits" (Qiddu-

26 See my "Returnable Gifts in Rabbinic and Sasanian Law."In: *Irano-Judaica VI*. Jerusalem 2008, pp. 150–195.

shin 6b), applies the principle not to the marriage itself, but to the money given to effectuate the engagement *(kesef qiddushin)*. He suggests that this would not work. It may be that Rava, who was apparently of middle-class origins as indicated by his prayer for wealth (M. Q. 28a), may indeed have reflected the disapproval of the practice, but since he does not allude to it explicitly, his attitude is not clear.

Two generations later, R. Ashi suggested *(ibid.)* that the problem arises because such an arrangement makes the marriage appear to be a form of barter *(halifin)*. Once again we must ask how R. Nahman effectuated these marriages—which, once again emphasizes the irregular nature of this union. An alternate possibility is that neither Rava nor R. Ashi had temporary marriages in mind, since there it was the marriage was that was "returnable," so to speak, and not the *kesef qiddushin*. But the possibility of "coded speech"—that is, that R. Ashi meant this as a veiled criticism of Rav or R. Nahman, cannot be ruled out.

This raises yet another question. We have only this report of two very prominent rabbis who practiced temporary marriage. Was the practice was more widespread than is reported in the Bavli? Did other rabbis contract temporary marriages, or non-rabbis? Given human nature, I assume that this was the case, though we have no evidence for it.

As noted, Rava's view of the practice is not clear, but Rava's view on matters Iranian was much more jaundiced than his teacher's. Thus, in an exchange with R. Nahman on why Hallel [= a selection from the Book of Psalms usually recited on a festival] is not recited on Purim, he observes that "we are still the slaves of Ahasuerus" (Megillah 14a), while R. Nahman suggests that the reading of the Megillah, or Scroll of Esther, substitutes for the recitation of Hallel.

We may wonder what more Rava would have expected from the Purim miracle. But it is clear that he expected more from the Sasanian government than it was prepared to give. For example, he considered the exemption from taxes for Jewish priests on the part of the Achaemenid government (Ezra 7:24) to apply to rabbis in the Sasanian period (Nedarim 62a). Likewise, he is reported to have had problems with the Iranian authorities (Hagigah 5a–b). His intense interest in the book of Esther—the Bavli preserves no fewer than 17 of his exegetical comments on the text—may indicate that he saw the book, as he apparently viewed the book of Ezra—as shedding light on his own era.[27] The controversial issue of the status of Hanukka as a non-Sinaitic festival may have had something to do with this interest as well.[28] By stressing the fact that Hallel was not instituted for Purim—for which we have an entire biblical book—while we do recite Hallel for Hanukka, for which there is no biblical mention, Rava once again (as in Makkot 22b) emphasized rabbinic authority over against that of the Bible.

27 See for now my comments in "Be-'Inyan Seruv Mordechai Lehishtahavot le-Hamam: Rava ba-Halakhah u-ba-Aggadah." In: *Beit Yitzhak* 5767 (2007), pp. 826–836.

28 See „Acculturation to Elite Persian Norms", pp. 31–56, esp. pp. 38–43.

Thus, the exchange in Megillah 14a indicates R. Nahman's positive view of the Sasanian government, and it may be that his naming of one of his daughters Dēnag (see Qiddushin 70a) was done in the knowledge that that was the name of the founding queen of the Sasanian dynasty; we might compare this to a British Jew naming his daughter Elizabeth.[29]

Beyond that, there is some indication that, though Rava formally approved of polygyny (Yevamot 65a)—given long Jewish tradition he could hardly have disapproved—he himself refrained from taking such a course, and would not take a second wife. Indeed, the contrast is striking, since the Palestinian R. Ammi ruled against the practice, while Rava permitted it with the proviso that the husband could afford to support both (Yevamot 65a).

Interestingly, in this passage Rava rejects R. Ammi's position that a man who takes a second wife must divorce his first, but he did not practice what he preached. There is a charming (etiological?) story (Bava Batra 12b) of Rava and his eventual second wife, Bat Rav Hisda. It seems that Rammi b. Hamma and he were sitting before R. Hisda in study and his daughter was in his lap. Playfully R. Hisda asked her which of the of these two students she preferred, and she replied "Both!" And Rava had the presence of mind to answer "And I will be last!"—as apparently he was.

Another charming story confirms the marriage of Rava and Bat Rav Hisda as having been a second marriage for both, and this reflects Rava's reluctance (refusal?) to take a second wife. This is from Yevamot 34b.

> When Rabin came [from the land of Israel] he stated in the name of R. Yohanan: A woman who waited ten years after [separation from] her husband, and then remarried, would bear children no more.
>
> Said R. Nahman: This was stated only in respect of one who had no intention of remarrying: if, however, one's intention was to marry again she may conceive.
>
> Rava said to Bat Rav Hisda's [who had waited ten years before marrying Rava]: The Rabbis are talking about you [that is, you were widowed for ten years, but when we married, we were blessed with children; how is this so if you were strictly celibate during that time?]. She answered him: I had my mind on you.

Why did she have to wait ten years (or more) between Rammi b. Hamma's death and her marriage to Rava? Presumably he was married to another woman, though it is possible that he felt that he could not afford a second wife. According to his own account at one point in his life he prayed for wealth—and it was given to him (Moed Qatan 28a). Did his wealth come only from R. Hisda's estate, since that same source notes that R. Hisda was wealthy? Again, we do not know, but there is at least the possibility that Rava could have afforded to marry his daughter but chose not to; the fact that polygyny does not seem to have been

29 Dēnag was wife of Pabag, see Philippe Gignoux: *Iranisches Personennamenbuch*. Vol. II: *Mitteliranische Personennamen*. Vienna 1986, p. 75 n. 312 s.v. *Dēnag*, 2–6. Current editions read "Donag", the Biblical Hebrew word for "wax", an unlikely name.

practiced by the Babylonian rabbis would lend credence to this possibility. This is all the more remarkable when we consider, as MICHAEL SATLOW and ADIEL SCHREMER have emphasized, that we must assume that Babylonian Jewish society was at least minimally polygynous.[30]

In sum, then, even Rava, whose attitude to Iranian mores was much more jaundiced than his teacher's, did not disapprove of the practice of temporary marriage even by even by rabbis. We now turn to the question of how the rabbis may have justified their adoption of this practice even while condemning and punishing fornication.

II

First of all, it must be understood that R. Nahman himself appears to have seen nothing wrong with it, and, indeed, considered himself an exemplary God-fearing individual, as we see from a comment he makes regarding the last *mishnah* of Sotah (on Sot 49b). Still, we must ask: But how did R. Nahman himself view the practice? How did he understand it in rabbinic terms?

First, let us look at R. Nahman's self-image (Sotah 49b).

> [The Mishnah states:] When Rabbi [Yehudah the Prince] died, humility and fear of sin ceased. R. Yosef said to the *tanna* [who recited this mishnah], Do not include [in this mishnah] the word 'humility', because there is I [who am humble]. R. Nahman said to the *tanna*, Do not include 'fear of sin', because there is I.

To our minds, this statement might be difficult to reconcile with R. Nahman's actions in contracting temporary marriages, even when we allow for the existence of polygamy and concubinage. What ever could R. Nahman have had in mind?

The clue comes from another statement of his regarding sin and thoughts of sin in Yoma 28b–29a:

> R. Nahman said: ... [29a] Thoughts of sin are more injurious [to one's health] (*qashu*) than the sin itself, your analogy being the odor of meat [which stirs the appetite more than eating it]. The end of the summer is more severe [i. e., hotter] than the summer itself, your analogy being a hot oven [in which it is easier to kindle a fire; at the end of summer it is so hot that any additional heat in intolerable]. A fever in winter is severer than in summer, your analogy being a cold oven [It requires a great deal of wood and effort to warm up the cold oven in the cold days of winter. Thus must a fever be very severe to afflict one on a cold day]. It is harder to remember well something old than to commit to memory a fresh thing,

30 See MICHAEL L. SATLOW: *Jewish Marriage in Antiquity*. Princeton 2001, pp 189–192, and ADIEL SCHREMER: *Male and Female He Created Them: Jewish Marriage in the Late Second Temple, Mishnah and Talmud Periods* [Hebrew]. Jerusalem 2003, pp. 204–210.

> your analogy being a cement made out of old cement [that has been used before; it is hard to dissolve it and re-make it].

Thoughts of sin are more injurious to health and conscience than the sin itself! To understand this idea, we must turn to David Brodsky's important paper, delivered at the Irano-Judaica conference in Jerusalem in October, 2010. Brodsky has pointed out in that this paradox is itself a very Zoroastrian idea. I quote from Brodsky's handout with his kind permission.

> Dēnkard 6:227 (transcribed and transl. by Shaul Shaked)
> *pad harw wināh ī menēd [ku] hān rōz pēšār* (?) **būd pad menišn gōwišn kunišn az-eš abaxš ud andar yazdān pad-padīd *bawišn.*
> "He (every person—DB) should be contrite and repentant to the gods for every sin he thinks he was guilty of that day in thought, speech and action."[31]

Here an evil thought is itself a sin. However, here we may add that R. Nahman's point is a bit different. As his analogy indicates, the thought alone—without the action—is more *injurious* than the action itself. As Rashi puts it, "the lust for women is harder [on the body in that] it weakens *[lehakhish]* the flesh more than the deed itself." This conforms to the usual meaning of *qasheh* in these sayings and proverbs, as Michael Sokoloff has pointed out in his *Dictionary of Jewish Babylonian Aramaic*, where he lists our passage under *qeshei*, "severe, serious".[32]

R. Nahman's point is illustrated by another Zoroastrian passage from the Dēnkard that Brodsky also lists:

> Dēnkard 6:236
> *xīr ī yazdān hagrez pad menišn az-eš be ne ēstēd, ud a'ōn abar ēstišn ku hān ī abārōn ciš hagrez pad menišn ne menīdan.... ce hamē tā mard kirbag ud ahālyīh menēd ēg yazd andar tan mānēnd ud dēwān staw bawēnd ud be šawēnd, ud ka ciš ī abārōn menēd ēg dēw andar ō tan dwārēnd.*
> "Never depart from the things of the gods in your thoughts. A man ought to be attached to them in such a manner that he should never think a sinful thing in his mind ... For as long as the man thinks good deeds and righteousness the gods stay in his body and the demons are made powerless and depart, and when he thinks sinful things, the demons rush into his body."[33]

And when demons rush in, the body is harmed.[34] It would seem that this is the essential meaning of R. Nahman's dictum, though, as Brodsky notes, other rabbinic statements do equate sinful thoughts with sin, in particular, one attributed to R. Nahman in Shabbat 64a–b. Here is Brodsky:

31 See Shaul Shaked: *The Wisdom of the Sasanian Sages (Dēnkard VI).* Boulder, CO 1979, pp. 88–89.

32 *A Dictionary of Jewish Babylonian Aramaic.* Ramat Gan 2002, p. 1049a.

33 Shaked 1979, pp. 92–93.

34 See my "Midrash Halakhah in Its Classic Formulation." In: Lieve M. Teugels/Rivka Ulmer (eds.): *Recent Developments in Midrashic Resarch*, Piscataway, NJ 2005, pp. 3–16.

> … That thoughts of the heart, need atonement can be found in several Babylonian *sugyot*.[35] In [Shabbat 64a–b], Rav Nahman quotes Rabbah bar Abuha as expounding: "Moses said to Israel, 'Perhaps you have returned to your original sinning ways.' R. Nahman said in the name of Rabbah b. Avuha: They said to him, 'Not one of us had intercourse' (Numbers 31:49). 'If so, what is this sacrifice for?' They said to him, 'If we have escaped from the hands of sin, from the hands of [sinful] thoughts we have not escaped.' At which point they said, 'We are offering the sacrifice of the Lord.' " (Numbers 31:50).
>
> The statement argues that the sacrifice offered in Numbers 31:50 was to atone for sinful thought. If such thought needed atonement, then it would seem to be sin.[36]

As Brodsky points out, such a sentiment is also attributed to Rav, who, as noted above, also contracted temporary marriages. The passage appears in Bava Batra 164b–165a.

> R. Amram said in the name of Rav: [There are] three transgressions which no man escapes for a single day: Sinful thought, [lack of concentration in] prayer, and slander.
> 'Slander'? [How] could one imagine [such a thing, can no one avoid slander every day?]![165a]
> — Rather, the fine shades of slander [were meant].
> R. Yehudah said in the name of Rav: Most [people are guilty] of robbery, a minority of lewdness, and all of slander.
> 'Of slander'? [How] could one imagine [such a thing]!
> — Rather, the fine shades of slander [were meant; that is, speaking well of someone, a comment which elicits a negative response].

From our point of view, it is important to note that R. Yehudah has replaced Rav's *hirhurei averah* with *arayot*, sexual transgressions, and has attributed the sin to a *minority* of people, as opposed to Rav's insistence that *everyone* transgresses the sin of having thoughts of sin every day. This is just as we would have expected. Rav, like R. Nahman, both members of the Babylonian rabbinic aristocracy with ties to the exilarch, express sentiments common among that acculturated class; R. Yehudah, who ran a wine shop, resists.[37]

Brodsky also notes that Rava, R. Nahman's disciple, also expresses this sentiment in Bava Batra 16a, where he suggests that though Job did not sin with his lips, he did sin in his heart. Furthermore, Brodsky shows that this doctrine was explicitly rejected in earlier rabbinic sources from Roman Palestine, as in Tosefta Peah 1:4, a passage which is cited in Qiddushin 40a, that is, in the Bavli itself!

It is significant to note that though the Toseftan source is quoted in the Bavli, just a page earlier, the Bavli's redactors, in analyzing the story of a young man

35 Zevahim 88b and Arakhin 68a.

36 My thanks go to Dr. Brodsky for sharing this article with me.

37 See "Socioeconomics", pp. 85–86.

who obeys his father and fulfills the *mitzvah* of sending away the mother bird before taking the chicks—and falls to his death while fulfilling the two *mitzvot* for which long life is promised—considered that he might have entertained thoughts of sin which caused him to fall to his death. Though ultimately the *sugya* rejects this notion too, the idea that protection against sinful thoughts is one of the rewards of Torah study is introduced by R. Yosef and further developed by Rava (Sotah 21a). What is particularly significant is that the *sugya* there opens with an exposition of Prov 6:23 by R. Menahem b. Yose that does not mention protection from evil thoughts, but rather protection from suffering. It is the Babylonians who introduce the notion of protection from evil thoughts.[38] I have already documented the influence of Zoroastrian thinking on R. Yosef's theology of divine anger;[39] here then is another index of the influence that Zoroastrian thought had on him.[40]

We have thus seen that Rav, Rava and R. Yosef all held to the idea that sinful thoughts were themselves sinful, as did R. Nahman. However, only Rav and R. Nahman went so far as to contract temporary marriages when away from home in order to prevent such thoughts. We have noted that they both associated with the exilarchs of their time, and presumably shared—knowingly or not—in the Iranized Jewish culture of their class. Thus while the problem posed by sinful thoughts was essentially rabbinic, it was exacerbated by the Zoroastrian notion that sinful thoughts were themselves a sin. Their solution was thoroughly in keeping with that Iranized culture: the adoption and adaptation of the Iranian institution of temporary marriage, not for its Sasanian and Zoroastrian purpose of providing offspring, but of keeping these rabbis from sinful thoughts.

What then may we say of Rava, who presumably would not express his disapproval of the practice when his own master contracted such marriages? His disagreements with R. Nahman are scattered throughout the Talmud, but this issue would have touched on personal matters. As we have seen, David Brodsky has made a strong case for Rava agreeing with Rav and R. Nahman on the basic premise that sinful thoughts constitute sins in themselves. At least one anecdote in the Bavli seems to reflect him acting on this premise: in Ketubot 65a he finds the sight of Homa, Abaye's beautiful widow, so attractive that he goes home immediately after dealing with her case in order to sleep with his wife.

38 See my "Righteousness as Its Own Reward: An Inquiry into the Theologies of the Stam." In: *Proceedings of the American Academy for Jewish Research* 57 (1991), pp. 35–67, esp. pp. 55–58.

39 See my "R. Yosef be-ʿIdan Ritha." In: *Bar Ilan Annual* 30–31 (2006). *Memorial Volume for Prof. M. S. Feldblum*, pp. 93–104.

40 This reification of thought within the halakhic system had far-reaching consequences; see (for the time being) my "Hercules Within the Halakhic Tradition, 7*–42*"; and Shanah Schick's dissertation, "Intention in the Babylonian Talmud: An Intellectual History" (Yeshiva University, 2011).

Nevertheless, this anecdote does not quite fit our needs; presumably Rava would not have run home had his wife been menstruating. Indeed, if we carry this thought further, we might well inquire as to why polygyny or temporary marriage were not the solutions to their wives' unavailability during those times of the month. However, this would be carrying the need to banish sinful thoughts to an absurd length; at some point self-control must be exercised. The purpose of temporary marriage would have been to limit those occasions as much as possible, since, as Rav observed (see above), no one is immune from *hirhurei averah* every day.

III

Having reached this point we may widen our inquiry, and consider the question of just how long a man (or woman) can resist *hirhurei averah* without damage to his or her health. MICHAEL SATLOW's prescient paper of 1994 may also be relevant here. SATLOW has suggested that the Bavli's view of seminal emission (which he sharply distinguishes from self-arousal and masturbation) was influenced by Zoroastrian notions, but he locates this idea in the Bavli's redactional layer.[41] However, he distinguishes that from masturbation, a practice that *tannaim* (second and third-century Palestinian sages) condemn. Indeed, they "condemn a man who touches his own penis, and self-arousal generally".[42] This applies to touching one's penis while urinating. However, there is a report that R. Nahman permitted this to a married man. To some extent, then, R. Nahman sees marriage—even when one's wife is unavailable—as mitigating one's vulnerability to *hirhurei averah*. How long one may go without marital sex is not clear, though the famous mishnah in mKetubbot 5:6 permits long periods of abstention from marital relations because of the pressure of occupational requirements, particularly for sailors and caravaneers. Presumably, the stresses of the job diminish one's libido.

This permission to limit one's marital obligations did not apply to rabbinic students, and the mishnah only allows them to leave their wives for periods up to thirty days, and not more, at least without their wives' permission. Nevertheless, as DANIEL BOYARIN has pointed out, the Bavli's discussions considers much longer periods of abstention. Thus, in the course of the Bavli's discussion of Ketubbot 5:6, we find much more flexible views regarding the marital obligations of members of the rabbinic class in Ketubot 61b–62a: they may go away for two or three years without their wives' permission, or, according to another

41 MICHAEL L. SATLOW: "'Wasted Seed,' The History of a Rabbinic Idea." In: *Hebrew Union College Annual* 65 (1994), pp. 137–175.
42 *Ibid.*, p. 144.

view, as long as they desire. However, under ordinary circumstances, R. Nahman is much less lenient.

> How often are scholars to perform their marital duties? –
> R. Yehudah in the name of Samuel replied: Every Friday night.
> "That brings forth its fruit in its season" [Psalms 1:3] R. Yehudah, and some say R. Huna, or again. as others say. R. Nahman, stated: This [refers to the man] who performs his marital duty every Friday night.[43]

Note that it is R. Nahman who requires (or limits) a scholar's marital obligation to once a week, aside, presumably, from the night when his wife visits the ritual bath after her menstrual period. Clearly, however, there were other exceptions as well, as when one's wife acts particularly lovingly as a signal that she wishes that her husband sleep with her; according to R. Shmuel b. Nahmani they will have children who the like of which had not been seen Moses' generation (see Eruvin 100b).

Nevertheless, DANIEL BOYARIN, in his study of rabbinic views on sexuality, *Carnal Israel*, pointed up the contradiction between the belief that sexual relief, or release, was a requirement of health, and the permission for rabbinical students to leave their wives for extended period. He rightly observed that it was implicit in the sources, and not a product of his own interpretation.[44] However, a closer look seems to indicate that what we have here is not so much a contradiction as a dispute, openly acknowledged. Rava notes that "The rabbis [=rabbinical students] have relied on R. Adda b. Ahabah and act accordingly at the risk of [losing] their lives." I have reproduced the Soncino translation, with a minor change; it in turn is based on Rashi's interpretation of *be-nafsheihu*, "at the cost of their lives" (lit., "by their souls" but more usually "regarding themselves") rather than the more usual "themselves". BOYARIN prefers this alternative and translates the sentence: "Rava said that our Rabbis have relied upon Rav Ada the son of Ahva and indeed practice in accordance with his view."[45] One might think that Rashi was influenced by the following story of R. Rehumi who lost his life by neglecting his wife's needs. However, in Yevamot 64b we have a similar situation, where Rava wonders at Abaye's adopting a view which eventually led to his death, by marrying Homa, who had already buried two husbands.

> When R. Yitzhak b. Yosef came he related: Such a case was once submitted to R. Yohanan in the Synagogue of Ma'on on Yom Kippur which fell on a Sabbath. A woman, it happened, had circumcised her child who died; her second [sister circumcised her child] and he also died, and her third sister appeared before him. He said to her, 'Go and circumcise him'. Said Abaye to him [=R. Yitzhak b. Yosef]: See, you have permitted a forbidden and a dangerous act.

43 This teaching is recorded in Bava Qamma 82a as well.
44 BOYARIN 1993, p. 145.
45 *Ibid.*, p. 144.

> Abaye, however, relying upon this statement [of R.Yohanan that it requires three occurrences to establish a presumption] married Homa the daughter of Issi b. R. Yitzhak b. R. Yehudah, although Rehavah of Pumbedita had married her and died, and R. Isaac son of Rabbah b. Hana had subsequently married her and also died. And after he had married her, he himself died also.
>
> Said Rava: Would anyone else acted so much [at the risk] of his life [*be-nafsheih*]?

Thus, we have two cases in which Rava uses the expression as a play on words, relating to the fatal results of adopting a certain halakhic position of which he disapproves.[46] Still, the expression is used again in Yevamot 22b (there it is perhaps redactional) and Boyarin's rendering may be defended on the basis of *be-nafsheih* there. If so, however, the very next sentence in Ketubot 62a (which is probably redactional) supports the view that the rabbis, in acting in accordance with the view of R. Adda b. Ahava, endangered themselves as in the case of R. Rehumai, who was a student of Rava. Thus, Boyarin's contention that "a relatively late Babylonian tradition" reverses the prohibition of extended absences is not quite accurate, unless he refers to R. Adda b. Ahava, who, as a disciple of Rava, and may be dated to the fifth generation of amoraim, that is the middle third of the fourth century, which is not all that late in talmudic terms. It is worth quoting Boyarin's searching analysis of this issue at length, though my understanding of the situation differs somewhat from his.

> We find here a relatively late Babylonian tradition, which, in contrast to all earlier authorities, reverses the ruling of Rabbi Eliezer that the married scholar may not absent himself for more than thirty days from his wife and permits absences of several years. The reversal demonstrates powerfully how much pressure the halakhic requirements that a husband must sleep regularly with his wife brought to bear on the entire socio-cultural system.
>
> There is here, to be sure, an apparently self-contradiction. On the one hand, I have claimed on the basis of fairly explicit Babylonian texts that these men held that adults cannot do without sex and that therefore they must marry early. On the other hand, I am arguing that to solve problems occasioned by those same early marriages, some of them promulgated a system of exceedingly long absence of husband from wife. The contradiction is, I think, internal to the system and not an artifact of my reading. Several solutions seem possible. One is that the understanding was that very early marriage would dampen sexual desire forever. A perhaps more plausible suggestion would be that the men were not expected to be celibate during these long absences from home. He goes on to discuss our cases of Rav and R. Nahman, and another in Taanit 16a]. If indeed there was a widespread practice of such temporary marriages for rabbinical students far from home (and this possibility is quite speculative), it is much easier to understand why the Talmud would have represented the primary problem here as being the wife's sexual

46 It should be remembered that he himself married Bat Rav Hisda as a widow and while he was a widower. Presumably burying several wives did not constitute a danger to the husband, given the mortality rate of women in childbirth.

> needs and not the husband's! Another possibility would be to read this as another example of "thinking with women," the notion that men often talk about women when referring in fact to their own sexuality, such that here the requirement of a certain frequency of intercourse because of the needs of women becomes, *ipso facto*, a means of giving men permission to enjoy that frequency of intercourse themselves. It is important, however, to note once more that at least in the rabbinic formulation, the need of women for sex is not described in pejorative terms.[47]

After suggesting that this practice became normative despite the many opposing voices—the Mishnah, Rav, R. Yohanan and Rava, that is, all the major authorities of the rabbinic world. He then concludes:

> The Babylonian Talmud's report of Rava's declaration—"our Rabbis have relied upon Rav Adda, the son of Ahva and indeed practice according to his view"—constitutes evidence for a change in social practice that is associated by the tradition with Rava, that is, with the leading Babylonian rabbinic authority of the fourth century, though to be sure, such attribution is not necessarily to be taken literally. It would seem, however, that the attempt to institute this change in marriage practice met with substantial opposition in spite of Rava's hegemonic prestige. The talmudic text that it is ostensibly recording the support for the innovation, reveals sharp dissension from it. These oppositional voices encoded within the text, I suggest, are intimations of the social conflict outside the text.[48]

It would seem that BOYARIN's assumption is substantially correct, but for one consideration. Human nature—men's sexual needs, plus the rationale suggested above, would have made temporary marriage a much more attractive possibility for rabbinical students, and so the possibility is not all that speculative, especially now that we know so much more about the acculturation of the Babylonian Jewish community to Iranian norms than we did when Boyarin published his study 20 years ago. It seems to me that in the light of all we know about Rava's understanding of human nature and his plea *(be-matuta minakh)* that his students maintain a relatively normal lifestyle (that is, he urged them to absent themselves from his lessons during the planting and harvest seasons, namely, at least during the months of Nissan and Tishrei,[49] that he managed to mitigate the worst effects of this new "pious practice". There is no way of knowing; certainly R. Rehumai did not listen to his master—and, according to Rava, paid for his mistake. In the nature of things, however, it is likely that at least a minority did stay away from home for a considerable length of time, and, in the end, there must have been a tension between the demand for immediate sexual release for health reasons (despite the ban on masturbation) and the reality of the absence of a spouse. That Rava's students were an independent lot may be discerned

47 *Ibid.*, pp. 145–146.
48 *Ibid.*, p. 147.
49 See Berakhot 35b.

from an exchange recorded between them in Bava Metzia 97a, where the students claim authority over the master in reference to the curriculum.

To return to the subject of rabbinical students absenting themselves from home for extended periods of time. How their wives coped is another question, a question for which rabbinic literature, no matter how subtly read, provides no clear answer. Could it be that when the rabbis condemn even touching one's penis, but praise a woman's examination of herself (Niddah 14a) they were really oblivious to the possibility of female sexual arousal and subsequent masturbation? After all, R. Huna was aware of the practice of tribadism, and declared that it made those women ineligible for marrying priests (Shabbat 65a–b). But what of women who were already married, and whose husbands were away? The rabbinic ideal may have been that women, in R. Yitzhak's words to Abaye—"who chase the sleep from their eyes [waiting for their husbands to return from study—in order to satisfy them?] in this world and achieve thereby the life of the world to come" (Ketubot 62a, see above)—but humans being humans, we may assume that some chose more immediate means of satisfaction when their husbands were not available.

In sum: temporary marriage, which was an important element in Sasanian family law to ensure a more fruitful use of women's fertility, entered rabbinic Jewish society as a defense against sinful thoughts. Ironically, both the institution and its rationale in rabbinic society were Iranian, though in a profound sense the justification was Jewish. Whether such a justification for its use existed in Zoroastrian society remains to be determined.

On Old Persian *tačara-* and its Elusive Meaning

Ela Filippone

1. Being rather scanty and repetitive, the royal Achaemenid corpus is in the main fairly intelligible. This is true especially for the OP texts.[1] Neverthless, many points still deserve attention, both in the field of syntax and lexicon. Suffice to think to the OP palatial terms, such as *t/dačara-*, *hadiš-*, *apadāna-*, *ardastāna-*, etc., whose full semantic implications are still far from being grasped, despite great efforts by scholars.

In what follows I will review the scholars' views on *t/dačara-* and advance some remarks on possible cognates in Modern Iranian languages.[2] My contribution will be modest and will provide no definitive solution. Inversely proportional to its scantiness is however the respect and affection with which these pages are dedicated to Maria Macuch for her sixty-fifth birthday, in recognition of the deep scientific value of her works on the Sasanian society and her natural cheerfulness and geniality, which always makes people feel good in her presence.

2. The first occurrence of *t/dačara-* is found in a multilingual inscription (DPa) attested in two copies in one of the oldest building in Persepolis, situated on the SW sector of the Terrace and commonly referred to as 'Palace of Darius' or 'Tachara'.[3] This building consists of a columned hall with a southern portico, flanked by rooms on its sides. A double reversed stairway connects it to the south court.

1 As well known, the Achaemenid royal inscriptions were written in three languages: Old Persians (OP), Achaemenid Babylonian (AB), Achaemenid Elamite (AE).

2 The present paper contains results of research conducted in the framework of a Project on Achaemenid epigraphy funded by the MIUR (PRIN prot. 2009JHSEE7_002); it also benefits from the results of former Projects funded by the MIUR (PRIN 2005105580_002, 2007ZKPPSM_003) and the DARIOSH Project for a new edition of the multilingual Achaemenid corpus (L'Orientale University, Naples—Tuscia University, Viterbo).

3 For the sake of convenience, the buildings at Persepolis and Susa will be referred to by the names frequently used in the literature; they will be written in inverted commas to stress the fact that I agree with the scholars who questioned these conjectural terms and the functions arbitrarily attributed to buildings (cf. Rossi 2003; Razmjou 2010).

The two copies of DPa are engraved on the jambs of the doorway connecting the portico with the hall, above the reliefs depicting the king with two attendants, one of which holding a parasol. They read as follow:[4]

DPa/OP	DPa/AE	DPa/AB
Dārayavauš xšāyaθiya vazarka [...] *haya imam tačaram akunauš*	*Dariamuš sunki iršarra* [...] *akka hi dazaram huttašta*	*Dariamuš šarru rabbū* [...] *ša bīta* (È) *agâ ipuš*
"Darius, the Great King [...] who built this *tačara*".	"Darius the Great King [...] who built this *dazarum*".	"Darius the Great King [...] who built this É/*bīt*".

In parallel to OP *tačara-* one finds: (1) in AE, *dazarum* (<h.tá-iz-za-ra-um>) a phonetic rendering of the OP word (a lw. in AE?); note that the phonetic value of AE <tá> is debated and some scholars opt for /t/ instead of /d/; (2) in AB, the logogram É for *bītu* "house, room, building, family, etc.", an alternative to the spelling *bi-it*. AB É/*bi-it* is regularly found in correspondence with OP *viθ-* "household, family" and OP *hadiš-*, for which see below.

To recover the meaning of *t/dačara-*, precious sources have been available since the very beginning: (1) the traditional Prs. lexicography records (a) *tajar* "winter house, with oven and heater" (also "treasury" in the dialect of Qazvin); (b) *tazar* "summer house; throne, platform"; (Arabicized form) *ṭazar* "summer house" (also *ṭarz* "id.");[5] (2) in Armenian one finds *tačar* (< Ir.) "temple", that in Classical Armenian occurs as "1. Tempel; 2. Palast; 3. Haus, Zimmer, wo das Gastmahl stattfindet, Gastmahl, Tafel" (HÜBSCHMANN 1897, p. 251).

If the connection of OP *t/dačara-* with the Prs. and Arm. forms appeared obvious (cf. already LASSEN 1845, p. 14), the semantic relation between them was hard to define. According to SPIEGEL (1881, p. 220), the meaning of *tačara-* "wird verschieden, je nachdem man die Bedeutung von neup. *tajar* (cella promptuaria, thesaurus) oder das armenische *tačar* (Tempel, Gotteshaus) zu Grunde legt". In HORN 1893, p. 84, where NPrs. *tajar* is given as "Winterhaus mit Heizvorrichtung; Magazin", *tazar* as "Sommerhaus" and Arm. *tačar* as "Haus, Tempel", the mention of OP *tačara-* is followed by the comment: "Bedeutung nicht sicher". To explain OP *tačara-*/AE *dazaram*, WEISBACH (1890, p. 95) resorted to NPrs. *tajar* ("Vorratskammer") and not to Arm. *tačar* ("Tempel") since for 'temple' different labels are used in the Behistun inscription.

4 All the examples come from the DARIOSH Archive and are given in transcription. Major reconstructions are in brackets.

5 Cf. DEHXODĀ s.vv. *tajar, tazar, ṭazar, ṭarz* for a collection of the definitions according to the different sources. See also LANE 1863 s.v. *ṭirz, ṭarz* "a house or chamber (= *bayt*) somewhat long; [said to be] a Pers. word arabicized; or a summer-house, summer-chamber".

The debate on the meaning of OP *t/dačara-* developed over time and expanded in different directions within an interdisciplinary framework; the linguistic argumentations interlocked with those concerning the functions of the 'Palace of Darius' and involving orientation, position, dimension and iconography of the building. An articulate analysis of the questions is in WÜST 1966, pp. 94–144 (q. v. for more details).

The orientation, e. g., provided support to the direct link with Prs. *tajar* "winter house": contrary to other buildings, the 'Palace of Darius' is south-oriented, securing light and warmth in winter. This was the first hypothesis advanced by HERZFELD ("Winterpalast"),[6] who subsequently dropped it in favour of another explanation (see below), also in view of the orientation to north of "a *tachara* of Xerxes" found east of the 'Hadish' (1941, p. 232). The fact that the building is behind the 'Apadana' was seen as in keeping with the traditional Iranian division of space, with public quarters distinct from private quarters. Similarly, the relatively modest dimension has been held as a proof of its private nature.[7] In general, scholars translate OP *t/dačara-* as "palace" (KENT 1953, p. 186, etc.), though some emphasize the residential character of the buildings called *t/dačara-* ("private/residential palace"): cf. LASSEN 1845, p. 14; BARTHOLOMAE 1904, p. 629; HINZ 1941, p. 237, MAYRHOFER 1964, p. 144, etc.

The origin of the word is controversial. Some scholars refrained from taking any position.[8] Some have pointed to a non-Ir. origin: GRAY (1932, p. 67 and fn. 3) thought of an Elam. borrowing into OP in view of the *t/d* alternation;[9] BRANDENSTEIN (1932, p. 25) excluded an original OP/AE origin; KENT (1953) presented *t/dačara-* as problematic, possibly a non-IE lw.;[10] EILERS (1959, pp. 249–250 fn. 3) conjectured a "voriranisch-elamischer Herkunft", traceable in the toponomastics already from the beginning of the 7th c. BCE.

The IE derivation theory has also found its advocates, who have increased over time. Favour has gained the connection of OP *t/dačara-* to Av. *tačar-* ("1. Lauf, Bahn; 2. ein Wegmass, eig. Länge einer Laufbahn", BARTHOLOMAE 1904, p. 629) and then to Ir. **tač-* "to flow, run", first proposed by FOY (1904, p. 456). MAYRHOFER (1964, p. 144) considered it as "[e]ine plausible Etymologie [...] trotz der auffallenden Nebenform *dačaram*".

6 HERZFELD 1908, p. 51. Occasionally, one finds authors still sticking at this semantic implication (cf. MATHESON 2001, p. 124, 'winter palace'), or to that recorded for Prs. *tazar* (cf. CUYLER YOUNG 1988, p. 25, 'summer palace').

7 The level of subjectivity of this kind of criteria produces conflicting statements; cf. "the Tachara is a small building and not suitable for the residence of a great king" (RAZMJOU 2010, p. 233) vs. "Given its modest dimensions, the Tachara was well suited to be a King's residence" (MOUSAVI 2012, p. 21).

8 Cf. MEILLET/BENVENISTE 1931, p. 158.

9 Accounted for by a peculiarity of the AE graphic system ("In Elamite, *t* stands for both *t* and *d*").

10 Cf. KENT 1953, p. 21 § 49, p. 31 § 76 V, p. 51 § 148 I.

Embracing the **tač*-derivation theory, Herzfeld put his first interpretation of *tačara-* ("Winterpalast") aside:

> the etymology of *tachara* is in fact 'stadium', as 'race-course' or 'measure'. Glossaries explain *tazar* also as 'treasure-house'. Possibly there were similar buildings, which served as tribunes for distinguished visitors and as places where requisites and prizes were kept, at the race-courses (1941, p. 232).

A semasiological motivation for the **tač*-derivation was offered by Hoffmann[11] who referred to Germ. 'Zimmer*flucht*' (and implicitly to similar technical words for succession of rooms in perspective found in some European languages).[12] As noted by Wüst (1966, pp. 109–110), however, such a motivation has shaky foundations: the 'Palace of Darius' does not have rooms in a series leading from one to the other. In view of the semantics of Prs. *tajar* and pointing to a link "avest. **takar-*, *tačar-*, /altiran. **taxra-* /altpers. *tačara-*" (< **tač-*), Wüst suggested for *t/dačara-* an original meaning "Roll-Ofen", accounting for the secondary development "Heizvorrichtung (als Herd und Haus), Palast (als Privat-Palais und Herren-Sitz)" (1966, p. 111ff.).

Particularly interested to the building lexicon, Itō has proposed his analysis of *t/dačara-* as a nomen agentis from **tač-* "to run" meaning " 'running out, flowing out' (of what may be regarded as main building), 'detached palace' " (1971, p. 22).

The **tač*-derivation was challenged by Pakhalina (1987, pp. 157–158), who analyzed *d/tačara-* as "a composite-word, i.e. * *d/ta-čara-*", originally "house-castle, house-fortress" (**d/ta-* < IE **dem-*, **dm̥-* "house", **-čara-* < IE *kăl* "to be fenced in"). Lecoq also admitted the lack of a conceptual link between 'run' and 'palace', but without discarding the current etymology, tried to settle the problem refining the word meaning: in view of the DPa location, *t/dačara-* could be "un lieu de passage, soit le corridor qui donne accès à la salle principale du palais, soit le portique d'entrée" (1997, p. 101).

The debate on the matter is far from being concluded.

3. The discussion on the meaning of OP *t/dačara-* paralleled that on *hadiš-*,[13] another OP word interpreted as "palace" on account of its etymology ("seat" < Ir. **had-* "to sit", IE **sed-*) and the royal nature of the 'owner' of the building ("seat" > "palace").

On two antae flanking the southern portico of the 'Tachara' and on the panels on the façade of the southern stairway, one finds three copies of an inscription

11 *apud* Mayrhofer 1964, p. 144 ("briefl.").

12 This motivation has sometimes influenced the translation of the term. See, e.g., "suite of rooms" in Llewellyn-Jones 2013, p. 98, where the word is given as a possible candidate for 'harem'.

13 Unlike *tačara-*, OP *hadiš-* is not accredited with cognates. For a possible one see now Filippone 2016, p. 69.

(XPc) where Xerxes ascribes to his own father the building of "this OP *hadiš* / AE *ulhi* / AB *É/bīt*". Since in one and the same complex one reads that Darius has built this *tačara-* (DPa) and that Xerxes' father has built this *hadiš-* (XPc), it has been deduced that the two words were semantically equivalent. Most scholars agree on their identical referential value,[14] with few dissenting voices.[15] In fact, this lexical interchangebility is not certain. DPa and XPc are engraved at a certain distance and the situational deixis (OP *ima-*, AE *hi*, AB *agâ* "this") might say something only if one already knows the meaning of the words they determine: 'this' might refer to the text carrier, but also to other realities, as the room/area where the carrier is found, the building inside which the room/area is contained, the complex of which the building is a part, the raised flat platform where the complex is situated. We cannot take for granted that *t/dačara-* and/or *hadiš-* were general terms for "palace"; the documentation in the other two Achaemenid languages is of little help.

4. Even less certain is the equivalence *t/dačara-* = *hadiš-* in other inscriptions found at Persepolis and Susa. In some spots at Persepolis, inside and outside the Terrace, dozens of fragments of column tori have been recovered that carry inscriptions ascribable to Xerxes. On the basis of these fragments, some still unpublished,[16] a number of inscriptions have been individuated, labelled according to content and/or finding spots: XPj, XPm, XPn, XPo, XPs (Schmitt 2009, pp. 21–22).

Among these inscriptions, the presence of OP *t/dačara-* is assured only for XPj and XPm; for the others it is only guessable (no fragment contains <tčr> or connected AB/AE forms).

In XPj/XPm one reads as follows:[17]

XPj/OP §2 = XPm/OP	XPj/AE §2 = XPm/AE	XPj/AB §2 = XPm/AB
imam tačaram adam akunavam	*hi dazara u hutta*	*É taššari agâ anāku etepussu*
"this *tačara* I have built"	"this *dazara* I have built"	"this *É taššari* I have built"

In parallel to OP *tačara-* one finds : (1) in AE, *dazara*; (2) in AB, É followed by <*ta-áš-šá-ri*>, the phonetic rendering of the OP word, translated "this house,

14 Cf. Schmidt 1953, p. 30; Eilers 1959, pp. 249–250 fn. 3; Vallat 1979, p. 148; Stronach 1985, p. 433 (*hadiš* and *taçara* "can be shown to have been of like (if by no means certain) meaning"); Steve 1987, p. 98; Schmitt 2009, p. 114, etc.

15 Cf. Wüst 1966, p. 98; Lecoq 1997, p. 101.

16 Several photos are kept in the DARIOSH Archive; they will be published in the catalogue of the inscribed objects stored in the Persepolis Museum depot.

17 The transcription of the three versions is based on a collation of different fragments; no account is given of possible orthographic variants.

tachara" in Schmidt 1953, p. 239 fn. 16 and "this palace" in ARI.[18] The behaviour of the AB redactors is remarkable; unlike the AE versions, usually teeming with OP words, the AB texts contain very few OP loans or OP words written according to the AB spelling.

Since the fragments carrying XPj were uncovered in the area of the 'Harem' thought to have once abutted the 'Hadish', Schmidt assumed that they "must belong" to the latter and concluded that, to designate his own residential palace at Persepolis, Xerxes would have used *hadiš-* in one set of inscriptions and *tačara-* in the text engraved on its column bases.[19] But in the light of the subsequent findings, Schmidt's arguments no longer hold: we cannot exclude the existence of more than one *t/dačara-* of Xerxes in Persepolis or even that one *t/dačara-* could contain more than one building.

Similarly, nothing is known about the structure referred to with OP *dačara-* in DSd/OP, an inscription on a column base structurally similar to XPj, one fragment of which has been found at Susa. There one reads:

DSd/OP	DSd/AE	DSd/AB
imam dačaram adam akunavam	*da[zaram hi u hutta]*	lost
"this *dačara* I have built"	"this *dazara* I have built"	

Worth mentioning is another OP text, of which scanty fragments exist, recently reconstructed by Schmitt (2009, p. 134) after XPj/OP, in contrast with previous reconstructions,[20] with <imm dcrm> in the passage:

DSg/OP	DSg/AE	DSg/AB
[imam dačaram adam akunavam]	lost	*[b]īti timmān agân anā[ku ētepussu]*
"This *dačara* I have built"		"This building with columns I have built"[21]

18 Achaemenid Royal Inscriptions Project (Chicago), directed by Matthew W. Stolper and discontinued by 2004 (<http://oi.uchicago.edu/research/projects/ari/>) and now accessible only via Internet Archive Wayback Machine (corpus catalogue: <http://web.archive.org/web/20031013091326/http://www-oi.uchicago.edu/OI/PROJ/ARI/ARI-Catalogue.html>).

19 Cf. Schmidt 1953, pp. 238–239. See also Schmitt 2009, p. 114 note to G^{6}.

20 Cf. *[viθiyā imā stūnā]* "in (my) house I made these columns", proposed by Brandenstein 1932, p. 39 (followed by Kent 1953, p. 144) and *[imam apadānam]* "diese Säulenhalle", proposed by Hinz 1941, p. 238 (followed by Schweiger 1998 I, p. 129, II, p. 395).

21 Rather than "le palais de ces colonnes" in Steve 1987, p. 78, not consonant with the usual this-X-I-built formula. See Lecoq 1997, p. 237 ("ce palais avec des colonnes") and CAD 2006, p. 419 s. v. *timmu* ("this house of columns").

If Schmitt's proposal were confirmed by new findings, we would have here the concomitance of OP *dačara-* and AB *bīti timmān* "building with columns", a label revealing a peculiarity of the referred structure, that of being columned;[22] at present, however, this is nothing more than a hypothesis (see also Schmitt, ibid. note to B³).

Particularly problematic is the last inscriptional attestation of OP *t/dačara-*, which is in fact indirect (an AE/AB phonetic rendering). In one of the inscriptions from Susa in the name of Artaxerxes, known as A²Sd, a multilingual inscription engraved on column bases of which some fragments survived amongst the debris of a building on the Shaur,[23] the structure denoted *hadiš-* in OP is apparently designated <tá-za-ra-um> and <tá-šá-ri> in the AE and AB versions. The simultaneous use of these terms would then confirm the equivalence *hadiš-* = *t/dačara-*. Too bad, though, that there is no agreement on the interpretation of the OP text, as clearly demonstrated by the many translations put forward,[24] in parallel to "this *dazara/dašari* I have built" in the AE and AB texts:

A²Sd/OP	A²Sd/AE	A²Sd/AB
imām hadiš taya jīvadi par(a)dayadām adam akunavam	*dazaram hi u hutta*	*agâ dašari [anāku epušu]*

- "ce palais, *Paradis de vie* (?), j'ai fait" (Scheil 1929, p. 92);
- "cette résidence (appelée) *jivadiy paradayadām* [...]" (Meillet/Benveniste 1931, p. 222);
- "this is the palace which I built in my life as a pleasant retreat" (Kent 1953, p. 155);
- "j'ai construit cette résidence, de mon vivant, en dehors des murs" (Steve 1987, p. 96);
- "j'ai construit ce palais que j'ai consacré de mon vivant" (Lecoq 1990, p. 211);
- "dies (ist) der Palast, den ich noch zu Lebzeiten als Lust/-Jagdschloß? errichtet habe" (Schmitt 2009, pp. 194–195)
- "this is the palace [which] I built indeed as a living place of pleasure" or "this is the palace (named) indeed 'Living Paradise' [which] I built up" (Panaino 2012, p. 147)

22 This motivates Hinz' reconstruction. As remarked in Steve 1987, p. 78 fn. 192, this conjuncture "perd sa probabilité du simple fait que l'inscription ne provient pas de l'Apadana". To be equipped with columns, however, is not an exclusiveness of that type of building commonly associated to OP *apadāna-*.

23 According to Vallat 1979, p. 148, there were at least 8 column bases carrying that inscription, that "auraient pu décorer les portiques ou la salles du bâtiment comme ceux du Taçara ou du Harem de Persépolis (8 colonnes) ou parteciper à un ensemble plus vaste" like those of other buildings at Persepolis and Susa.

24 For further translations proposed so far see Panaino 2012.

The debate concerns in particular <j^{i}vd^{i}iy> and <prdydam>, which according to some could be the only OP attestation of the word for 'Paradise', otherwise recorded in the AE Fortification texts; no proposed solution seems to me fully satisfactory. I am not going to get into the argument here; for a summary of related problems, see Panaino 2012. In view of the alleged equivalence *hadiš-* = *t/dačara-*, it is currently held that the AE/AB texts would be 'less' informative than the OP one. Furthermore, according to some of the proposed translations, the three versions would also differ in text structure: the pattern 'this X I have built' in AE and AB, peculiar to this type of inscription, would contrast with the presentational structure 'this is X' in OP. However, we cannot exclude that the divergence between them is less than held so far, and even that AE/AB *dazaram/dašari* is a technical term corresponding to *hadiš taya jīvadi par(a) dayadām*,[25] and not simply to *hadiš-*.

5. The AE Persepolis Fortification tablets provide three further occurrences of our word.[26] In PF-NN 602 and 696, reference is made to some quantities of flour, sent from Dakana and Apkištukkaš, and "received in the *dazara* (?) (<h.tá-za-ra>)"; in both a certain Zitekutra and his companion(s) are mentioned as the receivers. The third (PF-NN 1950) is more obscure but more intriguing.[27] From this tablet we know that in the 28th year of Darius Artamiša left from Matezziš and went to the king carrying three mules <da-za-ra-na-um sunki-na> "(from?/to?/of?), the *dazara*(s?) of the king". Awaiting for a final interpretation of this text, one might infer from the AE documentation that *t/dačara-* was not only used as an architectural term but could also refer to an administrative centre connected to the king.

6. The supporters of the thesis of the residential nature of the 'Tachara' base their arguments on the building's iconography. Particular attention is given to the figures carrying small animals, dishes and other goods up the southern and western stairways of the 'Tachara', the western and eastern stairways of the 'Hadish' and other spots on the Terrace.[28] Most scholars interpret them as servants bringing food; already Lassen (1845, p. 14) spoke of the hall of the 'Palace of Darius' as a "gewöhnliche Speisesale" for the king's daily meals. But

25 As already hinted at by Weissbach 1937, p. 651 ("Den altpers. Zusatz *tia jivadi paridaidam*, der anscheinend dem *hadiš* erst den Charakter eines *tačara* verleiht").

26 Hallock/Henkelman's draft transliteration, quoted with the permission of the Persepolis Fortification Archive Project directed by Matthew W. Stolper. I take here the opportunity to thank Matthew Stolper and Wouter Henkelman for their friendly help.

27 Many thanks are due to Gian Pietro Basello, who brough this important text to my attention.

28 This kind of climbing figures played a special role in the Achaemenid iconography. They were present in (at least) some buildings at Susa as well, as proved by a few orthostats found in the 'Donjon Palace' (photo no. 194 in Ghirshmann 1963, p. 144) and one in Building III of the Shaur complex (photo in Boucharlat 2010, p. 401).

the 'residential function' is not universally accepted; cf. e.g. BOUCHARLAT (2013, p. 513, 515), who presumes the royal residence was in the settled area outside the Terrace and all buildings on the Terrace had official and/or cerimonial functions.

GHIRSHMAN had a crucial role in spreading a theory that has prevailed for long, finding its way in many scholarly and amateur publications on Persepolis: according to him, the Terrace would have been planned as the venue for the Nowruz celebration, and the reliefs recorded the different festival stages.[29] In his narration, the 'Palace of Darius' was the official scene for the banquet served to the king's guests. The Nowruz theory has disappeared from scholarly publications;[30] nevertheless, the idea that the 'Palace of Darius' served as a banquet hall for the people participating to the 'royal table', is persistent; see CALMEYER 1980, p. 58, CANEPA 2013, p. 326 fn. 36, etc.

Identity and functions of the climbing figures are debated anyway. MUSCHE (1989, p. 144) wonders why the kings felt the need to represent so many servants (748), and in so many places; she prefers explaining them as "Volk" bringing gifts. Similarly, SANCISI-WEERDENBURG (1998, pp. 29–30) interprets them as ordinary people bringing their 'king's share' directly to the residential palaces.

Some scholars have attributed a religious character to the reliefs, and religious functions to the 'Tachara'. In relatively recent times, apart from FENNELLY (1980), who formulated a personal theory according to which the 'Tachara' would be the missing temple in Persepolis, a site purpose-built by Darius to celebrate the Babylonian New Year's ritual, one may cite LECOQ who stigmatized as "trop utilitaire" the interpretation of the building as a residence: the characters in the reliefs are in priestly attire and seem to carry what is needed for a sacrifice; the palace could have been used for cultual exercises (1997, pp. 102–103). That the carved figures, with their mouths covered, as if wearing the Zoroastrian *panām*, could represent priests[31] has also been underlined by SHAHBAZI (2004, p. 138).

The religious function of the 'Tachara' has been argued more systematically by RAZMJOU, who based his arguments on iconographical, archaeological and linguistic considerations. Going back to this theme in different papers,[32] he has mainly stressed the following points:

1. some peculiarities of the climbing figures, shared with other figures representing priests in Achaemenid religious contexts, would prove that the narrated scene is that of a ceremonial procession;

29 See e.g. GHIRSHMAN 1957.

30 See CALMEYER 1980, IMANPUR 2006, etc.

31 For a different explanation of the mouth covering (food defilement prevention) see e.g. KOCH 2006, p. 46.

32 RAZMJOU has devoted much of his scholarly work to this and related matters starting from his MA thesis (2002) up to his PhD thesis (2008), making public the results of his research in a number of papers (the last one being RAZMJOU/ROAF 2013). Here I mainly refer to RAZMJOU 2010, more specific on the matter.

2. Arm. *tačar* and Georgian *tadzari* "temple; sacred place" would provide the original sense of OP *tačara-* (Razmjou 2010); a 'Sasanian text' has also been hinted at, using "the word *tachara* as 'temple'" (Razmjou/Roaf 2013, p. 420 fn. 31);
3. an architectural adjunct added on the west side of the 'Tachara' (identified by Razmjou) could have been created for use in performing sacrifices in the reign of Xerxes, "at the same time as the figures for sacrificial ceremonies" (Razmjou 2010, p. 241).

The conclusions reached by Razmjou are that the building, built by Darius and named *tačara-*, would have been a place for ritual activities; it would have been subsequently enlarged by Xerxes, changed into a place for sacrificial ceremonies, and renamed *hadiš-*, which should be interpreted as "temple with sacrificial function" (cf. Lat. *aedes*), rather than "palace" (2010, p. 242). There is some inconsistency in this exposition. Apart from the alleged lexical meaning, on which I will come back below, the original religious nature of the 'Tachara' would have been supported by the relief carvings only, but, as rightly pointed out by the author, these are (or are held as) not contemporary to Darius.[33]

Razmjou's speculations have been accepted by some scholars (cf. Root 2010, p. 170, Curtis 2013, p. 65) and disputed by others, as Boucharlat 2013, p. 516 and Canepa 2013, p. 326 fn. 36, who pointed to the absence of religious scenes and other evidence on the ground. This is true beyond controversy, though one should admit that banqueting scenes are also absent and, anyhow, we have no idea of the complete decoration. But, in general, one might ask what can be inferred from the iconographical documentation about the real function of the buildings at Persepolis and how can one reconcile the symbolic function of the images with the description of reality. Calmeyer, e.g., disputed "the idea that the reliefs depict exact events and that these events used to take place within a palace" (1980, p. 56), stating that "the images [...] out of elements of everyday life [...] construct new, sometimes highly complicated symbols beyond reality" (1980, p. 61).

In the present state of our knowledge, we cannot exclude that cult activities could have taken place, among others, within the palace precincts, and, consequently, that the 'Tachara' and 'Hadish' could have been perceived as 'sacred spaces' (Canepa 2013, p. 334); this fact, however, has nothing to do with the meaning of OP *t/dačara-* and *hadiš-*. Some comments are required, in fact, on the kind of linguistic evidence produced by Razmjou in support of his thesis and, in general, on the lexical set to which OP *t/dačara-* belongs.

33 In view of the XPc copy on the panels, it is generally held that the southern staircase was added by Xerxes. The western staircase was added about 130 years later, though traces have been found of a more ancient one beneath it (Schmidt 1953, p. 238).

7. Razmjou's statement that "[i]n modern Persian this word no longer has its original meaning", (2010, p. 245 n. 21), while the meaning "temple" of OP *tačara-* would be endorsed by Arm. *tačar* is questionable since seemingly unsupported by any real linguistic documentation. Consider that in Classical Armenian the semantic range of *tačar* was not restricted to "temple"; interestingly, in the (anonymous) *Epic History*, commonly known as *History of Armenia* by Pʿawstos Buzand, the word is generally used in the sense of "hall" or "palace", apparently with no difference with *aparan* "palace", "though the *tačar*s may not have been as elaborate buildings as *aparankʿ* [...]. Occasionally the term is also used in its ecclesiastical sense [...], or quite often as a 'banqueting hall' " (Garsoïan 1989, p. 562).[34]

To my knowledge, no Sasanian text contains "the word tachara as 'temple' ". The quotations in Razmjou 2010, p. 241 and Razmjou/Roaf 2013, p. 420 fn. 31 refers to a passage in Wüst 1966 where the author brings to readers' notice the interpretation by some scholars of the final part of Middle Prs. *uzdēszār* <*'wc/zdysc'r*> "idol temple" as connected to OP *tačara-*[35] (already disputed by Herzfeld 1938, p. 131).

The only attested Middle Ir. cognate to OP *t/dačara-* is found in Manichaean Parthian; cf. *ṯcr* /*tažar*/ "palace, dwelling; (astronomical term) double hour, period of two hours" in Durkin-Meisterernst 2004, p. 323.[36] Only two occurrences of this word are available; the first in an astronomical context (M67 VII 8), which assures its belonging to the lexicon related to buildings; the second in a Middle Prs./Parth.-Sogd. lexical list in alphabetical order (M688 v 8(4)), whose Sogd. equivalent has been lost,[37] so we cannot say anything about its 'ordinary' meaning. That Parth. *tačar* could have been a designation for "temple" is only an inference by Widengren (1965, p. 191), based on Arm. *tačar*.[38] The latter, in any case, might have influenced other languages in the Caucasian area (cf. Georgian *tadzari* and Caucasian Albanian *çaṭar* "temple, shrine"[39]). To the religious sphere belongs *ṯzr* "a room in the Temple" in the Judeo-Prs. variety

34 Worth noting is III, 8 where an account is given of the forest plantation, the "paradise" creation and the erection of a rural residence called Tačar Mayri ("the Forest Palace") by order of King Xosrow Kotak (Garsoïan 1989, p. 75).

35 Nyberg (1974, p. 199) reads <'wcd'ystc'l> as *uzdaēs-tačār* instead of *uzdēst-z/čār*, explaining it as a "very archaic form of *uzdēs-čār*". In fact, this variant—not too rare—does not support the °*z/čār* < *tačara-* derivation; it rather provides an occurrence of the °*st*-variant of *uzdēs* (also found in *uzdēstparastišnī* "idolatry"); see also *uzd(i)st* in Horn 1893, p. 295).

36 Probably /tačar/; see Korn 2010 (OIr. *č* > Parth. *č*).

37 No Sogd. *tcr-* "palace" appears in this text; its presence in Gharib 1995, no. 9557 is probably due to a misfiling. Consequently, 'Sogd. *tačar*' has to be struck off the relevant lists in Hasandust 2004, p. 328 and Asatrian 2011, p. 773.

38 Differently, Wikander 1946, p. 97 suggested an inner development in Armenian. Cf. also Schmitt 1983, p. 95 (Arm. *tačar* "temple" ← Parth. *tažar* "Palast", the latter with a secular implication).

39 Cf. Gippert 2011, p. 4.

of the Tafsir of Jeremiah, recording a North-East Prs. dialect, some features of which are commented in SHAKED 2009, pp. 454–458.

But let's come back to Prs. *tağar/tazar*, recorded by classical lexicographical works and passed on to the bilingual dictionaries commonly used in the last centuries. In contemporary Persian, they are not in use and are not recorded in the modern dictionaries.

After HORN 1898–1901, p. 73, where *tağar* is given as "dialektisch", and even more after LENTZ 1926, p. 302, where NWIr. *tağar* is contrasted with SWIr. *tazar*, the form *tağar* "winter house" simply disappeared from the scholarly treatments of the OP word, leaving alone *tazar* "summer house" with the label 'New Persian'.[40] But the linguistic realities behind the lexicographical attestations remain unclear (except for the reference to the dialect of Qazvin ["treasury"]).

Apart from the definitions, which passed unchanged from one dictionary to another (with 'winter' associated to the *ğ*-form, and and 'summer' to the *z*-form), the only quotation (from *Farhang-e Ānandrāğ*) is a line by Hakim Nazāri Qahestāni, a poet born in Birğand in 650/1252, from which one may infer that the *tağar* could have had something similar to the vault of the sky (a domed roof ?): *miyān-e in tağar va gombod-e falak farq ast* "between this *tağar* and the vault of the sky there is a difference". One could recall here Birğandi *tazar* "big, long room, with a barrel-vaulted ceiling, especially built for animals"[41] and perhaps also Boxārāi *tazar* "large and deep roofed channel", if the latter is not to be connected to the Ir. **tač*-derived words for "river".

Certain is the persistence of the term in the toponomastics, with an unbroken chain of evidence from antiquity[42] up to nowadays: in the Provinces of Hamadān, Esfāhān, Kermānshāh, Lorestān, Semnān, Khorāsān, etc., one finds towns and villages named Tazar and/or Tağar, or whose names derive from, or contain Tağar/Tazar. Interestingly, Yāqūt al-Ḥamawī (12th/13th c.), in his *Muᶜğam al-buldān,* mentions Ṭazar as a small village one day journey off the main road to Khorāsān, lying in a plain where nothing can be found but the ruins of a portico *[eyvān]*.[43]

Here belong Tālеši *tağar* "veranda, portico"; Tāti *tağar* "portico"; (village of Lerd) *tağar* "fence"; *tačar* "palace, mansion" recorded as 'Gorāni' in SAFIZĀDE 2001. But here probably also belongs a consistent group of words widespread in WIr. languages/dialects and referring to different kinds of (movable) partitions of various materials (canvas, reed, wood, etc.), used to divide spaces in interiors (houses, rooms, etc.); roof-like canvas shelters to create 'roofed' open spaces (for weddings or the like); fences used to delimitate open areas; enclosures in

40 Cf. BARTHOLOMAE 1904, p. 629, MEILLET/BENVENISTE 1931, p. 158, MAYRHOFER 1964, p. 144, KENT 1953, p. 186, PAKHALINA 1987, p. 157, ASATRIAN 2011, p. 773, etc.

41 See also Birğandi *tazar puš* "barrel-vaulted".

42 Cf. Elamite *Parrudazaran* and *Dazzarakka* in HALLOCK 1969, pp. 682, 741.

43 See also EILERS 1959, pp. 249–250 fn. 3, HERZFELD 1968, p. 19, ASATRIAN 2011, p. 773.

the open (courtyards, pens for cattle, delimited areas round encampments, etc.).[44] In (mostly Colloquial) Persian, *tejir* means "partition; folding screen" (largely recorded in dictionaries); cf. *tejir* "partition used to separate women from men (e.g., during the commemoration of the martyrs of Karbala or for mourning)" (NAJAFI 1999).

See also Prs. of Afghanistan *tajīr* "fence round an encampment"; Sistāni *tajir* "fence; yard"; Xorāsāni (Mašhad, Kabul, Herat) *tajīr* "fence round the encampment; partition dividing inner spaces"; Lori *tajir, tažir* "summer sheepcote"; Baxtiāri *tejir* "fence, enclosure"; Lakki *tajir* "1) fence of wood, stones, etc. to protect gardens, cattle, houses, etc.; 2) sheepcote; 3) treasure chest, place for keeping money and antiques";[45] (South) Kurdish *tajīr* "partition; fence"; *tažīr* "sheepcote"; Širāzi *tajir, tejir* "cane trellis at the entrance of shops"; Marvdašti *tejir* "bamboo shades for windows"; Kermāni *tejir* "a canvas partition occasionally used to separate men from women"; Sirjāni *tejir* "partition dividing inner spaces"; Yazdi *tejir, tijir*, probably only used in the expression *parda-o-tijir* ("we say *parda-o-tijir*, but the meaning of *tijir* in today's Dari is not clear", MAZDĀPUR 2006, s.v. *tajir*); Nāini *tejir* "signals marking the possession in uncropped lands"; *tejir, tijir* "fence around gardens"; Bizovoi *tejīr* "roof like canvas shelter erected in courtyard for weddings"; Bādrudi, Čimei *tejīr* "tent, temporary house in the mountain"; Gilaki *tejil* "movable cloth partition"; Damāvandi *tajir* "tent used as ceiling and wall in houses"; Taleqāni *tejīr* 'fence or wooden partition dividing inner spaces", etc.

8. If we look for a conceptual link among the quoted words, that of *separateness* or *separated area* appears the most plausible. This notion, however, is of little help since *separateness* is a central issue of the spatial and representational divide of both traditional palaces and modest dwelling structures throughout Middle East, open to multiple applications. The referred entities are very different and have different functions, fit for manifold socio-cultural environments. There is no way to understand which kind of structure could be denoted with OP *t/dačara-* on the base of its possible cognates.

To conclude, one may say that no proposed etymology for OP *t/dačara-* is satisfactory; the OP *t/d* alternation has found no real explanation; the meaning is not definitely understood and the relationship with other palatial terms is not certain. Leaving aside the meaning, we have no idea of the functions performed by the structures called *t/dačara-* and if, and in which way, they were integrated into the economic-administrative system of the Achaemenid state, besides being a concentration of symbols communicating political power.

44 See also ASATRIAN 2011, p. 773. The connection with Ar. *taḥjīr* ("prohibition; petrification"), advanced by MONCHI-ZADEH 1975, p. 401 is untenable.

45 Cf. the sense "treasury" given in Prs. lexicography for the dialect of Qazvin.

As for the relation between OP *t/dačara-* and *hadiš-*, three options may still be brought up:

1. They were used interchangeably to denote the same structure; this could be possible since the Achaemenid palatial terminology was ambiguous, fluid and hardly restrictive, "risentendo della (ancora recente) localizzazione e stabilizzazione del potere achemenide" (Rossi 2003, p. 696).
2. They denote two different structures, somehow connected (one a part of the other). According to Mousavi 2012, p. 22, *t/dačara-* could denote the interiors or columned halls, with *hadiš-* being a general term, used for the whole building. Similarly, Basello/Filippone/Giovinazzo/Rossi 2014, p. 46 have suggested that OP *hadiš-* could "refer to the whole palatial complex, the external space (porticos, gardens etc.) included [...] while *tačara-* only referred to a closed/detached area with specific (but still unknown) functions". It is also possible that *t/dačara-* would denote the portico (Lecoq, see above); the royal figure going 'into the open'[46] could strengthen the point, with *imam tačaram* in DPa/OP written above the king referring to the outer part of the building. If so, one may liken AB *bīt taššari* to Akkadian *bīt ḫilāni* / *bīt appāti*, not native to Akkadian and occasionally used in the Neo-Assyrian royal texts to indicate a type of palace or structure with a columned portico, developed in the Syro-Anatolian area and adopted by the Assyrians.[47] One could assume that no Babylonian term was available to the royal chancellery to denote the Achaemenid columned portico since this was an innovation with no link with the Mesopotamian architecture.
3. They are connected by a hyponymic relation, with *t/dačara-* denoting a special kind of *hadiš-*, with a peculiar architectural form,[48] like, e.g., a palace with columned portico (see point 2 above).

Bibliography

Asatrian, G. 2011: *Humbābā: Farhang-e Guyešhā-ye Markazi-ye Irān.* Tehrān (1390).

Bartholomae, Chr. 1904: *Altiranisches Wörterbuch.* Strassburg 1904.

Basello, G.P./E. Filippone/G. Giovinazzo/A.V. Rossi 2014: "XPc". In: G.P. Basello/E. Filippone/G. Giovinazzo/A.V. Rossi: *DARIOSH Studies I.*

46 Though the parasol has acquired in the Achaemenid sculpture the symbolic value of the royalty of the figure shaded by it, the contexts in which it occurs prove that it was used as an iconographical device to indicate that the king was represented in the act of leaving the palace (Root 1979, p. 287–288).

47 See CAD 1956, pp. 184–185, 1968, p. 183. For a recent paper on the *bīt-ḫilāni* palace (with previous bibliography) see Osborne 2012. Note that *bītu* means also 'room', e.g. *bīt dannu* 'main room' (CAD 1965, p. 291, s.v. *bītu* 3a).

48 Cf. A²Sd/OP *hadiš taya jīvadi par(a)dayadām* above, p. 115.

The Achaemenid Royal Inscriptions in an Intertextual Perspective. Rome/Naples, pp. 1–98 [in print].

BOUCHARLAT, R. 2010: "Autres travaux de Darius et successeurs." In: J. PERROT: *Le palais de Darius à Suse. Une résidence royale sur la route de Persépolis à Babylone.* Paris, pp. 374–419.

— 2013: "Southwestern Iran in the Achaemenid period." In: D.T. POTTS: *The Oxford Handbook of Ancient Iran.* Oxford, pp. 503–527.

BRANDENSTEIN, W. 1932: "Die neuen Achämenideninschriften." In: *WZKM* 39, pp. 7–97.

CAD = *The Assyrian Dictionary of the Oriental Institute of the University of Chicago.* 1956: Vol. 6 Ḫ. 1965: Vol 2 B. 1968: Vol. I A Part II; 2006: Vol. 18 T.

CALMEYER, P. 1980: "Textual sources for the interpretation of Achaemenian palace decorations." In: *Iran* 18, pp. 55–63.

CANEPA, M.P. 2013: "The Transformation of sacred space, topography, and royal ritual in Persia and the ancient Iranian world." In: D. RAGAVAN (ed.): *Heaven on earth. Temples, rituals and cosmic symbolism in the ancient world.* Chicago, pp. 319–371.

CURTIS, J. 2013: *The Cyrus Cylinder and Ancient Persia. A New Beginning for the Middle East.* London.

CUYLER YOUNG, T. 1988: "The early history of the Medes and the Persians and the Achaemenid empire to the death of Cambyses." In: *The Cambridge Ancient History.* Vol. IV: *Persia, Greece and the Western Mediterranean, c. 525 to 479 BC.* Cambridge (2nd ed.), pp. 1–52.

DEHXODĀ, A.A.: *Loγātnāme.* Tehrān 1325/1946—1360/1981.

DURKIN-MEISTERERNST, D. 2004: *Dictionary of Manichaean Texts.* Vol. III, Part 1: *Dictionary of Manichaean Middle Persian and Parthian.* Turnhout.

EILERS, W. 1959: "Die Ausgrabungen in Persepolis." In: *Zeitschrift für Assyriologie* 53, pp. 248–260.

FENNELLY, J. M. 1980: "The Persepolis ritual." In: *The Biblical Archaeologist* 43/3, pp. 135–162.

FILIPPONE, E. 2016: "Arabic *ḥadd* in the Iranian languages: Notes on some cases of grammaticalization." In: D. GUIZZO/S. PELLÒ (eds.): *Borders.* Venezia (Safinè – serie speciale di Eurasiatica 1), pp. 53–76.

FOY, W. 1904: "Beiträge zur Erklärung des altpersischen Achaemenideninschriften." In: *Zeitschrift für Vergleichende Sprachforschung* 37, pp. 486–575.

GARSOÏAN, N.G. (tr.) 1989: *The Epic Histories (Buzandaran Patmutʿiwnkʿ).* Cambridge, Mass.

GHARIB, B. 1995: *Sogdian Dictionary (Sogdian—Persian—English).* Tehran.

GIPPERT, J. 2011: "The linguistic background of Caucasian Albanian literacy." In: V. SPRINGFIELD TOMELLERI/M. TOPADZE/A. LUKIANOWICZ (eds.): *Languages and Cultures in the Caucasus. Papers from the International Conference "Current Advances in Caucasian Studies" Macerata, January 21–23, 2010.* München/Berlin, pp. 3–21.

GHIRSHMAN, R. 1957: "Notes iraniennes VII. A propos de Persépolis." In: *Artibus Asiae* 20 (1957), pp. 265–278.

— 1963: *Perse : Proto-Iraniens, Mèdes, Achéménides.* Paris.

Gray, L.H. 1932: "Four Old Persian Etymologies." In: *The American Journal of Philology* 53/1, pp. 67–69.
Hallock, R.T. 1969: *Persepolis Fortification Tablets*. Chicago.
Hasandust, M. 2004: *Farhang-e riše-šenāxti-ye zabāne fārsi*. I. Tehrān (1383).
Herzfeld, E.E. 1908: "Pasargadae. Untersuchungen zur persischen Archäologie." In: *Klio* 8, 1–68.
— 1938: *Altpersische Inschriften*. Berlin.
— 1941: *Iran in the Ancient East. Archaeological Studies presented in the Lowell Lectures at Boston*. New York [reprint 1988].
— 1968: *The Persian Empire: studies in geography and ethnography of the ancient Near East*. Edited from the posthumous papers by Gerald Walser. Wiesbaden.
Hinz, W. 1941: "Zu den altpersischen Inschriften von Susa." In: *ZDMG* 95, pp. 225–257.
Horn, P. 1898–1901: "Neupersische Schriftsprache." In: W. Geiger/E. Kuhn (eds.): *Grundriss der iranischen Philologie*. Erster Band, 2. Abteilung. Straßburg, pp. 1–200.
— 1893: *Grundriss der neupersichen Etymologie*. Straßburg.
Hübschmann, H. 1897: *Armenische Grammatik. I. Theil. Armenische Etymologie*. Leipzig.
Imanpour, M.T. 2006: "The function of Persepolis: Was Nouruz celebrated at Persepolis during the Achaemenid period?" In: A. Panaino/A. Piras (eds.): *Proceedings of the the 5th Conference of the Societas Iranologica Europæa, held in Ravenna, 6–11 October 2003*. Vol I: *Ancient & Middle Iranian Studies*. Milano, pp. 115–121.
Itō, G. 1971: "On the function of Darius' Palace *(tacara-)* at Persepolis." In: *Memoirs of the Faculty of Letters, Kyoto University* 13, pp. 1–21 (Japanese), pp. 22–23 (English).
Kent, R.G. 1953: *Old Persian. Grammar, Texts, Lexicon*. New Haven (2nd ed.).
Koch, H. 2006: *Persepolis. Glänzende Hauptstadt des Perserreichs*. Mainz.
Korn, A. 2010: "Parthian ž." In: *BSOAS* 73/3, pp. 415–436.
Lane, E. W. 1863: *An Arabic-English Lexicon*. London.
Lassen, Ch. 1845: "Die altpersischen Keilinschriften nach Hrn. N.L. Westgaard's Mittheilungen." In: *Zeitschrift für die Kunde des Morgenlandes* 6, pp. 1–188, 465–580.
Lecoq, P. 1990: "Paradies en vieux perse ?" In: F. Vallat (ed.): *Contribution à l'histoire de l'Iran. Mélanges offerts à Jean Perrot*. Paris, pp. 209–211.
— 1997: *Les inscriptions de la Perse achéménide*. Paris.
Lentz, W. 1926: "Die nordiranischen Elemente in der neupersischen Literatursprache bei Firdosi." In: *ZII* 4, pp. 251–316.
Llewellyn-Jones, Ll. 2013: *King and Court in Ancient Persia 559 to 331 BCE*. Edinburgh.
Matheson, S. 2001: *Persia. An archaeological guide*. Tehran (3rd ed.).
Mayrhofer, M. 1964: "Lexicon." In: W. Brandenstein/M. Mayrhofer: *Handbuch des Altpersischen*. Wiesbaden, pp. 99–157.
Mazdāpur, K. 1995: *Vāženāme-ye guyeš-e Behdinān-e šahr-e Yazd. Fārsi be guyeš hamrāh bā mesāl. Jeld-e dovvom (t–x)*. Tehrān (1385).
Meillet, A./É. Benveniste 1931: *Grammaire du vieux-perse*. Paris.

Monchi-Zadeh, D. 1975: rev. to ʿAbd al-Ḥusain Nūšīn:, *Suḫan-ī čand dar bāra i Šāh-nāma*. Moskau. In: *ZDMG* 125 (1975), pp. 395–408.

Mousavi, A. 2012: *Persepolis. Afterlife of a world wonder.* Berlin.

Musche, B. 1989: "Das Mahābārata und die Reliefs von Persepolis." In: *AMI* 22, pp. 139–150.

Najafi, A. 1999: *Farhang-e fārsi-e ʿāmiāne*. 2 vols. Tehrān (1378).

Nyberg, H.S. 1974: *A manual of Pahlavi*. Part II: *Glossary*. Wiesbaden.

Osborne, J. F. 2012: "Communicating Power in the *Bīt-Ḫilāni* Palace." In: *Bulletin of the American School of Oriental Research* 238, pp. 29–66.

Pakhalina, T.N. 1987: "Iranian Etymologies." In: *Cahiers Ferdinand de Saussure* 41, pp. 153–158.

Panaino, A. 2012: "No room for the 'Paradise'? About Old Persian <p^{a}-r^{a}-d^{a}-y^{a}-d^{a}-a-m^{a}>." In: G.P. Basello / A.V. Rossi: *Dariosh Studies II. Persepolis and its settlements: Territorial system and ideology in the Achaemenid state.* Napoli, pp. 139–153.

Razmjou, Sh. 2010: "Persepolis: A Reinterpretation of the Palaces and their Function." In: J. Curtis / St.J. Simpson (eds.): *The World of Achaemenid Persia: History, Art and Society in Iran and the Ancient Near East.* New York, pp. 231–245.

Root Cool, M. 1979: *The King and Kingship in Achaemenid Art. Essays on the Creation of an Iconography of Empire.* Leiden (Acta Iranica 19).

Rossi, A. 2003: "Archeologia, storia e filologia a Susa." In: M. V. Fontana / B. Genito (eds.): *Studi in onore di Umberto Scerrato per il suo settantacinquesimi compleanno.* Napoli, pp. 681–700.

Safizāde, S. (Burakai) 2001: *Farhang-e Burakai-e kordi-fārsi.* 2 vols. Tehrān (1380).

Sancisi-Weerdenburg, H. 1998: "Bāji." In: M. Brosius / A. Kuhrt (ed.): *Studies in Persian history: Essays in memory of David M. Lewis.* Leiden (Achaemenid History XI), pp. 23–34.

Scheil, V. 1929: *Inscriptions des Achéménides à Suse.* Paris (Mémoires de la Mission archéologique de Perse 21).

Schmidt, R.F. 1953: *Persepolis I. Structures, reliefs, inscriptions.* Chicago.

Schmitt, R. 1983: "Iranisches Lehngut im Armenischen." In: *Revue des études arméniennes* 17, pp. 73–112.

— 2009: *Die altpersischen Inschriften der Achaimeniden. Editio minor mit deutscher Übersetzung.* Wiesbaden.

Schweiger, G. 1998: *Kritische Neuedition der achaemenidischen Keilinschriften.* I–II. Taimering.

Shahbazi, A.Sh. 2004: *The authoritative guide to Persepolis.* Tehran.

Shaked, Sh. 2009: "Classification of linguistic features in Early Judeo-Persian Texts." In: W. Sundermann / A. Hintze / F. de Blois (eds.): *Exegisti monumenta. Festschrift in Honour of Nicholas Sims-Williams.* Wiesbaden (Iranica 17), pp. 449–461.

Spiegel, F. 1881: *Die altpersischen Keilinschriften.* Leipzig (first ed. 1862).

Steve, M.-J. 1987: *Nouveaux mélanges épigraphiques. Inscriptions royales de Suse et de la Susiane.* Nice.

Stronach, D. 1985: "The Apadana: A signature of the line of Darius I." In: J.-L. Huot / M. Yon / Y. Calvet: *De L'Indus aux Balkans. Recueil à la mémoire de Jean Deshayes.* Paris, pp. 433–445.

VALLAT, F. 1979: "Les inscriptions du palais d'Artaxerxès II." In: *Cahiers de la DAFI* 10, pp. 145–154.
WEISBACH, F.H. 1890: *Die Achämenidenischriften zweiter Art*. Leipzig.
— 1911: *Die Keilinschriften der Achämeniden*. Leipzig.
— 1937: "Achäimenidisches (3.)." In: *ZDMG* 91, pp. 643–651.
WIDENGREN, G. 1965: *Die Religionen Irans*. Stuttgart.
WIKANDER, S. 1946: *Feuerpriester in Kleinasien und Iran*. Lund.
WÜST, W. 1966: *Altpersische Studien: sprach- und kulturgeschichtliche Beiträge zum Glossar der Achämeniden-Inschriften*. München.

Les ‹ Mémoires › dans l'archive pehlevie de Berkeley/Berlin

Philippe Gignoux

Au professeur Maria Macuch qui a tant travaillé pour analyser et nous faire connaître malgré sa complexité le droit sassanide et ses pratiques judiciaires, j'offre cet article dans lequel j'ai rassemblé la documentation d'un terme juridique, l'*ayādgār*, que l'on peut ajouter à la liste des mots qu'elle a étudiée dans l'ouvrage de D. Weber.[1] Il me plaît de rappeler que c'est elle qui, la première, a pensé que la collection de Berlin, désormais publiée par Weber, faisait partie de l'archive pehlevie de Berkeley.[2]

Dans l'introduction à la publication des documents en pehlevi de Berlin (2008), Dieter Weber a défini trois types, le troisième étant le groupe particulier des *ayādgār*, que l'auteur a traduit par ‹ memoranda ›. Deux documents de ce type font partie de la collection de Berlin (№ 13 et 34).[3] Mais dans l'ensemble de l'archive, neuf documents (dont deux à Berlin) appartiennent à ce même groupe. La liste que je mentionne n'est sans doute pas exhaustive. Cependant deux emplois différents du terme permettent de subdiviser les documents ainsi appelés en deux sous-groupes : comme le sens du mot l'indique, on doit s'attendre à un récapitulatif, à une liste de marchandises ou d'autres choses comme dans nos factures d'achat ou de vente. Or ce type est peu attesté (BERK. 46 et 97). Mais dans la plupart des documents le terme *ayādgār* ne conclut pas une liste, mais seulement une formule stéréotypée qui donne au document une certaine valeur juridique, sans que l'objet du ‹ memorandum › soit explicitement désigné. C'est curieusement le groupe le plus attesté.

1 Weber 2008b, « Zur juristischen Terminologie der Berliner Pahlavi-Dokumente », pp. 249–266.

2 Étant donnée l'étendue de l'œuvre de Maria Macuch, à commencer par sa magistrale édition du *Hazār Dādestān*, je me suis contenté de ne citer que quelques-uns de ses articles, et généralement de sélectionner les travaux qui concernent directement l'archive de Berkeley/Berlin. BERK = Berkeley ; BERL = Berlin.

3 Quelques autres documents contiennent le mot, mais le texte est trop lacunaire pour pouvoir en définir l'emploi : ainsi dans Weber 2003, P.152 V, et 317, mais il s'agit des documents d'Égypte, où le formulaire n'a pas été attesté.

Le formulaire est ainsi décliné :

man NN… ī abar čak (ou un autre mot) kē ēn ayādgār awiš wirāst ud nibišt ēstēd az NN padīrēm ud band ī ēn ayādgār NN pad gugāy-muhrīhā ī NN āwišt
« Moi, NN (telle chose) qui sur le document pour lequel ce mémoire a été préparé et écrit, de (un tel) je reçois et l'attache de ce mémoire, un tel [= je] l'ai scellé avec les sceaux qui en témoignent d'un tel (fils de un tel). »

Comme on le voit déjà et dans les documents qui vont suivre, un tel formulaire met en jeu quatre noms propres :

1. le receveur (celui qui dit ‹ je reçois ›) ;
2. le donateur ;
3. le scelleur qui est le même que le receveur ;
4. le possesseur du ou des sceaux avec lesquels le document a été scellé.

On reconnaît là une application très logique du droit : le receveur (1) doit apposer sa signature, (3) pour accord avec le donateur qui est une autre personne (2), mais avec le sceau (ou les sceaux) d'une autre personne (on ne peut être juge et partie). Il y a là une ‹ pratique › juridique, exprimée dans la sentence : « pad gugāy-muhrīh ī … » « par le scellement du témoin … », qui permet de dissocier celui qui déclare de celui qui atteste la véracité du déclarant.

Ce schéma qui ne souffre pas d'exception, permet de combler les lacunes où tel ou tel nom propre devrait se trouver. Une particularité de cette série, c'est que le sceau employé comporte avec le nom de son possesseur celui de son patronyme, ce qui n'est pas le cas avec les autres anthroponymes du même document dont le père n'est pas nommé.

La seconde série de deux documents comprend une liste de dix produits (№ 46) ou de onze (№ 97), « mémoire » qui s'achève par la formule : « Ud ēn ayādgār NN fils de NN et NN fils de NN l'ont scellé ».

Dans les deux documents il est question des mêmes personnes. Ces documents-là énumèrent manifestement les produits courants de la vie quotidienne (pour les humains et les bêtes de somme) :

- Berk. 46 : blé, orge, paille, luzerne, vin, jus de raisin (?), huile, miel, mouton, bois de feu.
- Berk. 97 : blé, orge, paille, luzerne, vin, jus de raisin (?), moût, bois de feu, miel, huile, mouton.

La particularité de ces documents est d'être datés (année 38). Il faut signaler enfin un document dont la datation (an 35) est précédée de la formule incomplète décrite ci-dessus :

NKSY' Y QDM ZNH 'b̲yd̲'ṭk'l npšṭ …
xwāstag ī abar ēn ayādgār nibišt …
« La propriété qui est écrite sur ce mémoire … »

Mais pourquoi ce type de documents n'est-il pas daté généralement ? On peut supposer que cela allait de soi ? Le ‹ mémoire › pouvait-il accompagner une autre sorte de document daté ? Il existe certes des variantes de mémoires où une datation est présente, comme les deux listes de produits que nous avons citées plus haut. Il existe un document № 41, qui contient aussi à côté de la datation (mois de Frawardīn de l'an 35), la mention « xwāstag ī abar ēn ayādgār nibišt », avec une réduction de la formule juridique attendue.

Catalogue

BERK. 13

Ce document, en tous points conforme à un *ayādgār* est publié dans un article destiné à honorer V. A. Livshits et qui s'intitule « Les documents de *Dādēn* dans l'Archive de Berkeley/Berlin ». C'est pourquoi il ne me paraît pas nécessaire de le reproduire ici, car il suffira de se reporter au volume indiqué (St. Petersburg, 2013).

BERL. 13

Ce document publié par Weber (2008b, pp. 60–63) est en tous points conforme aux *ayādgārs*. Seul le premier mot qui est un nom propre n'est pas d'une lecture très sûre : il pourrait aussi se lire : *z'ṭ'nwyh* = Zādān-weh.

BERK. 41

Ce document comprend trois textes : celui écrit verticalement en onze lignes et en haut du parchemin comprend une formule restreinte d'un *ayādgār* :

NKSY' Y QDM Z̲NH 'b̲yd̲'ṭk'l npšṭ 'L …
Xwāstag ī abar ēn ayādgār nibišt ō …
« La propriété qui est écrite sur ce mémoire pour… »

BERK. 43-1

Parchemin de couleur blanc crème, 9 × 18,5 cm, comportant une inscription de 12 lignes, avec une bulle attachée au haut du document. Les lignes 7 à 12 sont lacunaires à cause de la détérioration en bas à droite du document, mais celui-ci devait se terminer en pointe en sorte que la restauration des mots manquants peut être considérée comme assez sûre. De plus il fait partie d'un ensemble de cinq textes attachés ensemble. Ce premier est d'un grand intérêt. J'en donne ma lecture pour la première fois :

Translittération

1 Y̱LYDWNṭ hlṭwndʾṭ ʾwsṭʾndʾl
2 (zynynšnyh ?) Y QDM
3 čkyhʾ W pṭglwḇyhʾ Y
4 MNW ẔNH ʾḇyd̠ʾṭkʾl ʾw[bš]
5 wylʾsṭ W npšṭʾ YKʿYMWNyṭ
6 pṭʾ bhṭybʾl Y pṭʾ
7 [dsṭ]krṭʾ Y wndʾṭbwlčmṭrpʾṭ
8 [dʾlyk ?]… lʾd č[kʾ]
9 … Y pṭʾ
10 [gwkʾdmwdlyh Y m]ʾhpylwčʾ
11 [Y nhwsṭʾn ? ḤṬYM] WNṭ
12 …

Transcription

1 *zād xrad-windād ōstāndār*
2 *(zēnēnišnīh) ī abar*
3 *čakīhā ud padirāyīhā ī*
4 *kē ēn ayādgār awiš*
5 *wirāst ud nibišt ēstēd*
6 *pad Baxtiyār ī pad*
7 *dastgird ī Vindād-Burzmihr-ābād*
8 *dārīg … rāy čak*
9 *… ī pad*
10 *gugāy-muhrīh ī Māh-Pērōz*
11 *ī Naxustān āwišt*
12 …

BERK. 43-1

Traduction

(1) L'*ōstāndār* ‹ trouvé sage à la naissance ›, (2) la protection (mentionnée) sur (3) les documents et les reçus pour (4) lesquels ce mémoire (5) a été préparé et écrit, (6) pour Baxtiyār qui (est) possédant dans (7) le domaine de Vindād-Burzmihr-ābād, (8) le document … (9–10) avec le scellement de Māh-Pērōz (11) fils de Naxust, a scellé.

Commentaire

Ce texte manifeste la primauté de l'*ōstāndār* qui a la garde des ‹ chèques › et des ‹ reçus ›, et les scelle lui-même.

– 2: Le premier mot est lu conjecturalement comme un abstrait de la racine *zēnēn-* (CPD 99 : look after, preserve), et peut signifier la surveillance, ou la protection. Les pluriels des documents qu'il doit surveiller à la ligne 3 révèlent le contexte général de cette fonction.

- 4: Le formulaire d'un *ayādgār* est strictement respecté.
- 6: La locution *pad … rāy* doit signifier « en faveur de, pour », une distinction différente de celle des autres *ayādgārs*, à la place de *az*, car il ne s'agit pas ici d'un don particulier.
- 7–8: Ma restauration s'appuie sur les parallèles dans 43–2 à 5.
- 10–11: Le nom et son patronyme sont aussi connus dans BERK. 226.6–7.

BERL. 34

Ce document, publié par Weber (2008b, pp. 142–145), met aussi en scène un *ōstāndār*. C'est pourquoi je le place ici, en y apportant quelques corrections (en gras), car il présente pas mal de difficultés.

Translittération

1 Y̱LYDWNṭ hlṭwnd'ṭ 'wsṭ'nd'l hwmṭr' hwṭ'yk
2 **ẔK gwpṭ** Y QDM pṭglwḇ MNW ẔNH
3 'ḇyḏ'ṭk'l 'wbš **wyl'sṭ W** npšṭ' YK'YMWNyṭ
4 pṭ' **d'lyk ?** … mkl'n MNW ẔNH YWM 'L
5 bwn' YḤWWNṭ **hwslww'** l'd ẔNH BYRḤ ddw'
6 Y ŠNṬ 30-3-3 **dyn'pzwṭ'** plm'n YḤBWNṭ
7 W bnd Y ẔNH 'ḇyḏ'ṭk'l 'wsṭ'nd'l ḤṬYMWnṭ

Transcription

1 *zād xrad-windad ōstāndār humihr xwadāyīg*
2 *ān guft ī abar padīrāy kē ēn*
3 *ayādgār awiš wirāst ud nibišt ēstēd*
4 *pad dārīg (?) …. kē ēn rōz ō*
5 *bun būd Husraw rāy ēn māh Day*
6 *ī sāl 36 Dēn-Abzūd framān dād*
7 *ud band ī ēn ayādgār ōstāndār āwišt*

Traduction

(1) L'*ōstāndār* ‹ trouvé sage à la naissance ›, monsieur digne de confiance, (2) celui-là a dit au sujet du reçu pour lequel ce (3) mémoire a été préparé et écrit, (4) pour le … du possédant (?) … qui ce jour (5) a été dans le patrimoine de Husraw (?), ce mois de Day (6) de l'an 36, Dēn-abzūd l'a ordonné, (7) et l'attache de ce mémoire l'*ōstāndār* l'a scellé.

Commentaire

Ce mémoire est le plus développé du groupe auquel il appartient. Il a des affinités avec BERK. 43-1. Mais il a ceci de particulier : il est daté contrairement aux autres *ayādgārs*.

- 2: Le mot lu par WEBER **pāyēndān* est difficile à justifier paléographiquement, car le *p* initial a une forme non attestée.
- 4: Le nom en *-ān* devrait être à mon avis un toponyme.
- 5: Le nom que je lis Husrav demeure hypothétique en raison des trois traits qui le terminent.
- 6: On pourrait aussi penser à : W npšṭn, mais dans ce cas cet infinitif devrait suivre *framān dād*.

BERK. 65

Parchemin de couleur blanc crème, dont il manque une petite partie en haut à droite. 6,2×8,3 cm, comportant une inscription de huit lignes, avec une bulle attachée au sommet du document et deux cercles entrelacés en bas à gauche.

BERK. 65

	Translittération	Transcription
1	[wyhlw]č'n ḤS W šwpṭk'	*Wehrōzān may ud šuftag*
2	(Y) sl'd Y QDM čk' MNW Z̲NH	*(ī) srāy ī abar čak kē ēn*
3	'b̲yd̲'ṭk'l 'wbš wyl'sṭ'	*ayādgār awiš wirāst*
4	W npšṭ' YK'YMWNyṭ MN plhw'n	*ud nibišt ēstēd az Farroxān*
5	MKB̲LWNym W bnd Y Z̲NH	*padīrēm ud band ī ēn*
6	'b̲yd̲'ṭk'l wyhlwč'n pṭ' gw<k>'d-mwdl'n	*ayādgār Wehrōzān pad gugāy-muhrān*
7	Y 'šṭw'ṭ Y kṭkhwṭ'y	*ī Aštwād (?) ī kadag-xwadāy*
8	ḤṬYMWNṭ'	*āwišt*

Traduction

(1) Wehrōzān, le vin et le jus de raisin (?) (2) de la maison (?) qui (sont mentionnés) sur le document pour lequel ce (3) mémoire a été préparé (4) et écrit, de Farroxān (5) je reçois, et l'attache de ce (6) mémoire, Wehrōzān avec les sceaux qui en témoignent (7) de Aštwād (?) le maître de maison, (8) a scellé.

Commentaire

Ce document est un très bon exemple du ‹ mémoire › défini ci-dessus.

- 1: La première ligne est lacunaire au début puis cachée par la bulle, mais le nom attendu devrait être le même que celui de la ligne 6, le receveur étant aussi le scelleur. *šuftag* est aussi attesté associé à may dans le doc. 46.4, un texte défini à la fin comme un mémoire (cf. ci dessous). Il pourrait aussi se lire **guft'* mais il devrait être suivi de *'YK comme dans les autres documents.
- 2: Le premier mot dont il manque le commencement est lu de manière conjecturale.
- 7: Le nom propre ainsi lu n'est qu'une proposition incertaine. Le titre de *kadag-xwadāy* est surtout donné à Frāy (Berk. 105, 162 et 169).

BERK. 68

Déjà publié dans Gignoux 2010a, pp. 118–119. La traduction est à corriger légèrement lignes 6 et 7 comme suit :

> « Husrav le serviteur a dit : ‹ Moi, le seul qui (est mentionné) sur le document pour lequel ce mémoire a été préparé et écrit, de Dādēn-Vindād qui est possédant à Yazdān-abestān[4], je (le) reçois, et l'attache de ce mémoire, Husrav l'a scellée avec les sceaux qui en témoignent de Dēn-pānag. › »

4 D'après une correction récente de D. Weber (2012, p. 217).

BERK. 74

Parchemin de couleur blanc jauni, 7 × 4,5 cm, comportant une inscription de huit lignes et deux séries de cercles entrelacés au bas du document. L'attache de la bulle est encore présente au sommet du parchemin. Le coin droit de ce dernier en bas est manquant.

Translittération

1 pl'd gwpṭ' 'YK L b'ṭk'
2 10 dwlk' Y QDM čk' MNW ẔNH
3 'ḇyḏ'ṭk'l 'wbš wyl'sṭ W
4 npšṭ' YK'YMWNyṭ MN
5 'whrmzd'n-(z'ṭk') MKḆLWNym
6 W bnd Y ẔNH 'ḇyḏ'ṭk'l
7 [p]l'd pṭ' gwk'dmwdlyh
8 [Y] yzd'nplhw ḤṬYMWNṭ

Transcription

1 *Frāy guft kū man bādag*
2 *10 dōlag ī abar čak kē ēn*
3 *ayādgār awiš wirāst ud*
4 *nibišt ēstēd az*
5 *Ohrmazdān-(zādag) padīrēm*
6 *ud band ī ēn ayādgār*
7 *Frāy pad gugāy-muhrīh*
8 *ī Yazdān-Farrox āwišt*

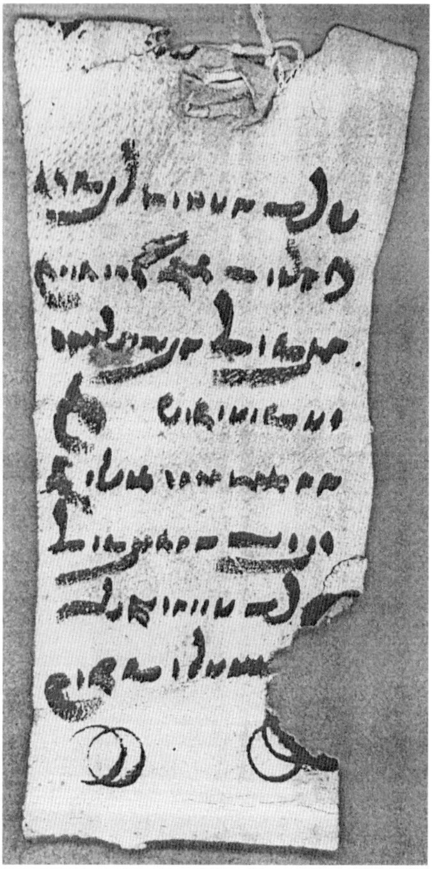

BERK. 74

Traduction

(1) Frāy a dit : « Moi, les dix cruches (2) de moût (mentionnées) sur le document pour (3) lequel ce mémoire a été préparé et (4) écrit, de (5) Ohrmazdān-(zādag) je (les) reçois (6) et l'attache de ce mémoire (7) Frāy avec le scellement qui en témoigne (8) de Yazdān-farrox l'a scellée.

Commentaire

Seuls les noms propres de ce document ne sont pas d'une lecture sûre.

– 5: Le deuxième élément du composé est assez difficile à lire. Ma proposition s'appuie sur les très nombreux noms se terminant en -zādag > zāde.

- 7: La première lettre doit être un *p* très élargi, car le nom du scelleur doit être le même que celui du receveur.
- 8: On pourrait penser au nom si fréquent de *Zādān-Farrox*, mais le premier élément du composé ne pourrait être écrit ainsi.

BERK. 226

Tissu en lin (?) de couleur blanc crème, 8,3 x 9 cm, comportant une inscription de huit lignes et deux cercles entrelacés au bas du document.

	Translittération	Transcription
1	mṭrbndk' gwpṭ' 'YK L grmk'	*Mihrbandag guft kū man garmak*
2	K 30 Y QDM čk' MNW Z̲NH	*kabīz 30 ī abar čak kē ēn*
3	'b̲yd̲'ṭk'l 'wbš wyl'sṭ W npšṭ'	*ayādgār awiš wirāst ud nibišt*
4	YK'YMWNyṭ MN mṭrwy MKB̲LWNym	*ēstēd az Mihrōy padīrēm*
5	W bnd Y Z̲NH 'b̲yd̲'ṭk'l mṭrbndk'	*ud band ī ēn ayādgār Mihrbandag*
6	pṭ' gwk'dmwdlyh' Y m'hpylwč'	*pad gugāy-muhrīhā ī Māh-Pērōz*
7	Y nhwsṭ'n W 'šṭp'ṭ'	*ī Naxustān ud Aštpād (?)*
8	ḤṬYMWNṭ	*āwišt*

BERK. 226

Traduction

(1) Mihrbandag a dit : « Moi, les melons (?), (2) trente kabīz (mentionnés) sur ce document pour lequel ce (3) mémoire a été préparé et écrit, (4) de Mihrōy je (les) reçois, (5) et l'attache de ce mémoire, Mihrbandag (6) avec les sceaux qui en témoignent de Māh-Pērōz (7) fils de Naxust et de Aštpād (?), (8) a scellé.

Commentaire

- 1: Les composés avec *-bandag* sont nombreux (Gignoux 1986, p. 209, où huit sont attestés), mais celui avec Mihr n'était pas jusqu'ici connu. Il est attesté aussi dans Berk. 177.1, sur un document malheureusement très effacé, de l'an 35. Le mot *garmak* est curieusement sur le doc. Berk. 160. écrit comme ici, mais il est bien connu de D. Weber (2008b, p. 217) qui mentionne plusieurs significations et annonce ses explications dans un livre à paraître *Studien zu den Dokumenten aus dem « Pahlavi-Archiv »*.
- 2: Le premier signe (K pour *kabīz*) semble lié à ce qui suit, mais S pour *satēr* ne donnerait pas de sens. Le formulaire est tout à fait conforme à ce qui est attendu. Une trentaine de kg paraît convenir pour une certaine quantité de melons.
- 6–7: *Naxust* semble convenir du point de vue paléographique, de plus il peut être donné au ‹ premier › d'une famille. Il ne semble pas être attesté jusqu'ici, mais il est présent comme patronymique de *Māh-Pērōz* sur le doc. Berk. 160.9–10. On peut se demander pourquoi le sceau d'un autre personnage doit lui être associé. Ce nom est écrit de la même manière dans Weber 2008b à plusieurs reprises, mais sa lecture n'est pas vraiment sûre. Du point de vue sémantique aussi, il n'est guère acceptable qu'il puisse signifier « protégé par Ašt(īh), la paix conçue comme une divinité ? ».

BERK. 228

Tissu en lin (?) de couleur blanc crème qui a jauni et qui a des franges à droite, troué et lacunaire à gauche pour les lignes 3–4, 4 x 12,5 cm, comportant une inscription de quatorze lignes.

	Translittération	Transcription
1	ʾpčṭr gwptʾ ʾYK L	*Ābčihr guft kū man*
2	NKSYʾ Y QDM čkʾ	*xwāstag ī abar čak*
3	MNW Z̲NH ʾb̲yd̲ʾṭkʾl	*kē ēn ayādgār*
4	[mot effacé] ʾwbš	*awiš*
5	wylʾsṭ W npšṭʾ	*wirāst ud nibišt*
6	YKʿYMWNyṭ MN	*ēstēd az*

7	'p'n' Y	*Ābān ī*
8	d'lyk MKB̲LWNym	*dārīg padīrēm*
9	W bnd [Y] Z̲NH	*ud band ī ēn*
10	'b̲yd̲'ṭkr'	*ayādgār*
11	'pčṭr	*Ābčihr*
12	pṭ'	*pad*
13	gwk'dmwdl('n)	*gugāy-muhr(ān)*
14	[ḤṬYMW]Nṭ	*āwišt*

Traduction

(1) Ābčihr a dit : « Moi, (2) la propriété (mentionnée) sur le document (3–4) pour lequel ce mémoire (5) a été préparé et écrit, (6–7) d'Ābān le (8) possédant je (la) reçois, (9) et l'attache de ce (10) mémoire, (11) Ābčihr (12) avec (13) les sceaux qui en témoignent (14) a scellé.

Commentaire

Il semble que le scribe ait manqué d'un support convenable en utilisant un morceau de tissu déjà délabré, à tel point qu'il n'a pu indiquer le nom du (ou des) possesseur(s) du sceau avec lequel le document fut scellé. Au demeurant certaines fins de mots semblent avoir manqué de place. Mais on ne peut échafauder des hypothèses sur cette négligence.

- 2: *xwāstag* employé isolément doit désigner un domaine plutôt que de l'argent dont la somme aurait été indiquée.
- 4: Le premier mot de cette ligne est sans doute une erreur, corrigée par le mot qui suit.
- 7–8: Le donneur a ici le titre de *dārīg*, comme ce peut être aussi le cas dans Berl. 34-4.

BERK. 228

Tableau des noms des quatre personnes des mémoires

numéros	déclarants	rédacteurs	scelleurs	possesseur du sceau
Berk. 13	Dādēn	Māh-Pērōz	Dādēn	Ardašīr fils de Farrox-Husraw
Berl. 13	Astvindād	Mihr-Panāh	Mihrōg	Māhdād-weh fils de Māhān
Berl. 34	ōstāndār	Husraw	ōstāndār	ōstāndār ?
Berk. 65	[Wehrōz ?]ān	Farroxān	Wehrōzān	...
Berk. 68	Husraw	Dādēnvindād	Husraw	Hupašnān
Berk. 74	Frāy	Ohrmazdān-...	Zādān-Farrox	Frāy
Berk. 160	Dādēnvindād	Ādur	Dādēnvindād	Māh-Pērōz fils de Naxust
Berk. 226	Mihrbandag	Mihrōy	Mihrbandag	Māh-Pērōz fils de Naxust
Berk. 228	Ābčihr	Ābān	Ābčihr	non mentionné

Index des inscriptions[5]

ʾb̲yd̲ʾṭkʾl *ayādgār* « mémoire » : Berk. 41.3 ; 43-1.4 ; 65.3, 6 ; 74.3, 6 ; 226.3, 5 ; 228.3, 10 ; Berl. 34.3, 7.
ʾpʾn *Ābān* : Berk. 228.7
ʾpčṭr *Ābčihr* : Berk. 228.1, 11.
ʾšṭpʾṭ (?) *Aštbād* : Berk. 226.7
ʾšṭwʾṭ (?) *Aštwād* : Berk. 65.7
ʾwbš *awiš* « à lui » : Berk. 43-1.4- ʾw[bš] ; 65.3 ; 74.3 ; 226.3 ; 228.4 ; Berl. 34.3
ʾwhrmzdʾnzʾṭkʾ (?) *Ohrmazdān-zādag* : Berk. 74.5
ʾwsṭʾndʾl *ōstāndār* : Berk. 43-1.1 ; Berl. 34.1, 7
ʾYK [*kū*] « qui, que » : Berk. 74.1 ; 226.1 ; 228.1
ʿL [*ō*] « à, pour » : Berk. 41.5 (vertical)
bʾṭkʾ *bādag* « moût » : Berk. 74.1
bhṭybʾl *Baxtiyār* : Berk. 43-1.6
bnd *band* « attache, lien » : Berk. 65.5 ; 74.6 ; 226.5 ; 228.9 ; Berl. 34.7
bwnʾ *bun* « patrimoine » : Berl. 34.5
BYRḤ [*māh*] « mois » : Berl. 34.5
čk *čak* « document » : Berk. 43-1.8 ; 65.2 ; 74.2 ; 226.5 ; 228.2
čkyhʾ *čakīhā* « documents » : Berk. 43-1.3
dʾlyk *dārīg* : Berk. 43-1.8 (?) ; 228.8 ; Berl. 34.4 (?)
ddwʾ *Day* nom de mois : Berl. 34.5

5 Berk. = Berkeley ; Berl. = Berlin.

[dsṭ]krṭ' *dastgird* « domaine » : Berk. 43-1.7
dwlk' *dōlag* : Berk. 74.2
dyn'pzwṭ' *Dēn-abzūd* : Berl. 34.6
grmk' *garmak* « melon ? » : Berk. 226.1
gwk'dmwdlyh *gugāy-muhrīh* « scellement qui en témoigne » : Berk. 43-1.10 (restauré) ; 65.6 – gw<k>'dmwdl'n ; 74.7 ; 226.6 – gwk'dmwdlyh' ; 228.13 – gwk'dmwdl('n)
gwpt *guft* « il a dit » : Berk. 74.1 ; 226.1 ; 228.1 ; Berl. 34.2
hlṭwnd'ṭ *xrad-windād* « trouvé sage » : Berk. 43-1.1 ; Berl. 34.1
ḤS [*may*] « vin » : Berk. 65.1
ḤṬYMWNṭ [*āwišt*] « scellé » : Berk. 43-1.11- [*ḤṬYM*]Wnṭ ; 65.8 ; 74.8 ; 226.8 ; 228.14 – [*ḤṬYMWN*]ṭ ; Berl. 34.7
hwmṭr' *humihr* « digne de confiance » : Berl. 34.1
hwslw'n' *Husrawān* : Berl. 34.5
hwslwy *Xusrōy* : Berk. 68.1, 9
hwṭ'yk *xwadāyīg* « monsieur » : Berl. 34.1
K *kabīz* : Berk. 226.2
kṭkhwṭ'y *kadag-xwadāy* « maître de maison » : Berk. 65.7
l'd *rāy* « pour, en faveur de » : Berk. 43-1.8 ; Berl. 34.5
L [*man*] « moi » : Berk. 74.1 ; 226.1 ; 228.1
m'hpylwč *Māh-Pērōz* : Berk. 43-1.10 ; 226.6
MKḆLWNym [*padīrēm*] « je reçois » : Berk. 65.5 ; 74.5 ; 226.4 ; 228.8
MN [*az*] « de (la part de) » : Berk. 65.4 ; 74.4 ; 226.4 ; 228.6
MNW [*kē*] « qui, que « : Berk. 43-1.4 ; 65.2 ; 74.2 ; 226.2 ; 228.3 ; Berl. 34.2, 4
mṭrbndk' *Mihrbandag* : Berk. 226.1, 5
mṭrwy *Mihrōy* : Berk. 226.4
nhwsṭ'n *Naxustān* « fils de Naxust » : Berk. 43-1.11 (restauré) ; 226.7
NKSY' [*xwāstag*] « propriété, argent » : Berk. 41.1 (vertical) ; 226.2
npšṭ *nibišt* « écrit » : Berk. 41.4 ; 43-1.5 ; 65.4 ; 74.4 ; 226.3 ; 228.5 ; Berl. 34.3
pl'd *Frāy* : Berk. 74.1, 7 – [*p*]*l'd*
plhw'n *Farroxān* : Berk. 65.4
plm'n *framān* « ordre » : Berl. 34.6
pṭ' *pad* « à, dans » : Berk. 43-1.6, 9 ; 65.6 ; 74.7 ; 226.6 ; 228.12 ; Berl. 34.4
pṭgl'ḇ *padīrāy* « reçu » : Berl. 34.2
pṭglwḇyh' *padīrāyīhā* « reçus » : Berk. 43-1.3
QDM [*abar*] « sur » : Berk. 41.2 ; 43-1.2 ; 65.2 ; 74.2 ; 226.1 ; 228.2 ; Berl. 34.2
sl'd *srāy* « maison » (?) : Berk. 65.2
ŠNṬ [*sāl*] « année » : Berl. 34.6
šwpṭk *šuftag* « jus de raisin (?) » : Berk. 65.1
wnd'ṭbwlčmṭrp'ṭ *Vindād-Burzmihr-ābād* : Berk. 43-1.7
wyhlwč'n *Wehrōzān* : Berk. 65.1 – [*wyhlw*]*č'n*, 6
wyl'sṭ *wirāsṭ* « préparé » : Berk. 43-1.5 ; 65.3 ; 74.3 ; 226.3 ; 228.5 ; Berl. 34.3
YḤBWNṭ [*dād*] « donné » : Berl. 34.6
YḤWWNṭ [*būd*] : Berl. 34.5
YK'YMWNyṭ [*ēstēd*] « a été (auxiliaire) » : Berk. 43-1.5 ; 65.4 ; 74.4 ; 226.4 ; 228.6 ; Berl. 34.3
Y̱LYDWNṭ [*zād*] « né » : Berk. 43-1.1 ; Berl. 34.1

YWM [*rōz*] « jour » : Berl. 34.4
yzd'nplhw *Yazdān-farrox* : Berk. 74.8
z'ṭ'nwyh *Zādān-weh* : Berl. 13.1
Z̲K [*ān*] « ce, celui-là » : Berl. 34.2
Z̲NH [*ēn*] « ce, celui-ci » : Berk. 41.2 ; 43-1.4 ; 65.2, 5 ; 74.2, 6 ; 226.2, 5 ; 228.3, 9 ; Berl. 34.2, 4, 5, 7
zynynšnyh *zēnēnišnīh* surveillance, protection » : Berk. 43-1.2

Bibliographie

Gignoux, Ph. 1986 : *Noms propres sassanides en moyen-perse épigraphique.* Wien (Iranisches Personennamenbuch II/2).
— 1991 : « Une nouvelle collection de documents en pehlevi cursif du début du septième siècle de notre ère. » In : *Comptes Rendus de l'Académie des Inscriptions et Belles-Lettres*, pp. 683–700.
— 2003 : *Noms propres sassanides en moyen-perse épigraphique. Supplément (1986–2001).* Wien (Iranisches Personennamenbuch II/3).
— 2009a : « Les comptes de Monsieur Friyag : Quelques documents économiques en pehlevi. » In: R. Gyselen (ed.) : *Sources pour l'histoire et la géographie du monde iranien (224–710).* Bures-sur-Yvette (Res Orientales XVIII), pp. 115–142.
— 2009b : « Les documents économiques de Xwarēn. » In : Ph. Gignoux/Ch. Jullien/F. Jullien (edd.) : *Trésors d'Orient. Mélanges offerts à Rika Gyselen.* Paris (StIr. Cahier 42), pp. 81–102.
— 2010a : « La collection de textes attribuables à Dādēn-Vindād dans l'archive pehlevie de Berkeley. » In : R. Gyselen (ed.) : *Sources for the History of Sasanian and post-Sasanian Iran.* Bures-sur-Yvette (Res Orientales XIX), pp. 11–134.
— 2010b : « Un nouvel ouvrage de référence de la papyrologie pehlevie : Note de lecture. » In : *StIr* 39/1, pp. 111–120.
Gignoux, Ph./Ch. Jullien/F. Jullien : *Noms propres syriaques d'origine iranienne.* Wien (Iranisches Personennamenbuch VII/5).
MacKenzie, D.N. 1971 : *A Concise Pahlavi Dictionary*, London 1971 ; repr. 1986.
Macuch, M. 2008 : « Zur juristischen Terminologie der Berliner Pahlavi-Dokumente. » In : Weber 2008b, pp. 249–266.
— 2009 : « Judicial and Legal Systems III. Sasanian Legal System. » In : *EIr* XV/2, pp. 181–196.
Weber, D. 1992 : *Ostraca, Papyri und Pergamente.* London (CII/III, vol. IV–V).
— 2003 : *Berliner Papyri, Pergamente und Leinen Fragmente in mittelpersischer Sprache.* London (CII/III, vol. IV–V).
— 2008a : « Einige Bemerkungen zur Paläographie des Pahlavi. » In : *Iranian Languages and Texts from Iran and Turan.* Berlin (Iranica 13), pp. 433–442.
— 2008b : *Berliner Pahlavi-Dokumente. Zeugnisse spätsassanidischer Brief- und Rechtskultur aus frühislamischer Zeit.* Wiesbaden (Iranica 15).
— 2012 : « New Arguments for Dating the Documents from the 'Pahlavi archive'. » In: *BAI* 22 (2008 [paru 2012]), pp. 215–222.

Onomastica Irano-Iberica

II. The Name of a Zoroastrian "Bishop"[1]

JOST GIPPERT

In his "Iranisches Namenbuch", still indispensable for investigations into the anthropononomastics of the Iranian peoples, FERDINAND JUSTI mentions a certain "Binkar, Oberpriester" who "spread the Zoroastrian religion in Georgia under Waxtang Gurgaslan (466–499)" and whose name he considered to represent an imperative form of the verb *nigarīdan* in the sense of "pay attention!".[2] The information on the high priest Justi relied upon was taken from a short notice in a numismatic article by BERNHARD DORN[3] and from MARIE-FÉLICITÉ BROSSET's "Histoire de la Géorgie", the French translation of the Georgian chronicle *Kartlis Cxovreba*, which refers three times to *Bin(a)kar*, styling him a "bishop of the fire worshippers".[4] Given that the name of the "bishop" exhibits remarkable variation in the manuscript tradition of the chronicle—apart from *Binkar* and *Binakar*, BROSSET himself mentions the forms *Binkarian* and *Bunakar* as well as *Binkaran* appearing in "the Armenian chronicle",[5] i.e., the 13th century Armenian translation of *Kartlis Cxovreba*, *Patmowtʿiwn Vracʿ*—, JUSTI's proposal deserves to be challenged. This is all the more true as the "bishop's" name can be shown to occur, in much more divergent forms, in other Old Georgian sources, too.

1 For part I of the present article see GIPPERT 2011.

2 JUSTI 1895, p. 68: "Binkar, Oberpriester, verbreitete die zoroastrische Religion in Georgien unter Waxtang Gurgaslan (466–499), vgl. Dorn, Bullet. Acad. Petersb. 1, 37. Brosset, Hist. 1, 149. 176. d. i. gib Acht (Imperat. von nigarīdan)?"

3 DORN 1844, p. 37: "Nun erzählt die georgische Geschichte, dass zur Zeit Gurgarslans viele aus dem niedern Volke dem Feuerdienste huldigten, welchen ein Oberpriester Binkar in Georgien predigte ..."

4 BROSSET 1849, p. 149: "Barzabod envoya donc à Mtzkhétha des serviteurs du feu, à la tête desquels il plaça l'évêque Binkar, et ils se fixèrent à Mogoutha. ... Cependant Binakar, évêque de Mtzkhétha pour la religion du feu, invitait les Géorgiens à embrasser ce culte ..."—p. 176: "Il jeta en prison Binakar, l'imposteur, évêque des adorateurs du feu, extermina et chassa tous ces derniers des domaines de la Géorgie".

5 BROSSET 1849, p. 149 note 2: "Ou Binakar, Binkarian, plus bas; Bounakar, p. 96, et Binkaran, dans la Chron. armén."—Cf. GIPPERT 1984, p. 38 and below for a more comprehensive list of variants.

1. The "bishop's" record in *Kartlis Cxovreba*

In the Georgian chronicle, a compilation of historiographical texts from the 11th up to the 18th century, the Zoroastrian "bishop" is mentioned within the account, attributed to a certain J̌uanšer, of the Georgian king Vaxṭang Gorgasali,[6] the legendary founder of the capital, Tbilisi, who ruled in the second half of the 5th century.[7] According to the chronicle, the "bishop" played an important rôle indeed in the controversy between the Christian king and his Zoroastrian coevals at the Sasanian court of Iran. For the sake of convenience, the relevant passages of the chronicle[8] are reproduced with an English translation here.

1.1 The Zoroastrian "bishop" is first introduced as being sent to the older Georgian capital, Mcxeta, as the head of a group of fire worshippers, by Barzabod, an Iranian general who was the governor of *Rani*, the region between *Kartli*, i. e. Eastern Georgia, and present-day Azerbaijan, and who was the father of Sagduxṭ, the wife of the Georgian king Mirdaṭ and mother of Vaxṭang Gorgasali. Binkaran (this is the name form adopted in the modern editions) is styled a "bishop" right from the beginning:[9]

> მაშინ ბარზაბოდ წარმოგზავნ{ნ}ა ცეცხლის-მსახურნი მცხეთას და მათ ზედა ეპისკოპოსად ბინქარან, და დასხდეს მოგუთას. და საგდუხტ დედოფალი განაგებდა მეფობასა ძალითა და შეწევნითა მამისა თჳსისა{ჲ}თა. და მოკუდა ბარზაბოდ, მამა{ჲ} საგდუხტისი, და მის წილ დაადგინა სპარსთა მეფემან {+ ადგილსა მისსა} ძევე მისი ვარაზ-ბაკურ, ძმა{ჲ} საგდუხტ დედოფლისა{ჲ}. და მოკუდა საურმაგ სპასპეტი, მამა-მძუძე ვახტანგისა.
>
> Then Barzabod sent out fire worshippers to Mcxeta, and Binkaran as a bishop over them, and they settled in Moguta. And Queen Sagduxṭ conducted the reign with the power and help of her father. And Barzabod, Sagduxṭ's father, died, and instead of him the king of the Persians appointed {+ in his stead} a son of his, Varaz-Baḳur, the brother of Queen Sagduxṭ. And Saurmag, the commander-in-chief, the warden of Vaxṭang, died.

6 JUSTI's *Gurgaslan* represents a later (Turkicized) form of the epithet of the king, which reflects a Persian **gurg-sar* "wolf's head"; cf. GIPPERT 1984, p. 40 with note 41.

7 The exact dating remains controversial. Cf. GIPPERT in print as to the difficulties met with in providing a reliable chronology of 5th century Georgia.

8 The chronicle is available in two modern scholarly editions (QAUXČIŠVILI 1955 = KCQ and MEṬREVELI 2008 = KCM). Divergences between the two editions mostly concern the attempt to restore a more standardized Old Georgian wording in the latter, which also takes into account an important manuscript that has only recently been found (Q = Q-1219, of 1697; cf. KCM, 23). The following transcripts reproduce the text of KCQ, with noteworthy text variants from KCM being added in curly braces.—The Armenian version of the chronicle, *Patmowtʿiwn vracʿ* = PV), is quoted after ABULAʒE 1953.

9 KCQ 145,4–8 / KCM 157,8–13.

1.2 Binkaran conducts Zoroastrian proselytism in Mcxeta, with much more success among the common people than the Georgian nobility:[10]

> მაშინ მეფემან დაადგინა სხუა{ჲ} სპასპეტი, რომელსა ერქუა ჯუანშერ. ხოლო ბინქარან, ეპისკოპოსი ცეცხლის-მსახურთა {მცხეთელთაჲ, რომელი იყო სპარსი ცეცლის-მსახური}, ასწავებდა ქართველთა სჯულსა თჳსსა, არამედ არავინ ერჩდა წარჩინებულთაგანი, გარნა წურილი ერი {წულილისა ერისაგანი} მიიქცა {მოაქცია} მრავალი {<} ცეცხლის-მსახურებასა. და შეერია ქართლს {+ შინა} წურილსა {<} ერსა {+ წულილსა} ცეცხლის-მსახურება{ჲ}.
>
> Then the king appointed another commander-in-chief, who was named Ǯuanšer. And Binkaran, the bishop of the fire worshippers {of the Mcxetians, who was a Persian fire worshipper}, taught the Georgians his faith, but none of the nobles submitted himself to it, but many {some} of the commoners were converted to fire worship. And (thus), fire worship invaded the commoners in Kartli.

1.3 Queen Sagduxṭ summons a Greek priest, Mikael, to support her in maintaining the Christian faith in Kartli. Mikael is appointed bishop in Mcxeta and performs his task with good success:[11]

> ამისთჳს {+ დიდად} მწუხარე იყო საგდუხტ დედოფალი, არამედ მძლავრებისაგან სპარსთა{ჲ}სა ვერას {+ ვინ} იკადრებდა. მაშინ მოიყვანა მღდელი ჭეშმარიტი საბერძნეთით, სახელით მიქაელ, და დაადგინა იგი ეპისკოპოსად ზემოსა ეკლესიასა, რამეთუ მობიდან ეპისკოპოსი გარდაცვალებულ იყო და ესე მიქაელ ეპისკოპოსი წინა-აღუდგა ბინქარან{ს} მაცთურსა, რამეთუ ასწავებდა ყოველთა ქართველთა სჯულსა ჭეშმარიტსა. ამან იპყრნა სარწმუნოებასა ზედა ყოველნი წარჩინებულნი ქართლისანი და ერიცა უმრავლესი, არამედ მცირედნი ვინმე წუ[რ]{ლ}ილისა ერისაგანნი მიიქცეს ცეცხლის-მსახურებასა.
>
> Because of this, Queen Sagduxṭ was {+ highly} distressed, but she {nobody} could not venture anything because of the superiority of the Persians. Then she summoned (*lit.* brought) a true priest from Greece, by the name of Mikael, and appointed him as the bishop of (*lit.* in) the upper church; for bishop Mobidan had passed away, and this Mikael stood up against Binkaran, the deceitful one, in that he taught all Georgians the true faith. He biased all nobles of Kartli towards the (Christian) belief, as well as most of the (common) people, but some of the commoners were converted to fire worship.

1.4 Binkaran is still alive and active some twelve years later when Vaxṭang Gorgasali has taken over rule in Kartli and has defeated the Ossetes, with strong support by Iranian troops. Binkaran acts as an envoy between Vaxṭang and the Persian king, Urmizd (= Hormizd III, ca. 457–9), who gives Vaxṭang his daughter Balenduxṭ[12] in marriage in preparation of a common war against the Byzantine emperor:[13]

10 KCQ 145,9–12 / KCM 157,13–17 .

11 KCQ 145,12–19 / KCM 157,17–158,6.

12 The correct form of the name can be restituted as **šāhēnduxt*; cf. Gippert 2011 and below.

13 KCQ 158,4–16 / KCM 171,5–16.

მაშინ ვახტანგ მეფემან შეწირა მადლობა{ჲ} ღმრთისა მიმართ მრავლითა ლოცვითა და ღამის-თევითა, და გლახაკთა მიცემითა. და გა{ნ}სცა ნიჭი ერსა თჳსსა, და წარჩინებულ-ქმნნა მჴედარნი, მსახურნი მჴნედ და {<<} გამოცდილნი წყობასა მას შინა ოვსთასა. და წარსცა ძღუენი ნატყუენავისა მისგან დედის-ძმისა მისისა თანა ვარაზ-ბაკურისა: მონა{ჲ} ათასი, ცხენი საჴედარი ათასი, ჯდალი ცხენი ათასი. და კუალად წარსცა წინაშე სპარსთა მეფისა მონა{ჲ} ათი ათასი, ცხენი საჴედარი ათი ათასი, ცხენი ჯდალი ათი ათასი. ესე ყოველი მიუძღუანა სპარსთა მეფესა ჴელითა ბინქარან ეპისკოპოსისა{ჲ}თა, და ითხოვა სპარსთა მეფისაგან ასული ცოლად; ხოლო სპარსთა მეფემან მოსცა ასული მისი ცოლად, {<<<<<<<} რომელსა ერქუა ბალენდუხტ. და მოსცა სომხითი და ყოველნი მეფენი კავკასიანნი ზითვად და მისწერა მის თანა წიგნი, რომელსა პატრუცაგსა {<} წერილ იყო ესრეთ:

"[უ]{ო}რმისდისგან, ყოველთა მეფეთა მეფისა, ვახტანგის მიმართ, ვარან-ხუასრო-თანგისა, ათთა მეფეთა მეფისა აჴოვანისა".

და მოუწერა მან ბრძოლა{ჲ} კეისრისა{ჲ}, რამეთუ კეისარი განსრულ იყო ბრძოლად სპარსთა.

Then King Vaxṭang showed his gratitude towards God by (performing) many prayers and night watches and by bestowing (alms) on the poor. And he gave present(s) to his people, and he ennobled the equestrians who had served bravely and with experience in the campaign against the Ossetes. And he gave gift(s) from his booty to his mother's brother, Varaz-Baḳur: 1,000 servants, 1,000 riding horses, 1,000 steeds. And to the Persian king again, he gave 10,000 servants, 10,000 riding horses, and 10,000 steeds. All this he sent to the Persian king by the hand of (= through) Binkaran, the bishop, and he asked the king of the Persians for (the hand of) his daughter in marriage. And the king of the Persians gave him his daughter, whose name was Balenduxṭ, in marriage. And he gave her Armenia and all the king(dom)s of Caucasia as her dowry, and he wrote him a letter in the head of which was written:

"From Urmizd, the king of all kings, to Vaxṭang, the Varan-Xuasro-Tang, the mighty king of the ten kings."

And he wrote to him about the battle against the (Greek) emperor, for the emperor had set out to fight against the Persians.

1.5 A few years later again, Vaxṭang has taken the side of the Byzantine emperor and is expecting a battle against the Persians. Binkaran is imprisoned and the Zoroastrians are thrown out of Kartli:[14]

ხოლო ვახტანგ მეფესა უშვნა ცოლმან ძე და ასული მარჩბივად, და მოკუდა შობასა შინა ბალენდუხტ დედოფალი, ასული სპარსთა მეფისა{ჲ}. ხოლო ვახტანგ უწოდა ძესა თჳსსა სახელი {<} სპარსულად დარჩილ და ქართულად დაჩი.

მაშინ ვახტანგ მეფემან ვერ მოიცალა {<} მოყვანებად {მოიყვანა} ცოლი ბერძენთა მეფისა ასული, და ვერცა კათალიკოსი[სა] და ეპისკოპოს[თა]{ნი}, რამეთუ მოელოდა იგი {+ მოსლვასა} სპარსთა მეფისა{სა} მოსლვასა {<}: ამაგრებდა ციხეთა და ქალაქთა, და ჰკაზმ{ვ}იდა მჴედართა, და განამზადებდა ბრძოლად სპარსთა. მაშინ შეაგდო საპყრობილესა შინა ბინქარან მაცთური, ეპისკოპოსი ცეცხლის-მსახურთა{ჲ}, და მოსრნა და განასხნა ყოველნი ცეცხლის-მსახურნი საზღვართაგან ქართლისათა.

14 KCQ 178,12–19 / KCM 193,6–13.

And king Vaxṭang's wife gave birth to twins, a son and a daughter, and she, Queen Balenduxṭ, the daughter of the king of the Persians, died during the birth. And Vaxṭang gave his son the Persian name Darčil, and in Georgian, Dači.

There was not enough time for Vaxṭang then to bring the daughter of the Greek emperor home to marry her, nor the catholicos and the bishops; for he was expecting an invasion by the king of the Persians. (So) he fortified the fortresses and cities, and he equipped the equestrians, and he prepared them for the battle against the Persians. Then he threw Binkaran, the deceitful bishop of the fire worshippers, into prison and he crushed all fire worshippers and expelled them from the borders of Kartli.

1.6 With the battle upcoming, Vaxṭang sends a letter to the Byzantine emperor in which he informs him about his deeds against the Zoroastrians, among them his treatment of Binkaran who is reported to have died when he tried to leave Kartli:[15]

ხოლო სპარსთა მეფე, შემდგომად სამისა წლისა, წარმოემართა ბრძოლად ვახტანგისად, და მოიწია ინდაბრიანთა, და დაიბანაკა მუნ {<}. ხოლო ვახტანგ წარავლინა ბერძენთა მეფისა თანა {<<<} და მიუმცნო {+ ბერძენთა}, ვითარმედ:

"აჰა დღე იგი, რომელ აღმითქუამს, ვითარმედ სპარსნი შემოვაწყუდივნე ჴელსა შენსა; აჰა ესერა, {+ იგინი} მომიყვანებიან იგინი {<} შუა საზღვართა ქართლისათა და ყოველი კაცი მათ თანა {მათთანაჲ} ვითარ სამასი ათასი. რამეთუ ჰგონებდა იგი განმრავლებასა სპათა მისთასა სომხითით და მეფეთაგან კავკასიანთა[სა], ხოლო მათ ვერ იკადრეს განრთვად მისა. რამეთუ რომელთამე მათგანთა აქუნდა სასოებაჲ ჯუარც{უ}მულისა{ჲ}, ხოლო რომელნი იძლი[ვ]ნეს ეშმაკისაგან, მეფენი დარუბანდისანი გა{ნ}ერთნეს. აწ {+ მე} აღმისრულებიეს აღთქ{უ}მა{ჲ} ჩემი, რომელი აღმითქუამს: რამეთუ {<} სადაცა მიპოვნიეს სახლი ცეცხლისა{ჲ}, დამივსია {დამივსიეს} ფსლითა, და მოგუნი და მზირნი მათნი მიმიცემიან სატანჯველსა ბოროტსა, და მაცთური ბინქარან მივეც საპყრობილესა, და სიკუდილისაგან გარდაიხუეწა. მან უკუე მოიყვანნა სპარსნი ქართლად, და დავსუ ეპისკოპოსად მიქაელ, კაცი სარწმუნო{ჲ}. ხოლო ბინქარან, ვითარცა მოიწია საზღვართა ქართლისათა, მოკუდა.

აწ სწრაფით წარმოემართენ სპანი შენნი, რათა აქა შინა დაეცნენ ყოველნი მტერნი ჯუარისანი, და მოიცალო შენ ყოველთა მტერთა შენთაგან, ხოლო უკეთუ {თუ} ჩუენ გუძლოს {გუძლევდეს}, განძლიერდეს იგი და შემოვიდეს {+ იგი} საზღვართა შენთა გზასა შიმშატისასა."

And after three years, the Persian king set out to fight against Vaxṭang, and he moved to Indabriani and encamped there. But Vaxṭang sent out (a message) to the Byzantine king and informed him:

"Look, this (is the) day for which I gave you my promise that I shall force the Persians into your hand(s). Look, (now) they are intruding into the borders of Kartli, altogether about 300,000 men with them. For he (the Persian king) had the intention to extend his troops (with people) from Armenia and the king(dom) s of Caucasia, but they did not venture to unite with him, for some of them set their hope on (Christ) Crucified. But some were overpowered by the devil, the kings of Derbent united with him. Now I have fulfilled the promise I gave: For

15 KCQ 178,20–179,15 / 193,14–194,11.

wherever I have found a fire temple, I have filled it with urine, and their Magis and spies I have delivered to bad torturings; the deceitful Binkaran I have thrown into prison, and (thus) he escaped from death. (It was) he (who) brought the Persians to Kartli. And I have appointed Mikael as bishop, a faithful man. Finally, Binkaran has died reaching the borders of Kartli.

Quickly now send out your troops so that they may defeat all the enemies of the cross (we have) here, and that you may preempt all your enemies; for if he overcomes us, he will gain strength and invade your borders via Šimšaṭi."

2. Binkaran as a "bishop"

2.1 It may appear strange at first sight that Binkaran is styled a "bishop" in the Georgian text, given that no other cases seem to be known of Zoroastrian high priests bearing that Christian title, neither in Georgian nor in any other language. As a matter of fact, not even the Armenian version of *Kartlis Cxovreba*, the *Patmowtʿiwn Vracʿ*, uses the epithet "bishop" in the given case. In the four passages relating to Binkʿaran in the Armenian version the term *kʿrmapet*, lit. "chief of pagan priests", is used instead. Note that the name itself, in the form Binkʿaran, appears only once:[16]

Եւ նոյնժամայն առաքեաց պաշտաւնեայ կրակի ի Մցխիթա, եւ քրմապետ մի Բինքարան կոչեցեալ. եւ եկեալ՝ նստան ի Մոգթա: …

Մեռաւ եւ սպայապետն Սայուրմակ, եւ առ զպատիւ նորա Ջեւանշէր: Իսկ քրմապետն ջանայր ի կրաւնն իւր դարձուցանել զՎիրս. եւ ոչ ոք հայէր ի նա, բայց ի սակաւուց յաննշան արանց, որք կորուսին զկեանս իւրեանց:

…

Եւ արձակեաց ընծայս Թագաւորին Պարսից՝ քսան հազար երիվարս, եւ ծառայս՝ տասն հազար ի ձեռն քրմապետին. եւ խնդրեաց զդուստր նորա իւր ի կնութիւն.

…

"Ահա գիտես, զի ամենայն Թագաւորք հարկս տային ձեզ, մինչեւ հաւատացին ի խաչեալն, եւ նովաւ զաւրացեալ յաղթեցին ձեզ, որք պաշտէք զկրակ, զոր ես չիջուցի աստ յաշխարհիս իմում, եւ առաքեցի առ քեզ զքրմապետ նոցա: Եւ արդ Քրիստոս Աստուած իմ է, եւ հուրն աստուած քո իցէ".

And then he (Barzabowtʿ) sent out fire worshippers to Mcxitʿa, and one *kʿrmapet* named Binkʿaran. And having arrived they settled in Mogtʿa. …

The commander-in-chief Sayowrmak died, too, and J̌owanšēr took over his honour. And the *kʿrmapet* tried to convert the Georgians to his faith, but no-one looked at him except for a few unimportant people, who lost their lives.

…

16 PV 144,2–5 ~ KC 145,5–7 / 157,9–10; PV 144,10–15 ~ KC 145,9–11 / 157,13–17; PV 152,2–6 ~ KC 158,7–11 / 171,8–13; the fourth passage (PV 169,7–15), in which Vaxṭang addresses the Persian king, has no exact equivalent in the Georgian text. The PV knows nothing about Binkʿaran's death.

And he sent gifts to the king of the Persians, 20,000 horses and 10,000 servants, by the hand of (= through) the *kʿrmapet*. And he asked for (the hand of) his daughter for marriage.

...

"Look, you know that all kings paid tribute to you while they were believers in (Christ) Crucified, and invigorated by him they defeated you who worship the fire, of whom I purged my country here, sending you their *kʿrmapet*, too. And now my God is Christ, and may the fire be your god!"

2.2 Nevertheless, the use of the word for "bishop", *episḳoposi*, is not due to mere awkwardness on the side of the Georgian author, J̌uanšer. On the contrary, the text passages show that he intentionally contrasts Binkaran with at least two Christian bishops, one, Mikael who was appointed by Queen Sagduxṭ as an opponent to Binkaran, and the other one, a certain Mobidan, the deceased predecessor of Mikael. These two bishops are mentioned in the Armenian version, too, where they are styled *episkopos*;[17] the divergence in the form of one of the names (Armenian *Mowšid* vs. Georgian *Mobidan*) explains itself, at least in part, by the notorious similarity of the characters <b> and <š> in the Georgian *nusxa-xucuri* script (ⴁ vs. ⴘ), which is also visible in variants such as *Šinkaran*, *Šinakran*, or *Šinakar* attested for the Zoroastrian "bishop's" name,[18] and variants with *š* for the name of Mobidan are also attested in manuscripts of the Georgian chronicle.[19]

Յաւուրսն յայնոսիկ մեռաւ Մուշիդ եպիսկոպոսն, եւ կալաւ զտեղի նորա Միքայէլ, որ էր ի Յունաց, որ ժրութեամբն իւրով պահեաց զերեւելի արսն ի հաւատս ճշմարիտս։

In those days bishop Mowšid died, and his place was taken by Mikʿayēl, who was from Greece and who, with his courage, protected the prominent people in the true faith.

Differently from the Georgian text, according to which Mikael "stood up against Binkaran", the Armenian version does not thematize the interrelation between the two bishops and the *kʿrmapet*, and it suggests that the succession from Mobidan/Mowšid to Mikael/Mikʿayēl was instantaneous. In the Georgian text, however, we read that it seems to have taken quite some time until Mikael appeared in Kartli, summoned there from Greece by Sagduxṭ, with a corresponding vacancy of the see. The Georgian wording further suggests that Binkaran might have abused the vacancy to establish himself as the "bishop" of Mcxeta—at least this is what we may assume is indicated by the epithet "deceitful" (Georgian *macturi*) which he is given more than once in the passages quoted above. This assumption is confirmed by external evidence.

17 PV 144,16–145,2 ~ KC 145,12–19 / 157,16–158,6.

18 Cf. Gippert 1984, p. 38 for a preliminary account of the confusion resulting from this and other pairs of similar characters in the transmission of historical names in Georgian sources, and further 4.1 below.

19 *Mošidan* in ms. B: KCQ 145,16 app.; *Mošidan* in ms. C: KCQ 142,16 app.; KCM 158,2 app.

3. The early Georgian bishops in the "Conversion of Kartli"

3.1 Bishop Mikael must have been an outstanding person in Georgian history indeed, given that he was not only the last bishop before the establishment of the office of a catholicos (Georgian *ḳataliḳosoba*) in Georgia[20] but also the spiritual teacher of Vaxṭang Gorgasali in his youth, as *Kartlis Cxovreba* tells us:[21]

> მაშინ ვახტანგ იზარდებოდა და ისწავლიდა მიქაელ ეპისკოპოსისაგან ყოველსა მცნებასა უფლისასა, და სიყრმისავე დღეთა შეიყუარა სჯული ქრისტესი უფროს ყოველთა მეფეთა ქართლისათა.
>
> Then Vaxṭang grew up, and he was taught by Mikael, the bishop, in all the knowledge of the Lord. And from his very childhood on he loved the faith of Christ, more than all (other) kings of Kartli.

In other sources, Mikael is even called an archbishop (Georgian *mtavar-ep̣isḳop̣osi*, lit. "head-bishop"). This is true, first of all, for the "Conversion of Kartli" *(Mokcevay Kartlisay)*, a compilatory text that comprises legendary material concerning the conversion of Georgia to Christendom by a female saint named Nino[22] as well as an annalistic type of account of the early centuries of Georgian Christianity, the so-called "Kings' List". The following synopsis of the passage in question contrasts the two major redactions of the Conversion (that of Šaṭberdi, 10th century, and that of Č̣eliši, 14th century)[23] with the corresponding passage from the fragmentary third redaction, which has recently been discovered among the manuscripts of the so-called "New Finds" of St. Catherine's Monastery on Mt. Sinai (ms. Sin.georg. N48),[24] as well as the two later "metaphrastic" versions of the Conversion.[25] In the Sinai manuscript and the metaphrasis by a certain Arsen Beri (NA), Mikael even receives the epithet *didi*, i. e., "the great":[26]

> MKS
>
> და შემდგომად რაოდენისამე ჟამისა მოიქცა, და მთავარებისკოპოსი იყო მიქაელ.
>
> And after some time he (Vaxṭang Gorgasali) returned (from Persia), and the archbishop was Mikael.

20 KCQ 197,9–14; KCM 213,10–14. The first catholicos was a certain P̣eṭre who was sent to Georgia by the Greek patriarch of Antioch; cf. 3.2.1 below.

21 KCQ 146,16–18; KCM 158,8–10.

22 Cf. GIPPERT 1997 and 2006 for an account of the historiographic value of the legend.

23 MKS 93,4–7 / 325,29–30 and MKC 93,4–6. Both redactions (MKS = Šaṭberd, MKC = Č̣eliši) are quoted after the edition in ABULAʒE 1963, pp. 81–163, that of Šaṭberd additionally after the edition in GIGINEIŠVILI/GIUNAŠVILI 1979, pp. 320–355.

24 MKN fol. 12v, line 14—13r, line 1; readings from the fragment (hereafter: MKN) are based on an autopsy undertaken on Mt. Sinai in May, 2009.

25 NA 47,20–22 and NB 81,9–11. The two metaphrastic redactions (of allegedly the 12th–13th cc.) are quoted after the edition in ABULAʒE 1971, pp. 7–51 and 52–83.

26 Note that the Sinai fragment exhibits the remarkable spelling *dit*, with final devoicing and no nominative ending as if it were a proper name.

MKC

და შემდგომად რაოდენისამე ჟამისა მოიქცა და მთავარებისკ[ო]პ[ო]სი იყო მიქაელ.

And after some time he returned, and the archbishop was Mikael.

MKN

და შემდგომად რავდენისამე ჟამისა მოიქცა და მთავარებისკოპოსი იყო მიქაელ დით.

And after some time he returned, and the archbishop was Mikael the Great.

NA

შემდგომად რაოდენისამე ჟამისა მოიქცა. და იყო მიქაელ დიდი მთავარეპისკოპოსად და შეასმინეს მის თანა, ვითარმედ ვახტანგ ქრისტეანობაჲ დაუტევა.

And after some time he returned, and Mikael the Great was the archbishop. And him they made aware (of the fact) that Vaxṭang had given up Christianity.

NB

და შემდგომად რაოდენისამე ჟამისა მოიქცა. და მაშინ ჟამსა მას იყო მიქაელ მთავარ-ეპისკოპოსად და დააჯერეს, ვითარმედ ვახტანგ ქრისტეანობაჲ დაუტევა.

And after some time he returned, and then, by that time, Mikael was the archbishop. And him they informed that Vaxṭang had given up Christianity.

3.2 More important in the given context is the fact that the "Kings' List" contains a consecutive register of all (arch)bishops of Mcxeta, from the conversion of Georgia under King Mirian (within the first half of the 4th century) up to Mikael. Just as in the example treated above, the church dignitaries are aligned with the reigns of the kings. Similar information can, of course, also be gained from *Kartlis Cxovreba*; however, both chronicles diverge to a certain extent, with respect to both the sequence of kings and the number of bishops.[27] Table 1 contrasts the data contained in the two chronicles (including the Armenian version of *Kartlis Cxovreba*).[28]

3.2.1 According to the three redactions of the "Kings' List" in *Mokcevay Kartlisay*, a total of ten (Christian) kings and thirteen archbishops passed away before the instalment of the first catholicos, Ṗeṭre. The synoptical arrangement of the three versions reveals that the Sinai fragment is closer to the Č̣eliši than to the Šaṭberdi version in its wording here:[29]

27 For a previous treatment of the lists cf. Winkler 1990 who, however, does not get into detail as to the latest bishops.

28 The legend of St. Nino within *Mokcevay Kartlisay* and the two metaphrastic versions mention only the first bishop, Iovane, under King Mirian. In MKS (157,21–27/353,26–30), archbishop Iaḳob is mentioned as the scribe of a letter sent by King Mirian to Salome of Užarma, the wife of King Mirian's son Rev, in the heading of chapter 15 of the legend; the corresponding heading in MKC (157,21–24) mentions neither the scribe nor the addressee of the letter.

29 MKS 93,30–33/325,36–37; MKC 93,30–35; MKN 13v,4–12.

Tab. 1

<table>
<tr><th colspan="2">King's Name</th><th colspan="4">(Arch)bishop</th></tr>
<tr><th>MK</th><th>KC</th><th></th><th>MK</th><th>KC</th><th>PV</th></tr>
<tr><td colspan="2">Mirian</td><td rowspan="2">Iovane</td><td rowspan="2">+</td><td rowspan="2">+</td><td rowspan="2">+</td></tr>
<tr><td colspan="2">Rev</td></tr>
<tr><td colspan="2">Bakur / Bakar</td><td>Iakob</td><td>+</td><td>–</td><td>–</td></tr>
<tr><td>Trdaṭ</td><td>Mirdaṭ</td><td rowspan="2">Iob</td><td rowspan="2">+</td><td rowspan="2">+</td><td rowspan="2">+</td></tr>
<tr><td colspan="2">Varaz-Bakur / Varaz-Bakar</td></tr>
<tr><td>Bakur</td><td>Trdaṭ</td><td>Elia</td><td>+</td><td>+</td><td>+</td></tr>
<tr><td colspan="2">Parsman</td><td rowspan="2">Swmeon[30]</td><td rowspan="2">+</td><td rowspan="2">+</td><td rowspan="2">–</td></tr>
<tr><td colspan="2">Mirdaṭ</td></tr>
<tr><td colspan="2" rowspan="4">Arčil</td><td>Iona</td><td>+</td><td>+</td><td>+</td></tr>
<tr><td>Grigor</td><td>?</td><td>+</td><td>+</td></tr>
<tr><td>Basili</td><td>?</td><td>+</td><td>+</td></tr>
<tr><td>Mobidan</td><td>?</td><td>+</td><td>+</td></tr>
<tr><td colspan="2">Mirdaṭ</td><td>Bolnokon</td><td>+</td><td>–</td><td>–</td></tr>
<tr><td colspan="2" rowspan="2">Vaxṭang Gorgasali</td><td>Iovel</td><td>+</td><td>–</td><td>–</td></tr>
<tr><td>Mikael</td><td>+</td><td>+</td><td>+</td></tr>
</table>

MKS
მეფენი გარდაცვალებულ იყვნეს ათნი, და მთავარებისკოპოსნი ათცამეტნი. ხოლო პირველი კათალიკოზი იყო პეტრე.

Ten kings had died, and thirteen archbishops. And the first catholicos was Ṗeṭre.

MKC
მაშინ გარდაცვალებულ იყვნეს მეფენი ათნი და კათალიკოზნი ცამეტნი. აქათგან იწყეს კათალიკოზთა მამად-მთავრობად. პირველი კათალიკოზი იყო პეტრე ვახტანგ მეფისა ზე.

Ten kings had died, and thirteen archbishops. From here on, the catholicoi began to rule as patriarchs (*lit.* heads of fathers). The first catholicos was Ṗeṭre, (still) under King Vaxṭang.

MKN
მეფენი გარდაცვალებულ იყვნეს ათნი და მთავარ-ებისკოპოსნი ცამეტნი და აქაჲთგ(ა)ნ იწყეს კათალიკოზთა მამად-მთავრობად და მწყემსა ერისა : პირველი კათალიკოზი იყო პეტრე ვახტანგ მეფისა ზე .

Ten kings had died, and thirteen archbishops. From here on, the catholicoi began to rule as patriarchs (*lit.* heads of fathers) and shepherds of the people. The first catholicos was Ṗeṭre, (still) under King Vaxṭang.

30 In MKN the name appears as *simon* (11v,12).

The number thirteen seems to contradict the data of the List itself as this mentions only twelve archbishops who had died before Pețre was sent to Georgia by the Greek patriarch at Antioch, upon Vaxțang's request. We arrive at thirteen, however, if we additionally count a monk named Samoel who came along with Pețre and who became, according to *Kartlis Cxovreba*, a bishop by his side. Interestingly enough, the Chronicle tells us that all in all twelve bishops accompanied Pețre:[31]

MKS

ხოლო მეფემან წარავლინნა მოციქულნი საბერძნეთა და ითხოვა მეფისაგან და პატრეაქისაგან კათალიკოზი. ხოლო მან მოსცა პეტრე კათალიკოზი. და თანა ჰყვანდა მას სამოველ მონაზონი, წმიდაჲ და ღირსი.

And the king sent out envoys to Greece and asked the king and the patriarch for a catholicos. And that one gave him Pețre, the catholicos. And with him he took Samovel, a monk, holy and worthy.

MKC

და მსწრაფლ წარავლინნა მოციქულნი საბერძნეთად და ითხოვა მეფის[ა]გ[ა]ნ და პატრიაქისა კათალიკოზი. და მოსცეს კათალიკოზი პეტრე. და თანა ჰყვანდა სამუელი მონაზონი, კაცი წმიდაჲ და ღირსი.

And the king sent out envoys to Greece and asked the king and the patriarch for a catholicos. And they gave him Pețre, the catholicos. And with him he took Samuel, the monk, a man holy and worthy.

MKN

ხ(ოლო) მეფემ(ა)ნ წარავლინა მოციქულნი საბერძნეთა და ითხოა მეფისაგ(ა)ნ და პატრიაქისა კათალიკოზი და მოსცეს კათალიკოზი პეტრე და თანა ჰყვანდა სამოელ მონაზონი კაცი წ(მიდა)ჲ და ღირსი :

And the king sent out envoys to Greece and asked the king and the patriarch for a catholicos. And they gave him Pețre, the catholicos. And with him he took Samoel, the monk, a man holy and worthy.

KC

"აწ მიგავლინო შენ პატრიაქისა კოსტანტინეპოლედ ..." და წარსცა იგი დიასპანთა ... და შეუთუალა, რათა კათალიკოსი და თორმეტნი ეპისკოპოსნი სწრაფით წარმოავლინენ. და მათ შორისმცა არს პეტრე კათალიკოსად და სამოელ ეპისკოპოსად ... და ანტიოქელმან პატრიაქმან აკურთხნა თორმეტნი ეპისკოპოსნი და პეტრე კათალიკოსად.

"Now I will send you to the patriarch at Constantinople ..." And he sent him out with messengers ... and let them convey that he (the patriarch) should send him quickly a catholicos and twelve bishops and that among them should be Pețre, the catholicos, and Samoel, the bishop. ... And the patriarch of Antioch consecrated the twelve bishops and Pețre, the catholicos.

The latter information may well be a later addition (possibly alluding to the twelve apostles); a view that agrees with the fact that it is only in *Kartlis Cxovreba*

31 MKS 93,21–26/325,31–34; MKC 93,21–26; MKN 13r,5–13; KCQ 197,7–198,6/KCM 213,10–214,13 (~ PV 180,19–181,19). NA (47,25–27) and NB (81,14–16) agree with MK.

that the patriarch of Constantinople is first approached by King Vaxṭang. On the other hand, it might also be interpreted as a misunderstanding of the information present in the Kings' List, with the number thirteen (archbishops before Ṗeṭre) being "corrected" to twelve (bishops accompanying him). This, however, would contradict the data contained in *Kartlis Cxovreba* itself as this chronicle omits at least three of the (arch)bishops named in the List, viz. Iaḳob, the second in the series, and the two bishops immediately preceding Mikael, who are indeed crucial for our topic.

3.2.2 Another major divergence consists in the fact that only *Kartlis Cxovreba* mentions the names of a total of four bishops for the time of King Arčil, viz. Iona, Grigor, Basili, and Mobidan. The Kings' List names only the first one explicitly, summarizing that "under King Arčil, four archbishops passed away". In the same context, the two older redactions of *Mokcevay Kartlisay* state that the Zoroastrians ("Magians") practised fire worship in Mogueta;[32] in the Chronicle, however, it is one of the four bishops themselves, Mobidan, who is blamed for having been a Magian, in accordance with his Persian provenance (and his name, cf. below), and who is therefore not counted among the bishops that died under Arčil:[33]

MKS

და მისა შემდგომად მეფობდა არჩილ, და მთავარებისკოპოსი იყო იონა. … და მოგუნი მოგუეთას მოგობდეს ცეცხლისა მსახურებასა ზედა. და მისვე არჩილის ზე ოთხნი მთავარებისკოპოსნი გარდაიცვალნეს.

And after him reigned Arčil, and the archbishop was Iona. … And the Magians practised fire worship in Mogueta. And under the same Arčil passed away four archbishops.

MKC

მერვე—არჩილ, და მთავარეპისკოპოსი იყო იონა. … მათ ჟამთა ოთხნი მთავარეპისკოპოსნი გარდაიცვალნეს.

The eighth (king after the conversion was) Arčil, and the archbishop was Iona. In those times four archbishops passed away.

MKN

და შემდგომად მისსა მერვე მეფობდა არჩილ, და მთავარებისკოპოსი იყო იონა. … და მოგუნი მოგუთას მოგობდეს ცეცხლის მსახურებასა ზედა. და მის ზევე არჩილისსა ოთხნი მთავარეპისკოპოსნი გარდაიცვალნეს.

And after him, (as) the eighth (king), reigned Arčil, and the archbishop was Iona. … And the Magians practised fire worship in Moguta. And under the same Arčil four archbishops passed away.

32 MA 92,24–34 / 325,19–24; MKC 92,24–31; MKN 11v,17–12r,16.
33 KCQ 139,11–142,18 ~ KCM 151,11–154,17 (~ PV 139,4–142,4).

KC

… დასუეს მეფედ მცხეთას ძე თრდატისი, ძმის-წული მირდატისი, მეფისა წარტყუენულისა, სახელით არჩილ. … ამის არჩილის ზე გარდაიცვალნეს სამნი ეპისკოპოსნი: იონა, გრიგოლი და ბასილი. და ბასილისა შემდგომად ამანვე არჩილ დასუა ეპისკოპოსი, რომელსა ერქუა მობიდან. ესე იყო ნათესავად სპარსი, და აჩუენებდა იგი მართლ-მადიდებლობასა. ხოლო იყო ვინმე მოგვ უსჯულო და შემშლელი წესთა, და ვერ უგრძნა არჩილ მეფემან და ძემან მისმან უსჯულოება მობიდანისი, არამედ ჰგონებდეს მორწმუნედ {სარწმუნოდ}…

… They appointed as king in Mcxeta the son of Trdaṭ, the nephew (*lit.* brother's child) of Mirdaṭ, the captured king, by the name of Arčil. … Under that Arčil three archbishops passed away: Iona, Grigoli and Basili. And after Basili, the same Arčil appointed a bishop whose name was Mobidan. This one was a Persian by provenance, and he pretended (to be) orthodox. But he was (rather) an unbeliever, a Magian, and a spoiler of morals, but Arčil and his son did not recognize Mobidan's infidelity but believed him to be faithful…

3.2.3 The most striking difference between the sources is met with in connection with the successor of King Arčil, Mirdaṭ, who was Arčil's son according to *Kartlis Cxovreba*:[34]

KC

და დაჯდა მეფედ {მეფე იქმნა} მის წილ ძე მისი მირდატ და მეფობდა იგი, ვითარცა მამა მისი, დიდსა სარწმუნოებასა შინა.

And in his stead his son Mirdaṭ was enthroned as king {became king}, and he reigned, like his father, in deep (*lit.* great) faith.

MKS

და მერმე მეფობდა მირდატ.

And then Mirdaṭ ruled as king.

MKC

და მეცხრე მირდატ.

And the ninth (king after the conversion was) Mirdaṭ.

MKN

მეცხრჱ მეფობდა მირდატ

(As) the ninth king Mirdaṭ ruled.

For this king, only *Mokcevay Kartlisay* provides the name of a contemporary archbishop, but in very divergent forms in the three redactions:[35]

MKS

და მთავარებისკოპოსი იყო გლონოქორ.

And the archbishop was Glonokor.

34 KCQ 143,2–3 ~ KCM 155,5–7 (~ PV 142,12–14); MKS 92,35 / 325,25; MKC 92,35; MKN 12v,1–2.

35 MKS 92,36–37 / 325,25; MKC 92,35–36; MKN 12v,2–3 (Fig. 1, with the name highlighted).

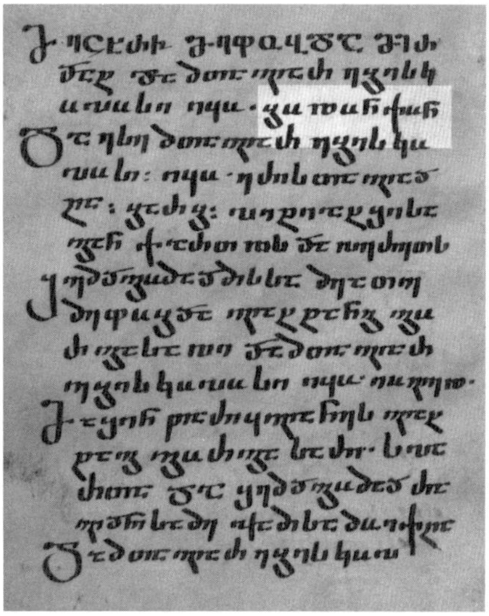

Fig. 1

MKC

მთავარებისკ[ო]პ[ო]სი იყო ბოლნოქონ.

The archbishop was Bolnokon.

MKN

და მთავარ-ებისკოპოსი იყო . ბოლონქონ.

And the archbishop was Bolonkon.

These divergences notwithstanding, the three redactions of the Kings' List agree in assigning to the archbishop a remarkable secondary function, viz. as an army commander appointed by a province governor whose name is not less divergent in the manuscripts:[36]

MKS

და ესე მთავარებისკოპოსი ერისთვადცა იყო ბარაზბოდ პიტიახშისაგან ქართლს და ჰერეთს.

And this archbishop was also an army commander (appointed) by Barazbod, the viceregent in Kartli and Hereti.

MKC

და ესევე იყო ერისთავ[ა]დცა ბარაბ პიტიახშის[ა]გ[ა]ნ.

And the same (person) was also an army commander (appointed) by Barab, the viceregent.

MKN

და ესე მთავარებისკოპოსი : იყო . ერის-თავადცა : ბარბ : პიტიახშისაგან ქართლს და ჰერეთს.

And this archbishop was also an army commander (appointed) by Barb, the viceregent in Kartli and Hereti.

Considering that the dominion of the viceregent[37] comprised *Kartli* and *Hereti*, i.e., Caucasian "Albania", and was thus essentially the same as later *Rani*, and taking the name *Barazbod* appearing in the Šaṭberd redaction as the most reliable form, we can easily assume that the person meant here is the same as Barzabod, the Iranian general and governor of *Rani* who sent the Zoroastrian "bishop" Binkaran to Mcxeta according to *Kartlis Cxovreba*. This further leads to the assumption that the archbishop mentioned in the Kings' List is identical with the very object of our study, the "deceitful" Zoroastrian "bishop" figuring among the Christian archbishops in *Mokcevay Kartlisay* in quite the same way as his "Magian" predecessor, Mobidan, does in *Kartlis Cxovreba*.

36 MKS 92,37–39 / 325,25–27; MKC 92,36–38; MKN 12v,4–7.

37 For the Georg. term *piṭiaxši* (~ Arm. *bdeašx*, Lat. *vitaxa* etc.) < Iranian **dwitīya-xšaya-* cf. Gippert 1991, pp. 207–216.

4. The name of the Zoroastrian "bishop"

4.1 If the Zoroastrian "bishop" of the Chronicle is indeed identical with the archbishop under Mirdaṭ in the Kings' List,[38] how then to account for the divergent forms of the name? As was stated above, it is not only the latter source that shows considerable variation here. In addition to the forms already listed by Brosset, we find at least five more in the manuscripts of *Kartlis Cxovreba*, including forms with an internal *o* vowel such as *Bonakran* and *Bonakaran* but also several forms with initial *š* instead of *b*. The evidence is gathered in table 2, in which the witnesses are arranged according to their (presumptive) age[39] (note that in some of the manuscripts several forms occur side by side).[40]

It is clear from the table that nearly all the forms attested in the manuscripts of *Kartlis Cxovreba* share a common skeleton comprising the consonants *n*, *k*, and *r* (the only exception is the form *Bakran* occurring once in ms. Q), while the initial letter alternates between *b* and *š*; major differences consist in the vowels of the first syllable and the existence or non-existence of a syllable ending in *-n* after the *r*. This picture can be summarized by the (vowelless) formula B/Š—N—K—R (—N). In contrast to this, the forms of the three redactions of *Mokcevay Kartlisay* add the variant g to the initial letter, the variation in word-final *r* and *n*, as well as an *l* letter occurring in the first syllable; including this, the formula would be G/B/Š (—L)—N—K (—R) (—N).

Concerning the alternation of the initial letter, we have already stated that the confusion between <b> and <š> in unknown words is a notorious feature of the Old Georgian *nusxa-xucuri* script (ⴁ vs. ⴘ); the alternation between <b> and <g>, though less frequently attested, is likewise based upon the graphical similarity of the corresponding characters, in both *(nusxa-xucuri)* minuscules (ⴁ vs. ⴂ) and *(mrglovani)* majuscules (Ⴁ vs. Ⴂ). There is no a priori means of deciding which character is primary; on the other hand, it should be noted that

38 The identification of the two bishops was first proposed by the Georgian scholar Ḳ. ḲEḲELIʒE (1955, pp. 37–39).

39 MK: S: ms. S-1141, 10th c.; N: Sin.georg. N48, ca. 11th c.; C: H-600, 14th c.—KC: A: ms. Q-795, 15th c.; C: Q-207, 16th c.; M: S-30, 1633–46 CE; Q: Q-1219, 1679 CE; T: SPb. no. 13, 18th c.; m: H-2135, 1736 AD; D: S-4770, 18th c.; E: A-131, 1718 CE, b: S-25, 1761 CE; p: H-988_2, 1761 CE; d: S-354, 18th c.; B: SPb. no. 41, 1839 CE; k: Kut. 441, 19th c.—For other mss. (here subsumed under "cet.") cf. the lists provided in KCQ, p. *2 and KCM, p. 23.

40 The two editions of *Kartlis Cxovreba* provide the following set of variants (in the sequence of the attestations treated above, with square brackets marking information only available from KCQ and curly braces, information only from KCM): I.: [ბინქარან C,] შინქარან Λ, შინაქარან Mm, {ბინაქარან Q,} [ბინაქარ Bdp, ბანქარ b, ბინქარ cet.]; II: [ბინქარან C,] შინქარან A, შიქრიან Mm, {ბაქრან Q,} [ბანქარიან b, ბინქარიან cet.]; III.: {ბინქარს C,} შინქარან A, შინაქარსა Mm, {ბინაქრსა Q}, [ბანაქარს Bdp, ბინქარს cet.]; IV.: ბუნქარან AC, ბონაქარან M, ბონაქრან {Q}m, [ბინქარ Dk, ბუნაქარ Bdp, ბუნქარ cet.]; V.: [ბინქარან A,] ბინაქრან M, ბინაქარ [Ed]m, ბინქარ {CQ}[cet.]; VI.: [ბინქარან AC,] ბინაქრან M{Q}m, [ბინქარ D, ბინაქრიანი Bdp, ბინქარიანი cet.]; VII.: [ბინქარან AC,] ბინქრან M[m], {ბინაქრან Qm,} [ბინაქარ BEdp, ბანქარ T, ბინქარ cet.].

Tab. 2

Source / Name	MK			KC													
	S	N	C	A	C	M	Q	T	m	D	E	b	p	d	B	k	cet.
Glonokor	×																
Bolonkon		×															
Bolnokon			×														
Šinkaran				×													
Binkaran				×	×												
Bunkaran				×	×												
Binkar					×		×			×						×	×
Bonakaran						×											
Binkran						×			×								
Šinakaran						×			×								
Šinakar						×			×								
Šikrian						×			×								
Binakran						×	×		×								
Bonakran							×		×								
Binakr							×										
Bakran							×										
Binakar									×		×		×	×	×		
Banakar													×	×	×		
Bunakar													×	×	×		
Binakrian													×	×	×		
Bankar								×				×			×		
Bankarian												×			×		
Bunkar																	×
Binkarian																	×

it is not easy to confuse <g> and <š> in Old Georgian majuscules (Ⴂ vs. Ⴘ); the confusion occurs only in minuscules (ⴂ vs. ⴘ).

In contrast to this, the alternation in the vowels requires a different explanation. Within Old Georgian, it may be due to an accidental restitution of abbreviations, given that the suspension of word-internal vowels was the most frequent method of abbreviating.[41] On the other hand, we may take non-Georgian

41 Cf. Gippert 1984, p. 38 for similar cases in forms of names occurring in the chronicles; Gippert 2007, pp. xxix–xxxi for the principles of abbreviation in pre-10th c. manuscripts; and Boeder 1987 for the general rules of Old Georgian abbreviation.

sources into account in the transmission of historical data, especially in the case of the "early centuries" of Georgian historiography; if these were written in a Semitic script (Syriac or, later, Arabic; Middle or, later, New Persian),[42] the omission of vowels would be natural.

4.2 Considering all this, we are forced to see the occurrence of the additional *-l-* in the forms of *Mokcevay Kartlisay* as a decisive factor. As a matter of fact, the evidence provided by the two sources is in this respect quite similar to the evidence of *Kartlis Cxovreba* concerning the name of Vaxṭang Gorgasali's Persian wife, which appears partly with a word-internal <l> as in *Balanduxṭ*, *Balenduxṭ*, *Balendoxṭ*, *Balenduṭ*, or *Šalenduxṭ*, partly without <l> as in *Bandoxṭ* or *Šanduxaṭ*. In a special treatise of this name, the present author proposed to derive it from a Middle Persian compound **šāhēnduxt*, interpretable as "daughter of a falcon". This proposal takes into account that in both the majuscule *(mrglovani)* script and its minuscule *(nusxa-xucuri)* successor, the character that was most often confused with <l> was <h> (cf. Ⴊ and Ⴠ, ⴊ and ⴠ), and that in intervocalic position, <h>, but not <l>, was often lost in the Georgian tradition.[43] Applying the same principles to the name of the Zoroastrian "bishop", we arrive at **šāhīnkār* as a possible source for the variants we find in the manuscripts.[44] A similar form *(šāhīnkār)* is well attested still today, as a family name, in Iran.[45]

4.2.1 Comparing **šāhīnkār* with **šāhēnduxt*, the reconstructed name of the daughter of Hormizd III who was married to Vaxṭang Gorgasali, we must not overlook the divergence in the vocalism of the second syllable, which would be noteworthy if both names contained MPers. *šāhēn* "falcon". The different reconstructions are nevertheless necessary, given that an <e> character is well attested in the variants of the latter name but in none of the former. We might still assume that the underlying etymon was the same, presupposing that the tradition concerning the Zoroastrian "bishop" entered Georgian later when MPers. *ē* had already developed into (NPers.) *ī*; however, given that the two persons were contemporary and are mentioned in the same contexts, this remains rather doubtful.[46] Instead we may rather take two different derivations from MPers.

42 Cf. Gippert 2006, pp. 114–117 for Syriac and Gippert 2004, pp. 110–111 for New Persian elements detectable in *Mokcevay Kartlisay*.
43 Cf. Gippert 2011, pp. 91–92 for the attestation of the name forms mentioned and 97–98 for the derivation of the reconstructed name.
44 The form *Blonkaran* established in Ḳeḳeliʒe 1955, p. 39 is untenable, as is the proposal by M. Andronikašvili (1966, p. 451) to derive *Binkar* etc. from MPers. *dīnkār* < OIran. **dainakāra* "believer", which presupposes a substitution of **d-* by **b-* otherwise unparalleled in Old Georgian.
45 Cf., e.g., the website of an artist named Rāmīn Šāhīnkār, http://www.raminshahinkar.com.
46 Cf. Gippert 1991, p. 91 and Bielmeier 2005, pp. 9–10 as to the problem of MPers. *ēmēd* "hope" being represented by *imed-* in Georgian.—A similar problem is raised by a second proposal by M. Andronikašvili (1966, p. 451), which proceeds from MPers. "Šīnkār <

šāh “king” into account here, one with the suffix *-ēn* denoting the “falcon” and one with *-īn*, a plain adjective formation meaning “royal”.[47] **sāhīnkār* would then have denoted somebody dealing with royal affairs, an epithet well suited for the “deceitful bishop” who acted as an envoy of the Persian king.

4.2.2 We still have to account for the forms ending in *-n* after or instead of the *-r* (*Bolnokon*, *Šinkaran* etc.). The variants of the Kings’ List seem to suggest that *-n* simply replaced *-r*, possibly by assimilation to the preceding *-n-*. This, however, cannot explain the emergence of forms with both *-r-* and *-n*. It is therefore appropriate to consider another solution, assuming a suffixal extension **sāhīnkār-ān* which might represent a hypostatic adjective formation built upon a former genitive plural (sc. “one of the *šāhīnkārs*”).[48] This solution has a good deal in its favour, given that a similar interpretation imposes itself for the name of the “bishop’s” predecessor, Mobidan, which occurs with and without *-an*, too. This name has for long been deduced from MPers. *mowbed*, the designation of high priests among the Magians (< **magu-pati*),[49] and the form in *-an* representing a plural formation (“one of the *mobeds*”) is possibly also attested as a common noun in Ǯuanšer’s account of Vaxṭang Gorgasali’s life, as the epithet of a certain Barzaban who was sent to the Georgian king from Persia. In the passage in question this is not totally certain, however, given the remarkable divergence in the manuscript tradition which is well reflected in the divergent wordings of the two editions:[50]

KCQ

ხვალისა დღე მოუვლინა მეფემან ვახტანგს ბარზაბან, საკუთარი მობიდანი, და რქუა ესრეთ გორგასალს …

On the next day, the king sent to king Vaxṭang (a certain) Barzaban, one of his own *mobeds*, and he spoke thus to the Gorgasali …

KCM

ხვალისა დღე წარმოავლინა ვახტანგსა ბარზაბან, საკუთარი, და მობიდან და ჰრქუა ესრეთ გორგასალსა …

On the next day, the king sent to Vaxṭang (a certain) Barzaban of his, and Mobidan, and he spoke thus to the Gorgasali …

---

*šainakāra ‘მშენებელი’”, i.e. “builder”. Given that the base in question (**šain-* “build”) is widely attested in Old Georgian in the forms *šēn-* and *šen-*, this is a priori unlikely; what is more, the etymology does not account for the name forms containing an <l>.

47 The formation in *-īn* will not contain a true adjective suffix but may represent, as in the formula *šāhīn šāh* “king of kings”, the original genitive plural of **xšāyaθiya*.

48 Cf. Gippert 2005, p. 157 with n. 80 (with further reference to G. Klingenschmitt apud Hoffmann 1967, p. 186 / 1975, p. 204 n. 15) on similar derivations.

49 Cf. Andronikašvili 1966, p. 341, referring to Hübschmann 1895, p. 195.

50 KCQ 183,22–184,1 ~ KCM 199,4–5. Cf. the critical apparatuses of the editions for the textual variation in the manuscripts, which also includes the name Barzaban.

Nevertheless, the passage raises serious doubts as to whether *Šahinkar(an) and Mobid(an) were at all the proper names of the two Zoroastrians denominated by them. It seems rather likely that they were designations of the functions they bore[51]—not as Georgian "bishops" but as officials of the Persian court. In any case, the etymology provided by HEINRICH HÜBSCHMANN for *Binkar* the "Oberpriester" must be given up.

References

ABULAӠE, I. 1953: *Kartlis cxovrebis ӡveli somxuri targmani.* Tbilisi.

— (red.) 1963: *Ӡveli kartuli agiograpiuli liṭeraṭuris ӡeglebi / Pamjatniki drevnegruzinskoj agiografičeskoj literatury.* I. Tbilisi.

ABULAӠE, I. (red.) 1971: *Ӡveli kartuli agiograpiuli liṭeraṭuris ӡeglebi / Pamjatniki drevnegruzinskoj agiografičeskoj literatury.* III. Tbilisi.

ANDRONIḲAŠVILI, M. 1966: *Narḳvevebi iranul-kartuli enobrivi urtiertobidan / Studies in Iranian-Georgian Linguistic Contacts.* I. Tbilisi.

BIELMEIER, R. 2005: "On West and East Iranian Loans in Kartvelian." In: D. HAUG / E. WELO (eds.): *Haptačahaptāitiš. Festschrift for Fridrik Thordarson on the occasion of his 77th birthday.* Oslo, pp. 1–18.

BOEDER, W. 1987: "Versuch einer sprachwissenschaftlichen Interpretation der altgeorgischen Abkürzungen." In: *Revue des études géorgiennes et caucasiennes* 3, 1987 [1989], pp. 33–81.

BROSSET, M. F. 1849: *Histoire de la Géorgie depuis l'antiquité jusqu'au XIXe siècle, traduite du géorgien.* 1re partie. S. Pétersbourg.

DORN, B. 1844: "Versuch einer Erklärung von drei Münzen mit Sasaniden-Gepräge." In: *Bulletin de la classe des sciences historiques, philologiques et politiques de l'Académie Impériale des Sciences de Saint-Pétersbourg* 1, pp. 33–43.

GIGINEIŠVILI; B. / E. GIUNAŠVILI (eds.) 1979: *Šaṭberdis krebuli X saukunisa / Šatberdskij sbornik X veka.* Tbilisi.

GIPPERT, J. 1984: "Zur historischen Onomastik des Georgischen." In: *Georgica* 7, pp. 37–42.

— 1997: "Marginalien zur Nino-Tradition." In: *Stimme der Orthodoxie* 3 (Sonderheft: Festschrift für Fairy von Lilienfeld), pp. 126–130

— 2004: "Iranians and Iranian Languages in Ancient Georgia." In: M. SAKHOKIA (ed.): *Indo-Iranica et Caucasica. Studies Volume in Honour of Prof. Mzia Andronik'ashvili.* Tbilisi (Perspective/Ṗerspeḳṭiva XXI, 6), pp. 106–113.

— 2005: "Das Armenische – eine indogermanische Sprache im kaukasischen Areal." In: G. MEISER / O. HACKSTEIN (eds.): *Sprachkontakt und Sprachwandel. Akten der XI. Fachtagung der Indogermanischen Gesellschaft.* Wiesbaden, pp. 139–160.

— 2006: "Çm. Ninos legenda: gansxvavebul çq̇arota ḳvali." In: *Enatmecnierebis saḳitxebi* 1–2, pp. 104–122; online English version under the title "St. Nino's

51 ANDRONIḲAŠVILI, l.c., treats *mobidan-i* in general as a common noun, not a proper name, in accordance with its occurrence in the passage treated above.

Legend: Vestiges of its various sources": http://titus.uni-frankfurt.de/personal/jg/pdf/jg1997je.pdf.

Gippert, J. 2011: "Onomastica Irano-Iberica. I. The Name of Vakhtang Gorgasali's Persian Wife." In: *Enatmecnierebis Sakitxebi / Issues of Linguistics* 2011, pp. 91–98.

— in print: "Nochmals zur Bauinschrift von Bolnisi." In: N. Reineck / U. Rieger (eds.): *Kaukasiologie heute – Festschrift für Heinz Fähnrich*. Wiesbaden.

Hoffmann, K. 1967: "Avest. *upa.mraōδəsca* N. 53." In: G. Wiessner (ed.): *Festschrift für Wilhelm Eilers. Ein Dokument der internationalen Forschung zum 27. September 1966*. Wiesbaden, pp. 177–188 (repr. in *Aufsätze zur Indoiranistik*, 1. Wiesbaden 1975, pp. 195–206).

Hübschmann, H. 1895: *Armenische Grammatik. I. Theil. Armenische Etymologie*. Leipzig.

Justi, F. 1895: *Iranisches Namenbuch*. Marburg.

Ḳeḳeliʒe, Ḳ. 1955: "Vin aris 'Mokcevay Kartlisays' Glonokor?" In: Ḳ. Ḳeḳeliʒe: *Eṭiudebi ʒveli kartuli liṭeraṭuris isṭoriidan III*. Tbilisi 1955, pp. 37–39.

Meṭreveli, R. (ed.) 2008: *Kartlis Cxovreba*. Tbilisi.

Qauxčišvili, S. (ed.) 1955: *Kartlis Cxovreba*. Ṭ. 1. Tbilisi.

Winkler, G. 1990: "Anmerkungen zu den georgischen Bischöfen nach Koriwn und georgischen Quellen." In: R. Schulz / M. Görg (eds.): *Lingua restituta orientalis. Festgabe für Julius Assfalg*. Wiesbaden, pp. 410–419.

Les données de géographie administrative sassanide dans le *Šahrestānīhā-ī Ērānšahr* : une réévaluation

RIKA GYSELEN

Introduction

Pendant de longues années, les études sur le droit et la jurisprudence sassanides ont été basées sur des sources textuelles, et plus particulièrement sur le *Mādigān-ī hazār dādestān (MHD)* « le recueil des mille jugements » auquel le récipiendaire de ce volume a consacré tant d'investigations. Ce n'est que depuis peu que des sources primaires de nature juridique sont apparues de telle sorte qu'il est désormais possible de vérifier la fidélité des données véhiculées par le *MHD*[1].

Une situation analogue s'est également présentée pour nos connaissances de l'administration du territoire sassanide et de son découpage spatial. Pendant longtemps les historiens se sont essentiellement appuyés sur des sources littéraires et en particulier sur un petit ouvrage traditionnellement désigné sous le titre de *Šahrestānihā-ī Ērānšahr* (*ŠĒ*) « les capitales provinciales de l'Ērānšahr (= pays des iraniens) »[2]. Toutefois la rédaction dans laquelle ce dernier nous est parvenu date au plus tôt du VIIIe siècle, ce qui peut faire craindre que les données fournies par ce texte s'appliquent à l'époque de la rédaction et non à la situation dans l'empire sassanide (224–651) du VIe siècle. Pour vérifier ce point il faut pouvoir disposer de sources primaires d'époque sassanide[3].

Il a fallu attendre la publication de suffisamment de sceaux sassanides, administratifs et officiels, pour enfin disposer d'une source primaire permettant d'aborder la géographie administrative de l'empire sassanide et de vérifier par la même occasion la véracité du *ŠĒ*. En nous appuyant sur les travaux de nos prédécesseurs qui avaient, avec plus ou moins de bonheur, déchiffré les inscriptions sur les sceaux administratifs sassanides, nous avions présenté en 1989 un

1 On peut mentionner ‹ l'archive du Tabaristān › dont plusieurs documents ont déjà été publiés par PHILIPPE GIGNOUX : GIGNOUX 2012.

2 On trouvera toutes les informations concernant les éditions du *ŠĒ* chez MARKWART 1931, GYSELEN 1988 et DARYAEE 2002, et nous n'y reviendrons pas ici.

3 Ce travail a été réalisé dans le cadre du projet CTESIPHON soutenu par l'ANR : ANR12-CORP-0012–01.

état des connaissances de la géographie administrative[4] et parallèlement nous avions procédé à une confrontation entre ces données sigillographiques et le texte du *ŠĒ*[5] dans l'édition de J. MARKWART[6]. Récemment, une nouvelle édition du *ŠĒ* a vu le jour[7]. Dans le commentaire de ce texte il n'est pas fait référence ni aux données sigillographiques présentées en 1989, ni aux nouvelles données apparues après 1989[8].

L'objectif du *ŠĒ* était de consigner des données que la tradition, principalement orale, véhiculait à propos de la fondation de certaines villes et les légendes qui entouraient cet événement, mais certainement pas d'être un témoin fidèle de la géographie administrative. On doit donc s'attendre à ne pas y trouver les noms de toutes les capitales provinciales que les données sigillographiques ont fait connaître. Pour des raisons éditoriales, la présente contribution se limite à l'examen des toponymes et de quelques termes présents dans le *ŠĒ* qui, à la lumière des inscriptions sigillaires, méritent un bref commentaire. Toutefois, n'étant pas philologue, aucune discussion d'ordre philologique n'accompagne cet examen du contenu et aucun avis n'est donné à propos du choix des lectures des divers éditeurs du *ŠĒ*. D'une manière générale c'est la lecture de DARYAEE 2002 qui a été retenue dans cet exposé sauf indication contraire.

L'épithète *hujadag* « bien fortuné »[9]

Le *ŠĒ* comporte en guise de titre la formule *pad nām ī dādār ī weh abzōnīg* « Au nom du créateur bienfaisant et généreux »[10], suivi par une autre formule : *pad nām ud nērōg ud ayārīh ī dādār Ohrmazd ī nēwak* (édition MARKWART 1931 avec une transcription adaptée à celle actuellement utilisée) et *pad nām <ī> ud nērōg ud ahlāyīh ī dādār ohrmazd [ud] jadag ī nēk* (édition DARYAEE 2002)[11]. On peut hésiter sur le choix de DARYAEE pour la lecture *ahlāyīh* « droiture », qui a bien sûr un sens compatible avec une telle formule, mais qui n'est pas habituelle. En témoigne par exemple le *Kār-nāmag ī Ardašīr ī Pābagān (KNA)*, un autre texte moyen-perse de rédaction post-sassanide, dans lequel on trouve *pad*

4 GYSELEN 1989.

5 GYSELEN 1988.

6 MARKWART 1931.

7 DARYAEE 2002.

8 NIKITIN 1994, LERNER/SKJÆRVØ 1997, GYSELEN 2001, 2002, 2006–2007, 2007 et 2012, GYSELEN/DARYAEE 2014, GYSELEN/JULLIEN 2015.

9 Si le terme *hujadag* se traduit assez fidèlement en anglais comme « well-omened », il est beaucoup plus difficile de le rendre d'une manière concise en français.

10 DARYAEE 2002, p. 17 : « In the name of the beneficent bountiful Creator ». MARKWART 1931, p. 8 traduit « In the name of the Creator, the good and munificent ».

11 MARKWART 1931, p. 8: « In the name and in the power and help of the Creator Ohrmazd, the good ». Daryaee 2002, p. 17: « In the name and power and righteousness of the Creator Ohrmazd and good omen ».

nām ud nērōg [ud] ayārīh (ī) dādār Ohrmazd [ī] rāyōmand [ī] xwarrahōmand « Par le nom et la force et l'aide du créateur Ohrmazd, le splendide et le glorieux »[12]. MARKWART lit *nēwak* « bon » à la fin de la phrase, alors que DARYAEE trouve dans le manuscrit *jadag ī nēk* « good omen » (bonne fortune). Toutefois cette traduction ne correspond pas tout à fait à celle proposée dans son commentaire[13]. À notre avis, il ne fait pas de doute que l'expression *jadag ī nēk* est la forme en néo-persan du terme moyen-perse *hujadag*, un épithète bien connu depuis l'apparition de douze sceaux de généraux d'empire qui portent tous ce terme[14]. Sur les sceaux, le terme *hujadag* « bien fortuné »[15] est systématiquement suivi du nom du souverain sous lequel servait le général. Chaque sceau porte ainsi soit *hujadag-Khusrō* (Khusrō I, 531–579), soit *hujadag-Ohrmazd* (Ohrmazd IV, 579–590). Il est bien possible que cette épithète s'applique aussi aux divinités, et en particulier au dieu suprême Ohrmazd. On peut considérer que *Ohrmazd jadag ī nēk* est une ‹ transposition › en persan de l'expression moyen-perse *hujadag-Ohrmazd* « well-omened Ohrmazd ».

Le terme *šahrestān*

Lors d'une édition ancienne, l'ouvrage reçut le titre *Šahrīhā-ī Ērānšahr* « Les provinces de l'Ērānšahr », titre considéré comme inexact par MARKWART qui a proposé *Šahrestānīhā-ī Ērānšahr* « Les capitales provinciales d'Ērānšahr »[16]. En effet le *ŠĒ* énumère explicitement des *šahrestānīha* comme la première phrase le montre :

> § 1. *šahrestānihā ī andar zamīg ī ēran-šahr kard estēd jud jud rōz*
> « les capitales provinciales (MARKWART)/les villes (DARYAEE) qui ont été construites sur la terre d'Ērānšahr à des jours différents (c'est-à-dire : à des moments différents) ».

Si DARYAEE choisit de traduire *šahrestān* par le terme neutre ‹ ville › (city), cela n'empêche évidemment pas qu'il s'agisse de villes qui ont probablement joué un rôle de capitale administrative de la province. On peut remarquer dans le *ŠĒ* que la manière de formuler les diverses capitales ne correspond que dans quelques rares cas à celle qu'on trouve sur les sceaux administratifs sassanides, c'est-à-dire un toponyme suivi du terme *šahrestān*. Dans le *ŠĒ* c'est uniquement le cas pour la première capitale : *Samarkand-šahrestān*. Sinon le nom du *šahrestān* est formulé : *šahrestān ī* (+ toponyme).

12 GRENET 2003, pp. 52–53.
13 DARYAEE 2002, p. 17.
14 GYSELEN 2001.
15 On doit à PHILIP HUYSE d'avoir reconnu le terme *hujadag* dans les lettres *hwjtk*.
16 Voir à ce propos le commentaire de MARKWART 1931, p. 24.

Le terme *šahrestān* est désormais bien attesté par la sigillographie et y apparaît dans deux expressions précises : 1) *kust ī šahrestān*, « côté de la capitale provinciale » et 2) un nom de lieu suivi du terme *šahrestān*. Dans le premier cas, l'expression est précédée par un toponyme qui correspond souvent à un nom de province connu. Il n'est pas impossible que cette manière de désigner une province – par exemple *Hamadān kust ī šahrestān* – soit symptomatique d'une réorganisation administrative qui va de pair avec l'octroi d'un nom qui le distingue de celui que la province portait auparavant. Dans ce cas précis, on peut suggérer que l'ancien nom de la province était tout simplement Hamadān. Mais ceci est un autre sujet. Dans le deuxième cas, le terme *šahrestān* qualifie une ville comme capitale provinciale. La sigillographie sassanide atteste que ce terme peut s'appliquer aussi bien dans le cas où la ville et la province portent le même nom – *Weh-Andiyōk-Šābuhr-šahrestān*, (province de) *Weh-Andiyōk-Šābuhr*, *Weh-Ardašīr-šahrestān*, (province de) *Weh-Ardašīr*, *Zarang-šahrestān*, (province de) *Zarang*[17] – que lorsque la capitale de la province porte un autre nom que celui de la province – *Tēsfōn-šahrestān*, (province de) *Husrō-šād-Kawād*[18], *Ganzag-šahrestān*, (province de) *Ādurbādagān*[19], *Rām-Pērōz-šahrestān*, (province de) *Ray*[20]. Mais on a aussi : *Gōr*, (province de) *Ardašīr-xwarrah*[21] alors qu'il est généralement admis que Gōr était la capitale de la province d'Ardašīr-xwarrah, ce qui est dit aussi explicitement dans le *ŠĒ* (§ 44). On est donc en présence soit d'une exception à la règle, soit Gōr n'était pas la capitale de la province comme il est coutume de le croire. A priori, l'utilisation du terme *šahrestān* n'est pas conditionnée par le statut de la province dont elle est la capitale. Ce statut est mis en évidence par le nom de l'administration qui gère la province : *šahrab* « celui qui protège le *šahr* », *ōstāndār* « celui <qui est> en charge d'un *ōstān* », ou encore *naxwār* « celui qui tient le premier <rang> »[22]. D'après les informations fournies par la sigillographie et les inscriptions monumentales, on connaît le statut de plusieurs provinces : Weh-Andiyōk-Šābuhr et Husrō-šād-Kawād sont des *šahr*[23], alors que Ray était administré par un *naxwār*[24]. Il est possible, mais pas prouvé, que le terme *šahrestān* s'applique à toutes les capitales provinciales quoi qu'ait pu être le statut de la province. Les capitales provinciales qui sont nommées sur les sceaux administratifs possèdent une administration de *mowūh* ou « bureau de mages » et ont le statut de canton. Dans ce cas, il s'agit d'une ville et de ses environs immédiats.

17 Gyselen 1989, *passim*.
18 Gyselen 1989, *passim*.
19 Gyselen 1989, *passim*.
20 Gyselen/Daryaee 2014.
21 Gyselen 1989, *passim*.
22 Gyselen 2004 ; Gignoux 2004, pp. 41–43.
23 Gyselen 1989, pp. 61–62.
24 Gyselen 2004.

Les termes pour ‹ provinces › et ‹ régions ›

Si dans la majorité des cas le *ŠĒ* utilise la formulation ‹ capitale de (la province) X ›, on rencontre aussi quelques autres formulations : § 8) *andar baxl ī *bāmīg šahrestān [ī] nawāzag...*, § 17) *andar gurgān šahrestān ī dahestān...*, § 27) *andar māh ud kust ī nīhāwand ud war [ī] wahrāmāwand šahrestān-e...*, § 28) *21 šahrestān ī andar padišxwārgar ...*

Grâce aux sceaux on sait que Baxl, Gurgān et Māh-kust-ī-Nēmāwand étaient des provinces qui avaient le statut de *šahr*. En revanche, les sceaux qui contiennent le nom de Parišxwārgar sont tous des sceaux d'*āmārgar*, une administration dont les circonscriptions sont fluctuantes et de superficie très diverse. Dans certains cas l'administration de l'*āmārgar* contrôle une seule province, mais la plupart du temps il s'agit d'un conglomérat de plusieurs provinces. Sur certains sceaux, la liste des provinces sous son autorité est explicitement mentionnée, mais lorsque ces provinces constituent une ‹ région ›, c'est le nom de la région qui y figure. Ceci est probablement le cas du Parišxwārgar. La sigillographie sassanide n'a pas livré le terme moyen-perse pour ‹ région › mais quelques sources secondaires comme l'Anthologie de Zādspram dont la rédaction date au plus tôt du IXe siècle contiennent des données à ce propos. Ce texte présente un passage qui a trait à la hiérarchie des diverses entités territoriales : § 23.5 : ... *rōstāg rōstāg dādwar ī dād-āgāh ud awestām* (= *ōstān*) *<awestām> mowbed ī rāst-kāmag ud kustag kustag rad ī abēzag* ... « ... il faut désigner dans chaque canton (*rōstāg*) un juge connaissant le droit, dans chaque province *(ōstān)* un mowbed à la volonté droite, dans chaque région *(kustag)* un rad pur »[25]. L'utilisation du terme *ōstān* pour désigner une province est typique pour les sources textuelles post-sassanides comme l'a montré l'étude de Morony sur la géographie administrative de l''Iraq à l'époque sassanide tardive et au début de la période islamique[26]. Les sources historiographiques post-sassanides que Morony cite utilisent systématiquement le terme *ōstān* pour désigner une province administrative. Ce n'est que dans des sources d'époque sassanide, en l'occurrence syriaques, qu'apparaît le terme *šahr* pour désigner une province. L'utilisation systématique du terme *ōstān* pour désigner une province est probablement consécutive à la réforme administrative de 'Abd al-Malek en 77 AH (= 696 AD) qui a uniformisé le statut des provinces. Si l'on sait qu'à l'époque sassanide les provinces pouvaient avoir des statuts différents, rien n'indique que cette règle s'appliquait aussi aux ‹ cantons › et aux ‹ régions ›.

Il faut se demander si les termes *rōstāg* « canton » et *kustag* « région » attestés dans les sources littéraires avaient cours à la période sassanide, s'ils désignaient un ‹ canton › ou une ‹ région › avec un statut particulier, ou si c'étaient des termes génériques sans connotation administrative. Quoiqu'il en soit, l'association des termes *kustag* et *rad* dans l'anthologie de Zādspram est particulièrement intéressante à la

25 Gignoux/Tafazzoli 1993, pp. 84–85. Voir à ce propos aussi Kreyenbroek 1987.
26 Morony 1982.

lumière des données apportées par ‹ l'archive du Tabaristān › qui comporte des documents dans lesquels est mentionné un Parišxwārgar-rad[27]. On peut en déduire que Parišxwārgar peut être considéré comme un *kustag*. Reste évidemment à savoir si le mot *kustag* avait un sens générique ou plutôt une connotation administrative précise. Le terme *kustag* apparaît encore dans d'autres textes en moyen-perse de rédaction post-sassanide. Ainsi dans le *Kārnāmag-i Ardašīr* le terme *kustag* est associé au Kermān, Makurestān, Fārs[28], ce qui n'est pas contredit par les sources primaires. En effet, l'étude des sceaux administratifs a mis en évidence que le Kermān et le Fārs sont des ‹ régions › et non des ‹ provinces ›[29]. Toutefois dans ce même ouvrage le terme *kustag* est aussi associé à Ray et à Dunbāwand alors qu'on sait que Ray a le statut d'une province. À première vue, on pourrait en conclure que le terme *kustag* est générique et désigne simplement un territoire sans aucune connotation annexe, mais il existe peut-être une raison précise pour que Ray et Dunbāwand aient été considérés comme un *kustag*. Cette question sera examinée ailleurs.

La notion de *kust* « côté, direction »

L'auteur du *ŠĒ* présente la liste des *šahrestān*s en quatre groupes selon le ‹ côté › – qui correspond à un point cardinal – auquel ils appartiennent : *kust-ī xwarāsān* « le côté de l'est », *kust-ī xwarbarān* « le côté de l'ouest », *kust-ī nēmrōz* « le côté du midi » et le *kust-ī Adurbādagān*[30] « le côté du nord ». Ce concept de quatre ‹ côtés › ou ‹ directions › a été amplement véhiculé par la littérature post-sassanide mais n'est apparu dans les sources primaires que récemment, sur douze sceaux de généraux de l'empire. Chaque sceau porte le nom du général, ses titres et la circonscription qui lui est attribuée. Chaque inscription se termine de la même manière : ... *ērān kust ī xwarāsān/xwarbarān/nēmrōz/ādurbādagān spāhbed*. Lors de leur publication nous avions associé le terme *ērān* à *spāhbed*. L'argument était que le pouvoir militaire unique incarné par l'*Ērān-spāhbed*[31] « général des iraniens » disparaît au VIe siècle pour céder la place à un système de quadripartition du pouvoir militaire avec quatre généraux qui ont chacun autorité sur un ‹ quart › de l'empire lequel est défini par un point cardinal. Nous avions préconisé que le titre *Ērān-spāhbed* ne disparaît pas, mais qu'on y ajoute respectivement *kust-ī xwarāsān*, *kust-ī xwarbarān*, etc. qu'on traduit comme « Ērān-spāhbed du côté de l'est », etc. Évidemment l'idée que le terme *Ērān* n'est pas associé au terme

27 GIGNOUX 2012, doc. Tab. 22 et 28.
28 GRENET 2003, pp. 74–75 : Ch. V, 10.
29 GYSELEN 1989, p. 64.
30 Comme le ‹ nord › est le pays des démons, le terme moyen-perse pour ‹ nord › n'est pas utilisé pour designer ce point cardinal. À la place est utilisé le terme Ādurbādagān, nom d'une des provinces de cette partie d'*Ērānšahr*.
31 Ce titre n'est pas attesté dans les sources primaires, mais il existe des titulatures analogues composées avec Ērān, par exemple *Ērān-anbaragbed* (BIVAR 1969, sceau AD1).

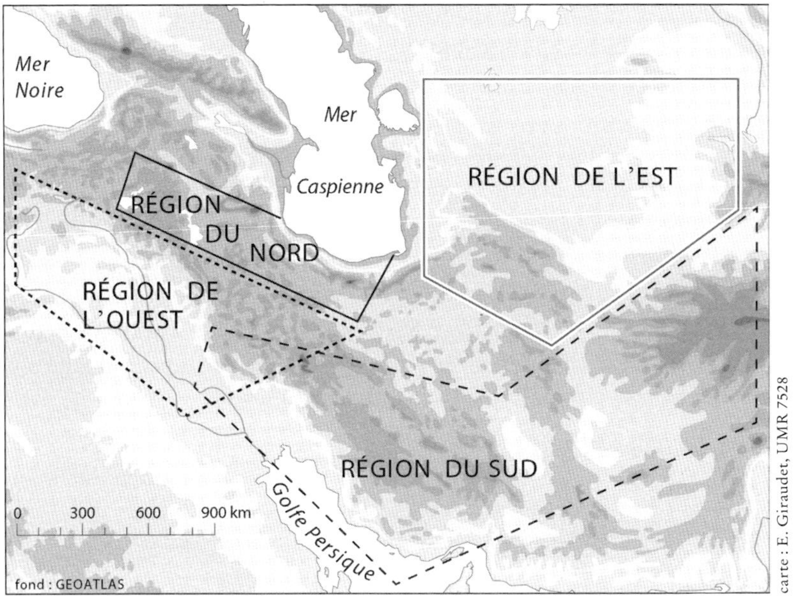

Carte : les quatre *kusts* d'Ērānšahr d'après le ŠĒ[32]

spāhbed, mais à l'expression *kust-ī xwarāsān*, *kust-ī xwarbarān*, etc. n'est pas à rejeter. On aura alors « spāhbed d'Ērān-coté-de-l'est », etc.

Si les sceaux des généraux confirment l'existence de quatre *kust*, ils ne nous apprennent presque rien sur leur étendue respective. La seule information que la sigillographie contient à ce propos est que le Sakastān, le Zāwulistān, et le Warāzigān font partie du *kust ī nēmroz* « le côté du sud » [33]. En revanche, pour connaître l'étendue de chaque *kust*, on peut faire appel au *ŠĒ* qui énumère les *šahrestānīhā* par *kust*. Dans la mesure où ces *šahrestānīhā* sont localisés, on peut cartographier l'étendue de chaque *kust*. Reste à savoir si cette répartition correspond à celle de l'époque sassanide.

À propos de quelques toponymes

La liste des *šahrestāns* mentionnés dans le *ŠĒ* a déjà été confrontée aux informations sigillographiques connues vers la fin des années dix-neuf cent quatre-vingt, et nous n'y reviendrons pas ici[34]. En revanche, on confrontera au *ŠĒ* les données

32 D'après Gyselen 1988, p. 195, fig. 1.
33 Voir à ce propos Gyselen 2007, p. 10.
34 Gyselen 1988.

sigillographiques qui sont apparues au cours des vingt-cinq dernières années en y consacrant un très bref commentaire.

§2. … Samarkand-*šahrestān* …
Samarkand-*šahrestān* ouvre la liste des *šahrestāns* du côté de l'est et bénéficie de maints commentaires (§2–7). Capitale de la Sogdiane, Samarkand ne fait pas partie intégrante d'Ērānšahr. Toutefois, à certains moments de l'histoire Samarkand tombe sous la coupe des Sassanides qui y auraient installé un atelier monétaire frappant monnaie sassanide[35].

§8. … *andar Bakhl ī *bāmīg šahrestān [ī] nawāzag* …
Dans le *ŠĒ* le statut de Baxl n'est pas énoncé, mais la sigillographie atteste qu'au IIIe siècle Baxl était gouverné par un *šahrab*[36]. Sur un sceau administratif d'*āmārgar* Baxl est associé à la province de Marw-rōd[37].

§11. *šahrestān ī marw-rōd*
Marw-rōd est attesté comme province, sans qu'on en connaisse le statut[38]. Marw-rōd fait partie de deux circonscriptions administratives d'*āmārgar* respectivement Marw-rōd et Baxl, et Marw-rōd, Harēy et Marw[39].

§12. *šahrestān ī marw ud šahrestān [ī] harē*
Marw est attesté pour l'administration d'un *āmārgar* dont la circonscription comporte Marw, Harī et Marw-rōd[40]. Mais aucune donnée sigillaire précise que Marw est une province, et à plus forte raison quel était son statut.

Harī est une province qui a le statut d'*ōstān*. Cette province est aussi attestée par deux sceaux d'*āmārgar* dont les circonscriptions sont respectivement la seule province de Harī, et Harī, Marw-rōd et Marw[41].

§13. … *šahrestān [ī] *pōšang* …
Nous avions suggéré que l'ancien nom de Pōšang pourrait être Pušagistān[42], mais il ne s'agit que d'une proposition.

§14. … *šahrestān [ī] tūs* …
Le nom de Tōs est connu grâce à un sceau administratif de *mowūh* [43].

§22. *šahrestān [ī] *nasībīn*
Dans le *ŠĒ* le nom de Nasībīn ou Nisibis est écrit *syn'*. C'est probablement sous la forme de *nsyn'*(?) que le nom figure sur un sceau administratif d'*āmārgar*,

35 MOCHIRI 1977 et 2009.
36 NIKITIN 1994.
37 GYSELEN 2002, pp. 137–138.
38 GYSELEN 2015.
39 GYSELEN 2002, p. 159.
40 GYSELEN 2002, pp. 158–159.
41 GYSELEN 2002, pp. 149–151.
42 GYSELEN 2002, p. 164.
43 GYSELEN 2002, p. 175.

et si notre hypothèse est exacte ce sceau comporte également le nom honorifique que Nisibis reçoit de Khusrō Ier : Ērān-abzūd-Husrō « Khusrō a augmenté Ērān »[44]. Sur ce sceau d'*āmārgar*, Nisibis est associé à deux autres provinces : Arzōn et Arwāyestān. La province d'Ērān-abzūd-Husrō (= Nasībīn ?) avait le statut d'*ōstān*.

§ 28. *21 šahrestān ī andar padišxwārgar …*
Cette phrase implique que la région du Parišxwārgar comporte 21 provinces. Récemment une contribution a été consacrée aux données sigillographiques concernant les provinces situées dans la région au sud de la mer Caspienne qui a pu porter le nom de Parišxwārgar. Nous n'y reviendrons ici que pour préciser que le nombre de provinces supposées appartenir à Parišxwārgar d'après les données sigillographiques n'atteint même pas la demi-douzaine, ce qui est très loin du nombre 21 avancé par le *ŠĒ*[45].

§ 37. *… šahrestān [ī] zāwalestān …*
Le nom de Zāwulistān est associé à celui de Warāzagān sur un sceau d'*āmārgar*[46]. Aucune donnée ne précise explicitement qu'il s'agit d'une province.

§ 41. *šahrestān [ī] staxr*
Si on soupçonnait bien que Staxr était une province, on en possède maintenant la preuve grâce à un sceau de l'administration de *mowūh*[47].

§ 42. *šahrestān [ī] dārāb-gird*
Le nom de Dārābgird n'était auparavant attesté que par un sceau d'*āmārgar*[48]. Désormais la sigillographie lui attribue le statut d'*ōstān*[49].

§ 46. *šahrestān ī ohrmazd-ardaxšīrān …*
Le sceau d'un *šahrab* d'Ohrmazd-Ardašīr[50] avait échappé à notre attention lors de la synthèse de 1989.

§ 52. *… šahrestān ī *āsūr*
Il n'existe pas de preuve que le nom d'Āsūr qui figure dans le *ŠĒ* soit synonyme d'Āsūrestān, toponyme qui représente la circonscription d'un *marzbān*[51]. Étant donné que le *marzbān*, tout comme l'*āmārgar*, peut être attaché à une circonscription qui représente une seule ou plusieurs provinces, il est impossible de déterminer si Āsūrestān était une province ou une région bien que cette dernière éventualité emporte notre préférence.

44 Gyselen 2002, pp. 140–142.
45 Gyselen 2012.
46 Gyselen 2002, pp. 177–178.
47 Gyselen 2015.
48 Gyselen 1989, p. 45.
49 Gyselen 2002, p. 139.
50 Mochiri 1983, p. 340, fig. 1126 et 1127.
51 Lerner/Skjærvø 1997.

§ 53. *šahrestān ī gay* ...
La province de Gay est désormais attestée par un sceau administratif de *šahrab*[52].

§ 54. *šahrestān ī ērān-āsān-kard-kawād* ...
Ērān-āsān-kar-Kawād était déjà attesté comme province, mais on en connaît maintenant le statut grâce à un sceau administratif d'*ōstāndār*[53].

§ 56. *šahrestān ādūrbādagān* ...
§ 58. *pad kust ādūrbādagān šahrestān ī ganzag* ...
On ne discutera pas ici du terme Ādurbādagān qui est utilisé une fois comme nom d'une province, une autre fois comme celui d'un *kust*. En outre, le *ŠĒ* place la ‹ province › Ādurbādagān dans le *kust* du sud et pas dans le *kust ī Ādurbādagān*. Quoiqu'il en soit, la sigillographie atteste que Ganzag est bien le *šahrestān* de la province d'Ādurbādagān qui bénéficie du statut de *šahr* [54].

Conclusions

La sigillographie sassanide fait connaître de plus en plus de toponymes qui sont également mentionnés dans le *ŠĒ*. Toutefois il reste quelques toponymes dans le *ŠĒ* pour lesquels aucune attestation sigillaire n'existe[55]. La raison peut être le hasard des trouvailles, ou le fait que la ville (et la province) était connue à l'époque sassanide sous un autre nom et que nous n'avons pas pu reconnaître ce nom dans les toponymes mentionnés sur les sceaux. Bien sûr, la sigillographie sassanide comporte beaucoup plus de noms de provinces et de régions que le *ŠĒ*. Mais comme on l'a déjà souligné : l'objectif du *ŠĒ* n'était pas de présenter un inventaire complet des provinces.

En combinant les données présentées en 1988[56] avec celles obtenues à partir des nouveaux matériaux sigillographiques on peut établir les concordances suivantes. Elles sont présentées sous forme de tableaux :

Tab. 1 : Les *šahrestāns* du côté de l'est

ŠĒ	Sigillographie		
šahrestān	*šahrestān* (?)	province	Statut de la province
Samarkand			
Nawāzag dans Balkh		Bakhl	šahr

52 Gyselen 2008.
53 Gyselen 2002, p. 142.
54 Gyselen 1989, pp. 43–44.
55 Ils sont faciles à reconnaître dans les tableaux (fig. 1–4) : la ligne comportant les attestations sigillaires est restée vide.
56 Gyselen 1988.

ŠĒ	Sigillographie		
šahrestān	*šahrestān* (?)	province	Statut de la province
Xwārazm			
Marw-rōd		Marw-rōd	?
Marw		Marw	?
Harē		Harī	ōstān
Pōšang		Pušagistān + Aspzār	ōstān
Tūs		Tōs	?
New-Šābuhr	Nēw-Šābuhr	Abaršahr	?
Kāyēn			
Dahestān dans Gurgān		Gurgān	šahr
Kūmiš		Kōmiš	?
Husraw-šād			
Husraw ī mūst-ābād			
Wisp-šād-Husraw			
Hu-bōy-Husraw			
Šād-farrox-Husraw			

Tab. 2 : Les *šahrestāns* du côté de l'ouest

ŠĒ	Sigillographie			
šahrestān	*šahrestān* (?)	province	Statut de la province	‹ Région ›
Tīsifōn	Tesfon-šahrestān	Husrō-šād-Kawād	šahr	
Nasībīn		Nasībīn = Ērān-abzūd-Husrō (?)	ōstān	
Ōrhāy				
Bābel	Bābīl	Weh-Kawād	šahr	
Hērt				
Hamadān		Hamadān	šahr	
Mā ud kust ī Nihāwand ud war wahrāmāwand		Mād, kust ī Nēmāwand	šahr	
21 šahrestān andar Padišxwārgar				Parišxwārgar
Mūsel		Nōd-Ardašīragān	?	

ŠĒ	Sigillographie			
šahrestān	*šahrestān* (?)	province	Statut de la province	‹ Région ›
9 šahrestān andar zamīg Gazīrag				
24 šahrestān andar zamīg Šām …				

Tab. 3 : Les *šahrestān*s du côté du midi (= sud)

ŠĒ	Sigillographie			
šahrestān	*šahrestān* (?)	province	Statut de la province	‹ Région ›
Kābul				
Raxwat				
Bast		Bost ud Kaš	ōstān	
Frāh		Frāx(-kar-Pēroz, kust ī šahrestān)	(naxwār)	
Zāwalestān		Zāwulestān	?	
Zarang	Zarang-šahrestān	Zarang	?	
Kermān				Kermān
Weh-Ardaxšīr				
Staxr		Staxr	?	
Dārāb-gird		Dārābgird	ōstān	
Weh-Šābuhr		Bišābuhr	šahr	
Gōr-Ardaxšīr-xwarrah	Gōr	Ardašīr-xwarrah	?	
Tūzag				
Ohrmazd-Ardaxšīrān		Ohrmazd-Ardašīr	šahr	
Rām-Ohrmazd				
Šūs ud Šuštar		Ērān-xwarrah-Šābuhr	?	
Wandōy-Šābuhr	Weh-Andiyōk-Šābuhr-šahrestān	Weh-Andiyōk-Šābuhr	šahr	
Ērān-kard-Šābuhr	(Ērān-xwarrah-Šābuhr ?)-šahrestān	Ērān-xwarrah-Šābuhr (?)	?	
Nahr-Tirag				

ŠĒ	Sigillographie			
šahrestān	*šahrestān* (?)	province	Statut de la province	‹ Région ›
Simrān				
*Arhēst				
*Āsūr				Āsurestān
Weh-Ardaxšir		Weh-Ardašīr	?	
Gay		Gay	šahr	
Ērān-āsān-kard-Kawād		Ērān-āsān-kar-Kawād	ōstān	
Aškar				
Ādurbādagān	Voir fig. 4			
Van				

Tab. 4 : Les *šahrestāns* du côté de l'Ādurbādagān (= le nord)

ŠĒ	Sigillographie		
šahrestān	*šahrestān* (?)	province	Statut de la province
Ganzak	Ganzak-šahrestān	Ādurbādagān	šahr
Āmōy		Āmūl	šahr
Rey ?	Rām-Kawād-šahrestān	Ray	(naxwār)
Baγdād			

Juillet 2013

Bibliographie

Daryaee, T. 2002 : *Šahrestānīhā ī Ērānšahr. A Middle Persian Text on Late Antique Geography, Epic, and History. With English and Persian Translations, and Commentary.* Costa Mesa.

Gignoux, Ph. 2004: « Aspects de la vie administrative et sociale en Iran du 7ème siècle. » In : R. Gyselen (ed.) : *Contributions à l'histoire et la géographie administrative de l'empire sassanide.* Bures-sur-Yvette (Res Orientales XVI), pp. 37–48.

— 2012 : « Une archive post-sassanide du Tabaristān (I). » In : R. Gyselen (ed.) : *Objets et documents inscrits en* pārsīg. Bures-sur-Yvette (Res Orientales XXI), pp. 29–96.

Gignoux, Ph. / A. Tafazzoli 1993 : *Anthologie de Zādspram. Édition critique du texte pehlevi, traduit et commenté.* Paris (StIr, Cahier 13).

Grenet, F. 2003 : *Kārnāmag ī Ardaxšēr ī Pābagān « La geste d'Ardashir fils de Pābag ».* Die.

Gyselen, R. 1988 : « Les données de géographie administrative dans le ‹ Shahrestaniha-i Eran ›. » In : StIr 17, pp. 191–206.

— 1989 : *La géographie administrative de l'Empire sassanide. Les témoignages sigillographiques.* Paris (Res Orientales I).

— 2001 : *The Four Generals of the Sasanian Empire: some Sigillographic Evidence.* Rome (Conferenze 14).

— 2002 : *Nouveaux matériaux sigillographiques pour la géographie administrative de l'empire sassanide. Collection A. Saeedi.* Paris (StIr, Cahier 24).

— 2004 : « L'administration ‹ provinciale › du *naxwār* d'après les sources sigillographiques. » Avec une note additionnelle sur la graphie du mot *naxwār* par P. Huyse. In : StIr 33, pp. 31–46.

— 2007 : *Sasanian Seals and Sealings in the A. Saeedi Collection.* Louvain (AcIr 44).

— 2006–2007 : « Gay, or the continuity of a Sasanian province's administrative status. » In : O. Tabibzadeh / T. Daryaee (edd.) : *Festschrift für Erich Kettenhofen* (= *Iranistik. Deutschsprachige Zeitschrift für iranistische Studien* 9–10), pp. 31–38.

— 2012 : « Le Tabaristān : lieu de mémoire sassanide. » In : R. Gyselen (ed.) : *Objets et documents inscrits en* pārsīg. Bures-sur-Yvette (Res Orientales XXI), pp. 109–122.

— 2015 : « Some Thoughts on Sasanian *mgwh*-Seals. » In : S. Farridnejad / R. Gyselen / A. Joisten-Pruschke (edd.) : *Faszination Iran. Beiträge zur Religion, Geschichte und Kunst des Alten Iran. Gedenkschrift für Klaus Schippmann.* Wiesbaden (Göttinger Orientforschungen. Iranica. Neue Folge 13), pp. 87–99.

— Gyselen, R. / T. Daryaee 2014 : « Rey dar ʿaṣr-e Sāsānīān bar asās-e manābeʿ-e pāyeh (Rayy during the Sasanian Period based on Primary Sources). » (en persan) In: *Iran Nameh* 29:2 (Summer 2014), A Special Issue Honoring Jaleh Amouzegar, pp. 36–48.

— Gyselen R. / C. Jullien 2014 : "Le Sakastān sous Husraw Ier. Approches croisées." In: C. Jullien (ed.) : *Husraw Ier : Reconstructions d'un règne. Sources et documents.* Paris (StIr, Cahier 53), pp. 85–113.

Kreyenbroek, G. 1987 : « The Zoroastrian Priesthood after the Fall of the Sasanian Empire. » In : Ph. Gignoux (ed.) : *Transition Periods in Iranian History. Actes du Symposium de Fribourg-en-Brisgau (22–24 mai 1985).* Paris (StIr, Cahier 5), pp. 151–166.

Lerner, J. A. / P. O. Skjærvø 1997 : « Some Uses of Clay bullae in Sasanian Iran. » In : R. Gyselen (ed.) : *Sceaux d'Orient et leur emploi.* Bures-sur-Yvette (Res Orientales X), pp. 67–78.

Markwart, J. 1931 : *A Catalogue of the provincial Capitals of Ērānshahr (Pahlavi Text, Version and Commentary).* Rome.

Mochiri, M. I. 1977 : *Étude de numismatique iranienne sous les Sassanides et Arabe-Sassanides.* Vol. II. Téhéran (édition révisée Leiden 1983).

— 2009 : « Une monnaie de Khusraw I de l'atelier de Samarcande. » In : Ph. Gignoux / C. Jullien / F. Jullien (edd.) : *Trésors d'Orient : Mélanges offerts à Rika Gyselen.* Paris (StIr, Cahier 42), pp. 237–244.

Morony, M. G. 1982 : « Continuity and change in the administrative geography of late Sasanian and early islamic al-ʿIrāq. » In : *Iran* XX, pp. 1–49.

Nikitin, A. B. 1994 : « The Sasanian Šahrab of Balkh. » In : *Ancient Civilizations from Scythia to Siberia* I/3, pp. 365–368.

Maria Macuch and Iranian Studies

ALMUT HINTZE

MARIA MACUCH is the daughter of the semitist RUDOLF MACUCH and IRANDOKHT SHAGHAGHI.[1] Her parents met during the years 1945–1947 when students in Paris, where RUDOLF studied Arabic and Semitic languages, and IRANDOKHT Hygiene at the Faculty of Medicine. Soon after their marriage on 31 March 1949 in Bratislava they transferred to Iran, and MARIA was born in 1 January 1950 in Tehran, where she spent the first six years of her life. In 1956 RUDOLF MACUCH received an invitation from Lady DROWER to work with her on the Mandaic Dictionary at the Oriental Institute in Oxford and the family moved there in October of the same year. MARIA remembers this trip as the most exciting journey of her life, travelling by train from Tehran via Turkey across the European continent and a stormy English channel (MACUCH 2008a, p. 13). In Oxford MARIA went to the SS Philip and James' Church of England Primary School, and her mother converted to Christianity. Life in Oxford has made an abiding impression on MARIA, and she never misses an opportunity to visit the city where she spent two very happy years of her childhood. After RUDOLF MACUCH's fellowship had come to an end, and since life in Iran seemed undesirable for a Christian convert, the small family moved to Windsor, Canada in 1958 and MARIA's father took up the position of a vicar. His dream of a university career eventually came true when he was invited to the Chair of Semitic and Arabic Studies at the Freie Universität Berlin. In 1963 the family moved to Berlin and MARIA went to school at the Droste-Hülshoff-Gymnasium in Zehlendorf. Growing up as the only child of the acclaimed scholar of the Mandaean, Samaritan and Syriac languages has deeply influenced MARIA's own professional outlook and choices. "With his background in Oriental Studies and his life and work as a scholar", she remembers in an interview (HINTZE 2014, p. 7),

> my father set the example for me of how to do scholarly work. He was the most important influence on me. I saw daily how he worked all the time, how intensely he studied the subjects he was interested in. It was all work and no play—except with me. I couldn't imagine doing anything else but scholarship because I hadn't

1 For MARIA's accounts of her father's life, see MACUCH 2008a, 2014a, 2015a.—I am grateful to DESMOND DURKIN-MEISTERERNST and MARIA MACUCH herself for helpful comments on an earlier version of the present article.

> seen anything else. My mother, Irandokht, influenced my choice of subjects through her Iranian background, although, being a Christian by choice, she was not typically Iranian.

After her *Abitur* in 1969 Maria enrolled at the Freie Universität in Iranian Studies, Semitic languages and Ancient History. She was soon captivated by the pre-Islamic tradition of her mother's homeland, and this has become a lifetime's fascination. Among the many teachers whose lectures she attended were, in Iranian Studies, CARSTEN COLPE, GÜNTER GOBRECHT, HANS KIPPENBERG, BERNFRIED SCHLERATH, and, as guest professor, RONALD EMMERICK, who taught an intensive course on Khotanese. In Semitic and Islamic Studies, she studied with ESTIPHAN PANOUSSI, BENNO POHL, ZUHAIR SHUNNAR, BABER JOHANSEN and FRITZ STEPPAT. However, the scholar who was the most influential on the direction she would eventually take was one whom she never could have met. This was CHRISTIAN BARTHOLOMAE (1855–1925), whose pioneering writings on Sasanian law drew MARIA into largely uncharted territory. Moreover, GÜNTER GOBRECHT introduced her to the linguistic and philological problems of Middle Persian legal texts, and it was in this area that she obtained her PhD in 1977 (with RUTH ALTHEIM-STIEHL as one of the examiners) and her Habilitation in 1990 (with WERNER SUNDERMANN and PHILIPPE GIGNOUX as referees). After a year spent as Visiting Professor at the National Taiwan University in Taipei, MARIA became Associate Professor (C3) at the Institut für Iranistik in Berlin in 1991. Having been offered the Chair in Iranian Studies (C4) at the Georg-August-Universität in Göttingen in 1994, she was able to take up the offer of the Chair in Iranian Studies at the Freie Universität Berlin in 1995 and held this position until her retirement in 2015. She now lives in Berlin and enjoys being able to focus on her research, free from administrative and teaching duties.

A Thousand Judgements

To date, MARIA's *magnum opus* is an edition in two volumes of the Sasanian law book 'A Thousand Judgements' *(Hazār Dādestān)*.[2] The transmission of this text is most precarious as it only survives in a single manuscript, which at some point in time was split into two parts. The first part consists of 55 folios published in facsimile by MODI in 1901 (usually abbreviated MHD), and the second part of 20 folios made available in facsimile by Anklesaria in 1912 (usually abbreviated MHDA).[3] MARIA's PhD thesis was concerned with the second part

2 On the title of the work, see MACUCH 1993, p. 10f.

3 ANKLESARIA's folios were copied by Dastur Erachji Sohrabji Meherji Rana of Navsari in AY 1247 (1878 CE). His copy is preserved in the Meherji Rana Library under the signature F25 and is described by DHABHAR 1923, p. 18. It was published in facsimile by JAMASPASA/NAWABI 1976.

and was published in 1981. She tackled the first part in her Habilitation thesis, published in 1993 as the first volume in the series *Iranica*, which she founded. Taken together, these two works provide a monumental edition of the complete text. It is transliterated from the manuscript, translated and accompanied by an extensive philological and legal commentary, and a dictionary. The text 'A Thousand Judgements' has also fuelled most of MARIA's other scholarship and is a constant point of reference in her research.

The *Hazār Dādestān* was compiled by Farroxmard ī Wahrāmān from court records and other documents, probably in the early seventh century CE, just a few decades before the Arab invasion of Iran. Constituting the only exclusively legal text which has survived from the pre-Islamic period, it is of supreme importance for the history of Iranian law in Zoroastrian and Islamic Iran, and for the influence of Sasanian law, especially on Talmudic and Islamic law. Moreover, this text provides unique insights into everyday life in Sasanian Iran and into its social institutions, by documenting how legal matters were discussed and law was practised in the law courts. The text discusses complex hypothetical and actual legal cases and legal judgements in the areas of family law, property rights and procedural law, and was designed as a reference work for specialists who were familiar with both the legal system and its terminology. The system gradually broke down when in the course of the Islamization of Iran Zoroastrian law was replaced by Islamic law, and the Zoroastrian jurisdiction became restricted to family law and the rules regulating dealings with members of other religions. As a result, the knowledge and understanding of the Sasanian legal terminology gradually became obsolete and eventually fell entirely into oblivion (MACUCH 2012a, p. 523f.). Although other contemporary iranists have also made important contributions to the study of Sasanian law, in particular the Russian (of Armenian origin) ANAHIT PERIKHANIAN (1928–2012) and the Danish BODIL HJERRILD (b. 1942), it was MARIA MACUCH who noticed most clearly that the Pahlavi legal texts use a very precise and compact terminology that needs to be unlocked before these texts can be translated. She identified it as her two-fold task to define the exact meaning of the numerous technical terms found in the Zoroastrian legal texts, and on that basis to reconstruct the underlying system of Sasanian law, the unwritten code which is a constant point of reference for the Sasanian jurists, but which is nowhere set out in a systematic fashion in our extant sources. Three major subject areas are particularly prominent in her publications: Sasanian Zoroastrian law, comparative law and Iranian literature. Her works on Sasanian law focus on legal terminology, Zoroastrian family law and the legal system, while those on Iranian literatures cover both Zoroastrian and Classical Persian literature.

Sasanian legal terminology

MARIA MACUCH's studies on Zoroastrian legal terminology aim at unlocking and extracting the meanings and definitions of individual legal technical terms from the various contexts in which they occur. She identifies three types of source, all of which need to be employed for this undertaking (MACUCH 2005a, p. 375f., 2012a, pp. 519–525). The first are Pahlavi texts which are translations, commentaries or summaries of the Avesta. They include the Pahlavi versions of the *Widēwdād* and *Hērbedestān*, the *Zand ī Fragard ī Juddēwdād* which was rediscovered by GÖTZ KÖNIG (KÖNIG 2010, p. 119), and the summary of the legal Nasks of the Avesta in Book 8 of the *Dēnkard*. The second group consists of Pahlavi law books, or *dādestān-nāmag*. These texts are exclusively concerned with legal matters and must have been numerous in Sasanian times, although the only surviving sample is the *Hazār Dādestān*. To this category also belong original Pahlavi documents written on leather, cloth and other materials, since some of these have legal content (MACUCH 2008c), and the unique original court records from Tabarestān, on which MACUCH has collaborated with DIETER WEBER (MACUCH 2016b, 2017b). Written in Pahlavi cursive script and dating from 737 CE, the documents testify to the legal practice of the Sasanian juridicial system. They provide unprecedented insights into the work of the law courts in Tabarestān and how law cases were recorded and documented. The third type is the Pahlavi literature, in particular the *Dādestān ī dēnīg*, the *Riwāyat ī Adur-farnbay and Farnbag-Srōš*, the *Riwāyat ī Ēmēd ī Ašawahistān* and other texts. Many of the Middle Persian legal terms originate from the Avesta and its translation and commentaries, the *Zand* while others come from the spoken language and have acquired a technical meaning in the legal context. Yet other technical terms were coined in the daily practice of the law courts (2005a, p. 385; 2009a, 2010b, p. 102f.).

MACUCH has published important editions of the Pahlavi version of chapters 5 and 12 of the *Hērbedestān*, the only Avestan text with a Pahlavi *Zand* which discusses matters relating to the religious education of Zoroastrians in greater detail (MACUCH 2009b, 2009c). The problems arising from the poor transmission of the text, which only survives in few manuscripts,[4] are compounded by the elliptical style of the Pahlavi commentary and the discrepancies in certain passages between the Avestan text, its Pahlavi translation, and the longer commentaries referring to the translated text. In spite of two relatively recent editions of this text, MACUCH maintains that a great number of legal terms occurring in it are still poorly understood.

She emphasizes that the Avesta constitutes the common foundation and constant point of reference of both Zoroastrian law and Zoroastrian religion. Moreover, Zoroastrian priests were trained in both disciplines to be legal and

4 For the transmission of the Hērbedestān, see HINTZE 2009, p. 171f.

religious experts, *rad* and *mowbed* in one person.[5] They had both juridicial and priestly authority, and their highest dignitaries were very influential at the top of the state's administrative hierarchy. Many of the Sasanian legal terms were formed in pre-Sasanian, indeed Old Iranian times and reflect an older stage of Zoroastrian law. MACUCH illustrates this point with the Av. expression *yō.hē pascaēta* 'who (succeeds) him afterwards', which is quoted in MHD 21.4 and elsewhere in Pahlavi texts from a lost Av. context. The petrified Av. phrase is used as a general technical term to denote the legal successor of the *paterfamilias* regardless of the successor's gender and the form of succession involved. It retains, MACUCH argues, the meaning of an earlier period predating the development of the precise terminology which distinguishes between the direct succession of the 'son according to the law' *(dādestān-pus)* and the intermediary succession of the 'daughter according to the law' *(dādestān-duxt)*, and which encodes the complex rules of succession as we know them from Sasanian times (MACUCH 2003b, p. 234; 2005a, p. 377f.; 2014c, p. 86f.).

While the Avesta and its *Zand* have always been the theoretical foundation of Sasanian law and the ties between law and religion have remained close throughout the Sasanian period, Macuch argues that over the years jurisprudence gradually developed into a discipline in its own right, detached from religion, as the law code and legal practice grew more complex and the language increasingly technical. As a result, towards the end of the Sasanian period the discipline of jurisprudence was only loosely connected with religion. Court procedures and decisions that deviated from the theoretical foundation of the Avesta and *Zand* were labelled *pad kardag* 'according to practice', while *pad čāštag* 'according to doctrine' designated the canonical law and its interpretation by priests and jurisconsults. Likewise, offences were divided into the two groups. One comprised 'offences against opponents' *(wināh ī hamēmālān)*, which were committed against fellow Zoroastrians, and the other 'offences against the soul' *(wināh ī ruwānīg)*, which were committed against religious norms and endangered the soul of the delinquent (MACUCH 2003a, p. 173ff.; 2009a, p. 181f.; 2012a, p. 520; 2014b, p. 50).

Among the many Pahlavi terms whose meaning MACUCH has clarified is the compound *pahikār-rad*, which WEST translated as 'magistrate in a dispute'. MACUCH 2002a, however, argues that in this compound the component *pahikār* has the technical meaning of 'legal dispute'. The compound *pahikār-rad* accordingly denotes a person 'involved in a judicial dispute', a 'litigant'. Moreover, she shows that it contrasts with *a-pahikār-rad*, which denotes a person who exercises the law himself without engaging in a judicial dispute. She identifies the antonymic pair as indicating the transition from the personal private law of blood feud and retaliation, to the formation of legal institutions at the early

5 MACUCH 2014b, p. 51 provides a succinct survey of the different functions of a *rad* in Sasanian society.

stages of the development of jurisprudence in Zoroastrian society. Another example of her detailed study of individual words is the examination of the Pahlavi term *adwadād*. She argues that its semantic range comprises not only the offence of 'abandoning (a person) on the road', which is the meaning of the term's Av. ancestor *aδβadāiti-*, but also the shortage of food and drink, and the offences of failing in one's duty to provide food and drink to a person or an animal, or fuel to the sacred fire, or spiritual nourishment to a pupil (Macuch 2012a, pp. 524–536; 2012b). Macuch's refined understanding of Pahlavi legal technical terms has also benefited the interpretation of the Pahlavi model contract of a *pādixšāy*-marriage, which is transmitted in the unique codex MK (Macuch 2007). Although the contract is dated 1278 CE and belongs to a time when jurisdiction of Zoroastrian communities was virtually confined to family law, Macuch argues that Sasanian technical terminology is used with full knowledge of all its legal implications. The article is an outstanding example of how the precise definitions of individual technical terms helps us to understand the text in the wider context of Sasanian jurisdiction. For example, she argues that the clause *pad rāh ī stūrīh (ud) ayōgānīh* in §2 means neither "by way of guardianship and submission" (MacKenzie) nor "... by way of being either a 'trustee' or an 'obligee'" (Perikhanian) but "by way of substitute succession *(stūrīh)* (or) intermediary succession *(ayōgānīh)*". The paragraph, Macuch concludes, states that the *pādixšāy*-bride transfers her reproductive capacity as both a *stūr* and an *ayōgēn* from her birth-family to the family of the bridegroom (Macuch 2007, pp. 186, 193–195).

Zoroastrian family law

In a range of studies on Zoroastrian family law, Macuch emphasizes the importance of the Zoroastrian religious ideas, promoted by the priesthood, which underpin the practice of marriage and inheritance in Sasanian Iran. She argues that the priesthood asserted and cemented its power in the state and its influence on the laity, by linking religious obligations with the social need and natural desire to preserve the basic structure of the family and of kinship groups. The entire system, she argues, served the dual purpose of maintaining the family property and of producing a male heir and successor. While the former is motivated by the material interests of powerful descent groups, the clergy and nobility in particular, the latter is underpinned by the society's patrilineal system and the religious doctrine that after death the soul of a man is unable to cross the bridge that connects this world and the next (*Činwad* Bridge) unless he has a male heir and successor whose duty it is to perform the death ceremonies for the soul of the deceased (2003b, pp. 235–236). The purpose of the Sasanian system of marriage is to ensure that it is virtually impossible for a man to die without leaving a son behind. Macuch maintains that the main reason for the overwhelming number of fictive ties lies in the obligation to ensure the continuity of a man's lineage *(nāmburdārīh)* and the performance of religious ceremonies in his name *(nāmgānīh)*.[6] Kinship practice and religion are thus linked together. Although such kinship practices are also found elsewhere, perhaps no other society has developed such a complex and elaborate system of constructed kinship to prevent the extinction of the male line. Showing the extent to which the two areas of inheritance law and family law are interrelated, Macuch reconstructs the complex Sasanian family structures as she extrapolates them from the Pahlavi legal texts.

Each Zoroastrian man was under the obligation to marry and have children and each woman was obliged to make her reproductive capacities available to the extended family. In the Pahlavi texts, endogamy and incest are promoted as the ideal means of keeping the family *(paywand)* 'pure' and guaranteeing the continuation of the race *(tōhmag)* of the Mazdaworshippers. The technical term *xwēdōdah*, which is absent from the *Thousand Judgements*, denotes various kinds of endogamous alliances, including those within the nuclear family (Macuch 2010a). While the Zoroastrian priesthood promoted *xwēdōdah*, Macuch finds evidence suggesting that there were reservations among laypeople concerning incestuous alliances between members of the nuclear family (Macuch 1991b, p. 151f.). One of the strategies used by the priests to make them a reality were temporary marriages, which were dissolved after a contractually agreed period of time (Macuch 1991b, p. 153; 2006, p. 593f.). The institution of temporary marriage, Macuch argues, was an integral part of Sasanian family law. In particular, she argues that temporary marriage provided additional options for procuring offspring, and was a means of using the female reproductive capacities to the full in the service of a patrilineal society. The general acceptance of incestuous alliances within the nuclear family is a fundamental prerequisite for the development of the elaborate system of intermediary succession *(ayōgēnīh)* and substitute succession *(stūrīh)*, in which real and fictive incestuous ties and consanguinity were key factors (2003b, pp. 236–238). Every Zoroastrian woman was obliged to act as *ayōgēn* or *stūr* when requested and enter a time-limited marriage in order to produce offspring for her deceased father, brother or husband (1995, pp. 153–155; 2006, p. 594f.).

Macuch 2014c examines four epic narratives of Ardaxšēr's genealogy in the light of Zoroastrian family law. In order to be accepted as a legitimate successor of the Achaemenid dynasty, Ardaxšēr had to be genetically linked to Sāsān while at the same time belonging to the line of his official father Pābag. With the

6 The meaning and function of the term *nāmgānīh* has been elucidated by Klingenschmitt 1971, pp. 145–150. Deriving the noun with suffix *-yh* from an adj. *n'mk'n 'belonging to the name, being in relation to the name', he argues that *nāmgānīh* denotes the death ritual.

exception of aṭ-Ṭabarī's account, which is clearly patrilineal (grandfather Sāsān, father Pābag, son Ardaxšēr), in the versions of the *Kārnāmag*, Agathias and the *Bundahišn* genetic ties between Sāsān and Pābag are constructed through Ardaxšēr's mother. The latter is either the daughter/wife of Pābag (*Kārnāmag*, Agathias) or the daughter of Sāsān *(Bundahišn).* In the various scenarios of Ardaxšēr's descent, MACUCH argues, the most interesting feature is that the constructions of Ardaxšēr's Achaemenid descent are based on Sasanian legal practice and involve the female line in a patrilineal society.

MACUCH emphasizes the significance of the system of Zoroastrian family law for our understanding of the social and political history of Sasanian Iran (MACUCH 1995). A case in point is her work on the legal implications of the revolt of Mazdak (2015b). Discussing the movement from the point of view of the accusations, preserved in the Dēnkard, made against the revolutionary by the Zoroastrian priesthood, she argues that when accusing the Mazdakites of overthrowing the complex rules of property and inheritance, the priests use precise legal terminology. She interprets this as indicating that the relevant passages (Dk 3.5.1–2 and 7.7.22–25) derive from an earlier Middle Persian text of the Sasanian period itself. Although the Dēnkard passages are short, the precise legal terminology used by the priests, and the accusations they make, speak of the existential threat which the movement posed to the Sasanian state. For by undermining all branches of jurisprudence and the institutions of marriage and inheritance, the Mazdakites attacked the very foundations of Sasanian society (1995, pp. 151f., 165f.).

The Sasanian legal system

Identifying the technical terms and meticulously studying their form and function constitutes the essential prerequisite for reconstructing the Sasanian law code. MARIA MACUCH explains her methodology as follows (HINTZE 2014, p. 6):

> From there [i.e. the study of the technical vocabulary] I proceed to putting the terms together into a system, trying to work out how they relate to one another. I aim at reconstructing the underlying legal system bit by bit, the unwritten code which is a constant point of reference for the Sasanian jurists but which nowhere in our extant sources is set out in a systematic fashion.

She presents her reconstruction of the Sasanian legal system in articles on "Vorislamisches iranisches Recht" (2013a) and on "Law in Pre-Modern Zoroastrianism" (2015c), and, as major contributions to the *Encyclopaedia Iranica*, in entries on "Charitable Foundations" (1991a), "Inheritance" (2005b), and, especially, on "Sasanian Legal System" (2009a). The most comprehensive discussion of the Sasanian legal system are her Ehsan Yarshater Lectures on *Sasanian Law in its Social Context*, delivered in the University of California at Los Angeles in November 2015. Arguing that the legal institutions were instrumental in consolidating the social status and power of Sasanian élites, notably the Zoroastrian clergy and the Iranian aristocracy, she discusses the Sasanian legal sources and instruments of law, kinship ties and fictive alliances, property and inheritance, civil and criminal proceedings, and the Sasanian law and other legal systems in general. The eventual publication of these lectures, which is currently under preparation, is bound to constitute a major milestone in the study of Sasanian law.

Comparative law

In the study of comparative law, MACUCH's research focuses on the relation between Zoroastrian Sasanian law, on the one hand, and Roman, Jewish, Eastern Christian, Byzantine and Islamic law, on the other. "There are certainly differences between Sasanian law and the legal systems of other cultures," she states (HINTZE 2014, p. 6), "in particular with regard to family law, inheritance and succession, but I also detect similarities." For example, in the field of property law, MACUCH compares the Iranian distinction between 'ownership' *(xwēšīh)* and 'possession, holding, tenure' *(dārišn)* with the distinction between *dominium*, *proprietas* 'ownership' and *possessio* 'possession, holding, tenure' in Roman law, although she also notes differences (MACUCH 2008b, p. 129f.; 2015d, p. 248f.). Moreover, by adducing a parallel from Roman law she elucidates the Pahlavi term *dastwar*. Previously it was widely thought that the term, which means 'authority, priest, minister' in non-technical language, denotes a 'lawyer' or an 'advocate' in a general sense in legal contexts. However, the word's technical meaning had remained unrecognized. Through comparison with the function of Latin *auctor* in ancient Roman law, Macuch has been able to establish that in addition to the non-technical meaning, *dastwar* also has two technical meanings. In the context of property law it denotes 'a person who holds the entitlement' to the substance, income and disposal of a certain object, while in procedural law it designates the 'legal predecessor'. The latter is a person who in a lawsuit guarantees that an object he previously owned or possessed did not belong to a third party and was transmitted legally to the defendant (MACUCH 1988, 2005a, p. 384f.; 2008b, p. 134f.; 2010b, p. 105f.; 2015d, p. 249f.).

During ca. 1,200 years of the Achaemenid, Parthian and Sasanian periods Jews in Babylonia lived under Iranian rule in close proximity to Zoroastrians. The importance of the Iranian legal sources for understanding the Babylonian Talmud, the chief source for Jewish law and theology, is increasingly appreciated by scholars, one of the foremost among them being MARIA MACUCH. This new evaluation is in stark contrast to JACOB NEUSNER's conclusion that Jews in Babylonia were little, if at all, influenced by the surrounding heterogeneous cultural environment (Macuch 2010b, p. 101). A substantial part of Macuch's work deals with the interactions of Zoroastrians and Babylonian Jews as reflected in the Babylonian Talmud. The latter employs a large number of Iranian loan words and loan translations taken from both everyday speech and the technical vocabulary of Iranian jurisprudence. Macuch 1999 and 2002b argues that the Rabbis were familiar with the technical meaning of Iranian legal terms and used them in the same way as their Iranian counterparts. As a result, Iranian technical terms are as little explained in the Babylonian Talmud as they are in the Iranian legal texts. A case in point is the term *dastwar*, whose meaning Macuch has elucidated with reference to Latin *auctor*, as discussed above, and its derivative *dastwarīh*. The latter term occurs as an Iranian loan word in two passages of the Babylonian Talmud and cannot be understood without considering the Iranian sources, from where it was borrowed. Macuch 2008b, p. 135f. argues that in the Babylonian Talmud *dastwarīh* denotes the 'entitlement' to the substance or income of a certain object and the power of its disposal, and is used with the same technical meaning which the term has in Sasanian property law.

During the second half of the first millennium CE a sizeable Christian community existed in Persis, with most of its members possessing a family background of conversion from Zoroastrianism. These Middle-Persian speaking Christians had their own law book, the *Corpus Iuris*, which was compiled in Pahlavi by the archbishop of Persis, Jesubōxt, in the eighth century CE for the local Christian community. The work was translated into Syriac under the East Syrian patriarch Timotheos I. (727–823 CE), who was Catholicos of the Church of the East in 780–823 CE. Only the Syriac version survives to the present day, whereas the Pahlavi original is lost. The significance of Jesubōxt's *Corpus Iuris* for our knowledge of Sasanian law was already noted by Eduard Sachau, its editor and translator (Sachau 1914). In an article published in the *Festschrift* for her father, Maria argues that the Syriac translation of Pahlavi legal terms is very precise, and that the translator makes every effort to find the equivalent expression in Syriac without using the Pahlavi word (1989, p. 150). There are, however, rare occasions when the Pahlavi term is not translated but transliterated in Syriac script. One of them is *abēsaxwanīh*, to which the entire chapter 6 of the *Corpus Iuris* is dedicated. Macuch links the Pahlavi word of the Syriac text with hitherto unnoticed attestations in the *Thousand Judgements* and defines its meaning as 'waiving of claims' ("Anspruchsverzicht", 1989, p. 157). Pointing out that the *Corpus Iuris* provides the key to our understanding of this term with regard to both its phonetic reading and its definition, she concludes that in the *Hazār Dādestān* the term chiefly occurs in contexts dealing with the law of obligations ("Schuldrecht"), while the meaning is more general in the *Corpus Iuris*, where it chiefly but not exclusively occurs in contexts concerned with the law of inheritance.

Macuch argues that the law code of the Persian Christians is based on Zoroastrian law, with the exception of Zoroastrian marriage law with its consanguineous and levirate marriages, which are vehemently rejected. She finds a clue for how deeply the law of the Persian Christians is rooted in Zoroastrian law in the same groupings of offspring. The categories of children denoted in the *Corpus Iuris* by Syriac (1) *b-nāmusā* 'according to law', (2) *b-kyānā* 'according to nature', and (3) *b-qūbālā* 'through adoption' correspond exactly to the Zoroastrian categories (1) *dādestān-pus/duxt* 'son/daughter according to law', (2) *frazand ī tanīg-zād* 'natural offspring' and (3) *pus/duxt ī padīriftag* 'adopted son/daughter' (Macuch 2003b, p. 242f.). The Syriac terms translate the Pahlavi ones and the Zoroastrian groupings of offspring are retained in the laws of the Persian Christians. Likewise, the evaluation of different types of seals found in Jesubōxt corresponds to that of the *Hazār Dādestān* (Macuch 1997, p. 84f.; 2010b, p. 104).

Macuch 2014b is an intriguing study of the charges brought by Zoroastrian priests against Mār Ābā, the catholicos of the Church of the East in 540–552 and a Zoroastrian convert to Christianity. Probably of aristocratic descent, he served as a major state official under Husraw I Anōšagruwān (ruled 531–579). That Mār Ābā had the legalistic mindset of a Zoroastrian jurisconsult emerges from the way he refutes Zoroastrian marriage customs in his Syriac tractate on marriage laws, edited and translated by Sachau 1914, pp. 255–285. This work includes a discussion of twenty types of conjugal alliances which were permitted by Zoroastrian law, but forbidden by Mār Ābā. Macuch notes that Mār Ābā's description of Zoroastrian marriage alliances fully accords with what we know from the Pahlavi legal literature, but surpasses the latter in detail. Moreover, she argues that by attacking individual Zoroastrian marriage customs, Mār Ābā critically undermined the legal institutions that upheld them, in particular *ayōgēnīh* 'intermediary successorship' and *stūrīh* 'substitute successorship', which constituted the backbone of the Sasanian social system (2014b, pp. 52–54). Consequently, he was prosecuted by the *mowbedān mowbed*, the head of the Zoroastrian clergy and judiciary, and charged with high treason which was 'worthy of death' *(margarzān)*.

Comparing the legal status of pious foundations in the Byzantine and Sasanian empires, Macuch 2004 detects a range of parallels, almost all of which are later also found in the laws that govern the establishment and management of Islamic charitable foundations, or *waqf*. Both Byzantine and Sasanian law distinguish between public and private foundations. These foundations had an inalienable endowment the income of which was used to cover the running costs of the establishment. While in Byzantine law the legal owner of public pious foundations was the Church, in the case of Zoroastrian fire foundations it was the fire itself (*xwēšīh ī ātaxš* 'ownership of the fire', p. 194). Certain fire-temples had huge possessions and played a significant role in the economy of Sasanian Iran. Macuch argues that Shiite Islamic charitable foundations are strikingly similar to religious charitable foundations of the Sasanian period, the most salient feature being a shared underlying structure. This includes the view that property consists of two parts: the substance (*bun* 'principle') and the increase (*bar* 'fruit'). At the root of this distinction lies the Sasanian requirement that the endowment, which is the substance, is inalienable and cannot be changed or spent. The distinction between the notions of *bun* and *bar* is deeply tied up with the Zoroastrian system of inheritance and succession and is also found in Talmudic law (MACUCH 2015d). Likewise, in Shiite Islam the institution designated with the Arabic term *waqf* represents fixed, inalienable property, while the interest or gain from this property may be spent and is at the disposal of the heirs and successors (MACUCH 1994, 2009d).

The institution of temporary marriage, which MACUCH has shown to have been an integral part of Sasanian family law, is also found up to the present day, as a distinct legal institution of a special form of marriage in Twelver Shiite jurisprudence, where it is called *mutʿa* 'enjoyment' and *ṣīġe* in Arabic and Persian sources respectively. Such a union may last between one hour and 99 years. Its practice is confined to Shiites in Iran and is not found among the Shiites outside Iran, while Sunni legal experts reject it as alien to Islamic law. Children born of the *mutʿa* are considered to be legitimate children of the father. MACUCH argues that temporary marriage adopted into Shiite jurisprudence has its origin in the Sasanian tradition. She supports this view with parallels which she identifies between different types of temporary marriage in Sasanian Iran and the Shiite *mutʿa* and concludes that these parallel are unlikely to be accidental (MACUCH 1985, 2006, p. 585f.). She also argues that the law of succession in Shiʿite jurisprudence is based to a considerable degree on Zoroastrian customary law (MACUCH 2017a). That Zoroastrian Sasanian law continued to be practised in Iran at least during the first two centuries of the Islamic period has been confirmed by the unique Tabarestān court records, whose legal context is examined by MACUCH 2016b and 2017b.

Iranian literature

MARIA MACUCH has provided two valuable surveys of Pre-Islamic Iranian literatures (2009e and 2013b). While women are usually represented in Pahlavi literature as lacking intellectual capacities that go beyond the standard religious knowledge, MACUCH 2009f discusses an episode related in the *Hazār Dādestān* that deviates from this stereotype. The story involves three women sitting at the roadside and engaging men passing by in a discussion about complex legal problems which, however, remain unsolved. Although the questions they raise are real questions, MACUCH argues that the woman represent a literary topos of symbolic rather than real persons. In demonstrating the limits of the discipline of law to the learned jurisconsults, they embody the enigmatic side of the discipline of jurisprudence.

Macuch examines the representation of the Turcs in Pahlavi literature against the background of the Zoroastrian world-view (Macuch 2016a), and the search for and experiences with God in Persian Sufi poetry (Macuch 2000). Her works on Persian poetry also include a study of the imagery in Persian mystical poetry (Macuch 1998) and of the pre-Islamic roots of Firdausi's *Šāhnāme* (Macuch 2011a and 2012c). In the latter article, which was published in German and in English, she points out that the *Šāhnāme* not only draws on Iranian traditions of individual figures, but also promotes Zoroastrian concepts and values, including the opposition between Good and Evil, truth and lie, and the concept of the legitimate, righteous ruler. The latter is defined by the king's patrilineal descent from the ruling dynasty and the possession of the aureole of kingship, the *xwarrah*, the king's charisma that is awarded to him by God.

Other academic achievements

For more than twenty years until her retirement in 2015, Maria Macuch taught Iranian Studies at the Institut für Iranistik of the Freie Universität Berlin with a focus on Middle and New Persian languages and literature. She was supported in her work by a competent team of colleagues, including Farifteh Tafakolli, Feryad Omar, Götz König, Iris Colditz and Maryam Mameghanian-Prenzlow. Many of us, students and colleagues alike, have benefited not only from her immense scholarship but also from her friendship and unstinting support. Thus, soon after the fall of the Berlin Wall in 1989, she arranged for Werner Sundermann to become an Honorary Professor of the Freie Universität to share his profound knowledge of Manichaeism and Iranian languages with the students. Several years later she made the same arrangements for Werner Sundermann's successor at the Berlin-Brandenburg Academy of Sciences, Desmond Durkin-Meisterernst. Together with the latter and other colleagues, she set up a structured three-year doctoral programme "Languages and Cultures of the Silk Road" at the Berliner Antike-Kolleg for PhD candidates in the fields of Iranian, Turkish and Central Asian Studies, and East Asian Art, enlisting the enormous resources of academic experts and source materials at the Berlin-Brandenburgische Akademie der Wissenschaften, especially the Turfan Studies project, the Staatsbibliothek zu Berlin, the Humboldt Universität, the Freie Universität, the Deutsche Archäologische Institut and the Staatliche Museen zu Berlin. Moreover, together with colleagues of the Freie Universität, she participated in the collaborative research project "Episteme in movement" ("Episteme in Bewegung"), which gave Iris Colditz and Benjamin Jokisch the opportunity to carry out research projects on the interactions between Zoroastrian and Islamic law. Furthermore, Maria Macuch has secured external funding for individual research projects and their publication in her series Iranica. Successful projects include the work of Dieter Weber on *Berliner Pahlavi-Dokumente* (Iranica 15), of David Buyaner on the *Patet* texts of the Khorde Avesta (Iranica 22) and of Miguel Ángel Andrés-Toledo on the Pahlavi *Widēwdād* (Iranica 23). All these activities, both within Iranian Studies and on an interdisciplinary level, have greatly contributed to the high standing which Iranian Studies at the Freie Universität enjoy both nationally and internationally. Being fully aware that it was nevertheless not to be taken for granted that Old and Middle Iranian Studies would continue to be covered at the University after her retirement, she successfully made every effort to defend the interests of our subject. With the appointment of her successor, Alberto Cantera, the continuity of Old and Middle Iranian Studies in Berlin has been secured at least for the foreseeable future.

To date 26 volumes have been published in the series *Iranica*, which Maria Macuch founded in 1993 and which she now co-edits with Alberto Cantera. The wide range of topics covered includes editions of Avestan and Middle Persian texts, studies of Iranian grammar, religion and society, conference volumes, festschrifts and memorial volumes. Layout and typesetting of the volumes are taken care of at the Institut für Iranistik and, since the series's inception have been the responsibility of Claudius Naumann, and in recent years also of Tatsiana Harting. Made to high specifications in outer appearance, and with high academic standards in their contents, the volumes constitute important contributions to Iranian Studies and are highly regarded internationally, with many libraries around the globe holding standing subscriptions. Moreover, Maria Macuch has served as co-editor of a Festschrift (Macuch 1989), a memorial volume (Macuch 2007), a collective work on Pre-Islamic Iranian literature (Macuch 2009e) and a conference volume (Macuch 2011b).

Maria Macuch is a member of a wide range of academic and professional organisations, including the *Corpus Inscriptionum Iranicarum*, the *Deutsche Morgenländische Gesellschaft*, the Advisory Board of the *Orient-Okzident-Gesellschaft*, and the *Societas Iranologica Europaea*, where she served as president from 2003 to 2007. In 2013 she was elected an Honorary Fellow of the Ancient India and Iran Trust (Cambridge, England).

References

Anklesaria, T.D. 1912: *The Social Code of the Parsis in Sassanian Times or Mādigān i Hazār Dādistān.* Part II. Bombay.

Dhabhar, B.N. 1923: *Descriptive Catalogue of all manuscripts in the First Dastur Meherji Rana Library, Navsari.* Bombay.

Hintze, A. 2009: "Disseminating the Mazdyasnian religion: An edition of the Avestan Hērbedestān Chapter 5." In: W. Sundermann / A. Hintze / F. de Blois

(eds.): *Exegisti monumenta. Festschrift in Honour of Nicholas Sims-Williams.* Wiesbaden (Iranica 17), pp. 171–190.
— 2014. "Meet our new Honorary Fellow. Professor Maria Macuch in conversation with Almut Hintze, 13 December 2013." In: *Indiran. The Newsletter of The Ancient India and Iran Trust* 9, pp. 6–7.
HJERRILD, B. 2002: *Studies in Zoroastrian Family Law: A Comparative Analysis.* Copenhagen (Carsten Niebuhr Institute Publications).
JAMASPASA, K.M./M. NAWABI 1976: *Manuscript F25. Matikan i Hazar Datastan, Ashem Vohu, etc.* Shiraz (The Pahlavi Codices and Iranian Researches vol. 31).
KLINGENSCHMITT, G. 1971: "Neue Avesta-Fragmente (FrA.)." In: *MSS* 29, pp. 111–174.
KÖNIG, G. 2010: "Der Pahlavi-Text *Zand ī Fragard ī Juddēvdād.*" In: M. MACUCH/ D. WEBER/D. DURKIN-MEISTERERNST (eds.): *Ancient and Middle Iranian Studies. Proceedings of the* 6th *European Conference of Iranian Studies, held in Vienna, 18–22 September 2007.* Wiesbaden (Iranica 19), pp. 115–132.
MACUCH, M. 1981: *Das Sasanidische Rechtsbuch "Mātakdān i Hazār Dātistān" (Teil II).* Wiesbaden (AKM XLV,1).
— 1985: "Die Zeitehe im sasanidischen Recht – ein Vorläufer der šī^{c}itischen *mut*^{c}*a*-Ehe in Iran?" In: *AMI* 18, pp. 187–203.
— 1988: "Der *dastwar*, ‚auctor', im sasanidischen Zivilprozeß." In: *AMI* 21, pp. 181–192.
— 1989: "Ein mittelpersischer *terminus technicus* im syrischen Rechtskodex des Īšōʿbōḫt und im sasanidischen Rechtsbuch." In: M. MACUCH/C. MÜLLER-KESSLER/B.G. FRAGNER (eds.): *Studia Semitica necnon Iranica Rudolpho Macuch septuagenario ab amicis et discipulis dedicata.* Wiesbaden, pp. 149–160.
— 1991a: "Charitable Foundations in the Sasanian Period." In: *EIr* V, Fasc. 4. Costa Mesa, California, pp. 380–382.
— 1991b: "Inzest im vorislamischen Iran." In: *AMI* 24, pp. 141–154.
— 1993: *Rechtskasuistik und Gerichtspraxis zu Beginn des siebenten Jahrhunderts in Iran. Die Rechtssammlung des Farroḫmard i Wahrāmān.* Wiesbaden (Iranica 1).
— 1994: "Die sasanidische Stiftung ‚für die Seele' – Vorbild für den islamischen *waqf*?" In: P. VAVROUŠEK (ed.): *Iranian and Indo European Studies: Memorial Volume of Otakar Klíma.* Praha, pp. 163–180.
— 1995: "Herrschaftskonsolidierung und sasanidisches Familienrecht: zum Verhältnis von Kirche und Staat unter den Sasaniden." In: CHR. RECK/P. ZIEME (eds.): *Iran und Turfan: Beiträge Berliner Wissenschaftler, Werner Sundermann zum 60. Geburtstag gewidmet.* Wiesbaden (Iranica 2), pp. 149–167.
— 1997: "The Use of Seals in Sasanian Jurisprudence." In: R. GYSELEN (eds.): *Sceaux d'orient et leur emploi.* Bures-sur-Yvette (Res orientales 10), pp. 79–87.
— 1998: "Zur Bildersprache der persischen mystischen Dichtung." In: A. HÖLSCHER/ R. KAMPLING (eds.): *Religiöse Sprache und ihre Bilder: Von der Bibel bis zur modernen Lyrik.* Berlin (Schriften der Diözesanakademie Berlin 14), pp. 175–199.
— 1999: "Iranian Legal Terminology in the Babylonian Talmud in the Light of Sasanian Jurisprudence." In: SH. SHAKED/A. NETZER (eds.): *Irano-Judaica IV: Studies Relating to Jewish Contacts with Persian Culture Throughout the Ages.* Jerusalem, pp. 91–101.
— 2000: "Gottes-Suche und Gottes-Erfahrung in der persischen Sufi-Dichtung." In: M. DELGADO/A.P. KUSTERMANN (eds.): *Gottes-Krise und Gott-Trunkenheit:*

Was die Mystik der Weltreligionen der Gegenwart zu sagen hat. Würzburg, pp. 134–158.
— 2002a: "A Zoroastrian Legal Term in the Dēnkard: *pahikār-rad.*" In: Ph. Huyse (ed.): *Iran : Questions et connaissances.* Vol. I: *La période ancienne.* Paris (StIr, Cahier 25), pp. 77–90.
— 2002b: "The Talmudic Expression 'Servant of the Fire' in the Light of Pahlavi Legal Sources." In: *JSAI* 26 (= *Volume in Honour of Shaul Shaked*), pp. 109–129.
— 2003a: "On the Treatment of Animals in Zoroastrian Law." In: A. van Tongerloo (ed.): *Iranica Selecta: Studies in honour of Professor Wojciech Skalmowski on the occasion of his seventieth birthday.* Turnhout (Silk Road Studies 8), pp. 167–190.
— 2003b: "Zoroastrian Principles and the Structure of Kinship in Sasanian Iran." In: C.G. Cereti/M. Maggi/E. Provasi (eds.): *Religious Themes and Texts of pre-Islamic Iran and Central Asia: Studies in honour of Professor Gherardo Gnoli on the occasion of his 65th birthday on 6 December 2002.* Wiesbaden (Beiträge zur Iranistik 24), pp. 231–246.
— 2004: "Pious Foundations in Byzantine and Sasanian Law." In: Gh. Gnoli (ed.): *La Persia e Bisanzio. Convegno internazionale, Roma, 14–18 ottobre 2002.* Roma (Atti dei convegni Lincei 201), pp. 181–196.
— 2005a: "On Middle Persian Legal Terminology." In: C.G. Cereti/M. Maggi (eds.): *Middle Iranian Lexicography: Proceedings of the Conference held in Rome, 9–11 April 2001.* Roma (Orientalia Romana 8), pp. 375–386.
— 2005b: "Inheritance. i. Sasanian Period." In: *EIr* XIII, pp. 125–131.
— 2006: "The Function of Temporary Marriage in the Context of Sasanian Family Law." In: A. Panaino/A. Piras (eds.): *Proceedings of the Fifth Conference of the Societas Iranologica Europaea held in Ravenna, October 6–11, 2003.* Vol. I: *Ancient and Middle Iranian Studies.* Milano, pp. 585–597.
— 2007: "The Pahlavi Marriage Contract in the Light of Sasanian Family Law." In: M. Macuch/M. Maggi/W. Sundermann (eds.): *Iranian Languages and Texts from Iran and Turan. Ronald E. Emmerick Memorial Volume.* Wiesbaden (Iranica 13), pp. 183–204.
— 2008a: "Rudolf Macuch." In: R. Voigt (ed.): *Und das Leben ist siegreich! / And Life is Victorious. Mandäische und samaritanische Literatur / Mandean and Samaritan Literature. Im Gedenken an Rudolf Macuch / In Memory of Rudolf Macuch (1919–1993).* Wiesbaden, pp. 9–16 (Mandäistische Forschungen 1).
— 2008b: "An Iranian Legal Term in the Babylonian Talmud and in Sasanian Jurisprudence: *dastwar.*" In: Sh. Shaked/A. Netzer (eds.): *Irano-Judaica VI: Studies Relating to Jewish Contacts with Persian Culture Throughout the Ages.* Jerusalem, pp. 126–138.
— 2008c: "Zur juristischen Terminologie der Berliner Pahlavi-Dokumente." In: D. Weber: *Berliner Pahlavi-Dokumente. Zeugnisse spätsassanidischer Brief- und Rechtskultur aus frühislamischer Zeit.* Wiesbaden (Iranica 15), pp. 249–266.
— 2009a: "Judicial and Legal System. iii. Sasanian Legal System." In: *EIr* XV, pp. 181–196.
— 2009b: "Disseminating the Mazdayasnian Religion: An Edition of the Pahlavi Hērbedestān Chapter 5." In: W. Sundermann/A. Hintze/F. de Blois (eds.): *Exegisti monumenta. Festschrift in Honour of Nicholas Sims-Williams.* Wiesbaden (Iranica 17), pp. 251–277.

– 2009c: "The Hērbedestān as a Legal Source: A Section on the Inheritance of a Convert to Zoroastrianism." In: BAI 19 (2005) [2009] (= *Iranian and Zoroastrian Studies in Honor of Prods Oktor Skjærvø*, ed. by C.A. Bromberg, N. Sims-Williams and U. Sims-Williams), pp. 91–102.

– 2009d: "Die sasanidische fromme Stiftung und der islamische *waqf*: Eine Gegenüberstellung." In: A. Meier/J. Pahlitzsch/L. Reinfandt (eds.): *Islamische Stiftungen zwischen juristischer Norm und sozialer Praxis*. Berlin, pp. 19–38.

– 2009e: "Pahlavi Literature." In: R.E. Emmerick/M. Macuch (eds.): *The Literature of Pre-Islamic Iran. Companion Volume I to A History of Persian Literature*. London 2009 (History of Persian Literature XVII), pp. 116–190.

– 2009f. "Gelehrte Frauen: ein ungewöhnliches Motiv in der Pahlavi-Literatur." In: D. Durkin-Meisterernst/Chr. Reck/D. Weber (eds.): *Literarische Stoffe und ihre Gestaltung in mitteliranischer Zeit. Kolloquium anlässlich des 70. Geburtstages von Werner Sundermann*. Wiesbaden (Beiträge zur Iranistik 31), pp. 135–151.

– 2010a: "Incestuous Marriage in the Context of Sasanian Family Law." In: M. Macuch/D. Weber/D. Durkin-Meisterernst (eds.): *Ancient and Middle Iranian Studies. Proceedings of the Sixth Europaean Conference of Iranian Studies of the Societas Iranologica Europaea in Vienna, Sept. 19–22, 2007.* Wiesbaden (Iranica 19), pp. 133–148.

– 2010b: "Allusions to Sasanian Law in the Babylonian Talmud." In: C. Bakhos/M.R. Shayegan (eds.): *The Talmud in its Iranian Context*. Tübingen, pp. 100–111.

– 2011a: "Die vorislamischen Wurzeln des Schāhnāme von Ferdausi." In: J. Gonnella/Ch. Rauch (eds.): *Heroische Zeiten. Tausend Jahre persisches Buch der Könige*. Berlin, pp. 22–27.

– 2011b (ed., with D. Weber and D. Durkin-Meisterernst): *Ancient and Middle Iranian Studies. Proceedings of the 6th European Conference of Iranian Studies, held in Vienna, 18–22 September 2007.* Wiesbaden (Iranica 19).

– 2012a: "Editing Pahlavi Legal Texts." In: A. Cantera (ed.): *The Transmission of the Avesta*. Wiesbaden (Iranica 20), pp. 519–540.

– 2012b: "The *adwadād* Offence in Zoroastrian Law." In: Sh. Secunda/St. Fie (eds.): *Shoshannat Yaakov. Jewish and Iranian Studies in Honor of Yaakov Elman*. Leiden/Boston (The Brill Reference Library of Judaism 35), pp. 247–269.

– 2012c: "The Pre-Islamic Roots of Firdausi's *Shahnama*." In: J. Gonnella/Ch. Rauch (eds.): *Heroic Times. A Thousand Years of the Persian Book of Kings*. Berlin, pp. 22–27.

– 2013a: "Vorislamisches iranisches Recht." In: L. Paul (ed.): *Handbuch der Iranistik*. Wiesbaden, pp. 123–132.

– 2013b: "Iranische Literaturen in vorislamischer Zeit." In: L. Paul (ed.): *Handbuch der Iranistik*. Wiesbaden, pp. 281–311.

– 2014a: "‚Behalte den Flug in Erinnerung …' – Leben und Werk von Rudolf Macuch." In: *Sláva šl'achetným III. Znalci vzdialeného Orientu a strážkyne národného ohniska. Slovenskí orientalisti a aktivity spolku Živena*. Liptovský Mikuláš, pp. 61–72.

– 2014b: "The Case against Mār Abā, the Catholicos, in the Light of Sasanian Law." In: *ARAM. Zoroastrianism in the Levant and the Amorites*, vol. 26.1&2. Oxford, pp. 47–58.

— 2014c: "Ardashir's Genealogy Revisited." In: P. POURSHARIATI/M. TAVAKOLI (eds.): *Iran Nameh* 29, *A Special Issue Honoring Jaleh Amouzgar*, pp. 80–94.
— 2015a: "Rudolf Macuch (1919–1993)." In: P. BUKOVEC (ed.): *Christlicher Orient im Porträt – Wissenschaftsgeschichte des Christlichen Orients. Kongreßakten der 1. Tagung der RVO (4. Dezember 2010, Tübingen).* Hamburg, Teilband 2, pp. 1035–1054.
— 2015b: "Legal Implications of Mazdakite Teaching According to the *Dēnkard*." In: CHR. JULLIEN (ed.); *Husraw Ier. Reconstructions d'un Règne. Sources et Documents.* Paris (Studia Iranica, Cahier 53), pp. 155–174.
— 2015c: "Law in Pre-modern Zoroastrianism." In: M. STAUSBERG/Y. S. D. VEVAINA (eds.): *The Wiley Blackwell Companion to Zoroastrianism.* Oxford, pp. 289–298.
— 2015d: "Substance and Fruit in the Sasanian Law of Property and the Babylonian Talmud." In: M.J. GELLER (ed.): *The Archaeology and Material Culture of the Babylonian Talmud.* Leiden/Boston, pp. 245–259.
— 2016a: "Türken in der zoroastrischen Literatur." In: I. HAUENSCHILD/M. KAPPLER/B. KELLNER-HEINKELE (eds.): *Eine hundertblättrige Tulpe – Bir ṣadbarg lāla. Festgabe für Claus Schönig.* Berlin, pp. 308–331.
— 2016b: "The Legal Context of the Tabarestan Court Records (Tab. 1–8,10)." In: R. GYSELEN (ed.): *Words and Symbols: Sasanian Objects and the Tabarestān Archiv Gyselen.* Bures-sur-Yvette (Res Orientales XXIV), pp. 145–169.
— 2017a: "Descent and Inheritance in Zoroastrian and Shiite Law: a Preliminary Study." In: *Der Islam* 94 (2), pp. 322–335.
— 2017b: "Pahlavi Legal Documents from Tabarestān on Lease, Loan and Compensation: the Juristic Context (Tab. 13,14, 15, 17, 18, 23)." In: R. GYSELEN (ed.): *Sasanian Coins, Middle-Persian Etymology and the Tabarestān Archive.* Bures-sur-Yvette (Res Orientales XXVI), pp. 165–195.
— MODI, J.J. 1901: *Mâdigân-i-Hazâr Dâdîstân. A Photozincographed Facsimile of a Ms. belonging to the Mânockji Limji Hoshang Hâtariâ Library in the Zarthoshti Anjuman Atashbeharâm.* Poona.
— SACHAU, E. 1914: *Syrische Rechtsbücher.* Vol.3: *Corpus juris des persischen Erzbischofs Jesubocht. Erbrecht oder Canones des persischen Erzbischofs Simeon. Eherecht des Patriarchen Mar Âbhâ.* Berlin.

Virginity and Water: Between the Babylonian Talmud and Iranian Myth

Tal Ilan and Reuven Kiperwasser

Who would be interested in the question whether a virgin can become pregnant? Most would answer this question with "Christians would". The Christian foundation myth has a betrothed virgin (Mary) become pregnant from someone other than her intended husband (Joseph), and the explanation the Gospels give to this phenomenon is that she was impregnated by the Holy Spirit and that she is, in fact, still a virgin (see in the canonic Gospels: Matthew 1:18–19; Luke 1:26–32; and in some apocryphal texts, e.g., Odes of Solomon 19:6–10 and Ascension of Isaiah 11:4–13).[1]

Yet it seems pretty obvious that the intention of the Christian myth was to combat accusations of adultery that had been, from very early on, leveled against Jesus' mother,[2] and that they were not really interested in proving the existence of biological/physical virginity in the body of the Virgin Mary. They were not concerned about how the Holy Spirit had planted a seed in the Virgin's womb or whether she was deflowered in the process or not.[3] Thus, scholars who devoted learned comparative studies to the question of the virgin birth in recent years, have concentrated on the similarity between the Jesus-birth-story and other miraculous birth stories in the Jewish tradition, which occurred without human intervention, rather than on the physical existence of a virginal hymen.[4]

Yet it seems that the question of a virginal pregnancy had been debated in the ancient world long before the Christian myth came into existence. For example, in a cuneiform tablet that lists a number of old Babylonian riddles the following can be read: "The deflowered (girl) did not become pregnant; the

1 R. E. Brown: *The Birth of the Messiah: A Commentary on the Infancy Narratives in Matthew and Luke*. New York 1993.

2 For a good summation of the issue see J. Schaberg: *The Illegitimacy of Jesus: A Feminist Theological Interpretation*. Sheffield 1995, pp. 145–178.

3 Later Christian sources (primarily the Protoevangelium Jacobi 11) are interested in proving that the Virgin's hymen had remained intact, not only in the impregnation process, but also in the actual birth of Jesus, but this is not the concern of the Gospels.

4 See e.g. R.D. Aus: *Matthew 1–2 and the Virginal Conception in Light of Palestinian and Hellenistic Judaic Traditions on the Birth of Israel's First Redeemer, Moses*. Lanham MD 2004; P. Zaas: "'Spirtus ex machina': Jewish Legal Aspects of the Matthean Birth Narrative." In: *Jewish Law Association Studies* 16 (2007), pp. 295–302.

undeflowered (girl) became pregnant (What is it?)"[5] The answer suggested for this riddle need not concern us here.[6] What it shows is that from ancient times, virginity as a physical feature of a woman had been noted, and the connection between virginity, sexual relations and pregnancy inspired awe.[7] It is against this background that we would like to present an enigmatic text found in the Babylonian Talmud which deals directly with pregnancy and virginity. At first blush, one would certainly assign this text to an interest in, perhaps even a polemic with Christianity, but we would like to suggest an additional Zoroastrian background against which such a text was produced and would have been read. By doing so, we touch on the deepest scholarly interest of the recipient of this book—Prof. MARIA MACUCH, who has over the years researched the Iranian background of the Babylonian Talmud, and the connections between its text and later Iranian compositions, that were put down in writing after the Muslim conquest but reflect earlier, Zoroastrian Iran.[8] This example can join the many others that are being diligently gathered by scholars in recent years, forming an important new trend in talmudic studies,[9] which draws Jewish studies and Iranian studies ever closer together.

5 M.P. STRECK/N. WASSERMAN: "Dialogues and Riddles: Three Old Babylonian Wisdom Texts." In: *Iraq* 73 (2011), p. 124.

6 The answer is 'Auxiliary forces'. The editors of the text do not fully understand this answer and they write: 'This riddle remains unclear. It might have a sexual connotation, like the riddle that precedes it.'

7 See a good summation of the topic in C. DELENEY: "The Meaning of Paternity and the Virgin Birth Debate." In: *Man* 21 (1986), pp. 494–513.

8 M. MACUCH: "Iranian Legal Terminology in the Babylonian Talmud in the Light of Sasanian Jurisprudence." In: *Irano-Judaica* 4 (1999), pp. 91–101; IDEM: "An Iranian Legal Term in the Babylonian Talmud and in Sasanian Jurisprudence—'dastwar(ih)'." In: *Irano-Judaica* 6 (2008), pp. 126–138; IDEM: "The Talmudic Expression 'Servant of the Fire' in the Light of Pahlavi Legal Sources." In: *Jerusalem Studies in Arabic and Islam* 26 (2002), pp. 109–129; IDEM: "Allusions to Sasanian Law in the Babylonian Talmud." In: C. BAKHOS/S.M. RAHIM (eds.): *The Talmud in Its Iranian Context*. Tübingen 2010, pp. 100–111.

9 See the pioneering work of Y.H. SCHORR. In: *Ha-Halutz* 7–8 (1865) (in Hebrew); and the rather sceptical approach of J. Neusner: "How Much Iranian in Jewish Babylonia?" In: *JAOS* 95 (1975), pp. 184–190. This field has recently undergone a renaissance, see e.g. Y. ELMAN: "'Up to the Ears' in Horses Necks (B.M. 108a): On Sasanian Agricultural Policy and Private 'Eminent Domain'." In: *Jewish Studies: An Internet Journal* 3 (2004), pp. 95–101; IDEM: "Acculturation to Elite Persian Norms and Modes of Thought in the Babylonian Jewish Community of Late Antiquity." In: E.B. HALIVNI/Z.A. STEINFELD (eds): *Neti'ot Le-David: Jubilee Volume for David Weiss Halivni*. Jerusalem 2004, pp. 31–56; IDEM: "The Other in the Mirror: Iranians and Jews View One Another: Questions of Identity, Conversion and Exogamy in the Fifth Century Iranian Empire." In: *Bulletin of the Asia Institute* 19 (2005), pp. 15–25; IDEM: "Who are the Kings of East and West in Ber 7a?: Roman Religion, Syrian Gods and Zoroastrianism in the Babylonian Talmud." In: S.J.D. COHEN/S. SCHWARTZ (eds.): *Studies in Josephus and the Varieties of Ancient Judaism*. Leiden 2007, pp. 43–80; IDEM: "Middle Persian Culture and Babylonian Sages: Accommodation and Resistance in the Shaping of Rabbinic Legal

1. The Babylonian text

The text we are interested in is found in no other rabbinic composition aside from the Babylonian Talmud. In this composition it is embedded in a very well-known episode, whose prototype was imported from Palestine.[10] The episode in question is the visit four sages paid to the Pardes, a mystical location, often associated with the abode of the divine. In this story, the encounter ended badly for three of the four would-be initiates. One—Ben Zoma—who interests us here, was smitten (הציץ ונפגע), which may imply that he lost his mind. This enigmatic story is told in a very concise version in the early, *tannai*tic Palestinian Tosefta (*tHagigah* 2:3–5), but is greatly embellished in both *talmudim* (*yHagigah* 2:1, 77b; *bHagigah* 14b-15a).[11] Both *talmudim* tell additional stories on the participants of this mystical journey but only the Babylonian Talmud reports the following about Ben Zoma:

Tradition." In: C. E. Fonrobert / M. S. Jaffee (eds.): *The Cambridge Companion to the Talmud and Rabbinic Literature*. Cambridge 2007, pp. 165–197; idem: "Toward an Intellectual History of Sasanian Law: An Intergenerational Dispute in 'Herbedestan' 9 and its Rabbinic and Roman Parallels." In: C. Bakhos / S. M. Rahim (eds.): *The Talmud in its Iranian Context*. Tübingen 2010, pp. 21–57; S. Secunda: "Talmudic Text and Iranian Context: On the Development of Two Talmudic Narratives." In: *Association of Jewish Studies Review* 33 (2009), pp. 45–69; idem: "Reading the Bavli in Iran." In: *Jewish Quarterly Review* 100 (2010), pp. 310–42; D. Sperber: "On the Unfortunate Adventures of Rav Kahana: A Passage of Saboraic Polemic from Sasanian Persia." In: *Irano-Judaica* 1 (1982), pp. 83–100; G. Herman: "The Story of Rav Kahana (BT Baba Qamma 117a–b) in Light of Armeno-Persian Sources." In: *Irano-Judaica* 6 (2008), pp. 53–85 ; idem: "David the Royal Hunter, Prison Adventures, and Rav Kahana's Silence: Persian Themes in the Babylonian Talmud." In S. Secunda / S. Fine (eds.): *Shoshannat Yaakov: Ancient Jewish and Iranian Studies in Honor of Professor Yaakov Elman*. Leiden 2012, pp. 111–136; R. Kiperwasser: "Rabba bar bar Hanna's Voyages." In: *Jerusalem Studies in Hebrew Literature* 22 (2008), pp. 215–243; R. Kiperwasser / D. Y. Shapira: "Irano-Talmudica I. The Three-Legged Ass and 'Ridyā' in B. Ta'anith: Some Observations about Mythic Hydrology in the Babylonian Talmud and in Ancient Iran." In: *Association of Jewish Studies Review* 32 (2008), pp. 101–116; idem: "The Misfortunes and Adventures of Elihoreph and Ahiah in the Land of Israel and in Babylonia: The Metamorphosis of a Narrative Tradition and Ways of Acculturation." In: R. Nikolsky / T. Ilan (eds.): *Rabbinic Traditions between Palestine and Babylonia*. Leiden 2013, pp. 250–268. This is a choice sample of this new and growing field

10 About the migration to and transformation of Palestinian traditions in Sassanian Babylonia see recently R. Nikolsky / T. Ilan: "Introduction." In: Nikolsky/Ilan 2013, pp. 1–36.

11 For discussions of this text see (among others) J. Liebes: *Elisha's Sin: Four Who Entered PaRDeS*. Jerusalem 1990 (in Hebrew). He deals with Ben Zoma on pp. 111–112 but ignores this text; A. Goshen Gottstein: *The Sinner and the Amnesiac: The Rabbinic Invention of Elisha ben Abuya and Eleazar ben Arach*. Stanford 2000. He deals with Ben Zoma in pp. 53–59. He too does not refer to our episode; P. Schäfer: *The Jewish Jesus: How Judaism and Christianity Shaped Each Other*. Princeton 2012, pp. 127–131. He completely ignores Ben Zoma.

bHagigah 14b–15a

	Ms München 61[12]	Translation
1	שאלו את בן זומא מהו לסרוסי כלבא	Ben Zoma was asked: Is it [permitted] to castrate a dog?
2	אמ' להן ובארצכם לא תעשו כל שבארצכם לא תעשו	He replied: "Neither shall ye do this in your land" (Lev 22). [This means:] to none that is in your land shall you do thus.
3	שאלו את בן זומא בתולה שעיברה מהו	Ben Zoma was asked: What [is the status of] a virgin who become pregnant?
4	מי חישינן לדשמואל	Do we [in such a case] worry about Shmuel's [statement]?
5	דאמ' שמואל יכולני לבעול כמה בתולות בלא דם	For Shmuel said: I can have sexual intercourse with several virgins without [causing] bleeding.
6	או דיל' דשמואל לא שכיחא	Or perhaps Shmuel's [statement about what he can do] is not common
7	וחישינן שמא בא{מ}בטי עיברה	And we consider that she may have become pregnant in a bathtub?
8	והאמ' שמואל	But did not Shmuel say:
9	כל שכבת זרע שאינה יורה כחץ אינה מזרעת	A spermatic emission that does not shoot forth like an arrow cannot inseminate?
10	ההיא נמי מעיקרא יורה כחץ הואי	That one had also shot forth like an arrow.

Apparatus Criticus
2 כל שבארצכם] in margin M95; missing O23 3 שאלו את בן זומא] missing V171 מהו] missing M95 4 מי חישינן] מ(אי) איתא O63 5 יכולני] יכול אני L400 O23 V171 6 לא שכיחא] missing O63 במה כמאבטי עיבירה א' להו added V134 7 וחישינן ושמא] אמ' ליה ושמא G3 באבטי V134 בא־ מבטי all mss. א"ל חיישינן שמא באמבטי עיברה in margin M95 8 האמ'] איני והאמ' M95 9 אינה מזרעת] אינו מוליד M95 10 נמי מעיקרא] נמי מעיקר' ההוא G3 V171 האי נמי מעיקרא הוא M95 הוא V134 הוה M95 הואי] V34 אימר מעיקרא O63 דילמא ההיא מעיקרה O23 מעיקרא

This tradition appears at first blush to have nothing to do with Ben Zoma's Pardes experience, and only to be related here because of the Babylonian Talmud's compilatory character. But as we will argue presently, perhaps this assumption is not quite as obvious as it appears. It is true that, while this tradition is found only in the Babylonian Talmud, it is formulated in the same way as are many authentic Palestinian traditions, beginning with "Ben Zoma was

12 12th–13th century, Spanish ms. Other mss used in the apparatus are G3—Göttingen 3, 13th century Spanish; L400—London 400 Harley 5508, 13th century Spanish; M95—Munich 95, 1342 European; O23—Oxford 366 (= Opp. Add. fol 23), 13th century Spanish; O63—Oxford—Bod. heb. d. 63 (2826) 32–32; V134—Vatican 134, 13th century Italian; V171—Vatican 171, 34, 1493, European.

asked" (שאלו את בן זומא) and continuing with a question formulated in Hebrew, to which the sage replies.[13] Thus, unless we have very good grounds to suspect otherwise, the question-and-answer session presented in the text cited above may very well derive from an authentic Palestinian tradition. There may have existed a Palestinian source which described how the sages interrogated Ben Zoma on whether it is permitted to castrate a dog, to which he answered, citing a verse forbidding the castration of beasts in the Land of Israel in general; and perhaps they also asked him something about a virgin becoming pregnant, but what they asked him exactly,[14] and what his answer was, have unfortunately not survived.

In its original Palestinian setting, the question posed to Ben Zoma could have been triggered by the virgin-birth stories circulated by Christians. Ben Zoma lived in the first half of the second century and Christianity was already making headway in Palestine at his time. However, if we follow the recent scholarly trend begun by Peter Schaefer[15] that the Babylonian Talmud was more interested than the Palestinian sources in early Christianity, we may speculate that this text is in fact a Babylonian pseudo-*baraita*[16] about early Christianity, and not one imported from Palestine.

In either case, Ben Zoma's answer has been lost in transmission and what now follows the question is a short give-and-take in Aramaic, typical of the literary activity usually assigned to the editors of the Babylonian Talmud (the *stamma*). How did this dialogical text land here? We wish to suggest a speculative reconstruction of the missing building blocks of the text: Ben Zoma was asked about a virgin becoming pregnant (perhaps in a Palestinian-Christian context; perhaps in a Babylonain pseudo-*baraita*), to which he replied (perhaps with the

13 The other traditions which are formulated in this way are: 1. *tBerakhot* 4:12 (cited in *yBerakhot* 6:6, 10d and *bBerakhot* 13a); 2. *tKippurim* 1:16 (cited in *yYoma* 3:3, 40b and *bYoma* 30a); 3. *tToharot* 6:17 (cited in *ySotah* 1:2, 16c). The Babylonian Talmud cites another tradition formulated in this way which also has no Palestinian parallel in *bBerakhot* 41b.

14 In the printed editions of the Babylonian Talmud the question asked is whether a virgin who became pregnant may marry a high priest. High priests, according to Leviticus 21:14–15, may only marry virgins. However, this is probably a later scribal addition. However in an old commentary on the Babylonian Talmud, that of Rabbenu Hananel (of Qairouan, Tunis 1057—see the Vilna printed edition to *bHagigah* 15a), the question asked is whether a virgin who became pregnant is required to bring a sin offering once she gives birth. All women who gave birth are expected, according to Leviticus 12:16, to bring a sin-offering. This author then relates the story of the miraculous conception of a virgin in a bath-house, an event of which he had once heard in his home-town. On such a tradition see in the Appendix to this article.

15 P. Schäfer: *Jesus in the Talmud*. Princeton 2007, pp. 113–122.

16 See for example L. Jacobs: "Are there Fictitious Baraitot in the Babylonian Talmud?" In: *The Hebrew Union College Annual* 42 (1971), pp. 185–196, and see also J. Hauptman: *Development of the Talmudic Sugya: Relationship between Tannaitic and Amoraic Sources*. Lanham 1988.

use of a biblical verse) that this is impossible. If she is pregnant, she is no longer a virgin. The editors of the Babylonian Talmud than ask: If this is so, what are we worried about, and why was Ben Zoma even asked this question? This is when they insert the text we have before us: "Do we [in such a case] worry about Shmuel's [statement]? For Shmuel said: I can have sexual intercourse with several virgins without [causing] bleeding."

This Shmuel was a prominent Babylonian rabbi, who died, according to Rav Sherira Gaon, in the year 253[17] and had thus lived at least a century after Ben Zoma. There is no dialogue between the two suggested here, and there never existed a text that had brought them in contact one with the other. We do not know whether Ben Zoma's original answer to the question about a virgin conceiving had involved the assumption that her physical hymen stayed intact. The Babylonians, in any case, shift the discussion to physical virginity, and to Shmuel claiming for himself an uncommon talent of impregnating women through actual sexual intercourse but without their defloration.

In investigating the editorial activity of the Babylonian editors here, it should be noted that Shmuel's answer to the question put to Ben Zoma has been imported from elsewhere.[18] *bNiddah* 64b discusses a first sexual intercourse with a presumed virgin, which does not produce bleeding, and a second intercourse, in which bleeding does occur. Should this blood, the editors enquire, be considered pure virginal blood of the torn hymen that had somehow remained intact in the first round? Or maybe something like this is considered impossible, and the woman was simply not a virgin to begin with, in which case the bleeding now is the result of impure menstrual blood? In the *sugya* in *bNiddah*, Shmuel is reputed to have said exactly what we find in the present discussion on the impregnated virgin (namely he would consider the blood pure, because sexual intercourse without defloration is possible). Yet, elsewhere in the Babylonian Talmud, within a discussion on virginal blood and the husband's rights, Shmuel (as cited by Rav Yehudah) asserts the opposite, namely that a husband may withhold the wedding contract from a woman who does not bleed at intercourse, because she was obviously not a virgin (*bKetubbot* 9b). It thus seems that Shmuel had won for himself the reputation of being something of an expert regarding virginity and its loss, and that is why his saying on his unique sexual performance was imported into our *sugya*.

The *stamma*, however, argues that Shemuel's claim, which he has just brought into play here, reflects a very unusual practice, and that a virgin who conceived, probably become pregnant in a bathtub. The actual process imagined in this argument is of a man having previously deposited his semen in bath water, of a

17 See N.D. Rabinowich: *The Iggeres of Rav Sherira Gaon*. Jerusalem 1988, p. 98.

18 See D. Weiss-Halivni: *Sources and Traditions: A Source Critical Commentary on the Talmud Seder Moed from Yoma to Hagiga.* New York 1973, p. 493.

girl sitting in them, and of the semen flowing naturally through her vagina into her womb and impregnating her, without any sexual intercourse.

To this suggestion the editors reply with another statement that is assigned to the same Shmuel, and which also originates in Tractate *Niddah* but in another section of it: "But did not Shmuel say: A spermatic emission that does not shoot forth like an arrow cannot inseminate?" (cf. *bNiddah* 43a). The original discussion centers on seminal emission and the extent to which a man is aware of it. There Shmuel is reported to have opined that in order for male sperm to be potent, it must issue forth like an arrow from a bow. The rabbis bring this saying here to suggest that perhaps, if a man had deposited his sperm in a bath, it had not issued forth with the necessary force, but they immediately reply that: "That one (i.e. the seminal emission deposited in the water of the bathtub) had also shot forth like an arrow." With these words the *gemara* closes the discussion of this topic and moves on to deal with other completely different issues.

Regardless of all that has transpired thus far in the talmudic discussion, and of whether we think the Babylonian editor is joking here (as we will be arguing presently), the image that this text conveys is very powerful, unexpected and innovative. Where has it come from, and why has the Babylonian editors found it necessary to insert it here? In the following section we suggest answering this question as far away as possible from the Christian foundation myth, about the birth of its messiah, namely in light of Zoroastrian mythology and its own version of the virgin birth of an alternative messiah.

2. The birth of the Messiah in Iranian myth

Surprisingly, ancient Iranian mythological narratives, like early Christian texts, nurture the notion of a saviour being born of a virgin. The following is a hypothesis of how the original Iranian myth may have looked, based on available textual remnants.

According to Dēnkard (= Dk) 7.10.15–19, which is a post-Sasanian Zoroastrian composition in Pahlavi, drawing on older Avestan and Pahlavi sources, a certain virgin will enter a lake; according to the Yasht 19.92, this is Lake Kansava. While in the water, she will conceive, and will then give birth to a miraculous son. He is mentioned in Yasht 19.88–96 as both Saušyant and Astuat-Ərəta the son of Vīspa.tauruuairī.[19] These are the relevant verses of this myth in the Dēnkard:

19 We thank our friend Dan Shapira for providing us these texts and translations (and graciously reading this paper and commenting on it, correcting errors and improving observations. For all errors that remain we are of course responsible.

15. ud ka ān ī dahom satōk-zim 30 zamistān arānāk kanīg[20] ō āb abar rawēd kē Gôbâk-pit[21] (ēd ku mād ī ōy ī Gōwāg Sōšans, ku Ēbgad-petyārag bē burd numūdar) u-š az Vahu-rōz ī Frahnyān ī andar dūdag ī Isatwāstr ī pus ī Zardušt az Arwaz zād ēstēd frāz tōhmag.

16. kē Harwisp-tarwēnīdār[22] nām, hān kanīg ēdōn harwisp-tarwēnīdār cyōn ān pad zāyišn zāyēd kē harwisp tarwānēd, ān-iz az dēwān bēš ud ān-iz az mardomān.[23]

17. ēg andar ān āb nišīnēd ka 15-sālag hast kanīk, ān andar dahēd kē hast ku Sūdōmand Pērōzgar nām Tan-kirdar[24]-iz nām (ēdōn sūdōmand cyōn harwisp axv ī astōmand sawēnēd[25] ud ēdōn (Tan) kirdār cyōn ham *tanōmand ud gyānōmand astōmandān mardomān asyazīh[26] abar xvāhēd).[27]

18. nē pēš az ān *abāg mardān nē nibast, nē ka pas ka ābustān bawēd pēš az ān tā ka ul zāyēd.

Translation

15. When in the last millennium more than thirty winters had gone by, a girl will come along to the river, Gôbâk-pit. She will be the mother of Sōšans who will teach how to eliminate the forces of evil. He will be the [foundation of the] family of Vahûrôč Frahnyân, born in the clan of Isatvâstr son of Zoroaster by Arvač.

16. Named "one who will dominate everything," this girl will be "the one who controls everything" because she has given birth to one who dominates all the malice, that of the *dēw*s as that of the men.

17. She sits in the water, this girl of fifteen, who will conceive the one named "Victorious Savior," who will be named "Maker of the body": "Savior" because he will bring salvation to everything material, "Maker of the body" because he will restore the pristine men endowed with body and breath.

18. She has never slept with men before or after, as she will be pregnant before he was born.

According to this text, the Zoroastrian saviour will be born of a fifteen-year-old virgin who has not engaged in sexual intercourse with any man, who will become pregnant in a lake. How she would become pregnant in this lake is not spelt out in this text, but an answer to this question is found in the Great Iranian

20 Ərədat-feδri, "Victorious Helper," and cf. Yasht 13.142.
21 Lake Kansava, according to Yasht 19.92.
22 *Vīspa.taurwairī.
23 This is based on a Pahlavi translation of Yasht 13.142, as noted in M. MOLÉ: *Le problème zoroastrien et la tradition mazdéenne*. Paris 1963, pp. 229–230.
24 *Astvat-ereta, see MOLÉ 1963, pp. 229–230.
25 Avestan **savayat*; cf. Yasht 19.37, see MOLÉ 1963, pp. 229–230.
26 Cf. MOLÉ 1963, p. 233: **aiθyejahya* (Yasht 13.129).
27 This is based on a Pahlavi translation of Yasht 13.129, as noted in MOLÉ 1963, p. 230.

Bundahishn. The following is a translation and reconstruction of the part of the text relevant to our inquiry, as suggested by Mary Boyce for verses 35:56–60 and 33:36–38 in this order[28]:

> Three times Zardusht [the Zoroaster] approached his wife, Hvovi. Each time his seed fell to the ground. The yazad Neryosang took all the light and power of that seed, and ... it was consigned to Lake Kayansih, in the care of the Waters ... It is said that even now three lamps are seen shining at night in the depth of the lake. And for each, when his own time comes, it will be thus: a virgin will go to Lake Kayansih to bathe; and the Glory (of Zardusht) will enter her body, and she will become with child. And so, one by one the (three) will be born thus, each at his own time.

In this, later, Zoroastrian tradition the one future Savior (Sōšans) has become three, one for the end of each of the three last millennia of the existence of this world. Like the one saviour in the earlier tradition in the Dēnkard, all three saviours in this tradition will be born of virgins who will miraculously become pregnant in a lake, in which they bath. Yet unlike the older Dēnkard, this version of the tradition definitely identifies the source of the pregnancy of the virgins. In this one pristine lake the semen of Zoroaster himself was deposited, and it is from this seed that they will all conceive. We are found on pretty safe ground when we assume that the earlier tradition in the Dēnkard had taken for granted the presence of Zoroaster's seed in the lake it describes, in which a virgin it mentions bathes.

Since both the Dēnkard and the Bundahishin were put down in writing even later than the Babylonian Talmud, the talmudic fantasy of a virgin conceiving in a body of water may be the earliest existing reflection of this myth. On a very basic level, what the Babylonian Talmud definitely accepts and internalizes from the Iranian mythical account is the medical information about what happens in the female body when conceiving. This way of acculturating the mythical knowledge of the "Other", especially in the Iranian context, is typical of the Babylonian Talmud.[29] But perhaps, on a deeper level, the acceptance of this mythical knowledge is not naïve at all, but rather reveals a complex dialogue with the theology of both Iranians and Christians, and their image of the virgin birth of their savior, as will be proposed in the following discussion.

28 See M. Boyce: *Textual Sources for the Study of Zoroastrianism*. Manchester 1990, p. 91.

29 As shown by R. Kiperwasser: " 'Three Partners in a Person': The Genesis and Development of Embryological Theory in Biblical and Rabbinic Judaism." In: *Lectio Difficilior* 9/2 (2009).

3. Christian and Zoroastrian myth and the Babylonian Talmud

The similarities between the Christian and Zoroastrian virgin-birth-of-the-messiah myths are too great to have gone completely undetected in antiquity.[30] A Christian composition preserved in Syrian-Aramaic,[31] *The Book of Scholia (k^e^ṯāḇā de-skōlyōn)*, composed in 791–792 by Theodore Bar Kōnay, a Nestorian sage from Kaškar in Babylonia,[32] tells, among other bits of information about diverse religions and sects, a story about Zoroaster and his disciples. Bar Kōnay's book has been thoroughly examined by Benveniste,[33] who claims that the biographical details about Zoroaster which it contains are based on earlier Christian sources, that are no longer extant.[34]

According to the story in which we are interested,[35] named "The Zoroastrian prophesy about the messiah" *(nebi'uta de Zardusht de-al-meshiha)*, once, when Zoroaster was sitting by a spring of water *('eina de-maya')*,[36] he said to his disciples, Gushtasp, Sasan and Meheman that before the end of times and the final destruction, in the womb of a virgin a child will be conceived, and all its limbs and organs will be perfected, despite the fact that no male will touch the

30 Although it does seem to have gone undetected in some circles of modern scholarship—see for example Schaberg 1995, p. 65: "It is rapidly becoming a scholarly consensus that the idea of divine begetting as a virginal conception is found in the biblical and intertestamental periods only in the Infancy Narratives of Matthew and Luke ... Critics generally agree also that there are no stories of virginal conceptions—in pre-Christian or non-Christian literature (ancient Greek or Roman, Hellenistic, Assyrian, Babylonian, **Zoroastrian**, Mithraic, Arabic, Egyptian or **Indian**)." (emphasis ours). On the virgin birth stories about Buddha see Z.P. Thundy: *Buddha and Christ: Nativity Stories and Indian Traditions*. Leiden 1993.

31 About the importance of these sources for the study of the talmudic historical setting see G. Herman: "'Bury my Coffin Deep!': Zoroastrian exhumation in Jewish and Christian sources." In: J. Roth/M. Schmeltzer/Y. Francus (eds.): *Tiferet leYisrael: Jubilee Volume in Honor of Israel Francus*. New York 2010, pp. 31–59; R. Kiperwasser/S. Ruzer: "Zoroastrian Proselytes in Rabbinic and Syriac Christian Narratives: Orality-Related Markers of Cultural Identity." In: *History of Religions* 51/3 (2012), pp. 197–218.

32 J.P. Asmussen: "Bar Kōnay, Theodore." In: *EIr* 3. London/New York 1989, pp. 737–738.

33 E. Benveniste: "Le témoignage de Théodore bar Kōnay sur le zoroastrisme." In: *MO* 26–27 (1932–1935), pp. 170–215.

34 And are possibly based on the writings of another prominent Nestorian church father, Theodore of Mopsuestia (ca. 360–428) in his now lost *Perì tēs en Persídi magikēs* [On the teaching of the Magians in Persia].

35 We read the text as published in A. Scher (ed.): *Theodorus bar Kōnī. Liber Scholiorum* vol. 2. (CSCO Syr. II.65–66). Paris 1912, p. 74. See also R. Hespel (ed.): *Théodore bar Koni. Livre des Scolies (recension d'Urmiah)*. Louvain 1983.

36 Which was probably a well-known place, because the narrator designates it "*di Glosha di Horin*" (?) and even adds that it is a place where the bath house *(bei mashuta)* of ancient kings stood.

girl. The story ends with Zaradusht sending these three disciples to Bethlehem to witness this miraculous birth.

This story is obviously a hybrid, produced from two different messiah birth stories and includes important elements from both of them. The Zoroastrian myth produced the source of water, by which this story takes place, and which plays no further role in it. The figure of Zoroaster himself, the Iranian prophet who predicts that the messiah will be born of a virgin, also derives from this angle. From the Christian story we encounter the virgin mother, the divine infant, and from the Gospel of Matthew we meet the Maggi, who in this version of the story are the disciples of Zoroaster. Bearing in mind that the possible intention of the Maggi story in Gospels was to persuade the readers that Jesus was the messiah of Persian mythological predictions, we can see here a new, probably unintentional, stage of Christian propaganda.[37] Not only their savior was in fact the Christian Messiah, but even Zoroaster was a sort of prophet of Christianity. Similar to the biblical Balaam, the heathen prophet who speaks in the name of the 'real' God, the impure Zoroaster predicts the birth of the 'real' messiah. This could possibly be the reason why Zoroaster is identified with Balaam by Syriac Christian authors.[38]

We think that the 8th century version of this story actually had much older antecedents, as is often the case in late Syriac narratology. We suspect that the unnecessary appendage of the source of water in this story, which, as we demonstrated above, had a significant mythical value in the Iranian story, had in the earlier versions an ironic character. We think that "impure" Zoroaster ("this filthy one"—*hnʾ ṭnpʾ*) was placed by the storyteller near the water source in order to hint at the location where his impurity could be removed.

This brings us back to our talmudic story. Is it mere chance that the Babylonian Talmud has chosen to relate a bizarre legal discussion about the possibility of a virgin conceiving, and suggesting that this could happen in a bathtub, or would it make more sense to connect it with the myths of the two neighboring religions among which the Jews lived, the Christians and the Zoroastrians, who both suggested a virgin birth for their savior? A central question in this context is whether religious texts like the Babylonian Talmud are always serious discussions of theological and legal concepts, or are they sometimes self reflective and able to view their religious adversaries' (and sometimes even their own) theological reflections in humoristic ways. Having observed that Christians treated the Iranian messiah myth with irony, this question is not inappropriate.

37 G. Messina: *I Magi a Betlemme e una predizione di Zoroastro.* Rome 1933, pp. 58–60.

38 R.J.H. Gottheil: "References to Zoroaster in Syriac and Arabic Literature." In: *Classical Studies in Honour of Henry Drisler.* New York/London 1894, pp. 24–51; Y. Abraham: "Another Old Syriac Reference to Zoroaster." In: *JAOS* 43 (1923), pp. 239–242. See also J. Neusner: "Note on Barukh ben Neriah and Zoroaster." In: *Numen* 12/1 (1965), pp. 66–69 and E. Barsky: "Zardusht and Barukh in the Book of the Bee by Solomon from Basra." In: *Symbol* 61 (2013), pp. 109–121 (in Russian).

Regarding the Babylonian Talmud, Daniel Boyarin has recently written:

> the *stamma* produces a real dialogism at one level even while shutting it down at another ... there are, in effect, two *stammas*, two authorial entities within the Babylonian Talmud (whether or not the same people are behind them historically is irrelevant here).[39]

In other words, not using stamma-terminology—there are two anonymous redactors (probably not personal but in the collective mind of the editors) of this text—the *Bavli*—one pious and conventional, the other a critical and self-reflecting skeptic, a wit with a good sense of humor. Boyarin continues:

> It is this second "author" who makes the Talmud both *spoudogeloios* and Menippean. ... the Talmud is the dialogue between the two anonymous authors, a monological voice that seeks to bring all under the purview of the system called oral Torah and another who allows cracks to appear in the fabric of that very system.[40]

Boyarin ascribes to the second voice carnival elements.[41] It seems that Boyarin wants to see in this asymmetry a kind of double-voiced editorial strategy combining serious and humoristic elements one with the other.

Applying to the text under discussion from Bavli *Hagigah* this humoristic and even parody-like intention we can see it as involved in a dialogue with the miraculous birth stories of both the Christians and Zoroastrians. As mentioned above, the discussion with Ben Zoma is located in the immediate context of the story of four sages who entered Pardes. Yet there is a larger context to the story of these four sages, namely the most complete collection of mystical speculations found in the Babylonian Talmud, both about the works of creation (Genesis 1–2) and about the chariot of God (Ezekiel 1–2—see *bHagigah* 11b-16a). Consequently, it is one of the hottest theological spots found in the entire Babylonian Talmud, and it contains many polemical utterances against views that are deemed heretical or marginal, or espoused by competing religions.

Thus, Daniel Boyarin has recently shown that a polemic against the Christian view of God the Father and God the Son is presented within this greater text. A few lines before the story of the four who entered Pardes is presented, Daniel 7:9 is cited ("until thrones were set up and the Ancient of Days sat", *bHagigah* 14a), and Boyarin suggests that the rabbis had to contend with the

39 D. Boyarin: *Socrates and the Fat Rabbis*. Chicago/London 2009, p. 173.

40 Ibid., p. 202.

41 Questions could be raised about this hypothesis: Because only a limited amount of, in Boyarin's words, "grotesque and harshly self-critical biographical legends" (ibid., p. 191) are found in the Babylonian Talmud, may we suppose that the second editor is suppressed? Or is there a strategy on the part of the redactor to keep these stories to a minimum, so as not to disturb the orderly sequence of the halakhic discourse in which they are included? For the purposes of this paper we will accept the presence of the skeptical voice as a given.

opinion of some, among them Rabbi Aqiva himself, that this verse is proof that there were two powers in heaven—a father and a son.[42] Thus, at least according to BOYARIN, Christianity is patently present in the greater *sugya* in which our episode of Ben Zoma is embedded.

We would like to draw the readers' attention to a further text, located a few lines after the episode of Ben Zoma, which may be a viewed as a polemic against well-recognized Iranian theology (*bHagigah* 16a):

> Our rabbis taught: Six things were said about demons—in three they are like angels and in three they are like humans. Three like the ministering angels: They have wings like ministering angels, and the fly from one end of the world to the next like ministering angels, and they know the future like ministering angels ... and in three they are like humans: They eat and drink like humans and they procreate like humans and they die like humans.

The preoccupation of Iranian theology with demons is widely recognized,[43] and the polemic against it in the definition of demons in this text is clear. While the Iranians viewed their demons as spiritual beings, without any material component, this text claims for them quite a number of human qualities, which the Iranians would have rejected, foremost among them—procreation.[44]

It seems to us not inconceivable that our small excerpt (which relates 1. the question posed to Ben Zoma about a virgin conceiving; 2. Shmuel's ability to engage in sex with virgins without causing them to bleed, or lose their hymen; and 3. a virgin's ability to become pregnant in a bathtub) is also engaged in a dialogue (nay polemic) with these two religions. The mythical context in which these religions tell the story of the conception of their savior draws our attention to the miraculous circumstances in which they occur. The Holy Spirit comes upon Mary and impregnates her. The sacred seed of Zoroaster is preserved in a lake for the insemination of the virgin at the end of time. Our rabbinic text ridicules these concepts. It argues that in order for a girl to conceive and remain a virgin, one needs no Holy Spirit. A skilled sage can do the job. And it argues that becoming pregnant in water requires no holy lake or the seed of a great ancestor. Anyone can deposit his seed in a bathtub and impregnate a virgin.

42 D. BOYARIN: "Beyond Judaisms: Metatron and the Divine Polymorphy of Ancient Judaism." In: *Journal for the Study of Judaism* 41 (2010), pp. 339–342.

43 See SCHORR 1865, p. 19. A. KOHUT: *Über die jüdische Angelologie und Daemonologie in ihrer Abhängigkeit vom Parsismus*. Leipzig 1866, p. 54.

44 See S. SHAKED: "The Notions of mēnōg and gētig in the Pahlavi Texts and their Relation to Eschatology." In: *AO* 33 (1971), pp. 59–107.

Appendix: *Alpha-Beta de-Ben Sira*

If, as we contend, this text is indeed a joke at the expense of the sister religions' mythology, this has not been recognized by traditional scholars, who all treated our episode as a serious halakhic discussion. We are not interested in tracing the reception history of this little talmudic annecdote in Jewish tradition through the ages,[45] but in order not to be charged with ignorance we would like to comment on the very next station in which we find this motif. A medieval literary work known as the *Alpha-Betha de-Ben Sira*, which purports to lay out the hagiography of the ancient Jewish sage Ben Sira, relates an episode in which insemination in a bathhouse takes place. The story is quite obscene. Ben Sira is said to be the son of the Prophet Jeremiah and Jeremiah's own daughter. Jeremiah is accosted in the bathhouse by hooligans who force him to masturbate in a bathtub. Later on, and unknowingly, his own daughter comes to the bathhouse and conceives of her father's seed. The offspring of this bizarre union is Ben Sira.[46]

With relation to this story, scholars have preceded us in identifying its inspiration in Zoroastrian myth. This is what ISRAEL LEVY wrote already in 1894:

> One searches in vain in Jewish literature for a reversal as curious as the one [between] the two legends, Christian and Persian, united by a single common trait: the miraculous birth of their hero. Our story is the last step in a religious myth that became a simple amusing tale, under the feather of an eclectic scribe of bad intentions.[47]

In other words, LEVY had already identified the common traits of the Christian and Iranian hero-birth myths, and bundled them together with a story of a woman conceiving in a bathhouse, as found in *Alpha-Betha de-Ben Sira*. Yet LEVY, who also knew our little talmudic episode, emphatically rejected any connection between it and the Iranian myth or the Christian virgin-birth story. He wrote:

> It is true that the Talmud also relates a myth of this genre, or rather it admits to the possibility of this sort of conception. The Talmud, however, speaks here

45 See now S. EMANUEL: "Pregnancy without Sexual Relations in Medieval Thought." In: *Journal of Jewish Studies* 62 (2011), pp. 105–120.

46 See E. YASIF: *The Tales of Ben Sira in the Middle Ages*. Jerusalem 1984, pp. 198–199 (in Hebrew). Incidentally, this text also claims that two other sages, Rabbi Zeira and Rav Pappa were also conceived in this manner, see *ibid.*, p. 197.

47 I. LEVY: "La nativité de Ben Sira." In: *Revue des Études Juives* 29 (1984), p. 205: "on chercherait vainement dans la literature juive une transposition aussi curieuse de deux legends chrétienne et persane unie par un seul trait commun: la naissance miraculeuse du héros. Notre roman serait la dernière étape d'un mythe religieux devenu simple conte amusant sous la plume d'un écrivain éclectique de mauvais goût."

> about a theoretical point of view, regarding a question of jurisprudence, and it is absolutely certain that our story does not derive from it.[48]

Instead LEVY promoted the idea that knowledge of this Iranian myth indicates a Persian provenance for *Alpha-Betha de-Ben Sira*.

It seems to us, however, that all the elements that LEVY identified in our story, as connected to the Persian and Christian myths, are already found in the talmudic episode of *bHagigah* 14b-15a, and that it is much more likely that this was *Alpha-Betha de-Ben Sira* inspiration for his story, since there is no doubt that the author of the latter was familiar with, and influenced by, the Babylonian Talmud.[49] If this is true, than the assumption that *Alpha-Betha de-Ben Sira* was composed in Iran (as suggested by ISRAEL LEVY), or at least in the domains of the erstwhile Sassanian Empire (ELI YASIF[50]) are unnecessary.

Moreover, we suspect that this story could have been composed in Christian Europe (where it is first attested[51]) because the hooligans who accost Jeremiah threaten him that they will sodomize him (מעשה סדום).[52] It is worthwhile noting that it is only Christian thinkers who identified the sin of Sodom with homosexuality.[53]

48 *Ibid*., p. 203: "Il est vrais que la Talmud semble connaître un mythe de ce genre, ou plutôt admet la possibilité d'une semblable conception. Seulement le Talmud n'en parle qu'à un point de vue théoritique, dans une question de jurisprudence, et il est absolument certain que notre récit n'en derive pas."

49 See especially YASIF 1984, pp. 41–43.

50 Ibid., pp. 28–29.

51 YASIF himself admits that the manuscripts of the text are Ashkenazi and Italian (not Spanish or Yemenite) and that the earliest references to the text are found in southern France. He also maintains that the first reference to the book is from the 11th century Italy (the *Arukh* composed in Rome), YASIF 1984, pp. 16–22; YASIF does mention a North African sage of the 11th century, who may also be referring to this book; in any case, according to SIMHA EMANUEL, the earliest citation of our story is found in a 13th century composition of Yehudah he-Hasid from Ashkenaz, i.e. Europe, see EMANUEL 2011, p. 109.

52 YASIF 1984, p. 199.

53 See J. L. KUGEL: *Traditions of the Bible: A Guide to the Bible as it Was at the Start of the Common Era*. Cambridge MA 1998, pp. 332–333.

The Technical Term *tarkīb* "Compound" in the Indigenous Persian "Scientific" Literature

Éva M. Jeremiás

1. Introduction

In the Persian scientific or scientific-like literature the technical term *tarkīb*[1] is a genuine cover-term or, using a metaphoric designation from earlier linguistic terminology, an umbrella term or blanket word, which might cover a wide range of phenomena used in various fields. The term means "compound" or rather "compounding" indicating the act of compounding itself; hence, the compounded items so produced must consist of more than one constituent. In Persian, this word is an Arabic loan as its shape clearly indicates: it appeared with the infiltration into Persia of various Arabic sciences such as logic, grammar or literary sciences—to mention only disciplines of the humanities—in the early Islamic period.

At first glance, *tarkīb* seems to be a practical tool which served to handle the compounded forms of any sort called *murakkab* in Arabic grammar, and which was used as an antonym of the term *mufrad* which indicates the (morphologically) indivisible simple forms. The term *tarkīb* was employed to designate compounded words in most cases, but more complex units at a higher level such as phrase or sentence structures (including also logical propositions[2]) were also considered *tarkīb*. If it is considered a practical tool to treat compounded phenomena, its employment presupposes the existence of smaller constituents

1 In the transcription of Arabic and Persian words I follow the instructions of the editor. This means that the terms shared by Arabic and Persian traditions appear in two differing transcriptions depending on the context where they appear (e.g. Arabic *mufrad* vs Persian *mofrad*). I must add, however, that the suggested Persian transcription (DMG-Umschrift) of the vowel system (a, e, o, ā, (ō), ū, (ē), ī) is a mixture of the Classical and Modern Persian phonological systems. Classical Persian is supposed to have preserved the quantity opposition of the short and long vowels (a, i, u, ā, (ō), ū, (ē), ī) consequently, the two-vowel-sequences, traditionally called diphthongs, are (ay, aw), but in Modern Persian the opposition is based on quality (a, e, o, â, i, u and ey, ow).

2 For instance, al-Fārābī treated *tarkīb* as a general term of logic for "classification" in his *Alfāẓ*, and as a specific term referring to various types of compounded constructions such as phrases and (declarative) sentences *(alfāẓ murakkaba)*, vs simple expressions *(alfāẓ mufrada* in *Fuṣūl*, cf. Jeremiás 2003, p. 54, note 17).

of compounded items. And it is the *ḥarf* "letter" at word level which always designates a consonant in the Semitic system of writing. This basic term permeated the whole edifice of Arabic grammar, especially morphology and lexicography, by identifying the so-called "meaningful letters" *(ḥurūf al-maʿānī)* used in various functions. In the indigenous Persian literature, where both theoretical and didactic grammatical literature as *ars* were completely missing in the first centuries of the Muslim period, the *ḥarf* played a central role.[3] It may have functioned as a kind of basic principle—together with other principles of Arabic grammar such as the parts of speech (*esm, feʿl* and *ḥarf*) or the concept of the word consisting of a base *(aṣl)* and a suffixed element *(zāʾed)*. In the sources I have scrutinized so far, where ideas about linguistic thinking or analyses occur, the systematic employment of the *ḥarf* helped elicit and formalise rules of theory and practice (*ʿelm* and *ʿamal*) at all levels of grammatical analysis, by means of which certain specific characteristics of Persian could be spelled out.[4] This is why in the non-formalised grammatical system of Persian this term might be regarded as a basic principle, not merely as a tool of description. This fundamental role of the *ḥarf* is revealed in the phenomenon called *tarkīb*; therefore, in the following study I will examine some theoretical and practical issues arising from this term, in an effort to interpret the Persian case.

What was said above concerns primarily morphologically "compounded" *(morakkab)* words, that is, inflected and derived verbs and nouns; but constructions at a higher level, such as verbal and nominal phrases or simple declarative sentences, are also included. Moreover, in Persian, a huge amount of real *composita* of the Indo-European type occur which are equally regarded as *morakkab* entities which—when exposed to analysis—have no similar instances in Arabic. These true compounds are treated together with derived words and phrases in this indigenous literature, even though they are dissimilar in nature and quality: the true compounds are words consisting of two equally independent constituents, although the relations between these constituents and their degree of independency vary.

3 Jeremiás 2016, pp. 62–64.

4 On the *ḥarf* as organizing principle see Jeremiás 2000, p. 330; id. 2012a, pp. 97–103: cf. the rules of more general scope such as "the two-letter rule" *(qāʿede-ye do-ḥarfī)* regarded as the minimal word-rule or, the rule of the sequence of two *sāken* letters in caesura or pause (*kalemāt-e mosakkenat al-avāḫer*, see Šams-e Qeys [1338/1959], p. 209); see also the restrictions of these "rules" by poetical necessity *(żarūrat-e šeʿr)*, rhetorical devices (*ḥosn-e kalām* "embellishment") or by the social standards of common usage *(kas̱rat-e esteʿmāl)*, cf. Jeremiás 2012a, p. 100.

2. Šams-e Qeys' poetical manual

Historically, the problem of analysing *tarkīb* appeared first in the early 13th century poetical manual of Šams-e Qeys, who used this term with linguistic and non-linguistic references.[5] The final chapter of his manual shows how important he considered this phenomenon. Here he enumerated all the necessary requirements for making verse:

> A poem has tools *(adavāt)* and versification has prerequisites *(moqaddamāt)*, without which no one will be ornamented with the title of poet and no poem will be rightly regarded as good.

Then, he described the process of verse-making, listing the fields of linguistic knowledge a poet must acquire. He says—among other things—that

> the poet must be well acquainted with the details of vocabulary of the language in which he is to make a verse, and he must also learn the differences between its proper and improper compounds *(tarkībāt-e ṣaḥīḥ va fāsed)*.[6]

Šams laid special emphasis on the treatment of compounds in his rhyme section *(ʿelm-e qāfiye)*. Here his aim was to clarify whether certain verse-final sequences could create matching rhymes or not. This was a complicated matter in Persian, because grammatically the verse-final parts and the rules of rhyme-science which prescribed proper rhyme-making, differed fundamentally from those of Arabic. As is well-known, rhyme in Persian means that the core of the rhyme section, that is, the *ravī* (the last letter of the base form) and the letters preceding it must have the same spelling, but their meaning must be different.[7] "Meaning", however, was not a purely grammatical or semantic matter, when the verse-final segment was a compounded word, that is a *tarkīb*.[8] In general, the employment of the term *tarkīb* had to meet certain general conditions: on word level it was necessary to indentify the base form *(aṣl)*, that is, a word with "full meaning" (in

5 Šams used it as a prosodic term *tarkīb-e arkān-e ʿarūżī* or *tarkīb-e owzānī* ([1338/1959], p. 43) or, occasionally as a term of rhetoric which might have referred to the figure *tağnīs* as in the case *tağnīs-e morakkab* in the rhyme-pair *āftāb / āfat-e āb* ([1338/1959], p. 340), cf. Jeremiás 2003, p. 54; Dehḫodā uses this term with the meaning "compounded verb" or "phrasal verb" constructed with the verbs such as *gereftan, dādan, kardan* (1377/1998, vol. 5, p. 6663).

6 *šeʿr-ra adavatī-st va šāʿerī-rā moqaddamātī ke bī-ān hīč kas-rā laqab-e šāʿerī na-zībad va bar hīč šeʿr nām-e nīk dorost na-yāyad … ammā moqaddamāt-e šāʿerī ān ast ke mard bar mofradāt-e loghatī ke bar ān šeʿr ḫʷāhad goft voqūf yābad va aqsām-e tarkībāt-e ṣaḥīḥ va fāsed-e ān-rā mostaḥżar šavad* ([1338/1959], p. 445). There are other requirements as well, but here our concern is the compound. Clinton's translation lays more emphasis on aesthetic considerations than on exact equivalents of linguistic terms (1989, p. 103).

7 In rhyme sequence, the section that occasionally follows the *ravī* (the suffix-like *zāʾed* elements or the *radīf* or both) have the same meaning.

8 Further details see in Jeremiás 1999, pp. 22–23.

Arabic *kalimat tāmm al-maʿnā*), and the attached element *(zāʾed)*, with a clearly definable meaning *(maʿnā va ʿellat-e elḥāq)*, that is, the *ḥorūf-e aṣlī* and *ḥorūf-e zāʾed* or, in other terms, the *aṣlī* and *vaṣlī* letters.[9] Consequently rhymes, if they were compounded words, had to be analysable or "transparent" constructions, that is, *mašhūr al-tarkīb*[10] or, as Šams summarized the issue: the compounds had to be transparent lexically and functionally. This "transparency-principle" seems to be a special Persian phenomenon which helped analyse compounded words of various kinds, such as finite verbal forms consisting of verbal stem and personal suffix (*goft-am* "I spoke", *gūy-ad* "he/she says"[11]), plural nouns (*asb-hā* "horses"), verbal nouns (*goft-ār* "speech") or verbal forms with prefixes (*be-*, *na-*, *ma-*). True compounds (e.g. *māh-tāb* "moon-light") had also to comply with this condition. In this case the properness of rhyme was judged according to the meanings of the two constituents of the compounds which had to consist of independent, meaningful lexical units, that is, words of nominal character in most cases.[12]

In Šams' manual there are two passages where compounds were treated. First, in a separate chapter all derivational and inflectional suffixes (*zāʾeds*) were listed according to their last letter which itself could be *mofrad* "simple" or *morakkab* "compounded". This helped to clarify whether the verse-final sequence was a clearly analysable, transparent compound consisting of a base word and a suffix-like element. But there were cases where transparency was defined in a different way: in these compounds—the true compounds—both constituents were independent words with their own lexical meanings. These sorts of rhyming pairs were discussed in an attached commentary inserted after each letter in the section on *ravī*.[13] For example, such a commentary can be found under the letter *b*, where in the list of examples the part shared by true compounds is the component in second position, the noun *āb* "water" (p. 214). According to Šams' analysis there are two groups: one of them is able to rhyme

9 Šams-e Qeys defines clearly the difference between these two sorts of letters when he discusses the letter *hāʾ*: *hāʾ-e aṣlī ān ast ke kaleme bī-ān maʿnā-e ḫwīš na-dehad* (note 8 on the page 242: *be-dehad?*) *va vaṣlī ān ast ke kaleme-rā dar aṣl-e maʿnā bedān eḥteyāğ na-bāšad*. ([1338/1959], p. 242). There was, however, much debate on the matter of whether certain word-final or word-initial letters were to be regarded as *aṣlī* or *vaṣlī*. See Šams-e Qeys or the author of the *Farhang-e Ğahāngīrī* (1359/1980, I, pp. 38–40).

10 See Šams-e Qeys [1338/1959], p. 205; Jeremiás 2003, p. 54.

11 This is the reason why Šams says that the verbs in the third person singular of the simple past are simple words, but the present/future forms are compounds (*ṣiyagh-e māżī kalemāt-e mofrade-and va ṣiyagh-e mostaqbal morakkab-and* ([1338/1959], p. 221). The author of the *Borhān-e qāṭeʿ* did not understand the rationale and said that "the sign of the simple past at the end of the words are the letters *tā* and *dāl*" (*ʿalāmat-e māżī-ye mofrad tāʾ-e qarašat va dāl-e abğad bāšad ke dar āḫer-e kalemāt āyad*), cf.1341/1962, p. 22.

12 In this native tradition the concept of the stem is missing. The constituents of the old-style compounds might have been stems, the phonological shapes of which were identical with existing lexical items, that is, they were words. See note 37.

13 In rhyme-science this term designates the last letter of the base word (without extension).

with *āb* (*kūd-āb*[14] "date-water, syrup of dates", *dūl-āb* "wheel-water", *sīm-āb* "silver-water, quicksilver, mercury", *sapīd-āb* "white-water, lead", *gol-āb* "rose-water"), while the other is not (*šūr-āb* "salt-water", *tīz-āb* "sharp-water, aqua-fortis", *panīr-āb* "cheese-water, whey from new cheese", *sar-āb* "head-water, fountain-head, mirage",[15] *bon-āb* "bottom-water", *zeh-āb* "running-water", *seyl-āb* "flowing-water, flood", *ḫūn-āb* "blood-water, bloody water", *zard-āb* "safflower-water, bile"). In this commentary there is no discussion of why these words were grouped in the way they were, except in a few cases. For instance, Šams says (p. 215) that there is a controversy about the properness of the rhyme-pair *āb* and *gol-āb* "rose-water", which is regarded as a proper rhyme pair by the "modernists",[16] because although the two rhyming segments (*āb* and the second constituent of the compound *gol-āb)* have the same meaning, and therefore would not normally be judged a proper rhyming pair, nevertheless the meaning of the compound is literally "rose-water", that is, it is not water, materially. Consequently, the "meanings" of the two words are not to be considered identical, if their references are not the same. A similar reasoning must have made the words *pāy* "foot" and *čahār-pāy* "having four feet, quadruped"[17] an acceptable rhyme, otherwise, on the basis of the two principles they would not make a proper rhyme-pair. There is another interesting example among the unfitting rhyme-pairs under the letter *b*: Šams says that *tāb* and *bar-tāb* may rhyme, because the second member is not considered a transparent compound in his interpretation. This indicates that the preverbal *bar-* is conceived to be an indivisible unit with the verb *tāb* (p. 215). In another example of matching rhymes, there is a new argument: the words *āftāb* and *māh-tāb* may rhyme, because *māh-tāb* "moonlight" is a transparent compound with the meaning *tāb-e māh* "the light of the moon", while *āftāb* is not, because its first part *(āf-)* has no independent meaning in itself (p. 215). A similar, but even more sophisticated explanation is given in the following text:

> Some poets allow the words *rūz* "day" and *now-rūz* to rhyme, because *nowrūz* "Nowruz" is the name of a special day [and its meaning is not *rūz-e now* "new day"].[18]

There is yet another type of argument: the words *ko-ǧā* "where" and *ān-ǧā* "there" may also rhyme, even though they share the same second constituent *ǧā* "place", but the two compounds belong to different word classes: one is a

14 Cf. Dehḫodā 1377/1998, vol. 12, p. 18687.
15 According to Dehḫodā *sar-āb* is a synonym of *kūr-āb* (vol. 12, p. 18693).
16 Called *mota'aḫḫerān* by Šams; the quotation is by Anvarī ([1338/1959], p. 215).
17 As a compound, however, *čahār-pāy* "four-foot, having four feet, quadruped" is an exception in comparison to the previous compounds; it represents the classical *bahuvrīhi* or attributive Compositum (cf. Horn 1898–1901, p. 198) or "possessive adjectival compound" (Skjaervo 2009a, p. 168); cf. also "les composés « possessifs » (généralement adjectives)" (Lazard 2006, p. 268).
18 Cf. ([1338/1959], p. 225. The text in square brackets might be an interpolation.

question-word *(estefhām)* and the other is a demonstrative *(ešāre).*[19] Following the same argument, Šams considers the pairs *ān-ǧā* "there" and *īn-ǧā* "here" improper rhymes (p. 214).

Šams mentions several dubious cases, where ancient and younger poets passed different judgements. The reason for this was not only that the youngsters were more casual about rhyme-prescriptions. The examples quoted above demonstrate that there was no fixed norm for analysing compounds that fits into a broader framework of linguistic norms. This is why right at the beginning of the section on rhyme, Šams elucidated an important point saying that "there is no exact norm in the rules of Darī on the basis of which correct or corrupt usage *(ṣaḥīḥ va fāsed)* could be defined".[20]

Obviously, Šams' aim was to find matching rhyme-pairs and to define criteria by which they may or may not create such pairs. But his grouping seems to have been made randomly, based on heterogeneous criteria. Nevertheless, despite the lack of a consistent system, a certain degree of logical thinking might be assumed based on various branches of sciences such as grammar, logic or rhetoric, as terminology testifies.

In the above list, the compounds represent a clearly defined group: they consist of two nominal constituents, where the second member is always a noun which dominates the first, while the first can be a noun, an adjective or a numeral, and the compounds so produced are all nouns except one.[21] The meanings of the compounds are accounted for in various ways, for instance, based on reference *(gol-āb, čahār-pāy)* or on word class-membership *(ān-ǧā – ko-ǧā)*. Incidentally, however, Šams hinted at the structural disparity of his examples, pointing out that the compound *māh-tāb* is the equivalent of the possessive *eżāfe*-construction *tāb-e māh*, whereas *nowrūz* cannot be converted into such an equal structure. Obviously, these two examples represent different types of compound with differing inner relations. The examples which share the word *āb* may have either noun or adjective as a first member and all of these are of a determinative type.[22] The compounds consisting of an adjective and a noun are clearly analysable (*sapīd-āb* "white water", *tīz-āb* "quick water", *zard-āb* "yellow water"), but the compounds where both first and second members are nouns may belong to different types, and the relations between the two constituents may vary. The most transparent compounds are those which can be converted into a possessive

19 Here Šams' argumentation is not correct: *koǧā* cannot be regarded as a transparent compound, because the first part consists of one letter *k* and therefore it cannot constitute a word (cf. note 4).

20 *qavānīn-e loghat-e darī-rā meqyāsī dorost nīst ke maʿrefat-e ṣaḥīḥ va fāsed-e ān az ū ṭalaband va dar šarḥ-e ḫaṭā va ṣavāb-e kalām-e pārsī aṣlī moʿtamad elayh na ke be vaqt-e ḥāǧat bedān morāǧaʿat konand* ([1338/1959], p. 205; cf. Jeremiás 1999, p. 21, note 3; id. 2012a, p. 95, note 39).

21 See note 17.

22 Cf. Lazard 2006, §245.

eżāfe-construction (see *panīr-āb* → *āb-e panīr*, also the words *kūd-āb*, *bon-āb*, *zeh-āb*). Šams' examples, however, do not represent all the possible kinds of compound which occur in Classical Persian literary sources: they are simply the types which were exposed to analysis by this early author.

3. Ottoman commentary literature: Moḥammad Sūdī (d. 1000/1591)

This kind of linguistic analysis did not change much in subsequent centuries. Grammar-like short descriptions of Persian and lexicography both follow this traditional approach in most cases. Without detailing all the possible sources where one can find traces of compound analysis, I would like to quote some examples from the Ottoman commentaries on Classical Persian literary works. The most famous representative of this genre was without doubt "the Ottoman Persianist",[23] the Bosnian Moḥammad Sūdī. From among his commentaries on Persian Classical poetry,[24] some relevant data will be quoted that deal with compounds. The terminology that he uses in his comments suggests that he may have been well-versed in a Classical Arabic background.[25] But a knowledge of Arabic grammar and earlier Persian lexicography was not enough to treat this subject. The first point to be noted is that his commentaries, although the majority are of a philological nature, differ from one another in varying degrees in their linguistic relevance. In his Ḥāfeẓ commentary, for example, the explanations deal with textual problems, while his Saʿdī commentaries are mostly of a philological-linguistic nature. These latter commentaries, however, differ from one another in their aim: the *Golestān* contains more data on Persian clause and phrase syntax when explaining the prosaic parts, while the *Būstān* deals more fully with compounds.[26]

In his grammatical comments Sūdī applies two terms to designate true compounds: *tarkīb-e vaṣfī* "descriptive compound" and *vaṣf-e tarkībī* "compounded description". Obviously, the first specifies the compound as a descriptive entity, while the other specifies the manner of the description *(vaṣf)* made by a compound element. It is difficult to judge whether Sūdī employs these terms consciously or not. There is, however, one passage in which he seems to make a distinction between a true compound *(vaṣf-e tarkībī)* and a syntactic nominal phrase *(tarkīb-e towṣīfī)*, when commenting on the compounded word

23 Algar 2003.

24 He wrote commentaries on Ḥāfeẓ's ghazals and Saʿdī's *Būstān* and *Golestān*. Here I quote those commentaries which were published in Persian translation in Iran (cf. Bibliography *Gol*, *Bū*, *Ḥāfeẓ*).

25 Supposedly he translated Ibn al-Ḥāǧib's *Kāfiya* into Turkish.

26 The texts used for the following comments are: *Bū* pp. 1–155, *Gol* pp. 1–350, *Ḥāfeẓ* pp. 1–79.

nīkū-nām.[27] But the meanings of the terms *tarkīb-e vaṣfī* and *vaṣf-e tarkībī* appear to be the same, even though the first term occurs more often in the *Būstān* while the *Golestān* prefers the second. It seems that the choice between these terms might have been made randomly, under the impression of the moment.

According to my classification, the true compounds regarded by Sūdī as *tarkīb* belong to various types. A large group consists of the constituents ADJ + N,[28] which create either a noun (ADJ + N → N) or an adjective (ADJ + N → ADJ). Sūdī himself occasionally indicates this disparity by giving the equivalent structure or periphrasis of the compound under discussion, for instance, *nīk-mard* is unfolded as an attributive phrase *mard-e nīk*.[29] Obviously, *nīk-mard* is a traditional determinative type made by juxtaposition of the two constituents (put in "inverse order"—as Sūdī says) creating a noun. However, the other type of compounds having the same constituent structure (ADJ + N) and also called *tarkīb-e vaṣfī* or *vaṣf-e tarkībī*, differs essentially from the first type in that the two constituents create an adjective, for instance, *nekū-nām* "of good reputation",[30] whose meaning is further extended to designate someone who has good reputation. Sūdī must have been aware of this difference, as his comment testifies. This type represents the possessive or the ancient *bahuvrīhi* compound (see note 17). There are many such compounds, some with further extension (ADJ + N → ADJ → N) and some without further extension. For instance, *nīk-baḫt-ān* "of good disposition" → "persons having good disposition" (*Gol* 77), *nīk-baḫt-ī* "having a good luck" → "fortune" (*Gol* 228), *nīk-ḫāh* "of good-will" (*Gol* 326[31]), *nīk-farǧām* "of happy end" (*Gol* 329), *nīk-maḥżar* "of

27 See *vaṣf-e tarkībī ast, tarkīb-e towṣīfī nīst* (*Gol* 101). That is, *nīkū-nām* is a compound meaning "a person having good reputation", but the other is the equivalent to the adjectival phrase *nām-e nīk(ū)* "good reputation".

28 I use the following abbreviations: ADJ = adjective, N = noun, PRO = pronoun, V_{stem} = verbal stem, PP = past (passive) participle, $V_{presstem}$ = present stem, $V_{prespart}$= present participle.

29 *dar aṣl mard-e nīk bovad, qalb karde tarkīb-e mazǧī namūde-and* "its underlying structure is *mard-e nīk*, but it was converted into a "condensed (?) compound" (*Bū* 33)". The expression *tarkīb-e mazǧī* seems to be a casual label whose reference seems to be similar to *tarkīb-e towṣīfī*. The latter, however, is referred to as a possessive *eżāfe*-construction, for instance, in the phrase *došman-e zūr-āvar* "violence-doing enemy" *zūr-āvar* is called *vaṣf-e tarkībī*, and the whole phrase is conceived as *tarkīb-e towṣīfī* (*Gol* 179). Similarly, the phrase *asb-e lāgher-miyān* "slender-waisted horse" is called *towṣīf-e tarkībī* and the adjective *lāgher-miyān* "slender-waisted" is considered *vaṣf-e tarkībī* (*Gol* 141).

30 *tarkīb-e vaṣfī ast be maʿnā dārande-ye nām-e nīk* "it is a descriptive compound which means having a good name" (*Bū* 114); cf. also *nīk-nām-ī: "nīk-nām" yaʿnī kasī ke dārā-ye nām-e ḫūb ast; īn az aqsām-e tarkīb-e vaṣfī ast va yāʾ ḥarf-e maṣdar ast* "the person is called *nīk-nām* who has a good name and it is one of the descriptive compounds and the *yāʾ* is the letter [sign] of the *maṣdar*" (*Ḥāfeẓ* I: 46).

31 *nīk-ḫʷāh-ān-rā: "nīk-ḫʷāh" vaṣf-e tarkībī va morād-e "nīk ḫʷāhande" ast be maʿnā dūst va alef va nūn adāt-e ǧamʿ va rā adāt-e mafʿūl* "the word *nīk-ḫʷāh* is a compounded description intending to mean a person of good-will and signifies a friend and the letters *alef* and *nūn* are the plural sign and *rā* is the sign of the object" (*Gol* 326).

good nature" (*Gol* 51[32]), *pārsī-gū* "Persian-speaker",[33] etc. Here again, Sūdī describes the transformation clearly.

Sūdī also comments on the so-called "inverted" *bahuvrīhi* compounds: both *del-tang* (*Gol* 92) and *tan-āsān* (*Gol* 229) are described as *vaṣf-e tarkībī*, that is, he does not make any distinction between the two types of compound which were clearly distinguished by Telegdi.[34]

There are rare occurrences of another type, where the first constituent is a pronoun (PRO + N → ADJ), such as *ḫʷod-kām* "self-willed" which is explained by means of a paraphrase.[35] It is interesting to note that in this type of compound the first constituent is a Persian word in most cases. However, there are a few examples which were not analysed properly by Sūdī in the texts I have investigated.[36]

The compounds with the same first constituent (*nīk-mard* and *nīk-nām*), however, recall another observation: the semantic value of the second constituent (*-mard* or *-nām*) defines the species of the compound (determinative or possessive) and also the status of the part of speech of the compound, even though they have the same surface structure. That is, as compounds they behave differently. This difference, however, is disguised by their structural homonymity (ADJ + N), but becomes manifest in their syntactic behaviour.

The second large group of determinative compounds consists of the constituents $N + V_{presstem}/V_{prespart}$, where N is the complement of the verb which is expressed in stem or participial forms.[37] This compounding creates either an

32 *vaṣf-e tarkībī be maʿnā dārande-ye ḫūy-e nīk* "a descriptive compound with the meaning [the person] having a good nature" (*Gol* 51).

33 *tarkīb-e vaṣfī ast yaʿnī kasī ke fārsī mī-gūyad dar aṣl gūyande-ye pārsī būde* "it is a descriptive compound which means [the person] who speaks Persian and its underlying structure is the speaker of the Persian language" (*Ḥāfeẓ* I: 50). The interpretation by which compounds are unfolded is called *taqdīr* in Arabic grammar and Sūdī also knows this term, cf. Jeremiás (forthcoming).

34 Cf. Telegdi on structural homonimity (1962, 1964, 1970); he argues for the structural disparity of the compounds *tang.del* "ein bedrücktes Herz zu haben": ADJ + NOUN → ADJ (compound) and *del.tang* (1962, p. 327 = 2006, I, p. 326), the true character of which was dismissed by Lazard (1957, p. 276; id. 2006, p. 271) and also by Windfuhr/Perry 2009, p. 528.

35 *ḫʷod-kām-ī az aqsām-e tarkīb-e vaṣfī aṣt va ḫʷod-kām kasī rā gūyand ke hame-ye kārhā-ra be moqtażā-ye meyl …angām dehad* "Self-willing is a sort of *tarkīb-e vaṣfī* and the person is called *ḫʷod-kām* who behaves according to his own wish" (*Ḥāfeẓ* I: 13).

36 For instance, the *bahuvrīhi* compounds *boland-aḫtar* "high-starred" is glossed as *dar aṣl aḫtar-e bolandt bā eżāfe* "high star" (*Bū* 120) or, *ṣalāḥ-kār* "of pious behaviour" is glossed as *ʿamal-e ṣāleḥ va nīk* "pious and good behaviour" (*Ḥāfeẓ* I: 18). Haïm gives the synonym *nīkū-kār* "a righteous person". Similarly, Sūdī does not consider *šīrīn-kār* "of agreeable manner" a *tarkīb-e vaṣfī* arguing against the opinion of other commentators (*Ḥāfeẓ* I: 26).

37 See this type in Middle Iranian in Skjaervo (2009b, p. 263) who interprets them as compounds of noun + verbal noun, e.g. *gyān-abespār* "surrounding one's life" or noun/adj + PP, e.g. *yazd-āfarīd* "God created". He also adds that the compounds consisting of more than two constituents are "not of an inherited type" (2009a, p. 168).

adjective (ADJ + N→ ADJ) or a noun (ADJ + N→ N), in a similar way to the previous compound type, but the reason for changing the status of the parts of speech in the compound is different. When Sūdī tries to explicate this compound, that is, to transform it into its equivalent underlying structure, he says that *ʿeyb-ǧūy* "fault-seeking" is *ʿeyb-ǧūyande* (*Bū* 94), but *pūzeš-pazīr* "excuse-accepting" is *pazīrande-ye pūzeš*[38] or *dast-gīr* "hand-taking" *gīrande-ye dast.*[39] In the first case, Sūdī interprets the present stem form *(ǧūy)* as an equivalent of the present participle, but in the latter two cases he went further, saying that the underlying structures of these compounds *(dar aṣl* or *dar taqdīr)*[40] are possessive *eżāfe*-constructions, in which the present participles have to be conceived as nouns. The interpretation of this N, however, differs somewhat from the N which appeared in the *bahuvrīhi* constructions: in Arabic and Persian indigenous grammatical literature both present and past participles, and also the infinitive or verbal noun are considered nouns *(esm-e fāʿel, esm-e mafʿūl* or *maṣdar)* and consequently, they may figure as the first member of the *eżāfe*-construction. The difference, however, is not a matter of theory, but of terminology: in the explication of these compounds, Sūdī skips the transformation ADJ → N interpreting the participle (and also the infinitive) as a noun.[41] This type is one of the most commonly used compounds in Persian poetry which occurs rarely with an Arabic word as a first constituent.[42]

The group of compounds with the past participle as the second constituent (N/ADJ/ADV + $V_{pastpart}$), however, seems to be of unclear character in most cases. Interestingly, Sūdī regards only some of them as *tarkīb.* The examples *vāqeʿe-dīde* "accident/misfortune + seen/experienced" with its synonym *kār-dīde* "work-experienced" or, *ǧang-āzmūde* "war-experienced" with its synonym *ǧang-dīde* (*Gol* 149) are not considered *tarkīb.* There is only one exception in the texts I

38 *tarkīb-e vaṣfī ast; pūzeš esm-e maṣdar ast az pūzīdan be maʿnā ʿoẕr; pazīr esm ast az pazīrīdan , dar aṣl pazīrande-ye pūzeš bovad* (*Bū* 4).

39 *gīr dar aṣl gīrande bovad, dar taqdīr gīrande-ye dast, az qabīl-e eżāfe-ye esm-e fāʿel be mafʿūl-aš* (*Bū* 3–4).

40 This term refers to the reconstruction of the underlying sentence of compounds, the term for which was first *aṣl* "principle, origin", but later its common label became *taqdīr* (cf. Versteegh 1997, p. 50; Bohas etc. 1990, pp. 62–63). The terms *taqdīr* and *aṣl* are interpreted slightly differently by Baalbaki 2008, p. 108. Sūdī seems to have used both terms to refer to the underlying sentence of a compound, or simply, to a compounded verb where the copula is missing, see his comment on *sāḫte: qesmatī az feʿl-e māżī-ye mofrad-e ġāʾeb va taqdīr-aš sāḫte būdand ast "sāḫte* is abbreviated from the Past Singular third person verbal form and its underlying structure is *sāḫte būdand*" (*Gol* 145). Cf. Jeremiás (forthcoming).

41 The status of these participles and infinitives caused Lumsden many head-aches when he was dealing with the problems of the parts of speech in indigenous systems (Jeremiás 2012b, p. 135). The *Loghatnāme*, however, uses the term *naʿt* or *ṣefat* to designate these participles, see ن مف in the list of abbreviations (Dehḫodā 1377/1998, vol. 1, p. [2]).

42 Cf. *ǧahān-āfarīn* "world-creator" (*Bū* 120, *Gol* 100, etc.) vs *ḥaqīqat-šenās* "truth-knowing" (*Bū* 144).

analysed: *setam-dīde* "oppression-experienced" with its synonyms *ẓolm-dīde* or *maẓlūm* "injured" is labeled as *tarkīb* (*Gol* 272). Disregarding Sūdī's uncertain opinion, these examples might be conceived as inflected participial forms made of verbal phrases or simple verbs, and not as true compounds, rather like to the examples *now-damīde* "newly sprung up" and *now-rasīde* "newly-arrived"[43] which are analysed by Sūdī as inflected verbs preceded by an adverb (*Gol* 151), where the copula *ast* must be implied. It is also to be noted that the past participle occurring in the compounds made from *dīde* "seen, experienced" seems to have lost its passive meaning, while in the compound *mār-gazīde* "snake-bitten" it has retained its passive sense. This rare determinative type is interpreted as "the snake-bitten person" (*Gol* 235),[44] but the example *keštī-nešaste-gān* "(who are) sitting on shipboard" is not commented on by Sūdī.[45]

4. Post-classical Indian lexicography

The well-known Indian *Farhang-e Ǧahāngīrī* written by Mīr Ǧamāl al-dīn Ḥoseyn Īnǧū (completed in 1608) contains a large amount of lexica used in literary language, that is, in the *fors-i qadīm* "ancient Persian" as the author called it.[46] From the 17th century onwards, however, chapters on various problems of the language were prefixed to this kind of genre. These introductory chapters dealt with valuable issues of linguistic relevance including orthography, morphology or a skeleton-like syntax, even though their treatment was carried out in a non-grammatical way in most cases. In these analyses the technical term *tarkīb* also appeared referring to compounded items in general, but the main term for this specific issue was the *ḥarf* ('letter'): its various functions in the semantic-morphological structure of the word, both in its archaic or modern shapes. True compounds, however, occur only sparsely in the lexicographic section, and the author never indicated or even hinted at their compounded character. The only way he described them in his huge œuvre was by a reference to their *ḥarf* character.[47]

43 *now*: *be fatḥ-e nūn be maʿnā ǧadīd* "the letter *nūn* has a *fatḥ* with the meaning fresh"; *rasīde: qesmatī az māżī-ye mofrad-e ġāʾeb lafẓ-e būd moqaddar ast* "the word *rasīde* is abbreviated from the Past Singular third person and its underlying structure (*moqaddar*) is *rasīde būd*" (*Gol* 151). Cf. *taqdīr* in note 40.

44 *vaṣf-e tarkībī va taqdīr-aš mardom-e mār-gazīde* Cf. LAZARD 2006, p. 269.

45 Sūdī did not make any grammatical comment, but misunderstood the phrase: *keštī-šān dar daryā nešaste yaʿnī ḥarakat namī-konad* "their ship has foundered and does not move" (*Ḥāfeẓ* I: 41). The *Loghatnāme* recognises both *keštī-nešaste* and *keštī-nešīn* (vol. 12, p. 18361), but the first might be a misspelling of *keštī-šekaste*.

46 See JEREMIÁS 2012a, pp. 94–103.

47 This was my general impression while using this dictionary, but I could not judge all the lexical items. See the indication of the *maǧhūl* and *maʿrūf* vowels in the body of lexicographic items.

5. Īravānī's "Persian rules" (1846)

Īnǧū's work, especially his "grammatical" chapters, seems to have been the most important source of the so-called "oldest" grammar of Persian[48] written by Īravānī in the mid-19th century. The question arises, however, whether this work represented a new genre, the so-called first grammar of Persian or, as I think, it was the last representative of the old indigenous tradition, even though there were traces in it of real grammatical thinking. The treatment of true compounds of the Indo-European type might be regarded as one of the author's novelties. This issue was not a completely new topic, as we have seen, but post-classical lexicography seems to have paid no attention to it. In Īravānī's grammar, however, the last short chapter[49] deals with this subject.

Īravānī starts this last chapter with the general statement that *vaṣf-e tarkībī* is a widely used type of compound and because of its importance a special chapter is dedicated to it.[50] He describes the compounded entities as follows: Persians combine two words *(lafẓ)*, the meaning[51] of which is considered to be derivate *(moštaqq)*; the compounds so produced can be *esm-e fāʿel*, *esm-e mafʿūl*, *ṣefat-e mošabbahe*[52] and *esm-e mansūb*, that is, present or past participles and derived (or secondary) adjectives (used occasionally as nouns),[53] and also derived nouns. Then, he tries to give a classification of the types of compound, dividing them into two main groups in terms of *taḫfīf* "lightening",[54] *taqdīr*,[55] *ḥaẕf* "deletion, omission"[56] and *taqdīm* "anteposition, fronting"[57].

The compounds of the first group are produced purely and simply for the sake of "lightening" called *taḫfīf*, such as *golāb* "rose-water", the underlying structure (*dar aṣl*) of which is *āb-e gol* "the water of rose". These compounds are created by the operation of "fronting" (*taqdīm*) of the *mużāf ilayh*[58] producing a sort of "lightened" [more easily pronounced] form *(nowʿ-e taḫfīfī)*. The items of the other group are also produced by *taḫfīf*, but they create new meaning [that

48 See Īraǧ Afšār's bibliography 1333/1954, p. 30.
49 Ch. XIV: *dar bayān-e vaṣf-e tarkībī* "On the explanation of the descriptive compound" (ff. 56r–57r). See Jeremiás 2012a, p. 112.
50 *vaṣf-e tarkībī dar tarākīb-e pārsī kaṯīr al-esteʿmāl ast* "The descriptive compound is the most frequently used type of compound" (f. 56r).
51 For the meaning of "meaning" see note 59.
52 Cf. Afšār 1388/2009, vol. 2, p. 1827; Carter 1981, p. 483: *ṣifa mušabbaha bi-l-fāʿil* "quasi-participial adjective".
53 The last two categories might be conceived as subcategories of the *esm* interpreted in terms of *tašbīh* "formal similarity" (cf. Bohas etc. 1990, pp. 51–53).
54 See "lightening" in terms of phonological processes (Bohas etc. 1990, pp. 91–93; Baalbaki 2008, p. 59; "phonetic ease" (Carter 1981, p. 484). See Jeremiás (forthcoming).
55 See note 40. In this passage both *taqdīr* and *aṣl* are used.
56 Cf. Bohas etc. 1990, pp. 62–63, 91–93; Baalbaki 2008, p. 31.
57 Versteegh 1997, p. 16; Baalbaki 2008, p. 284.
58 This is the first nominal member of the possessive *eżāfe*-construction.

is, a different part of speech] and this type is called *vaṣf-e tarkībī*.[59] This latter group may be divided into three subgroups:

a) The first group is created only by the operation called "deletion" *(ḥaẕf)*,[60] such as *ḫūn-āb* "bloody water"[61] the underlying structure *(dar aṣl)* of which is *ḫūn va āb* "blood and water"; in this case the letters *vāv* and *alef* are dropped and *ḫūn-āb*, a new part of speech *(esm-e mansūb)* is created. This latter may be supplied by the letter *hā-ye nesbat* "the letter of relation/correlation" producing a word like *ḫūn-ābe* "id." by means of secondary word-formation.
b) The second type is created by the operation of "fronting the element which should be the last" *(taqdīm mā ḥaqqahu al-ta'ḫīr)*, such as *soḫan-dān* "eloquence-knowing, eloquent", the underlying structure *(dar aṣl)* of which is *dān-e soḫan*. In this case the object *(maf'ūl)* of the imperative is fronted and the compound becomes an *esm-e fā'el*. The interpretation of *soḫan-dān* is twofold: one is the aforementioned, and the underlying structure *(taqdīr)* of the other is *dānande-ye soḫan*. In this case both *ḥaẕf* and *taqdīm* have operated. The *taḫfīf* and the fluency owing to the lack of *taqdīr* gives a priority to first case *(dān)* over the second[62] *(dānande)*, while the second interpretation is to be preferred due to its [formal] analogical proximity [to present participles]—as Īravānī says.
c) The third type is created by means of both *ḥaẕf* and *taqdīm*, such as *šaqāvat-pīše* "of cruel behaviour" which is transformed from the underlying structure *(dar aṣl) pīše konande-ye šaqāvat* and yields the meaning of a *ṣefat-e mošabbahe*, in the same way as the compounds *żalālat-andīše* "of deviation thinking/deviating thought", *siyāh-čašm* "black-eyed", and *tar-dāman* "of wet-rock, immortal, polluted"; and *vaṣf-e tarkībī* is also created when *mużāf* is fronted to *mużāf ilayh* and the *kasre-ye eżāfe* is omitted, such as *sa'ādat-ḫāne* "felicity-mansion" which is deduced from the underlying structure *(dar aṣl) ḫāne-ye sa'ādat* "mansion of felicity". Īravānī adds, however, that this latter compound-type which created the meaning *esm-e mansūb* by means of *taqdīm* occurs in words which are not regarded as *vaṣf-e tarkībī* but simply as a *taḫfīf*, a "lightened" form as in the case of *gol-āb* mentioned above.

59 This classification is rather ambiguous: I interpret the passage *fāyede-ye dīgar az ḥeysiyyat-e ma'nā maqṣūd mī-bāšad* (f. 56r) as referring to the part of speech, that is, the "meaning" of the word. Cf. the various interpretations of *ma'ānī*: "the meaning or function of a word, which is what the grammarians are concerned with" (Versteegh 1997, p. 59).

60 Cf. the deletion of elements "in their speech in order to be as concise as possible" (Versteegh 1997, p. 146); see Baalbaki 2008, p. 108.

61 See in Ferdowsī "Blut; Tränen" (Wolff 1965, p. 344).

62 This passage indicates that the terms *aṣl* and *taqdīr* might have different meanings.

6. Summary

The most striking feature of this classification is its heavy reliance on Arabic linguistic tradition which surpasses Sūdī's approach, whose commentaries were in most cases restricted to indicating simply the compound-like character of the words concerned. Even though Sūdī's compounds represented more numerous types than those listed by Īravānī, the difference between them was not a matter of quantity, but of quality. Occasionally, Sūdī also indicated the alleged underlying structures *(dar taqdīr* or *dar aṣl)* of compounds;[63] but Īravānī went further: he not only listed various types, but also tried to describe the process of how they became transformed into one-word-compounds derived from underlying structures. For that purpose he used Arabic technical terms selected from various fields of linguistic description. His most general term seems to be the *taḫfīf* "lightening", an uncommon term in Persian sources, on the basis of which the two main groups of his classification were specified. This term had been well-known since Sībavayhi's time referring to "phonetically tolerable or more syntactically economical" forms, as Baalbaki argues, but its adaptation to the process of creating compounds seems to be unique: it suggests that the author's focus was directed towards the *operation* itself which generated new meanings. Meaning, that is, the part of speech as I interpret this term, played an essential role in specifying the three subgroups which can be equated more or less with the copulative, determinative and possessive compounds of the European tradition. This does not mean, however, that compounding was carried out under the influence of that tradition; on the contrary, it was rooted deeply in Oriental teaching. This doctrine, however, failed to have been followed in earlier or later elaborations of Persian, therefore it must be regarded as Īravānī's own contribution. I think I am not mistaken if I consider this *taḫfīf* "lightening" term a special tool by which the compact and compound-like character of Persian poetical language may be grasped.

Bibliography

Afšār, Ī. 1954: "Ketābšenāsī-ye dastūr-e zabān-e fārsī." In: *Farhang-e Īrānzamīn* 2 (1333/1954), pp. 19–45.

Afšār, Ṣ. (ed.) 2009: *Farhangnāme-ye Fārsī.* 3 vols. Farhang-e Moʿāṣer, Tehran 1388/2009.

Algar, H. 2003: "Bosnia and Herzegovina". In: *Encyclopaedia Iranica*, http://www.iranicaonline.org/articles.

Baalbaki, R. 2008: *The Legacy of the Kitāb. Sībawayhi's Analytical Methods within the Context of the Arabic Grammatical Theory.* Leiden.

63 See notes 29–33, etc.

Bohas, G./J.-P. Guillaume/D.E. Kouloughli: *The Arabic Linguistic Tradition.* London/New York 1990.

Borhān-e Qāṭeʿ see Moḥammad Ḥoseyn ben Ḫalaf Tabrīzī.

Bū see Moḥammad Sūdī: *Šarḥ-e Sūdī bar Būstān-e Saʿdī.*

Carter, M.G. 1981: *Arab Linguistics: An introductory classical text with translation and notes.* Amsterdam.

Clinton, J.W. 1989: "Shams-i Qays on the Nature of Poetry." In: *Edebiyât* 1, pp. 101–127.

Dehḫodā, ʿA.A. 1998: *Loghatnāme.* Ed. by M. Mo'īn, Ǧ. Šahīdī. 16 vols. Tehran 1377/1998.

Farhang-e Ǧahāngīrī see Īnjū, Mīr Ǧamāl al-dīn Ḥoseyn.

Gol see Moḥammad Sūdī: *Šarḥ-e Sūdī bar Golestān-e Saʿdī.*

Ḥāfeẓ see Moḥammad Sūdī: *Šarḥ-e Sūdī bar Ḥāfeẓ.*

Haïm, S. 1985: *New Persian-English Dictionary.* 2 vols. Tehran.

Horn, P. 1898–1901: "Neupersische Schriftsprache." In: W. Geiger/E. Kuhn (eds.): *Grundriss der iranischen Philologie.* Vol. I, 2, IV. Straßburg, pp. 1–198.

Īnǧū, Mīr Ǧamāl al-dīn Ḥoseyn 1980: *Farhang-i Ǧahāngīrī.* Ed. by Raḥīm ʿAfīfī. 2 vols. 2nd ed. Mašhad 1359/1980.

Īravānī, ʿAbd al-Karīm [1846]: *Qavāʿed-e fārsiyya.* [Tabrīz], lithograph.

Jeremiás, É.M. 1999: "Grammar and linguistic consciousness in Persian." In: Ch. Melville (ed.): *Proceedings of the Third European Conference of Iranian Studies.* Part II. Wiesbaden, pp. 19–31.

— 2000: "Arabic influence on Persian linguistics." In: S. Auroux/E.F.K. Koerner/H. Niederehe/K. Versteegh (eds.): *History of the Language Sciences.* Vol. 1, IX. *The Establishment of Arabic Linguistics.* Ch. 57. Berlin, pp. 329–334.

— 2003: "The Formation of Early New Persian Poetry." In: L. Paul (ed.): *Persian Origins—Early Judaeo-Persian and the Emergence of New Persian.* Wiesbaden (Iranica 6), pp. 49–66.

— 2012a: " ʿAbd al-Karīm Īrawānī's 'Persian Rules'." In: É.M. Jeremiás (ed.): *At the Gate of Modernism.* Piliscsaba, pp. 85–116.

— 2012b: "*Matthew Lumsden's Persian Grammar (Calcutta, 1810), Part I.*" In: *IRAN, BIPS*, 50, pp. 129–140.

— 2016: "The history of grammatical ideas in Persian: *kitābatan–lafẓan* in Classical Persian sources." In J. Gomesh/C. Jahani/A. Lenepveu-Hotz (eds): *Further Topics in Iranian Linguistics. Proceedings of the 5th International Conference on Iranian Languages (ICIL5), held in Bamberg on 24–26 August 2013.* Paris (StIr Cahier 58), pp. 55–70.

— (forthcoming): "The technical terms *taqdīr* and *taḫfīf* in Persian Classical sources."

Lazard, G. 1957: *Grammaire du Persan contemporain.* Paris (new ed. Téhéran 2006).

Moḥammad Ḥoseyn ben Ḫalaf Tabrīzī 1962: *Borhān-e Qāṭeʿ.* Ed. by M. Moʿīn. 2nd ed., Amīr Kabīr, Tehran 1341/1962.

Moḥammad Sūdī 1970: *Šarḥ-e Sūdī bar Golestān-e Saʿdī.* Transl. Ḥ.Kh. Ṭīnat, Zeynolʿābedīn Čāvošī, ʿAlī Akbar Kāẓemī. Tabrīz (Tehran) 1349/1970.

— 1973: *Šarḥ-e Sūdī bar Būstān-e Saʿdī.* Transl. Akbar Behrūz. 2 vols. Tabrīz 1352/1973.

— 1999: *Šarḥ-e Sūdī bar Ḥāfeẓ*. Transl. ʿESMAT SETTĀRZĀDE. 4 vols. 5th ed. Tehran 1378/1999.

ŠAMS-E QEYS: *al-Muʿǧam fī maʿāyīr ašʿār al-ʿaǧam*. Ed. by M. QAZVĪNĪ/M. RAŻAVĪ. [Teheran 1338/1959].

SKJAERVO, P.O. 2009a: "Old Iranian." In: G. WINDFUHR (ed.): *The Iranian Languages*. London/New York, pp. 43–195.

— 2009b: "Middle West Iranian." In: G. WINDFUHR (ed.): *The Iranian Languages*. London/New York, pp. 196–278.

SŪDĪ see MOḤAMMAD SŪDĪ

TELEGDI, Zs. 1962: "Zur Unterscheidung von Substantiv und Adjektiv im Neupersischen." In: *Acta Orientalia Acad. Scient. Hung.* 15, pp. 325–336 (= *Opera omnia* I, pp. 324–335).

— 1964: "Über einen Fall von struktureller Homonymie im Persischen." In: *Acta Lingu. Acad. Scient. Hung.* 14, pp. 237–261 (= *Opera omnia* I, pp. 350–375).

— 1970: "La construction abrūi mūhoyaš daroz en tadjik." In: M. BOYCE/I. GERSHEVITCH (eds): *W.B. Henning Memorial Volume*. London, pp. 427–446 (= *Opera omnia* I, pp. 437–458).

— 2006: *Opera omnia*. Ed. by É.M. JEREMIÁS. 2 vols. Piliscsaba-Budapest.

VERSTEEGH, K. 1997: *The Arabic Linguistic Tradition*. London/New York (Landmarks in Linguistic thought 3).

WINDFUHR, G./J.R. PERRY 2009: "Persian and Tajik." In: G. WINDFUHR (ed.): *The Iranian Languages*. London/New York, pp. 416–544.

WOLFF, F. 1965: *Glossar zu Firdosis Schahname*. Hildesheim.

Aristotle's Theory of the Elements and Zoroastrian Dualism

Judith Josephson

1. Introduction

In this paper I would like to present a short text in Pahlavi in which logical reasoning is used to demonstrate the existence of two creative principles at work in the world.[1] In this text, essay § 119 of the third book of the Denkard (henceforth Dk III), the author uses Aristotle's theory of the elements in the process of generation and destruction as the basis for his argumentation that the Zoroastrian form of dualism provides a rational explanation of how evil arises in the world and who is responsible. Among the issues which were heatedly debated in the Hellenized Near East from the sixth to the tenth centuries we find two prominent ones, namely, the proof of creation and refutation of the eternity of the world and the question of responsibility for destruction and evil in a world created by a good creator. These problems were presented within a complex of related ideas in which philosophy was seen as an aid to revelation in elucidating the actual workings of creation. It provided theories concerning the finite quality of the world, the existence of a creator, the nature of the constituent parts of the cosmos, the role of the four elements and their properties, the processes of genesis and destruction, the relations between the creator, nature and man. This in turn led to questions about who is responsible for deviation and ensuing destruction in nature and evil in man.

If one postulates a creator and a beginning for the world then the relation of the creator to the further evolution and change among objects in the world is also important. This leads to the core question: when things go wrong as they often do, for example in nature with catastrophes in weather, predatory instinctual behavior of animals and in man voluntary evil-doing, who can be said to bear the final responsibility?

In essay § 119 of Dk III, the author has constructed a loosely syllogistic reasoning in which he speaks of the creator but never identifies him as Ohrmazd and suggests that there is also a second principle at work in the world which would explain harm, strife and evil and who corresponds to Ganāg Mēnōg but

1 Denkard MS B 749.18–747.7; Madan 114.6–115.20; essay nr. 119 in Sanjana. The text has been translated by de Menasce (1973, pp. 121–122).

who is never identified by name either. This is entirely in keeping with the rules of discussion between the representatives of the various religions in which appeal could only be made to reason, never to the sacred texts containing revelation.[2] In this spirit the author postulates a creative principle or even two. He affirms that the cosmos is made up of four elements which change from one to the other in a cycle of generation and destruction. In this process they generate the forms which constitute nature and man. However, also different or deviant forms in nature and in man are generated which tend toward evil and cause harm and destruction. He discusses the construction and purpose of the cosmos which was also generally believed to play a role in man's salvation.

In a series of arguments the Zoroastrian scholar postulates one creative principle for change and another which he calls a "giver of different forms" for destruction. He has construed his argument as follows: A. The elements can change from one to another to constitute new forms in the process of genesis and destruction. B. Genesis requires a creative principle while destruction suggests that there could be a giver of deviant forms. C. Constructive compounding leads to beneficial forms in nature and good men in society while destruction leads to deviancy in men and contrariety in nature. D. One maker cannot be responsible for both construction and destruction. E. Therefore there must be more than one maker. F. Additional proof is found in the organization of the cosmos which is perfectly suited to the plan of the maker.

The text is highly rhetorical in its composition and is designed to persuade and to please. As to the technical vocabulary it seems more simplified and general than the essays in Dk III which are more empirical in content.[3] The four elements *āb* 'water', *wād* 'air', *zamīg* 'earth' and *ātaxš* 'fire' are named in lines 3–6 and in line 15 are called *zahagān* which is the term usually used when speaking of the four of them together.[4] Their transformation from the *cihr* 'nature' of the one to the *cihr* 'nature' of the other suggests that here the term *cihr* refers to composites consisting of an element together with one of its properties, i.e. hot, cold, dry and wet. In line 9 we learn that when the *cihr* 'natures' of the elements work together they produce *dēsagān* 'forms'.[5] In the present context it can be suggested that the term *bawišn* means 'generation, becoming'.[6]

The verb *sāxtan/sāz* 'make, construct, prepare, tolerate' with further nuances of 'accommodate, bring into harmony' is used repeatedly and serves to weave

2 KRAEMER 1986, p. 59.

3 I. e. essay § 123. It is not clear whether the two texts were intended for different audiences or if § 119 was taken from a different source and included in Dk III.

4 BAILEY 1943, p. 89 notes that it translates Greek *stoikheion*.

5 BAILEY 1943: pp. 88, 91 notes that the Pahlavi equivalent of Greek *eidos* 'form' is sometimes *dēsag* as above or *cihr* 'visible form' but observes that the latter can also mean 'nature' as in the present text.

6 *bawišn* in this context does not appear to be part of the series *bawišn, bawišn-rawišnīh, bawišn-astišnīh* of essay § 123.

the central argument of the text together. We find the verbal nouns based on the simple present tense *sāz-*, in line 9 *āgenēn sāzišnīh* 'working together, cooperating' contrasted with the negated form of the verbal noun *asāzagīh* 'dysfunction, destruction'. Further in line 12 we find *abāg sāzēnāgīh* 'work in conjunction' and negated **asāzēnāgīh* 'disjunction, decomposition' in line 13. In line 18 *abāg sāxtārīh* 'cooperation, building together' is opposed to the term *wizūdārīh* 'harmfulness' while in line 22 *āhang-sāxtārīh* 'inclination to cooperate' is opposed to *asāxtārīh* 'lack of cooperation' in the same line while in line 24 we find *zyānōmand asāxtārīh* 'harmful dissociation' contrasted with *ān ī sūdōmand sāxtārīh* 'beneficial association' in line 25.

2. The text,[7] translation and a short commentary

abar paydāgīh ī dō bunīštagīh ōh-iz ī xīrān gēhān {w}dōīh bun
On the demonstration of the two principles indeed of the two foundations of the things of the world

az nigēz ī weh dēn
according to the teaching of the Good Religion

The text begins by stating the thesis that there are two creative principles underlying the things of the world and that this is evident from their ability to change into different natures.

1. *hād dō bunīštagīh ōh-iz ī xīrān gēhān*
2. *ī paydāg az-iz wihīrišnīgīh ī ī-šān ō jud-cihr abar*

1. Now there are indeed two principles for the things of the world
2. as is evident from their transformations into different natures.

In lines 3–6 the author enumerates the changes of the four elements water, air, earth and fire into one another in a cyclical series of movements. While he does not mention the properties hot and cold, humid and dry they are implied in the manner in which he has organized the changes. Thus water which is cold and moist can become air which is warm and moist in which cold has been replaced by warm or it can become earth which is cold and dry and it is the quality of moist which has given way to dry and so on in a cycle beginning with water and ending with water. The cycle of changes corresponds to Aristotle's theory of the elements as delineated in the *Physics*. In this set of changes only one quality at a time is replaced by an opposite in a cyclic process of genesis and destruction in

7 The signs < > indicate a word added to the text and ( ) a word added to the translation and { } a word deleted from the text.

which the coming into being of one element is the occasion of the destruction of the other.[8]

3. *āb ast ka ō cihr ī wād ud ast ka ō cihr ī zamīg wardēd*
4. *ud wād-iz ast ka ō cihr ī āb ast ka ō cihr ī ātaxš wardēd*
5. *ātaxš-iz ast ka ō cihr ī <wād>ast ka ō <cihr ī> zamīg wardēd*
6. *ud zamīg-iz ast ka ō cihr ī ātaxš ud ast ka ō cihr ī āb wardēd*

3. Sometimes water changes into the nature of air and sometimes into the nature of earth;
4. sometimes also air changes into the nature of water and sometimes into the nature of fire;
5. sometimes also fire changes into the nature of (air) and sometimes into the (nature) of earth;
6. and also earth sometimes changes into the nature of fire and sometimes into the nature of water.

After this introductory statement the author maintains in line 7 that change indicates the presence of a principle but that also becoming different or deviant as a result of destruction suggests a principle of differentiation. In line 11 he draws his conclusion: it is not possible to postulate one wise principle as responsible for both construction which brings forth the forms by means of generation and also for the destruction of other forms.

7. *u-šān az wardišn ī pad cihr ī bunīstagīh*
8. *az jud*[9]*-cihrīh jud-cihrēnīdār bunīšt*
9. *az āgenēn sāzišnīh ī pad bawišn azišīh ī dēsagān*
10. *ud asāzagīh-iz ō didān ī dēsagān*
11. *dahišn wihān nē sazīdan ī az ēk dānāg bun*

7. From the changes in their nature (is) a principle,
8. (and) from deviant nature, a principle of giver of deviancy.
9. From the working together in generation (there is) the derivation of forms
10. and also the dysfunction of other of the forms.
11. It is not possible for the cause of creation to be from one wise principle.

In line 12 he introduces a key point in his argument which is that the cooperative construction of the producers of natures is beneficial and bringing about discordance or dissociation is harmful and therefore (line 14) postulation of more than one principle should not be seen as an impossibility. It can be seen

8 Solmsen 1960, p. 338f. On discussion of the role of the elements as constituent parts of man see Bailey 1943, pp. 89–92 and Gignoux 2001, pp. 31–48 who emphasizes that the element theory came to Iran primarily through the Syriac translations of Galen's works on medicine.

9 *jud* 'separate, different, anti-'. In some texts it renders Greek *alloiosis* 'alteration' (Bailey 1943, p. 92). In § 119 it is used repeatedly to indicate changes which lead to destruction, harmful forms or evil in men. It indicates something that deviates from the norm of moderation and has a pejorative nuance.

from other texts that generation was envisaged as a series of smooth transitions from one state to another based on harmonious cooperation between constituent parts whereas other types of combination came about by means of direct encounter of contraries or collision leading to the production of extremes in nature and in man.[10]

12. *xwēš *cihrēnāgān*[11] *abāg-sāzēnāgīh ī ō sūdōmand bawišn*
13. **asāzēnāgīh-iz*[12] *ī ō zyānōmand dahišn*
14. *paydāg nēst az šāyēn ēdōn sazīdan ī-z ī buništ wēš az ēk*

12. The mutual cooperation of their producers of natures [leads] to beneficial generation.
13. Likewise destruction [leads] to a harmful creation.
14. Clearly it is not impossible to find fitting that indeed there is more than one principle.

Lines 15–28 expand on and illustrate the postulation of line 14 and form the main argument of the text. This section is rhetorically dense with a number of rhetorical devices over and above the grammatical parallelism and synonyms and antonyms which tightly weave the whole text together. The author begins by pointing out (line 15–17) that just as it is evident that the generative activity of the elements precedes the existence of the resulting forms in time so also the resulting product of the activity of the elements is even more evident and thereby also the existence of an agent who made them. In other words he suggests that, although the activity of the elements is hard to observe but becomes evident by reasoning, the generated forms can be observed and are therefore even more evident. That there is a someone or a something who has made them follows logically.

15. *ciyōn zahagān kardagīh pēšīh ī az dēsagān ī az-iš paydāg*
16. *kardag ī az zahagān kardagīh paydāgtar-iz*
17. *ud az kardagīh-išān kardār*

15. Just as the anteriority of the work of the elements in relation to the forms (resulting) from it is manifest
16. so the product of the work of the elements is even more evident
17. and from their work a maker.

He reiterates that working together is beneficial and that harmfulness is damaging (line 18). In line 19 he continues the theme of harmfulness, reminding us that there are two kinds, one which is found in nature like the wolf who attacks the sheep and one found in the will of man in his relations with other men. He adds that there are deviant men as well as contrariety among the forms (line 21). This

10 See for example essay § 162 of Dk III which describes how *spenāg mēnōg* the 'holy spirit' mitigates the potential harm caused by the direct confrontation between cold and hot or dry and moist.
11 MS B: *cylʾnʾkʾn*.
12 Emendation by de Menasce 1973, p. 120. MS B: *ʾsʾcʾkʾn' gwʾkyhc*.

is repeated in line 22 with a slight variation of wording but reiterates the ability to cooperate of the one and the lack of cooperation of the other.

18. *ud az-iz abāg-sāxtārīh ī gēhān sūd wizūdārīh-iz ī-šān zyān*
19. *ī ast ī pad cihr ciyōn gurg ō gōspand*
20. *ud ast ī pad kām ciyōn mardōm ō mardōm*
21. *ud jud az mardōm jud-tarīh ud hambadīgīh-iz ī andar dēsagān*
22. *āhang-sāxtārīh ī-šān ō āgenēn az ān ī asāxtārīh ī-šān ēk ō did*

18. And just as from the cooperative building of the world (comes) benefit so also their harmfulness is damaging.
19. It happens in nature like the wolf toward the sheep
20. and sometimes by will like one man toward another.
21. Besides differences in men (there is) also contrariety among the forms (and)
22. their inclination to associate with one another (stands) against their disassociation of one from another.

In line 23 he continues his theme by pointing out that some men are law-abiding and others fail to observe the law. Finally in lines 24 to 27 he reaches his rhetorical climax with a very elaborate proposition in four segments the first of which describes lack of cooperation as the cause of destruction (line 24), the second describes beneficial association as the cause of help (line 25), leading to virtue and reward in the hereafter (line 26) and finally in segment four we find how destruction in the long run leads to evil-doing and finally to punishment in hell (line 27). The purport of this long sentence is to emphasize that beneficial construction helps law-abiding men to become virtuous and likewise harmful destruction is one reason why non-law-abiding men become evil. The believer will become blessed if virtuous or if he keeps to lawlessness he will become one of the wicked. In line 28 the author concludes this argument with a strong undertone that there can no longer be any doubt there must be more than one principle.

23. *ud andar mardōm *āhang*[13] *ī dād az ān ī adād {w} nē spōxtan*
24. *ī andar dēsagān zyānōmand asāxtārīh wizūdārīh wihān*
25. *az ān ī sūdōmand sāxtārīh {w} ayārīh wihāngar*
26. *ōh-iz ān ī dādīgīh andar mardōm kē rāy-išān kār kirbagīhēd padiš ahlawīhēnd*
27. *az ān ī adādīh kē rāy-išān kār bazagīhēd padiš druwandīhēnd*
28. *sazīdan paydāg ī buništ wēš az ēk*

23. Among men the inclination to abide by the law (stands) against non-rejection of lawlessness.
24. And among the forms harmful non-cooperation is the cause of damage
25. while from beneficial cooperation (comes) the causer of help.
26. So indeed law-abidingness among men who because of it their work is virtuous and through it they become blessed
27. (is in contrast) to lawlessness because of which their work is sinful and through it they become evil

13 MS B: *w'hn y*.

28. It ought to be obvious that there is more than one principle.

The author still has one more argument to present in support of his postulation and so he now turns to the role of the cosmos. He begins by stating in line 29 that the making of the sky, earth, sun, moon and stars shows that there is an active principle or agent at work in constructing the cosmos. He recapitulates this in line 30 stating that constituting and construction come after the constructor. Lines 31–32 explain how the sky and the heavenly bodies are essential parts of the ongoing struggle against evil. The sky protects the earth while the star station provides a battlefield for the struggle and every aspect of creation from the most intimate inner self of the individual to the star station is engaged in the struggle.

29. *asmān ud zamīg xwar māh starān kardagīh-išān paydāg ī buništ*
30. *az passāxtīh ud passāxtagīh pas {w} az passāxtār*
31. *ud asmān ō drubuštīh zamīg*
32. *ī star pāyag ō kōxšišn gyāg ī kōšagān razm kardagīh*
33. *ud kōšāgān az andartom ī tan tā star pāyag*

29. The sky, earth, sun, moon and stars, the making of them is evidence of a principle:
30. from composition and the activity of composition after the composer.[14]
31. The sky is for the defense of the earth,
32. the star station is the battlefield of the doing battle of the combatants
33. and the combattants [range] from the innermost self to the star station.

The final argument (lines 34–39) is that it would be incorrect to believe that these luminaries which protect the individul could be harmful or that the creator would stir up murderous strife between his own creatures and allow them to do battle with each other. In conclusion the Zoroastrian author argues that one is obliged to assume that there is more than one fundamental creative principle.

34. *ud padiš paydāgīh rōšnān-iz ī abardar*
35. *kē pad tan *a-wizōn*[15] *ēstēnd kār-išān wizūdagīh*
36. *ud dādār xwad ō xwēš dahišn wizūdan*
37. *ud andar xwēš dām razm *rēzīdan*[16]
38. *ud dām āgenēn kōšēnīdan nē sazēd*
39. *sazīdan paydāg ī buništ wēš az ēk*

34. From this evidence it is not possible that the work of the uppermost luminaries,
35. which are not harmful toward the body, could be to cause injury
36. nor that the Creator would himself harm his own creation
37. and instill strife in his own creatures
38. and cause his creatures to do battle against each other.
39. It must be obvious that there is more than one principle!

14 This is a reiteration of line 12 using the verb *passāxtan* 'fashion, prepare' instead of *kardan*.

15 Skjærvø, private communication.

16 MS B: *l'cytn'*.

3. The text in the context of interfaith discussion

Both the form and wording of essay § 119 suggest that it could have been a model on how to reason with non-Zoroastrians about the problem of theodicy. The text is filled with expressions which echo those found in works by the learned representatives of the Christian Nestorians and Monophysites, the Muslim Mu'tazila and the Jewish Rabbanites and Karaites of the 6th to 10th centuries. All were agreed upon the fact that certain concepts like creator, creation, constituent elements, nature, man, choice and responsibility could be known by reason. The dogma that creation was *ex nihilo* had been reconciled with Aristotle's theories of matter and form and the elements by the 6th century Christian Neoplatonist John Philoponus. Philoponus' ideas were widely spread in the Near East and his arguments appear in different variations in Christian, Jewish and Muslim works, even taking on a life of their own when detached from their original context and attached to other arguments on related issues.[17]

It seems to me that this is what we see in the argumentation of essay § 119 and it can be suggested that the Zoroastrian Hellenist was not only familiar with some form of Philoponus' arguments but also invokes them indirectly by echoing certain expressions common in the discussion of the period. This is perhaps most obvious in lines 15–17 where the Zoroastrian author states that the elements are prior to and have produced the forms and that prior to this activity there must have been an agent. This formulation recalls that of the Jewish writer Saʿadia's (d. 942) second proof of creation "Bodies consist of combined parts and composed members and thus reveal ... signs of generation and of the art of an artisan." It has been noted that Saʿadia's statement is parallel to but not identical to Philoponus' proposition that the creation of the universe can be inferred from its composition.[18]

In the context of the Zoroastrian's argument it is obvious that already at the level of the elements it can be maintained that not only an all-wise good creator has been at work but also a principle of evil and chaos has succeeded in polluting parts of creation. He builds his argument by contrasting the positive results of the joining, combining and composing activity of the elements and their properties *(āgenēn sāzišnīh, abāg-sāzēnāgīh, āhang-sāxtārīh)* which produces the good things in nature and men of moral stature with examples of destruction and contrariety. Originally arguments from the conjunction and composition of things in the universe were also part of Philoponus' arguments that the creation of the universe can be inferred from its composition.

In naming the opposing failed things, whether they are from destruction in the process of generation and degeneration or collision in the combining of opposites described as *asāzagīh, asāzēnāgīh, asāxtārīh* 'decomposition, disjunc-

17 DAVIDSON 1969, p. 391.
18 Quotation and comment by DAVIDSON 1969, p. 364.

tion, lack of cooperation' he points out that they result in *wizūdārīh* 'harmfulness' and *hambadagīh* 'contrariety'. He sees them as signs that there is a second creative principle with destructive power which is active in the universe. This argument is used by authors like al-Kindi (ninth century) following John of Damascus (d. ca 750) as proof of the existence of an all-powerful god who is able to allow such contrary natures as fire and water, etc. to combine and control them so that they remain undissolved.[19]

The discussion about the role of the elements, the shape of the heavens and the cosmos in the question of man's salvation raged from the sixth century onward until the tenth and eleventh centuries and even later. This can be observed already in the sixth century in the sharp exchange of opinions between the Nestorian Cosmas Indicopleustes and the Monophysite Philiponus in a quarrel which basically concerned the elements and their properties and the construction of the cosmos.[20] The question of destruction in nature and evil in man was perhaps even more central in the following centuries and on this question leading Christian scholars were in agreement that man has a free will and is responsible for his deeds. The Nestorian stance had been formulated already in the sixth century in the words of Narsai, "In making him (man) the Creator accumulated in him all science and made him master of his liberty and guide to his will"[21] while evil was seen as the absence of good.

The question of man's free will and the nature of evil figures largely in one of John Philoponus' arguments against the uncreatedness of the universe. He maintained against Aristotle that the prime mover sets an object in motion with a force which is impressed in the object. This gives it a capacity for spontaneous movement by which it is able to move independently.[22] With this theory it was possible to postulate a God who had set things in motion and then allowed them to develop according to their natures until the energy which had been impressed upon them was exhausted. He applied this theory of spontaneous motion not only to animals but also to the human soul and moral and ethical questions. He defends the fact that man has a free will and maintains that it must be possbile voluntarily to depart from the good and then repent. Philoponus considers that free will is the origin of good and evil. He claims that evil has no substantial properties but is a misuse of physical forces based on our free choice.[23]

19 Davidson 1969, p. 374.

20 Although no names are mentioned it is thought that Cosmas Indicopleustes is defending the theology of Theodore of Mopsuestia who had absorbed a good deal of combined Stoic and other philosophical schools into his teaching while Philoponus represented Alexandrian neoplatonism and defends the Ptolomaic formation of the heavens. See Wolska 1962, p. 147f..

21 Homily IV 304–305 quoted by Wolska 1962, p. 55f.

22 See the account by Wolff 1987, p. 97 based on the passage from *On Aristotle's Physics* 384.35–385.4 which is a commentary on *Physics* 3.3.

23 See *De Opificio Mundi* Book 7.10 quoted by Wolff 1987, p. 117f.

The question of the creator in relation to man and man's responsibility for his own actions was also central to the Muslims of this period. Especially the early Muʿtazila maintained that God has created in man the accidents of will, knowledge and the power of autonomous action and that through knowledge man can know the universal principles of moral judgement. They postulated a complex relation between God and man maintaining that freedom of choice is necessary for human responsibility while at the same time God dominates and determines the cosmos entirely through his initial and continuing creation.[24]

To return to the Zoroastrian text, the author touches only briefly on the fact that man has a choice to be law-abiding or not to reject lawlessness (line 23) and that this will lead either to the state of blessedness or to existence among the evil ones (lines 26–27). Although this is one of the main themes of Dk III he does not go into the question in detail here but goes on to treat of the cosmos and its position as the location of the struggle between good and evil. This final argument shows how the creator has built up a cosmos in which all things are designed to combat and ultimately to defeat the unnamed second principle which is responsible for the evil in the world.

To the author of Dk III the arguments by the monotheistic religions concerning the nature of evil were highly unsatisfactory and many essays end by pointing out that their dilemma is that their dogmas lead them to attribute responsibility for evil to the creator. In most cases the essays are directed toward monotheists in general but sometimes a particular identifiable belief is being targeted. Several essays appear to comment on certain postulations which were typical of the early Muʿtazila.[25] It seems to me however that in § 119 the author maintains a general tone by using the language of philosophy to demonstrate the rationality of the Zoroastrian solution to this problem in an argumentation meant to appeal to monotheists irregardless of whether they be Christians, Jews, or Muslims.

4. Conclusion

Essay § 119 is unique in that it presents a succinct summary of the main beliefs of Zoroastrianism without ever mentioning Ohrmazd or Ganāg mēnōg 'the evil spirit' by name. Its purpose is to demonstrate the rationality of the Zoroastrian explanation of evil in the world. The author begins with the foundational elements which constitute the material world and shows how already at this level there is positive generation of forms and harmful destruction of other forms. The effects of both generation and destruction can be observed in nature and in

24 VAN ESS 1987, p. 227 and FRANK 1971, p. 12f.

25 DE MENASCE (1973) identifies essays § 138, 147, 172, 253 and 294 as containing criticism of the Muʿtazila.

man who are in turn part of a cosmos designed by a good creator for the purpose of defeating exactly this evil spirit.

The context of this essay is that of the interreligious debate with roots in the 6th century Christian Neoplatonic criticism of Aristotle's thesis of the uncreatedness of the universe. During the subsequent centuries which saw, among other things, the advent of Islam, emphasis shifted from the issue of creation to questions concerning how to preserve the creator from responsibility for the destruction and evil found in nature and caused by man. Essay § 119 responds to both issues by proving the existence of a creative principle which is good and arguing for the existence of a second creative principle to whom evil should be attributed.

5. References

BAILEY, H. W. 1943: *Zoroastrian Problems in the ninth-century books.* Oxford.

DAVIDSON, H. A. 1969: "John Philoponus as a source of Medieval Islamic and Jewish Proofs of Creation." In: *JAOS* 89, pp. 357–391.

Dēnkard MS B = *Dēnkart, A Pahlavi Text.* A Facsimile Edition of the Manuscript B of the K.R. Cama Oriental Institute Bombay. Ed. by M. J. DRESDEN. Wiesbaden 1966.

FRANK, R. 1971: "Several Fundamental Assumptions of the Baṣra School of the Muʿtazila." In: *SI* 33, pp. 5–18.

GIGNOUX, PH. 2001: *Man and Cosmos in Ancient Iran.* Roma (SOR XCI).

KRAEMER, J. L. 1986: *Humanism in the Renaissance of Islam.* Leiden.

MADAN = The complete text of the Pahlavi Dinkart. 2 vols. Ed. by D. M. MADAN. Bombay 1911.

DE MENASCE, J. 1973: *Le Troisième livre du Dēnkart. Trad. du pehlevi.* Paris.

SANJANA – *Dinkart. The original Pehlwi text.* 19 vols. Ed. by P. B. SANJANA and D.P. SANJANA. Bombay (1874–1928).

SOLMSEN, F. 1960: *Aristotle's System of the Physical World.* Ithaca.

VAN ESS, J. 1987: "Muʿtazila." In: *Encyclopedia of Religions* 10, pp. 220–229.

— 1991–1993: *Theologie und Gesellschaft im 2. und 3. Jahrhundert Hidschra.* Vols. II–III. Berlin / New York.

WOLFF, M. 1987: "Philoponus and the Rise of Preclassical Dynamics." In: R. SORABJI (ed.): *Philoponus and the rejection of Aristotelian science.* London, pp. 84–120.

WOLSKA, W. 1962: *La topographie chrétienne de Cosmas Indicopleustès, théologie et science au VIe siècle.* Paris.

Normative and Theological Dissent in Early Zoroastrian Law: Pahlavi *Nīrangestān* 23

Yishai Kiel and Prods Oktor Skjærvø

Introduction

The scholarly discussion about individual nonconformity to and dissent from traditional Zoroastrian law and doctrine[1] has largely centered on medieval responses in Pahlavi and New Persian focusing on the legal status of apostates, typically in the form of converts to Islam.[2] The treatment of apostasy and conversion by medieval Zoroastrian jurists reflects, for the most part, legal concerns typical of Zoroastrianism as a religious minority under Islamic dominance,[3] some of which were shared by their Jewish, Christian, and Islamic contemporaries.[4] The Zoroastrian responses from the early ninth century onward concern questions such as the marital status of the wife of an apostate, the legal status of his *ayōgēn* ("levirate") sister, the inheritance privileges of the apostate, the conditions of his return and readmission to Zoroastrianism, the issue of performing mourning rituals for the salvation of his soul, and concerns pertaining to members of the clergy who apostatized.[5]

1 This article is concerned with the issue of nonconformity of Zoroastrians to traditional Zoroastrian law and doctrine. For Zoroastrian views on non-Zoroastrian adherence to other religious systems and the question of whether or not non-Zoroastrians are expected, at least in theory, to convert to Zoroastrianism or abide by Zoroastrian law and doctrine, see Elman (2005 [pub. 2009], 2010b).

2 The conversion of Zoroastrians to Islam during the first few centuries of the Islamic period is, in some respects, part of a broader cultural phenomenon termed the "Islamic age of conversions" (see, e.g., Wasserstein 2010; de Menasce 1967a; Morony 1990; Hoyland 1997, pp. 336–342).

3 The legal status of Zoroastrians under Islam was subject to some controversy among Muslim jurists (see Friedman 2003, pp. 72–76).

4 For comparative discussions of apostasy in Zoroastrian, Islamic, Christian, and Jewish law during this period, see, e.g., Simonsohn 2013, Irshai 1984–1986, and Kiel/Skjærvø 2011, p. 11, and 2017.

5 See, e.g., REA 4, 26 (JamaspAsa/Nawabi 1978, pp. 324, 338–339; cf. Safa-Isfehani 1980, pp. 19–24, 183–188); RAF 2–3, 5, 52–53 (JamaspAsa/Nawabi 1978, pp. 323–325, 348–349; Anklesaria 1969, vol. 1, pp. 47–49, 70–71); *Pahlavi Rivāyat* 7 (Williams 1990,

The legal concerns pertaining to individuals' nonconformity to Zoroastrian law and doctrine did not, however, originate as a reaction to the large-scale conversions to Islam in the early Islamic period. In fact, the issue of religious dissent from Zoroastrian norms and views is systematically treated in the Pahlavi commentary on the Avestan *Nīrangestān*, which was redacted orally probably in the late Sasanian period. The extensive medieval discussion of apostasy and conversion is, therefore, not only a reflection of the religious and legal encounter of Zoroastrianism with Islam, but also represents earlier Zoroastrian traditions, which were redacted in their final form before the advent of Islam.

Here, to honor Maria Macuch's inestimable contributions to the study of Zoroastrian law, we shall discuss the twenty-third chapter of the Pahlavi *Nīrangestān* (N.)[6] along with its commentary against the backdrop of Islamic laws of apostasy, on the one hand, and Talmudic (particularly Babylonian) law and other sources, on the other hand. We shall see that the discussions concerning religious dissent in this Pahlavi text are significantly illuminated by a comparison with Talmudic law and, particularly, with the Babylonian Talmud's discussions of normative and theological dissent, which are situated in the intellectual world of the Sasanian period.

We shall also see that, after the redaction of the *Nīrangestān*, some of the legal concerns in our text continued to occupy the minds of the medieval Zoroastrian jurists, who appropriated and repackaged earlier discussions by applying them to the new reality of large-scale conversions to Islam. Here, the traditions of the Pahlavi *Nīrangestān* together with their later incarnations in medieval Zoroastrian responses on apostasy and conversion can be significantly illuminated by a comparison with Islamic legislation.

vol. 2, p. 9); *Dādestān ī dēnīg* 40 (Jaafari-Dehaghi, pp. 168–171); *Persian Rivāyats of Hormazyar Framarz* (Dhabhar 1932, pp. 197–198).

6 Beginning of the second section *(fragard)* of the *Nīrangestān* (cf. Kotwal/Kreyenbroek 2003, pp. 30–35). The text is on HJ 64r5–66r2 (= Sanjana 1894) and TD 44r12–45v4 (= Kotwal/Boyd 1980; in the Iranian reprint [n.p., ca. 1970] of Sanjana 1894, on pp. 127–131). Here it is normalized to some degree, and only variants that might impact on the discussion are mentioned. Parenthesis (...) = editorial additions. An asterisk = slightly restored form and its translation/uncertain translation. For manuscripts and previous editions, see Kotwal/Kreyenbroek's edition. Our interpretation of the text differs from theirs in various respects.—Here and elsewhere, all texts cited are based on inspection of the manuscripts and, in the case of the *Questions (Pursišnīhā)* of Ēmēd son of Ašwahišt (REA), Ādurfarrbay (RAF), and Frīy-srōš (RFS), on new editions prepared by the authors.

Nīrangestān chapter 23

N.23.1
yō gāθå asrāuuaiiō ąstā vā tarōmaiti vā tanūm piriieiti.
kē gāhān nē yazēd *anastīh[7] rāy ka gōwēd ay dēn nēst (ayāb tar-menišnīh rāy)
ka gōwēd ast u-š nē ābādīh dādār bē (guft?) *[TD 44v]* tanābuhl bawēd

N.23.2
*kō ąstō kā *tarōmaitiš*
kadār *anastīh kadār tar-menišnīh *[HJ 64v]*

N.23.3
yā haca daēnaiiāṯ māzdaiiasnōiṯ apastūitiš ::
kē dēn ī mazdēsnān abāz stāyēd ::

N.23.4
ēd gōwišn ī tan ī xwēš wizīr hād Abestāg ān gōwēd
bawēd ka pad ēd gōwišn menišn gōwēd hād dēn nēst pad gyāg tanābuhl
sāl-drahnāy margarzān
tanābuhl az ēn gyāg paydāg 3 gōwišn
sāl-drahnāy ōh margarzān az ān gyāg paydāg
*yō haca daēnaiiāṯ māzdaiiasnōiṯ apastōiṯ θriš vaγžibiš *hakərəṯ vīpaiticiṯ*

N.23.5
ka nē menišnīg gōwēd margarzān nēst nē bawēd
ka pad menišn abēr was menēd pad guftan nē gōwēd margarzān nē bawēd

N.23.6
Rōšn *[HJ 65r]* guft hād ēn griftārīh āmār
tā 3 bār pad menišn menēd margarzān ōh bawēd
ka 3 gowišn *ēwāz[8] pad gōwišn gōwēd margarzān
pad anīy zamān bawēd ka-š kerd ēw abāg bē kunēd
kerd abāg kunišn drāyān-jōyišnīh pad *[TD 45r]* bun

N.23.7
ka sāl pad petītīgīh bawēd *ā-š[9] yašt ī nōg nāywar abāg kunišn u-š tanabuhl ī
ruwānīg bē wizārišn
u-š kār kerbag pēš az ān kerd *abaz[10] rasēd
ān ī andar ān ēw xwēš nē bawēd

7 For *anastīh* (Bartholomae 1904, col. 361) TD has <'wytwds> (= *xwēdōdah*!), H <'wytw's> in §1 and <'wytyh> in §2 [w = n].
8 Mss.: <'ywp>, the common *ayāb* "or," is not unusual for the rarer <'yw'c> *ēwāz* "only."
9 Mss. u-š.
10 Mss. <LWTE> *abāg* for <LAWHL> *abāz*, cf. RAF 53 cited below.

N.23.8
ka pad petītīgīh nē bawēd rad-iz (nē?) pādixšāy škastan
kū pad petīt bawēd *radīhā
ka škast[11] rad rāy bē mīrēd margarzān

N.23.9
ka Zardušt rāy gōwēd u-š dēn rāy guft bawēd
ka Ohrmazd rāy gōwēd *[HJ 65v]* xwārtar nē bawēd ma agar grāy bawēd
abārīg dād rāy gōwēd ā-iz pad ēd šōn

N.23.10
dād ī wattar pad ēč meh-dādestānīh nē pādixšāy stāyīdan
ka xwadāy-gāh xwāstag rāy stāyēd margarzān
ka bīm ī tan rāy stāyēd ā-m nē rōšnag

N.23.11
(Rošn guft?) hād čē *dād ī weh kē-š ōh stāyēd u-š menišnīg stāyēd
kē az dād ī weh ō wattar šawēd margarzān
(az) ān ī wattar ō ān ī wattar margarzān nē bawēd
Wehšābuhr guft hād pad ān zamān nē bawēd ka ān gyāg *ōh šawēd *[TD 45v]* (ī) ēk wattar kū *anīy[12] nēst

N.23.12
az jud-ristagān wāz nē gīrišn u-š ōh nē dahišn
ka ān gyāg ōh šawēd ka šāhān šāh gōwēd kū drōn ēw ma yaz *[HJ 66r]* ā nē yazišn
ka gōwēd ay nē abāyēd yaštan ā-š pad gōš dārišn

Translation

N.23.1
*He who (because) not reciting the Gāθās, either out of *evil or out of disdain, forfeits his body.*
He who does not sacrifice the *Gāθās*[13] either out of *deceit—when he says: there is no *dēn*
(or out of disdain)—when he says there is, but he has not (said) the 'prosperity of the Creator', becomes *tanābuhl* (his body is forfeit).

N.23.2
*What *evil? What disdain?*
Which is *deceit? Which is disdain?

11 TD has *rad ka škast*; not in HJ.
12 For **ōh* and **anīy*, the mss. have <OL> and <ZK>.
13 I.e., recite during the *yasna* "sacrifice" or other rituals.

N.23.3
The 'back-praising' from the Mazdayasnian daēnā.
He who praises 'back' the *dēn* of the Mazdayasnians.

N.23.4
This speech is a decision (about?) his own body. That is, that is what the *Avesta* says.
It happens when he utters in this[14] speech and thought: "No, there is no *dēn*," (then) he is *tanābuhl* on the spot and, after a year, *margarzān* (worthy of death).
(His being) *tanābuhl* is manifest from this place: "three utterances,"
(and) "after a year (his being) *margarzān* in the usual way" is manifest from that (other) place: *he who stands back from the Mazdayasnian* daēnā *three times with words (and) once with just *remorse.*[15]

N.23.5
When he does not say it (while also) thinking (it), there will be no "there is no *margarzān*."
When he thinks it in his thought very much, (but) does not say it in speech, he will not be *margarzān*.

N.23.6
Rōšn said: Yes, but count this as being 'seized':
As long as he thinks it three times in his thoughts, he becomes *margarzān* in the usual way.
When he utters the three utterances *only in speech, (he becomes) *margarzān*.
When it happens at some other time that he does an action in addition, (then) 'done together with an action' (and) 'chewing while chattering'[16] (accrues) to his account.[17]

N.23.7
When he remains in repentance for a year, he should perform a *nōg-nāywar* ritual together with (it) and (thereby?) resolve (~ expiate) the *tanābuhl* (sin) to his soul.
And the work and good deeds he has done before that come *back.
What (happened) during that period[18] does not become his own.

14 Mss <HNA>, but perhaps for <’ḏ – 3> (common in many Pahl. mss.) as in the following "in three utterances and thoughts."
15 For **vīpaititi*?
16 See Skjærvø 2012, p. 37.
17 *pad bun* is usually "at the beginning/bottom," but it is also used similarly to *ō bun* "to (his) account": e.g., *Dēnkard* 9.12.15 *ān āsrō kē-š nē frāy az xwar-ēw pad bun* "that priest who has no more than one *xwar* to his account" (Dresden 1966, p. [MR154]; Madan 1911, pp. 798–799); similarly *Dādestān ī dēnīg* 11.2, 12.3 (Jaafari-Dehaghi 1998, pp. 58–61).
18 *Mādayān ī hazār dādestān* 34.8 *andar ān ēw ka* "at the time when" (cf. Macuch 1993, p. 554: "zu einem Zeitpunkt, da ..."; also in RAF 94.2 (JamaspAsa/Nawabi 1978, p. 378; Anklesaria 1969, vol. 1, p. 57).

N.23.8
When he is not in repentance, he is also (not?) authorized to break the *rad*.
When he is repentant (it should be done?) *according to the *rad*.
When (he says it?) with a view to breaking the *rad* (and) he dies, he is *margarzān*.

N.23.9
When he says it with regard to Zarathustra, then he will (also) have said it with regard to the *dēn*.
When he says it with regard to Ohrmazd, it is not a lighter (sin), but rather a 'heavier'[19] one.
(When) he says it with regard to the rest of the Law, then too it is in this way.

N.23.10
By no 'higher' law is he authorized to praise a 'worse' law.
When he praises (it) with a view to lordly position (or) property, he is *margarzān*.
When he praises (it) for fear of his body, it is not clear to me (what the legal position is).

N.23.11
(Rōšn said?)[20] Yes,[21] for he who praises the good Law in the usual way, he praises it in thought.
He who goes from the good Law to a worse one is *margarzān*.
(From) a worse to a worse, he does not become *margarzān*.
Wehšābuhr said: Yes, but he does not become so when he goes to that place in the usual way, where one is no worse than *another.

N.23.12
One should not take the *wāj* from 'those with different ways', and one should not give it in the usual way.
When one goes to such a place in the usual way, when the king of kings says: Do not sacrifice any *drōn*, then one should not sacrifice any.
When he says, "One must not sacrifice"—then one should keep it in the ear.

19 Pahl. *grāy* is the old comparative of *garān* "heavy," commonly used of a grade of sin; we also find sins that are *garāntar* "more 'heavy'" and *grāytar* "more 'heavier'"; cf., e.g., *Pahlavi Videvdad* 13.24c *ēn tanābuhl-ēw rāy grāy bawēd čē pad adwadād ōzad estēd* "for this one *tanābuhl* it becomes a 'heavier' (sin), for it was killed by *adwadād* (abandonment)" (cf. JAMASP 1907, p. 471).

20 The phrase *ā-m nē rōšnag* "is not clear to me" is frequently followed by the opinion of Rōšn (lit. "light") in legal texts; contrast *Pahlavi Videvdad* 5.62 *tam kū gyāg tārīk Rōšn guft* "*tam*, i.e., a dark place. Rōšn said …" (cf. JAMASP 1907, p. 202).

21 On the use of *hād* and other particles, see SKJÆRVØ 2010, pp. 182–190.

Commentary

N.23.1–3

The Avestan text says that a person forfeits his body for not reciting the *Gāθās* when it is done out of *ąsta* "*evil" or *tarōmaiti* "scorn/disdain." The two Avestan terms are then defined: *ąsta* is when he denies the existence of the *dēn* out of "deceit" (?) and "scorn" when he says the *dēn* exists, but he has not (said?) "the prosperity of the Creator." The last item may refer to notions such as that expressed in *Yasna* 37.1, where Ahura Mazdā's creations are enumerated, concluding with *vīspācā vohū* "all good things," Pahl. *harwisp-iz ābādīh ī bun ud bar* "and all prosperity, root and fruit,"[22] but also, perhaps, to the *aṣ̌əm vōhū vahištəm astī* "*aṣ̌a* is the best good (thing/reward) there is," Pahl. *ahlāyīh ābādīh ī pahlom ast*. If so, the implication may be that he says the *dēn* exists, but he does not say the *aṣ̌əm vohū*.

On Pahlavi *an-astīh*

The exact meaning of Avestan *ąsta* is not known, other than that it is something negative. The word *anastīh* was not understood by the copyist in N.23.1, but he got it almost right in N.23.2. MacKenzie (1971) lists *an-ast* spelled <'nAYT'> "non-existent" and *ānāst* <'n'st' = 'n'yyt'> "spoilt,"[23] but *an-ast* is also spelled <'n'st'>. There appear to be two different meanings of *anast/anastīh* in the literature. One is based on the analysis as *an-ast/an-astīh* "non-existent/non-existence, e.g., from the *Dēnkard*:

> Dk.6.231 *ka ahlomōyān ō dēn āyēnd ud abar astīh* <AYT'yh> *ud an-astīh* <'n-AYT'yh> *ī dēn ud yazdān pahikār kunēnd* "when the heretics come to the *dēn* and argue about the existence and non-existence of the *dēn* and the gods";
>
> Dk.6E.31c *harw rōz 3 bār … astīh ud hamēyīgīh ī yazdān ud an-astīh ud abesīhišnīgīh ī Ahrimen ud dēwān bē gōwišn* "three times every day, one should utter the existence and eternal being of the gods and the non-existence and annihilation of Ahrimen and the demons";[24]
>
> Dk.3.114.2 *tan az judāgīh ī gyān nē an-astīh bē a-kārīh* "the body does not get non-existence from being separated from the soul, but non-functioning";

22 Note also *ābādīh ī weh dādār* "the prosperity of the good Creator" in the colophons of the Pahlavi Yasna mss. Mf4 (K. M. JamaspAsa/Nawabi 1976, vol. 1, p. 2) and Pt4 (http://ada.usal.es/paginas/ver/17198).

23 This possible meaning is found in *Dādestān ī dēnīg* 36.13 *ud ham druz hamist dēwān ālūdagīhā ud* <'n'st>*-īhā … bērōn abgandan* "and to cast out said Lie together with the demons so as to be polluted, <'n'st> …," but the reading *an-astīha* "so as to be non-existent" is just as, if not more, likely (thus Jaafari-Dehaghi 1998, p. 115).

24 Dresden 1966, pp. [411, 461]; Madan 1911, pp. 523, 581; cf. Shaked 1979, pp. 90–91, 198–199.

Dk.3.238.4 *ag-dēnīh sāmān an-ast-mēnīdārīh ī dēn* "the definition of 'having an evil *dēn*' is being somebody who thinks about the *dēn*'s being non-existent."[25]

The other, spelled <'n'st'> and <'n'stk>, has to do more specifically with falsehood in speech, e.g.:[26]

Bundahišn 27.41 *Anāst dēw ān kē zūr gōwēd* "the demon Anāst is the one who speaks wrongly";

Bundahišn 31.9 *ašomōγān ud anāst-gōwišnān ud ahlaw-bēšān* "the heretics, those who speak *anāst*, and those who harm the righteous";[27]

Dk.6C.30 *anāstag ud drōw abar kas nē gōwišn* "one should not speak *anāst* and lies about somebody";[28]

RAF 61.1 *mard-ēw kē anāst ēw abar mard ēw gōwēd wināh čē* "what is the sin of somebody who speaks *anāst* about another?";[29]

Zand ī Wahuman Yasn 4.38 *zūr ud anāst(ag) abar man Ohrmazd gōwēnd* "they utter falsehood and *anāstag* about me, Ohrmazd."[30]

In the *Pahlavi Yasna*, <'n'st-> renders *ąsta-*, but appears to be used once in the sense of *an-ast-* and once in the sense of *an-ast-* or *anāst*:

PY.34.8 *ān ī ōzōmand ahlomōγ ... pad ēd ī tō Ohrmazd* <'n'st>*-īh wurrōyēd pad dēn ī tō* "the strong one, the heretic, believes in your, Ohrmazd's, non-existence, in (that of) your *dēn*";

PY.44.14 <'n'st>*-gar kū gōwišn ī kasān a-kār kunēnd* "the one who does <'n'st>, i.e, who invalidates what people say."[31]

Note also *Aogəmadaēca* 48, where *ąstəm* "for the body" is rendered as Pazand *anahastīh*, Pahl. *an-ast*, Sanskrit *tanu-nāstikatvaṃ* "non-existence of the body."[32]

N.23.2–3

The Avestan text then asks explicitly what the two terms mean and answers that they refer to the "praising back" of the Mazdayasnian *daēnā*. This statement has two important aspects. Firstly, it evokes the Evil Spirit's word to Zarathustra in *Videvdad* 19.6: *apa.stauuaŋᵛha vaŋᵛhīm daēnąm māzdaiiasnīm*, Pahl. *abāz*

25 DRESDEN 1966, pp. [82, 197]; MADAN 1911, pp. 111, 262; cf. DE MENASCE 1973, pp. 117, 248.
26 Compare, perhaps, Khotanese *hu-nāśa-salāva-* "of very agreeable speech" (SKJÆRVØ 2004, vol. 2, p. 370), which suggests a reading *a-nāst*.
27 Cf. PAKZAD 2005, pp. 325, 353.
28 DRESDEN 1966, p. [411]; MADAN 1911, p. 559; cf. SHAKED 1979, pp. 156–157.
29 JAMASPASA/NAWABI 1978, p. 354; ANKLESARIA 1969, vol. 1, p. 33.
30 Cf. CERETI 1995, p. 138.
31 Cf. Dk.3.114.2, above.
32 See JAMASPASA 1982, pp. 34–35.

stāy weh-dēn ī mazdēsnān "praise back the good *dēn* of the Mazdayasnians," which underscores the severity of the transgression. Secondly, *apa-stu-* has as its opposite *fra-stu-* "send forth with one's praise", which is how the performance of the *yasna* begins: "I praise forth with good thoughts, etc.," that is, presumably, Ahura Mazdā and the Life-giving Immortals, as suggested by *Zand ī Wahuman Yasn* 7.22, where, at the end of the world, this is what Pišišōtan and his men will do: *frāz stāyēnd man Ohrmazd abāg amahrspandān*.[33] In N.30.11, the direct object is *yasna*s and *vahmas* "sacrifices and hymns of praise."[34]

The implication of these passages is that *deceitful, that is, deliberate, and disdainful neglect[35] to recite the *Gāθās* is equated with the "back-praising" of the (entire) *dēn*.[36]

The theological significance of N.23.1–3 lies in the explicit association of normative and doctrinal dissent. The practical failure to perform a ritual (the recital of the *Gāθās*), when done out of (deliberate) *deceit or disdain, is equated with the theological denial of the (entire) *dēn*. In other words, the question addressed in this passage is whether and to what extent deliberately neglecting a religious command (which amounts to performing the forbidden act of omission)[37] equals theological dissent. The commentary teaches us in this context that when a religious commandment is deliberately neglected out of disdain, the act must not be regarded as a "regular" offence requiring atonement, but as a form of theological dissent. See also on N.23.9, below.

Similar issues were raised already by Palestinian rabbis, who used the term *meshumad* (lit. "one who is destroyed," from the noun *shemad* "destruction") to denote the destruction of the soul or the body by deliberately and systematically committing a religious crime,[38] but the legal concerns distinctly characteristic of the Babylonian rabbis are even more similar to those of the Zoroastrian *dastwar*s. Thus, in its discussion of *meshumad*, the Babylonian Talmud, on the one hand, distinguishes between different motivations for deliberately and systematically neglecting a religious command: there are those who neglect

33 Cf. Cereti 1995, p. 143.

34 Note also *ā-stu-* "ally oneself to … by one's praise" in Av. *ā-stauuana-*, Pahl. *āstawān* (see below).

35 Cf. N.18.3 *pad sūdagīh* "out of carelessness", *pad nigerišn* "deliberately", *pad tarmenišnīh* "out of scorn".

36 For Pahlavi *dēn* as the totality of the oral tradition, see, most recently, Skjærvø 2012; cf. Vevaina 2010 p. 114, n. 8.

37 See examples in Skjærvø 2012, pp. 38–41.

38 Originally in the context of religious persecutions. See, e.g., Petuchowski 1959; Zeitlin 1963; Lieberman 1975, pp. 228–229 and notes 103, 106; Wagner 1982, pp. 198–227; Arad 2009, with detailed references to earlier scholarship. The term *mumar* (lit. "one who has been changed") was used by sixteenth-century censorship to replace the term *meshumad* in the Talmudic manuscripts, see Sussman 1990, p. 46, n. 153; Arad 2009, pp. 242–243. For the history of this term in Second Temple and early rabbinic literature, see Arad 2009, pp. 238–251.

a command for the sake of provocation (להכעיס), while others do so only for the sake of pleasure or desire (לתיאבון);[39] on the other hand, it distinguishes between religious dissent with regard to a particular command (משומד לדבר אחד) and with regard to the entire Torah (משומד לכל התורה כולה).[40]

Of interest here is also the clear distinction maintained between *meshumad* (apostate) and *min* (heretic) in the Palestinian sources—the former denotes dissidence in religious practice, while the latter refers to heretical beliefs[41]—a distinction blurred in the Babylonian Talmud, cf.:

> Rav Aha and Ravina disagreed on this matter: one said: (a dissident) for the sake of desire (לתיאבון)—is regarded as an apostate (משומד), for the sake of provocation (להכעיס)—is regarded as a heretic (מין). And one said: (a dissident) even for the sake of provocation (להכעיס) is regarded as an apostate (משומד). Which is the heretic (מין)? One who worships idols (העובד עבודה זרה).[42]

Again, the connection made by the Babylonian rabbis between normative and theological dissent—"an apostate for the sake of provocation is regarded as a heretic"—recalls the Pahlavi assertion that the *practical* neglect of a religious command out of disdain equals *doctrinal* denial (invalidation) of the religious tradition.

The attempt to define normative nonconformity as a form of apostasy was subject to extensive discussion among Islamic jurists, too. For instance, according to a tradition recorded by IBN QUDĀMA,[43] not only heretical beliefs or the denial of Allah and his prophet constitute apostasy; the neglect of essential Islamic norms may be regarded as an act of apostasy punishable by death, as well:

> Vilifying Allah the Exalted or His Prophet, falsely impugning the honor of the Prophet's mother, denying the book of Allah or a part of it, (denying) one of His prophets or one of His books, rejecting a manifest and agreed upon commandment such as the five pillars (of Islam), or making licit a well-known and agreed-upon prohibition, such as wine, pork, carrion, blood, illicit intercourse and the like.[44]

39 Babylonian Talmud, Gittin 47a; Hullin 4a; Horayot 11a; ʿAvodah Zarah 26b. See, e.g., the translations in EPSTEIN 1936.

40 Babylonian Talmud, Eruvin 69a–b; Hullin 4b–5a. In this regard, we also encounter a category of religious dissent with regard to specific religious commandments, such as the "apostate with regard to the desecration of the Sabbath" (משומד לחלל שבת). See Babylonian Talmud, *ibid.*

41 This distinction is mentioned in SCHIFFMAN 1985, pp. 41–49, but cf. the definition proposed by SUSSMAN 1990, p. 54 n. 176, and the discussion in ARAD 2009, pp. 246–251.

42 Babylonian Talmud, Horayot 11a.

43 IBN QUDĀMA, vol. 4, p. 60; see FRIEDMAN 2003, pp. 122–123.

44 Other Islamic jurists disagree with the notion that the transgression of eating or sexual taboos constitutes apostasy. See, e.g., NAWAWĪ, vol. 18, p. 7; SHĪRĀZĪ, vol. 3, p. 256; and FRIEDMAN 2003, pp. 121–133.

N.23.4

The degree of sinfulness for "back-praising" the *dēn*, here (apparently) interpreted in terms of verbal or mental denial of the *dēn*, is twofold: in itself, it amounts to a *tanābuhl* sin, but, if the crime is not "resolved"[45] within a year, the sinner becomes *margarzān*, which is common with *tanābuhl* sins, cf.:

> *Pahlavi Videvdad* 7.52
> aδaca hən̨ti parətō.tanunąm šiiaoθənanąm uzuuarštaiiō
> *ānōh paydāg kū wizārišn tanābuhl-ēw rāy margarzān bē estēd ā-š tanābuhl-ēw wizārd bawēd*
> *Then there will be the 'working up' of actions for which one's body is forfeit.*
> From there [= the text cited] it is manifest that for the resolving of a *tanābuhl* sin, the *margarzān* sin remains.[46] Then, for him a *tanābuhl* sin has been resolved.[47]

Pahlavi *tanābuhl* is from Av. *tanu-pərəθa* "whose body is forfeit" (cf. *tanūm piriieiti* in N.23.1), while the term *margarzān* is not in the *Avesta*.[48] Sometimes, *margarzān* is used simply to interpret Avestan *tanu-pərəθa* (e.g., N.20.1, 21.1), but the above distinction is common already in the *Pahlavi Videvdad*.

Some medieval Zoroastrian jurists, among them the tenth-century Ēmēd son of Ašwahist, in his *Questions*, reaffirmed this decision of the Pahlavi *Nīrangestān* and applied it to the case of apostasy by conversion to Islam:[49]

> REA 4.2[50]
> *mard kē az weh-dēnīh ō ag-dēnīh šawēd ud pad ag-dēnīh bē rasēd pad gyāg tanābuhl ēw wināh ka andar sāl-drahnāy pad rāh ī weh-dēnīh hišt margarzān*
> A man who goes from adhering to the good *dēn* to adhering to an evil *dēn* and comes to adhering to the evil *dēn* on the spot has a sin of one *tanābuhl*. When he (remains) for a year on the path of leaving the good *dēn*, he (becomes) *margarzān*.[51]

Not all Zoroastrian jurists, however, were in agreement that a grace period of one year should be extended to an apostate who converted to Islam, cf.:

45 On repentance and atonement of sin in Zoroastrian law and theology, see Asmussen 1965, pp. 26–112; Kiel 2008 (pub. 2012) and 2014.
46 I.e., the atonement for a *tanābuhl* sin does not resolve a *margarzān* crime.
47 Cf. Jamasp 1907, p. 276.
48 See *Šāyist nē šāyist* 1.1–2 (Tavadia 1930, pp. 27–28); *Supplementary Texts to Šāyist nē šāyist* 11.1–2, 16.1–4 (Kotwal 1969, pp. 22–23, 68–69); RAF 72 (Anklesaria 1969, vol. 1, p. 40). On the classification of sins, see also Jany 2007, pp. 347–361; Macuch 2003, pp. 109–129.
49 On this sage, see Modi 1931, pp. 275–288; Safa-Isfehani 1980, pp. i–xiii.
50 JamaspAsa/Nawabi 1978, p. 246; cf. Safa-Isfehani 1980, pp. 21–22.
51 A similar position is advocated in the *Persian Rivāyats of Hormazyar Framarz* (Dhabhar, pp. 197–198).

Pahlavi Rivāyat 7.2[52]
kē az dād ī-š andar estēd bē ō dād ī didīgar šawēd margarzān ēd rāy kū dād weh-dēnīh bē hamē hilēd kē[53] *dād ī wad hamē gīrēd*
dād ī wattar grift rāy ēd rāy margarzān hamē bawēnd
He who goes from the law in which he stands to another law (is) *margarzān* for the reason that he who takes up a bad law abandons the law of the good *dēn*.
For this reason they are always *margarzān* for taking up a worse law.

While this response may refer to the ultimate *margarzān* that takes effect only after a year, it is also possible that the author simply did not believe the grace period should be extended in this case.

The opinion of the high priest Mānuščihr (2nd half of the ninth-century)[54] differs from both of the above: an apostate essentially deserves the death-penalty,[55] but he can repent for as long as he is alive:

Dādestān ī dēnīg 40.5[56]
*bē *agar-iš andar zīndagīh az ān grāy petīt bawēd*
awēšān kē-š ō ān ī duš-dādīh frēbēnīd ō weh-dādīh hāzēnēd
ud ān ī-š abārōnīhā pad dād nihād az rawāgīh kunēd
rawāg-wināhīhā abāz bandēd čē raft abāz wirāyēd
nōg pad dēn mazdēsnān menišnīg ud abar-estišnīg ud āstawān bawēd
wināh ī-š rawāgēnīd bandēnēd
ud pad xīr ud ranj ud tuwān ud kār-framān tōzēd
ēd čē pad tan pad sidōš pādifrāh widārēd ēg āmurzišn windēd u-š ruwān bōzīhēd
But, if during his lifetime, he repents from that 'heavier' (sin),
brings those whom he had deceivingly brought to that evil law (back) to the good *dēn*,
and stops propagating that which he has wrongly laid down as law,
and 'ties back' the sins being propagated, redresses what has gone out,
again thinks according to the *dēn* of the Mazdayasnians, stands firm (in it), and professes (it),
and makes (people) 'bind' the sins which he has propagated
and atones for (them) by material things, toil, ability, and hard work—
(for all) this (for) which he suffers bodily punishment at the *sidōš* ("third dawn," i.e., after death), he then finds forgiveness, and his soul is saved.[57]

52 See Williams 1990, vol. 2, p. 9.
53 Mss. <ME> *čē*.
54 See Jaafari-Dehaghi 1998, pp. 23–26.
55 *Dādestān ī dēnīg* 40.2, cf. Jaafari-Dehaghi 1998, pp. 168–169.
56 Cf. Jaafari-Dehaghi 1998, pp. 170–171.
57 With the above passages, cf. from the inscriptions of Kerdīr (after 276 CE): KKZ 14–15 *ud was mardōm ī anāstawān būd ān āstawān būd ud was ān būd kē kēš ī dēwān dāšt u-š az man kerd ān kēš ī dēwān hišt u-š kēš ī yazdān grift* "and much people who did not profess (the *dēn*), they professed (it); and there was many a one who held the teaching of the demons, but by my endeavor he abandoned that teaching of the demons and took up the teaching of the gods" (cf. MacKenzie 1989, § 17 pp. 55, 59 [transl. defective]).

Also, some medieval Islamic jurists argue that an apostate must be immediately executed, while others recommend various periods of grace, giving the apostate the opportunity to renounce his sins and return to Islam.[58] It must be stressed, however, that, while the ninth- and tenth-century Zoroastrian responses correspond in many details with contemporary Islamic decisions, the *Nīrangestān* probably reflects an earlier layer of traditions, which was in turn adapted by the medieval jurists so as to apply to the case of conversion to Islam, too.

Compare also the requirement in N.23.4 that the denier of the *dēn* repeat his denial three times, whether in speech or in thought, to become *tanābuhl* (and, eventually, *margarzān*), with the prevailing positions among Muslim jurists that the apostate be asked to repent three times (or for three days) and that he be put to death only after he denies Islam three times.[59]

N.23.4 On the Avestan quotation

The verb used here, *apastōit̰*, is surprising, since it cannot be from *apa-stu-* as one might expect (the construction with *haca* here is the same as in N.23.3 *haca ... apastūitiš*), although corruption of **apa.stauuōit̰* is possible, cf. *upa.stauuōiš* in V.19.22 (the missing syllable may have been lost, e.g., at a line break in an ancestor ms.).

An alternative solution might be to posit a thematic (aorist?) stem *apa-sta-* from **apa-stā-* "stand back (from)," cf. thematic *axštat̰* in *Yasna* 51.4 and *fraxšta-* "stand forth," e.g., imperfect/injunctive *fraxštata* "stood forth" in *Yašt* 13.97 (cf. Greek *aphistēmi* < *apo-stā-*).[60] Such an analysis is supported by *Mēnōy xrad* 14, 22–23 *hu-pādixšāyīh ān bawēd kē ... agar ast kas kē az rāh ī yazdān bē estēd ēg-iš wirāyišn padiš kardan framayed u-š griftār kunēd ud abāz ō rāh ī yazdān āwarēd* "being a good ruler is he who ... if there is someone who stands away from the road of the gods, then he orders him to be restored and makes him 'seized' and brings him back to the road of the gods."

Here, Pahlavi *bē est-* + *az* "stand away from" is the perfect equivalent of *apa-sta-*.

N.23.5–6

According to N.23.5, the denial of the *dēn* must be in both speech and thought. If one merely utters a denial of the *dēn*, but does not deny it in thought, or if one denies the *dēn* in thought, but does not utter a statement to that effect, he does not become *tanābuhl* (and *margarzān* after a year). According to the position attributed to Rōšn in N.23.6, however, even an utterance or thought alone, when

58 See Friedman 2003, pp. 121–133.

59 See, e.g., Abū Yūsuf Ya'qūb, p. 182; Mālik b. Anas, vol. 2, p. 737, no. 16; Friedman 2003, p. 131, n. 62.

60 Cf. Kellens 1984, p. 192.

repeated three times, renders the denier of the *dēn margarzān*. Rōšn's reasoning is that a person who repeatedly denies the *dēn* (even in thought or speech alone) is regarded as *griftār* "seized" by the sin.

The question debated by the Zoroastrian jurists in these passages, therefore, is whether a heretical thought alone or an utterance that is not accompanied by denial in thought is sufficient to render a person *margarzān*. While Rōšn argues that an utterance or a thought alone is sufficient to render a person *margarzān*, other jurists insisted that a thought of heresy must be accompanied by an utterance in order for the sinner to become *margarzān*. The particular legal matter of the status of heretical thoughts is, of course, intertwined with the broader issue of the role of intent and mental cognizance as opposed to verbal utterances and actions in assessing religious merit, on the one hand, and criminal liability, on the other.[61] Although legal issues relating to mental awareness and intent emerge in the earliest stages of rabbinic thought and pervade the rabbinic corpus from then on,[62] recent studies have shown that certain legal issues relating to intent are conceptualized in the Babylonian Talmud and the Pahlavi literature in a distinctly similar way.[63]

The positions of Rōšn and his interlocutors on the legal status of thoughts and utterances (or acts) recall those of the Babylonian rabbis Ravina and Rav Hisda, who debated the essential legal question of whether or not thoughts are akin to utterances:

> Ravina said, this means that a thought is akin to an utterance... Rav Hisda said: a thought is not akin to an utterance.[64]

N.23.6 On Pahlavi *griftār*

Kotwal/Kreyenbroek understood *griftār* as "becoming involved (in an offence)," which would also fit the following passage:

> RFS 1.8 *ōy kē ... dēn ud dastwar a-passand ... ud kas pad-iš wiyābānīhēd ud mardōm az rāh ī rāst passandišnīg abāz dārēd harw wināh ī az-iš uzīhēd pad-iš griftār ud āstārōmand*
> "he whom ... the *dēn* and the *dastwar*s do not please ... and somebody is led astray by him and he holds people back from the straight and pleasing path, every sin that arises therefrom—he (becomes) 'seized' by it and full of sins."[65]

Another passage, however, suggests that we are dealing with the regular *griftār* "seized":

61 On the role of intent in Zoroastrian law, see Macuch 2003, pp. 109–129; Elman 2010a; Shaked 2012, pp. 403–414.

62 The importance of intent and mental awareness in rabbinic literature is widely documented, see, e.g., Bazak 2004; Jackson 1971; Balberg 2011; Rosen-Zvi 2011; Schick 2011.

63 See e.g. Kiel 2013.

64 Babylonian Talmud, Berakhot 20b. See also Berakhot 12b; Yoma 28b–29a, Bava Batra 16a, 164b, Shabbat 64a–b.

65 JamaspAsa/Nawabi 1978, p. 404; cf. Anklesaria 1969, vol. 1, p. 83.

Mēnōy xrad 1.39–41 *az pāy pēšārwār ma kun kū pad dād ī dēwān griftār nē bawē u-t ān wināh rāy dēwan ō dōšox nē kešēnd*
"do not urinate standing, so that you do not become seized by/caught in the law of the demons and the demons do not drag you to hell for that sin!"[66]

This use is also confirmed by the passage from *Mēnōy xrad* 14, 22–23 cited above, p. 235: *u-š griftār kunēd ud abāz ō rāh ī yazdān āwarēd* "and makes him 'seized' and brings him back to the road of the gods," as well as *Dēnkard* 7.1.43 *mardōm pad xwāyišn pursišn ī ān tis ēdōn griftār būd hēnd čiyōn nūn pad xwāyišn pursišn ī dēn* "people were 'seized' by seeking and studying that thing in the same way that (they are) now by seeking and studying the *dēn*."[67]

The proximity of *apa-stōiṯ/bē estēd* and *griftār* in both the *Nīrangestān* and the *Mēnōy xrad* passages strongly suggests the passages are related, perhaps drawing on one and the same phraseology in the oral Zoroastrian tradition.

N.23.7

According to N.23.7, if a person is "in repentance" for a year after denying the *dēn* (and not yet *margarzān*), he is authorized to perform rituals and thereby atone for the *tanābuhl* sin. While a *tanābuhl* sinner cannot be credited at the final judgment for good deeds performed previously, upon expiating the sin, all the good deeds performed before the sinful act will go back to his account. Good deeds performed while *tanābuhl*, however, and before atoning for the crime do not go to the sinner's account in the usual way. This decision is informed by the following text, which deals with the issue of repentance:

Pahlavi Videvdad 7.52[68]
ay harw ān gyāg kū abestāg paititəm u vacō uruuaitiš u yauuaēca *gōwēd ēn az garzišn wināh tanābuhl-ēw bē kunēd ud kerbag ōh estēd*
That is, in every place one utters the *Avesta*: "repented, a word of vow, and for ever"—this (is) from the confession of sins[69]—it cancels one *tanābuhl*, and the good deeds 'stand' in the usual way.

66 Anklesaria 1913, p. 13.
67 Dresden 1966, p. [476]. The *Mēnōy xrad* passage also appears to provide the explanation of the Manichean phrase *yazdān pand grift hēm* "I was seized by the 'path/advice' of the gods" (cf. *hām-pand* "companion of the road, fellow traveler") in M49/II/V/4 (*Šābuhragān*; cf. Boyce 1992), which has sometimes been adduced as an example of the modern Persian past tense construction in early Middle Persian, but which Boyce (1975, p. 31) correctly translated as "I was seized by the counsel of the gods." The evidence of the *Mēnōy xrad* passage suggests that *pand grift hēm* is yet another Zoroastrian idiom used by Mani. Cf. also *Šābuhragān* 355–356 *pad yazdān pand raft hēd ud hām-pand ud hayār būd hēd* "you have gone in the path of the gods and have been fellow travelers and friends" (cf. MacKenzie 1979, pp. 518–519).
68 Cf. Jamasp 1907, p. 276.
69 Cf. Shaked 1979, p. 264, on *māndag garzīdan*.

The theology expressed in N.23.7 is also applied by Ādurfarrbay (first half of the ninth-century), *hudēnān pēšōbāy* "leader of those of the good *dēn*,"[70] to the case of an apostate who converted to Islam, but now seeks to revert to Zoroastrianism:

RAF 53[71]

pursišn: mard ēw kē kustīg bē wišāyēd andar sāl bē mīrēd ud az ān wināh pad petīt bawēd ān wināh bē šawēd ayāb nē

passox: ka andar sāl pad petīt bawēd kār ud kerbag (ī) pēš az ān kerd abāz rasēd ud ān ī pas az ān ī petīt kunēd ōh bawēd ud ān ī pas az kustīg-wišādagīh ud pēš az petītīgīh kunēd nē bawēd

Question: A man who unties the *kustīg* (sacred girdle) and dies within a year, but repents that sin: does that sin go away or not?

Answer: When he repents within a year, the works and good deeds done before that come back, and those he does after he repents will be in the usual way. But those he does after untying the *kustīg* and before his repentance, will not.

The trend of apostatizing and reverting to one's original denomination is well documented in Muslim, Jewish, Christian, and Zoroastrian sources of the early Islamic period.[72] According to this passage, leaving the good *dēn* (to join Islam) is symbolized by untying the *kustīg*, which Zoroastrians are to wear at all times.[73] While the removal of the girdle was considered a symbolic act of apostasy not only in Zoroastrian sources, but also in Christian documents,[74] the removal of the girdle clearly had particular significance for Zoroastrians, for whom girding was a religious percept.[75] While the particular symbolism of the removal of the *kustīg* probably belongs to the Islamic period, the theological core of Ādurfarrbay's response appears to be derived from N.23.7.

N.23.8

Here, *rad* refers not to the official, but to the 'ritual model', Av. *ratu*, seen in *ratu-friš* "satisfying the ritual model," Pahl. *radīhā* "according to the ritual model," glossed as *dastwarīhā* "according to the *dastwars*" in the Pahlavi

70 His title may be the Zoroastrian equivalent of the Islamic *amīr al-mu'minīn*. He is said to have participated in interreligious disputations in the presence of the Caliph *al-Ma'mun* (815–833) and is remembered as one of the first redactors of the *Dēnkard*. See Anklesaria 1969, vol. 2, pp. 1–25.

71 JamaspAsa/Nawabi 1978, p. 349; Anklesaria 1969, vol. 1, p. 28.

72 Friedman 2003, pp. 143–144; Simonsohn 2013.

73 See, e.g., de Menasce 1967b; Stausberg 2004, pp. 9–29; Shaked 2010; Kiel 2012.

74 On the significance of girding in other religious denominations, see Herman 2014. On the removal of the girdle as an act of apostasy, see Hoyland 1997, pp. 337–338.

75 On Islamic polemics against the *kustīg*, see also the Pahlavi *Gizistag Abāliš*, cf. Tafazzoli 1985; Cereti 2001, pp. 188–189; Secunda 2010, pp. 310–334.

Ahunwar (cf. *dādīhā* "according to the law"). Compare *Dādestān ī dēnīg* 47.20 *gōwišnīg petītīg(īh) radīhā ōšmurdan* "to enumerate the repentance in speech according to the 'models'";[76] *Pursišnīhā* 10.2 Av. *aiβiiāstō aθa ratufriš* "(when) girded, thus it satisfies the 'model'," Pahl. *ka aibyāst kū šabīg kustīg dārēd ēdōn radīhā* "when one is girded, i.e., one wears the shirt and girdle, in this way it is according to the 'model'."[77]

With "breaking the *rad*," cf. *stūr(īh) škastan* "break the *stūr(īh)*,"[78] *xwēdōdah škastan* "break the *xwēdōdah*."[79] The implications of these statements are unclear, however, and the text may not be in order.

N.23.9

These far-reaching theological implications of denying the *dēn* of Zarathustra and Ohrmazd, with whom the *dēn* originates, or any other part of the Law are strikingly reminiscent of the Islamic definition of apostasy, which centers on the denial of Allah, his prophet Muhammad, or the religious law. In Islam, retracting from either part of the *shahāda* pertaining to Allah or his prophet Muhammad is regarded as a form of apostasy.[80]

N.23.10

This passage introduces the term *meh-dādestānīh* (application of a) "greater law/judgement," denoting the prioritization of a 'higher' law (often pertaining to the preservation of life) over other laws in a case of conflicting religious obligations. The term is widely attested in the Pahlavi literature and has been subjected to various interpretations. Recently, Maria Macuch has suggested equating this term with *weh-dādestānīh* (application of a) "better law," which she interprets as "*going beyond* the law" or "exceeding the minimum requirements of the law."[81] In several contexts, however, it would seem rather to refer to a 'higher' law, that is, one which *overrides* the regular law.

The principle according to which the preservation of life takes precedence over the fulfillment of other legal requirements is most clearly articulated in *Pahlavi Videvdad* 7.71, where it is taught that a woman who has given birth but suffers from fever or severe thirst may consume water despite its inevitable defilement,

76 After the manuscripts.
77 Cf. JamaspAsa/Humbach 1971, pp. 20–21.
78 E.g., *Mādayān ī hazār dādestān* II 4.28 (Macuch 1981, p. 161 n. 62).
79 E.g., REA 24.3 (JamaspAsa/Nawabi 1978, p. 292; cf. Safa-Isfehani 1980, pp. 177–178).
80 See Friedman 2003, pp. 121–133.
81 We would like to thank her for generously making this article available to us. See also Macuch 2005 (pub. 2009), p. 95, and Agostini/Kiesele/Secunda 2014.

since the preservation of her life is the 'higher' law *(meh-dādestānīh)*.[82] Similarly, the Pahlavi texts often refer to "fear for the body" *(bīm ī tan)* and "death and injury" *(margīh ud rištagīh)* to indicate life-threatening circumstances, in which a person is authorized to save his own life at the expense of transgressing the law.[83]

The rabbis similarly maintained that saving a life (פקוח נפש) overrides the fulfillment of other religious commandments.[84] While this concept has been long acknowledged as a clear expression of the sanctity of life endorsed by both Palestinian and Babylonian rabbis, in three cases, one is expected to give up one's life and not transgress the law: idolatry, sexual crimes, and murder.[85]

Thus, N.23.10 appears to say that no appeal to a 'higher' law can save one for becoming *margarzān* for praising a "worse law," especially, the redactor adds, when it is for material gain. He is not certain, however, whether this trumps the principle of fear for one's body, but another authority (Rōšn?) confirms that he will indeed become *margarzān*. The limits of the general principle of the precedence of life are debated also elsewhere, as we see in a dispute concerning the obligation to carry a corpse out of water in a case of self-endangerment.[86] In other words, despite this general principle, there were *dastwar*s who held that in the case of severe transgressions such as heretical utterances (praising another religion), one may not transgress the law even when one's life is in danger.

82 A similar principle is reflected in *Pahlavi Videvdad* 5.16–21(JAMASP 1907, pp. 159–164), as well as in the *Zand ī fragard ī jud-dēw-dād* (JAMASPASA/NAWABI 1978, pp. 448–449), in which Ohrmazd is said to bring rain so as to nourish his creatures despite the fact that it might fall on corpses and defiling substances. Ohrmazd, too, seems to follow a 'higher' law.

83 See, e.g., *Hērbedestān* 2.9, 3.6 (KOTWAL/KREYENBROEK 1992, pp. 32–35); *Pahlavi Videvdad* 5.4 (cf. JAMASP 1907, pp. 144, 149–150; see ELMAN 2010a, pp. 30–31; KIEL 2011, pp. 55–58; KIEL/SKJÆRVØ 2011, pp. 9–10).

84 Mekhilta de-Rabbi Ishmael, Masekhta de-Shabta 1 (HORVITZ-RABIN 1970, pp. 340–341; cf. KAHANA 2005, p. 151); ibid., Nezikin 13 (HORVITZ-RABIN 1970, pp. 292–293); Mekhilta de-Rabbi Shimon b. Yohai, Exodus 21:14 (EPSTEIN 1956, p. 171); Tosefta, Shabbat 15:16 (LIEBERMAN 1975, pp. 73–74); Palestinian Talmud, Yoma 8:5 45b; Sanhedrin 8:8 26c; Babylonian Talmud, Yoma 85a-b; Shabbat 132a. SHEMESH (2013, pp. 481–505, and 2009, pp. 70–71) discusses this legal principle in rabbinic, Qumranic, and early Christian texts.

85 Some rabbis disagreed. R. Ishmael, for one, held that preserving life overrides even the prohibition of idolatry, as long as it is not in a time of persecution. See Sifra, Ahare Mot, Mekhilta de-'Arayot 14, 86b; Tosefta, Shabbat 15:17 (LIEBERMAN 1975, pp. 74–75); Palestinian Talmud Shevi'it 4:2 35a; Sanhedrin 3:6 21b; Babylonian Talmud, Sanhedrin 74a; Keritot 19a.

86 See *Šāyist nē šāyist* 2.79–81 (TAVADIA 1930, pp. 59–60); *Pahlavi Videvdad* 6.29 (cf. JAMASP 1907, p. 220).—Cf. also *Hērbedestān* 19.8–9, where, according to the redactor, a Zoroastrian may teach a heretic in the case of danger of death and injury, while Farrox disagrees (see SKJÆRVØ 2009, pp. 489–490).

Again, compare a Talmudic debate between two fourth-century Babylonian authorities:[87]

> It was stated: one who worships idols out of love (of a person)[88] or fear: Abaye said he is liable. Rava said he is exempt; only if he accepted the idol as his god is he held liable, but if not he is exempt.

N.23.11

When a person converts "from a worse law to a worse law," i.e., from one non-Zoroastrian law to another, he does not become *margarzān* according to the redactor. Exactly what Wehšābuhr argues (if our reading is correct) is not clear, but the implication seems to be that there is a hierarchy of legal systems even among non-Zoroastrians and that some legal systems are regarded as better than others.[89]

Similarly, according to ABŪ HANĪFA, MĀLIK B. ANAS, and others, there is no death penalty for converting from one non-Islamic religion to another, since it is immaterial for Islam whether a person belongs to one wrong religion or another. AḤMAD B. HANBAL, however, views the issue of religious conversion between non-Islamic religions from the perspective of the social and economic interests of the Muslim community. If a Jew or a Christian converts to an 'inferior' religion (e.g. Zoroastrianism or Manicheism), this person will no longer pay the *jizya*, the product of his slaughter will now be forbidden to Muslims, and so on. This situation cannot be tolerated by the Muslim community and, therefore, a convert who seeks to downgrade his religious affiliation may be subjected to the death penalty. Moving up in the religious hierarchy, however, supports the interests of the Muslim community and is thus tolerated.[90] The different positions of the Islamic jurists on the issue of converting from one non-Islamic religion to another seem to match the positions in N.23.11.

87 Babylonian Talmud, Sanhedrin 61b; cf. Shabbat 72b; Keritot 3a.

88 This interpretation follows R. Shlomo Itzhaqi in his commentary on Sanhedrin 61b. Cf. Maimonides, *Mishneh Torah*, Laws of Idolatry, 3:6.

89 Cf. the assertion of Gōgušnasp in *Pahlavi Videvdad* 3.42, 5.38: *ce andar harw dād-ēw mardōm ahlaw ōh bawēnd čē az* tūiriianąm daxiiunąm *paydāg* "For people become righteous in every law in the usual way, which is manifest from "(the law?) of the Turian lands" (cf. JAMASP 1907, pp. 100, 180). In other words, if a certain religious system contains proper laws (in this particular case, the law of avoiding corpse-contamination), a non-Zoroastrian can become (relatively) righteous through that law. This position contradicts the positions of *Sōšāns* and the anonymous redactor, who argue: PV.5.38 *ēn az abestāg paydāg an-ēr margarzān hamāg ēdōn bawēd čiyōn ag-dēn* "This is manifest from the Avesta: The non-Iranian is *margazān*; it is all like someone with an evil *dēn*" (cf. JAMASP 1907, p. 179; see ELMAN 2005 [pub. 2009], pp. 15–26).

90 See FRIEDMAN 2003, pp. 146–148.

N.23.12

The chapter concludes with two examples of what Zoroastrians should not do in encounters with "those of different ways" *(jud-ristagān)*: taking the *wāj*[91] and sacrificing the *drōn*.[92]

In the case that there is a contradiction between a religious obligation to sacrifice the *drōn* and a royal edict issued by the king of kings forbidding the sacrifice, the redactor distinguishes between two different circumstances: if the king says "do not sacrifice any *drōn*", one must obey the king; but, when the king says "one should not sacrifice", one must keep it in mind(?).[93] Here, the former case appears to address a specific occasion *hic et nunc*, while the latter may refer to this and future occasions. A similar issue is raised in the *Dēnkard*:

Dēnkard 6.233[94]
ān ī ka dahibed pursēd kū drōn yazišn ayāb nē ēg ka bazag pad bazag brīnēnd ēg-iz nē gōwišn kū nē yazišn
bē ka ān dahibed mard-ēw framān dād kū drōn ma yaz ka yazēd nē yazišn bē wināh bawēd
When a ruler asks: "Ought one to sacrifice the *drōn* or not?," then one ought not to tell him not to perform it, even when they cut an evil deed with an evil deed.[95]
But, when that ruler has commanded a man: "Do not sacrifice the *drōn*," if he does, it will not be a 'sacrifice', but a sin.

Thus, if a ruler gives a direct order, his order must be upheld. The legal decision in the *Dēnkard* seems to rely on the former case of the *Nīrangestān*, in which the ruler merely forbids the sacrifice of the *drōn* on a specific occasion, but the latter case is not addressed in the *Dēnkard*.

91 See BOYCE/KOTWAL 1971; WILLIAMS 1988; KARANJIA 2010.
92 On the *drōn*, see CHOKSY 1995; BOYCE/KOTWAL 1971; JAMASP-ASA 1918; JAMASPASA 1985.—A similar matter to that of taking the *wāj* from and giving it to a religious deviant is whether or not one may study *Avesta* and *zand* from, or teach it to, persons who practically or theologically differ from the *dēn*, see *Hērbedestān* 18–19 (KOTWAL/KREYENBROEK 1992, pp. 76–83); SECUNDA 2005 (pub. 2009). Educational encounters with a broad range of 'others', including non-Iranians, demon-worshippers, sinners, and heretics, are discussed throughout the *Hērbedestān*.
93 The meaning of "keep it in the ear" is not certain. According to STEINGASS's Persian dictionary, *dar guš dāštan* means "keep in mind, remember."
94 *Dēnkard* 6.233 (DRESDEN 1966, pp. 411–412; MADAN 1911, p. 523; cf. SHAKED 1979, pp. 90–91); cf. *Dēnkard* 3.197.9 (DRESDEN 1966, p. 166; MADAN 1911, p. 213; DE MENASCE 1973, p. 206), according to which a decision of the ruler is considered to be of a lower rank than religious law. See also JANY 2012, pp. 48–49.
95 SHAKED (p. 91) suggests the phrase may mean "come what may."

Final remarks

The similarity between the Babylonian rabbinic and Zoroastrian discussions of religious dissent need not necessarily point to cultural *exchanges* between rabbis and *dastwars*, but these connections at least suggest that the Babylonian rabbis and the Zoroastrian authorities were part of a distinct "intellectual atmosphere" (not shared by the Palestinian rabbis), in which they confronted similar legal issues—whether of practical or theoretical nature—and sought to resolve these issues by considering similar legal taxonomies.

Bibliography

Abū Yūsuf, Yaʿqūb b. Ibrāhīm 1352 ah: *Kitāb al-kharāj*. Cairo.

Agostini, D./E. Kiesele/Sh. Secunda 2014: "Ohrmazd's Better Judgment (meh-dādestānīh): A Middle Persian Legal and Theological Discourse." In: *StIr* 43, pp. 177–202.

Anklesaria, B.T. 1969: *The Pahlavi Rivāyat of Āturfarnbag and Farnbag-Srōš*. 2 vols. Bombay.

Anklesaria, T.D. 1913: *Dânâk-u Mainyô-i Khard*. Bombay.

Arad, M. 2009: *Sabbath Desecrator with Parresia: A Talmudic Legal Term and Its Historical Context*. New York/Jerusalem.

Asmussen, J.P. 1965: *Xᵘāstvānīft: Studies in Manichaeism*. Copenhagen.

Balberg, M. 2011: "Recomposed Corporealities: Purity, Body, and Self in the Mishnah." (PhD dissertation, Stanford University).

Bartholomae, C. 1904: *Altiranisches Wörterbuch*. Strassburg.

Bazak, J. 2004: "The Element of Intention in the Performance of *Mitsvot* Compared to the Element of Intention in Current Criminal Law." In: H. Gamoran (ed.): *The Jewish Law Association Studies 14: The Jerusalem 2002 Conference Volume*. Binghamton, pp. 9–15.

Boyce. M. 1975: *A Reader in Manichaean Middle Persian and Parthian*. Téhéran/Liège.

Boyce. M./F. M. Kotwal 1971: "Zoroastrian *bāj* and *drōn* I–II." In: *BSOAS* 34, pp. 56–73, pp. 298–313.

Cereti, C. G. 1995: *The Zand ī Wahman Yasn: A Zoroastrian Apocalypse*. Rome.

— 2001: *La letteratura pahlavi*. Milan.

Choksy, J.K. 1995: "Drōn." In: *EIr*, vol. 7,5, pp. 554–555.

de Menasce, J.P. 1967a: "Problèmes des mazdéens dans l'Iran musulman." In: G. Wiessener (ed.): *Festschrift für Wilhelm Eilers*. Wiesbaden, pp. 220–230 (repr. in: Hoyland 2004, pp. 331–341).

— 1967b: "Early Evidence for the Symbolic Meaning of the Kustīk." In: *Sir JJ Zarthoshti Madressa Centenary Volume*. Bombay, pp. 17–18.

— 1973: *Le troisième livre du Dēnkart*. Paris.

DHABHAR, B.N. 1932: *The Persian Rivayats of Hormazyar Framarz and Others.* Bombay.

DRESDEN, M.J. 1966: *Dēnkart: A Pahlavi Text. Facsimile Edition of the Manuscript B of the K. R. Cama Oriental Institute, Bombay.* Wiesbaden.

EILBERG-SCHWARTZ, H. 1986: *The Human Will in Judaism: The Mishnah's Philosophy of Intention.* Atlanta.

ELMAN, Y. 2005: "The Other in the Mirror: Iranians and Jews View One Another: Questions of Identity, Conversion, and Exogamy in the Fifth-Century Iranian Empire, Part 1." In: *Bulletin of the Asia Institute* 19 [pub. 2009], pp. 15–26.

— 2010a: "Toward an Intellectual History of Sasanian Law: An Intergenerational Dispute in *Hērbedestān* 9 and Its Rabbinic Parallels." In: C. BAKHOS/M.R. SHAYEGAN (eds.): *The Talmud in Its Iranian Context.* Tübingen, pp. 21–57.

— 2010b: "The Other in the Mirror: Iranians and Jews View One Another: Questions of Identity, Conversion, and Exogamy in the Fifth-Century Iranian Empire, Part 2." In: *Bulletin of the Asia Institute* 20, pp. 25–46.

EPSTEIN, I. 1936: *The Babylonian Talmud.* London.

EPSTEIN, J. N. (ed.) 1956: *Mekhilta de-Rabbi Shimon b. Yohai.* Jerusalem.

FRIEDMAN, Y. 2003: *Tolerance and Coercion in Islam: Interfaith Relations in the Muslim Tradition.* Cambridge.

HERMAN, G. 2014: "Like a Slave Before His Master: A Persian Gesture of Deference in Sasanian, Jewish, and Christian Sources." In: *ARAM* 26, 1/2, pp. 93–100.

HOROVITZ H.S./I. A. RABIN (eds.) 1970: *Mekhilta de-Rabbi Ishmaʿel.* Jerusalem.

HOYLAND, R. 1997: *Seeing Islam as Others Saw It: A Survey and Evaluation of Christian, Jewish, and Zoroastrian Writings on Early Islam.* Princeton.

— 2004: *Muslims and Others in Early Islamic Society.* Aldershot.

IBN QUDĀMA, ʿABD ALLAH B. AḤMAD B. MUḤAMMAD 1994: *Al-Kāfī fī fiqh al-imām Aḥmad b. Hanbal.* Ed. M. FĀRIS/M.ʿA. AL-SAʿDANĪ. Beirut.

IRSHAI, O. 1984–1986: "The Apostate as an Inheritor in Responsa of the Ge'onim: Foundations of the Ruling and Parallels in Gentile Law." In: *Shenaton ha-mishpaṭ ha-ʿivri* 11–12, pp. 435–461.

JAAFARI-DEHAGHI, M. 1998: *Dādestān ī Dēnīg, Part 1: Transcription, Translation and Commentary.* Paris.

JACKSON, B. 1971: "Liability for Mere Intention in Early Jewish Law." In: *Hebrew Union College Annual* 42, pp. 197–225.

— 1990: review of EILBERG-SCHWARTZ 1986. In: *JQR* 81,1–2, pp. 179–188.

JAMASP, H. 1907: *Vendidâd. Avesta Text with Pahlavi Translation and Commentary. Vol. I—The Texts.* Bombay.

JAMASP-ASA, K.J. 1918: "On the Symbolism of the Darun." In: *The Dastur Hoshang Memorial Volume.* Bombay, pp. 201–205.

JAMASPASA, K.M. 1982: *Aogəmadaēcā. A Zoroastrian Liturgy.* Vienna.

— 1985: "On the Drôn in Zoroastrianism." In: *AcIr* 24, pp. 335–356.

JAMASPASA, K.M./H. HUMBACH 1971: *Pursišnīhā: A Zoroastrian Catechism.* Wiesbaden.

JAMASPASA, K.M./Y.M. NAWABI (eds.) 1976: *Manuscript D 90: Yasnā with Its Pahlavi Translation.* 2 vols. Shiraz.

— 1978: *MS. TD_2. Iranian Bundahišn & Rivāyat-i Ēmēt-i Ašavahištān, etc.* Shiraz.

JANY, J. 2007: "Criminal Justice in Sasanian Persia." In: *Iranica Antiqua* 42, pp. 347–361.
— 2012: *Judging in the Islamic, Jewish and Zoroastrian Legal Traditions: A Comparison of Theory and Practice*. Farnham, Surrey, England / Burlington, Vermont, pp. 48–49.
KAHANA, M. 2005: *Kit'ei midreshei halakha min ha-genizah*. Jerusalem.
KARANJIA, R. P. 2010: *The Bāj-dharnā (Drōn Yasht): A Zoroastrian Ritual for Consecration and Commemoration: History, Performance, Text, and Translation*. Mumbai.
KELLENS, J. 1984: *Le verbe avestique*. Wiesbaden.
KIEL, Y. 2011: "Selected Topics in Laws of Ritual Defilement: Between the Babylonian Talmud and Pahlavi Literature." Ph.D. Dissertation, The Hebrew University.
— 2008 [pub. 2012]: "The Systematization of Penitence in Zoroastrianism in Light of Rabbinic and Islamic Literature." In: *Bulletin of the Asia Institute* 22, pp. 119–135.
— 2012: "Redesigning Tzitzit in the Babylonian Talmud in Light of Literary Depictions of the Zoroastrian Kustīg." In: SH. SECUNDA / S. FINE (eds.): *Shoshanat Yaakov: Jewish and Iranian Studies in Honor of Yaakov Elman*. Leiden, pp. 185–202.
— 2013: "Cognizance of Sin and Punishment in the Babylonian Talmud and Pahlavi Literature: A Comparative Analysis." In *Oqimta* 1, pp. 319–367.
— 2014: "Penitential Theology in East Late Antiquity: Talmudic, Zoroastrian, and East Christian Reflections." In: *Journal for the Study of Judaism* 45, pp. 551–583.
KIEL Y. / P. O. SKJÆRVØ 2011 [pub. 2015]: "The Sabbath Was Made for Humankind: A Rabbinic and Christian Principle in Its Iranian Context." In: *BAI* 25, pp. 1–18.
— 2017: "Apostasy in Early Medieval Zoroastrianism: A Response by Ādurfarrbay in Its Historical and Legal Contexts." In: *JAOS* 137, 2, pp. 221–243.
KOTWAL, F. M. 1969: *The Supplementary Texts to the Šāyest nē Šāyest*. Copenhagen.
KOTWAL, F. M. / J. W. BOYD: *Ērbadistān ud Nīrangistān: Facsimile Edition of the Manuscript TD*. Cambridge, Mass. 1980.
KOTWAL, F. M. / PH. G. KREYENBROEK: *The Hērbedestān and Nērangestān*. Vol. 1: *Hērbedestān*. Paris 1992.
— 2003: *The Hērbedestān and Nērangestān*. Vol. 3: *Nērangestān, Fragard 2*. Paris.
LIEBERMAN, S. 1975: "Redifat dat Israel." In: *Jubilee Volume in Honor of Shalom Baron*. Jerusalem, pp. 213–245.
MACKENZIE, D. N. 1971: *A Concise Pahlavi Dictionary*. London / New York.
— 1979: "Mani's *Šābuhragān*." In: *BSOAS* 42,3, pp. 500–534.
— 1989: "Kerdir's Inscription." In: *The Sasanian Rock Reliefs at Naqsh-i Rustam. Naqsh i Rustam 6*. Berlin (Iranische Denkmäler. Lief. 13. Reihe II: Iranische Felsreliefs I), pp. 35–72
MACUCH, M. 1981: *Das sasanidische Rechtsbuch „Mātakdān i hazār dātistān" (Teil II)*. Wiesbaden.
— 1993: *Rechtskasuistik und Gerichtspraxis zu Beginn des siebenten Jahrhunderts in Iran: Die Rechtssammlung des Farroḫmard i Wahrāmān*. Wiesbaden (Iranica 1).
— 2003: "On the Treatment of Animals in Zoroastrian Law." In: A. VAN TONGERLOO (ed.): *Iranica Selecta: Studies in Honour of Professor Wojciech Skalmowski on the Occasion of His Seventieth Birthday*. Turnhout, pp. 109–129.

– 2005 [pub. 2009]: "The Hērbedestān as a Legal Source: A Section on the Inheritance of a Convert to Zoroastrianism." In: *Bulletin of the Asia Institute* 19, pp. 91–102.
– forthcoming: "A Pahlavi Legal Term in Jesubōxt's *Corpus Iuri*." In: *Irano-Judaica* 7.
MADAN, D.M. 1911: *The Complete Text of the Pahlavi Dinkard*. I–II. Bombay.
MĀLIK B. ANAS 1951: *al-Muwaṭṭā'*. Ed. M.F. ʿABD AL-BĀQĪ. Cairo.
MCGRATH, S. 2003: "Elias of Heliopolis: The Life of an Eighth-Century Syrian Saint." In: J.W. NESBITT (ed.): *Byzantine Authors: Literary Activities and Preoccupations: Texts and Translations Dedicated to the Memory of Nicolas Oikonomides*. Leiden, pp. 85–107.
MAHNAZ, M. 2014: *Wrestling with the Demons of the Pahlavi Widēwdād: Transcription, Translation, and Commentary*. Leiden.
MODI, J.J. 1931: "The Mōbadān Mōbad Referred to by Hamzeh Isfehani." In: *Studia Indo-Iranica: Ehrengabe für Wilhelm Geiger zur Vollendung des 75. Lebensjahres 1856–21. Juli 1931*. Leipzig, pp. 275–288.
MORONY, M. 1990: "The Age of Conversions." In: M. GERVERS/R.J. BIKHAZI (eds.): *Conversion and Continuity: Indigenous Christian Communities in Islamic Lands: Eighth to Eighteenth Centuries*. Toronto, pp. 135–150.
NAWAWĪ, MUḤYĪ AL-DĪN ABŪ ZAKARĪYĀ YAḤYĀ B. SHARAF 1966: *al-Majmūʿ sharḥ al-Muhadhdhab*. Cairo.
PAKZAD, F. 2005: *Bundahišn: Zoroastrische Kosmogonie und Kosmologie*. Tehran.
PETUCHOWSKI, J.J. 1959: "The Mumar—A Study in Rabbinic Psychology." *Hebrew Union College Annual* 30, pp. 179–190.
ROSEN-ZVI, I. 2011: *Demonic Desires: "Yetzer Hara" and the Problem of Evil in Late Antiquity*. Philadelphia.
SAFA-ISFEHANI, N. 1980: *Rivāyat ī Hēmīt ī Ašawahistān: Edition, Transcription and Translation: A Study in Zoroastrian Law*. Cambridge, Mass.
SANJANA, D.P. 1894: *Nirangistan: A Photozincographed Facsimile*. Bombay.
SCHIFFMAN, L.H. 1985: *Who Was a Jew? Rabbinic Perspectives on the Jewish-Christian Schism*. Hoboken, New Jersey.
SCHICK, SH. 2011: *Intention in the Babylonian Talmud: An Intellectual History*. PhD Dissertation, Bernard Revel Graduate School at Yeshivah University.
SECUNDA, SH. 2005 [pub. 2009]: "Learning from a Magus/Like Giving a Tongue to a Wolf." In: *Bulletin of the Asia Institute* 19, pp. 151–157.
– 2010: "Reading the *Bavli* in Iran." In: *JQR* 100,2, pp. 310–334.
SHAKED, SH. 1979: *The Wisdom of the Sasanian Sages* (Dēnkard VI) *by Aturpāt-i Ēmētān*. Boulder, Colo.
– 2010: "'No Talking During a Meal': Zoroastrian Themes in the Babylonian Talmud." In: C. BAKHOS/M.R. SHAYEGAN (eds.): *The Talmud in Its Iranian Context*. Tübingen, pp. 161–177.
– 2012: "Religious Actions Evaluated by Intention: Zoroastrian Concepts Shared with Judaism." In: SH. SECUNDA/S. FINE (eds.): *Shoshanat Yaakov: Jewish and Iranian Studies in Honor of Yaakov Elman*. Leiden, pp. 403–414.
SHEMESH, A. 2013: "The History of the Halakhic Concept 'Saving Life Overrides the Sabbath'." In: *Tarbiz* 80,4, pp. 481–505.
– 2009: *Halakhah in the Making: The Development of Jewish Law from Qumran to the Rabbis*. Berkeley, Calif.

SHĪRĀZĪ, ABŪ IṢḤĀQ IBRĀHĪM B. ʿALĪ B. YŪSUF AL-FĪRŪZĀBĀDĪ 1995: *al-Muhadhdhab fī fiqh al-imām al-Shāfiʿī*. Ed. Z. ʿUMAYRĀT. Beirut.
SIMONSOHN, U. 2013: "'Halting between Two Opinions': Conversion and Apostasy in Early Islam." In: *Medieval Encounters* 19, pp. 342–370.
SKJÆRVØ, P. O. 2004: *This Most Excellent Shine of Gold, King of Kings of Sutras. The Khotanese Suvarṇabhāsottamasūtra*. Cambridge, Mass.
— 2009: "OL' News—ODs and Ends." In: W. SUNDERMANN / A. HINTZE / F. DE BLOIS (eds.): *Exegisti Monumenta. Festschrift in Honour of Nicholas Sims-Williams*, Wiesbaden (Iranica 17), pp. 479–495.
— 2010: "On the Terminology and Style of the Pahlavi Scholastic Literature." In: C. BAKHOS / M. R. SHAYEGAN (eds.): *The Talmud in Its Iranian Context*. Tübingen, pp. 178–205.
— 2012: "The Zoroastrian Oral Tradition as Reflected in the Texts." In: A. CANTERA (ed.): *The Transmission of the Avesta*. Wiesbaden (Iranica 20), pp. 3–48.
STAUSBERG, M. 2004: "The Significance of the Kusti: A History of Its Zoroastrian Interpretations." In: *East and West* 54, pp. 9–29.
SUSSMAN, Y. 1990: "Heker toldot ha-halakhah u-megilot midbar yehudah: hirhurim talmudiyim rishonim le-or megilat miktzat maʿase ha-torah." In: *Tarbiz* 59, pp. 11–76.
TAFAZZOLI, A. 1985: "Abāliš." In: *EIr*, vol. 1,1, p. 58.
TAVADIA, J. C. 1930: *Šāyast-nē-šāyast. A Pahlavi Text on Religious Customs*. Hamburg.
VEVAINA, Y. 2010: "Enumerating the Den: Textual Taxonomies, Cosmological Deixis, and Numerological Speculation in Zoroastrianism." In: *History of Religions* 50,2, pp. 111–143.
WAGNER, S. M. 1982: "The Meshumad and Mumar in Talmudic Literature." In: *The Jacob Dolnitzky Memorial Volume*. Skokie, pp. 198–227
WASSERSTEIN, D. J. 2010: "Conversion and the *ahl al-dhimma*." In: R. IRWIN (ed): *The New Cambridge History of Islam*. Cambridge, pp. 184–208.
WILLIAMS, A. V. 1988: "Bāj." In: *EIr*, vol. 3,5, p. 531.
— 1990: *The Pahlavi Rivāyat Accompanying the Dādestān ī Dēnīg*, 2 vols. Copenhagen.
ZEITLIN, S. 1963: "Mumar and Meshumad." In: *JQR* 54, pp. 84–86.

Die Pahlavi-Literatur des 9./10. Jahrhunderts und ihre frühe Kodex-Überlieferung (I)

Götz König

Nur wenige Iranisten außerhalb Indiens haben ihre Schaffenskraft der Erforschung der für die Kenntnis des Zoroastrismus wie des vorislamischen Iran so wichtigen Pahlavi-Literatur gewidmet. Maria Macuch zählt zu ihnen. Ihren Studien zur mittelpersisch-zoroastrischen Rechtsliteratur ist es wesentlich zu danken, daß wir uns heute diesem Schrifttum mit dem Anspruch nähern müssen, nicht nur dessen Wörter, sondern auch Terminologien verstehen zu wollen. Vor wenigen Jahren hat die Geehrte schließlich einen höchst prägnanten Überblick über die gesamte Pahlavi-Literatur veröffentlicht.[1] Daran anknüpfend wollen die folgenden Zeilen versuchen, deren frühe Tradierungslinien bis ins 17. Jh. nachzuzeichnen.

Iranische Literatur im 9./10. Jahrhundert

Ungewöhnlich ist die literarische Konstellation Irans in den beiden letzten Jahrhunderten des 1. Jt. n. Chr.[2] Nach literaturhistorisch nur verzerrt faßbaren Perioden – die einstmals umfangreiche Literatur der Sasanidenzeit ist heute weitgehend auf eine Rekonstruktion aus vereinzelten oder bruchstückhaften späteren Zeugnissen angewiesen, die literarische Aktivität der ersten 150 Jahre der Heğra erscheint weitgehend als ein Versuch der Rettung eben dieser Literatur durch ihre Übersetzung ins Arabische – treten uns im 9./10. Jh. zwei sprachlich ungleichzeitige und in ihrer Gattungszugehörigkeit einander kaum berührende Textgruppen entgegen. Entwickelte sich im iranischen Osten, vor allem in Sīstān, Xorāsān und Baktrien, unter den dort vom Kalifat sich lösenden Dynastien und ihren Höfen die ehemalige Sprache „of everyday oral communication“[3], das *darī(g)*, zu jener neuen Literatursprache Irans, die dann für eintausend Jahre das iranische Geistesleben mitbestimmen sollte, so beschränkte sich das (später *pahlawī* genannte) *pārsī(g)*, dem solch übergreifende Funktion einstmals unter den Sasaniden zukam, nun weitgehend darauf, als

1 Macuch 2009.
2 Aus der Betrachtung schließe ich hier die Literaturgeschichte des ‚zentralasiatischen Iran‘ aus.
3 Lazard 1984, S. 599.

theologisch-juristische Prosa der zoroastrischen Priester zu fungieren. Gleichwohl scheint mit der Distribution in eine in Fārs beheimatete, priesterliche Literatur bzw. Tradition in Mittelpersisch und in eine dem iranischen Osten zugehörige, eher ‚nationale' Überlieferung in Neupersisch, an welcher zoroastrischer Klerus nur noch bedingt teilhatte (so im Falle des bzw. der *Xwadāy-nāmags*[4]), keineswegs eine ideologisch-ästhetische Spaltung der iranischen Welt in eine alte und neue verbunden zu sein. Erst im 11. Jh., nach Irans „Summa" seiner großen, nun verlorenen Zeit, dem *Šāhnāme* Ferdousīs, beginnt die neupersische Literatur, sich ästhetisch und geistig neu zu formulieren. Wo sie indes, wie in Asadīs *Geršāspnāme* (458 H. = 1065/66 n. Chr.), den Rückgriff auf die Vorzeit noch länger zu gestalten sucht, ist sie ästhetisch zum Scheitern verurteilt. Denkwürdig ist es darum auch, daß nicht nur die Anfänge der np. Literatur mit einer (offenbar neuerlichen oder gesteigerten) Schriftaktivität der zoroastrischen Priester zusammenfallen, sondern letztere wiederum ungefähr zu jenem Zeitpunkt versiegt, da die neupersische Literatur das alte Erbe Irans allmählich hinter sich läßt. Auf das Jahr 1028 n. Chr. – ein Jahr vor Beendigung des *Šāhnāme* – datiert das *Riwāyat* des Hohepriesters Farrbay-Srōš Wahrāmān, möglicherweise ein Bruder des Farroxmard ī Wahrāmān, dem Kompilator des MHD.[5] Sehen wir von einigen späteren Ergänzungen ab – aus dem 12. Jh. (1158) stammt z. B. Kap. 36 des GrBd (= IndBd [Justi] Kap. 34[6]) –, so sind diese beiden genannten Rechtswerke vielleicht (beim MHD zumindest in seiner finalen Fassung) die spätesten Erzeugnisse jener verspäteten Blüte der Pahlavi-Literatur des 9./10. Jh. Ein Ms. wie MU29[7] dürfte Texte einer wesentlich späteren Zeit fassen, und deren Pahlavi zeigt wie alles Pahlavi, das die Priester bis ins 19. Jh. am Leben zu erhalten suchten, deutlich die Züge einer sekundär erworbenen Sprache.[8]

Die Pahlavi-Literatur des 9./10. Jahrhunderts

An datierbaren Materialien der Pahlavi-Literatur konnte PH. KREYENBROEK nachweisen, daß die zoroastrische Gemeinde von Fārs in der zweiten Hälfte des

4 Man beachte besonders GrBd 35A7.

5 Anders MACUCH 1993, S. 1, die den Kompilator auf das frühe 7. Jh. datiert.

6 Im IndBd fehlt auffällig die entscheidende Schlußbemerkung *nūn panj <sad> ud wīst <ud> haft sāl ī pārsīg* „nun <schreiben wir> das persische Jahr 527". Den kalendarischen Bestimmungen in GrBd 15A10 zufolge ist GrBd 15A auf die Zeit „A.Y. 480 to 600" (ARDESHIR 1956, S. 8) (= 1111–1231 n. Chr.) zu datieren.

7 JAMASPASA, K. M. / M. NAWABI 1976; MAZDAPOUR 1990.

8 Man siehe z. B. den Brief SANJANAS an den Duke of Edinburgh (PESCHUTUNJEE BEHRAMJEE SUNJÁNA: *An Address in Pahlvi and Zend with its English and Gujerati Translations presented to H. R. H. Prince Alfred Ernest Albert Duke of Edinburgh.* Bombay 1871. Siehe auch das im 19. Jh. von E. D. SANJANA geschriebene Pahlavi-XA-Ms D.

9. Jh. unter zunehmenden ökonomischen Druck geriet.[9] Dieser „Druck" bilde, so Kreyenbroek in einer späteren Studie, „after a lengthy oral transmission"[10] das Movens zur schriftlichen Abfassung des Großteils der auf uns gekommenen Pahlavischriften. Gleichwohl ist aber festzustellen, daß der zoroastrische *Hudēnān pēšōbāy* Ādurfarrbay ī Farroxzādān, auf dessen Schriften große Teile des *Dēnkard*-Buches, dessen erster Redakteur er zugleich war (s. Dk 3.420), beruhen, in der Zeit des al-Maʾmūn (813–833) und seines an rationalistischer Theologie ausgerichteten, Willensfreiheit (zumindest theoretisch) zugestehenden Kalifenhofes an der Bagdāder Diskussionskultur partizipierte (s. GizAb 0.1–6). Und noch in den späteren Jahrzehnten des 9. Jh. bzw. im 10. Jh. besaßen persische Zoroastrier die Mittel und die Freiheit zu großen Forschungsreisen,[11] die zum einen in eine Apologetik des Zoroastrismus und eine Kritik aller anderen, auch der islamischen Glaubenslehren mündete, zum andern auf editorische Großprojekte (Dk; Bd) führte, die wir vielleicht als in einem Wettbewerb mit den islamischen Universalgeschichten und dem aufblühenden islamischen Forschungseifer stehend betrachten dürfen. Auch wenn Teile der Pahlavi-Literatur in ihrer starken Orientierung an *Abestāg ud Zand ud Pōryōtkēšān gōwišn* „Avesta und Zand und den Worten/Schriften der *Pōryōtkēšān*" (so benennt Dk 3.420 die Arbeitsgrundlage des Ādurfarrbay ī Farroxzādān) vielfach Lehrinhalte aufweisen, die weit vor das 9./10. Jh. zurückgreifen, und methodologische Äußerungen insbesondere des Hohepriesters Manuščihr (Dd Intr.; NM) explizit machen, welch hoher Wert der gelehrten Tradition beigemessen wurde, so sind gleichwohl zeitspezifische Wandlungen, z. B. im Bereich der Erkenntnislehre bzw. Metaphysik, weithin zu bemerken.

Verfaßt oder redigiert wurden die großen Pahlavi-Traktate von Mitgliedern des höchsten Klerus, der sich spätestens im 9. Jh. in Landeskongregationen aufzulösen schien.[12] Auch wenn literarische Aktivitäten in den Gemeinden des NO und SO anzunehmen ist – tatsächlich waren die xorāsanischen[13] und sīstānischen Gemeinden bis in das 16. Jh. hinein existent,[14] und von ihnen

9 Kreyenbroek 1987a und 1987b. Dem gesellte sich bisweilen religiöse Verfolgung bei: „There are a number of passages in various sources claiming that the Tahirids, as good Muslims, were indeed hostile towards anything Iranian, and that they ordered Pahlavi books to be thrown in the water or burned since the reading of the Qurʿan and hadiths suffices for everyone." (Frye 1975, S. 192; vgl. Browne 1903, S. 2; Browne 1902, S. 346f.).

10 Siehe Kreyenbroek 2002, S. 47f., vgl. S. 50.

11 ŠGW 1.35–57; vgl. das schwierig zu datierende MX 1.14–61.

12 Masʿūdī berichtet noch für das 10. Jh., daß Feuertempel in ʿIrāq, Fārs, Kirmām Sīstān, Xurāsān, al-Ǧibāl, Āẕarbāyǧān, Arrān sowie in Hind, Sind und Ṣīn unterhalten wurden (s. Barbier de Meynard vol. iv, S. 86).

13 Von Kohistān (Xorāsān) ging den Emigrationsberichten (QS [Hodivala 1920, S. 2, 7, 97ff.); QZH [Cereti 1991, S. 109]) zufolge die Exilierung nach Indien aus. Kreyenbroek 1987a, S. 162, gibt für diese „probably around 917". Nach Kolophon M50 geschah die Exilierung bereits im frühen 7. Jh.

14 Noch 1511, im *Riwāyat* des Narīmān Hōšang, sind die Gemeinden in Xorāsān und Sīstān die mit Abstand größten Irans: Šarfābād/Turkābād 400 Seelen (MU II, 396.16),

gingen wesentliche Impulse in der manuskriptgeschichtlichen Überlieferung der Pahlavi-Literatur aus (s. u.) –, so scheinen gleichwohl alle uns bekannten Theologen des 9./10. Jh. in der Persis[15] bzw. in Mesopotamien[16] beheimatet und tätig gewesen zu sein. Farrbay, Redakteur des (Gr)Bd, sagt möglicherweise in GrBd 35a8, alle iranischen Mowbeds seiner Zeit führten ihren Stammbaum auf den berühmten Ādurbād Māraspandān, also auf eine Persis-Tradition, zurück.[17] Tatsächlich läßt sich fast die gesamte Pahlavi-Literatur im Rahmen eines nahezu geschlossenen Stammbaums der iranischen Hohepriester notieren (s. Tab. 1).[18]

So ist für eine Rekonstruktion der Geschichte der an historischen Personen, Orten und Geschehnissen unergiebigen Buch-Pahlavi-Literatur die Genealogie ihrer Autoren ein wichtiges Hilfsmittel. In dieser Hinsicht sind auch einige wenige interne Textbezüge von Wert. Zum Beispiel verweist das ŠGW, die bedeutende Schrift des Mardān Farrox – ein offenbar dem hohen persischen Klerus nicht zugehöriger, diesem jedoch intellektuell weit überlegener Autor – mehrfach auf das bereits zu seiner Zeit herausragende Werk *Dēnkard*,[19] aber auch auf andere Schriften, s. besonders

> ŠGW 10.50–58
> „durch die vereinte *(ham)* Kraft der <Schriften> „*Dīn-dānāī*“[20], durch das „*Xvaškār*-Buch“[21] der Weisen und die unvergleichlichen Schriften des weisen *Adar-Pādyāwandą* (= *Adūrbād ī Jāvandān*), durch das Buch, welches vom gesegneten *Rōšan Adar-Farōbagą* verfaßt wurde und den Titel „*Rōšan Nißə*“ („Das Buch des Rōšan“) trägt, und durch das <Buch>, welches der höchste Weise (*aγrə. faržąnaa.*[22]), der selige *Adar-Farōbag i Frōxzādą*, Führer der Mazdayasnier, redigierte *(vazārd(an))*, <und das> das Buch *Dīn-Kard* genannt wird …“

Yazd 500 Seelen (MU II 390.1), Kirmān 700 Seelen (MU II 390.2), Sīstān 2700 Seelen (MU II 390.4), Xorāsān 1700 Seelen (MU II 390.7). Im *Riwāyat* des Kāmdīn Šāpūr von 1559 finden wir dann 3000 „Behdīns“ aus Xorāsān in Kirmān.

15 Einem Bericht des Abū Zayd al-Balxī (850–934) zufolge sollen die Zoroastrier nirgends zahlreicher als in Fārs gewesen sein. (Boyce 1979, S. 152f.).

16 Ādurfarrbay beantwortet in Dk 5 Fragen eines Yākob ī Xālidān, der dem Volk von Sml'c/Slm'c zugehört (zur Lesung des Volksnamens s. den Forschungsbericht Amouzgar/Tafazzoli 2000, S.109).

17 „Und ich Farrbay [den man nennt D/Jādagīh], <Sohn> des Ašawahišt, <Sohn> des +Juwānjam, <Sohn> des Wahrām-šād, <Sohn> des Zarduxšt, <bin Nachkomme?> des Ādurbād Māraspandān; Zādsparam, <Sohn> des +Juwānjam; Ādurbād +Ēmēdān und Ašawahišt, <Sohn> des Frāy-Srōš und die anderen <zeitgenössischen (?)> Mōbeds, <alle> waren aus dergleichen Familie.“ Ādurbād ist nach GrBd 35a3 Abkömmling des Manuščihr, dem Stammvater aller Mowbeds.

18 Siehe besonders Anklesaria 1969 II, S. 1ff.

19 ŠGW 4.106f., 5.92, 9.1–4, 10.57, 12.1.

20 Vgl. den Ausdruck „*Zand-āgāhīh*“.

21 Anders West 1885, S. 169, de Menasce 1945, S. 117. In MHD sind erwähnt a) das *Xwēškārīh-nāmag ī mōwbedān* (MHD 26.15) und b) das *Xwēškārīh-nāmag ī kārfarmān ī šahrīhā* (MHD 38.16–39.1). In Dd 74.3–4 scheint aus einem Werk *Xwēškārīh* ein Rechtssatz zitiert zu werden.

22 Vgl. NM 1.10.8 (s. Fn. 76).

Tab. 1

(**Ādurbād ī Māraspandān** [4. Jh.] (Schüler des Mihr-Ohrmazd [s. PRDD 62])

Ādurbād ī *Jāwandān (s. ŠGW)

Ādurfarrbay ī Farroxzādān
ca. 750(?)–?; lebte unter al-Ma'mūn (Kalif 813–833; s. GizAb). Erster *hudēnān pēšōbāy*[23] – PRĀF; Dk *1,*2 (verl.), 3,4,5; (*)Ēwēn-Nāmag (verl., Reste in den PT, Dk 6)

Rōšn
(† vor ŠGW [< 847 (?)])
– *nißə̄.* (s. ŠGW)

Zartošt ī Ādurfarrbay
hudēnān pēšōbāy, um 847[24]

Wāhramšād
hudēnān pēšōbāy (? s. MHD)

Juwānjam ī Šābuhrān (in Bd 35A8 ī Wāhramšād)
hudēnān pēšbāy (s. NM 1.3.10)

Zurwāndād

Manuščihr ī +Juwānjamān
Pārs ud Kirmān rad ...
– Dd, NM (881)

Ašawahišt

Zādsparam ī J.
Hērbed in Sīrgān
– WZ; Verlorenes

***Frāy-srōš <ī Ašawahišt (?)>**

Ašawahišt ī Frāy-srōš <ī Ašawahišt (?)>
(Zeitgenosse d. Farrbay)

Farrbay ī Ašawahišt[25]
– Redakteur des Bd

Ādurbād ī Ēmēdān[26]
hudēnān pēšōbāy (Zeitgenosse d. Farrbay)
– Redakteur des Dk.

Isfandyār ī Ādurbād ī Ēmēd
† 936 (erm.) Bagdād, Mowbed über Iran

Farroxmard ī Wahrāmān
– MHD

Farrbay-Srōš Wahrāmān[27]
Mōwbedān mōwbed
– Riwāyat (1028)

Ēmēd ī Ašawahištān
hudēnān pēšōbāy,
Mowbed über Iran (955?)
– RĒA

23 Siehe dazu Anklesaria 1969 II, S. 5, vgl. Kreyenbroek 1987a, S. 160 (*hudēnān pēšōbāy* „Führer der Rechtgläubigen" ≈ Bezeichnung des Kalifen als *ʿamīr ul-muʾmanīn* an; Asha o. D., Fn. 30 verweist auf aram. *rēš gālūṯā* „Haupt des Exils; Exilarch"). Der *pēšōbāy* war zugleich auch „*Pārs āsrōnān pēšag framādār*" bzw. „*mōbedān-iz ī Pārs sālār*" (DD 44.5; s. Kreyenbroek 1987, S. 201f.; zu den Titeln s. a. Macuch 1993, S. 58f.).

24 Zu diesem und zum Datum s. West 1892, S. xxxii (Dk 3.420); Browne, 1902, S. 323–336 (Beteiligung am Afšīn-Prozeß); Anklesaria 1964, S. vii, xxi; Anklesaria 1969 II, S. 13. Asha o. D. bezweifelt, daß Zartošt konvertiert sei und denkt eher an ein Martyrium. Seine Interpretation von Dk 3.420 läßt sich m. E. dadurch stützen, daß die Passage pṯʿ škptʿ ʾlm W wznd y ʿI, zltwhšt darauf weist, daß Zartošt etwas zugestoßen ist, nicht von ihm bewirkt wurde.

25 Nach B. T. Anklesaria 1964, S. 3 Neffe des Ēmēd ī Ašawahištān (?).

26 Von Farrbay in GrBd 35a8 als Zeitgenosse erwähnt. Die arab. und np. Quellen zu Ādurbād und Ēmēd ī Ašawahištān sind zusammengestellt in Modi 1931, sodann in de Menasce 1958, S. 10f. mit Lit. Es sind die verschiedensten Lösungsvorschläge hinsichtlich des genealogischen Zusammenhangs vorgebracht worden, s. Tavadia 1930, S. 5; Tavadia 1943, Sp. 61; Anklesaria 1962, S. 3 ; Anklesaria 1969 II, S. 5 und 21 („Âṭarfrenabag's sixth descendant"); Boyce 1968, S. 46 (Ēmēd ī Ašawahištān eventuell Enkel des Ādurbād ī Ēmēdān); Shaki 1998

27 Zu diesem s. Anklesaria 1969 II, S. 23.

Die Referenzen auf das *Dēnkard* des Ādurfarrbay und das „Buch" seines Sohnes Rōšn geben für das ŠGW ein Datum *post quem*. Ādurfarrbay wird als *ašō*, Rōšn als *hufraward* bezeichnet, d.h. beide sind zum Zeipunkt der Abfassung des ŠGW bereits tot. Da die Hohepriester Manušcihr (späteres 9. Jh.) und Ādurbād ī Ēmēdān (spätes 9. Jh./frühes 10. Jh.?) von ŠGW noch nicht erwähnt werden,[28] mag das Werk auf die Mitte des 9. Jh. zu datieren sein. Mardān Farrox dürfte sich auf die Redaktion des *Dēnkard* beziehen, die Ādurfarrbay im 9. Jh. selbst unternommen hatte, und von der der Zweiteditor Ādurbād ī Ēmēdān in Dk 3.420 berichtet. Dieses Ur-*Dēnkard* wird in seiner Stoffsammlung jenem „*Dēnkard* der 1000 Kapitel" ähnlich gewesen sein, welches Ādurbād ī Ēmēdān erwähnt und das offenbar die Bücher 1–3 des *Dēnkard* umfaßte. So zitiert ŠGW denn auch aus Materialien, die heute verloren sind.[29]

Ein anderes umfangreiches Werk der Pahlavi-Literatur ist bis heute nicht gemäß seinem Wert für die Rekonstruktion der kirchlichen, religiösen und geisteshistorischen Situation der Zoroastrier in der zweiten Hälfte des 9. Jh. bearbeitet und herangezogen worden, die Briefe des Manušcihr von 881 n. Chr. (250 Y).[30] Wir wollen an dieser Stelle den drei Briefen, die einen (historisch bekanntlich vergeblichen) Versuch darstellen, die Auflösung der komplizierten und langwierigen zoroastrischen Reinigungsprozeduren zu verhindern, nur den Verweis darauf entnehmen, daß es auch im 9. Jh. (wie noch Jahrhunderte später[31]) ein in Austausch stehendes Netz von entfernten Gemeinden „der Distrikte des Landes Iran"[32] gab. So nennen die Briefe Saraxs im fernsten Xorāsān, wo Manušcihrs Bruder Zādsparam offenbar zeitweise wirkte,[33] Šīrāz in der Persis, das Sitz des Manušcihr[34] und von besonderer Wichtigkeit war, Sīrkān und Kirmān in Ost-Persien, sowie Ray in Medien (NM 2.1.13). An diesen Orten ist möglicherweise von priesterlichen Konventen die Rede (NM 2.1.8,11,12), die insgesamt noch mehr als „1000 Priester" zählten (so NM 2.1.8[35]).

28 Auch die für die zoroastrische Gemeinde schwierige Zeit unter Ādurfarrbays Sohn Zartošt, der offenbar Kirchenoberhaupt unter den Kalifen Muʿtaṣim (833–842) und Wāṯiq (842–847), d.h. in der Spätzeit der Muʿtazila war (im Jahr 849 beendete Mutawakkil die Miḥna und kehrte zum orthodoxen Dogma zurück), wird von ŠGW nicht erwähnt. Gegen die Muʿtazila bezieht ŠGW 11.280 Stellung, s. Rose 2011, S. 165.

29 Siehe ŠGW 9.1–4/Dk 3.239 (B 197.16); dazu West 1885, S. 162f. Fn. 4.

30 Eine (problematische) Gesamtübersetzung stammt von West 1882, S. 277–366; Teilübersetzungen von M.F. Kanga 1966, 1967, 1968, 1971, 1974. Zwei wesentliche Handschriften, TD4a und K35, sowie das spätere D7(= M/MR1) liegen faksimiliert vor.

31 Siehe Dhabhar 1932, S. liii.

32 NM 3.3 (*kustagīhā ī Ērānšahr*, K35 231 r 11f.).

33 Siehe NM 2.1.12 (dort werden die [türkischen] Tuġazġuz [pāz. tuγzγuzʿ, K35 221 v 9] genannt [zu diesen s. Golden 2000]), NM 2.5.3.

34 Siehe Dd Intr. 17; NM 1.3.13, 2.1.11, 2.5.10.

35 K35 221 r 11–13 *pad … hanjaman ī pārs dar <ud> abārīg was ham-rasišnīh <ī> uskārdan ud 1000 hudēn mōwbed* (mgwwd) *padiš ham-sahišnīh* „durch … die Versammlung am Tempel in Pārs und zahlreiche andere Zusammenkünfte der Beratschlagung und den <gedanklichen> Gleichklang von 1000 Mowbeds".

Dunkle Jahrhunderte: die erste Hälfte des 2. Jahrtausends

Im 11. Jahrhundert scheint nicht nur die literarische Aktivität der Zoroastrier zum Erliegen zu kommen, auch verlieren sich für drei Jahrhunderte nahezu alle Spuren von ihnen. Die vermutlich immer kleiner werdenden Gemeinden, von denen politisch weder Hoffnung noch Gefahr ausging, gerieten aus dem Blickfeld muslimischer Historiker und Geographen. Von den Revolten des 8./9. Jh., die gewisse reaktionäre, ‚zoroastrisierende' Züge aufwiesen,[36] hatte sich die orthodoxe Kirche bereits frühzeitig distanziert.[37] Hegten die Ziyāriden im 10. Jh. unter Mardāwīǧ noch „phantastische Pläne zur Wiedererrichtung eines (offenbar zoroastrischen) persischen Reiches"[38], so mußte Qābūs (977–1013) bereits die Oberhoheit der Ghaznawiden anerkennen, und Falak al-Maʿālī Manucihr (1013–1030) war sogar Schwiegersohn des Maḥmud von Ghazna geworden. Auch bei den Ziyāriden sollte der alte Iran nur noch als Literatur, so im *Qābūsnāme* vom Ende des 11. Jh., überleben.

Kurz vor dem Mongolensturm kommt uns dann eine erste Nachricht aus Sīstān zu. Für die Zeit des frühen 13. Jh. bezeugt das bekannte, kopierte 1. Kolophon von K1[39], das uns von der Abschrift eines *Vīdēvdād* in Sīstān durch Erdašīr Wahman Rōzweh Šahburzēn Šahmard[40] berichtet, den religiösen Austausch der Sīstāner Gemeinde und jener von Uca im Indus-Tal, von der wir aus späterer Zeit keine Kenntnis mehr haben. Das *Vīdēvdād*-Ms. wurde geschrieben

> auf Befehl des ... Māhdād Ādurweh, dem *Sālār*, der es auf eigene Kosten hergestellt hat für Māhyār Māhmihr, Ērbad aus Indien, aus der Stadt Uzag, die am Ufer des Indusflusses <liegt> [den man in der Religion Weh-rōd nennt]. 6 Jahre lebte dieser unter den Ērbads von Sīstān, und durch ihn kamen die gelehrten religiösen Gegenstände nach Indien. Und dieses Buch des *Juddēwdād* mit *Zand* war durch ihn in dieses Gebiet <in Indien gelangt> ...

36 Bihʾāfrīd (al-Maǧūsī az-Zauzanī), 746/747–749, der selbst ein „Zamzami", d.h. ein Mager, gewesen sein soll (s. Haarbrücker 1850–1851, I, S. 283f.), Nēšābuhr; Sunpad/Sinbad (genannt Pērōz Ispāhbad), 755, Nēšābuhr; Isḥāq der Türke, 755–757, Transoxanien; Ustād Sīs, 767 Bādġēs; Yusuf ben Ibrahim 776–778, Sīstān; al-Muqannaʿ („der verschleierte Prophet von Xorāsān"), 775–783, Merw bis Transoxanien; Bewegung der al-Muḥammira ("Rotgekleideten"?), 778–783, Gurgān; Babag Xurramdēn, 816–838, bes. Azerbaidschan.

37 Siehe Spuler 1952, S. 196.

38 Spuler 1952, S. 90.

39 K1 fol. 338 v 2–339 r 4; zu dem Kolophon s. Sanjana 1896, S. xxxvi–xl; Unvala 1940, S. 123; Kreyenbroek 1987a, S. 163; Cereti 1996, S. 449f., Cereti 2007, S. 218; dasselbe Kol. in IM mit kleineren Varianten, abgedruckt in Jamasp 1907, S. xxv–xxix, ebenso im Ms. Bh11, transkribiert und übersetzt von Cereti 1996, S. 447–450.

40 Geschrieben nach dem Ms. des Hōmast Šādān Ohrmazd, „kontrolliert (?) und korrigiert" *(rāyēnīd ud drust kard)* durch den „Spāhbed all jener dortigen <Priester>, Ērbad Šahmard <ī> Māhyār Šāhmard ī Māhyār ī Šahzād ī Mihrjī(w)".

Aus der 2. Hälfte des 13. Jh. stammt sodann der nach allgmeiner Ansicht älteste erhaltene Kodex, das Kopenhagener Ms. K7.[41] Kolophone und Kodices bieten uns im späteren 13. und dann 14. Jh. zunehmend bessere Einblicke in die Tradierungsgeschichte der zoroastrischen Literatur. Auch die Kontaktsuche Europas zu den neuen Mächten Asiens zeitigt erste kurze europäische Reisenotizen.[42] Doch erst seit dem späten 15. Jh. begegnen uns wieder umfangreiche Textzeugnisse, Produkte des religiösen Verkehrs der zoroastrischen Gemeinden von Fārs mit der Exilgemeinde der indischen Parsen. Deren älteste gehen unter dem Namen des indischen Boten Narīmān Hōšang († < 880 Y)[43], der u. a. Texte iranischer Priester[44] nach Indien brachte, die von diesen in avestischen Charakteren (also im Pāzand) geschrieben wurden, „because the Persians were informed by Nariman that the Herbads and Behdins of Cambay, Navsari, Broach, Surat and Anklesar were not versed in Pahlavi."[45] Die Kommunikation der Jahre 847[46], 855[47], 880[48] Y (= 1478, 1486, 1511) faßt zahlreiche wertvolle Nachrichten über den Zustand der indischen, vor allem aber der iranischen Gemeinden der Zeit, über welche sonst nur wenige Informationen existieren. Die für die Rekonstruktion der Überlieferung der Pahlavi-Literatur wichtige Nachricht in diesen frühen Sendschreiben ist die Mahnung der iranischen Dastūren an ihre indischen Glaubensbrüder, Pahlavi zu erlernen,[49] bzw. das Angebot, nach Iran gesandte Ērbeds darin zu unterweisen.[50]

41 VrS + PVr; Kol. nach K7b fol. 107 r – 108 r, 107 r 15 gibt *637 pārsīg* (Geldner 1886–1896, 1886 *Prol.*, S. xxxviiif. „627"); Barr 1944, S. XIII; Cereti 2007, S. 214.

42 Carpine (†1252; Reise 1245–1247) wie Rubruk (†1270; Reise 1253–1255) reisten beide durch das Mongolenreich auf einer Nordroute, die Iran nicht berührte. Marco Polo (†1324; Reise 1271–1295) reiste indes durch Persien von Hormuz aus über Kirmān nach Xorāsān/Baktrien (also wohl auf jener Route, die die xorāsānischen Zoroastrier bei ihrer Exilierung nach Gujarāt in umgekehrter Richtung wählten). In Gujarāt (Broach, Gegend von Sūrat) finden wir 1321–1324 den Dominikaner Jordanus Catalani (s. Yule 1863, zu den Pārsī dort Kap. 4.23), eben in den Jahren, als dort auch der Kopist Mihrābān Kayxusrō tätig war. Allerdings haben Jordanus wie sein Zeitgenosse Odoric von Pordenone (Yule 1866), ein Franziskaner, dessen Weg über die Gebiete von Kāšān (Yule 1866, S. 50), Yazd (S. 51f.), Westpersien, Xūz, Mesopotamien und Hormuz (S. 53) nach Ṭhāṇa (S. 57ff.) in Gujarāt ebenfalls in den frühen 20er Jahren des 14. Jh. führte, nur kurze Nachrichten hinterlassen (Firby 1988, S. 23; Hodivala 1920, S. 128). Von der Hafenstadt Ṭhāṇa (von Polo als Hafen für Baumwolle erwähnt, s. Yule 1866, S. 57 Fn. 3), das unter muslimischer Herrschaft stand, weiß Odoric zu berichten: „The people thereof are idolators, for they worship fire, and serpents, and trees also." Die Nachrichten beider Mönche über die Zoroastrier sind jedoch wenig ergiebig.

43 Dhabhar 1932, S. 607.

44 Siehe Dhabhar 1932, S. li und S. 595ff.

45 Dhabhar 1932, S. li.

46 Dhabhar 1932, S. li f., S. 595–602; MU II 354–382; T33 (MRL/Navsari; Kopie des Dastūr Kaus Sohrab 1129 AY).

47 Dhabhar 1932, S. lii, S. 602–606; MU II 383–388.

48 Dhabhar 1932, S. lii, S. 606–610; MU II 391–397.

49 Dhabhar 1932, S. li, S. 608; vgl. das *Riwāyat* des Kāūs Kāmdīn (< 1553) (Dhabhar 1932, S. liii).

50 Siehe Dhabhar 1932, S. 604.

Daraus folgt, daß Indien an der Tradierung der Literatur in Pahlavi zumindest in der ersten Hälfte des 2. Jt. keinen namhaften Anteil hatte (s. jedoch Kol. II, K43a 176v). Tatsächlich beweisen ja die Übersetzungen des Nēryōsang des 11. oder 12. Jh., daß im zoroastrischen Indien Sanskrit das Pahlavi als Kirchensprache abgelöst hatte. Die Nachricht impliziert aber zugleich, daß in Iran zumindest bis ins 16. Jh. Pahlavi nicht nur abgeschrieben, sondern für ‚Originalwerke' verwendet wurde (vermutlich reicht eine kontinuierliche Tradition bis ins 19. Jh.), z. B. bei der Anfertigung der XA-Avesta-Übersetzungsliteratur. Gleichwohl vollzog sich auch bei den iranischen Zoroastriern im frühen 2. Jt. ein Schriftwandel. Wie spätestens die *Riwāyat*s seit dem 15. Jh. zeigen, diente ihnen als Sprache der Dogmatik wie der Erzählung das Neupersische. Bereits im 13. Jh. (1278)[51] komponierte der aus Xorāsān stammende[52] Zartošt Bahrām Paždu u. a. sein *Zartošt-Nāme* in Neupersisch (in der modernen Masnawi-Form und im Metrum Motaqāreb), das der Vorrede zufolge das Werk eines Mūbed-ē Mūbedān zur Grundlage hatte, und zwar *be-xaṭṭ-ī ke xwānī we-rā pahlawī* „in der Schrift, die Du Pahlavi nennst". Möglicherweise hängt mit diesem sich im 2. Jt. schließlich auch unter den Zoroastriern vollziehenden Wechsel zur arab.-np. Schrift u. a. zusammen, daß nur relativ wenige Kodices der eigentlichen Pahlavi-Literatur existieren, deren Alter 300 Jahre übersteigt.[53] Diese alten Kodices befinden sich zumeist in indischem Privatbesitz, einige wenige jedoch auch in den Bibliotheken von München und Kopenhagen. Während die alten Kodices die Vermischung mit Texten in anderen Sprachen/Schriften eher vermeiden, ist eine solche in den Pahlavi-Kodices des 19. Jh., in welchem Jahrhundert die Kopienzahl stark ansteigt, häufig (Tab. 2[54]).

Die Pahlavi-Kodices des 14.–17. Jahrhunderts

Der Großteil der Pahlavi-Kodices des 14.–17. Jh. stammt erwartungsgemäß aus Iran. Allerdings sind die drei ältesten erhaltenen Kodices (MK, K20, M51) bzw. deren Vorläufer in Indien entstanden (vgl. zum Jahr 1321 die Kermaner Vorlage zum *Wizīgart ī dēnīg*), und zwar durch aus Iran (Sīstān) stammende Schreiber, die Jahre, wenn nicht Jahrzehnte ihres Lebens in den

51 Siehe Wilson 1843, S. 77 (Wilson gibt das Jahr 1277); West 1896–1904, S. 122. Nach Lazard 1984, S. 624, der einer Lehrmeinung von Rempis folgt, sei das Zartošt Nāme kurz vor 978 entstanden und das Werk eines Kai Kāūs, Sohn eines Kai Xusrō aus Ray.

52 Siehe sein Vorwort zu seinem AWN.

53 Der Hauptgrund für deren geringe Anzahl dürfte jedoch darin zu suchen sein, daß die großen theologischen und juristischen Traktate der alten Dastūren immer weniger von Bedeutung waren und auch nicht, wie das *Bundahišn*, den Anspruch erheben konnten, dem Avesta zuzuzählen.

54 Die Liste ist keineswegs vollzählig. Bei einigen Hss. ist die Identifizierung schwierig, s. z. B. die jüngeren Mss. der PT (JJ von 1867, DP, TD, TDa [19. Jh.], Ta von 1887, JU [1. Hälfte 19. Jh.]) die sich teilweise vielleicht im COI oder in der MRL befinden.

Tab. 2

	1300–	1350–	1400–	1450–	1500–	1550–	1600–	1650–	1700–	1750–	1800–	1850–	o.D.
privat	MK				TD1, TD4a	DH[55], BK	TD2	B; P+D[56]			Ka20[57], 21, 23*; Bh13	Ka754d, 764, 765, 766, 767	Ka22*, 239b, 311a, 313e, 342*, 354e, 372, 402*, 418, 455b, 596, 602, 603, 686, 688, 807e*
M[58]		51									86, 52, 53, 54	58, 59a+b, 60, 61, 62, 74, 77	
K[59]	20, 20b[60]		27(?)			35, 43a	20b(?)[61]	43b		K21			24, 25, 31–33; 22, 28
IO[62]									L15				
BM										Add. 22.378, *22.379	Add. 24.413		
Paris									SP40*, 417*	SP33, 42, SP1186		SP1216	
Cama							Ms. des MHD					R1, 44, 49, 50, 54, 55	R124 (Hindust.), (R241)
MRL									E26*; T66; G17	T23*; T8	E18; T21, 22, 60; G33, 59; F28*, T5	13×F, 7×G, 2×T, 9×E; 5×F	T44 (77Hindust), 61, 62, 63; G1, 9, 46, 56
Bh[63]													Bh13

*FP

Gemeinden von Gujarāt zubrachten. Ob sie dabei auf dem Landweg (über Kandahār, wie dies im späten 15. Jh. dem Narīmān Hōšang empfohlen wurde) oder dem Seeweg (man denke etwa an Ǧāmāsp Dastūr Ḥakīm Dastūr Ardašēr aus Dār-al-ʿabādat[64]/Yazd, der 1722 im Hafen von Monbahi [Bombay] ankam)[65] reisten, ist nur im Fall des Mihrābān zu rekonstruieren. War die Pahlavi-Literatur im 9./10. Jh. in Persien, wohl teilweise auch in Mesopotamien beheimatet, so ver-

55 Cama Athornan, Bombay; ehemals Dr. HOSHANGJI JAMASPJI.
56 Mss. des KN.
57 Ka = KATRAK 1941
58 München.
59 Kopenhagen
60 1 Folio (s. CHRISTENSEN 1931, S. 15).
61 18 beschriebene Folios, nach CHRISTENSEN 1931, S. 16, 16. oder 17. Jh.
62 India Office. Seit 1982 im British Museum (BM).
63 Bhandarkar.
64 Siehe dazu UNVALA 1940, S. 58 N.1.
65 Siehe das Kolophon von M50 (UNVALA 1940, S. 56—59).

lagerte sich der Schwerpunkt der Pahlavi-Kodex-Produktion im 13./14. Jh. auf Xorāsān und Sīstān (und von dort aus auch nach Gujarāt), seit dem 15./16. Jh. dann aber auf Nordpersien (Yazd, Kirmān).[66] Die nachstehende Tabelle (Tab. 3) ist eine Zusammenstellung der zehn ältesten und umfangreichsten Pahlavi-Kodices.[67]

Tab. 3

<table>
<tr><th>Siglum</th><th>Inhalt</th><th>Schreiber</th><th>< Schreiber</th><th>< Schreiber</th></tr>
<tr><td>MK</td><td>Handarz-Kodex + Epische Texte</td><td>Mihrābān Kayxusrō, 1322 Ṭhāṇa u. a.</td><td>Rustam Mihrābān, 1278, Indien</td><td>Dēnpanāh ī Hērbed Dēnpanāh, 1255 Broach</td></tr>
<tr><td>K20</td><td rowspan="2">AWN/JFr & IndBd Tradition; in K20 auch ZWY</td><td>Mihrābān Kayxusrō 1321, (1331, 1351)</td><td></td><td>Hērbed Mihrpānāg Srōšayār/ Nēšābūr</td></tr>
<tr><td>M51</td><td>Pišōtan Rām Kāmdēn 1397[68], Broach</td><td>Rustam Mihrābān Šahriyār[69], 1269 Dizūg (?)</td><td>Hērbed Mihrpānāg Srōšayār/ Nēšābūr</td></tr>
<tr><td>TD1</td><td>GrBd</td><td colspan="3" rowspan="4">Familie des Rustam Bundār Šāhmardān/Kirmān, 16./17. Jh.

TD1 zwischen ca. 1531 und (vermutlich) 1664 begutachtet von Rōstām Guštāsp Erdašīr[70] (TD1 207.6–10) und noch einmal begutachtet von dem turkābāder Dastūr Ǧamšēd Dastūr Ǧāmāsp Dastūr Hakīm[71] 7/3/1113 Y (vermutlich 1744[72]) (TD1 207.11–16)

Av. Mss. des für die Dēnkard- Überlieferung wichtigen Šahriyār Ardašēr Ērīz Rostām Ērīz gelangen seit dem späten 16. Jh. in die Bundār Šāhmardān-Familie (s. die Mss. IM, Jp1, Ave 1001)</td></tr>
<tr><td>TD2</td><td>a) GrBd
b) jur.-theol. Lit.</td></tr>
<tr><td>DH (vgl. K43b)</td><td>a) 159 Folios Ø
b) GrBd
c) ZWY
d) Teile des Dk[73]</td></tr>
<tr><td>TD4a, K35, BK</td><td>PRDd-Dd-NM-WZ</td></tr>
<tr><td>K43a</td><td>a) GrBd
b) MX
c) Teile des Dk[74]
d) ZWY; JN</td><td>Mihrābān[75] Anōšagruwān[76] Rostam Šahriyār Wahrām Šahriyār Mihrābān/ Turkābād (bei Yazd), 1587–1594, Großonkel von s. Ms. B</td><td>< Baxtfīrūz Isfandiyār Baxtfīrūz < Šāhriyār Bīžan Xosrōšāh</td><td>Māhwindād Narimāhān (MX[77]; Dk); vgl. Ms. B</td></tr>
<tr><td>B</td><td>Dk 3–9</td><td>Māhwindād[78] Wahrām Ardašēr, 1659 Turkābād (bei Yazd), geprüft von Wahrām[79] Māhwindād Rostahm Anōšagruwān[80] Rostam, 1669 Turkābād</td><td>< Šahriyār Ardašēr Ērīz Rostām Ērīz Kawād Ērānšāh aus (Kirmān)[81] 1486 < Marzbān Spanddād Marzbān Mihrābān Spanddād Mihrābān Marzbān Šahriyār Rōzweh Šāhmardān Šāhdān Kūšād[82] (Sīstān)</td><td>Māhwindād Narimāhān, 1020 Bagdād</td></tr>
</table>

66 Sīstāner Traditionen (im Falle von Avesta-Mss.) lassen sich vereinzelt in Iran nachweisen. So schrieb mir Alberto Cantera am 15.6.2012 bei einem Aufenthalt in Kirmān: „Im Kerman habe <ich> eine ganze Reihe von illuminierten Handschriften (zwei Yasna, ein Wisperad und ein Xorde Abastag) von einem Dastūr A<s>fandyār usw. Sīstānīg <gesehen>. Sie datieren alle um 1180 Y.E., aber Nērangs fast ausschließlich im Pahlavi."

67 Schwarze Umrandungen in der Tabelle zeigen Verbindungen der Texttradierung an, die durch Verwandtschaftsverhältnisse gestiftet sind.

68 Dr. David Buyaner wies mich darauf hin, daß M51aII +b sehr wahrscheinlich dieselbe Hand wie K27 (Hampel 1974) zeigt, eine Beobachtung, der ich zustimmen möchte.

69 Auch Dahišnayār gelesen.

70 Dieser schrieb auch das XA Mf28 (1706), das Ms. 15286 der Mağles Library, das Ms. Ave 1072 (1703) und ein weiteres Ms. von 1087 Y (1718) (s. Mazdapour 2012, S. 168); Katrak 1941, S. 227 führt noch ein XA von 1069 Y und ein Yasna mit Nērang vpn 1090 Y auf. West 1880, S. xxxiii Fn. 1 sagt, von diesem Dastūr heiße es, er entstamme der Laizität und nicht einer priesterlichen Familie.

71 Sohn des Ǧāmāsp Dastūr Ḥakīm Dastūr Ardašēr Dastūr Nōšērwān Dastūr Zarātošt Dastūr Ǧāmāsp Dastūr +Šāpūr Dastūr Baxt-āfrīn (s. Kol. M50, K13 u.a.m.)

Das *Dēnkard*, das zweimal, im frühen 9. Jh. von Ādurfarrbay ī Farroxzādān, im späten 9./frühen 10. Jh. von Ādurbād ī Ēmēdān, ediert und bei der Zweitedition offenbar in zwei Portionen redigiert wurde (Dk 1–3 = *Dēnkard <ī> hazār darag* „*Dēnkard* der 1000 Kapitel"), dürfte spätestens in der 1. Hälfte des 10. Jh.

72 Im Kol. von M50 sagt sein Vater, sein Sohn Ǧamšēd sei im Jahr 1091 oder 1093 *mowāfeq-e rawāǧ-e īrāniyān*, d.h. nach dem „*Kadīmī* calendar" (Unvala 1940, S. 58) 1722–24, 14 Jahre alt, folglich 1708–1710 geboren.

73 Dk 3.417, 419, 420; Dk 5; Dk 9 bis Kap. 60.

74 Dk 6; Dk 3.158, 285.

75 Bruder des Xusrō Anōšērwān Šahriyār Wahrām Šahriyār Mihrābān aus Turkābād, der 1618 das VS Mf2 schrieb. Ein weiterer Bruder könnte der Yazder Dastūr Māhwindād Anōšērwān sein, der im Brief des Kaus Mahyār (1599–1601) unterschrieb (Dhabhar 1932, S. 615 Fn. 2), wenn nicht eine Namenkonfusion herrschen und im Brief tatsächlich Mihrābān Anōšērwān unterzeichnet haben sollte (s. Hodivala 1920, S. 323). Mihrābān wird im undatierten *Riwāyat* des Šāpūr Bharuci (Dhabhar 1932, S. lxiv) genannt und vielleicht als 10. Unterzeichner (noch ohne Dastūren-Würde) im Brief des Kaus Kāmdīn (Dhabhar 1932, S. liv). An ihn soll später der Dastūr Qyamuddīn 1598 schreiben, wenn sich auf seiner Reise Probleme ergeben (s. Dhabhar 1932, S. 616).

76 Dieser Anōšagruwān Rustam Šahriyār dürfte der *Dastūr-e Dastūrān Dastūr* aus Turkābād sein, der als Unterzeichner im „Maktūb-e Manek Cangā" (1535) genannt wird (Dhabhar 1932, S. 629). Den Namen finden wir auch im Brief des Kaus Kāmdīn (s. Dhabhar 1932, S. lii–liv; ca. 1553–1559, s. Dhabhar 1932, S. liv), gefolgt von seinem Bruder Māhwindād Rustam (dieser wird auch im Brief von 885 Y [Dhabhar 1932, S. lv] genannt). Er ist der Ur-Ahne des Xusrō, der ein VS schrieb (s. Kol. K9) und einen Vorläufer von K4.

77 Māhwindād ī Narimāhān ī Wahrām ī Mihrābān schrieb 369 + 20 AY das *Dēnkard*. Das Ms. des MX wurde ihm aus Indien zugeschickt (K43 177 r 3: *ud az kišwar ī hindūān be ō amā rasīd* „Und sie [die Kopie) gelangte aus dem Land der Inder zu uns"), s. dazu West 1885, S. xviii f.; Anklesaria 1969, S. 24.

78 Von diesem Māhwindād stammt der Brief für Bahman Asfandyār von 995/996 Y (1626/27), s. Dhabhar 1932, S. 594 (MU II, S. 160f.). Der Vater Bahrām Ardašēr war Hohepriester von Yazd, der erste der den Brief von 1627 unterzeichnenden Dastūren (Dhabhar 1932, S. 594). 1650, im Brief des Barzo Kāmdīn, wird Māhwindād dann als *Dastūr-e Dastūrān* und „Dastūr der Epoche" (*dastūr-e zamān* [MU II 445.12; vgl. Hodivala 1920, S. 331]) bezeichnet (Dhabhar 1932, S. lxii und Fn. 4, S. 611; vgl. damit NM 1.10.8 die Titel des Ādurfarrbay und Ādurbōzīd *rāst-dēn kišwar-dastwar ud āwām-frazānag* „Landes-Dastūren der Rechten Religion und Weisen der Zeit" [K35 218 v 16f.]; in MU II, S. 150.2 wird der Ausdruck *ṣāḥeb-e zamān* mit *peyġambar* glossiert). Ein Sohn Rustom Māhwindād Wahrām wird im Brief an die Priester in Sūrat von 1670 erwähnt (Dhabhar 1932, S. 624, 625). Māhwindād scheint zu diesem Zeitpunkt bereits verstorben zu sein.

79 Vermutlich ist er derselbe, der 1650 im Brief an Barzo Kāmdīn als *Dastūr-e Dastūrān* zeichnet (Dhabhar 1932, S. 611) und um 1600 geboren sein dürfte.

80 Ein Nōšīrwān D. Rustam findet sich im Brief von 996 Y (1627) (Dhabhar 1932, S. 594), doch ist es wesentlich wahrscheinlicher, daß es sich hierbei um den Bruder des Māhwindād D. Rustom (= Vater des Wahrām) handelt, der vor ihm unterzeichnet, als um den Urahnen. Māhwindād D. Rustom finden wir noch im Brief an Barzo Kāmdīn (1650), während sein Bruder verstorben zu sein scheint.

vorgelegen haben. Aus dem Jahr 1020 stammt der in Bagdād[83] von Māhwindād Narimāhān[84] geschriebene Vorläufer des Ms. B (Tūrkābād 1659), ist also nur ca. 100 Jahre nach der Redaktion des Ādurbād ī Ēmēdān entstanden. Möglicherweise ist es kein Zufall, daß Māhwindād den Kodex in Bagdād schrieb, an eben jenem Ort, an dem auch der Ersteditor des *Dēnkard*, Ādurfarrbay ī Farroxzādān, seine (oder eine) Wirkungsstätte hatte, sondern mag eher einer bis ins 11. Jh. währenden politischen Kontinuität geschuldet sein. Nach dem Untergang der an den Zoroastriern interessierten Buyiden[85] werden wir im übrigen von keiner Schriftaktivität von Zoroastriern in Mesopotamien mehr hören.

81 Im *Riwāyat* des Kāmah Bohrah begegnet Šahriyār Ardašēr Ērīz Rostām Ērīz Kowād Ērānšāh als Schreiber (s. Dhabhar 1932, S. 627), und zwar in *hampursagīh* mit dem Gīw Esfandiyār Gīw Māhiyār. Behdīn (!) Gīw kennen wir auch aus dem Kolophon von Suppl. pers. 47 (954+20 Y, aus einem Ms. des Gīw kopiert), von ihm stammt die Vorlage des (verlorenen) ir.VS Jp1 von 1618/1638 des Frēdōn Marzbān. Als Mitarbeiter (*az hampursagīh*) am *Dēnkard*, das auch unter Mithilfe (? [s. dazu Unvala 1940, S. 155]) des Wīzan Dastwars Šahriyār Wīzan entstand, begegnet Gīw wiederum in dessen 2. Kolophon (Šahriyār Ardašēr) von 835 + 20 Y (= 1486) (DkM 949.18–951.14; vgl. Add. 328.329 [Unvala 1940, S. 154–158]), wo er ein noch junger Mann gewesen sein muß. Im *Riwāyat* von 1527 weist sein Beiwort *anūšrowān* darauf hin, daß er während der Arbeit verstorben ist (s. Dhabhar 1932, S. lvi–lix, S. 627; HF f. 1–3, 70f.). Das Kolophon des *Riwāyat*s des Kāmah Bohrah gibt nach H.F. (pāz.) *sāl. hašta. sat̰. navat̰. šaš. pas. aj. sāl. man. bi. ōi. yazdagardi.* (s. dazu mit Lit. Dhabhar 1932, S. lvi–lix, S. 627). Die Zeichenfolge *man.* dürfte für L/20 stehen, wie aus phraseologischen Parallelen hervorgeht. Demzufolge wäre das *Riwāyat* des Kāmah Bohrah erst 896+20 Y (= 1547) geschrieben. Das würde gut zu der Nachricht stimmen, daß Gīw auch der Schreiber des Ms. Z&P 8 (Unvala 1940, S. 89f.) von 896+20 Y (= 1547) war. Dastūr Šahriyār Ardašēr hingegen ist (wie die beiden Dastūren Bahram und Gōbedšāh Rustam Bundār Šāhmardān [s. TD1, TD4a]) auch im *Riwāyat* von 880 Y (1511) bezeugt, und zwar als Mitglied der xorāsāner Gemeinde (s. Dhabhar 1932, S. 610). Aus dem *Riwāyat* von 880 geht nicht ganz eindeutig hervor, ob diese Gemeinde bereits in die Persis (Kirmān) übergesiedelt war, wie es dann deutlich ist im Brief Kāmdīn Šāpūrs von 1559 (Dhabhar 1932, S. 620). Während die xorāsāner Kongregation im Jahr 1511 1700 Personen umfaßte, so 1559 mehr als 3000. Es muß also im Verlauf des 16. Jh. zu einer kontinuierlichen Exilierung aus Xorāsān gekommen sein. Bloß namensgleich wird der im „Maktūb-e Manek Cangā" (1535) genannte Schreiber Šahriyār Ardašēr aus Yazd sein (Dhabhar 1932, S. 629 [2 Erwähnungen]; vgl. S. 626 Fn. 2).

82 Ein Großcousin des Mihrābān Kayxusrō (s. Unvala 1940, S. 192), geboren also ca. 1400–1420.

83 *pad Asūrestān andar farrox-ābād ud hubōy ud huwahāg ud hubadisn* (?) *xwarrahōmand ahrišwang Bagdād* (Kol.1 des Ms. B).

84 Tavadia 1956, S. 50. Māhwindād Narimāhān Wāhrām Mihr(ābān) (zum Namen s. das Kol. von Pt4 [Cantera/de Vaan 2005, S. 36f.]) schrieb neben Dk und MX (> K43; s. Christensen 1936, S. 11f.) auch ein PY (s. Geldner, *Prol.* xxxiv; West 1896–1904, S. 84).

85 In Persepolis findet sich eine arabische Inschrift, die darüber informiert, daß der Buyide ʿAdad 955 von dem Mowbed Marasfand verlangte, ihm Pahlavi-Inschriften vorzulesen (eine Abbildung in Herzig/Stewart 2012, S. 110; zu zwei weiteren Inschriften s. R. P. Mottahedeh in Herzig/Stewart 2012, S. 154). Im 11. Jh. (ungefähr derselbe Horizont wie die Kaṇheri-Inschriften [1009]) finden sich in den Kaspi-Provinzen Arabisch-Pahlavi-Bilinguen auf den Türmen Mil-i Radkan und Lajim, „showing that

Māhwindāds Ms. (oder eine Abschrift davon) könnte in den Folgejahrhunderten den Weg nach Sīstān genommen haben. Das war zumindest der Wanderungsweg von Māhwindāds *Pahlavi-Yasna*, das zunächst in die Gegend von Isfahān und Kāzerūn gelangte (frühes 13. Jh.), und das wir dann bei (dem vermutlich in Dizūg ansässigen) Mihrābān Spanddād, Großvater des Mihrābān Kayxusrō, vorfinden. Eine Kopie des Ms. des Māhwindād geht auf Marzbān Spanddād (2. Hälfte 14. Jh.), den Großcousin des Mihrābān Kayxusrō, zurück. Wohl in den folgenden 250 Jahren kam das *Dēnkard* in die Kirmān-, dann Yazd-Gegend. Von zentraler Bedeutung für die *Dēnkard*- wie *Vīdēvdād*-Überlieferung in Kirmān um 1500 war Šahriyār Ardašēr Ērīz Rostām (s. Fn. 79), der mit der Familie des Šahriyār Wīžan in Verbindung stand (s. die Mss. Ave 1001; IM; Jp1), die offenbar auch über einen *Dēnkard*-Kodex verfügte (s. Dk Kol. 2). In Turkābād schließlich wurde im Jahr 1659 das Ms. B von Māhwindād Wahrām Ardašēr geschrieben und dieses 10 Jahre später vom Dastūr-e Dastūrān Wahrām Māhwindād Rostahm Anōšagruwān Rostam wohl anhand der Vorlage überprüft. Letzterer ist wiederum der Großneffe des Mihrābān Anōšagruwān Rostam, aus dessen Hand der Kodex K43 stammt, der Texte integriert, die sich bis auf Māhwindād Narimāhān zurückverfolgen lassen.

Der Kodex K43a[86] ist unvollständig. Fol. 130 r 1–130 v 2 zeigen das letzte Kapitel des GrBd (Kap. 36), eine Chronologie der iranischen Weltgeschichte, die auf das Jahr 527 *pārsīg* datiert. Die verwandtschaftlichen Beziehungen zu den drei anderen Mss. des GrBd, TD1 (ca. 1531), TD2 (1606/9 oder 1626/9) und (das verschiedene Kapitel auslassende[87]) DH (1577 oder 1597) lassen sich nicht exakt bestimmen. Im Falle des ZWY stammen DH und K43 von einem gemeinsamen Vorfahren ab, der wie K20 auf den Subarchetyp zurückgeht.[88] K43 ist aber nicht wie TD1, TD2 und DH in der Kirmān-, sondern in der Yazd-Gegend entstanden (der Bruder wie der Großneffe des Kopisten Mihrābān Anōšagruwān waren beide in Turkābād/Yazd ansässig).[89] Anders als im Falle von K20 (s. u.) haben die drei Kolophone von K43 eine zeitliche Folgerichtigkeit. Kol. 1 (1587 [4/9/936 *pārsīg*, 20 Jahre nach Y]) folgt dem GrBd nach (fol. 130 v 2–131 r 4),[90] Kol. 2 (1589 [6/8/938 Y]) dem MX (fol. 176 v 9–177 r 4), Kol. 3 (1594 [14/7/943 *pārsīg*, 20 Jahre nach Y]) den Dk-Auszügen (fol. 259 r 6–260 r 12[91]). Der Kodex ist fortlaufend geschrieben (MX beginnt verso, Dk 6 direkt nach Kol. 2, ZWY direkt

even at this late time people existed in the Caspian area who could read Pahlavi." Ebenfalls zeigen „medals struck by the Boyids" solche Bilinguen (Frye 1975, S. 210, 211).

86 Christensen 1936.

87 Eine Konkordanz in Michlik 1994.

88 Siehe Cereti 1995, S. 6.

89 Modi („Preface", S. iv, in Anklesaria 1908) hält es für möglich, daß Mihrābān Anōšagruwān der Kirmāner Bundār-Familie angehört. In einer genealogischen Tabelle S. v wird er zum Neffen des Gōbedšāh Rustam Bundār, der TD1 (und TD4a) schrieb. Das scheint aber aufgrund der differenten Urgroßvaternamen eher unwahrscheinlich.

90 Es folgt ein np. Masnawī von 7 Versen, das den *Vanitas*-Gedanken formuliert.

91 K43a 260 r 13ff. = Kol. 1 B 641.17ff.

nach Kol. 3). Mihrābān hat ihn offenbar selbst, vielleicht auf Betreiben seines Auftraggebers Xwarr(ah)-pērōz Spanddār Xwarr-pērōz (Kol. 1), zusammengestellt. Aus dem Besitz dieses Xwarr(ah)-pērōz stammte wiederum die Vorlage des MX (s. Kol. 2), die nach der Kopie des Šahriyār Bīžan Xosrōšāh angefertigt worden war.[92] In inhaltlicher Hinsicht zeigen sich gewisse Ähnlichkeiten mit dem ungefähr gleichzeitigen Ms. DH: K43a a) GrBd; b) MX; c) Teile des Dk; d) ZWY & JN; DH (vgl. K43b) a) 159 ff. Ø; b) GrBd; c) ZWY; d) Teile des Dk.

Die erst im 19. Jh. bekannt und berühmt gewordenen Hss. des GrBd (TD1, TD2, DH)[93] sind wiederum mit drei weiteren großen Pahlavi-Hss. des 16./17. Jh. verbunden, die die Texte PRDd, Dd, NM und WZ – die drei letztgenannten sind Schriften der Juwānjam-Söhne – führen. Sie alle wurden von denselben Schreibern der sehr aktiven Bundār-Šāhmardān-Familie geschrieben. Die Kodices TD4a, K35 und BK stammen von dem (nach 880 AY) aus Xorāsān nach Kirmān übergesiedelten Gōbedšāh Rostam/Kirmān (TD4a; auch Schreiber von TD1), von dessen Großneffen Marzbān Frēdōn (BK oder K35; auch Schreiber von DH[94]), sowie von dessen Sohn Frēdōn Marzbān, der auch das Ms. TD2 schrieb.

Während alle bislang erwähnten Kodices in der Safawidenzeit, insbesondere in der Zeit ʿAbbās I (DH, BK und/oder K35, TD2), gefertigt wurden, gehören die Kodices MK, K20 und M51 einer älteren, bis in die Mongolenepoche reichenden Zeit an.[95] Mit den Mss. des GrBd bzw. des ZWY sind die Hss. M51 und K20 inhaltlich verbunden. Beide führen die sog. „indische" Rezension des Bd, an welche sich in K20 mit thematischer Folgerichtigkeit ein (fragmentarisches) ZWY anschließt (vgl. den Aufbau in DH). Die Hss. MK, M51 und K20 sind aber vor allem über eine gemeinsame Herkunfts- und Wanderungsgeschichte verbunden. Dabei stehen zwei Schreiber im Zentrum des Interesses, Rustam Mihrābān Marzbān Kayxusrō (so Kol. I M51b) (= Rustam Mihrābān Marzbān Šahriyār [sic!] in Kol. 2 von K1 und Kol. K7b) und dessen Urgroßneffe Mihrābān Kayxusrō Mihrābān Spanddād[96] Mihrābān Marzbān Bahrām (sic!) aus Dizūg/ Sīstān.[97] Während Rustam Mihrābān offenbar nur für wenige Jahre in Indien

92 Dieser Šahriyār Bīžan war möglicherweise der Vater des Dastwar Wīžan Šahriyār Wīžan, der eine der Vorlagen der Dk-Kopie des Šahriyar Ardašer/Gīw Esfandiyār schrieb (Dk, Kol. 2).

93 Zu den Hss. s. besonders B. T. Anklesaria in seiner „Introduction" zum Faksimile von TD2, wiederabgedruckt in Anklesaria 1956, S. 1–30.

94 Die Schriftanalyse scheint auf zwei verschiedene Hände in DH und K35 hinzuweisen, so daß wir annehmen müssen, daß das (verschollene) Ms. BK und DH von Marzbān Frēdōn stammen.

95 Zu den älteren Pahlavi-Mss. s. West 1896–1904, S. 113 und bes. Cereti 2007.

96 Mihrābān Spanddād schrieb ein PY (ca. 1290; vgl. West 1896–1904, S. 85 „1280"; Cantera/de Vaan 2005, S. 37), das Vorläufer des Ms. des Hōšang war, welches wiederum als Vorlage von Pt4, Mf4 und Mf1 diente (so Geldner, *Prol.* xxxiv). Die wesentlichen Passagen des Kolophons von Pt4 gibt West 1896–1904, S. 84f., eine Neulesung findet sich in Cantera/de Vaan 2005, S. 35–37.

97 Zum Ort s. Kol.1 K5; Unvala 1940, S. 128f.; Hintze/Kotwal 2008, S. 15.

arbeitete (1269–1278?), ist die Rekonstruktion von Mihrābān Kayxusrōs Wirken schwierig. Die Kolophone nennen seinen Namen vor allem in einer Periode von 1321–1324, jedoch erscheint sein Name auch mit den Jahreszahlen 700, 720 und 732 *pārsīg* (= 1331, 1351 und 1363 bzw. 1351, 1371, 1383 n. Chr.[98]). Diesen Kolophonen zufolge müßte Mihrābān Kayxusrō sein gesamtes Leben in den indischen Gemeinden zugebracht haben. Auffällig ist, daß beide Schreiber teilweise dieselben Kodices kopierten:[99]

Rustam Mihrābān (13. Jh.)[100]				Mihrābān Kayxusrō (14. Jh.)			
*M51(b)	7/6/618 p[101] (Kol.1)	Broach?	< Mihrpānāg Srōšayār/ Nēšābūr[102]	**K20**	18/10/690 Y (Kol.1)	Ort?	< Mihrpānāg Srōšayār/ Nēšābūr
					18/9/720 p (Kol.2)	Kombāyad	
					9/7/700 p (Kol. 3)		
K7b (PVr)	27/12/637 p	Anklēsar					
*MK	627 + 20 Y	Broach?	< Dēnpanāh H.Dēnpanāh, 324/624(?) <Y>, Broach[103] *pad ātaxš kadag.*	**MK**[104]	11/6/691 <Y> & 19/9/691[105] Y	Ṭhāṇa[106]	< Rustam Mihrābān, Für Kaufmann Cāhil Sangān (CS)/ Kombāyad. Darin ein *Rōznāmag*[107]
*M74 (KN) (< D[108]?)	Zeit?	Ort?	> M74[109]				
*M60[110](KN)	Zeit?	Ort?	> M60				
				J2[111] (PY)	2/1/692 Y[112]	Ort?	

98 Nehmen wir die späteren Daten an, so müßte Mihrābān Kayxusrō als sehr junger Mann nach Indien gegangen sein, während sein Urgroßonkel bei seinem Indienaufenthalt schon in höherem Alter gestanden haben dürfte.

99 Zu den Mss. beider Schreiber s. a. KATRAK 1941, S. 245f. Zu den Kolophonen des Mihrābān Kayxusrō s. WESTERGAARD 1993, S. 3 N.1, S. 11, N.1; SANJANA 1896, S. XXX–XXXV; HODIVALA 1920, S. 118–133; TAVADIA 1933, Kol. 569, 1944, S. 317ff. Schon WESTERGAARD schloß aus der Kolophonfolge in K20, daß K20 nur eine Kopie von Mss. des Mihrābān sein könne (während TAVADIA K20 weiterhin für ein Originalwerk des Mihrābān hielt).

100 Verlorene Vorgänger-Mss. sind mit * gekennzeichnet (*M51 = Vorläufer von M51).

101 p = pārsīg.

102 > M51aII + M51b, Pēšyōtan Rām Kāmdēn Šahriyār, 29/9/766 Y (M51aII Kol.), 19/11/766 Y (M51b Kol. II), Brōhac (Broach).

103 Siehe JAMASP-ASANA 1897, S. 4f., zur Diskussion des Datums S. 5 Fn. 1.

104 Die Pahlavi-Kolophone in MK (Kol. 1 nach AZ [Nr. 1), Kol. 2 und Kol. 3 nach Nr. 19; Kol. 4 am Werkende) in JAMASP-ASANA 1897, S. *16f., 4f., S. *83, 5, S. *83, 6, S. *167f., 6f. Vgl. dazu SANJANA 1896, S. XXX. In einem 5. Kolophon (JAMASP-ASANA 1897, S. *168, 7) ist nur ein Datum 15/4 genannt und Mihrābān Kayxusrōs Auftraggeber Cāhil. Das Skr.-Kolophon (JAMASP-ASANA 1897, S. *169, 7; SANJANA 1896, S. XXXI f.) folgt dem *Rōz-nāmag* nach, von dem Teile verloren sind.

105 Nach HODIVALA 1920, S. 120 690 Y; siehe dazu aber JAMASP-ASANA 1897, S. 7 Fn. 1. Yazdegird-Datum = Samvat 1377, Mittwoch, Kārtikka Sudi 14.

Rustam Mihrābān (13. Jh.)[100]				Mihrābān Kayxusrō (14. Jh.)			
				L4 (PV)	6/8 *wihēzag*/692 Y[113]; 732 p	Navsārī	
* K5 (PY)			< Māhpanāh Azādmard (Hs., die Rustam nach Indien brachte.)	K5[114] (PY)	27/10 *wihēzag* /692 Y (= 8. Mārga 1379 Saṃvat) (Kol. 1+2)	Kombāyad; im Feuertempel (s. Skr.-Kol.)	< Rustam Mihrābān < Māhpanāh Azādmard[115]/ Kāzerūn (ca. 1200). Für CS.[116]
*K1 (PV)	5/1 *wihēzag*/? (Kol. 2)	Indien	Für den eigenen Besitz.	K1 (PV)	24/4/693 Y (Kol. 3)	Kombāyad	Für CS

Rustam Mihrābāns und Mihrābān Kayxusrōs berühmteste Kodices, *M51 und K20, sind sowohl stofflich als auch in der Textdeszendenz eng miteinander verwandt. Die im Wortlaut identischen und lediglich im Schreibernamen unterschiedenen Kolophone führen beide Kodices auf „das Ms. *Jošt ī Fryān* samt

106 Kol. 3 štr' t'mnk pṯ' gzylk <y> zlyy̱; Kol. 4 štr' t'nk pṯ' 'thš BYTA; Skr.-Kol. Ṭhāṇām. Sanjana 1896, S. XXX vermutet in der von ihm *Dāmōī* gelesenen Ortschaft „perhaps Damaun". Die Schreibungen der Kolophone weisen aber auf Ṭhāṇa, das heutige Ṭhāne im Norden der Bombayer Peninsula (s. die Angabe in Kol. 3 „auf der Insel"; = Skr.-Kol. *velākūle* „an der Küste"), s. die Diskussion bei Hodivala 1920, S. 118–133. Mihrābān Kayxusrō dürfte dann über das Meer nach Bombay (Kanheri) und von dort weiter nach Norden gereist sein. Auch Odoric reiste in denselben Jahren von Hormuz nach Ṭhāna, auf der „customary missionary route to China" (Firby 1988, S. 23). Eine Seereise in entgegengesetzter Richtung führte den Behdīn Bahman Asfandyār später nach Turkābād (1627), wofür er sich eines Barəšnum unterziehen mußte (s. Dhabhar 1932, S. 593). Zu der Problematik der Seereise siehe auch den Brief von 1486 (Dhabhar 1932, S. 604).

107 Jamasp-Asana 1897, S. 169.

108 Sanjana verwendete für seine Edition des KN Hss. mit den Siglen P (datiert 1054 Y, s. Sanjana 1896, S. XXIX f. und S. 68) und D (undatiert). Letzteres führt im Kolophon den Namen des *Rostam Mihrābān*. Das Kolophon ist bemerkenswert, weil es Segenswünsche an die Helden des abgeschriebenen Werkes äußert (apud Sanjana 1896, S. 68). Dieselbe Art der Referenz finden wir im Kol. 1 von MK, welches nach dem AZ steht und auf dessen Personage sich bezieht (s. Jamasp-Asana 1897, S. 4).

109 1871 von Peshotanji Byramji <Sanjana> für Haug aus einem Ms. des Dastūr Edalji. Siehe dazu Unvala 1940, S. 76f.; Bartholomae 1915, S. 292–294.

110 Bartholomae 1915, S. 217–219.

111 J2 (Bodleian Library/Oxford) wurde von Mills 1893 veröffentlicht (elektronisch unter: http://ada.usal.es/paginas/buscador_obra#).

112 Nach Geldner 1896–1904, S. 13 = 26. 1. 1323.

113 Sanjana 1896, S. XXXIII („PB").

114 Christensen 1937–1939.

115 Zu diesem s. Geldner 1896–1904, S. 13f. sowie *Prol.* xxxiv; West 1896–1904, S. 85; Cantera/de Vaan 2005, S. 35f., 40.

116 Im Anhang an Kol. 2 auf fol. 327 v ein *Rōznāmag* von Mihrābān für die Vorfahren des Cāhil, jedoch „most probably in a later hand" (Unvala 1940, S. 129). Zu den *Rōznāmags* (MK, K5) s. Jamasp-Asana 1897, S. *169; Hodivala 1920, S. 126f.; Cereti 1996, S. 449f.; Cereti 2007, S. 217.

dem Ms. des *Ardā-Wīrāz*" (*ēn mādayān Jošt ī Fryān abāg ēn Ardā-Wīrāz*) des Mihrpānāg Srōšayār aus Nēšābūr zurück. Mihrpānāgs Lebenszeit läßt sich (mit einiger Unsicherheit) auf einen Zeitraum von ca. 150 Jahren eingrenzen. Soweit sein Kodex, von dem Rustam Mihrābān und Mihrābān Kayxusrō abzuhängen behaupten, außer JFr/AWN auch das sog. IndBd geführt haben sollte, dessen Kap. 34 – legen wir hier die Datumsangabe von GrBd Kap. 36 zu Grunde – nicht vor 1158 entstanden ist, Rustams Kopie aber auf das Jahr 1249 bzw. 1269 datiert, muß Mihrpānāg Srōšayār ca. zwischen 1100 und 1250 gelebt haben. Vermutlich ist er Rustam Mihrābān und Mihrābān Kayxusrō als Wanderschreiber, vielleicht in Folge der Mongoleneinfälle in den iranischen Nordosten nach 1220, vorangegangen. Sein Name wird im *Dībācha* von E2 erwähnt.[117] Solches Gedenken in der indischen Gemeinde ist wohl nur dadurch zu erklären, daß Mihrpānāg dieser nicht nur als ein xorāsānischer Schreibername, sondern *in persona* bekannt gewesen ist.

Neben den Handschriften des „Buches *Jošt ī Fryān* und *Ardā-Wīrāz*" schrieben sowohl Rustam Mihrābān als auch sein Urgroßneffe Mihrābān Kayxusrō ein „book called Shâh-Nâmâ Gushtâspa and Pand-Nâmâ Âdarbâd Mârâspand",[118] und zwar aus einem mutmaßlich 624 Y in Broach angefertigten Manuskript des Dēnpanāh ī Hērbed ī Dēnpanāh. Die Kopie des Mihrābān Kayxusrō, das Ms. MK,[119] entstand zwar ca. ein Jahr nach der Abschrift des AWN/JFr, die der Kodex K20 führt; da der erhaltene Kodex K20 aber eine spätere Kompilation von Abschriften des Mihrābān darstellt, die offenbar nicht von Mihrābāns Hand selbst stammt[120] und „most probable ... dates from the latter half of the 14th century"[121], ist MK heute als der älteste Kodex anzusehen, der ausschließlich Pahlavi-Stücke enthält.

Wie das Ms. M51 des Pēšyōtan Rām Kāmdēn[122] von 1397 führt MK zwei Kolophone des Schreibers, die uns Kenntnis über seine Schreibgeschwindigkeit vermitteln. Im Falle von M51 liegen 58 Tage und 151 Folios zwischen beiden Kolophonen, was ein Arbeitspensum von ca. 3 Folios pro Tag ergibt.[123] Tatsächlich können wir Mihrābān Kayxusrōs Wanderung und seine – soweit er nicht noch andere, verlorene Kodices in dieser Zeit geschrieben haben sollte – recht geringe Arbeitsleistung (bzw. gute Bezahlung durch den Cambāyer Kaufmann) gut nachvollziehen (Tab. 4).

117 KOTWAL/HINTZE 2008, S. 15.
118 SANJANA 1896, XXXII; vgl. HODIVALA 1920, S. 124.
119 JAMASP-ASANA 1897, S. 1–8; WEST 1896–1904, S. 111, 113; CERETI 2007, S. 213f., 215.
120 Von Mihrābān Kayxusrōs Hand stammt jedoch das eine alte Blatt in K20b.
121 CHRISTENSEN 1931, S. 11.
122 Im Jahr 1595 kopierte in Broach ein Ērbed Ardašēr Mōbed Zīwāk Vīkāk Ardašēr Rām Kāmdīn ein *Vīdēvdād* aus einer Hs. des Mihrābān Kayxusrō (JAMASP 1907, S. x–xi), doch scheint aus zeitlichen Gründen der hier genannte Rām Kāmdīn nicht mit dem Schreiber Rām Kāmdīn identisch zu sein.
123 Siehe dazu HAUG/WEST 1872, S. v; BARTHOLOMAE 1915, S. 59.

Tab. 4

	AWN/JFr (K20)	MK (a)	MK (b)	J2 (PY)	L4 (PV)	K5 (PY)	K1 (PV)
Ort	Ṭhāṇa?	Ṭhāṇa		?	Navsārī	Kombāy	
Datum	18/10/690	11/6/691	19/9/691	2/1/692	6/8/692	27/10/692	24/4/693

Zeitabstand		238	58	108	214	81	182	
Folios		MK 1–74 (12 Z)	MK 74–160 (12 Z)	J2 385 (15 Z)	L4 304 (15 Z)	K5 328 (15–17 Z)	K1 340 (16 Z)	
Folios tägl.		0,3	1,5	3,5	1,4	4	1,9	

Vergleichen wir abschließend die Geschichte der Pahlavi-Literatur des 9./10. Jh. mit deren Tradierung im 14.–17. Jh., so tritt als eine Gemeinsamkeit zutage, daß sich beide Prozesse in einem engen Familiennetz (meist) hoher Priester vollziehen. Während jedoch die Textkomposition der Pahlavi-Schriften des 9./10. Jh. auf Fārs beschränkt zu sein scheint, sind für deren Texttradierung zunächst vor allem Bagdād, Xorāsān und Sīstān von Bedeutung. Erst im 16. Jh. scheint Nordost-Persien diesbezügliche eine Vorrangstellung erhalten zu haben. Die Graphik auf der folgenden Seite versucht, die Wanderungsbewegungen der Pahlavi-Kodices zwischen dem 11. und 17. Jh. nachzuzeichnen.[124]

Literatur

ANKLESARIA, T.D. 1908: *The Bûndahishn. Being a Facsimile of the TD Manuscript No.2 brought from Persia by Dastur Tîrandâz and now preserved in the late Ervad Tahmuras' Library.* With an Introduction by B.T. ANKLESARIA. Bombay.

ANKLESARIA, B.T. 1956: *Zand-Ākāsīh. Iranian or Greater Bundahišn. Transliteration and Translation in English.* Bombay.

— 1962: *Rivāyat-ī Hēmīt-ī Ašavahištān.* Vol. I: *Pahlavi Text.* Bombay.

— 1964: *Vichitakiha-i Zatsparam.* Pt. 1. Bombay.

— 1969: *Pahlavi Rivāyat of Āturfarnbag and Farnbag-Srōš.* 2 vol. Bombay.

ASHA, R. (o.D.): „The traditional history of the Zoroastrian Scriptures" (Elektron ische Publikation. http://www.rahamasha.net/uploads/2/3/2/8/2328777/dk_iii__420.pdf)

BARR, K. 1944: „Preface." In: *Selections from Codices K7 and K25 (Vispered and Frahang i Pahlavīk) and Tracings of the Avesta Codex K1.* Codices Avestici et Pahlavici Bibliothecae Universitatis Hafniensis, vol. XII. Copenhagen.

124 Unterstrichen sind die Ortsnamen, die in NM (881 n. Chr.) genannt werden.

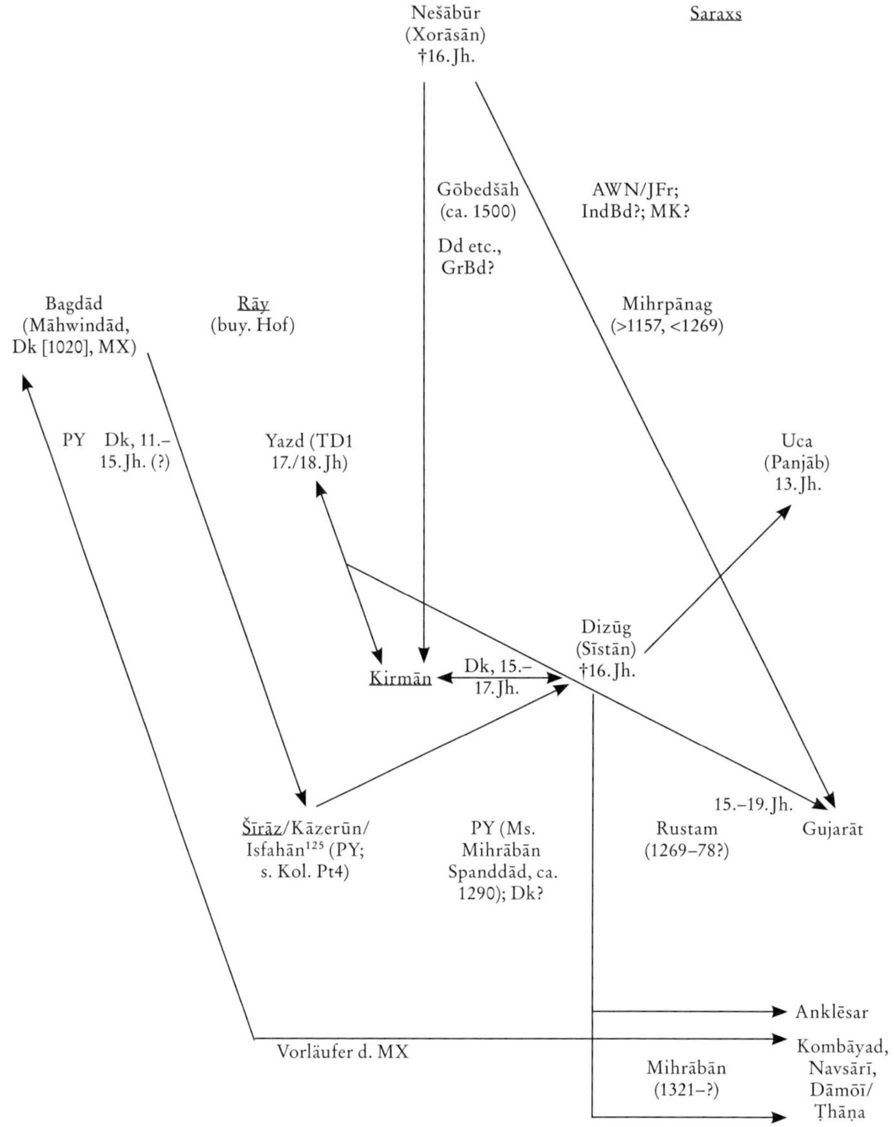

125 Zum Rūddašt-Gebiet, aus dem der im Kolophon von Pt4 genannte Rūstaxm Dādohrmazd stammte, s. SCHWARZ 1969, S. 637f. Zum problematischen „*deh*" wlcwk s. CANTERA/DE VAAN 2005, S. 36 Fn. 22.

Bartholomae, Ch. 1915: *Die Zendhandschriften der K.Hof- und Staatsbibliothek in München*. München.

Boyce, M. 1968: „Middle Persian Literature." In: HdO 1.4.2.1, S. 31–66.

– 1979: *Zoroastrians. Their Religious Beliefs and Practices*. London.

Browne, E. G. 1903: *The Lubábu'l-albáb of Muḥammad 'Awfí*. Vol. II. London.

– 1902 (Reprint 1951): *A Literary History of Persia. Volume I: From the Earliest Times until Firdousí*. Camebridge.

Cantera, A. / M. de Vaan 2005: „Remarks on the Colophon of the Avestan Manuscripts Pt4 and Mf4." In: *StIr* 34, S. 31–42.

Cereti, C. G. 1991: *An 18th century account of Parsi history. The Qesse-ye Zartoštiān-e Hendustān*. Napoli.

– 1995: *The Zand ī Wahman Yasn. A Zoroastrian Apocalypse*. Roma.

– 1996: „Zoroastrian Manuscripts Belonging to the Bhandarkar Institute Collection, Pune." In: *East&West* 46, S. 441–451.

– 2007: „Some Primary Sources on the Early History of the Parsis in India." In: F. Vahman / C. V. Pedersen (eds.): *Religious Texts in Iranian Languages. Symposium held in Copenhagen May 2002*. København, S. 211–221.

Christensen, A. 1931: *The Pahlavi Codices K20 & K20b. Containing Ardāgh Vīrāz-Nāmagh, Bundahishn etc. Published in facsimile by the University Library of Copenhagen. With an Introduction*. Codices Avestici et Pahlavici Bibliothecae Universitatis Hafniensis vol. I. Copenhagen.

– 1936: *The Pahlavi Codex K43 First Part. Published in facsimile by the University Library of Copenhagen. With an Introduction*. Codices Avestici et Pahlavici Bibliothecae Universitatis Hafniensis vol. V. Copenhagen.

– 1937–1939: *The Avesta Codex K5. Containing The Yasna with its Pahlavi Translation and Commentary. 3 Parts. Published in facsimile by the University Library of Copenhagen. With an Introduction by K. Barr*. Codices Avestici et Pahlavici Bibliothecae Universitatis Hafniensis vol. VII–IX. Copenhagen.

Dhabhar, E. B. N. 1932: *The Persian Rivayats of Hormazyar Framarz and others. Their version with introduction and notes*. Bombay.

Firby, N. K. 1988: *European Travellers and their Perceptions of Zoroastrians in the 17th and 18th Centuries*. Berlin.

Frye, R. N. 1975: *The Golden Age of Persia. The Arabs in the East*. London.

Geldner, K. F. 1886–1896: *Avesta. The Sacred Books of the Parsis*. Part I: *Yasna* (1886); Part II: *Vispered and Khorda Avesta* (1889); Part III: *Vendīdād* (1896). Stuttgart.

Golden, P. B. 2000: „Toghuzghuz." In: *EI*, New Ed. X, S. 555–557.

Haarbrücker, Th. 1850/1851: *Abu-'l-Fath' Muh'ammad asch-Schahrastâni's Religionspartheien und Philosophen-Schulen*. I, II. Halle.

Hampel, J. 1974: *Die Kopenhagener Handschrift Cod. 27. Eine Sammlung von zoroastrischen Gebeten, Beschwörungsformeln, Vorschriften und wissenschaftlichen Überlieferungen*. Wiesbaden (Göttinger Orientforschungen, III. Reihe: Iranica, Bd. 2).

Haug, M. / E.W. West 1872: *The Book of Arda Viraf*. Bombay/London [Nachdruck Amsterdam 1971].

Herzig, E. / S. Stewart 2012: *Early Islamic Iran. The Idea of Iran*. Vol. V. London.

Hodivala, Sh.H. 1920: *Studies in Parsi History*. Bombay.

Jamasp, D.H. 1907: *Vendidād. Avesta Text with Pahlavi Translation and Commentary, and Glossarial Index*. With the Assistance of M.M. Gandevia. Vol. I: *The Texts*. Bombay.

JamaspAsa, K.M./M. Nawabi 1976: *MU 29*. Shiraz (PCIR 26).

Jamasp-Asana, J.M. 1897: *The Pahlavi Texts*. With an Introduction by B.G. Anklesaria and a Preface by M. Nawabi. Bombay (Iranian Culture Foundation 112).

Kanga, M.F. 1966: „Epistle I, Ch. IV of Manuščihr Gōšnjamān: A Critical Study." In: *Indian Linguistics* 27, S. 46–57.

— 1967: „A critical study of Chapter III, Epistle I of Manuščihr Gōšnjamān." In: *Sir J.J.Zarthoshti Madressa Centenary Volume*. Bombay, S. 147–161.

— 1968: „A study of the first two Chapters of the first Epistle of Manuščihr Gōšnjamān." In: *Proceedings of the XXVI International Congress of Orientalists*. Vol. 2. New Delhi, S. 218–225.

— 1971: „A critical study of Ch. V of Epistle I of Manuščihr Gōšnjamān." In: *Journal of the Ganganatha Kendriya Sanskrit Vidyapeetha* 27, S. 303–313.

— 1974: „A critical study of Epistle I Ch. 6 and 7 of Manuščihr Gōšnjamān." In: P. Gignoux/A. Tafazzoli (eds.): *Memorial J. de Menasce*. Louvain, S. 252–262.

Katrak, J.C. 1941: *Oriental treasures being a condensed tabular descriptive statement of over a thousand manuscripts and of their colophons written in Iranian and Indian languages and lying in private libraries of Parsis in different centres of Gujarat*. Bombay.

Kotwal, F.M./A. Hintze 2008: *The Khorda Avesta and Yăst Codex E1. Facsimile edition*. Wiesbaden.

Kreyenbroek, Ph.G. 1987a: „The Zoroastrian Priesthood." In: StIr 1987, Cah. 5, S. 151–166.

— 1987b: „The Dâdestân î Dênîg on Priests." In: *IIJ* 30, S. 185–208.

— 2002: „Millennialism in the Zoroastrian Tradition." In: A. Amanat/M. Bernhardsson: *Imaging the End: Visions of Apocalypse from the Ancient Middle East to Modern America*. London/New York, S. 33–55, 339–344.

Lazard, G. 1984: „The rise of the New Persian language." In: *Cambridge History of Iran* 4, S. 595–633.

Macuch, M. 1993: *Rechtskasuistik und Gerichtspraxis zu Beginn des siebenten Jahrhunderts in Iran. Die Rechtssammlung des Farroḫmard i Wahrāmān*. Wiesbaden (Iranica 1).

— 2009: „Pahlavi Literature." In: R.E.Emmerick/M.Macuch: *The Literature of Pre-Islamic Iran. Companion Volume I to A History of Persian Literature*. London/New York, S. 116–196.

Mazdapour, K. 1378 H 1990: *Barrasī-i dastniwīs MU 29*. Tehrān.

— 2012: „Twelve Newly Found Avestan Manuscripts in Iran." In: A. Cantera (ed.): *The Transmission of the Avesta*. Wiesbaden (Iranica 20), S. 165–172.

de Menasce, J. 1945: *Une apologétique mazdéenne du IXe siecle. Škand-Gumānīk vičār. La solution décisive des doutes. Texte pazend-pehlevi transcrit, traduit et commenté*. Fribourg.

— 1958: *Une encyclopédie mazdéenne: Le Dēnkart. Quatre conférences données à l'université de Paris*. Paris.

DE MEYNARD, B./P. DE COURTEILLE 1861–1877: *Abu-ʿl-Ḥasan ʿAlī Ibn-al-Ḥusain. al- Masʿūdī Les Prairies d'Or*. 9 Vols. Paris.
MICHLIK, D. 1994: „Konkordanz zu Handschriften und Textausgaben des Bundahišn." In: *Studia Iranica, Mesopotamica & Anatolica* 1, S. 71–100.
MILLS, L.H. 1893: *The ancient manuscript of the Yasna, with ist Pahlavi translation (A.D. 1323) generally quoted as J2, reproduced in facsimile*. Oxford.
MODI, J.J. 1931: „The Mobadān Mobad Omîd bin Ashavast referred to by Hamzā Ispahāni. Who was he?" In: *Studia Indo-Iranica, Ehrengabe für Wilhelm Geiger*. Leipzig, S. 274–288.
ROSE, J. 2011: *Zoroastrianism. An Introduction*. London / New York.
SANJANA, P. 1896: *The Kârnâmê î Artakhshîr î Pâpakân, being the Oldest Surviving Records of the Zoroastrian Emperor Ardashîr Bâbakân, the Founder of the Sâsânian Dynasty in Irân. The Original Pahlavi Text edited for the first time with a Transliteration in Roman Charakters, Translations into the English and Gujerati Languages, with Explanatory and Philological Notes, an Introduction, and Appendix*. Bombay.
SCHWARZ, P. 1969: *Iran im Mittelalter nach den arabischen Geographen. 9 Teile in einem Band*. Reprogr. Nachdr. der Ausg. Leipzig (T.8: Zwickau; T.9: Stuttgart [u. a.]) 1896 – 1935. Hildesheim.
SHAKI, M. 1998: "Ēmēd ī Ašawahištān." In: *EIr* VIII, S. 413–414.
SPULER, B. 1952: *Iran in frühislamischer Zeit. Politik, Kultur, Verwaltung und öffentliches Leben zwischen der arabischen und seldschukischen Eroberung*. Wiesbaden.
TAVADIA, J.C. 1930: *Šāyast-nē-šayast. A Pahlavi text on religious customs edited, transliterated and translated with introduction and notes*. Hamburg.
— 1933: Rezension von Christensen, A.: „The Pahlavi Codices K20 & K20b ..." In: OLZ 8/9, Kol. 567–569.
— 1943: „Zum iranischen Feuertempel." In: OLZ, Kol. 57–66.
— 1944 : „Zur Pflege des iranischen Schrifttums im Mittelalter." In: *ZDMG* 98, S. 313–332.
— 1956: *Die mittelpersische Sprache und Literatur der Zarathustrier*. Leipzig (Iranische Texte und Hilfsbücher 2).
UNVALA, E.M.R. 1922: *Dârâb Hormazyâr's Rivâyat*. With an introduction by J.J. MODI. 2 vols. Bombay.
UNVALA, J.M. 1940: *Collection of Colophons of Manuscripts bearing on Zoroastrianism in some Libraries of Europe*. Bombay.
WEST, E.W. 1882: *Pahlavi Texts*. Part II: *The Dādistān-ī Dīnīk and the Epistels of Mānūśkīhar*. Oxford (SBE 18).
— 1885: *Pahlavi Texts*. Part III: *Dīnā-ī Maīnōg-ī Khirad, Sikand-Gūmānīk Vigār, Sad Dar*. Oxford (SBE 24).
— 1892: *Pahlavi Texts*. Part IV: *Contents of the Nasks*. Oxford (SBE 37).
— 1896–1904: „Pahlavi Literature." In: GrIrPh II.3, S. 75–129.
WESTERGAARD, N.L. 1993: *Zendavesta or the Religious Books of the Zoroastrians*. Neu herausgegeben mit einem Essay über Niels Ludvig Westergaard und seine Avesta-Ausgabe von RÜDIGER SCHMITT. Vol. I: *The Zend texts*. Wiesbaden [Erstausgabe Copenhagen 1852–1854].
WILSON, J. 1843: *The Parsi Religion*. Bombay.

YULE, H. (ed.) 1863: *Mirabilia Descripta. Wonders of the East, Friar Jordanus, of the order of preachers and Bishop of Columbum in India the Greater (circa 1330). Tr. from the Latin original as publ. at Paris in 1839 ... with the addition of a commentary.* Hakluyt Society, London. (Elektronisch unter: http://ia700308.us.archive.org/7/items/mirabiliadescrip00jord/mirabiliadescrip00jord.pdf)

— (ed.) 1866: *Cathay and the Way Thither*, being a collection of Medieval Notices of Notice of China. vol. I. Hakluyt Society, London. (Elektronisch unter: http://archive.org/stream/CathayAndTheWayThitherVol1/Cathay_and_the_way_thither_a_collection#page/n327/mode/2up/).

Ignatius Pietraszewski – ein polnischer Iranist in Berlin

MANFRED LORENZ †

Polnische Wissenschaftler haben seit Jahren einen würdigen Beitrag zur Erforschung von Sprache, Geschichte und Kultur Irans sowie der sprachlich und kulturell anverwandten Staaten (Afghanistan, Tadshikistan, Nord-Ossetien) und auch der Völker der Kurden , Baludshen, Pamiris u. a. geleistet.

Während einer Einladung zu iranistischen Vorlesungen an der Krakauer Jagiellonen-Universität wurde ich mit vielen Kollegen bekannt, die wertvolle Arbeit auf dem Gebiet der Iranistik vorzuweisen haben. Als Beispiel könnte man die Festschrift für den Krakauer Iranisten WLADYSLAW DULĘBA nennen[1], in der interessante Beiträge von ANDRZEJ PISOWICZ, ANNA KRASNOWOLSKA, KINGA MACIUSZAK, BARBARA MEKARSKA und JADWIGA PSTRUSIŃSKA zu finden sind, neben einer Arbeit des in Belgien tätigen und 2008 verstorbenen Professors WOJCIECH SKALMOWSKI, der übrigens in Berlin bei Prof. H.F.J. JUNKER promoviert wurde.

Bei meiner Arbeit über die Entwicklung der Berliner Iranistik[2] stieß ich auf den Namen IGNATIUS PIETRASZEWSKI. Die eingehendere Untersuchung des Berliner Vorlesungsverzeichnisses und einer polnischen Internet-Studie ergab interessante Informationen: IGNACY (IGNATIUS) PIETRASZEWSKI wurde am 31.12.1796 in Biskupiec (Warmia/Ermland) geboren.[3] Von 1807 bis 1813 besuchte er das Gymnasium der Dominikaner in Grodno. Danach verdiente er mehrere Jahre seinen Lebensunterhalt als Hauslehrer, bis er im Jahre 1822 nach Wilna übersiedeln konnte, wo er sich in der Fakultät für Literatur einschrieb. Bei Prof. WILHELM MÜNNICH hörte er Vorlesungen über Persisch und Arabisch.

Im Jahre 1826 , so liest man in der Internet-Studie, übersiedelte er nach Sankt Petersburg, um dort am Institut für Orientalische Sprachen zu studieren. Nach Auskunft russischer Kollegen gab es in Sankt Petersburg damals nur ein Asiatisches Museum und eine Filiale des Moskauer Orient-Instituts. Es bestehen für mich also noch Unklarheiten, was mit dem „Institut języków wschodnich" gemeint ist. Dank seines Fleißes und der Unterstützung von Gönnern bekam

1 *Iranica Cracoviensia. Cracow Iranian Studies in memory of Wladyslaw Duleba.* Cracow 1996.

2 In: *Spektrum Iran, Zeitschrift für islamisch-iranische Kultur* 2 (2013), S. 44–67.

3 Nach anderen Quellen ist sein Geburtsdatum der 1. Januar 1797.

er im Jahre 1830 ein Stipendium an diesem Institut für Orientalische Sprachen und erhielt zur gleichen Zeit eine Arbeitsstelle im Innenministerium und später im Ministerium für Auswärtige Angelegenheiten Russlands. 1831 legte er sein Abschluss-Examen ab. Er konnte fließend Persisch, Türkisch und Arabisch sprechen. Mit dem Ziele der Vervollkommnung seiner Kenntnisse in Türkisch wurde er im Jahre 1832 nach Konstantinopel geschickt, wo er als Dolmetscher tätig war. Aus dieser Zeit rührt auch seine Vorliebe für das Sammeln orientalicher Münzen. Es folgte eine Reihe von Anstellungen im diplomatischen Dienst: Dolmetscher im Konsulat von Jaffa, Sekretär im Konsulat von Saloniki, 1837 Dolmetscher im Konsulat Alexandria und in den Jahren 1838 bis 1840 Konsul in Jaffa. 1840 wurde er nach Sankt Petersburg versetzt, dort erhielt er eine Stellung im Ministerium für Auswärtige Angelegenheiten. Im Jahre 1842 übernahm er eine Professur an der Petersburger Universität, wo er sich vorwiegend der türkischen Sprache widmete. Aufgrund einer Krankheit gab er 1844 (nach anderen Quellen 1843) seine Stellung auf und verzog nach Berlin, um sich dort kurieren zu lassen. Im selben Jahr erhielt er den Titel eines Doktors der Philosophie der Universität Berlin. Von 1847 an übernahm er an der Universität Berlin die Stellung eines Lektors für orientalische Sprachen, vorwiegend für Türkisch, daneben aber auch für Arabisch und Persisch.

Er war immer bemüht, seine Kenntnis orientalischer Sprachen auch in der Praxis anzuwenden und lenkte auch seine Schüler auf diesen Zweck hin. So findet man in einer Ankündigung für eine Lehrveranstaltung im Jahre 1863 die Bemerkung: „Denjenigen, die Vorkenntnisse in Persisch und Türkisch haben und die die Absicht hegen, sich im Orient nützlich zu machen, erbietet sich Dr. Pietraszewski zu unentgeltlichen Privatissimis."

Im Jahre 1859 hatte die preussische Regierung beschlossen, eine offizielle Gesandtschaft nach Persien zu senden. Ihr Leiter war der Diplomat Minutoli (der Name Minutoli taucht übrigens in der polnischen Internet-Darstellung über Pietraszewski nirgends auf). Dolmetscher dieser Gesandtschaft war Ignatius Pietraszewski. Es gibt darüber Erinnerungen von Heinrich Brugsch, dem Teilnehmer dieser Gesandtschaft und späteren bedeutenden Ägyptologen.[4] In dem Buche *Im Reich des Königs der Könige (Berichte deutscher Persienreisender aus dem 17. bis 19. Jahrhundert)*[5] nennt Brugsch Pietraszewski als Dolmetscher und schreibt:

> Der Freiherr von Minutoli ... erlag auf der grossen Rundreise durch Persien, nach kaum siebenmonatlichem Aufenthalte in diesem Lande, mitten in der Erfüllung seiner Dienstpflicht, den klimatischen Einflüssen. Fünf Monate später erfolgte die amtliche Abberufung der übrigen Mitglieder der K. Mission, deren Leitung Brugsch übertragen worden war. Nach einem Aufenthalte in Persien von einem

4 H. Brugsch: *Reise der k. preussischen Gesandtschaft nach Persien 1860 und 1861.* 2 Bde. Leipzig 1862–1863.

5 Verlag der Nation, Berlin 1976, S.323

> Jahr und sieben Tagen überschritten dieselben erleichterten Herzens am 19. April 1861 die persisch-russische Grenze am Araxes, um über Tiflis und den Kaukasus nach der Heimat zurückzukehren.

In der Internet-Studie wird erwähnt, dass der persische Schah Náser-ed-din (1848–1896) dem Dolmetscher IGNATIUS PIETRASZEWSKI im Jahre 1860 eine Stellung an seinem Hofe angeboten habe. Jedoch dieser habe abgelehnt.

Mit dem Wirken FRANZ BOPPS an der Berliner Universität [6] erhöhte sich auch das Interesse an den alten iranischen Sprachen, wie dem Awestischen. Auch PIETRASZEWSKI wollte sich hier einschalten. Nach seiner Rückkehr nach Berlin (1861) gab er einige Schriften zum Awesta heraus, z. B. *Deutsche verbesserte Übersetzung der Bücher des Zoroaster* (1864).

PIETRASZEWSKIS wissenschaftliche Ansichten hinsichtlich des Altiranischen werden jedoch allgemein abgelehnt, zum Beispiel wenn er versucht eine Verwandtschaft des Awestischen mit seiner Muttersprache Polnisch zu beweisen. Als Exoticum kann man seine in Berlin erschienene Schrift ansehen: *Das slavische Eigenthum seit dreitausend Jahren, oder nicht Zendavesta, aber Zendaschta, das heisst das lebensbringende Buch des Zoroaster* (Berlin 1857).

Als Kenner und Förderer des Persischen ist seine Bedeutung aber unumstritten. Im Vorlesungsverzeichnis der Berliner Universität wird auch erwähnt, dass er eine seiner Vorlesungen in seiner polnischen Muttersprache hielt. Wer seine Hörer waren, konnte ich nicht feststellen.

6 Manfred Lorenz. Franz Bopp und die Berliner Iranistik. In: Bopp-Symposium 1992 der Humboldt-Universität. Heidelberg 1994, S. 159–161.

Annotations on the *Book of Zambasta*, V: Indian Parallels to 2.139 and the Musk of Khotan

Mauro Maggi

I am pleased to offer these notes on a rule of conduct found in a fifth-century text of the Iranian-speaking Buddhists in ancient Khotan, and on its roots in Indian wisdom literature and law books as a sincere tribute to Maria Macuch, whose works have shed new light on Middle Persian texts concerning the beliefs of the Zoroastrians as mirrored in their legal customs in innermost Iran.[1]

Even in the case of such a long studied and well-known text as the Old Khotanese *Book of Zambasta*, the identification of textual parallels can prompt one to rethink the interpretation of a problem passage. The single first hemistich of verse Z 2.139, which presents us with as many as three hapax legomena (*malstä*, *jūṣḍānyau* and *ttäṣḍä*) is one such case:

139
kye mamä śśau bāysū malstä . śśau mä jūṣḍānyau ttäṣḍä .
hamaggä mä haṃ väte badrra śśäri aysmū hūdva vīri 8

The verse occurs in the materials discovered by Vladimir S. Vorob'ëv-Desjatovskij in 1955.[2] Mainly following Harold W. Bailey, Ronald E. Emmerick translated the verse thus: 'Whoever has crushed [*malstä*] one of my arms (or) cuts [*ttäṣḍä*] one with thongs [*jūṣḍānyau*], towards both is my mind always equally well-disposed, Bhadra'.[3]

Chapter 2 of the *Book of Zambasta* is a translation of a sūtra narrating the conversion of Bhadra the magician, who failed to deceive the Buddha and was then predicted by him to achieve awakening *(Bhadramāyākāravyākaraṇa).* In the Chinese and Tibetan canons, the sūtra corresponds to the twenty-first part

1 I am grateful to Anya H. King for having generously made available to me her unpublished dissertation on "The musk trade and the Near East in the early medieval period" (King 2007, see now King 2017), to which I am indebted for much information and many a reference. It is a pleasure to thank Sergio Basso, Ching Chao-jung, Federico Dragoni, Jens-Uwe Hartmann, Douglas A. Hitch, James McHugh and Nicholas Sims-Williams for the comments and suggestions they made after reading the first draft of this article. The *Book of Zambasta* is quoted after Emmerick's edition and translation (Z). For the dating of the text see Maggi 2004 and Martini 2013.

2 See Skazanie 21 (facsimile), 33 (transcription) and 49 (incomplete translation).

3 Cf. KT 6.274–275, 105 and 91.

of the collection known as *Mahāratnakūṭa*.[4] The Khotanese version is an at times expanded paraphrase if compared with the Chinese and Tibetan ones. The Tibetan was edited and translated by KONSTANTY RÉGAMEY in comparison with the two by and large parallel Chinese translations.[5] Unfortunately, the Tibetan and Chinese versions lack parallels to the Khotanese verse. In the absence of bilingual evidence, BAILEY's and EMMERICK's renderings of the hapaxes it contains can only be regarded as provisional.

Verse Z 2.139 is uttered by the Buddha in forgiveness for Bhadra the magician, who, in a vain attempt to show the Buddha's fallibility, has disguised a cemetery as a luxurious palace and has invited him and his retinue for a feast, but has been eventually unable to turn the palace back into a cemetery. The translation of the first hemistich is not entirely convincing because one would expect that an evil and a good action are contrasted in order to stress the Buddha's equanimity, as is the case with the immediately following verses Z 2.140–141:

140
kye mamä käḍe buljse hvāñi kye vā pharu ggaṃjse vicitre
ṣa ju näśtä buljsā ggaṃjsa kama jsa mamä uī' hamyāro 9

141
trāmä mamä aysmū badra tteri asaṃkhälstu bihīyu
bipajsama buljso vīrä samu kho viysavārgyo ūtca

'(140) If anyone should greatly proclaim my virtues or if anyone should speak of many various faults, there is not a virtue, a fault by which my wits might be changed[6]. (141) My mind, Bhadra, is such, so very unsullied with regard to dishonours, to praise, as the water in a lotus-leaf (pool)'.

NICHOLAS SIMS-WILLIAMS enhanced the interpretation of Z 2.139 by showing that the verb *malstä* cannot be 3 sg. pres. 'crushes' from a present stem *malys-* 'to rub' as BAILEY thought[7], nor is it 3 sg. pf. tr. m. from a present stem **mal-* from the root **mard-* 'to crush' as was suggested by EMMERICK[8], but that it is "3 sg. pres. mid. of **maljs-* 'to destroy, injure' < **marča-*" and "attests the transitive present corresponding to the Late Khotanese passive *maich-* 'to miscarry' < Old Khotanese **mulch-* < **mr̥čya-*"[9].

A safe way out from the uncertainties about the meaning of the other two hapax legomena is provided by close parallels which are to be traced not only in Buddhist, but also in Brahmanical and Jain texts. The parallels confirm SIMS-WILLIAMS' interpretation of *malstä* on the one hand and, on the other,

4 See Taishō 310(21) and 324 for the Chinese; Tōhoku 65 and Ōtani 760(21) for the Tibetan.
5 See RÉGAMEY 1938 and cf. the translation of Taishō 310(21) in CHANG 1983, pp. 3–23.
6 EMMERICK: 'are changed'.
7 BAILEY (KT 6.274–275 and Dict. 325) follows tacitly the analysis in Skazanie 84.
8 EMMERICK 1967, pp. 92–93.
9 SIMS–WILLIAMS in Studies 3.122–123 with references.

show that the meanings of the hapaxes *jūṣḍānyau* 'with thongs' and *ttäṣḍä* 'he cuts', which were tentatively established on etymological grounds, are wrong.

Starting with the Pali texts, a partial parallel is found in the *Milindapañha* in a stanza which is said to have been pronounced by the female believer Cūḷasubhaddā when praising the followers of the Buddha. Since the stanza closes the section where the good qualities that characterise Buddhist monks are compared to those of the earth, it is significant that soon after the Khotanese verse under consideration Bhadra says to the Buddha: Z 2.177 *tterä kṣamovī brya balysa samu kho śśandā ne ju oysa* 'So forgiving are you, beloved Buddha: like the earth, you do not get angry'. In Vilhelm Trenckner's edition the Pali stanza appears as follows:[10]

> *Milindapañha* 383.3–6
> *Ekañ c' evāhaṃ vāsiyā taccheyya' kupitamānasā,*[11]
> *ekañ c' evāhaṃ gandhena ālimpeyya' pamoditā,*
> *Amusmiṃ paṭigho natthi, rāgo asmiṃ na vijjati,*
> *paṭhavīsamacittā te, tādisā samaṇā mamā.*

This may be translated 'Should I ever, with an angry mind, hack one with an axe (or), delighted, anoint another one with scent, there is no hatred (for me) in that one, nor is there affection (for me) in this one: their mind is impartial like the earth, such are my monks' with Andrej V. Paribok and Édith Nolot.[12] However, the reading *c' evāhaṃ*, with *ahaṃ* 'I', may be a mistake induced by the fact that Cūḷasubhaddā herself is speaking and the feminines *kupitamānasā* 'angry in mind' and *pamoditā* 'delighted' may have been adopted by the editor as a consequence, though all manuscripts used by Trenckner had °*mānaso* and three of them had *pamodito* (BC) or *pamodiko* (M) in the masculine. Thus, Thomas W. Rhys Davids, the first translator of the text into a Western language, may have been right in departing from Trenckner's text and following the Sinhala translation by the eighteenth-century Buddhist scholar Hīnaṭikumburē Sumaṅgala and the underlying Pali text:

10 Ed. Trenckner 1928. In this and the following Pali and Sanskrit quotations I have standardised the sandhi.

11 The hemistich is hypermetrical: read *tacche* (cf. CST4).

12 Cf. Paribok 1989, p. 344: 'Odnaždy na monaha ja / So zlosti podnjala topor, / Drugim byla dovol'na tak, / Čto blagovon'em umastila. / Ničut' ne rasserdilsja tot, / A ėtot laskoj ne prel'stilsja. / Vot kakovy moi monahi – / Zemle podobny bespristrast'em!'; and Nolot 1995, pp. 296–297: 'Dans un accès de colère, je pourrais débiter l'une d'eux à la hache, / Réjouie, je pourrais oindre l'autre de parfum : / Celui-là n'a pas d'adversion, celui-ci est sans passion ; Telle la terre, leur pensée reste égale : ainsi sont mes ascètes'. The translation 'If I, angry in mind, were to hack one person with an axe; / If I, rejoicing, were to anoint another with scent— / There is no repugnance for that one; no attachment to this one exists: / These thoughts are like the earth—such are my recluses' by Horner 1963, vol. 2, p. 255 does not make much sense.

Ekañ ce bāhaṃ vāsiyā, tacche kupitamānaso,
Ekañ ce bāhaṃ gandhena, ālimpeyya pamodito,
...

'Were one, enraged, to cut their one arm with an axe, / Another, pleased, to anoint the other with sweet scent, / No ill-will would they bear the one, nor love the other. / Their hearts are like the earth, unmoved are my recluses'.[13]

The interchange of *b* and *v* in *bāhaṃ/°vāhaṃ* is as trivial in Sinhalese script as it is in Devanāgarī and other Indian scripts and the division of words is irrelevant because of the scriptio continua. Mention of the arms in TRENCKNER's and HĪNAṬIKUMBURĒ SUMAṄGALA's reading not only makes the Pali passage closer to the Khotanese, but also brings it decidedly into line with a virtually identical passage which occurs twice in *Mahāniddesa* in a listing of what characterises an Arhant and the Buddha as such, including imperturbability with respect to what is agreable and disagreable.[14] Here, the order is inverted and anointing precedes cutting:

Mahāniddesa 114.22–26 and 459.13–16 *ekañ ce bāhaṃ gandhena limpeyyuṃ, ekañ ce bāhaṃ vāsiyā taccheyyuṃ, amusmiṃ* (459 *amukasmiṃ*) *n' atthi rāgo, amusmiṃ* (459 *amukasmiṃ*) *n' atthi paṭighaṃ*[15] 'Should one anoint one arm of his with scent or cut one arm of his with an axe, he has no affection for that one, nor has he hatred for the other one'.

Among Brahmanical Sanskrit texts, close parallels are to be found, with only slight differences, in one of the two major epics of ancient India, the *Mahābhārata*, and in the *Yājñavalkyasmr̥ti* and the *Viṣṇusmr̥ti*, two works on dharmaśāstra, the Hindu religious and legal code. In the *Mahābhārata*, the maxim first occurs in the chapter on the origins *(Sambhavaparvan)* of book 1 among the vows taken by King Pāṇḍu before leaving his two wives and taking up a life of ascetism in the woods and again, with a minor lexical variant, in the chapter on instruction in a king's duties *(Rājadharmānuśāsanaparvan)* of book 12 among the vows which Yudhiṣṭhira proposes to take, thus renouncing kingship and withdrawing from the world:

13 See RHYS DAVIDS 1890–1894, vol. 2, p. 309 with n. 1 ("Hînati-kumburê reads ekañ ke bâham (twice) and mânaso, pamodito; and he is no doubt right") and cf. vol. 1, pp. xi–xii for information on the Sinhala translation. NYANATILOKA 1985, §7.3.1 translates similarly 'Ob einer ihnen da im Zorn / Den Arm mit einem Beil zerhackt, / Ob einer da in voller Freude / Mit duft'gen Salben sie bestreicht: // Kein Groll erfüllt sie zu dem einen, / Zum andern kein Gefühl des Danks; / Der Erde gleich bleibt ihr Gemüt. / Ja, solche Mönche haben wir'.

14 Cf. the middle way chosen by the editors of CST4 with *Ekañ ce bāhaṃ* but with the feminines *°mānasā* and *pamoditā*.

15 Ed. DE LA VALLÉE POUSSIN/THOMAS 1978. The first occurrence of the passage is explained in the commentary *(aṭṭhakathā)* on the *Niddesa* (*Saddhammapajjotikā* 245.15–21, ed. BUDDHADATTA 1980) and is repeated twice in the *Sīlakkhandavaggābhinavaṭīkā* I and II (ed. CST4).

Mahābhārata 1.110.14 and 12.9.25
vāsyaikaṃ takṣato bāhuṃ candanenaikam ukṣataḥ
nākalyāṇaṃ na kalyāṇaṃ pradhyāyann (12.9.25 *cintayann*) *ubhayos tayoḥ*

'If a man hacks off my arm with a hatchet, and another anoints the other arm with sandal, I shall think neither good nor ill of either'.[16]

In the *Viṣṇusmṛti*, a work later not only than the *Mahābhārata* but also than the *Book of Zambasta* if Patrick OLIVELLE's dating to the sixth to eight centuries with a preference for the seventh century is correct, the maxim is similarly inserted, virtually identical, among the rules for wandering ascetics:

Viṣṇusmṛti 96.23 *vāsyaikaṃ takṣato bāhuṃ candanenaikam ukṣataḥ nākalyāṇaṃ kalyāṇaṃ ca cintayet* 'Should one man cut off one of his arms [with an axe] and another man sprinkle sandal on his other arm—he should not think unkindly of the one and kindly of the other'.[17]

Among the dharmaśāstra parallels to *Viṣṇusmṛti* 96.23[18], the only close one is found in the earlier *Yājñavalkyasmṛti* (first or second century CE[19]), again in the section on ascetic life in the woods. The wording differs, however, and the parallel is less close to the Buddhist passages than the *Mahābhārata* and *Viṣṇusmṛti* ones:

Yājñavalkyasmṛti 3.53
yaḥ kaṇṭakair vitudati candanair yaś ca limpati
akruddho 'parituṣṭaś ca samas tasya ca tasya ca

'He is not angry with one who pricks him with thorns, nor is he delighted with one who anoints him with sandal: he is impartial towards that one and this one'.[20]

In Buddhist Sanskrit texts, one finds the compound adjective *vāsī-candana-kalpa-* in e.g. *Divyāvadāna* 282.2 *vāsī-candana-kalpo* 'He didn't distinguish between being cut by a blade and being anointed with sandalwood paste'[21]. FRANKLIN EDGERTON points out that this is "a stock ep[ithet] of an arhat", which occurs "only in a cliché list of such epithets" and corresponds to Ardhamāgadhī *vāsī-candaṇa-kappa-* in Jain canonical texts.[22] The Sanskrit adjective is frequently to be found in Buddhist edifying narrative literature

16 Ed. SUKTHANKAR 1933–1966, trans. VAN BUITENEN 1973, p. 248 (1.110.14).
17 See OLIVELLE 2009, pp. 14–15 (dating), 156 (trans.) and 472 (ed.) with a note where he remarks that "most mss. present this as a verse" but that "it is unusual for a verse to appear within prose sections of a chapter". The gnomic nature of the sentence, as well as the pressure from the epic, may have brought about the verse form.
18 Cf. OLIVELLE 2009, p. 528.
19 See KANE 1968, pp. 443 and 447.
20 Ed. ACHARYA 1949.
21 Ed. COWELL/NEIL 1886, trans. ROTMAN 2008, pp. 94 and 407 n. 294 (references from JAMES MCHUGH).
22 See BHSD 479 and cf. p. 478 s.v. *vāśī-candana-kalpa*.

(*Divyāvadāna*, *Avadānaśataka*, *Vinaya* of the Mūlasarvāstivādins) and also occurs in Jain works. It was appropriately interpreted by MAURICE BLOOMFIELD as 'he for whom the (cooling) sandal is not different from a (painful) sword'.[23] Its Ardhamāgadhī counterpart occurs in *Uttarajjhayaṇa* 19.93[24] in a description of ascetic life and is glossed as '(one) who is neither angry with one who causes pain nor glad with one who soothes; (one) who has neither hatred nor love' in RATNACANDRA's dictionary.[25] KENNETH R. NORMAN's translations of *vāsī-candaṇa-kappa-* as 'like the (saying about the) sandalwood tree and the axe' and 'like the sandalwood tree (in the presence of) the axe' stress the function of the compound as an epitome of a traditional saying, though he refers to a different saying comparing a noble man, who still keeps his morality and goodwill when destroyed, with the sandalwood tree, which keeps its smell and even perfumes the axe when cut by it.[26] EDGERTON adopts "the Jain traditional interpretation" and translates 'indifferent alike to being cut with a hatchet ... or anointed with sandalwood paste', but remarks that °*kalpa-*, °*kappa-* at the end of a compound means 'like, resembling ...' (cf. NORMAN's translations) and suggests that the adjective means, "possibly, *resembling a knife or sandalwood* in 'coldness', dispassionate nature?".[27] Such a hypothesis is unnecessary, as °*kalpa-* can be taken in its common meaning 'manner of acting' and the compound translated simply 'having (one) attitude towards (one who cuts with a) hatchet and (one who anoints with) sandal', which brings it in line with the pan-Indian saying discussed above. This is confirmed by the more precise Amg. *vāsī-candaṇa-samāṇa-kappa-* lit. 'having the same *(samāṇa-)* attitude towards hatchet and sandal', which occurs, with reference to ascetics and Mahāvīra himself, the founder of Jainism, in the virtually identical passages *Uvavāiya* 29[28] and *Jiṇacaria* 119[29] that significantly share some epithets with the *Divyāvadāna* list.

To our modern mind, sandalwood stands out because of its fragrance and the same must have to some extent applied in ancient India. However, sandalwood also had other connotations, which are not incompatible with each other. DOUGLAS A. HITCH suggests to me that it is the medicinal quality of sandalwood which is originally important in the contrast with axe, since the axe damages while sandalwood promotes healing. This complements the fact that, as

23 BLOOMFIELD 1920, pp. 339–343 (esp. 342), and 1923, pp. 260 n. 3, 286 with n. 89 and 306 ad 7.94 (references from FEDERICO DRAGONI).

24 Ed. PUṆYAVIJAYAJI/BHOJAK 1977, p. 187.6, and CHARPENTIER 1922, p. 151.21 (as 19.92).

25 RATNACHANDRAJI 1923–1938, vol. 4, p. 385; cf. VIJAYARĀJENDRASŪRI 1913–1925, vol. 6, pp. 1108–1009.

26 See the discussion in NORMANN 1959–1960, pp. 269–271, and cf. NORMAN 1989, p. 396, and 1999, pp. 10–11 (= NORMAN 1990–2007, vol. 1, pp. 16–18; vol. 4, p. 268; and vol. 8, p. 9) (references from JENS-UWE HARTMANN).

27 BHSD 479 with references to previous, superseded interpretations.

28 Ed. LEUMANN 1883, pp. 37.26–38.1.

29 Ed. JACOBI 1879, p. 53.23–24, and MUNICHANDRASOORI 2012, p. 61.16.

stressed by JAMES MCHUGH, sandalwood was first of all felt as cool and pleasant to touch:

> what all sandalwoods seem to have in common in the early South Asian understanding is their quality of coldness ... And in the story of Purṇa from the *Divyāvadāna* ... the coldness ... is directly implied on at least two occasions: when the man carrying the wood is shivering, and also when the King needs sandalwood to cure his fever. Even when sandalwood is used in an aphorism in the *Divyāvadāna*, the application of sandalwood paste is contrasted with the *tactile* pain of being cut with a knife *[vāsī-candana-kalpa-]*, as it is in other contexts.[30]

As for the source of the maxim in the *Book of Zambasta*, it may be recalled that its author had some knowledge of the *Mahābhārata*, as he refers polemically to its contents in Z 5.2–3, and that the contents of the *Mahābhārata* were known in Central Asia, as is attested by the list of its books and sections *(parvan)* contained in the Spitzer manuscript, which was found in Turfan but may have been produced in Greater Gandhāra, possibly Bāmiyān, in the second half of the third century CE.[31] One can reasonably presume, however, that Z 2.139 derives from some Buddhist work rather than from the *Mahābhārata* itself or other non-Buddhist works. Due to its nature the maxim under consideration is likely to occur also elsewhere in Buddhist, Brahmanical and Jain literature. Its inclusion in the *Book of Zambasta* recalls what MORIZ WINTERNITZ wrote with reference to the *Dharmapada*:

> in the collection such sayings have been included, as are originally non Buddhistic but have been taken from that inexhaustible fountain of Indian sayings of wisdom, from where also they found their way into Manu's lawbook, into Mahābhārata, into the texts of the Jainas and into the tales of the Pañcatantra etc. It is generally almost impossible to decide where such sayings were placed originally.[32]

Actually, other more or less close correspondences can be observed in the contexts where the listed Khotanese, Pali and Sanskrit passages occur, though they need not to detain us here, e.g.:

> Khotanese: Z 2.141 *trāmä mamä aysmū badra tteri asaṃkhälstu bihīyu bipajsama buljso vīrä samu kho viysavārgyo ūtca* 'My mind, Bhadra, is such, so very unsullied with regard to dishonours, to praise, as the water in a lotus-leaf (pool)';
>
> Pali: *Milindapañha* 382.7–9 *yoginā yogāvacarena iṭṭhāniṭṭhe ... nindāpasaṃsāya ... sabbattha tādinā yeva bhavitabbaṃ* 'the yogin, the ernest student of yoga should be simply such a one in all circumstances of what is agreeable or disagreeable, ... of reproach and praise, ...';[33] *Mahāniddesa* 114.21–23 and 459.11–13

30 See MCHUGH 2012, pp. 212 and 290 n. 43 and cf. BLOOMFIELD 1920, p. 342, and EDGERTON's reference above to coldness as a characteristic of sandalwood.
31 See FRANCO 2004, esp. pp. 8–10 and 17 on the *parvan* list, with reference to earlier works by DIETER SCHLINGLOFF.
32 WINTERNITZ 1983, p. 81 with n. 2 (German ed., p. 65 with n. 2).
33 Ed. TRENCKNER 1928, trans. HORNER 1963, vol. 2, p. 254.

> *Katham arahā* (459 *Bhagavā*) *iṭṭhāniṭṭhe tādī? Arahā* (459 *Bhagavā*) ... *pasaṃsāya pi tādī, nindāya pi tādī,* ...[34] 'How is an Arhant/the Blessed One such a one in agreeable or disagreeable circumstances? An Arhant/the Blessed One ... is such a one in case of praise and is such a one in case of reproach, ...';
>
> Sanskrit: *Mahābhārata* 1.110.9 = 12.9.14 *na śocan na prahr̥ṣyaṃś ca tulyanindātmasaṃstutiḥ* 'neither grieving nor delighting, holding praise and blame to be equal value'.[35]

As for the first hemistich of Z 2.139 *kye mamä śśau bāysū malstä . śśau mä jūṣḍānyau ttäṣḍä*, it should be noted that only by chance *malstä* was erroneously assigned to a present stem *malys-* 'to rub' and *ttäṣḍä* was tentatively etymologised as a continuation of the Ir. root **taš-* 'to cut'. This might suggest that the order of the bad action of cutting and the good action of smearing an arm with perfume was reversed in Khotanese, as it was in the *Mahāniddesa*. In actual fact, this possibility is ruled out by SIMS-WILLIAMS's unquestionable explanation and interpretation of *malstä* 'he injures'. This and the identified parallels indicate clearly that (1) *malstä* 'he injures' parallels Pali *tacch-* 'to cut', Skt. *takṣ-* 'to cut' and *vitud-* 'to prick'; (2) *ttäṣḍä* means 'he anoints, smears' (cf. Skt. and Pali *(ā)limp-*), 'he sprinkles' (cf. Skt. *ukṣ-*) or the like; and (3) *jūṣḍānyau* means 'scent' (cf. Pali *gandha-*) or refers to a particular perfume (cf. Skt. *candana-* 'sandal').

The verb *ttäṣḍä* has been so far regarded as the 3 sg. pres. indic. mid. of *täṣ-* 'to cut' < Ir. **taš-* 'to cut, create (by cutting)' (cf. Skt. *takṣ-*) but this interpretation cannot be retained. Two analyses of *ttäṣḍä* are theoretically possible: either it is parallel to *malstä* and is, thus, 3 sg. pres. indic. from *ttäṣ-* ; or it is 3 sg. pres. opt. act. like *hvāñi* 'he should proclaim' in the immediately following verse Z 2.140 (see above), in which case it would be from a present stem *ttäṣḍ-*. My preference too goes to *ttäṣ-* but, whatever the verbal stem, no self-evident etymology is readily at hand.

As one of the meanings indicated by the Indian parallels is 'to sprinkle', the possible relationships between *ttäṣ-* and the infrequent but well-attested compound verb *vatciṣ-* : *vatcäṣṭa-* 'to besprinkle' < Ir. **au̯a-čaš-* to **čaš-* 'to drip; to drink'[36] should be investigated. The 3 sg. pres. indic. mid. of *vatciṣ-* occurs in Z 22.140 *ūtco vatciṣḍe* 'he will sprinkle water' and the meaning of the verb is assured by its use as an Old Khotanese equivalent of Skt. *sic-* 'to pour out; sprinkle etc.' in the *Suvarṇabhāsasūtra*[37]. The verb *vatciṣ-* contains the simplex **tcäṣ-* 'to sprinkle'. This is homophonous with the verb **tcäṣ-* 'to perceive' < Ir. **čaš-* 'to

34 Ed. DE LA VALLÉE POUSSIN/THOMAS 1978.

35 Ed. SUKTHANKAR 1933–1966, trans. FITZGERALD 2004, p. 186 (12.9.14).

36 See SGS 117 and, for the etymology, Dict. 141 s.v. *-tcäṣṭa-* and CHEUNG 2007, pp. 35–36 s.v. *čaš²*.

37 See SKJÆRVØ 2004, vol. 2, pp. 337 and 370 s.v. *huvatcäṣṭa-*.

teach, show',[38] which is only attested in OKh. Z 22.319 *tcäṣā'ri* 3 pl. pres. indic. mid. (where either -*ṣ*- or the subscript hook -'- is redundant). When combined with the preverb *va*- (< Ir. **aṷa*-), the two verbs are treated differently, in that the initial dental voiceless affricate *tc*- [ts] in *tcäṣ*- 'to perceive' is voiced to -*js*- [dz] in *vajsäṣ*- 'to perceive, see', while the voiceless affricate in **tcäṣ*- 'to sprinkle' is retained in *vatciṣ*- 'to besprinkle'.[39] This may be due to the greater frequence of *vajsäṣ*- 'to perceive' (with the expected voicing in juncture) combined with the need to differentiate the two potentially homophonous compound verbs. It is reasonable to suppose that the same need caused **tcäṣ*- 'to perceive' to be kept unchanged and the originally homophonous verb **tcäṣ*- 'to sprinkle' to undergo dissimilation with dropping of the sibilant component in the initial affricate before the stem-final sibilant to obtain *ttäṣ*-, i. e. **tc...ṣ* > *tt...ṣ* [ts...ʐ > t...ʐ]. In this particular case, the change **tc*- > *tt*- may have been favoured by the initial of the semantically not too far verb *ttajs*- 'to flow'.[40] This might sound as an ad hoc explanation, but one should take into account that such phonological irregularities and deviations from normal linguistic change are one of the means to which speakers of a language may resort when clarity is at risk due to homonymy and which Jules Gilliéron termed "thérapeutique verbale" (therapy of words)[41]. Alternatively, as Sims-Williams suggests to me, *vatciṣ*- retained the voiceless affricate because it was a recent formation and is, thus, indirect evidence that the simplex **tcäṣ*- 'to sprinkle' was in use in Khotanese and coexisted with *tcäṣ*- 'to perceive', in which case one can suppose that dissimilation took place just in forms with -*ṣḍ*- such as *ttäṣḍä* 'he sprinkles' and the homophonous but unfortunately unattested **ttäṣḍe* 3 sg. pres. indic. mid. of *tcäṣ*- 'to perceive', i. e. **tc...ṣḍ* > *tt...ṣḍ* [ts...ʐɖ > t...ʐɖ]. In either case, the postulated dissimilation is comparable to the one suggested by Gert Klingenschmitt to explain the irregular development of Iranian **dzasta*- 'hand' (< Indo-Iranian **ǰʰasta*-, cf. Vedic *hásta*-, Avestan *zasta*-, Old Persian *dasta*-) to **dasta*- outside Southwest Iranian, as in Kh. *dasta*-, Sogdian *δst*, Pashto *lās* etc., instead of expected **zasta*-.[42] Curiously enough, a different but likewise irregular phenomenon affects the verb *vajsäṣ*- 'to perceive', whose dental voiced affricate -*js*- [dz] is frequently changed into a palatal before the subsequent voiced retroflex sibilant, whether this is kept or eventually lost, e.g. *vajäṣḍe* 3 sg. pres. indic. mid. (Z) beside original *vajsäṣḍe* (Z) and *vajäte'* 1 sg. pres. indic. mid. < **vajsäṣe*[43]: i. e. *js...ṣ* > *j...ṣ* [dz...ʐ > dʒ...ʐ]. Of course, one cannot exclude the possibility that *ttäṣḍä* was written in error for **tcäṣḍä* 'he sprinkles' with *tt*- instead of the comparatively

38 See SGS 40 s. v. *tcäṣ'*- and cf. Cheung 2007, p. 35 s. v. *čaš¹*.
39 See SGS 117 for both compound verbs.
40 Cf. SGS 38.
41 Cf. Lauwers 2002, pp. 93–94: "Quant à l'aspect *phonétique* ..., la langue peut estropier un vocable, dans le but de le différencier de façon artificielle ... d'un homonyme".
42 Klingenschmitt 1975, p. 77 n. 2.
43 Cf. Dict. 372 s. v. *vajäṣṭe* and Canevascini 1993, p. 279.

similar *tc-*.[44] Such an emendation, however, is as good as the phonological explanations above. So, in the absence of further documentation, I find it is advisable to keep to the manuscript reading and to regard *ttäṣḍä* provisionally either as a form of *ttäṣ-* 'to sprinkle' (derived irregularly by dissimilation from **tcäṣ-*) or as a dissimilation of **tcäṣḍe* directly from **tcäṣ-* 'to sprinkle'.

All the above is rather speculative, however, and a different etymology is probably to be preferred. Several Khotanese verbs beginning with *ttä-*, *tti-*, *ttu-* etc. contain the Ir. prefix **ati-*, but they, unlike *ttäṣ-*, are disyllabic, unless the preverb is reduced to *t(t)-* when followed by *r-* or *v-* as in *ttrām-* 'to cross over; enter' and *t(tu)vāy-* 'to convey across'.[45] Nevertheless, it is worthwhile checking possible connections of *ttäṣ-* with Ir. **ati-šaik/č-*,[46] since the root **haik/č-* 'to pour out, moisten' (cf. Skt. *sic-*) is widespread in Iranian[47] and is also continued in the OKh. 3 sg. pres. indic. mid. Z 14.79 *häste* 'besprinkles' < Ir. **hičatai* to Kh. **häjs-* with past participle *hīya-* < Ir. **hixta-* (cf. Ved. *siktá-*).[48] It is unlikely that *ttäṣḍä* goes back to **atišičatai*, because one expects **ati-šič-a-* to develop through **tiẓidz-* to Kh. **tei'js-* with 3 sg. pres. indic. mid. **ttei'ste* [taə'ste] parallel to *häste* and because simplification of an intermediate form **tiẓidzide* or the like to *ttäṣḍä* by haplology or dissimilatory loss would be unparalleled and hardly motivated. It is conceivable, instead, that *ttäṣ-* is an *-s-* "inchoative" from **ati-šaik/č-*, i.e. Ir. **ati-šix-sa-* (where **-sa-* represents conventionally the reflex of Indo-European **-sḱe/o-*[49]). The similarly sounding Ir. root **raik/č-* 'to leave, let, abandon'[50] is continued in the Khotanese inchoatives *pars-* 'to escape' < Ir. **pari-rix-sa-* and *hars-* 'to be left, remain' < Ir. **fra-rix-sa-* with zero grade of the root.[51] Taking *pars-* as an example, the development is as follows: Ir. **pari-rix-sa-* > **par-rīs-* (with **-ixs-* > **-īs-* by simplification of the consonant cluster and compensatory lengthening of the vowel, cf. the simplex Ir. pp. **rix-ta-* > Kh. *rrīya-* to *rrīj-* 'to leave behind, excel'[52]) > **pár-ris-* > **par-rs-* (by weakening and subsequent loss of **-ī-* due to prehistoric shift of the accent to the prefix, cf. the Ir. pp. **pari-rixta-* > **parrīta-* > Kh. *parräta-*[53]) > Kh. *pars-* (by simplification of the resulting consonant cluster). The same development can be observed

44 See DRESDEN 1955, p. 405 § 9(2) for an example of subscript *-t-* instead of *-v-* (ms. *ptạṇe* for **pvạṇe*), whose shape is almost identical with that of *-c-* (cf. § 9(1) for the comparatively common interchange *c/v*).

45 See SGS 231 and cf. pp. 40–41 and 39.

46 As NICHOLAS SIMS-WILLIAMS suggested to me.

47 See CHEUNG 2007, pp. 127–128.

48 See KT 6.417 and Dict. 488.

49 But cf. LUBOTSKY 2001.

50 See CHEUNG 2007, pp. 307–308.

51 See TEDESCO 1925, pp. 59–62, SGS 76 and 150, and WEBER 1970, pp. 256–259 and 286–288.

52 SGS 115.

53 Cf. LEUMANN 1926, pp. 77–78. Loss of **-i-* did not occur in *haspäs-* 'to strive' < Ir. **fra-spix-sa-* to **spaik/č-* (SGS 151) possibly because the root already began with a consonant cluster.

in Ir. **ati-šix-sa-* > **ti-ẓīs-* > **tí-ẓis-* > **ti-ẓs-* > *ttäṣ-* [təʐ], where the change -*ẓs-* > -*ṣ-* [ʐ] has scarcely any parallel but is quite straightforward in itself. As far as the inflection is concerned, it may be noted that the vast majority of the -*s*- inchoatives are intransitive verbs usually inflected in the active and very rarely in the middle. A few of them, however, are transitive and are likewise inflected in the active. Thus, the intransitive verb *pars-* 'to escape' has 3 sg. pres. indic. *parśtä* and the transitive verb *vamas-* 'to experience'[54] has 3 sg. pres. indic. *vamaśtä*, both with the unambiguous active, palatalising ending -*ⁱtä*. Since -*s*- inchoatives are usually inflected in the active, interpreting *ttäṣḍä* 'he (be)sprinkles' as an -*s*-inchoative makes it possible to regard final -*ä* as a genuine spelling rather than a variant for -*e* in the middle ending -*te*. Of course, the theoretically voiceless dental consonant -*t*- of the active ending -*ⁱtä* is voiced and changed into a retroflex -*ḍ*- after -*ṣ*- [ʐ], and palatalisation does not show because retroflex consonants are indifferent to palatalisation and -*ä*- is already palatal.

As for the hapax *jūṣḍānyau*, this does not seem to match exactly the generic Pali *gandha-* 'scent; perfume', whose Skt. equivalent *gandha-* is translated by Kh. *busi-* (with irregular nom. pl. *buśśañä* etc.) in the *Saṅghāṭasūtra* and the *Suvarṇabhāsasūtra*[55], nor the specific Skt. *candana-* 'sandal', which is rendered by the Kh. loanword *candana-* in the *Saṅghāṭasūtra* and by *cuṇa-* (a Prakrit form ultimately from Sanskrit *cūrṇa-* '(sandal) powder') and again *busi-* in the *Suvarṇabhāsasūtra*.[56] Accordingly, *jūṣḍānyau* probably denotes some other particular perfume.

In his *Dictionary of Khotan Saka*, Bailey has the following three entries:[57]

1. *jūṣḍa-* 'ibex, mountain goat', which he derives from "**yaužda-* " and compares with Waxi *yukš*, *yukṣ̌* 'wild goat, ibex' < "**yauždaka-*", as well as with a couple of marginally attested Western Iranian words for 'ass';[58]
2) *jūṣḍānyau* 'with thongs (?)', whose meaning he postulates from the context and which he regards as a derivative "[f]rom *jūṣḍa-* 'goat' with adjectival -*āna-*";[59]
3) *jūṣḍyāna-* 'terebinth, pistachio seed', which he derives from "**yaužda-dāna-* in N.Pers. *vušk-dānah* 'terebinth nut'".[60]

The meanings of all three words were established by Bailey on etymological grounds and only in the case of Z 2.139 *jūṣḍānyau* he could rely on a comparatively clear, albeit incorrectly understood context. As for *jūṣḍa-*, Ivan

54 SGS 119.
55 See Canevascini 1993, p. 275 s. v. *busi-* and Skjærvø 2004, vol. 2, pp. 130 (3.88) and 319 s. vv. *buśśañä* and *busi-*.
56 See Canevascini 1993, p. 261 and Skjærvø 2004, vol. 2, pp. 264 and 319 s. v. *buśśañä*.
57 Dict. 112.
58 See also Bailey 1968a, p. 16, 1968b, esp. pp. 157–158, and 1982, pp. 35 and 55.
59 Cf. KT 6.91.
60 See also Bailey 1968b, esp. pp. 157–158.

M. STEBLIN-KAMENSKIJ has stressed in his etymological dictionary of Waxi that the Khotanese word denotes an unknown animal and prefers to keep to Georg MORGENSTIERNE's etymology of Waxi *yukš̌* 'four- or five-year old male mountain goat, ibex [gornyj kozël, kiik (četyrex, pjati let)]' from Iranian "**āsuka-*" (i.e. **ātsuka-*, cf. Kh. *āska-* 'deer', Sogdian *ʾʾs(ʾ)wkʾ* 'gazelle', Middle Persian *āhūg* 'id.' etc.), thus rejecting the connection with Kh. *jūṣḍa-* suggested by BAILEY.[61] Kh. *jūṣḍa-* occurs four times only in the Late Khotanese commercial document from Dunhuang P 2024.61 (§59) and 62b (§§66, 69 and 71) KT 2.78 in the phrase *jūṣḍi kaga-*, which HIROSHI KUMAMOTO translates 'antelope skin'. He arrives at the meaning 'antelope' for *jūṣḍa-* on account of the "long, backward-curving horns" which characterise the ibex (a goat antelope) as identified by BAILEY and of the "[f]ive pairs of horns of antelopes (*lingyang* 羚羊) … mentioned as tribute in a Dunhuang Chinese document P 4638 (early tenth century)".[62] However, since BAILEY's identification is no longer supported by comparison with Waxi *yukš̌* 'mountain goat, ibex', there are no cogent grounds for the meaning 'antelope', which is, thus, largely hypothetical.

BAILEY is presumably right in positing a connection between Z 2.139 *jūṣḍānyau* and *jūṣḍa-*. However, we now know that the instr.-abl. pl. *jūṣḍānyau* does not mean 'with thongs' but denotes some specific perfume. If the perfume referred to by *jūṣḍānyau* is connected with an animal, then it is likely to be musk, and *jūṣḍa-* to be the musk deer. Of course, other perfumes like castoreum and civet were obtained from animals. However, the sources for castoreum and civet were more far removed from Khotan than those for musk, which is obtained from the musk deer (*Moschus moschiferus* or *sibiricus*), native to Chinese Central Asia (Xinjiang), Northwest China (Gansu) and farther to the north-east, and above all from the alpine musk deer *(M. chrysogaster)*, native to the Himalayan regions and the source of the "musk of Tibet",[63] renowned among Persian poets *(mošk-e tabbat)*. Moreover, Khotan had a long association with the musk trade in the past, as ANYA H. KING explains with reference to the early medieval period, though the picture most likely applies to earlier centuries as well, including Sasanian Iran:

> While musk deer are not found in Kāshgar or Khotan, these important trade cities came to be associated with the source of musk, for it was there that the caravans heading across the mountains into Khurāsān bringing musk must have

61 See STEBLIN-KAMENSKIJ 1999, p. 431 s.v. *yukš̌* and cf. MORGENSTIERNE 1938, p. 465: "*yukš̌* 'male ibex' may have been influenced by the ending of these two names of male, horned animals [*vrokš̌* 'male Ovis Poli' and *drukš̌* 'bull'], and go back through **yuks* to **yusk* < **āsuka-*".

62 KUMAMOTO 1995, pp. 234–235 (ed. and trans. of §§59, 66, 69 and 71) and 238 (commentary on §59).

63 See KING 2017, pp. 12–13, who lists also other species found in Southeast Tibet and Northwest Yunnan *(M. fuscus)*, in Tibet, Nepal, Sikkim and Bhutan *(M. leucogaster)*, in Kashmir *(M. cupreus)* etc., and KING 2011, esp. pp. 145–147 with references.

> originated. Musk destined for the Muslim world from China and the Altai as well as Tibet was obviously gathered in Kāshgar and Khotan and then transshipped. Khotan became proverbial in Persian poetry for its abundance of musk.[64]

Musk is most probably to be recognised also behind the *bwy ʾy cyny (būi i čīnī)* 'Chinese perfume' mentioned in the recently published eighth-century Judaeo-Persian letter from Khotan (Du II 15).[65] The different designation mirrors the changed standpoint: as musk was "the musk of Khotan" to Persians in Iran, so it was "the perfume of China" to a Persian in Khotan, who was aware if its real provenance.

The musk deer is not a fur animal and its skin is not especially valued and is not traded, though it may be used locally. However, it may be recalled that musk pods (i.e. the pouches of skin in front of the preputial orifice in the male deer which contain the glands producing the musk) were cut from the animal with the skin of the belly and then dried keeping their hair, and could be stored and shipped in that form, so much so that they were probably referred to as skins in Jerome and the Syriac Alexander Romance.[66] Accordingly, P 2024 61 and 62b *jūṣḍi kaga-*, lit. 'musk-deer skin', may be taken to mean 'musk pod', a translation that apparently suits better the context of the tenth-century Khotanese commercial document from Dunhuang. In P 2024 there is no mention of coins and sheep are bought by exchange with *pvaica* 'rolls (of cloth)'[67] as the main currency, as well as with other goods.[68] So, we read that *[pā]tca śai jūṣḍi kaga vī pasa śau* 'Then [we bought?] one sheep for one *jūṣḍi* skin' (§ 66) and *u pātca dvāṃ jūṣḍi kagāṃ vī pasa gīryāṃdū dva* 'And for two *jūṣḍi* skins we bought two sheep' (§ 69):[69] that is, one sheep was exchanged for one *jūṣḍi* skin, but a

64 King 2017, p. 206. See also the detailed study by Wang 1993: "Persia did not produce musk, but the Persians began to use it as early as in the ancient Sasanian dynasty. The so-called 'Khotan musks' were very famous in Persian literature. Nevertheless, musks were not produced in Khotan. They came from different regions in China … and Tibet. Through the famous silk roads … musks were brought to Khotan and then to Persia" (summary on p. 128). On musk in Iran and Persian culture, see Newid 2010, pp. 62–103.

65 See Zhang/Shi 2008, pp. 84–85 and 94.

66 See King 2017, pp. 15–17 for a brief description of the pods, and pp. 31 and 134 for references to Jerome and the Syriac Alexander Romance. Cf. Markham 1854, pp. 84–85: "Its skin being worthless from its small size, the flesh alone would hold out no inducement for the villagers to hunt it"; and 97: "The musk pods which reach the market through the hands of the native hunters are generally enclosed in a portion of the skin of the animal, with the hair or fur left on it. When they have killed a musk-deer, they cut round the pod, and skin the whole of the belly. The pod comes off attached to the skin, which is then laid with its fleshy side on a flat stone previously heated in the fire, and thus dried without singeing the hair. The skin shrinks up from the heat, into a small compass, and is then tied or stitched round the pod, and hung up in a dry place until quite hard."

67 Kumamoto 1995.

68 I am indebted to Ching Chao-jung for sparing me shortcomings in the use of economic data in Dunhuang and Turfan documents.

69 Ed. and trans. Kumamoto 1995, p. 234 (I have substituted *jūṣḍi* for his 'antelope').

musk-deer skin (or an ibex or antelope skin, for that matter) would have been in all likelihood too low a price for a sheep. In § 46, one roll of cloth is said to have been paid for one sheep. Though the values of sheep and musk pods—the average weight of whose content may be considered to be 25 g—cannot be determined precisely for tenth-century Dunhuang, 25 g of costly musk seem to be a more realistic price for one sheep rather than a virtually worthless musk-deer skin, so that *jūṣḍi kaga-* probably denotes the traded 'musk pod'.

The solution of deriving OKh. *jūṣḍānyau* 'musk' from *jūṣḍa-* 'musk deer' through the adjectival suffix *-āna(a)-*, as suggested by BAILEY with reference to his 'ibex, mountain goat' and 'thongs (?)',[70] and, thus, seeing it as a substantivised adjective ('what is from the musk deer' → 'musk') is attractive because of its simplicity. There are good reasons, however, for regarding the word as a compound. The second member could theoretically be Ir. **-dāna-* 'vessel, receptacle' with loss of intervocalic *-d-* as in *khāysāna-* 'stomach' < **xāza-dāna-* with *khāysa-* 'food' and *phiysgāna-* 'urinary bladder' < **mizga-dāna-* with **mizga-* 'urine'[71], but this would refer to the musk pod rather than to musk. A second member *dānā-* 'grain, corn'[72] is much more to the point, because musk scraped out in grains from the dried musk pods is traded as "grain musk"[73]. Though OKh. *jūṣḍānyau* may be either masculine or feminine instr.-abl. pl., the proposed etymology indicates a feminine *-ā-* stem *jūṣḍānā-* < **jūṣḍa-dānā-* 'musk grain' (lit. 'musk-deer grain').

This is exactly the analysis which BAILEY proposed for LKh. *jūṣḍyą̄nāṃ* gen.-dat. pl. ("formed from *jūṣḍa-* and *dānā-* 'grain'"), though he compared the Khotanese word with "NPers. *vušk-dānah* explained as *granum terebinthinum*"[74] and translated the verse P 2891.23 KT 3.80 *jūṣḍyą̄nāṃ khaiṇḍä saga dī pai baysgä* as 'stones under the feet thick as the nuts of the pistachio tree'.[75] The text contained in P 2891 belongs to the literary genre of "letters in verse" identified by KUMAMOTO.[76] These present themselves as letters of travellers on the road, but are elaborate literary works of at times lofty poetic mode, which develop the theme of separation from the family, teachers and friends in the homeland. The P 2891 verse under consideration is part of a passage where the poet describes a mountain landscape. I regard LKh. *jūṣḍyą̄nāṃ* as a variant spelling of *jūṣḍānā-*, since comparison of gravel with grains of musk fits the lyric character of the poem: 'The stones under the feet are as thick as musk grains'.

70 On the suffix see DEGENER 1989, pp. 83–87.
71 See Dict. 72 s. v. *khays-* and 262.
72 Cf. Dict. 156.
73 See KING 2017, p. 16 and WATT 1908, p. 786; cf. MARKHAM 1854, p. 88: "The musk itself is in grains, from the size of a small bullet to small shot, of irregular shape, but generally round or oblong".
74 BAILEY 1968b, pp. 157 and 158.
75 Dict. 112; cf. BAILEY 1968b, p. 157: 'stones beneath the feet thick as *jūṣḍa-* seeds'.
76 See MAGGI 2009, pp. 408–410 with references and a list of manuscripts containing letters in verse.

Since no other instances of an alternation *-ḍ-/-ḍy-* are known, the gen.-dat. pl. *jūṣḍyą̄nāṃ* is in all likelyhood a misspelling for **jūṣḍą̄nyāṃ* with displaced *-y-* and the occasional Late Khotanese interchange of the gen.-dat. pl. ending *-ā(ṃ)* (OKh. *-ānu*) with the instr.-abl. pl. ending *-yau/-yā(ṃ)* (OKh. *-yau*): cf. e.g. gen.-dat. pl. Rāma P 2801.59 KT 3.67 *ttūryāṃ* m. from *ttūra-* 'that', P 2783.169 KT 3.72 *tcarkyāṃ* f. from *tcarkā-* 'play, sport'; and, conversely, instr.-abl. pl. Rāma P 2781.137 KT 3.71 *makalā* m. from *makala-* 'monkey' and P 2783.182 KT 3.73 *mā'vāṃ* m. from *mā'va-* 'bee'.

Kh. *jūṣḍānā-* can thus be set beside *yausa-, yą̄sa-,* the other Khotanese word for 'musk', which only occurs in Late Khotanese texts.[77] It is no surprise that Khotanese possessed two words for 'musk', possibly referring to different forms of it, let alone a name for the animal from which musk is obtained *(jūṣḍa-)*, for the Khotanese were actively involved in the musk trade, as we have seen. Of course, musk was not actually used in grain form, but as powder or tincture to be employed in perfumery and medicine. One might suppose that *jūṣḍānā-* was generalised, already in Old Khotanese, as the common term for 'musk' without specific reference to grain musk. This hypothesis is contradicted, however, by the Late Khotanese use of *jūṣdyą̄nāṃ* in its literal meaning of 'musk grains' in the comparison with gravel. Moreover, it is the word *yausa-, yą̄sa-* which is used for musk as an ingredient in medicinal prescriptions, e.g. *Jīvakapustaka* § 57 97v3 KT 1.179 *yausa* = corrupt Skt. 97v2 KT 1.178 *kastūra* (i.e. *kastūrī*) 'musk'. Thus, it may be surmised that the word *jūṣḍānā-* 'musk grain' denoted the raw form of the product, the plural referring to 'grain musk' collectively, and was used in the *Book of Zambasta* in a deliberately hyperbolic way to mention a large amount of musk in its pure quality, while *yausa-, yą̄sa-* denoted 'musk' in general, including powder and tincture.

Going back to Z 2.139, where this inquiry started, it appears that the author of the *Book of Zambasta* expanded the text of the *Bhadramāyākāravyākaraṇa* through the insertion of a widespread maxim, but replaced the generic reference to perfume that we have observed in the Pali parallels *(gandha-)* or the specific mention of sandal as in the Sanskrit parallels *(candana-)* by referring to the highly valued and more typically Central Asian musk *(jūṣḍānā-)*:

> 'Whoever injures one arm of mine (or) sprinkles one with grain musk, towards both is my mind always equally well-disposed, Bhadra'

77 See Dict. 343 s.v. *yausa*. A LKh. *yāsa* occurs also in P 2024.62b (§ 68) KT 2.78 in the vicinity of *jūṣḍi kaga-* (see above) and "is either Turkish 'damage, harm, destruction, loss ..., or Khotanese 'musk'" according to Kumamoto 1995, p. 238.

References

Acharya, N. R. (ed.) 1949: *Yājñavalkyasmṛti of Yogīśvara Yājñavalkya: with the commentary Mitākṣarā of Vijñāneśvara, notes, varient* [!] *readings etc.* 5th ed. Bombay.

Bailey, H. W. 1968a: *Corpus inscriptionum Iranicarum*, 2: *Inscriptions of the Seleucid and Parthian period and of Eastern Iran and Central Asia*, 5: *Saka documents. Text volume*. London.

— 1968b: "Saka of Khotan and Wakhān." In: J. C. Heesterman / G. H. Schokker / V. I. Subramoniam *Pratidānam: Indian, Iranian and Indo-European studies presented to Franciscus Bernardus Jacobus Kuiper on his sixtieth birthday*. The Hague, pp. 157–159.

— 1982: *The culture of the Sakas in ancient Iranian Khotan*. Delmar.

BHSD = F. Edgerton: *Buddhist Hybrid Sanskrit grammar and dictionary*. 2: *Dictionary*. New Haven 1953.

Bloomfield, M. 1920: "Notes on the Divyāvadāna." In: *JAOS* 40, pp. 336–352.

— 1923: "The Śālibhadra Carita: a story of conversion to Jaina monkhood." In: *JAOS* 43, pp. 257–316.

Buddhadatta, A. P. (ed.) 1980: *Saddhammapajjotikā. The commentary on the Mahā-niddesa*. 2 vols. in 1. London.

van Buitenen, J. A. B. (trans.) 1973: *The Mahābhārata*. 1: *Book 1, the book of the beginning*. Chicago.

Canevascini, G. 1993 (ed. and trans.): *The Khotanese Saṅghāṭasūtra: a critical edition*. Wiesbaden.

Chang C. C. (ed.) 1983: *A treasury of Mahāyāna sūtras: selections from the Mahāratnakūṭa Sūtra*. New York (repr. Delhi 1991).

Charpentier J. (ed.) 1922: *The Uttarādhyayanasūtra, being the first* mūlasūtra *of the Śvetāmbara Jains: edited with an introduction, critical notes and a commentary*. Uppsala.

Cheung, J. 2007: *Etymological dictionary of the Iranian verb*. Leiden.

Cowell, E. B. / R. A. Neil (eds.) 1886: *The Divyāvadāna: a collection of early Buddhist legends*. Cambridge.

CST4 = Vipassana Research Institute: *Chaṭṭha Saṅgāyana Tipiṭaka*. Version 4.0. Igatpuri.

Dict. = H. W. Bailey: *Dictionary of Khotan Saka*. Cambridge 1979.

Emmerick, R. E. 1967: "Notes on the 'Tale of Bhadra'." In: *BSOAS* 30.1, pp. 83–94.

Fitzgerald, J. L. (trans.) 2004: *The Mahābhārata*. 7: *Book 11, the book of the women; Book 12, the book of peace, part one*. Chicago.

Franco, E. 2004: *The Spitzer manuscript: the oldest philosophical manuscript in Sanskrit*. 2 vols. Wien.

Horner, I. B. (trans.) 1963: *Milinda's questions*. 2 vols. London.

Jacobi, H. (ed.) 1879: *The Kalpasūtra of Bhadrabāhu, edited with an introduction, notes and a Prākṛit-Saṃskṛit glossary*. Leipzig.

Kane, P. V. 1968: *History of dharmaśāstra: ancient and mediaeval religious and civil law in India*. 1. Poona (2nd ed. rev. and enl.).

King, A. 2007: "The musk trade and the Near East in the early medieval period." Unpubl. diss., Indiana University.

— 2011: "Tibetan musk and medieval Arab perfumery." In: A. Akasoy / C. Burnett / R. Yoeli-Tlalim (eds.): *Islam and Tibet: interactions along the musk routes*. Aldershot, pp. 145–161.

— 2017: *Sent from the garden of paradise: musk and the medieval Islamic world*. Leiden.

Klingenschmitt, G. 1975: "Altindisch *śaśvat-*." In: *MSS* 33, pp. 67–78.

KT 1–7 = H.W. Bailey (ed.): *Khotanese texts*. Cambridge: 1: 1945; 2: 1954; 3: 1956 (1–3, 2nd ed. in one vol., 1969; repr. 1980); 4: *Saka texts from Khotan in the Hedin collection*. 1961 (repr. 1979); 5: 1963 (repr. with corrections 1980); 6: *Prolexis to the Book of Zambasta*. 1967; 7: 1985.

Kumamoto, H. 1995: "Miscellaneous documents from the Pelliot collection." In: *Tokyo University linguistic papers* 14, pp. 229–257.

de La Vallée Poussin, L. / E.J. Thomas (eds.) 1978: *Mahāniddesa*. 2 pts. in 1 vol. London.

Lauwers, P. 2002: "Jules Gilliéron: contrainte et liberté dans le changement linguistique." In: P. Lauwers / M.-R. Simoni-Aurembou / P. Swiggers (eds.): *Géographie linguistique et biologie du langage: autour de Jules Gilliéron*. Leuven, pp. 79–112.

Leumann, E. (ed.) 1883: *Das Aupapātika Sūtra, erstes Upānga der Jaina*. 1: *Einleitung und Glossar*. Leipzig.

— 1926: "Nordarische Verba mit und ohne Präfix." In: W. Kirfel (ed.): *Beiträge zur Literaturwissenschaft und Geistesgeschichte Indiens: Festgabe für H. Jacobi zum 75. Geburtstag (11. Febr. 1925) dargebracht von Freunden, Kollegen und Schülern*. Bonn 1926, pp. 74–88.

Lubotsky, A. 2001: "Reflexes of Proto-Indo-European **sk* in Indo-Iranian." In: *Incontri linguistici* 24, pp. 25–57.

McHugh, J. 2012: *Sandalwood and carrion: smell in Indian religion and culture*. New York.

Maggi, M. 2004: "The manuscript T III S 16: its importance for the history of Khotanese literature." In: D. Durkin-Meisterernst et al. (eds.): *Turfan revisited: the first century of research into the arts and cultures of the Silk Road*. Berlin, pp. 184–190 and 457.

— 2009: *Khotanese literature*. In: R.E. Emmerick / M. Macuch (eds.): *The literature of pre-Islamic Iran: companion volume I to A History of Persian Literature*. London.

Markham, F. 1854: *Shooting in the Himalayas: a journal of sporting adventures and travel in Chinese Tartary, Ladac, Thibet, Cashmere, &c.* London.

Martini, G. 2013: "Bodhisattva texts, ideologies and rituals in Khotan in the fifth and sixth centuries." In: *Multilingualism and history of knowledge*. Ed. by J.E. Braarvig et al. 1: *Buddhism among the Iranian peoples of Central Asia*. Ed. by M. de Chiara, M. Maggi and G. Martini. Wien, pp. 13–69.

Morgenstierne, G. 1938: *Indo-Iranian frontier languages*. 2: *Iranian Pamir languages: Yidgha-Munji, Sanglechi-Ishkashmi and Wakhi*. Oslo.

MUNICHANDRASOORI (= MUNICANDRASŪRI), V. (ed.) 2012: *Uvavāi suttaṁ (Aupāpatika sutraṁ).* Mumbai.

NEWID, M. A. 2010: *Aromata in der iranischen Kultur unter besonderer Berücksichtigung der persischen Dichtung.* Wiesbaden.

NOLOT, É. (trans.) 1995: *Entretiens de Milinda et Nāgasena.* Paris.

NORMAN, R. K. 1959–1960: "Middle Indo-Aryan studies I." In: *Journal of the Oriental Institute* (Baroda) 9, pp. 268–273 (= NORMAN 1990–2007, vol. 1, pp. 15–20).

— 1989: "Common terminology in early Buddhist and Jain texts". In *Jainology: manifold facets: Pt. Jaganmohanlal Shastri sadhuvad grantha.* Rewa, pp. 393–397 (= NORMAN 1990–2007, vol. 4, pp. 264–270).

— 1990–2007: *Collected papers.* Vols. 1–7, Oxford; vol. 8, Lancaster.

— 1999: "Early Buddhism and Jainism: a comparison." In: *Chūō gakujutsu kenkyūjo kiyō* 中央学術研究所紀要 = *Memoirs of the Chūō Academic Research Institute* 28, pp. 3–30 (= NORMAN 1990–2007, vol. 8, pp. 1–29).

NYANATILOKA (trans.) 1985: *Die Fragen des Königs Milinda: Zwiegespräche zwischen einem Griechenkönig und einem buddhistischen Mönch = Milindapañha.* Hrsg. und teilweise neu übersetzt von NYANAPONIKA. Interlaken.

OLIVELLE, P. (ed. and trans.) 2009: *The law code of Viṣṇu: a critical edition and annotated translation of the Vaiṣṇava-Dharmaśāstra.* Cambridge, Mass.

Ōtani = *Ōtani Daigaku Toshokan zō eiin Pekimban Chibetto daizōkyō sō-mokuroku, sakuin* 大谷大学図書館蔵影印北京版西蔵大蔵経総目録・索引 = *The Tibetan Tripiṭaka, Peking edition kept in the Library of the Otani University, Kyoto: catalogue and index.* Tokyo 1962 (quoted by catalogue number).

PARIBOK, A. V. (trans.) 1989: *Voprosy Milindy = Milindapan'ha: perevod s pali, predislovie, issledovanie i kommentarij.* Moskva.

PUṆYAVIJAYAJI (= PUṆYAVIJAYA) / A. M. BHOJAK (eds.) 1977: *Dasaveyāliysuttaṁ, Uttarajhayaṇāiṁ and Āvassayasuttaṁ.* Bombay.

RATNACHANDRAJI (= RATNACANDRA) 1923–1938: *An illustrated Ardha-Magadhi dictionary, literary, philosophic and scientific, with Sanskrit, Gujrati, Hindi and English equivalents, references to the texts and copious quotations.* With an introduction by A. C. WOOLNER. London (repr. Delhi 1988), 5 vols.

RÉGAMEY, K. (ed. and trans.) 1938: *The Bhadramāyākāravyākaraṇa.* Warsaw (repr. Delhi 1990).

ROTMAN, A. (transl.) 2008: *Divine stories: Divyāvadāna.* 1. Somerville, Mass.

RHYS DAVIDS, T. W. (trans.) 1890–1894: *The questions of King Milinda.* 2 vols. Oxford.

SGS = R. E. EMMERICK: *Saka grammatical studies.* London 1968.

Skazanie = V. S. VOROB'ËV-DESJATOVSKIJ / M. I. VOROB'ËVA-DESJATOVSKAJA (eds. and trans.): *Skazanie o Bhadre: novye listy sakskoj rukopisi "E": faksimile teksta, transkripcija, perevod, predislovie, vstupitel'naja stat'ja, glossarij i priloženie.* Moskva 1965.

SKJÆRVØ, P. O. 2004 (ed. and trans.): *This most excellent shine of gold, king of kings of sutras: the Khotanese Suvarṇabhāsottamasūtra.* 2 vols. [Cambridge, Mass.]

STEBLIN-KAMENSKIJ, I. M. 1999: *Ėtimologičeskij slovar' vahanskogo jazyka.* Sankt-Peterburg.

Studies 3 = R. E. EMMERICK / P. O. SKJÆRVØ: *Studies in the vocabulary of Khotanese.* 3. Wien 1997.

SUKTHANKAR, V.S. 1933–1966 (ed.): *The Mahābhārata*. For the first time critically ed. by V.S. SUKTHANKAR with the co-operation of B.P. PRATINIDHI et al. 19 vols. in 22. Poona.

Taishō = *Taishō shinshū daizōkyō* 大正新脩大藏經. 100 vols. Tokyo 1924–1934 (quoted by text number).

TEDESCO, P. 1925: "Les rapports sogdo-saces." In: *Bulletin de la Société de linguistique de Paris* 25.1, pp. 52–63.

Tōhoku = *Chibetto daizōkyō sō-mokuroku* 西蔵大蔵経総目録 = *A catalogue-index of the Tibetan Buddhist canons (Bkaḥ-ḥgyur and Bstan-ḥgyur)*. Sendai 1934 (quoted by catalogue number).

TRENCKNER, V. (ed.) 1928. *The Milindapañho, being Dialogues between King Milinda and the Buddhist sage Nāgasena: the Pali Text*. General index by C.J. RYLANDS and index of gāthās by [C.A.F.] RHYS DAVIDS. London.

VIJAYARĀJENDRASŪRI 1913–1925: *Abhidhāna Rājendra koṣa*. 7 vols. Ratalāma.

WANG YIDAN 王一丹 1993: "Bosi, Hetian yu Zhongguo de shexiang 波斯、和田与中国的麝香 [Persia, Khotan and China's musk]." In: *Beijing daxue xuebao* 北京大学学报 1993.2, pp. 78–88 (English summary on p. 128).

WATT, G. 1908: *The commercial products of India: being an abridgement of "The dictionary of the economic products of India"*. London.

WEBER, D. 1970: *Die Stellung der sog[enannten] Inchoativa im Mitteliranischen*. Göttingen.

WINTERNITZ, M. 1983: *A history of Indian literature. 2: Buddhist and Jaina literature*. Trans. by S. SARMA. Delhi (German ed.: *Geschichte der indischen Litteratur. 2: Die buddhistische Litteratur und die heiligen Texte der Jainas*. Leipzig 1920).

Z = EMMERICK, R.E. (ed. and trans.): *The Book of Zambasta: a Khotanese poem on Buddhism*. London 1968.

Zhang Zhan 張湛 / Shi Guang 時光 2008: "Yijian xin faxian Youtai Bosiyu xinzha de duandai yu shidu 一件新發現猶太波斯語信劄的斷代與釋讀 [Dating and interpretation of a newly discovered Judaeo-Persian letter]." In: *Dunhuang Tulufan yanjiu* 敦煌吐魯番研究 11, pp. 71–99, 1 colour plate.

Vom ersten bis zum 30. Tag: Ein Blatt mit soghdischen prognostischen und medizinischen Kalendertexten

Enrico Morano und Christiane Reck

Hiermit präsentieren wir zwei bisher nicht veröffentlichte Texte, die einen gewissen Bezug zum Lebensalltag im alten Kočo haben und so den Kulturtransfer auf der Seidenstraße beleuchten. Mögen sie ein gutes Vorzeichen für die Lebens- und Schaffenskraft der Jubilarin sein.

Eine vielfältig bekannte manichäisch-soghdische Sammelhandschrift, deren vollständig erhaltene Doppelblätter, So 14410 und MIK III 200 = So 14411, auch bekannt unter dem Fundsigel T II D II 169, an verschiedenen Stellen besprochen und teilweise auch publiziert wurden, enthält Texte in verschiedenen Sprachen, Schriften und unterschiedlichen Charakters.[1] MIK III 200 (So 14411) beinhaltet auf dem zweiten Blatt alttürkischen Text.[2] Die meisten anderen Texte sind in soghdischer Sprache und Schrift verfasst. Einige Hymnen sind in parthischer bzw. mittelpersischer Sprache, aber in soghdischer Schrift geschrieben. Die Überschriften sind zumeist alttürkisch, einige davon in Runenschrift. Auf dem oberen Rand des Fragmentes So 14415 II/r/ glossierte Eigennamen sind teilweise in manichäischer Schrift geschrieben. So 14430 bewahrt vermutlich Reste von baktrischen Buchstaben, während auf So 14468 syrische Schrift erkennbar ist.[3]

Diese Sammelhandschrift scheint eine Art *Reader's Digest* darzustellen, ein manichäisches Erbauungsbuch, das Ausschnitte aus den unterschiedlichsten Textgattungen vereint. Neben kanonischen Texten wie Manis Psalmen und bedeutsamen Teilen aus dem Ersten Canto des Hymnenzyklus *Huyadagmān*, einem Hymnus auf den Sonnengott, verschiedenen anderen Hymnen und dem Schluss des Laienbekenntnistextes *Xwāstwānīft* gehörte zu diesem Buch auch ein umfangreicher Text mit Omina (So 14410 I), die vermutlich in der Art des *Irk bitig* durch Würfelwurf erlost wurden.[4] Magische und mantische Texte sind vielfach in der manichäischen Literatur vertreten. Die Funde in Kellis belegen eine offenbar einträgliche Praxis der Erstellung von magischen Texten, wie sie

1 Über die Formalien und die Publikationen der einzelnen Textteile dieser Sammelhandschrift sei hier auf Reck 2011, S. 133–136 und 154–157 verwiesen.

2 Wilkens 2000, S. 283–284, #311, und Wilkens 2009.

3 Sims-Williams 2013, S. 194, # E53.

4 Reck 2010, S. 72.

in Briefen bestellt wurden.[5] Wir kennen die mittelpersischen Zaubersprüche gegen Fieber und um böse Geister vom Haus fern zu halten (M 781) und das parthische Amulett (M 1202)[6], mittelpersische Amuletttexte (M 389 und M 8430 I)[7] und andere Beschwörungstexte[8], wie auch die Beschwörungsschalen mit manichäischer und syrischer Schrift aus Mesopotamien[9].

Einige Fragmente lassen sich aufgrund der Tatsache, dass sie sehr kleinteilige Faltungsspuren aufweisen und als Einzelblätter vorliegen, als in Amulettbehältern aufbewahrt und benutzt vorstellen, so auch das baktrische Fragment M 1224.[10] Das illustrierte mittelpersische Omenfragment M 556 enthält eine Reihe von Vorhersagen für ein nicht bekanntes Ereignis anhand von ungewöhnlichen Erscheinungen.[11] Das alttürkische Orakelbuch *Irk bitig*, dem nicht nur das o. g. soghdische Textstück aus dieser Handschrift sowie zwei weitere soghdische und zahlreiche andere sogenannte „Losbücher“ in verschiedenen Sprachen[12] im Charakter entsprechen, wird aufgrund der Verwendung der Runenschrift ebenfalls mit manichäischer Tradition verbunden.[13] Diese magischen und mantischen Praktiken erscheinen etwas verwunderlich, da Magie zu den den Manichäern verbotenen Dingen zählt. Wie sind diese Texte in die manichäische Literatur gelangt?

SHAUL SHAKED hat resümiert, dass die manichäischen Gläubigen ihre Beschwörungen offenbar nicht als magisch angesehen hätten, sondern als alltägliche Heil- und Schutzpraktiken. Die als magisch angesehen Tätigkeiten seien vielmehr auf vergleichbare Aktionen der Anhänger anderer Religionen bezogen worden.[14] DESMOND DURKIN MEISTERERNST erklärt die Existenz magischer Texte innerhalb des manichäischen Schriftgutes damit, dass „some Manichaeans at least, reconciled popular religious practices with their Manichaean beliefs and placed texts from both spheres in their books.“[15]

Allerdings ist die manichäische Lehre selbst durchaus astrologisch und fatalistisch geprägt. Sonne und Mond sind Lichtschiffe, in denen sich Gottheiten aufhalten. Die Planeten dagegen gehören zu den Archonten des Reiches der Finsternis. Das Böse ist dem Menschen immanent und muss durch Befolgen der Gebote in den Schranken gehalten werden. Die Lichtelemente werden durch rituelle Mahlzeiten, Gebete, Gesänge und beim Sterben eines Erwählten erlöst. So waren manichäische Gläubige möglicherweise magischen Ritualen wie Be-

5 MIRECKI/GARDNER/ALCOCK 1997.
6 HENNING 1946, S. 39–66, repr. in: HENNING 1977 II, S. 273–300.
7 DURKIN-MEISTERERNST 2004.
8 MORANO 2004.
9 MONTGOMERY 1912 und SHAKED 2000.
10 SIMS-WILLIAMS 2009. Zur Nachnutzung schreibt er auf S. 246: „The fragment seems to have been used to wrap round some small rectangular object, with the verso inwards, ...“
11 RECK/SUNDERMANN 1997.
12 RECK 2010, S. 72.
13 KLJASHTORNYJ 2004.
14 SHAKED 2000, S. 74.
15 DURKIN-MEISTERERNST 2004, S. 152.

schwörungen und Schutzzaubern gegenüber aufgeschlossen. Der Handel mit Amuletten und magischen Texten mag auch Teil der missionierenden Geschäftstätigkeit gewesen sein. Die Bemühung um Schutz vor Unglück und Krankheit ist ein menschliches Bedürfnis, das auf diese Weise leicht zu befriedigen ist.

In Zentralasien mussten sich die manichäischen Gemeinden zudem mit der wachsenden Bedeutung der buddhistischen Klöster auseinandersetzen und sich schließlich geschlagen geben, wie wir aus der Umwidmung ursprünglich manichäischer Klöster in buddhistische wissen.[16] In dieser Zeit fanden volkstümliche magische Praktiken ebenfalls ihren Weg in die buddhistische Literatur. Vermutlich haben die Manichäer auch magische Heil- und Schutzmethoden benutzt, um sich die Unterstützung durch die Hörerschaft, auf die sie angewiesen waren, zu sichern.

Das Blatt So 14425 + So 14427 + So 14428 + So 14460 + So 14461

Dieses aus fünf Einzelbruchstücken rekonstruierte Blattfragment (Abb. 1 und 2)[17] der oben beschriebenen Handschrift bewahrt nur wenige vollständige Zeilen.[18] Zumeist fehlen die Zeilenanfänge und es bleiben viele Lücken im Text. Ein Blatt dieser Sammelhandschrift umfasste 20 Zeilen, wovon auf unserem Blatt nur 19 Zeilen erhalten sind und die 20. Zeile fehlt. Dies stimmt auch mit der Textlücke im Seitenübergang überein. Auf diesem Blatt befinden sich Teile von zwei Texten. Die Zeilen v/5/ und /7/ sind rot geschrieben. Daher werden sie in der Transliteration und in der Übersetzung kursiv gesetzt. Sie enthalten die Unterschrift zum vorhergehenden und die Überschrift zum folgenden Text. Die Zeile v/6/ ist frei gelassen.

Text 1 reicht von r/1–v/5/. Text 2 beginnt v/7–19/. Beide Texte sind nicht vollständig erhalten. Der Beginn des ersten Textes fehlt ebenso wie das Ende des zweiten. Der erste Text wurde von Christiane Reck bearbeitet, der zweite von Enrico Morano. Der erste Text hat prognostischen Charakter. Er stellt ein Kalendarium mit Voraussagen für einen Monat von 30 Tagen dar. Der erhaltene Teil beginnt beim Schluss des sechsten Tages. Der zweite Text zählt zwar ebenfalls die Tage eines Monats auf, verbindet sie aber mit dem Lauf eines göttlichen Wesens im menschlichen Körper, der im Chinesischen als *rén shén liù zhù* 人神流注 bezeichnet wird.[19]

In China waren divinatorische Kalender mit Prognosen besonders für die Landwirtschaft bereits in der Han-Zeit (206 v. Chr.–222 n. Chr.) verbreitet.[20]

16 Moriyasu 2004, S. 174–184.

17 Reck 2006, #155, S. 124–126.

18 Wir danken an dieser Stelle Paolo Melis für die hervorragende virtuelle Rekonstruktion des Blattes. Die einzelnen Fragmente können im Digitalen Archiv des Akademienvorhabens Turfanforschung der Berlin-Brandenburgischen Akademie der Wissenschaften eingesehen werden.

19 Wang Shumin, S. 415.

20 Kubny 2000, S. 17.

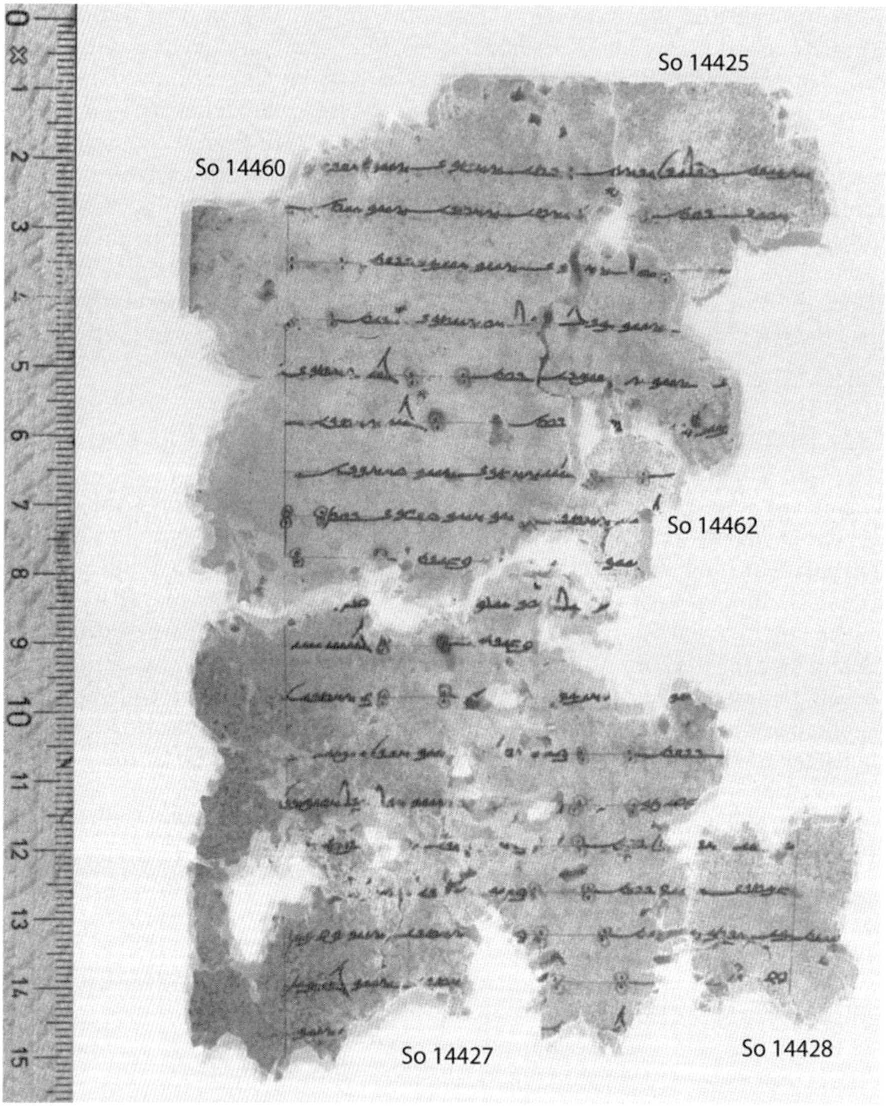

Depositum der Berlin-Brandenburgischen Akademie der Wissenschaften in der Staatsbibliothek zu Berlin – Preußischer Kulturbesitz, Orientabteilung. Fotos: Fotostelle der Staatsbibliothek zu Berlin. Virtuelle Zusammensetzung: PAOLO MELIS.

Abb. 1: So 14425 – So 14427 + So 14428 + So 14460 + So 14462/recto

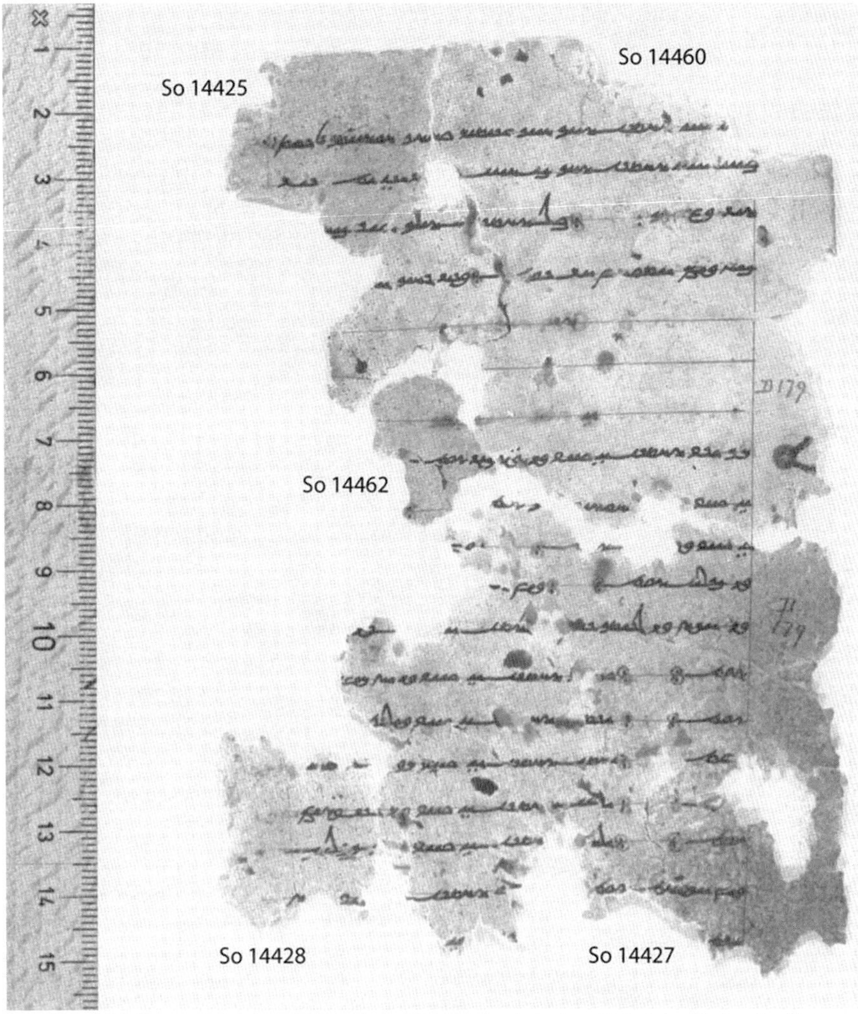

Depositum der Berlin-Brandenburgischen Akademie der Wissenschaften in der Staatsbibliothek zu Berlin – Preußischer Kulturbesitz, Orientabteilung. Fotos: Fotostelle der Staatsbibliothek zu Berlin. Virtuelle Zusammensetzung: Paolo Melis.

Abb. 2: So 14425 – So 14427 + So 14428 + So 14460 + So 14462/verso

Durch die Erfindung des Buchdrucks verbreiteten sich die Volkskalender besonders in der Tang-Zeit (618–907 n. Chr.) stark. Es sind zahlreiche uigurische und mongolische Kalenderfragmente aus Turfan und Dunhuang bekannt, die die chinesische Tradition des Volkskalenders und der Verknüpfung mit medizinischen Inhalten fortsetzten.[21] Für einige der uigurischen Kalendertexte kann aufgrund der Schrift und des Formats ein manichäischer Hintergrund angenommen werden (Mainz 153, MIK III 34b und Ch/U 6932 und U 495).[22] Sie werden jedoch prinzipiell als volkstümliche Tradition bewertet.

Der mantische Kalendertext r/1/–v/5/

Im Gegensatz zum zweiten soghdischen Text, für den sowohl mehrere chinesische Vorlagen als auch eine soghdische und eine uigurische Parallele nachgewiesen werden können, steht der soghdische Kalendertext bisher ohne direktes Muster da. Die chinesischen Kalendertexte sind viel ausführlicher. Sie beinhalten nicht nur das dem Tag zugeordnete Element, sondern auch sehr konkrete Angaben, was an diesem Tag günstig oder ungünstig ist. Dies ist auch der Fall bei den uigurischen Kalenderfragmenten. Die soghdischen Texte dagegen enthalten nur die Nummer des Tages und eher allgemein gehaltene Aussagen über einen prognostizierten Umstand, z. B. darüber, dass Friede im Haus sei. Allerdings muss hier auch die Lückenhaftigkeit der Texte berücksichtigt werden.

Die chinesischen Kalenderprognosen werden mittels komplizierter Berechnungen ermittelt und können daher aber auch zurückverfolgt und datiert werden. Dies ist bei den soghdischen Texten aufgrund der mangelhaften Angaben nicht der Fall. Bemerkenswert ist, dass auch die soghdischen Namen der Tage eines Monats nicht angeführt werden. Auf den chinesischen Kalenderrollen aus Dunhuang ist ein kleines rot geschriebenes Zeichen 密 hinzugefügt, das *mì* gelesen wird und als Umschrift für soghdisch myhr bzw. myr „Sonne" (mp. Lehnwort) verstanden wird.[23] Dieses Zeichen erscheint im Text P.ch. 3247 und in anderen Texten aus Dunhuang im Abstand von sieben Tagen und bezeichnet den Sonntag, s. Abb. 3. In der Überschrift von P.ch. 3247 wird der Verfasser des

21 Rachmati 1936/1937, Cerensodnom/Taube 1993 und Matsui 2012. Zu den uigurischen magischen Texten siehe auch Zieme 2005, dessen Texte aber fast ausschließlich nach dem 11. Jh. anzusetzen sind. Zur Verbindung dieser Texte mit buddhistischen Vorstellungen, s. Eberhard 1937.

22 Wilkens 2000, # 432–436, S. 376–379. Das unter #*434 irrtümlich als verloren angegebene Fragment *T I 601 ist unter der Signatur Ch/U 6932 erhalten, s. auch Knüppel 2013, S. 87, #75.

23 F. W. K. Müller 1907, S. 2 [459] und Chavannes/Pelliot 1913, S. 164. Wir danken Ching Chao-jung, Chang Wen-ling und Hu Ching-san für ihre Hinweise zu den chinesischen Texten. Die Texte aus Dunhuang sind publiziert in Liu 1925, und einsehbar in http://gallica.bnf.fr/.

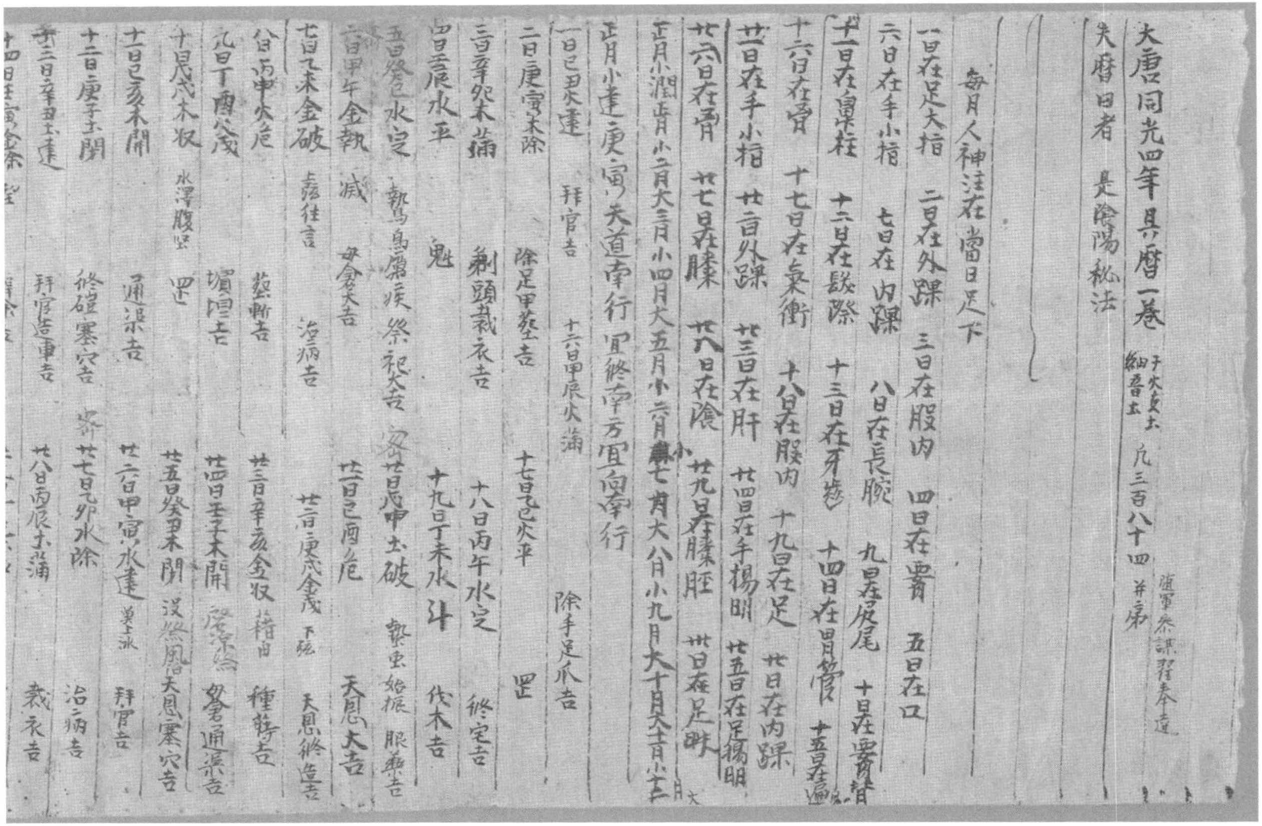

Photo: Bibliothèque nationale de France, Paris

Abb. 3: P.chin. 3247, Versoseite, Beginn des Textes

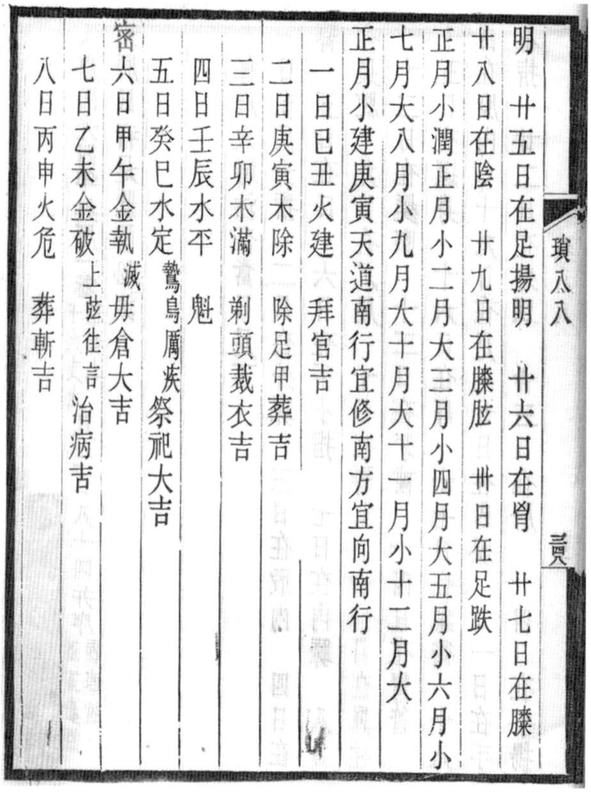
明 廿五日在足揚明 廿六日在脊 廿七日在膝
廿八日在陰 廿九日在膝脛 卅日在足趺
正月小潤正月小二月大三月小四月大五月小六月小
七月大八月小九月大十月大十一月小十二月大
正月小建庚寅天道南行宜修南方宜向南行
一日己丑火建 拜官吉
二日庚寅木除 除足甲葬吉
三日辛卯木滿 剃頭裁衣吉
四日壬辰水平 魁
五日癸巳水定 鸛鳥厲疾 祭祀大吉
蜜 六日甲午金執 滅 毋倉大吉
七日乙未金破 上弦 往言 治病吉
八日丙申火危 葬斬吉

Abb. 4: Publikation von P.ch. 3247 in Liu 1925, als Ms. 88, S. 372

Kalenders mit Namen *Dí* oder *Zhái Fèngdá* 翟奉達 genannt, s. Abb. 3.[24] *Dí* bzw. *Zhái* ist einer der Namen, die soghdische Familien trugen.[25] Die Kalenderblätter aus Dunhuang repräsentieren auf diese Weise soghdischen Einfluss und unterscheiden sich somit von den Kalendern aus Zentralchina.

Schwierig zu interpretieren ist die mit roter Tusche geschriebene Unterschrift des Textes v/5/, die den Titel des Kalendertextes darstellt. Sie ist trotz der verblassten roten Schrift sicher lesbar als sry s'ny (βẓ)-n'. Alle drei Wörter können unterschiedlich übersetzt werden. Das erste Wort sr- ist ein leichtstämmiges Nomen „Kopf" mit einer Deklinationsendung für Nom.-Akk. -y. Es kann auch als Ordi-

24 Er entstammte einer berühmten Familie in Dunhuang und wird in fünf Kalendertexten aus Dunhuang genannt, vgl. Deng Wenkuan 2002, S. 179. Wir danken P. Zieme für das Buch und Li Xue, dass sie uns über die relevanten Passagen dieses in Chinesisch verfassten Buches informiert hat.

25 Siehe Rong Xinjiang: „The surname Zhai could be from Sogdiana or from another nomad kingdom Gaoche", Rong 2006, S. 156. Zur Lesung *Dí* s. Rong 2009a, S. 413 und 2009b, S. 156.

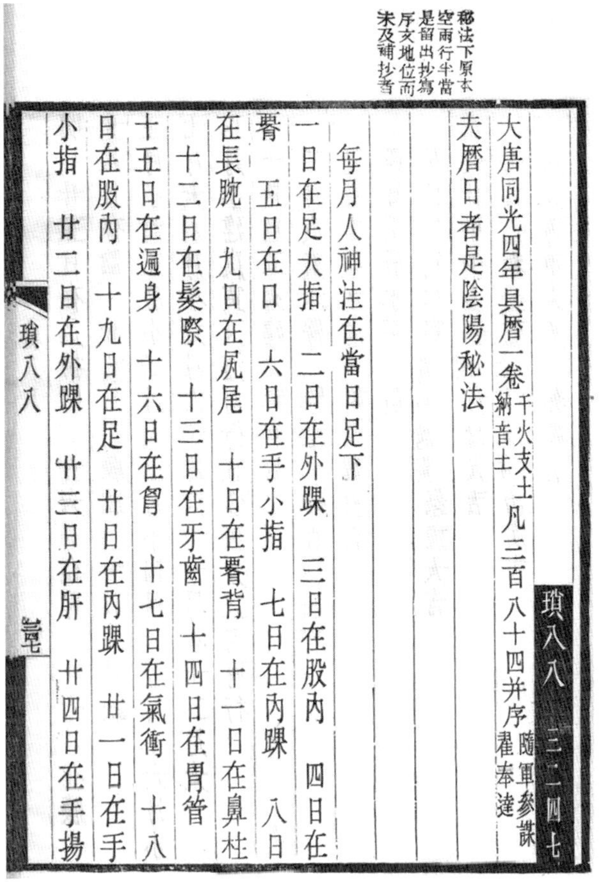
秘法下原本空兩行半當是留出抄寫序文地位而未及補抄者

大唐同光四年具曆一卷 干火支土 納音土 凡三百八十四并序 隨軍參謀翟奉達

瑣八八 三二四七

夫曆日者是陰陽秘法

每月人神注在當日足下

一日在足大指 二日在外踝 三日在股內 四日在

髆 五日在口 六日在手小指 七日在內踝 八日

在長腕 九日在尻尾 十日在髆背 十一日在鼻柱

十二日在髮際 十三日在牙齒 十四日在胃管

十五日在遍身 十六日在胷 十七日在氣衝 十八

日在股內 十九日在足 廿日在內踝 廿一日在手

小指 廿二日在外踝 廿三日在肝 廿四日在手揚

瑣八八

Abb. 5: Publikation von P.ch. 3247 in Liu 1925, als Ms. 88, S. 371.

nalie verwendet werden im Sinne von „Anfang, Erstes“.[26] Das zweite Wort s’ny hat mehrere Bedeutungen, s. DMT III/2, S. 173: 1. obl. von s’n „Feind“, 2. türk. Lehnwort „Nummer“, s. Fn. 26, und 3. „Buch, Schrift“. Diese dritte Bedeutung ist unsicher. Es findet sich als s’nk in So 10900/r/6/, einem *Xwāstwānīft*-Fragment, das auch zu dieser Sammelhandschrift gehört. Es steht dort ebenfalls in einer rot geschriebenen Zwischenüberschrift. Möglicherweise kann dieses Wort hier ebenso im Sinne von „Buch, Kapitel“ verstanden werden. Das dritte Wort βẕn’ könnte man in Verbindung bringen mit βzn- „gratitude, benediction“, s. DMT III/2, S. 62. Wahrscheinlicher ist aber wegen der Schreibung -ẕ- für ž, was in der manichäischen Schrift -j- entspricht, βjn- „mark, sign“, s. DMT III/2, S. 53, heranzuziehen.

Die Möglichkeiten der Übersetzung wären also: „Beginn der Nummer-Zeichen“, d. i. des „Zeichen-Kalenders“ oder „Erstes Buch der Zeichen“.

26 DMT III/2, S. 177 s. v. sr- und 178 s. v. sr’yk.

Transliteration und Übersetzung des mantischen Kalendertextes (r/1/–v/5/):

r/1/ ʾšmʾrt wyδʾβ ʾyst ○○ βtʾ sγty-ʾ sʾny[27] γry(w) (ʾp)[w]
/2/ [pc]xwʾk βwt ○[○] (○○) ʾštʾ sγtyʾ sʾny rʾt
/3/ [6]○○ ○○ nw(ʾ) (sγt)y-ʾ sʾny γrʾmy βyrt ○○ ○○
/4/ [δsʾ sγtyʾ] sʾny my-δ (xy)δ[28] xwsʾnty-ʾ wβʾt ○○ ○○
/5/ [XI sγty]-ʾ sʾny š-(.)rʾkyʾ/n[29] βwt ○○ ○○ XII (s)γty-ʾ
/6/ [sʾny 4]mʾ/n(.) (..)[3](.)[3] βwt ○○ ○○ XIII sγtyʾ
/7/ [sʾny 3 βw/βyr](t)[30] ○○ ○○ XIV sγty-ʾ sʾny wγškyn
/8/ βwt ○○ ○○] (XV) sγty[ʾ] (s)ʾny xʾny wrcy-ʾ βwt ○○ ○○
/9/ [XVI sγty-ʾ](s)ʾny[6](.)[3](..) pcʾyt ○○ ○○
/10/ [XVII sγty-ʾ sʾny](.)[1](ʾ)δ (ʾ)wy rʾ(δ)p[ntʾk[31] 6] (w...)[3](.)
/11/ [XVIII sγty-ʾ sʾny 6]pcʾy(t) ○○ ○○ XIX
/12/ [sγty-ʾ s](ʾny)[4](.) γʾm(k)[yn βw](t) ○○ ○○ XX sγtyʾ
/13/ [sʾny 3] βyrt ○○ ○○ XXI (sγt([yʾ](s)ʾny γrβ z-nkʾn
/14/ [6](p)cwz-ty ○○ ○○ (XX)[II sγtyʾ](s)ʾny xyδ myδ xwʾkry-ʾ
/15/ (nm)[2](.)n [1](γy)[1–2](ʾ) βwt ○○ ○○ (XXIII) [sγ](t)yʾ s[ʾny 4]ft[2?]
/16/ cmty-ʾ[32] (γ)[r]ʾnw βwt ○○ ○○ XXIII-[I][33] (sγ)[t]yʾ (sʾny) [5]
/17/ {auf dem Rand:} [β](β/y)rʾnt[34]

27 sʾny ist offenbar Teil der Tagesangabe. Es gibt im Alttürkischen *san* als „Nummer, Anzahl", vgl. J. Hamilton: „Calendriers Manichéens Ouïgours de 988, 989 et 1003." In: *Mélanges offerts à Louis Bazin*. Paris 1992, S. 12. Die Endung -y/-ı kann eine soghdische Deklinationsendung (Nom., Akk., Gen., Dat. oder Abl.) sein oder ein türkischer Possessivsuffix. Die Verbindung beider Worte sγtyʾ und sʾny ist bisher nicht belegt. *Sanı* wird im Alttürkischen nicht in Verbindung mit Tageszählungen benutzt. Für die Beratung zum Alttürkischen danken wir Peter Zieme und Simone-Christiane Raschmann.

28 Vermutlich Fehler für xyδ myδ, s. r/14/.

29 Das š am Wortanfang scheint isoliert geschrieben zu sein. Allerdings ist auch die Oberfläche zerstört, so dass eine Verbindung zum folgenden Buchstaben nicht ganz ausgeschlossen werden kann. Von diesem Folgebuchstaben sind nur zwei kleine Spitzen erhalten. Der Finalbuchstabe kann sowohl als -ʾ als auch als -n gelesen werden. Es sind bisher nur δβrʾkyʾ „das Geben" und šmʾrʾkyn „gedankenvoll" (Hinweis Yoshida) mit dieser Buchstabenkombination -rʾkyʾ/n belegt. Ersteres ist durch den Wortanfang nicht möglich und zweiteres mit den Buchstabenresten schwierig zu vereinbaren.

30 In der Lücke ist Raum für ein sehr kurzes Wort und vermutlich entweder βwt oder βyrt.

31 Ich danke Y. Yoshida für seinen Ergänzungsvorschlag.

32 Gen. Pl. (?) von cšm „Auge" s. DMT III/2, S. 66.

33 Ganz offensichtlich sind hier nur drei Zacken zu erkennen. Hier wäre die Zahl 24 zu erwarten. Möglicherweise liegt ein Schreiberfehler vor. Nicht völlig ausgeschlossen ist, dass ein einzelnes Häkchen isoliert stand. Die Oberfläche ist an dieser Stelle beschädigt. Die Lücke zum folgenden Beginn von (sγ)[t]yʾ, wäre aber dafür etwas klein.

34 Es ist nicht klar, ob und wie viele Buchstaben am Anfang möglicherweise fehlen. Vermutlich kann man βyrʾnt „sie erlangen" oder βrʾnt „sie tragen, erdulden" lesen.

MN ryty t[ys'](n)t[35] ○○ ○○ XX[V] (s)γty' s'ny pw m'/r(n/c?)[36]
/18/ pw[1](y') [βw]t[37] ○○ ○○ XXIII-[I] (sγ)[t]y' (s'ny) [5]
/19/ [9](δ') [βw](t)[○○ ○○ XXVII sγty-](') s'ny
/20/ {fehlt}

v/1/ [XXV]III (s)γty' s'ny x'ny cynt'r w(γ)šy xws'nty-' βwt ○○○
/2/ XXIX sγty' s'ny MN x'n'[s']r nyẓ̈-'t y'r[38]
/3/ s'r pc(wzt)y ○○ ○○ XXX sγty['] s'ny (nw)'y m'x [3]
/4/ m'x prm 'ntwxc-n'k βwt ○○ ○○ py'r[39] βγ'y 'n[7]
/5/ *sry s'ny (βẓ̈)-n'*
/6/ {frei gelassen}

r/1/ [un]erwarteter[40] Schaden kommt. Am siebenten Tag: Die Person[41] ist (ohne)
/2/ Hindernis. Am achten Tag: Die Gabe
/3/ [ ]. Am neunten Tag: Er erlangt Besitz.
/4/ [Am zehnten] Tag: Tag für Tag wird Zufriedenheit wird sein.
/5/ [Am 11.] Tag: Es ist … Am 12. Tag:
/6/ Es ist [ ]. Am 13. Tag:
/7/ [Es ist]. Am 14. Tag: Es ist freudig.
/8/ Am 15. Tag: Im Hause ist es friedlich.
/9/ [Am 16.] Tag: [ ] ist günstig.
/10/ [Am 17. Tag: [ ] (auf dem Weg) [ ].
/11/ [Am 18. Tag:] ist günstig. Am 19.
/12/ [Tag:] (wird) reich. Am 20. Tag:
/13/ Er erlangt [ ]. Am 21. Tag: Viele Arten von
/14/ [ ] erlangt er. Am (22. Tag): An diesem Tag wird der Handel
/15/ [ ]. Am (23. Tag:) [ ]
/16/ beider Augen ist schwer. Am 24.[42] (Tag:) [ ]
/17/ {auf dem Rand:} sie erlangen/tragen/erdulden[43]

35 Ich danke Y. Yoshida für seinen Ergänzungsvorschlag.
36 Die sehr gedrängten Buchstaben am Zeilenende sind nicht sicher zu identifizieren. So kann man das Wort als m'n „Sinn“, mrn „Herr“ (Lesung Yoshida, Übersetzung nach Sundermanns Wortliste) oder mrc „Tod“ lesen.
37 Bei der Restaurierung dieser Blattbruchstücke muss ein Stück mit Interpunktion verrutscht sein und befindet sich nun über dem βwt.
38 Ich danke Yutaka Yoshida für seine Lesung und Interpretation.
39 Zu 'py'rh, bzw. βy'r'k, s. Gharib 1995, S. 55 (# 1396) und S. 117 (# 2964).
40 „[un]erwartet“ bei einer angenommenen Ergänzung von [L'] am Ende des nicht erhaltenen vorangegangenen Blattes. Für den Hinweis danken wir N. Sims-Williams.
41 Vgl. DMT III/2, S. 88 kann γryw sowohl als Person, Selbst, Seele oder Körper übersetzt werden.
42 Zu lesen ist 23. Siehe Fn. 26.
43 Zur Lesung s. Fn. 27.

sie kommen vor [ ]. Am (25.) Tag: Ohne Geist/Herrn/Tod[44]
/18/ (ohne) [ist?]. Am (26.) Tag: Die Ehefrau
/19/ [ist? . Am 27.]Tag:
/20/ {fehlt}

v/1/ Am (28.) Tag: Im Haus ist Freude und Zufriedenheit.
/2/ Am 29. Tag: Wenn jemand aus dem Haus geht, wird er auf Ärger
/3/ treffen. Am 30. Tag: Neuer Mond/Monat [ ]
/4/ bis Mond/Monat ist mühsam. Am Abend Herr [ ][45]
/5/ *Beginn der Nummer-Zeichen / Erstes Buch der Zeichen*

Der medizinische Kalendertext (v/7–19/)

Der zweite Text beginnt, wie oben erwähnt, in v/7/. Eine rote Überschrift *'ẓ-w'nw šw'(m)[n]ty* „Der Gang des Lebens(geistes)" fungiert als Titel. Der Text spricht demnach von „dem Weg" (šw'mnty, wörtl. „das Gehen") des Leben(s-geistes) ('ẓ-w'nw, wörtl. „das Leben") und bestimmt seine wechselnden Positionen in den verschiedenen Körperteilen für die einzelnen Tage eines Monats. In unserem Fragment sind nur die Tage vom ersten bis zum elften erhalten.

Dieser Text hat eine Parallele in einem von RACHMATI veröffentlichten uigurischen Fragment der Berliner Turfansammlung, *U 9228.[46] Die chinesische Vorlage für diese kalender-medizinischen Texte wies W. EBERHARD in einer Rolle aus Dunhuang (Pelliot Chinois 3247) nach, die heute in der Bibliothèque Nationale de France in Paris aufbewahrt wird.[47] Die Vorderseite der Rolle trägt einen chinesischen Vinaya-Text mit dem Titel *sì fēn lǜ jiē mò* 四分律羯磨.[48] Auf der Rückseite der Rolle befindet sich ein Almanach für das vierte Jahr des *Tóng Guāng*-同光 Herrschaftszeitraums der neueren Tang-Dynastie, d. h. 926 n. Chr., dem ein medizinischer Text vorangeht. (Abb. 3–5) Dieser medizinische Text befasst sich mit dem Lebensgeist 人神 *rén-shén* („Geist des Menschen"). Solch ein Text ist ein substantieller Bestandteil im Vorspann der chinesischen Kalendertexte.[49] Er beschreibt die Positionen dieses Geistes im Laufe eines Monats in

44 Zur Lesung s. Fn. 30.

45 Diese Passage scheint bereits auf den neuen Monat Bezug zu nehmen. Möglicherweise richtet sich βγ'y „Herr" an Jesus als Mond-Gott im manichäischen Mythos. Für den Hinweis danken wir N. SIMS-WILLIAMS.

46 RACHMATI 1936/1937, S. 32 N. 20. (als T. I 602). Dieses Fragment ist jetzt verloren, s. KNÜPPEL 2013, S. 92, # 82. Es ist eins von drei inhaltlich sehr ähnlichen Fragmenten, die diesen „Lebensgeist" und seine Positionen behandeln.

47 W. EBERHARD in RACHMATI 1936/1937, S. 95–96 zu Ms. Nr. 20 mit der Übersetzung des chinesischen Textes vom 1. bis zum 11. Tag. Ähnliche Texte findet man auch als Präambel zu anderen Kalendertexten.

48 WANG SHUMIN 2006, S. 415.

49 DENG WENKUAN 2002, S. 53 und 249.

verschiedenen Körperteilen.[50] Man muss ihm ausweichen, wenn ein Patient mit Moxibustion behandelt wird bzw. zur Ader gelassen wird.

Eine weitere soghdische Fassung wurde auf einem Blatt in manichäischer Schrift M 142[51] gefunden. Dieser Text ist nur vom ersten bis zum siebenten Tag erhalten und hat auch keine Überschrift oder Titelangabe. Auf diesem Blatt wird r/3–7/ die Folge der Behandlung genau angegeben: „an diesem Tag darf man nicht die Moxibustion anwenden (und) zur Ader lassen: derjenige, der das tut, lebt 3 Jahre“. Auf solche medizinischen Zusammenhänge geht auch der alttürkische Text *Ch/U 9001 (T II Y 49) ein.[52]

Die vier Versionen, die chinesische, die uigurische und die beiden soghdischen, stimmen im Wesentlichen überein. In einigen Punkten sind sie aber divergent. So geht z. B. am 10. Tag „der Lebensgeist“ in dem chinesischen Text in die Lenden, im uigurischen in die Lippen, und im soghdischen in soghdischer Schrift in [...] zwischen die 5 Finger. Der soghdische Text in manichäischer Schrift bricht nach der Nennung des siebenten Tages ab.[53]

Die Natur dieses Wesens, das hier mit „Lebensgeist“ bezeichnet wird, ist nicht sicher bestimmbar.[54] Der chin. Begriff 人神 *rén-shén* setzt sich aus zwei Begriffen zusammen: „Mensch“ und „Geist, Bewusstsein“.[55] *Shén* 神 gehört mit *qì* 氣 und *jīng* 精 zu den „drei Schätzen“ *sānbǎo* 三寶, den drei zentralen Termini der chinesischen Medizin.[56] *Rén-shén* steht für das menschliche Sich-bewusstsein.[57] In den alttürkischen Texten heißt dieses Wesen *öz konuk*. *Öz* heißt „Wesen, Selbst“. *Konuk* ist „Gast, Gastfreundlichkeit, Aufenthaltsort“. Die Verbindung *öz konuk* wird mit „Seele“ übersetzt.[58] Der soghdische Text in soghdischer Schrift nennt das Wesen ʾẕwʾn *(əžwān)* „Leben“, und spricht vom „Gehen, Gang“

50 Diese Positionen variieren nicht in den chinesischen Kalendertexten aus Dunhuang, s. Deng Wenkuan 1996, S. 744 und 2002, S. 278. Wir danken Li Xue für die Informationen zu den relevanten Passagen dieser in Chinesisch verfassten Bücher.

51 Siehe Boyce 1960, S. 12.

52 Rachmati 1936/1937, Nr. 21, S. 32–33, Knüppel 2013, S. 92 # 83. Vgl. z. B. Z. 11f. in Rachmati 1936/1937 S. 33: „wenn man an diesem Tage zur Ader lässt oder ausbrennt, so wird man an diesem Tage sterben“.

53 Vgl. Harper 2006, S. 152–153: auch in ähnlichen chinesischen Texten sind manchmal die Positionen des Geistes im Körper an denselben Tagen abweichend.

54 Harper 2006, S. 150–151, Ricci, Bd. 3, S. 478.

55 Mathews' *Chinese-English Dictionary*, rev. American edition, # 3097 und # 5716.

56 Kubny 1995, S. 1, 183 und 406.

57 Needham 1974, S. 87–88 und Kaptchuk, S. 57–58.

58 Vgl. Rachmati 1936/1937, S. 113 und *Drevnetjurkskij slovar'*, S. 394 und 456. P. Zieme übersetzt *konuk* (s. v. *qonuq*) als „Wohnort“ (Zieme 1985, S. 227) und verbindet wie Rachmati beide Begriffe zusammen zu „Selbst(=Seelen)-Aufenthalt, Seele“. *Öz konuk*-kommt in einem Text über die Ehrerbietung gegenüber den Eltern und Ahnen vor, Zieme 1985, S. 78 (Text 12, Z. 60). Im Kommentar führt P. Zieme neben den von Rachmati veröffentlichten zwei weitere Belege in unveröffentlichten Fragmenten an: Ch/U 6016/v/13/ und Nr. 1114+1374/a/3/ in der Ōtani-Sammlung der Ryūkoku-Universität in Kyōto. In beiden Fragmenten geht es ebenfalls um „den Aufenthaltsort der Seele“ in den Gliedern. Wir danken Yukiyo Kasai für ihren Hinweis auf diese Übersetzungsmöglichkeit.

šwʾmnty *(šwāmandē)*. Der chinesische Text bezeichnet die Bewegung als „Strömen, Fließen“ 流注 *liù zhù*.[59] Der alttürkische Titel nennt dafür *käzigi* „Reihenfolge von“. So entsprechen „die Reihenfolge des Aufenthaltsortes des Geistes“ (zu interpretieren als „der Gang der Seele“) und „der Gang des Lebens(geistes)“ dem chinesischen Titel „das Fließen des Menschengeistes“.

Bemerkenswert ist das Zeichen am äußeren Rand der Versoseite: ⌀. Es sieht wie ein Kreis mit einem Winkel aus und ist bisher nicht sicher bestimmbar. Möglicherweise ist es ein Tamga, oder ein gedrehtes alttürkisches Runenzeichen für „B“: 𐰉. Es hat große Ähnlichkeit mit dem Brāhmī-Zahlzeichen für 10. Es lässt sich auch mit dem Brāhmī-Buchstaben „ma“ ♉ in Verbindung bringen, oder der Devanāgarī-Ziffer 4: ८. Dann wäre es auch seitlich gedreht. Alle diese Erklärungen sind bisher nicht befriedigend. Auch der Vergleich mit sogenannten „glücksbringenden“ Verzierungen, die in verschiedenen chinesischen Texten auftauchen, brachte keine Lösung.[60] Es könnte auch eine Bezugnahme auf die in den alttürkischen Turfantexten aufgezeichneten Mondstationen mit ihren Sternbildern erwogen werden. In Frage käme eventuell das Z. 27 *Aśvinī* aus *U 9227 (T II Y 29).[61] Allerdings ist es etwas unproportioniert, weil in der Handschrift nur ein Kreis gezeichnet ist, und es fehlt die dritte Verbindung. Ein alttürkisches Dokument weist am Textanfang ein Symbol auf, dessen Funktion ebenfalls unklar ist.[62] Einige alttürkische Texte weisen chinesische Zeichen auf, die wie in den o. g. chinesischen Texten „glückbringend“ sein sollen und von Rachmati 1937, S. 96 als Amulettzeichnungen bezeichnet werden. So scheinen solche Zeichen der damaligen Leserschaft vertraut gewesen zu sein.

Transliteration und Übersetzung von So 14460 + So 14427 + So 14428 + So 14462/v/7–19/

/7/ *ʾz̤-wʾnw šwʾ(m)[n]ty*
/8/ ky ʾyw sγtyʾ ʾz̤-wʾnw pr fšpʾr[63] šwt [○○ ○○ ʾδwʾ sγtyʾ]
/9/ ʾz̤-wʾnw [pr …](.x/γw)šʾ(y)[…](m)[64] šwt)[○○ ○○ δry sγtyʾ]
/10/ ʾz̤-wʾnw pr [rʾnt] š[w]t ○○ ○○ c[tβʾr sγtyʾ ʾz̤-wʾnw]
/11/ pr myδʾn šwt ○○ ○○ pnc (sγ)[tyʾ ʾz̤-wʾnw]

59 Wang Shumin 2006, S. 415.
60 Vgl. T. Nishiwaki: „Chinesische und mandschurische Handschriften und seltene Drucke, Teil 6“, in Vorbereitung. Wir danken Simone-Christiane Raschmann für ihren Hinweis auf diese Verzierungen.
61 Rachmati 1937, S. 14, s. auch Knüppel 2013, S. 83–84, #65.
62 Raschmann 2007, S. 136 (# 117, U 5399v + U 6068 v). Wir danken Simone-Christiane Raschmann für ihren Hinweis auf dieses Zeichen.
63 Unbekanntes Wort, warscheinlich mit *pšpʾry* ‚Fortschritt‘ und *pšpr* ‚place the feet‘ verbunden, s. DMT III/2, S. 150.
64 M 124 hat *pšnʾ* ‚Ferse‘. Hier vielleicht ‚Ohren‘?

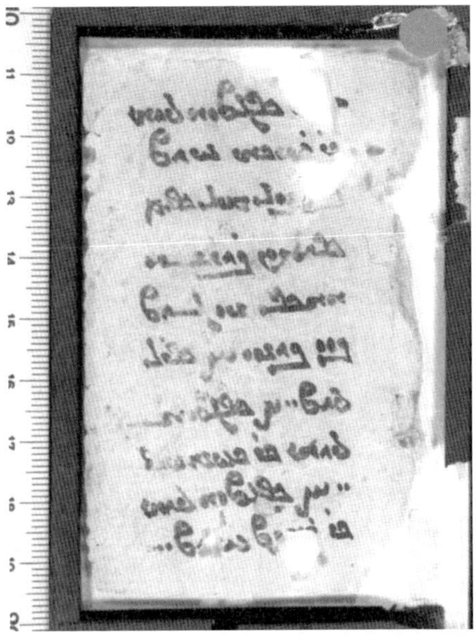
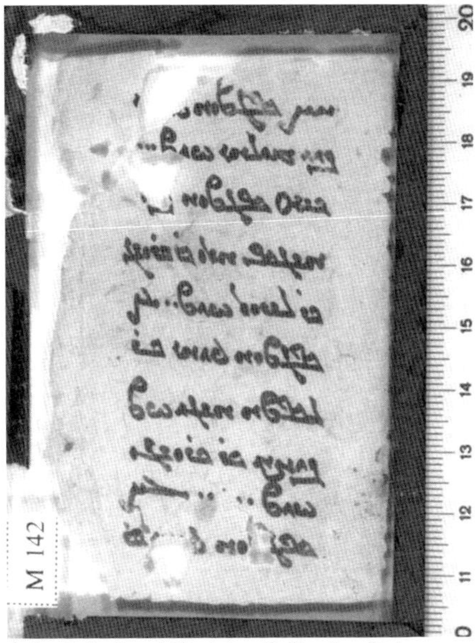

Depositum der Berlin-Brandenburgischen Akademie der Wissenschaften in der Staatsbibliothek zu Berlin – Preußischer Kulturbesitz, Orientabteilung. Fotos: Fotostelle der Staatsbibliothek zu Berlin

Abb. 6: M 142/recto

Abb. 7: M 142/verso

/12/ pr ʾnks[65] pr δynty β(.)[....] δstʾ ʾn[kwšt]pr[...][66]
/13/ šwt ○○ ○○ w(x)wšw sγtyʾ ʾz̤-wʾnw pr ns kwc(ʾ)
/14/ šwt ○○ ○○ ʾβt[ʾ] sγ[ty](ʾ) ʾz̤-wʾnw pʾδyt [pyxt (?)]
/15/ [š]wt [○○] ○○ ʾštʾ sγtyʾ ʾz̤-wʾnw kw [.](.)tγʾ/n[..]
/16/ [šw](t) ○○ ○○ nwʾ sγtyʾ ʾz̤-wʾnw pr (β)yk fšrm[67]
/17/ šwt ○○ ○○ ʾδs[ʾ s]γtyʾ ʾz̤-wʾnw [p](r) myδʾn
/18/ pnc ʾnkwšt šwt [○○ ○○] XI sγtyʾ [ʾz̤-w]ʾnw [pr n]s
/19/ (šwt)[○○ ○○ XII sγt](yʾ)[ ] ʾz̤[-wʾnw ....]

/7/ Der Gang des Leben(sgeistes)
/8/ Am ersten Tag geht der Leben(sgeist) in den großen Zeh. Am 2. Tag /9/ geht der Leben(sgeist) in [...] Am 3. Tag /10/ geht der Leben(sgeist) in die Waden. Am 4. Tag geht der Leben(sgeist) /11/ in die Taille. Am fünften Tag geht [der

65 Siehe Reck 2005, S. 339, Fn. 30.
66 An diesen Stellen (5. und 6. Tag) verwechseln beide soghdischen Texte die Positionen des Geistes oder wiederholen sie.
67 Buddh. *šfʾrmʾk* ‚pudenda' (Gharib 1995, S. 371), cf. aw. *fšarəma-* ‚Scham' (Bartholomae 1904, Sp. 1029), pahl. *šarm* (*-gāh*) ‚Genitalien', np. *šarm* ‚id.' (Horn 1893, S. 172). Im uigurischen Text könnte vielleicht das Hapax *korklık* aus *kork-* ‚fürchten' stammen, also ‚furchtbar', ‚schamhaft', ‚pudenda', s. Clauson 1972, S. 651 und 128, wo *uvutka bolup korklık alplık kılur* wird ‚out of shame a coward performs brave deeds' übersetzt.

Leben(sgeist)] /12/ ins Kinn, in die Zähne, ins [Zahnfleisch?], in die Hände, die F[inger,]in […]. /13/ Am 6. Tag geht der Leben(sgeist) ins Nasenloch(?)[68]. /14/ Am 7. Tag [geht] der Leben(sgeist) in den Fuß(knöchel). /15/ Am 8. Tag geht der Leben(sgeist) in […]. /16/ Am 9. Tag geht der Leben(sgeist) in die äußeren Genitalien. /17/ Am 10. Tag geht der Leben(sgeist) zwischen die /18/ fünf Finger. Am 11. Tag geht der Leben(sgeist) in die Nase. /19/ [Am 12. Tag geht] der Le[ben(sgeist) …]

Transliteration und Übersetzung von M 142 (Abb. 6 und 7)

/r/		
/1/	(‘)[yw] sγṯy’ jw’n	Am ersten Tag geht
/2/	pr fšp’(r) šwṯ	der Leben(sgeist) in den großen Zeh,
/3/	(kyw)yδ myδ s(w)m	am diesem Tag darf man nicht die
/4/	s(w)cy xwrnyy	Moxibustion anwenden (und) zur Ader
/5/	’’s nyy γwṯ	lassen:
/6/	kyy kwnyy III srδ	derjenige, der das tut, lebt 3 Jahre.
/7/	jwt ○○ II sγṯy’	Am 2. Tag geht
/8/	jw’n pr pšn’ šwt	der Leben(sgeist) in die Ferse.
/9/	○○ III sγṯy’ jw’*n*	Am 3. Tag geht der Leben(sgeist)
/10/	pr r’nṯ šwṯ ○○	in die Waden.
/v/		
/1/	IV sγṯy’ j[w’]n	Am 4. Tag geht der Leben(sgeist)
/2/	kww myδ’n šwṯ ○○○	in die Taille.
/3/	pnc sγṯy’ k[w](w)	Am fünften Tag geht er ins
/4/	’ngs ’ty pr pryng	Kinn, ins Zahnfleisch (und)
/5/	pr δndyt šwṯ ○○ VI	in die Zähne. Am 6.
/6/	sγṯy’ jw’n pr	Tag geht der Leben(sgeist) in die
/7/	δsṯ’ ’ngwšṯ	Hände, in die Finger,
/8/	kwc’ pr pryng	in den Mund und ins Zahnfleisch.
/9/	šwṯ ○○ ○○ VII	Am 7.
/10/	sγ(ṯ)y’ j(w’n) pr	Tag [geht] der Leben(sgeist) in

68 kwc’ wörtl. „Mund“, hier als „Loch“, ns kwc’ also als „Nasenloch“ verstanden.

Tabelle

Tag	Körperteil	Soghdisch in manich. Schrift M 142	Soghdisch in soghd. Schrift So 14460+	Uigurisch	Chinesisch
1.	großer Zeh	fšp'r	fšp'r	[...]	足大指 *zú dà zhǐ* ‚großer Zeh des Fußes'
2.	äußere Fußknöchel	pšn'	[...](.x/γw) š'(y)[...](m)) (?)	*taš tobık*[67] ‚äußere Fußknöchel'	外踝 *wài huái* ‚äußere Knöchel'
3.	Waden	r'nṯ		*baltır* ‚Waden'	股 *gǔ* ‚Waden'
4.	Mitte, Taille	myδ'n	myδ'n	*uča* ‚Kreuz '	腰 *yâo* ‚Taille'
5.	Kinn, Zahnfleisch, Zähne, Hände, Finger	'ngs 'ty pryng δndyt	'nks δynty β(.) [....] δst' 'n[kwšt] [..]?	*agız* , Mund '	口 *kǒu* Mund
6.	Hände, Finger/ Nasenloch, Zahnfleisch, Mund	δsṯ' 'ngwšṯ kwc' pr pryng	ns kwc' ‚Nasenloch'?	*elig* ‚Hände'	手小指 *shǒu xiǎo zhǐ* ‚kleiner Finger der Hand'
7.	innere Fußknöchel	–	p'δyt [pyxt(?)] ‚Fuß[gelenk?]'	*ič tobık* ‚innere Fußknöchel'	內踝 *nèi huái* , innere Fußknöchel'
8.	Handflächen/ Gelenk	–	(.)ιγ'/n	*aya* ‚Handflächen'	長腕 *cháng wàn* ‚langes Gelenk'
9.	Genitalien	–	βyk fšrm ‚äußere Genitalien'	*korklık* ‚Genitalien'	尻尾 *kāo wěi* ‚Ende der Wirbelsäule'
10.	Lippen/ Lende/zwischen den 5 Fingern	–	[p](r) myδ'n pnc 'nkwšt ‚zwischen den 5 Fingern'	*irin* ‚Lippen'	腰背 *yāo bèi* ‚Rücken-Taille = Lende'
11.	Nase	–	ns	–	鼻柱 *bí zhù* ‚Nasenrücken (*wörtl.* Nasen-Pfeiler)'

69 Über *tobık* s. Clauson 1972, S. 437.

Literatur

BARTHOLOMAE, CH. 1904: *Altiranisches Wörterbuch.* Straßburg.

BOYCE, M. 1960: *A Catalogue of the Iranian Manuscripts in Manichean Script in the German Turfan Collection.* Berlin.

CERENSODNOM, D./M. TAUBE 1993: *Die Mongolica der Berliner Turfansammlung.* Berlin (Berliner Turfantexte 16).

CHAVANNES, É./P. PELLIOT 1913: „Un traité manichéen retrouvé en Chine (Deuxième partie)." In: *JA* 1, S. 99–199.

CLAUSON, G. 1972: *An Etymological Dictionary of Pre-Thirteen-Century Turkish.* Oxford.

DENG WENKUAN 1996: 敦煌天文曆法文獻輯校 = *Dunhuang tian wen li fa wen xian ji jiao* = Collected Collations of the Astronomical Texts and Calendars from Dunhuang. Jiangsu.

— 2002: 敦煌吐魯番天文曆法研究 = *Dunhuang Tulufan tian wen li fa yan jiu.* Gansu.

DMT III/2 = N. SIMS-WILLIAMS/D. DURKIN-MEISTERERNST: *Dictionary of Manichaean Sogdian and Bactrian.* Turnhout 2012 (Corpus Fontium Manichaeorum: Dictionary of Manichaean Texts, vol. 3: texts from Central Asia and China, Part 2).

Drevnetjurkskij slovar'. Leningrad 1969.

DURKIN-MEISTERERNST, D. 2004: „The apotropaic magical text M 389 and M 8430/I/ in Manichaean Middle Persian." In: ARAM 16, S. 141–160.

EBERHARD, W. 1937: „Chinesische Volkskalender und buddhistisches Tripiṭaka" In: OLZ 40, S. 346–349.

GHARIB, B. 1985: *Sogdian Dictionary. Sogdian-Persian-English.* Teheran.

HARPER, D. 2006: „Dunhuang iatromantic manuscripts P. 2856 R° and P. 2675 V°." In: V. LO/CH. CULLEN (Hrsg.): *Medieval Chinese Medicine: The Dunhuang medical manuscripts.* New York, S. 134–164.

HENNING, W.B. 1946: „Two Manichaean Magical Texts, with an Excursus on the Parthian ending -ēndēh." In: *BSOAS* 12, 1, S. 39–66, repr. In: *Selected Papers* II, S. 273–300.

— 1977: *Selected Papers II.* Téhéran/Liège (Acta Iranica 15).

HORN, P. 1893: *Grundriß der neupersischen Etymologie.* Straßburg.

Instituts Ricci (Hrsg.) 2001: *Grand dictionnaire Ricci de la langue chinoise.* Paris.

LIU PAN-NUNG 1925: *Tun-huang to-so.* Shanghai.

KAPCHUK, T.J. 1988: *Das große Buch der chinesischen Medizin: Die Medizin von Yin und Yang in Theorie und Praxis.* Bern/München/Wien.

KLJASHTORNYJ, S.G. 2004: „The Manichaean Text T II D and *Ïrq bitiq* XIX." In: D. DURKIN-MEISTERERNST et. al. (Hrsg.): *Turfan Revisited: The First Century of Research into the Arts and Cultures of the Silk Road.* Berlin, S. 147.

KUBNY, M. 1995: *Qi, Lebenskraftkonzepte in China: Definitionen, Theorien und Grundlagen.* Heidelberg.

— 2000: *Traditioneller chinesischer Mondkalender: Das chinesische Mondjahr und das westliche Sonnenjahr von 1910–2020.* Heidelberg.

KNÜPPEL, M. 2013: *Alttürkische Handschriften, Teil 17: Heilkundliche, volksreligiöse und Ritualtexte*. Stuttgart (VOHD 13,25).

Mathews' Chinese-English Dictionary. Rev. American edition. Cambridge (Mass.) 1972.

MATSUI DAI 2012: "Uighur Almanac Divination Fragments from Dunhuang." In: I. POPOVA / LIU YI (Hrsg.): *Dunhuang Studies: Prospects and Problems for the Coming Second Century of Research*. St. Petersburg, S. 154–166.

MIRECKI, P. / I. GARDNER / A. ALCOCK 1997: „Magical Spell, Manichaean Letter." In: P. MIRECKI / J. BEDUHN (Hrsg.): *Emerging from Darkness: Studies in the Recovery of Manichaean Sources*. Leiden / New York / Köln (Nag Hammadi and Manichaean Studies 43), S. 1–32.

MONTGOMERY, J. A. 1912: „The original script of the Manichæans on texts in the museum." In: *University of Pennsylvania: The Museum Journal* 3, 1, S. 25–29.

MORANO, E. 2004: „Manichaean Middle Iranian incantation Texts from Turfan." In: D. DURKIN-MEISTERERNST et. al. (Hrsg.): *Turfan Revisited: The First Century of Research into the Arts and Cultures of the Silk Road*. Berlin, S. 221–227.

MORIYASU, T. 2004: *Die Geschichte des uigurischen Manichäismus an der Seidenstraße: Forschungen zu manichäischen Quellen und ihrem geschichtlichen Hintergrund*. Wiesbaden (Studies in Oriental Religions 50).

MÜLLER, F. W. K. 1907: „Die ‚persischen' Kalenderausdrücke im chinesischen Tripiṭaka." In: SbPAW, S. 458–465 (repr.: *Ergebnisse der deutschen Turfanforschung*. Teil 3. Leipzig 1985, S. 131–138).

NEEDHAM, J. 1974: *Science and Civilisation in China*. Vol. 5, Part II. Cambridge.

RACHMATI, G. R. 1937: *Türkische Turfan-Texte VII*. Mit sinologischen Anmerkungen von W. EBERHARD. Berlin (APAW 1936, Phil.-hist. Kl., Nr. 12).

RASCHMANN, S.-CH. 2007: *Alttürkische Handschriften Teil 13: Dokumente, Teil 1*. Stuttgart (VOHD 13, 21).

RECK, CH. 2005: „The Tribulations of Human Existence: a Sogdian Fragment Corresponding to a Passage of Burzōy's Preface to *Kalīlah wa Dimnah*?" In: A. VAN TONGERLOO / L. CIRILLO (Hrsg.): *Il Manicheismo. Nuove prospettive della Ricerca*. Turnhout, S. 331–341.

— 2006: *Mitteliranische Handschriften. Teil 1: Berliner Turfanfragmente manichäischen Inhalts in soghdischer Schrift*. Stuttgart (VOHD 18, 1).

— 2010: „Some remarks on the Manichean fragments in Sogdian script in the Berlin Turfan Collection." In: I. TAKASHI (Hrsg.): *"The Way of Buddha" 2003: the 100th Anniversary of the Otani Mission and the 50th of the Research Society for Central Asian Cultures*. Kyoto, S. 69–74.

— 2011: „Fragmente von Büchern – Zwei Sammelhandschriften im Vergleich." In: Z. ÖZERTURAL / J. WILKENS (Hrsg.): *Der östliche Manichäismus: Gattungs- und Werksgeschichte. Vorträge des Göttinger Symposiums vom 4./5. März 2010*. Berlin, S. 133–159.

RECK, CH. / W. SUNDERMANN 1997: „Ein illustrierter mittelpersischer manichäischer Omen-Text aus Turfan." In: *Zentralasiatische Studien* 27, S. 7–23.

RONG XINJIANG 2006: „New Light on Sogdian Colonies along the Silk Road: Recent Archaeological Finds in Northern China." In: *Berichte und Abhandlungen der Berlin-Brandenburgischen Akademie der Wissenschaften*. Band 10. Berlin, S. 147–160.

— 2009a: „Further Remarks on Sogdians in the Western Regions.“ In: W. SUNDERMANN/ALMUT HINTZE/FRANÇOIS DE BLOIS (Hrsg.): *Exegisti monumenta: Studies in Honour of Nicholas Sims-Williams*. Berlin (Iranica 17), S. 399–416.
— 2009b: „Sabao and Sabo: On the Problem of the Leader of Sogdian Colonies During the Northern Dynasties, Sui and Tang Period.“ In: YE YILIANG (Hrsg.): *Collection of Papers on Iranian Studies in China*. Beijing, S. 148–162.
SHAKED, SH. 2000: „Manichaean Incantation bowls in Syriac.“ In: *Jerusalem Studies in Arabic and Islam* 24, S. 58–92.
SIMS-WILLIAMS, N. 2009: „The Bactrian fragment in Manichaean script (M 1224).“ In: D. DURKIN-MEISTERERNST/CH. RECK/D. WEBER (Hrsg.): *Literarische Stoffe und ihre Gestaltung in mitteliranischer Zeit. Kolloquium anlässlich des 70. Geburtstages von Werner Sundermann*. Wiesbaden (Beiträge zur Iranistik 31), S. 245–268.
— 2013: *Mitteliranische Handschriften Teil 4: Iranian manuscripts in Syriac script in the Berlin Turfan collection*. Stuttgart (VOHD 18, 4).
WANG SHUMIN 2006: „Abstracts of the medical manuscripts from Dunhuang“, transl. by P. Barrett. In: V. LO/CH. CULLEN (Hrsg.): *Medieval Chinese Medicine: The Dunhuang medical manuscripts*. New York, S. 374–434, Appendix 2.
WILKENS, J. 2000: *Alttürkische Handschriften Teil 8: Manichäisch-türkische Texte der Berliner Turfansammlung*. Stuttgart (VOHD 13, 16).
— 2009: „Ein manichäischer Alptraum?“ In: D. DURKIN-MEISTERERNST/CH. RECK/D. WEBER (Hrsg.): *Literarische Stoffe und ihre Gestaltung in mitteliranischer Zeit. Kolloquium anlässlich des 70. Geburtstages von Werner Sundermann*. Wiesbaden (Beiträge zur Iranistik 31), S. 319–348.
ZIEME, P. 2005: *Magische Texte des uigurischen Buddhismus*. Turnhout (Berliner Turfantexte 23).

The Liturgical Daēnā

Speculative Aspects of the Next-of-Kin Unions

Antonio Panaino

In the framework of a research already made public, but unfortunately not yet published in its complete version,[1] I have entered a detailed discussion concerning the 2nd chapter of the *Widēwdād* and in particular the interpretation of the role there played by the Daēnā in (her interrupted) meeting with Yima. Very briefly I have suggested that it would be misleading to maintain the basic interpretation of this episode as whether the Daēnā already represented *sic et simpliciter* the standard embodiment of the "Zoroastrian theology", the "Religion" *par excellence*. The framework of the myth is patently more primitive. The "poor" Yima is placed in front of the mighty Ahura Mazdā. Then, I wonder how it would be possible that the highest God were presenting a primitive man (as Yima is normally described in order to justify his *"gran rifiuto"*)[2] with the "Religion", i.e. with an abstraction, exactly as whether Ahura Mazdā were speaking with Rudolph Bultmann, Martin Buber or Hans Jonas. And more: was Yima actually in the condition to answer Ahura Mazda with a bold, radical refusal, opposing his own religion, i.e. that of the Daēuuas to that of Ahura Mazdā?

In a further study I have shown[3] how Ahura Mazdā can be very harsh, violent and also "bad" against his enemies. Would Lord Wisdom have accepted a refusal from a primitive man with a so fair reaction? After this amazing (negative) answer, would Mazdā have offered Yima with the seminal role of increasing the earth and that of civilizing[4] hero as well? Something seemed to me at least escaping, if not highly improbable. For this reason, I tried to turn the chessboard around in order to see the situation from a different point of view; then,

1 The first contribution on this subject was presented at Liège during the Colloquium "Démons Iraniens" (February, 5th and 6th 2009), and for it see Panaino 2015. Some important arguments derived from this article have been elaborated and already edited in Panaino 2013. During the final preparation of the present study I have benefitted of the presence in Ravenna of Jean Kellens, who delivered a seminar entitled "La restitution du rituel gâthique" (April, 16th, 18th, 19th 2013).

2 The verse-line *Che fece per viltade il gran rifiuto* ("Who by his cowardice made the great refusal") is the 60th of the Third *Canto* in Dante's *Inferno*; it was referred to the abdication's act signed by Pope Caelestinus V (December 13th 1294). Cf. Frugoni 2005.

3 Panaino 2009a.

4 See Kellens 1984.

I suggested that instead of the "Religion" we should start imagining just the Daēnā as the prototype of the animical twin, like a feminine partner of Yima, his "sister" who, in fact, is never expressly mentioned in Avestan sources, but that appears only in few Pahlavi documents (so that we are sure of her existence not only from the Indian framework, but also from the Iranian one).[5]

According to this different picture, I thus explained the presence of the Daēnā and her apparently peculiar refusal not as a declaration of Pagan endurance in a Daēvic cult by Yima himself (a stupid decision after which he would have been hammered for ever), but as a sort of trial, as an initiatory test, in which the simple man decided (as Ahura Mazdā knew in advance he would have actually done) to postpone his own future "beatification" in order to be helpful according to the general project of his highest God. Only after this "right" decision (according to my reconstruction), Ahura Mazdā entrusted to him the duty of civilizing the world and enlarging (three times) the earth.[6] Thus, the Daēnā is here the "double", the twin and the sister of Yima; but because she was also referred to as the *āhūiri-* one (i. e. "belonging to Ahura [Mazdā]"[7] as one of his wives or as his daughter [if we want to see in this secondary adjectival *vr̥ddhi*-formation in -*i*- a patronymic]),[8] we must suppose that she was closely and directly related to Ahura Mazdā himself, probably as one of his closest "relatives" and in particular as his feminine double. This peculiar situation seems to reflect an esoteric doctrine in which human beings were considered as given with a "soul-vision" spiritually consubstantial or, in any case, as directly (we could say ontologically) linked with the supreme God. This animical double appears, in fact, to be in common with Ahura Mazdā himself. Then, the way in which the Daēnā *āhūiri-* is presented in this brief mythical event suggests that we could have to do with a sort of divinity or, at least, with a divinization of an image of the afterlife beatification, which will be identified (but only in later times) with the "Mazdean Religion" *(Daēnā Māzdaiiasni)*, not in crude terms of an ideal abstraction, as we modern people would be immediately compelled to imagine, but as a "prize" representing the final state of re-composition of the soul.[9]

5 See the detailed discussion of this problem in Panaino 2013.

6 Panaino 2012.

7 Cf. Debrunner 1954, p. 303: *āhuiri-* (sic) "zu Ahura in Beziehung stehend".

8 See Kellens 2007, pp. 150–151. In any case, if this is a patronymic, the Daēnā would be "the one daughter of Ahura (Mazdā)", a fact that does not forbid this Dēn to be his wife. In my opinion, it is very improbable that in this context *āhūiri-* could be strictly referred to *ahura.ṯkaēša-*, as, may be, it was in other passages, as suggested by Kellens *(ibidem)*. On the other hand, I cannot exclude that the earlier ritual speculations considered Yima as a man acting along this correct line, so that the reinterpretation of the passage in which he was demonized should have completely reversed a previous liturgic assessment. This shows that a great theological change (or corruption) took place in the framework of the Mazdean tradition. For the patronymic see again Debrunner 1954, pp. 301–303.

9 On the later ichonography of the Dēn in Mazdean manuscripts see Choksy 2002, pp. 70–73, *passim*.

I must underline the fact that also KELLENS[10] has suggested that in the earliest times the Daēnā did not mean "Religion"[11] and that, contrariwise, she should be considered as: "l'allégorie d'une force de vision, non de la vision mystique, mais de la vision eschatologique qui permet de trouver et de suivre le chemin de l'au-delà". I share this reconstruction as the following logical implication that the Daēnā appears in the sacrifice and that she was considered as one of its direct productions.[12] This new evidence produces some compelling implications. The first is that the framework in which Yima had the opportunity to see the Daēnā (without joining her) is doubtless ritual; it cannot be considered as a profane meeting, just happening because of a "magic" apparition of Ahura Mazdā in front of him.

Furthermore, KELLENS[13] has shown that *Y.* 11, 16 – 13, 8, contain a particular section in the whole *Yasna* liturgy, where a great importance was attributed to the exegesis of the *Frauuarānē* prayer. Here a particular esoteric interplay among different subjects took place; the sacrificer, having offered his own *uštāna-* to Ahura Mazdā, give thanks to the direct involvement of his *frauuaṣ̌i-* (evoked through the recitation of the *Frauuarānē*), and can finally obtain his *daēnā-* in order to became a *saošiiaṇt-*.[14] It is clear that this doctrine establishes a strong link between the eschatological dimension and that of the sacrifice; then, the link between them is not, so to say, of moral or finalistic order, but intrinsic. The union of the *uruuan-* and of the *daēnā-*, thus, is not only an event *post mortem*, but also a process,[15] which can be evoked in the ritual as an esoteric access to the divine (uncontaminated) dimension through the sacrifice of the sacrificer's *uštāna-*. We must actually consider that the "imaginal" framework in which the *uruuan-* and the *daēnā-* were supposed to meet together and join, as in a sort of *post mortem* hierogamy (as shown by KELLENS),[16] represents the re-composition of a duality, the victory over a symbolic condition of alienation (i. e. "separation"), and that it constituted a very archaic model for the next-of-kin marriages, because it embodies the type of union as close as actually possible in nature, i. e. the one between two twins, as it was, in fact, that of Yima/Yama with his sister, and as it was the one between Mašyē (or Mahlē) and Mašyānē (or Mahlyānē) according to ch. 14 of the *Iranian Bundahišn*.[17]

10 KELLENS 2007, p. 153.

11 The existence of two entries as ¹*daēnā-*, f. "Religion" and ²*daēnā-*, f. "inneres Wesen, geistiges Ich, Individualität", established by BARTHOLOMAE (1904, pp. 662–667), was rightly criticized by NYBERG (1938, pp. 114–120; cf. also SCHMIDT 1975, pp. 164–168, *passim*). See also LANKARANY 1985.

12 KELLENS 2007, p. 154.

13 KELLENS 2007, pp. 93–155.

14 Kellens 2007, pp. 149–155.

15 Cf. also KELLENS in HERRENSCHMIDT/KELLENS 1994, pp. 49, 51–51.

16 KELLENS 1996.

17 See PAKZAD 2005, p. 181.

The new suggestions proposed by Kellens about the sacrificial framework of this doctrine demonstrate the extraordinary evolution of the Zoroastrian liturgical speculations that would have been already taken place between the redaction of the *Gāθās* and the formation of the speculative sections of the *Yasna*, particularly those in "Middle Avestan",[18] which offer a comment on its earlier parts. If so, the refusal of the Daēnā by Yima can be interpreted nor as a repudiation of the "Religion", as we have already suggested, neither as a manifest declaration of opposition to the Mazdean sacrifice, but as a decision to endure in the "living", earthly, human (contaminated) dimension, while the power of the sacrifice, in which the sacrificer's *uštăna-*, but in other texts also explicitly the *uruuan-*, had been sacrificed[19] (and, at the same time, liberated), would have given him the possibility to leave the world for the Paradise of Ahura Mazdā. We must consider that according to the frame of the myth attested in the *Widēwdād* (which remains a myth, and we must not forget this aspect), it is Ahura Mazdā who just mentions to Zoroaster who was the only mortal man to "see"[20] the Daēnā "other then him" (i.e. "before him" according to the "historical" or *gaēiθiia-*, i.e. "living", chronology, but "after him" from the point of view of the first recitation of the *Ahuna Vairiia*).[21] This fact implies that, if the Mazdean doctrine of the sacrifice were the one reconstructed by Kellens,

18 Kellens 2007, pp. 104–110, *passim*.

19 On the concept of self-sacrifice see already Panaino 2004a; 2004b.

20 The Daēnā was revealed, shown, to Yima: the verb used is *fra-daēs-*, in Pahlavi *fraz-nimūdan* "to show" (Panaino 2015, pp. 115–117).

21 This is the standard interpretation of *Widēwdād* 2, 1, if we follow the textual analysis suggested by Bartholomae, who considered as adverbs the forms *paoiriiō* ("zuerst"; 1904, p. 876) and *aniiō* (1904, p. 139:, see also *parą̄š* "bei Seite", nom.sg.m. of *parą̊ŋk-*, adj., "weg"; 1904, p. 860, n. 1), This kind of adverbs would obviously derive from earlier forms of nominative singular (cf. Delbrück 1893, pp. 627–629). Contrariwise, already Alberto Cantera suggested to me an alternative solution, where *paoiriiō* and *aniiō* must be analyzed as real nominative forms in agreement with the name of Ahura Mazdā. According to this interpretation, Zaraθuštra would be in the position to ask Ahura Mazdā to whom God himself had shown or would like to show the *daēnā-* precisely *after* he had already done or would like to do it with Zoroaster, and not *before* this event. Thus, *aniiō mana* would be interpreted not as "other than me", "except me", in the presumable meaning of "before me", but, on the contrary, as "after me". This solution would be illogical, and then unacceptable, from the chronological point of view, if we frame (as it has been normally done in the past) the sequence of these events in the historical time, where the era of Yima is older than that of Zoroaster. But another possibility, which I must consider, after a deeper discussion with J. Kellens, is at hand. In fact, if the dialogue between Ahura Mazdā and Zoroaster takes place outside the historical time, i.e. in the *mainiiauua-* dimension, as it was the case of the first recitation of the *Ahuna Vairiia* (*Y.* 19), it would result possible. But while during the Conference of Liège (2009), my colleague Philippe Swennen suggested that the dialogue happened between Ahura Mazdā and Zoroaster's *frauuaši-*, the new scenario emerging from a more careful examination of *Yasna* 19, is that it would have been Zaraθuštra to be present at the first recitation of the *Ahuna Vairiia*, and not his *frauuaši-*. In any case, these facts clearly

as I think, Yima (as Zaraθuštra) would have made a correct sacrifice, which produced (together with Ahura Mazdā) also the manifestation of the Daēnā, who, in her turn, was offered to him as a prize for his (immolated) *uštăna-*.[22] This means that there all the references to the Daēnā are strictly ritual, and do not strictly concern the matter of a "conversion", as the "presentation of the Religion" would imply. But in that mythical framework, the effects of the sacrifice could have been radical, real death and beatification (with the Daēnā and Ahura Mazdā).[23] It is this definitive solution that has been (mythically) refused (or postponed) by Yima, who, contrariwise, offered a suitable prototype for all the future sacrifices in which the *daēnā-* would appear as the liturgical divinity introducing the sacrificers to God, but without falling in the risks of a (sudden) death for the officiant priests. Probably, this strongly esoteric and speculative doctrine was transformed during the process of textual re-interpretation that affected the image of the Daēnā, now reduced to the standard representative of the "Religion". Contrariwise, she was originally the visible form of the efficacy of the ritual, a sort of feminine *viaticum*, which offered to the *uruuan-* the missing "password" for the unmixed divine dimension, ritually opened after the sacrificer had "offered" his own *uštăna-*.

In close connection with these problems it would be useful also to pay the necessary attention to the pertinent contents of a very important Semitic inscription, in which the "Dēn Mazdayasniš" was presented as the wife and sister of Bēl, i.e. of Ahura Mazdā (according to an interpretation proposed by C.F. Andreas and generally accepted).[24] This source[25] normally considered as still written in Imperial Aramaic (although Reichelt claimed that this text should be considered as already composed in Chaldaeo-Pahlavi),[26] was found in Arebsun and it is generally known as the Inscription of Arabyssos (i.e. the

open a different perspective. Presently, we can reasonably say that both possibilities are open, one compatible with the existence of Zoroaster already in the *mainiiauua-* dimension, the second and more standard one, compatible with the historical, *gaēiθiia-*, chronology of the world. I cannot exclude that the first was the original one, but that in the course of time, it was the second that was considered as true by the Mazdean clergy, as it also happened with the secondary interpretation of the refusal of the Daēnā by Yima himself.

22 Cf. Kellens in Herrenschmidt&Kellens 1994, p. 52.

23 On the dangerous, mortal, aspects of the sacrifice see, for instance, Malamoud 1989, pp. 60–61, passim, and Heesterman 1993, p. 53, *passim*.

24 With the exception of Reichelt (see below).

25 According to the catalogue by Chabot (*Répertoire d'Épigraphie Sémitique*, III, pp. 228–291). The first news about it were given by Smirnov 1896.

26 We may recall that Reichelt (1901, p. 52, n.1) explicitly proposed this interpretation in open polemics with F.C. Andreas, whose expertise had been asked for by Lidzbarski (1902, pp. 67–69). Lidzbarski himself (1902, pp. 321–323) rejected on linguistic grounds Reichelt's hypothesis.

ancient Arebsun). According to palaeographical criteria it has been attributed[27] to the 2nd century BC[28] or to the 4th or the 5th century BC.[29]

The Aramaic text declares as follows:

(1) [...] this (?) is the Dēn Mazdayasniš
(2) the Queen (?), the sister and wife of Bēl,
(3) so spoke: "I am the wife of the king Bēl".
(4) Then, Bēl so spoke to the Dēn-Mazdayasniš:
(5) "You, O my sister, are very wise,
(6) and you are beautiful as (my) wife,
(7) and I have made (or: 'I desire you')[30] you
(8) [... ... ...] for wife of
(9) [... ... ...] Bēl (or: 'the wife of my heart')[31]."

Although the text does not represent an earlier witness of a form of aramaeographic Proto-Middle-Persian (or of Late-Old-Persian), however, it clearly refers to a Mazdean background, as we can expect in early Cappadocia. The relative antiquity of this source also shows that the Dēn, here denominated "Mǟzdayasniš", with an (apparently nominative feminine) ending, very close to Avestan *māzdaiiasniš* (usually attested in the syntagmatic sequence *daēna māzdaiiasniš*),[32] is doubtless the Iranian goddess of the "Religion", but also the sister and wife of Bēl/Ahura Mazdā. The insistence of this inscription on her role of queen, wife and sister (or spouse) of the highest divinity emphasizes the speculative dimension existing behind the *x^{v}aētuuadaθa-* "next-of-kin marriage",[33] a subject on which Maria Macuch has given very remarkable contributions,[34] to which ones this article would just bring a little improvement as a modest gift and deep expression of friendship in Her honour.

Albeit all the exact implications of this matrimonial institution are still unclear in the Avestan literature, it is evident in front of the conspectus of the Classical sources and of the later statements attested in the Pahlavi documents that we have to do with a consanguineous union. In this precise case, already

27 On the inscription and its dating see CHABOT (s.d.), pp. 283–292, n. 1785; BIDEZ/CUMONT 1938, I; p. 95, n. 2; p. 133; II, p. 85, 5; DUCHESNE-GUILLEMIN 1962, p. 29; LIDZBARSKI, 1902, p. 66 (II sec. a.C.); DONNER-RÖLLIG 1968, p. 311; 1971, p. 51 (2nd c. BC; V–IV BC?); REICHELT 1901; MARQUART 1905, pp. 96–121; SCHAEDER 1930, p. 201; ROSENTHAL 1939, pp. 28–29. Cf. also HALÉVY 1898; CLERMONT-GANNEAU 1898; 1900; BOYCE 1982, pp. 274–275.
28 See in particular LIDZBARSKI 1900–1902, p. 66.
29 SCHAEDER 1930, p. 201; ROSENTHAL 1939, pp. 28–29.
30 Interpretation proposed by CHABOT (no date, p. 289).
31 *Ibidem*. Cf. also DONNER/RÖLLIG 1968, p. 311.
32 See PANAINO 1993; 2003.
33 HÜBSCHMANN 1889; BARTHOLOMAE 1904, p. 1860; KLÍMA 1966; MACUCH 1981; D'ARX 2005. In another much longer work I will discuss this problem in a systematic way. Here I have limited my considerations on a particular aspect of the next-of-kin unions.
34 MACUCH 1991.

CUMONT emphasized the inclusion of the inscription of Arabyssos in the list of the sources pertinent to the Mazdean next-of-kin unions.[35]

A new reflection on the importance of the esoteric doctrines concerning the Daēnā constitutes a very useful and supportive pillar for a correct interpretation of the meaning to be attributed to the *x^vaētuuadaθa-*. In fact, the speculative, hierogamic model of the union between Ahura Mazdā and Anāhitā, that between Yima and his Daēnā (which, although postponed, remains in the *proscenium*, and reappears in later sources, while a direct echo of it becomes manifest through the union of Mašyē and Mašyānē), and the third one between Spəṇtā Ārmaiti and Gayōmart, if not completely attested in Avestan literature, cannot be the later fruit of a Sasanian or post-Sasanian elaborations. They are rooted in the earliest Iranian background. In its turn, the doctrine of the union between the *uruuan-* and the *daēnā-* belongs to the same framework and cannot be taken aside from a reflection about the origins of the next-of-kin unions, so that we must imagine that the positive impulse to these matrimonial strategies (although preferred among leading and priestly classes at a certain stage of Iranian history, but no more exclusively in Sasanian times) was strongly connected with a deep eschatological perspective, in its turn, strongly rooted in the sacrificial doctrine. Then, the hypothesis that such a peculiar pattern might be (also) related to a ritual origin[36] should not be ruled out. In other term it would have been a sort of anticipation/simulation/reproduction of the eschatological union of the twin-components of the soul, the masculine and the feminine one, but also a practical ritual hierogamy of enormous religious and anti-demoniac power, as also Pahlavi theological sources continuously affirm.[37] Thus, the suspect that originally the *x^vaētuuadaθa-* ought be part of a liturgy, should be prudently taken into consideration.

I would like also to remark that the comparison between the Inscription of Arabyssos and the contents of the second chapter of the *Widēwdād* confirms the idea that a representation of the Daēnā as a living, good-looking woman, wife of Ahura Mazdā, but also as a potential ritual spouse of Yima (at least in the *post mortem*), includes two aspects, the one connected with the soul-vision to be seen in the afterlife process of beatification, and the one representing the completeness of the sacrifice, the efficacy of the religious wisdom, i.e. the sacrifice, which later became a personification of the Religion, its (beautiful) body.

As KELLENS has remarked, one of the most plausible meaning for the compound *māzdaiiasni-* could be literally "(la daena de quand on est *mazdaiiasna*)"[38] or, as I prefer in normal contexts, "the one (which belongs to) those who worship Mazdā".[39] The same scholar has also suggested that, while the *daēnā-māzdaiiasni-* belongs to the sacrificer who is *mazdaiiasna-* (i.e. who has

35 CUMONT 1924, pp. 60–61.
36 See already HERRENSCHMIDT in HERRENSCHMIDT/KELLENS 1994, pp. 49, 51–51.
37 See MACUCH 1991, pp. 149–152, *passim*.
38 KELLENS 2007, pp. 150–151, *passim*.
39 See DEBRUNNER 1954, pp. 303: *māzdayasni-* "den Mazdaverehren *(mazdayasna-)* zugehörig".

worshipped Mazdā), she is also denominated as *zaraθuštri-* and *āhūiri-*, probably because this priest was acting as Zaraθuštra and had already assumed the wisdom of an *ahurō.tkaēša-*. Although these solutions word very fittingly within the textual commentary of *Y.* 12, 9, we must verify whether the technical meaning postulated by Kellens for all the occurrences of these *-i-* adjectives can be endorsed without any *caveat*. For instance, in the case of Yima, if we assume that the Daēnā appearing (more precisely shown by Ahura Mazdā)[40] to him should be *āhūiri-* because he had previously acted in quality of an *ahurō.tkaēša-*, this means, as I remarked before, that the framework was ritual and that in this mythical passage there is no reference to a (failed process of) conversion; Yima was already Mazdean. But we can say more. Also the definition of the Daēnā as *zaraθuštri-* (*Vd.* 2, 2) would constitute *per se* an interesting anachronism according to the perspective we assume. In fact, Yima should not see something "Zoroastrian", if his time was much older than that of Zaraθuštra. Thus, one possible interpretation is the one that postulates here a simple reference to a standard formulary pattern, which cannot be taken literally, although it might imply that the "revelation" of the Daēnā was possible because Yima was behaving, *ante litteram*, as Zoroaster himself. Another solution, which I presently prefer, is the one assuming that Zoroaster was already present at the first recitation of the *Ahuna Vairiia*,[41] (together with the Aməṣ̌a Spəṇtas,[42] in particular Aṣ̌a, Vohu Manah and Xšaθra, as already stated by KELLENS[43] in his revision of *Y.* 19), so that his existence, at least in the *mainiiauua-* dimension, was presumed to be earlier than that of Yima himself. In any case, the illusion of a Barbarian and Pagan Yima has thus definitively sunken.

Coming back to the discussion of the Arabyssos Inscription, it would be also useful to recall that against ANDREAS' identification of Ahura Mazdā with Bēl, REICHELT,[44] proposed a different one, exactly with Miθra, so making reference to *Yt.* 17, 16 (where the Daēnā Māzdaiiasniš and Miθra are presented as siblings) and fittingly also to (the already quoted) *Y.* 12, 9 (where the Daēnā Māzdaiiasniš appears in a framework in which the next-of-kin marriage is clearly meant).

40 *Vd.* 2, 1: *kahmāi fradaēsaiiō daēnąm yąm āhūirīm zaraθuštrīm*; 2, 2: *ahmāi fradaēsaēm daēnąm yąm āhūirīm zaraθuštrīm.*

41 KELLENS 2010, pp. 27–51.

42 According to Y. 19, 1, and 3, Ahura Mazdā recited the *Ahuna Vairiia* for Zaraθustra *(mē frāuuaocō / tē frāuuaocəm)* before the existence of the material living (*gaēiθiia-* world; *Y.* 19, 2 and 4–5); according to *Y.* 19, 8, the text of the *Ahuna Vairiia* was recited before the creation of the heaven, the water, the earth, the plants, the cow, the human being, the sun, but after that of the Aməṣ̌a Spəṇtas *(ape aməṣ̌anąm spəṇtanąm dāhīm)*. See KELLENS 2010, pp. 28–32.

43 The presence in particular of Vohu Manah and Xšaθra has been fittingly suggested by KELLENS (2010, pp. 40–43) in the framework of his interpretation of *Y.* 19, 2 and 4, to which I confer. With regard to the presence or absence of the feminine Aməṣ̌a Spəṇtas during the first recitation of the Ahuna Vairiia I leave at the moment the answer open.

44 1901, p. 55.

We can see more in detail these passages:

Yt. 17, 16:[45]

pita tē yō ahurō mazdå	"Your father (is) Ahura Mazdā
yō mazištō yazatanąm	who (is) the greatest among the divinities
yō vahištō yazatanąm	who (is) the best among the divinities
māta ārmaitiš spəṇta	(Your) mother (is) Spəṇta Ārmaiti
brāta tē yō vaŋhuš sraošō aṣ̌iiō	your brother (is) the good Sraoša given with reward
rašnušca bərəzō amauuå	and the high powerful Rašnu
miθrasca vouru.gaoiiaoitiš	and Miθra having wide pastures,
yō baēuuarə.spasanō hazaŋra.gaošō	who disposes of ten thousand spies and of thousand ears,
x^{v}aŋha daēna māzdaiiesniš	(your) sister (is) the Daēnā Māzdaiiasniš.

This stanza, clearly dedicated to Aṣ̌i, simply confirm that the Daēnā Māzdaiiasniš is not only the sister of Miθra, but also of Sraoša and Rašnu, and that she is presented as the daughter of Ahura Mazdā. This statement could be used in order to confirm (or simply to better evaluate) the interpretation of the compound *māzdaiiasni-* as a patronymic. In any case, the potential matrimonial relation between the Daēnā and Ahura Mazdā is not countered by the fact that she was represented as his daughter, particularly in a context in which the *x^{v}aētuuadaθa*-union was normal.

More interesting appears another passage, which has been recently translated and commented (as already underlined) also by Kellens and which results very pertinent for our discussion:[46]

Y. 12, 9:

āstuiiē daēnąm māzdaiiasnīm	"I wish with a praise (my) Daēnā belonging to the Mazdean worshippers (or: "daughter of [Ahura] Mazdā", or "when I worship Ahura Mazdā"),
fraspāiiaoxəδrąm niδā.snaiθišəm	who makes the harness fall down,[47] who (makes one) deposit the weapons,[48]

45 Cf. Lommel 1927, p. 162.

46 See Kellens' translation: "D'un éloge, je salue mon âme-voyance maintenant que je rends le sacrifice à (Ahura) Mazdā. Elle fait tomber le harnachement, fait déposer l'équipement, soutient l'Agencement en contractant mariage dans la lignée-familiale. Elle est la plus grande, la meilleure et la plus belle des (déesses) qui sont et seront maintenant que je professe la doctrine sur Ahura (Mazdā) comme le fit Zaraθuštra (en disant) « je crois tout ce qui est bon appartient à Ahura Mazdā ». Tel est l'éloge *(Āstūiti)* adressé à mon âme-voyance maintenant que le sacrifice est rendu à (Ahura) Mazdā." (2007, pp. 137–138, *passim*).

47 But "qui fait suspendre l'attaque", according to Duchesne-Guillemin 1936, p. 75 (§104), p. 199 (§237).

48 Translation according to Kellens 2007, p. 138. Kellens (orally) reminds me the study of Klingenschmitt (1967) concerning the Avestan compounds with a root noun (and a preverb) in the first member; cf. Duchesne-Guillemin 1936, p. 59 (§85), 199 (§237).

x^{v}*aētuuadaθąm aṣ̌aonīm*	supporting the Order through a wedding in her own family-line,
yā hātinąmcā būšiieiṇtinąmcā	who among those (goddesses) who are and who shall be
mazištācā vahištācā sraēštācā	is the greatest, the best, and the most beautiful one,
yā āhūriš zaraθuštriš	who is the one who belongs to Ahura (Mazdā and) to Zaraθuštra.
ahurāi mazdāi vīspā vohū cinahmī	I attribute all good things to Ahura Mazdā
aēšā astī	This is the praise
daēnaiiå māzdaiiasnōiš āstūitiš.	of the Daēnā belonging to the Mazdean worshippers (or: "daughter of [Ahura] Mazdā", or "when I worship Ahura Mazdā")".

The complexity of the eulogy offered to the Daēnā Māzdaiiasniš in the framework of the *Yasna* liturgy and in close connection with the commentary of the *Frauuarānē* has been already mentioned.

Here I would like only to insist again on the fact that the reference to the *daēnąm māzdaiiasnīm* in her quality of x^{v}*aētuuadaθąm aṣ̌aonīm* is very important and cannot be underestimated. There is a sort of "transitivity" linking the *daēnā-* with the (ritual) thoughts, words and actions of the sacrificers, so that the reference to the x^{v}*aētuuadaθa-* must be observed also from a more technical, ritual, point of view. The implications that inevitably follow seem to be strongly rooted in a liturgical context and cannot be generic,[49] so that we should deduce that the next-of-kin marriage was not limited to the "imaginary" (or "imaginal" *à la* Corbin) dimension of the meeting of the soul-vision with her *uruuan-*, but directly involved the sacrificer, probably on both levels, one symbolic, the latter, perhaps, more practical. We can, in fact, suspect that in some liturgical occasions also a certain eroticism, or a mimic of sexual unions, was possible, as we may suspect in the case of the so-called "matrimonial" *Gāθā*, the *Vahištōišti*

49 Kellens (2007, pp. 151–154) has critically re-opened the discussion about the potential (etymological and semantic) connections between Av. *daēnā-* and Ved. *dhénā-*, without a definitive reversal of perspectives and a refusal of the standard doctrine (see Schmidt 1975), but with a series of stimulating suggestions. Although it would be impossible to enter here this complex problem for an evident lack of space, I think that it is important at least to remark that also the simple thematical comparison between the "nourishing (woman or cow)" and the "vision-soul" would offer some new perspectives of investigation with close regard for the new psychological implications now inevitably emerging from the relation between the *uruuan-* and the *daēnā-*. In fact, if a thematic relation (thus, not necessarily a close etymological derivation or link) with the "milk" or the "cow" as *nutrix*, would be proved (as Kellens has implicitly shown), the image would be that of a "moving-soul" joining his "*nutrix*", i.e. a myth of reintegration of the child with(in) his mother. This pattern could represent another speculative form of incest, but also satisfy a deeper unconscious desire of supreme spiritual wellness. It is a matter on which it would be necessary to meditate more.

(*Y.* 53).[50] The presence of more or less crude erotic connotations cannot be a surprise in the liturgical context of the Indo-Iranian world, in particular if we take into serious consideration and without any taboo or *pruderie* the explicit, sometimes "lurid", characters appearing during the conclusive moments of the *Aśvamedha* ceremony, the obscenity of which has put a high number of past scholars in embarrassment.[51]

In any case, we have the right to wonder if through an act of x^{v}*aētuuadaθa-* any (ritually prepared) man could perform the role of Ahura Mazdā with his *āhūiriš Daēna Māzdaiiasniš*, and if the consanguineous marriages had also a ritual (real or symbolic we are no more in condition to say) correspondent performance in earlier liturgic traditions. The hypothesis that a strong impulse to the diffusion of such a matrimonial strategy started from the enormous importance it assumed in the framework of the Mazdean ritual symbolism and its speculative perspectives (aiming at an anticipated "vision" of the "unmixed" [afterlife] dimension), results to be something more than a simple guess.

Bibliographical references

d'Arx, B. 2005: "Le mystère du choix de la deuxième vertu. Courte réflexion sur l'inceste à l'iranienne." In: *Barbares et Civilisés dans l'antiquité.* Paris (Cahiers Kubaba VII), pp. 249–266.

Bartholomae, Chr. 1904: *Altiranisches Wörterbuch.* Strassburg.

Bidez, J./F. Cumont 1938: *Les Mages Hellénisés.* 2 vols. Paris.

Boyce, M. 1982: *A History of Zoroastrianism.* Vol. II. *Under the Achaemenians.* Leiden/Köln.

Chabot, J.-B. (no date): *Répertoire d'épigraphie sémitique, publié par la Commission du Corpus Iscriptionum Semiticarum.* In 7 vols., 1900–1950. Vol. III. Paris, pp. 283–292.

Choksy, J.K. 2002: *Evil, Good, and Gender: Facets of the Feminine in Zoroastrian Religious History.* New York (Toronto Studies in Religion 28; reprinted in 2009).

Cumont, Fr. 1924: "Les unions entre proches à Doura Europos et chez les Perses." In: CRAI, 15 fév., 27, pp. 53–62.

Debrunner, A. 1954: *Die Nominalsuffixe.* Göttingen (Jakob Wackernagel: *Altindische Grammatik.* Band II, 2).

Delbrück, B. 1893: *Vergleichende Syntax der indogermanischen Sprachen.* Strassburg (*Grundriss der vergleichenden Grammatik der indogermanischen Sprachen.* Bd. 3: *Vergleichende Syntax der indogermanischen Sprachen.* Theil 1).

Donner, H./W. Röllig 1968: *Kanaanäische und aramäische Inschriften.* Mit einem Beitrag von O. Rössler. Band II. *Kommentar.* Zweite, durchgesehene und erweiterte Auflage. Wiesbaden.

50 See Kellens/Pirart 1991, pp. 265–274, in particular pp. 272–273 about the sexual symbolism of *Y.* 53, 7.

51 See Jamison 1996, pp. 65–72 with the pertinent bibliography.

Duchesne-Guillemin, J. 1938: *Les Composés de l'Avesta*. Liége/Paris (Études de Morphologie Iranienne I; Bibliothèque de la Faculté de Philosophie et Lettres de l'Université de Liège – Fascicule LXXIV).

— 1962: "L'étude de l'iranien ancien au vingtième siècle." In: *Kratylos* 7/1, pp. 1–44 (reprinted in Duchesne-Guillemin 1974, pp. 7–52).

— 1974: *Opera Minora*. Vol. I. *Philologie et Histoire de l'Iran*. Téhéran.

Donner, H./W. Röllig 1968: *Kanaanäische und aramäische Inschriften*. Mit einem Beitrag von O. Rössler. Band II. *Kommentar*. Zweite, durchgesehene und erweiterte Auflage. Wiesbaden.

— 1971: *Kanaanäische und aramäische Inschriften*. Mit einem Beitrag von O. Rössler. Band I. *Texte*. Dritte, durchgesehene Auflage. Wiesbaden.

Frugoni, A. 2005: "Celestino V." In: *Enciclopedia Dantesca*. Vol. VI. *Av–Ce*. Milano (Istituto della Enciclopedia Italiana. Ristampa in edizione economica allegata al settimanale *Panorama*), pp. 665–668.

Halévy, J. 1898: "Une inscription araméenne d'Arabissos." In: *Revue sémitique d'épigraphie et d'histoire ancienne* 6, pp. 271–273.

Heesterman, J.C. 1993: *The Broken World of Sacrifice. An Essay in Ancient Indian Ritual*. Chicago/London.

Herrenschmidt, Cl./J. Kellens 1994: "La question du rituel : le mazdéisme ancien et achéménide." In: *Archives des sciences sociales des religions* 85/1, pp. 45–87.

Hübschmann, H. 1889: "Über die persische Verwandtenheirath." In: *ZDMG* 43, pp. 308–312.

Jamison, St.W. 1996: *Sacrificed Wife/Sacrificer's Wife. Women, Ritual, and Hospitality in Ancient India*. New York/Oxord.

Kellens, J. 1984: "Yima, magicien entre les dieux et les hommes." In: *Orientalia J. Duchesne-Guillemin emerito oblata*. Leiden (Acta Iranica 24), pp. 267–281.

— 1996: "L'ame entre le cadavre et le paradis." In: *JA* 283, pp. 19–56.

— 2007: *Études avestiques et mazdéennes*. Vol. 2. *Le Hōm Stōm et la zone des déclarations* (Y7.24–Y15.6, avec les intercalations de Vr3 à 6). Paris (Persika 10).

— 2010: *Études avestiques et mazdéennes*. Vol. 3. *Le long préambule du sacrifice (Yasna 16 à 27.12, avec les intercalations de Visprad 7 à 12)*. Paris (Persika 15).

Kellens, J./E. Pirart 1991: *Les textes vieil-avestiques*. Vol. III. *Commentaire*. Wiesbaden.

Klíma, O. 1966: "Zur Problematik der Ehe-Institution im Alten Iran." In: *ArOr* 34, pp. 554–569.

Klingenschmitt, G. 1967: "Avestan Possessive Compounds with a Root Noun in the First Member." In: *Sir J. J. Zarthoshti Madressa Centenary Volume*. Bombay, pp. 120–122.

Lankarany, F.-T. 1985: *Daēnā im Avesta, eine semantische Untersuchung*. Reinbek (Studien zur Indologie und Iranistik, Mon. 10).

Lidzbarski, M. 1900–1902: "Aramäische Inschriften aus Kappadocien." In: *Ephemeris für semitische Epigraphik*. Bd. I. Giessen, pp. 59–74; pp. 319–326.

Lommel, H. 1927: *Die Yäšt's des Awesta übersetzt und eingeleitet*. Göttingen/Leipzig (Quellen der Religionsgeschichte 15, Gruppe 6).

Macuch, M. 1991: "Inzest im Vorislamischen Iran." In: *AMI* 24, pp. 141–154.

Malamoud, Ch. 1989: *Cuire le monde. Rite et pensée dans l'Inde ancienne.* Paris (= *Cuocere il mondo. Rito e pensiero nell'India antica*, Milano 1994, traduzione italiana a cura di A. Comba).

Marquart, J. 1907: *Untersuchungen zur Geschichte von Eran. Philologus.* Supplementband 10.

Nyberg, H.S. 1938: *Die Religionen des alten Iran.* Deutsch von H.H. Schaeder. Leipzig (Mitteilungen der Vorderasiatische-Ægyptischen Gesellschaft 43).

Pakzad, F. 2005: *Bundahišn. Zoroastrische Kosmogonie und Kosmologie.* Band I: *Kritische Edition.* Tehran (Ancient Iranian Studies Series 2).

Panaino, A. 1993: "Philologia Avestica III. Av. *mazdaiiasna-/māzdaiiasni-/māzdaiiasna-*. M.P.I. *mazdēsn* (?)/Part.I. *mazdēzn*/Pahl. *māzdēsn*/M.P.Man. *māzdēs*/ Sogd.Man. °*mzt'yzn*." In: *Annali di Ca' Foscari* (Serie Orientale) 32, 3, pp. 135–173.

— 2003: "Once again upon Middle Persian *māzdēsn*." In: *Paitimāna. Essays in Iranian, Indo-Iranian and Indian Studies in Honor of Hanns-Peter Schmidt.* Volumes I, II. Ed. by S. Adhami. Costa Mesa (California), pp. 321–327.

— 2004a: *Rite, parole et pensée dans l'Avesta ancien et récent.* Quatre leçons au Collège de France (Paris, 7, 14, 21, 18 mai 2002), édité par Velizar Sadovski avec la collaboration rédactionnelle de Sara Circassia. Wien (Sitzungsberichte der ÖAW. Philosophisch-historische Klasse, 716. Band / Veröffentlichungen zur Iranistik, Nr. 31).

— 2004b: "Aspects of the 'Interiorization' of the Sacrifice in the Zoroastrian Tradition." In: *Zoroastrian Rituals in Context.* Ed. by M. Stausberg. Leiden/Boston (Numen Book Series. Studies in the History of Religions 102), pp. 233–252.

— 2009a: "Anche il migliore si arrabbia. A proposito di Y. 19,15." In: *Trésors d'Orient. Mélanges offerts à Rika Gyselen.* Publié par Ph. Gignoux/Ch. Jullien/F. Jullien. Paris (StIr 42), pp. 269–281.

— 2009b: "Ahreman and Narcissus." In: *Literarische Stoffe und ihre Gestaltung in mitteliranischer Zeit. Kolloquium anlässlich des 70. Geburtstages von Werner Sundermann.* Hrsg. von D. Durkin-Meisterernst/C. Reck/D. Weber. Wiesbaden (Beiträge zur Iranistik 31), pp. 201–209.

— 2009c: "The Mental Dimension of Evil: Psychoanalytic Remarks on the Image and Behaviour of Ahreman in the Framework of Zoroastrian Cosmology." In: *Geist, Gehirn, Verhalten. Sigmund Freud und die modernen Wiessenschaften.* Hrsg. von P. Gianpieri-Deutsch. Würzburg, pp. 143–158.

— 2012: "The Triadic Symbolism of Yima's *vara-* and Related Structures and Patterns." In: *Yama/Yima. Variations indo-iraniennes sur le geste mythique / Variations on the Indo-Iranian Myth of Yama/Yima.* Édité par S. Azarnouche/C. Redard. Paris (Collège de France. Publications de l'Institut de civilisation indienne 81), pp. 111–130.

— 2013: "Mortality and Immortality. Yama's/Yima's Choice and the Primordial Incest. (Mythologica Indo-Iranica I)." In: *Disputationes Iranologicae Vindobonenses II.* Theil II. Herausgegeben von V. Sadovski/A. Panaino. Wien (Sitzungsberichte der Akademie der Wissenschaften, Philosophisch-Historische Klasse, Veröffentlichungen zur Iranistik 65), pp. 47–164 (plus bibliograpy).

— 2015: "Yima ed il 'rifiuto' della *daēnā-* ovvero dell'incestualità, della beatitudine e della morte tra ostacoli e seducenti trasparenze." In: *Démons Iraniens. Actes du*

Colloque international organisé à l'Université de Liège, le 5 et le 6 février 2009 à l'occasion des 65 ans de Jean Kellens. Ed. par PH. SWENNEN. Liège, pp. 97–123.

REICHELT, H. 1901: "Aramäische Inschriften aus Kappadocien." In: *WZKM* 15, pp. 51–56.

SCHAEDER, H.H. 1930: *Iranische Beiträge I*. Halle (Schriften der Königsberger Gelehrter Gesellschaft. 6 Jahrgang, Geisteswissenschaftliche Klasse, Heft 5).

SCHMIDT, H.-P. 1975: "Is Vedic *dhénā* related to Avestan *daēnā*?" In: *Monumentum H.S. Nyberg*. Vol. II. Téhéran/Liège (Hommages et Opera Minora, AcIr 5), pp. 165–193.

SMIRNOV, JA.I. 1896: [no title for the article] In: *Zapiski Imperatorskogo Russkogo arxeologičeskogo obščestva*, tom VIII, Vyp. 3–4, Novaja Serija, *Trudy otdelenija arxeologii drevne-klassičeskoj, vizantijskoj i zapadno-evropejskoj* (Kniga pervaja 1895, S. Peterburg), pp. 444–446.

Iranian Words in *čam*°*

Adriano V. Rossi

1. Walter Bruno Henning published in *Sogdica* (as Glossary "g") a fragmentary page from a MP-Sogdian Glossary (M835) which presents in the last lines of the column written on the *verso* the following set of words containing <cmb> (<cmb°>):

(26) cmbyyšn
(27) (cm)b oo tγ'(m)
(28) cmb oo wyn'ẖ
(29) cmb oo cmxwy oo
(30) cmb oo cyngry' oo

Henning annotated: "I do not know a single MPers. or NPers. word *čamb*, and the number of words that begin in *čamb-* is small".[1]

Durkin-Meisterernst's *Dictionary* contains the following articles:[2]

cmb MP /*čamb*/ *n.* 1. 'ford' (?); 2. *čemb* 'guitar, lute' (?); 3. 'repentance' (?)
cmbyyšn MP /*čambišn*/ *n.* Variant for *čamišn* 'urination; lavatory' ?

The number of question marks (concentrated in two lines of his *Dictionary*) inserted by Durkin-Meisterernst is remarkable, and this is a valid reason to verify the available documentation on the whole lexical set.

2. On the premise that occlusion of a final nasal is not infrequent in Iranian, Henning widens his survey of possible cognates to the Parth. verbal base *čam-* 'to walk, stride, run', connecting it, without further explanations, to Parth. *čām-* 'to come', NP *čamidan* 'to step', Arm. *čem* 'walk'.

To build the article "*čam* ? 'to walk' "[3], whose high doubtfulness is clear already by the query following its headword, *EDIV* could rely, besides Parthian,

* The following scattered remarks on matters involving Middle Persian and Parthian lexical features are dedicated to Maria Macuch as a token of deep admiration for her outstanding contribution to Middle Iranian studies, and also for the aspects of her human personality which make so pleasant her attitude towards colleagues and young students from all parts of the world. For the sake of space full references for minor dialects and languages are not given in the *Bibliography* at the end of this article, and the reader is referred to the Archive of the *Balochi Etymological Dictionary Project*, L'Orientale University, Naples. I am deeply indebted to Ela Filippone for her generous advice on Iranian dialectology.

1 Henning 1940, p. 38.

2 Durkin-Meisterernst 2004, p. 125.

3 *EDIV* s.v.

on few further parallels: (?) Khot. *tcāma-* 'leaping insect, either locust or grasshopper',[4] NP *čamidan* 'to walk proudly' and Bal. *čam-* 'to shake, dance, prance, dangle';[5] in the miscellaneous section of the article a Parachi base (whose connection to Parth. *čam-* had been already doubted by MORGENSTIERNE[6]), and the Arm. LW *čem* 'walk' (on which see below) are added.

As regards the Parthian documentation, *EDIV* quotes *čam-* but not *čām-*[7]; note that HENNING[8], BOYCE[9] and DURKIN-MEISTERERNST all consider the latter as distinct from *čam-*.[10]

Parth. *čām-* occurs in the following hymnic passages[11]:

M 10 R 7
pd drwd c'm'h̲ 'w šhr (r)wšn 'may you go in well-being to the realm of light'

A.R. vii /3a/ M 91 R II = M175 V 9
's'h̲ tw gy'n || 'wd fr'c c'm'h̲ 'come, spirit, step forth!'[12]

DURKIN-MEISTERERNST's recent reinterpretation is accompanied by the following note: "Henning's 'come' should rather be 'go' which fits both occurrences"[13].

4 *DKS* s.v. The Khotanese denomination of the insect, whose identification remains doubtful (MAURO MAGGI, Sapienza/Rome, kindly attracts my attention on the fact that SKJÆRVØ in his *Khotanese Manuscripts from Chinese Turkestan in The British Library*, pp. 34 and 556, does not translate the two occurrences of this word in the Khotanese Buddhist Texts), is hardly linkable to the alleged base because of semantic and morpho-structural reasons; *EDIV* 32 connotes this connection by "?"; *EWA* 3, pp. 180–181 seems rather sceptical; only *ESIJ* 2, p. 262 considers it as certain.

5 SHAHBAKHSH 2004, p. 118, but see below §4.2.

6 In addition to "*č(h)īm-, č(h)em-* 'to go, move, wonder' ", MORGENSTIERNE 1929, p. 246a records a nominal form *čīmȫ* (*čhīmō*?) 'walking, gait' with the comment: "Cf. Prs. *čamīdan* 'to walk proudly', *čaman* 'walking'?", and providing an example not easily analyzable; KIEFFER 1979, pp. 99–101 does not mention any nominalizations from this base. GARNIK ASATRIAN (pers. comm. from his archive) quotes MORGENSTIERNE 1929 and adds this word to the 'walking'-set.

7 GHILAIN distinguishes between *čām-* 'venir' (classified among the "thèmes radicaux au degré allongé de racines à vocalisme *a*", 1939, p. 72) and *čam-* 'courir' (considered among the "thèmes radicaux au degré plein de racines avec voyelle *ă*", 1939, p. 56).

8 Loc.cit.

9 BOYCE 1954, Glossary, s.vv., BOYCE 1977 s.vv.

10 Also *ESIJ* 2, p. 262 apparently point to two autonomous verbs: *čam-* 'bežat′, bystro dvigat′sja', *čām-* 'prixodit′'.

11 A third passage (M 507 R 4a–4b: cw'gwn kd hwyn || 'dwr z'dg'n o tmyg'n (pd? h)w c'mynd 'as when the children of the Fire run against him in the manner of the beings of Hell') is too obscure to be useful in this circumstance; on it cf. BOYCE 1952, pp. 440–441; BOYCE 1975, pp. 96–97; KLIMKEIT 1989, p. 65.

12 Note DURKIN-MEISTERERNST (2006, p. 178, commentary, l. 145): "Boyce's translation above suggests she was thinking of something like 'to get going, step out' indicating the start of a movement or a journey".

13 DURKIN-MEISTERERNST 2006, p. 178, commentary, l. 145: "in M 10 it has the advantage of not suggesting that those speaking are then not placed in the realm of light but rather here and encouraging the freed light to go away from them to that realm" (ibid.). In the

However, in my opinion it is not the direction of the movement and its perception perspective which is encoded by *čām-*, but the modality of motion: 'to step in a solemn way' would perfectly fit both contexts, while *čam-* could point to an undetermined walking[14] and, at least in two cases,[15] to the human faculty of 'walking'.

As far as the Parth. name *čamag*[16] is concerned, the astronomical meaning 'course' seems prevailing[17], even if with it a 'course of river' (rwd'n cmg, M 6 R ii 2[18]) may also be referred to; see below § 6, *in fine*.

3. A preliminary inspection on texts and dictionaries shows that a verb †*čamīdan* seems not to occur in the MP documentation. Consequently, one should assume—unless they are represented in Phl texts that I do not know—that both †*čamītan* appearing in the Pahlavi-Persian[19] and Persian-Pahlavi[20] dictionaries by Bahrâm Faravaši, and Phl. †*čamīdan* quoted by Mengal (1990, p. 145) in connection with Bal. *čam-* 'to shake, dance, prance, dangle' (see below, § 4.2) derive from the correlated article in Kapadia's *Glossary*[21]. There Kapadia only gives the meaning 'to ricreate, to walk proudly waving from side to side', mentioning NP *čamidan* and giving no indication of Phl. sources. There a paretymological explanation is given: "hence in the allegorical sense to make water". From Kapadia's subsequent article "*chamaš* 'urine'; fr[om] *chamîṭan* see above", the reader gets the impression that Phl. †*čamīdan* would be a deverbal noun derived from the preceding verb, which is not the case, because the alleged verb is reconstructed without any textual attestation on the basis of a phonetic confusion between NP *šâšidan*, *čamidan*, *čâmidan*[22], 'to urinate'.

While Kapadia's "*chamaš* 'urine'" is Phl. *čamišn* id., a noun with limited textual attestations[23] but confirmed by Middle Arm. LW *čemiš* 'lavatory' (also in modern Arm. dialects)[24], there is another unattested noun †*čamišn* appearing

same note the author comments upon the divergences between Henning and Lentz on the interpretation of this passage.

14 Quotations of the passages containing *čam-* in Durkin-Meisterernst 2004, p. 125 s. v.

15 M248+V 10 = M275+V ii 14 (*Gyān Wifrās* § 53, Sundermann 1997, pp. 78–79) and $_0$M5561+M5562 V 6 = M847 V 7 (*Gyān Wifrās* § 79, Sundermann 1997, pp. 80–81).

16 This formation type is uncommon with present stems of intransitive verbs in Parthian, cf. Rastorgueva/Molčanova 1981, p. 194 § 4.

17 Durkin-Meisterernst 2004, p. 125 s. v. translates 'course, movement'.

18 Andreas/Henning 1934, p. 866, l. 32.

19 Faravaši 1967, p. 89 s. v., with the following NP equivalents: *čamidan*, *tafarroǰ kardan*, *bâ nâzu kerešme râh raftan*, *dar mowqe'-e râh raftan benâz-e andâm-e xodrâ pičotâb dâdan*, followed by a gloss from the *Borhan-e qâteʿ*.

20 Faravaši 1979, s. v. *tafarroǰ kardan* (p. 145), *čamidan* (p. 180).

21 Kapadia 1953, p. 515 s. v. *chamîṭan*.

22 Moʿin, Steingass etc.

23 Tavadia 1930, p. 75 fn. 9. On the Phl. expression *abastāg ī pad čamišn* cf. Shaked 1979, pp. 265 *ad* 125.

24 As kindly suggested by Garnik Asatrian (priv. comm.), cf. also Ačaṙyan 3, p. 196.

in the *Pahlavi-Persian Dictionary* by BAHRÂM FARAVAŠI[25] with the NP translation *'čameš, tafarroǰ, xarâmân râh raftan, benâz râh raftan'*, followed by a gloss from the *Borhan-e qâte*ʿ; it seems probable that FARAVAŠI has attributed to the MP phase a word whose only (late) attestation was the *Borhan* quotation.

4.1 The only effective source material adduced by *EDIV* to support the article "*čam ? 'to walk'" stands therefore on NP *čamidan* 'to walk proudly' and Bal. *čam-* 'to shake, dance, prance, dangle'.

Modern Persian *čamidan* preserves the meaning 'to walk proudly'[26] as attested uninterruptedly since *Šâhnâme*.[27] *Šâhnâme* also documents a sporadic usage of its causatives *čamândan* and (rarely) *čamânidan* 'gängeln, in Bewegung setzen',[28] and two different forms of (original) participles to indicate two different horsy gaits: *čamân* and *čamande*, with reference to a horse gaiting slowly and gracefully (= *xarâmande*),[29] *čamand* with reference to a lazy and sluggish *(tondraftâr va kâhel)*[30] horse. Remarkable is that also in the Cambridge *Tafsir* (x–xi c., probably from Khorâsân[31]), *čamand* is used with reference to walking animate beings in opposition to not walking ones (*moryân va čamandegân va čahârpâyân*[32]), as in the ManParth. passages quoted above. In formal Tajik *čamidan* means 'to move slowly, graciously, move from side to side on the march';[33] the most recent dictionary[34] isolates in a special article labelled as 'literary' the military meaning 'to trot on the battlefield as a sign of defiance'. In some Tajik dialects specializations of the notion of 'walking' can be found, e.g. high Matchin *čamidan* ~ low Matchin *čambidan* 'to limp' *(xromat')*;[35] Yaghn. *čamak* 'to limp, be lame'[36] could result from the pressure by Tajik dialects.

NP *čam* is also in current usage for 'gait, pace, walk, strut'[37]; similarly Taj. *čam* according to NAZARZODA[38].

25 FARAVAŠI 1967, p. 89 s.v.; see also FARAVAŠI 1979, s.v. *tafarroǰ* (Phl. *čamišn*) p. 145, *čameš* (Phl. *čamišn*) p. 180, *xarâmân râh raftan* (Phl. *čamišn*) p. 199.
26 LAZARD 1990 s.v., MOʿIN, 1, s.v., ARYANPOUR s.v., RUBINČIK s.v., HAÏM s.v. The verb is not in common use.
27 WOLFF 1935 s.v., DEHXODÂ 41, s.v.
28 WOLFF 1935 s.vv.
29 WOLFF 1935 s.v. *čamidan*, DEHXODÂ 41, s.v.
30 DEHXODÂ 41, s.v.
31 LAZARD 1963, p. 57.
32 BROWNE 1894, p. 454.
33 SAJMIDDINOV 2006 s.v.
34 NAZARZODA 2010 s.v. *čamidan* II.
35 XROMOV 1962, p. 191 s.v. The author quotes in this connection literary Tajik *čamidan* glossed as 'to vacillate, stagger' *(pokačivat'sja, kolebat'sja)*.
36 MIRZOZADA 2008 s.v.
37 LAZARD 1990 s.v., HAÏM s.v., RUBINČIK s.v., not in ARYANPOUR.
38 NAZARZODA 2010 s.v. *čam* I.

A specialization of *čam* in the sense of 'dance' is attested in the Eastern Persian area (but not the verb *čamidan*, apparently not attested) specialized to mean 'to dance' in Afghan Persian[39], Khorâsâni[40] and Minâbi area (Banderi *čamak*, Angohran *čamak*, Miršekâli *čamak* all 'to dance', cf. Kahnuji, Jirofti *čamâki* 'dancer'); *čamiden* 'to dance' is found practically everywhere in Hormozgan[41]; a different metonymical change produced Birjandi *čam*[42] 'behaviour, moral profile'.

Arm. *čemim* 'to walk in a solemn manner' has been borrowed in an undetermined Parthian phase; the Armenian lexical family is supplemented by *čem* 'walk', *čem-aran* 'schola peripatetica, academy', *čem-akan* 'peripatetic', which may be Armenian calques from underlying MIr. formations or Armenian original formations from the borrowed verbal base.[43]

4.2 If one excludes recent borrowings from Persian,[44] Balochi seems to be the only modern Iranian language to preserve *čam-* with reference to the gracious gait of animals or stepping of human beings. However, it is not sure that all the semantic nuances contained in the available Bal. dictionaries ('to shake, dance, prance, dangle')[45] are really in full use today.[46]

5.1 Justi[47] linked NP *čamidan* to the Kurdish verb *čam-* 'to curve', which since Justi's mention entered the etymological debate about WIr. *čam-*.

39 Afghaninevis 1961 s. v.
40 Šâlči 1991 s. v.
41 Data from Hormozgan have been recently gathered by my former pupil Gerardo Barbera, PhD in Iranian dialectology from L'Orientale, Naples, to whom I am much indebted.
42 Rezâi 1984 s. v., Rezâi 1998, p. 381 s. v. This same meaning is also traceable in contemporary formal Persian and further WIr. languages.
43 Hübschmann 1897, p. 189; Bolognesi 1962, p. 134 (also for oscillation in the vocalism of LWs from Iranian with *e* < *a*); Ačaṙyan 1977, pp. 195–196; Asatrian (pers. comm.). The first to link up Arm. *čem* with Iranian *čam-* was Justi 1880, p. 233, no. 381; but see already de Lagarde 1854, p. 19, l. 471–472.
44 This is certainly the case with Psht. *čam* 'walk, gait' recorded by Raverty 1860 s. v. and Aslanov 1966 s. v. (in Raverty erroneously recorded in the article *čam* 'division, district'); Bellew 1901 s. v. has only *čam-u-xam* 'graceful gait, strut, waddle', LW from the relevant NP compound.
45 The quotations of the main Balochi dictionaries are gathered in Shahbakhsh 2004, p. 118.
46 Eastern Balochi varieties apparently do not have the verb *čam-*. Mengal 1990, p. 145 had already remarked a connection between (Rakhshani, his own dialect) Bal. *čamag*, NP *čamidan* and "Phl. *čamīdan*", evidently found by the scholar in one of the dictionaries quoted at § 3 above. His annotation in the margin *baločia bor čo kauk-at* 'In Balochi the mare is like a partridge' (with a reference to the poet Gul Khan Nasir, who evidently praises somewhere in his poems the elegance of the bird) let us think that Mengal had in mind a core meaning of (Rakhshani) Bal. *čamag* centred on the elegant gait of certain paradigmatic animals. I am indebted to Dr. Badal Khan, specialist of Balochi and Urdu at L'Orientale, Naples, for his kind advice.
47 Justi 1880, p. 233, no. 381.

The verb under focus is represented both in Northern Kurd. as *čamyān*[48], *čamīn*[49] and Central Kurdish as *čamān*[50], with the intransitive meaning 'to bend, curve'; it becomes transitive by adding *-ān-* (NKurd., CKurd. *čamāndin*, NKurd. *čaw°*[51] 'to bow, bend (tr.)'). In Lakki *čæmein* means 'to be bent' *(do tâ o dollâ šodan)*[52].

In addition to the verb, a noun *čam* 'curve'[53], 'courbure'[54] (also Awrāmānī and Gurānī according to Mokri)[55] is documented, possibly only in Central[56] and Southern Kurdish[57]—but consider *čam* 'club-foot' *(kosolapyj)* in the Kurmanǰi variety described by Orbeli[58].

The nominal *čam* is widely attested throughout Iran, as seen in the following, non-exhaustive sample: Azari *čam* 'bending', Gilaki *čam* 'crooked', Tehrân area *čam* 'curve of street or hairpin bend'[59], Baxtiâri 'bending', Lakki *čam* 'curve of street', Davâni *čam* 'curve of street or river', Gavkošaki *čam* id., Kermâni *čam* 'wrinkle, fold', 'curve of street', Khorâsâni *čam* 'curved', *čam-gerdeš* 'curve of street', etc.[60]

5.2 While Justi had been in search of an Iranian base for 'to bend' linking NP *čamidan* to Kurd. *čamī-* 'to curve' (§ 5.1 above), Henning pointed to a base **kamb-* 'to bend' to explain ManSogdian °kmb, Budd. °k'np-[61] and Khwarezmian 'kβd(k) and 'kfs-[62], a base that already Horn[63] had proposed to see in NP *xam(m)* 'crooked, twisted'. This base and its Middle Iranian outcomes appear in the IE dictionaries (**kam-p-* Pokorny, **kamp- LIV*, cf. **kamp EDIV*) with major or minor doubts. Mayrhofer[64], against Kellens's[65] stand, maintains a

48 MacKenzie 1961, p. 235.
49 Chyet 2003 s.v.
50 MacKenzie 1961, p. 227. Cf. also Mokri 2003, p. 393.
51 Wahby/Edmonds 1966 s.v., Chyet 2003 s.v.
52 I am indebted for this information to my former pupil Dr. Sara Belelli, specializing in Southern Kurdish and Lakki at L'Orientale, Naples.
53 Wahby/Edmonds 1966 s.v.
54 Mokri 2003, p. 134 s.v.
55 Hakem 2012, pp. 223–224 shows that the relevant lexical field (especially in Sorani) is rather rich, with many derivatives around the basic notion 'to bend'.
56 Kurdoev, based on Kurmanǰi, marks his articles ⁴*čam* 'fold' and ⁵*čam* 'manner' as 'Southern Kurdish'.
57 Hazhar 1991, s.v. *čam*; sense no. 5 seems to derive from NP *čam*.
58 Orbeli 2002, p. 55 s.v.
59 Adib Tusi 1963–1964, p. 488 s.v.
60 In formal Persian *čam* in the meaning of 'curve of street' appears sporadically. It is not recorded in Moʿin, Lazard, Haïm etc. In Steingass s.v. *čam* 'curved, crooked, bent' and 'a lane full of windings' are the fifth and sixth sense in a list of sixteen. Analogously NP *čamidan* is recorded in Steingass also as 'to twist, turn, bend, curve'. Both should derive from the dialectal material incorporated in the Dictionary.
61 Henning 1940, pp. 43–44.
62 Henning-MacKenzie 1971, s.vv. 'kβd(k) and 'kfs-.
63 Horn 1898–1901, p. 60: "*xamm* 'krumm, Krümmung' (Schahn. 207, 1412) *xammīδan* (673, 2654) neben *xam*, etwa aus **xanb*, ap. **ka(n)pa-* vgl. gr. *κάμπυλος*?".
64 *EWA* 1, p. 306.
65 Kellens 1986, especially p. 347.

sceptical attitude ("Verbindung mit gr. κάμπτω 'biege, krümme' u.a. (s. Frisk I 774f.) bleibt aus semantischen Gründen zweifelhaft") and does not include √*kamp*- among his certain Indo-Iranian etymologies.

MacKenzie's remarks[66] on the article *cambule* in Bailey's *Prolexis* caused the addition of NP *čamidan* to the series 'bent, crooked, curved' in the subsequent literature, even if the meaning 'to bend'[67] seems to have been assigned to NP *čamidan* only by the lexicographers.[68]

A possible relationship between WIr. *čam*° and EIr. *kam*° is pointed out by Bailey, who proposed that: "the base could here be *čamp*-, palatalised to *kamp*- to shake".[69] *ESIJ* points to a Proto-Iranian contamination among different bases (**kam(p)-*, **kam(b)-* : *čam(p)-*, **čam(b)-*)[70]; similarly, Steblin-Kamenskij holds that "dlja dr.-ir. dialektov sleduet vosstanovit′ 'defektnuju' osnovy **k(h)am(b)-* // **čam-* 'izgib', 'naklon' ".[71]

6.0 At this point, we can deal with the central core of our study, i. e. the answer to the implicit question contained in Henning's remark: "There is [...] the possibility of *mb* replacing *–m*, so that *cmb* 'ford' (27) could belong to *cm*- 'walk, stride, run' (31), cf. *cm- Mir. Man.*, iii, Arm. *čem*-, NPers. *čam*-, etc."[72]: is there any connection between MP *cmb* 'ford' and MWIr. *čam*- 'to walk, to step' (cf. §§2–4 above) ?

6.1 We should emphasize that MP *cmb* 'ford' (whose meaning is assured by the Sogdian gloss *tγ'(m)* in Glossary "g") is not an isolated term, as possibly Henning deemed, but fits into the wider nominal network of the WIr. type *čam* whose core meaning seems to be 'ground at both sides of a river, humid and verdant, especially in the neighbourhood of a river bight'.

Members of this lexical family are: Azeri, Taleši *čam* 'flat round with trees at both sides of a river', Daštestâni, Lirâvi-Daylami *čam* 'river-bank', Sor. Kurd. *čam* 'verdant ground at both sides of a river', Kermânšâhı Kurd. *čam* id., Lakki *čam* 'verdant ground at both sides of a river which previously was part of the river-bed', Baxtiâri *čam* id., Lori *čam* 'verdant ground at both sides of a river',

66 MacKenzie 1969, p. 398: "*cambule* : add NP *čamīdan*, Kurd. *čamān* 'curve, bend', Chor. *nknby*-, *'knby*- 'bend', *'kfs*- 'be bent'". Bailey in his *Dictionary* only partially accepted MacKenzie's suggestion, not mentioning NP *čamidan* but adding two NP words with *č*°: *čamba* 'large bar' (but why here?) and *čafte* 'curved' (already circulated by Morgenstierne in connection with Psht. *cəvda* 'nook under overhanging rocks, cave', *EVP* s. v.).

67 Cf. e. g. MacKenzie 1970, p. 62: "*nk'np*-: bend, bow [...] cf. M *''kmb*- [...], Xwar. *nknby*- [...] NP *čamīdan* 'bend'". From *DKS* and MacKenzie 1970 transferred e. g. to Samadi 1986, p. 129 and probably to *EDIV*, p. 229 s. v. **kamp* : "NP *čamīdan* 'to twist, bend' ".

68 Anyhow an accurate survey is needed before the last word can be said on this matter.

69 Bailey 1967, p. 81 s. v. *cambule*; *DKS* s. v.

70 *ESIJ*, 4, pp. 196–198.

71 *ESVJ*, p. 405 s. v. *xam(b)*-. Morgenstierne (1930, p. 167, also Tremblay 2005, p. 179) proposed (dubitatively) to explain Wanetsi *čamba* 'back of the hand' < **kampyā*- 'bent', but this kind of palatalization is very common in Eastern Iranian.

72 Henning 1940, p. 38.

Gavkošaki *čam* 'flat river-banks', Širâzi *čam* 'area in which the river deviates', Zarqâni *čam* 'verdant ground at both sides of a river', Bušehri *čam* 'area in which the river makes a bend, or deviates'.

In New Persian, *čam* with the meaning 'verdant ground at both sides of a river' appears mostly in local toponym systems, predominantly in the area of the Zagros[73], while NP *čamâb* designates the 'meander, bight' also in the literary language.[74]

6.2 In connection with HENNING's ideas on ManParth. *cmb* 'ford' and phonetic oscillations °*mb* ~ °*m*, particularly interesting is the existence of the following terms related to the semantic field 'verdant ground at both sides of a river': Southern Baškardi (Molkigal) *zamp* 'soft and washed sand', Southern and Northern Baškardi *čamp*, *čambi* 'dimples on the side of the course of a river', Minâbi *čambi* id.[75]; to these one could tentatively add Kermâni *čombol*[76] 'sequence of pits' (PURHOSEINI, s. v.), implying a strip of humid ground.

In his interpretation of a term of possible Iranian origin occurring in four Late Babylonian texts, reconstructed as Ir. **zamba-* 'silt, loam'[77], TAVERNIER[78] compares the following Iranian words: MP *dnb* 'bank, shore', Parth. *znb*, Sogd. *zmb*[79], Bšk. *zamb/p* 'silt, loam', Shughni *zimb* 'bank, shore'. The scholar thus implicitly proposes to connect also Parth. *znb* to the Eastern Iranian series : Sogd. *zmb* 'bank, shore', Shughni *zimb* 'side, flank', already identified by REICHELT (1926, p. 239), as hinted by HENNING in his *List.*[80] Without mentioning Parth. *znb*, MORGENSTIERNE, who accepts SOKOLOVA's etymology (< **zambya-*, cf. Skt. *ǰambhya-* 'incisor tooth'[81]) had already proposed a link between Sogd. *zmb* 'bank, shore' and Shughni *zimb* 'side, flank, riverbank', with possible extension to further Pamir languages.[82] TAVERNIER also connects to the series MP *dnb* and Parth. *znb*.

73 EILERS 1971, p. 299 fn. 19, EILERS 1977, p. 299, 301, EILERS 1982, p. 41.

74 In many of NW Iranian regions where *čam* means the 'verdant ground at both sides of a river', it also designates the 'river' *tout court*: e.g. Lakki, Lori, Sorani Kurd., Kurm. Kurd. *čam* 'river', Gurani *čam* 'brook, river', Zaza *čam, ǰam, cam* [tsam] 'river', Azari *čam* id., Baxt. *čam* id. (see fn. 89 below).

75 On some of these words a pressure from NP *ǰamb* 'side' < Arabic *ǰamb* id. is more than probable; in the Minâb area the Arabic terminology for geographic features is particularly in use. For the sources from this area see fn. 41 above.

76 Derivative with *-ol,-ul*, on the same pattern as Hazaragi *čombul* 'curved' (DULLING 1973 s. v.), 'crooked back' (TÂRIQ MÂLISTÂNI 1993 s. v.).

77 VON SODEN 1981, p. 1528 s. v. *zimbānu* marks as "iran. Fw.?" and translates "etwa ‚Lehen'?".

78 2007, p. 413 (4.4.5.13).

79 TAVERNIER 2007, p. 413 (4.4.5.13) does not provide a gloss for the Parthian and Sogdian words.

80 HENNING 1937, p. 82.

81 SOKOLOVA 1967, p. 33 § 38.

82 Both had in mind a semantic development 'cut off, cleft' > 'bank'. *EWA* 1, pp. 572–573 s. v. *ǰámbha-* only acknowledges as Indo-Iranian the sense 'jaw'.

6.3 Sub voce MP *dnb* in his *Glossary*[83], Back mentions the relevant literature on the matter and reconstructs a 'Proto-MP' form **damba-*, but this does not permit to get a closer view of his conception of the relationship between MP *dnb* and Parth. *znb*.

In the Man. documentation, Parth. *znb* is attested only in the small, incomprehensible fragment M2029 V 4 and in the toponym *Zamb* (M5815 II R i 20), probably designating a city in Sogdian territory (on the Oxus left bank = Arab. *zam(m)*[84]), if Henning's identification is correct. It also occurs as a *hapax* in the inscriptional Parthian of the ŠKZ where mention is done of Narseh's possessions delimitated by the sea (MP, line 24 : OD YMA dnb = Parth., l. 19 : OL YMA znb = Greek, ll. 42–43 : ἕως χείλους θαλάσσης 'bis ans Meeresufer'[85]).

MP *dnb* and Parth. *znb* have been discussed in many occasions also by Eilers, with no definitive statement; his hint to Iranian locative expressions involving parts of the body as 'lips, mouth'[86] shows that he may have appreciated Sprengling's suggestion to interpret *znb* as 'lip', in view of the corresponding Greek word (and also the semantic extensions of NP *lab*)[87].

Unto this day, the variance MP *d*° ~ Parth. z° in the couple MP *dnb* ~ Parth. *znb* has been tacitly understood with reference to a different outcome of Ir. *z° < IE *ĝ°.

But a possible interpretation of Parth. *znb* with reference to the series of Bšk. *zamb/p* 'silt, loam' discussed above could induce us to reanalyze Inscr. MP *dnb* 'shore'[88] as a 'hyper-Persianism' operating on an old word, perhaps pre-Iranian, attested as *čam(b)*, *zamb* in various areas of the Western and Eastern Iranian domain to denominate strips of ground in the surroundings of rivers and seacosts and, particularly in NW Iran, the river as a whole, especially in its mountain form of 'brook'.[89]

The variance °*m* ~ °*mb* may have a purely phonetic background (cf. high Matchin *čamidan* ~ low Matchin *čambidan* 'to limp', §4.1 above, ENP *ǰum(m)īδan* ~ *ǰunbīδan* 'to move'[90]), and/or be limited to some areas of Western and/or Eastern Iranian.

83 Back 1978, p. 207 s.v. *dnb-y*.

84 Marquart 1901, p. 81; Andreas/Henning 1934, p. 858 fn. 2.

85 Huyse 1999, p. 47.

86 Eilers 1954, p. 355. See also Eilers 1956, p. 197: "Man kann *damb* dann als eine SW-Form ansehen, die sonstigem *zamb* entspricht mit idg. *ĝ* oder *ĝh*- im Anlaut". Sprengling 1940, p. 386 quotes unconvincingly MP *zamīg* 'earth'.

87 Sprengling 1940, p. 386.

88 Of limited attestation in inscriptional MP, seemingly absent from the Phl. documentation.

89 Andreas/Christensen et al. 1939, p. 297—who ignored the series of *čam* 'silt, loam'—treated widely Kurd. *čam* 'river, brook' and considered as possible a connection between this word and Parth. *čamag* 'course of river' (cf. rwd'n cmg, M 6 R ii 2, see above §2). Cabolov 2001, p. 249 s.v. *ĉam* is uncertain if Kurd. *čam* 'river' should be connected to Parth *čam*- 'walk' or *čam* 'silt, loam'; *ESIJ* 2, p. 262 does not exclude this latter; Asatrian (priv. comm.) seems rather to favour Eilers 1982, p. 41 ("*čam* [...] bezeichnet ein Stück Land rechts und links der Fluß- oder Kanalseite, das dessen Wasser 'schlürft oder trinkt' (pers. *čamīdan*)", where NP *čamidan* 'to drink' is hinted at.

90 Lazard 1963, p. 164 §82.

It is hard to establish if these terms related to water economy and irrigation are somehow connected to a possible Ir. base **čam-* 'to stride, step', which appears in any case limited to Iranian with no sure IE check.

Bibliography

AČAṘYAN, H. 1971–1979: *Hayerēn gawaṙakan baṙaran*. 4 vol. Erevan (second edition).
ADIB TUSI, M. A. 1963–1964: "Farhang-e loγât-e bâzyâfte (mostadarak)." In: *Našrie-ye dâneškade-ye adabiât-e Tabriz* 15–16.
AFGHANINEVIS, 'A. 1961: *Loγât-e 'âmiâne-ye fârsi-ye Afγânistân*. s. l.
ANDREAS, F. C. / A. CHRISTENSEN et al. 1939: *Iranische Dialektaufzeichnungen aus dem Nachlass von F. C. Andreas*, zusammen mit K. BARR und W. HENNING bearb. und hrsg. von A. CHRISTENSEN. Berlin.
ANDREAS, F. C. / W. B. HENNING 1934: "Mitteliranische Manichaica aus Chinesisch-Turkestan, iii." In: SPAW, pp. 848–912.
ÂRYÂNPOUR KÂŠÂNI, 'A. & M. 1979: *Farhang-e ǰibi fârsi be englisi*. Tehrân.
ASLANOV, M. G. 1966: *Afgansko-russkij slovar´*. Moskva.
BACK, M. 1978: *Die sassanidischen Staatsinschriften*. Leiden.
BAILEY, H. W. 1967: *Indo-Scythian studies; being Khotanese texts*. Vol. VI: *Prolexis to the Book of Zambasta*. Cambridge.
BELLEW, H. W. 1901: *A Dictionary of the Pukkhto or Pukshto Language*. Lahore.
BOLOGNESI, G. 1962: "Studi armeni." In: *Ricerche linguistiche* 5, pp. 105–147.
BOYCE, M. 1952: "Some Parthian abecedarian Hymns." In: *BSOAS* 14, pp. 435–450.
— 1954: *The Manichaean Hymn cycles in Parthian*. London / New York / Toronto.
— 1975: *A Reader in Manichaean Middle Persian and Parthian*. Téhéran/Liège.
— 1977: *A Word-list of Manichaean Middle Persian and Parthian*. Téhéran/Liège.
BROWNE, G. G. 1894: "Description of an Old Persian Commentary on the Ḳur'án." In: *JRAS*, pp. 417–524.
CABOLOV, R. L. 2001: *Ėtimologičeskij slovar´ kurdskogo jazyka*. 1. Moskva.
CHYET, M. L.: *Kurdish-English Dictionary*. New Haven / London 2003.
DEHXODÂ, A. A. 1958ff.: *Loqâtnâme*. Tehrân.
DE LAGARDE, P. A. 1854: *Zur Urgeschichte der Armenier. Ein philologischer Versuch*. Berlin.
DKS = H. W. BAILEY: *Dictionary of Khotan Saka*. Cambridge 1979.
DULLING, G. K. 1973: *The Hazaragi dialect of Afghan Persian: A preliminary study*. London.
DURKIN-MEISTERERNST, D. 2004: *Dictionary of Manichaean Texts*. III, 1: *Texts from Central Asia and China (Texts in Middle Persian and Parthian)*. Turnhout.
— DURKIN-MEISTERERNST, D. 2006: *The Hymns to the Living Soul*. Turnhout.
EDIV = J. CHEUNG 2007: *Etymological Dictionary of the Iranian Verb*. Leiden.
EILERS, W. 1954: *Der Name Demawend*. In: *ArOr* 22, pp. 267–374.
— 1956: "Der Name Demawend." In: *ArOr* 24, pp. 183–224.
— 1971: "Mongolische Ortsnamen in Iran." In: *Atti del Convegno internazionale sul tema: La Persia nel medioevo*. Roma, pp. 449–464.

— 1977: "Einige Prinzipien toponymischer Übertragung." In: *Onoma* 21, pp. 277–317.
— 1982: *Geographische Namengebung in und um Iran. Ein Überblick in Beispielen.* München.
ESIJ 2 = V.S. Rastorgueva/D.I. Èdel'man 2003: *Ètimologičeskij slovar' iranskix jazykov.* II. Moskva.
ESVJ = I.M. Steblin-Kamenskij: *Ètimologičeskij slovar' vaxanskogo jazyka.* Sankt-Peterburg 1999.
EVP = G. Morgenstierne: *Etymological vocabulary of Pashto.* Oslo 1927.
EVSG = G. Morgenstierne: *Etymological vocabulary of the Shughni group.* Wiesbaden 1974.
EWA = M. Mayrhofer: *Etymologisches Wörterbuch des Altindoarischen.* 1. Heidelberg 1992; 2. Heidelberg 1996; 3. Heidelberg 2001.
Faravaši, B.: *Pahlavi-Persian Dictionary.* Tehrân 1967.
— 1979: *Persian-Pahlavi Dictionary.* 2nd ed. Tehrân.
Ghilain, A. 1939: *Essai sur la langue parthe.* Louvain/Leuven.
Haïm, S. 1992: *Farhang-e ǰâmeʿ fârsi-englisi.* Tehrân.
Hakem, H. 2012: *Dictionnaire kurde-français (sorani).* Paris.
Henning, W.B. 1937: "A List of Middle-Persian and Parthian words." In: *BSOS* 9, pp. 79–92.
— 1940: *Sogdica.* London.
Henning, W. B./D. N. MacKenzie 1971: *A Fragment of a Khwarezmian Dictionary,* by the late W.B. Henning, edited by D.N. MacKenzie. London.
Horn, P. 1898–1901: "Neupersische Schriftsprache." In: W. Geiger/E. Kuhn (ed.): *Grundriss der iranischen Philologie.* I, 2. Strassburg, pp. 1–198.
Huyse, Ph. 1999: *Die dreisprachige Inschrift Šābuhrs I. an der Kaʿba-i Zardušt (ŠKZ).* 1. London.
Hübschmann, H. 1897: *Armenische Grammatik.* I. Teil: *Armenische Etymologie.* Leipzig.
Justi, F. 1880: *Kurdische Grammatik.* St-Petersburg.
Kapadia, D.D. 1953: *Glossary of Pahlavi Vendidad.* Bombay.
Kellens, J. 1986: "La racine sanscrite *kamp* à la lumière des faits iraniens." In: *Proceedings of the Fourth World Sanskrit Conference of the International Association of Sanskrit Studies, Weimar, May 23-30, 1979.* Berlin (Schriften zur Geschichte und Kultur des Alten Orients 18), pp. 344–347.
Kieffer, Ch.M. 1979: "Études parāči. Le lexique parāči: Glossaire, IV.a." In: StIr 8, pp. 67–106.
Klimkeit, H.-J. 1989: *Hymnen und Gebete der Religion des Lichts.* Opladen.
Kurdoev, K.K. 1960: *Kurdsko-russkij slovar'.* Moskva.
Lazard, G. 1963: *Les plus anciens monuments de la prose persane.* Paris.
— 1990: *Dictionnaire persan-français.* Leiden/New York/København.
LIV = H. Rix (ed.): *Lexikon der indogermanischen Verbe, die Wurzeln und ihre Primärstammbildungen.* Wiesbaden ²2001.
MacKenzie, D.N. 1961: *Kurdish Dialect Studies.* 1. London.
— 1969: review of H.W. Bailey: *Indo-Scythian studies; being Khotanese texts.* Vol. VI. *Prolexis to the Book of Zambasta.* Cambridge 1967. In: *BSOAS* 32, pp. 397–401.
— 1970: *The 'Sūtra of the Causes and Effects of Actions' in Sogdian.* Oxford.
Marquart, J. 1901: *Ērānšahr nach der Geographie des Ps. Moses Xorenacʿi.* Berlin.

Mengal, A.K. 1990: *A Persian-Pahlavi-Balochi Vocabulary. 1 (a–c)*. Quetta.
Mirzozada, S. 2008: *Farhangi yaynobī-tojikī-anglisī*. Dušanbe.
Moʿin, M. 1963: *Farhang-e fârsi*. 6 vol. Tehrân.
Mokri, M. 2003: *Grammaire et lexique comparés des dialectes kurdes. Éléments de linguistique iranienne*. Paris.
Morgenstierne, G. 1929: *Indo-Iranian Frontier Languages*. 1: *Parachi and Ormuri*. Oslo.
— 1930: "The Waṇetsi dialect of Pashto. A preliminary note." In: *NTS* 4, pp. 156–175.
Nazarzoda, S. et al. 2006: *Farhangi tafsirii zaboni tajikī*. 1–2. Dušanbe.
Purhoseini, A. 1991: *Farhang-e loγât va estelâhât-e mardom-e Kermân*. Tehrân.
Rastorgueva, V. S./E.K. Molčanova 1981: "Parfianskij jazyk." In: *Osnovy iranskogo jazykoznanija*. II: *Sredneiranskie jazyki*. Moskva, pp. 147–232.
Raverty, H.G. 1860: *A Dictionary of the Puk'hto, Pus'hto or Language of the Afghans*. London.
Reichelt, H. 1926: "Soghdisches." In: *ZII* 4, pp. 239–250.
Rezâi, J. 1984: *Vâženâme-ye guyeš-e Birjand*. Tehrân.
— 1998: *Barresi-e guyeš-e Birjand*. Tehrân.
Rubinčik, Ju.A. 1970: *Persidsko-russkij slovar'*. I–II. Moskva.
Sajmiddinov, D. et al. 2006: *Tadžiksko-russkij slovar'*. Dušanbe.
Samadi, M. 1986: *Das chwaresmische Verbum*. Wiesbaden.
Shahbakhsh, A. 2004: *The Balochi Verb: An Etymological Study*. London (PhD Thesis, SOAS).
Shaked, Sh. 1979: *The wisdom of the Sasanian sages (Dēnkard VI)*. Boulder, Colo.
Sokolova, V.S. 1967: *Genetičeskie otnošenija jazguljamskogo jazyka i šugnanskoj jazykovoj gruppy*. Leningrad.
Sprengling, M. 1940: "Kartir. Founder of Sassanian Zoroastrianism." In: *American Journal of Semitic Languages and Literature* 57, pp. 197–228.
Steingass, F. 1892: *A comprehensive Persian-English dictionary*. London.
Šâlči, A. 1991: *Farhang-e guyeš-e Xorâsân-e bozorg*. Tehrân.
Sundermann, W. 1997: *Der Sermon von der Seele. Eine Lehrschrift des östlichen Manichäismus. Edition der parthischen und soghdischen Version mit einem Anhang von Peter Zieme. Die türkischen Fragmente des „Sermon von der Seele"*. Turnhout.
Târiq Mâlistâni, 'A.H. 1993: *Hazaragi-Dari/Farsi-English. A Preliminary Glossary*. s.l.
Tavadia, J.C. 1930: *Šayast-nē-šayast. A Pahlavi Text on Religious Customs*. Hamburg.
Tavernier, J. 2007: *Iranica in the Achaemenid period (ca. 550–330 B.C.). Lexicon of Old Iranian Proper Names and Loanwords, Attested in Non-Iranian Texts*. Leuven et al.
Tremblay, X. 2003: review of G. Morgenstierne: *A New Etymological Vocabulary of Pahto*. Compiled and edited by J. Elfenbein, D.N. MacKenzie and N. Sims-Williams. Wiesbaden.
von Soden, W. 1981: *Akkadisches Handwörterbuch*. 3. Wiesbaden.
Wahby, T./C.J. Edmonds 1966: *A Kurdish-English Dictionary*. Oxford.
Wolff, F. 1935: *Glossar zu Firdosis Schahname*. Berlin.
Xromov, A.L. 1962: *Govory tadžikov matčinskogo rajona*. Dušanbe.

Some Interlinguistic Iranian Conundrums

MARTIN SCHWARTZ and ALEXIS MANASTER RAMER

This modest tribute to MARIA MACUCH's Iranistic scholarship and service is the result of a series of exchanges between MARTIN SCHWARTZ (MS) and ALEXIS MANASTER RAMER (AMR).

I

Herodotus (*Histories* 4, p. 127) gives an account (which we condense drastically) of the exchange of angry words between Darius and the Scythian king Idanthyrsus. Darius challenges the Scythian either to stand and fight (instead of constantly retreating) or else acknowledge Darius as *his master*. In response, Idanthyrsus says he will fight only if the Persians desecrate the Scythian royal graves, declares his only masters to be Zeus and Hestia, and concludes with words which, though famous, struck AMR as not making much sense, and, as a retort, oddly flat in the Greek: ἀντὶ δὲ τοῦ ὅτι δεσπότης ἔφησας εἶναι ἐμός, κλαίειν λέγω "And in return/exchange[1] for your saying that you are my master, I say (you should) weep". But of course the two Iranian monarchs did not communicate in Greek. In fact, though this is likely an interpolation, some Greek (even if not Herodotus himself) seems to have believed that, as the text goes on to say, τοῦτο ἐστὶ ἡ ἀπὸ Σκυθέων ῥῆσις "This is Scythian speech". AMR, having previously observed (in an article awaiting publication) that the dying words of Anacharsis (Idanthyrsus' uncle as it happens), while also transmitted to us in Greek, seem to yield a very nice pun in Old Iranian, likewise suspected some sort of paronomasia in Idanthyrsus' address to Darius, a paronomasia that would make these words both a cry of defiance and a put-down of the aggressor's puffery. If so, we could thus now have two early examples of (the Greek topos of) "Scythian speech", showing that this was not, as usually assumed, merely blunt and direct but rather involved the use of punning, and perhaps some other forms of verbal humor as well. (AMR)

MS, consulted about this hypothesis, immediately pointed out that Greek δεσπότης, thrice translated as 'master' above but also meaning 'absolute ruler, tyrant', would correspond quite well to Sogdian *xšēwan* 'king, ruler', which

1 This is the correct translation of Greek ἀντί. (AMR)

is *mirabile dictu* homophonous with Sogdian *xšēwan* 'weeping, lamentation' (from the root *xšī* 'to lament, weep') corresponding to Greek κλαίειν above.

We see several possibilities, under the rubric of "Scythian speech", for explaining the relationship of Herodotus' report of Idanthyrsus' response, and Iranian linguistic realities. MS points out that at least Sogd. *xšēwan* 'lamentation, weeping', in view of MPers. *šēwan* id., indicates that there was a Proto-Iranian **xšaiwan-* from which an equivalent form in Scythian could have come. However, one cannot reconstruct a single Proto-Iranian form for the institutional term 'king', since the relevant root is manifest in varied nominal forms referring to such persons: OPers. <x-š-a-y-θ-i-y> 'king', along with the likely reading *πατιξειθης for Herodotus' πατιζειθης, apparently the title—or perhaps (nick)name (AMR)—of Cambyses' successor (cf. elaborate recent discussion in Werba 2010), Sogd. *xšēwan*, but also *xšēδ* designating rulers, the latter form corresponding to Av. *xšaēta-* in *Yima- Xšaēta-*, cf. Bactrian *iamšo* *'King Yama', probably with the postpound from **xšāwan-* (Sims-Williams 2010, p. 68; note also **pāti-xšāwan-*, reflected in Sogd. *pātxšāwan*, MPers. *pādixšā(y)* 'rul(er), authority'), and Av. *xšōiθnī-* 'mistress, lady'. Furthermore, MS notes, OAv. *xšaiia-* 'able one, master' corresponds formally to -ξαϊς in the triad of mythical royal brothers Λιπόξαϊς, Ἀρπόξαϊς, and Κολάξαϊς, of which the middle one may well be reflected also in the Biblical Hebrew name ארפכשד (ʾrpkšd) via a simple miscopying of the י of hypothetical *ארפכשי (*ʾrpkšy) as ד, giving us a second witness besides Herodotus to the existence of such names.[2] Thus it cannot be assumed that Scythian had an exact formal correspondent of Sogd. *xšēwan* 'king, ruler' (MS). Note that AMR has found notable differences, not the least phonological, between Scythian and the East Middle Iranian languages; cf. fn. 6 (MS).

Nevertheless, it is possible that some Saka language in which the communication took place to begin with did in fact have a homophony formally paralleling the Sogdian. It is also possible that the pun did not involve exact homophones but instead two forms close in sound. (AMR)

Finally, since the paronomasia of 'ruler' and 'lamentation' was latent in Old Sogdian **xšaiwan-*, it is almost inevitable that there was punning on the two words. An originally Sogdian pun could have been approximated in Scythian, or attributed to Idanthyrsus if there was already a topos of "Scythian speech". The phonic similarity of Σογδ- and Σκυθ- may have contributed to such a confusion. (MS)

2 This name anyway does not look native, but a specific argument for it being of foreign (Iranian) origin is that the last vowel in most occurrences of the name in the Masoretic tradition is a short *a (pataḥ)* rather than a long *ā (ḳameṣ)*. (AMR)

II.

The name Ἰδάνθυρσος (*Idánthursos*) goes well with the ethnonym Ἀγάθυρσοι (*Agáthursoi*), dwellers on the borders of Scythia (Herodotus 4:119, 125). The two are analyzable in parallel, from respectively OIran. **hiϑām-ϑr(a)uš(a)-* 'prospering the ally'[3] (AMR,[4] MS) and **haxā-ϑr(a)uš(a)-* 'prospering the friend/*socius*' (MS). For the semantics and pragmatics of these names, we may broadly compare the name of Achaemenes, OPers. /haxā-maniš-/ 'friend-minded'. One may suppose that the Greeks modified the postpound to -θυρσος[5] 'thyrsus, the composite vegetal wand of Bacchus', via an association of Scythians with Bacchic rites; see esp. Herodotus 4:79.[6] (MS)

III.

The obscure hapax *ārštiiō.barəza* 'to (the) height of an *ārštiia-*' (*Yašt* 19:40 = *Yasna* 9:11) is glossed in Pahlavi as *asp bālāy* 'the height of a horse' (for a recent discussion of the many difficulties of this entire passage, see Hintze 1994). The hapax *ārštiia-* has long been recognized as the vṛddhi of *aršti-* 'spear', but the long-unchallenged idea of Bartholomae (1886, p. 274) that this specifically meant 'fathom' struck AMR as immediately impossible because Iranian spears were far longer than that[7] (though that would be approximately the height of a large horse). Furthermore, whereas the Pahlavi version often gets the translation exactly right or else errs in various rather obvious ways (see Cantera 2004,

3 Bartholomae's *hiϑa-* alongside *hiϑāu-* (1904, p. 1813) is rendered dubious by two facts. First, if the alleged fem. acc. sg. *hiϑąm* (Y. 34:10), with its ms. variants, is taken as a miscopying of **haiϑīm* 'real', then it supplies the obligatory ring-compositional concentric concatenation for Y. 34:6 *haiϑīm*. Second, Y. 34:6 *šiiaoϑanā vaocaṯ gərəbąm … dąmīm vīduuå̄ *haiϑīm aṣ̌ahiiā* becomes parallel to 31:8, and the Avestan words *hə̄m … grabəm haiϑīm aṣ̌ahiiā dąmīm … šiiaoϑanaēšū*. The majority of mss. actually have *haiθąm*. In **hiϑām-ϑrauša-*, **hiϑām-* would be the acc. sg. of *hiϑāu-*, attested in the hapax *hiϑāuš* (nominative! — *pace* Bartholomae [ibid.] but in agreement with Bartholomae 1895–1901, p. 115). In short, Av. *hiϑāuš* is to our **hiϑām* as Av. *gāuš* is to Av. *gąm* (MS).

4 AMR would like to thank Michael Weiss for constructive criticism of his various earlier attempts at this etymology.

5 That the Greeks indulged rather freely in such folk-etymological retouching of Iranian name has long been evident, e.g., Μεγα- for *Baga-* (see further Schwartz 1986, p. 384). For Scythian specifically consider, e.g., *Πρωτοθύης*, whose real etymon must be reflected in the Assyrian transcription *Bartatua* (Vasmer 1923 [1971, p. 118]).

6 AMR hopes to discuss at some point in the future the historical phonology of the Scythian underlying the Greek forms of these names.

7 Bartholomae's (1886, p. 338) "‚von Klafterhöhe' […] ‚von Pferdeshöhe' (was aufs Gleiche hinauskommt)" is correct, but he does not explain how a "Klafter" can be derived from the basic meaning of the vṛddhi as "auf Speere bezüglich, davon herrührend, daraus gemacht".

pp. 98–99 and passim), one would not expect to find there this kind of fanciful metaphor.

Consulted on this matter as well, MS suggested that *asp* may have written aramaeographically as <SWSYA> in the passage at issue and that perhaps this was simply a misreading of a word unfamiliar to later copyists but either identical (given the massive homography characteristic of Pahlavi) or at least sufficiently similar to <SWSYA>. AMR then found that it in fact was so written in two mss. studied by Mills (1900, p. 525 n. 17) and one by Davar (1904, p. 19 n. 35.1, 38 n. 35.1), while one ms. studied by both had *asp*, and one known only to Davar had <SWSA>. He then realized, first of all, that <SWSYA> looks suspiciously similar to <snyh> *sneh*, whose meaning, as kindly pointed out to us by William Malandra (personal communication)[8] was at least sometimes[9] (generic) 'weapon'; second, that it would look even more similar to some hypothetical (but morphologically and semantically well-formed) word derived from *sneh*; and, third, that <SWSA> (otherwise unattested) is indistinguishable from *sneh* (though of course we cannot assume that this was the original reading).[10]

Now, the basic idea is simply that the exact meaning of *āržtiia-* must have been as unclear to the original Pahlavi glossator (and *a fortiori* his successors) as it is to us,[11] but perhaps its connection to the semantic domain of armament *(sneh)* was still perceived. If, more specifically, the older reading is not <SWSA> but <SWSYA>, then it may be that the glossator had written, generically, *<snyhyk> **snehīg* '(something) pertaining to a weapon'. This unfamiliar, presumably nonce, form (written without an otiose stroke or else with one but taken, as so often, to be *W* 'and' and then removed), especially if executed care-

8 *Pahlavi Rivāyat* to the *Dādestān ī Dēnīg* 48:7, to wit: *aštar ud kārd ud warz ud šafšēr ud nēzag ud tigr ud abarīg snēhīhā* 'whip, knife, mace, sword, lance, arrow, and other weapons'.

9 It is of course possible that in other contexts the same word could have referred to a particular kind of weapon, perhaps the same as that suggested for the Avestan *snaiθiš* by Malandra (1973, p. 286), that is, some sort of club or the like. For Pahlavi *sneh*, MacKenzie (1986, unpaginated, logical p. 3 of the "Addenda and Corrigenda") lists precisely this combination of both a generic and a specific meaning: 'club, weapon'.

10 Davar (1904, p. 14) himself commented about this manuscript: "though it often gives the better preserved reading, I am inclined to think that the copyist has, at times, meddled with the text". We cannot, therefore, rely on this <SWSA>. For, if it is an example of the "meddling", then this copyist has simply anticipated (part of) our proposal and changed the text to suit it rather than providing evidence of a transmitted original reading.

11 It is rather clear that *-arštiia-* with a short first vowel (attested only as a postpound) meant 'shaft (of a spear)', but it is not at all obvious that this is the same word. In fact, if the meaning really was some unit of measurement, as argued by Bartholomae and apparently unquestioned since, then the long-vowel form was presumably the vṛddhi of the short-vowel one. But once this is granted, then we can see that the latter could have referred to any number of other things, as long as they were 'pertaining to a (spear) shaft'.

lessly, might easily have been miscopied as *<snyhydy>,[12] a form that because of the multiple homographies would be indistinguishable from <SWSYA> = *asp*.[13] (AMR)

If so, this could be a case somewhat similar to the "rätselhaft" <dytk> (or <zytk> etc.[14]) in V. 3.29, which according to Cantera (2004, p. 98 n. 125) our honoree has proposed as possibly a miscopying of *<stdk> *stadag* 'weggenommen'. Interestingly in this case the copying error would have created a nonexistent form, hence a reversal of the more common principle that the *lectio difficilior* is the original one, whereas in our example this principle is duly observed. It is a pleasure to conclude this article by mentioning this thought-provoking idea, among the many contributions of Maria Macuch.[15]

Bibliography

Bartholomae, C. 1886: "Beiträge zur altiranischen Grammatik. IV." In: *Beiträge zur Kunde der indogermanischen Sprachen* 10, pp. 267–280.

— 1895–1901: "Vorgeschichte der iranischen Sprachen." In: W. Geiger/E. Kuhn (eds.): *Grundriss der iranischen Philologie*, I.1. Strassburg, pp. 1–151.

— 1904: *Altiranisches Wörterbuch*. Strassburg.

Cantera, A. 2004: *Studien zur Pahlavi-Übersetzung des Avesta*. Wiesbaden.

Davar, M. 1904: *Die Pahlavi-Version von Yasna IX*. Berlin.

Hintze, A. 1994: *Der Zamyād-Yašt. Edition, Übersetzung, Kommentar.* Wiesbaden.

MacKenzie, D.N. 1986: *A Concise Pahlavi-English Dictionary*. London.

Malandra, W.W. 1973: "A glossary of terms for weapons and armor in Old Iranian." In: *IIJ* 15, pp. 264–289.

Mills, L. 1900: "The First preparers of the Haoma (Indian Soma). The Pahlavi translation and commentary on Yasna IX, 1–48 inclusive, for the first time edited with the collation of MSS., and now prepared from all the MSS. also deciphered." In: JRAS 32, pp. 511–528.

Schwartz, M. 1986: "Coded sound patterns, acrostics, and anagrams in Zoroaster's oral poetry." In: R. Schmitt/P.O. Skjærvø (eds.): *Studia Grammatica Iranica. Festschrift für Helmut Humbach*. Munich, pp. 327–392.

12 If it were possible that <-ydy> could be a valid spelling of *-īg* (as seems to be implied by MacKenzie 1986, p. 36 and passim), then of course the solution would be that much simpler: no miscopying, just the misinterpretation of a homograph. However, Skjærvø (2009, p. 480 n. 8) makes this appear quite unlikely.

13 Davar (1904, pp. 38–39 n. 35.1) anticipated this general approach, "conjectur[ing] the original word to have been *arišnic* [sic!] = arm, or arm's length [...] but being badly written in the original MS. and part of the word being moth-eaten, a not very intelligent copyist deciphered it to be the common word *asp*".

14 The correct transcription is of course uncertain given the multiple homographies together with the fact that we do not know the correct reading.

15 The authors thank Agnes Korn for kindly sending us meticulous comments on a preliminary version of this article.

Sims-Williams, N. 2010: *Bactrian Personal Names.* Vienna (Iranisches Personennamenbuch 2.7).

Skjærvø, P. O. 2009: "OL' news: ODs and ends." In: W. Sundermann et al. (eds.): *Exegisti monumenta. Festschrift in Honour of Nicholas Sims-Williams.* Wiesbaden, pp. 479–495.

Vasmer, M. 1923 (1971): *Untersuchungen über die ältesten Wohnsitze der Slaven*: I. *Die Iranier in Südrußland.* Leipzig (Veröffentlichungen des baltischen und slavischen Instituts an der Universität Leipzig 3). Reprinted in his *Schriften zur slavischen Altertumskunde und Namenkunde*, I. Wiesbaden, pp. 106–170.

Werba, C. 2010: "The title of the Achaemenid 'King'. Etymology, Formation and Meaning of Old Persian *xšāyaϑiya-*." In: M. Macuch et al. (eds.): *Ancient and Middle Iranian Studies. Proceedings of the 6th European Conference of Iranian Studies, held in Vienna, 18–22 September 2007.* Wiesbaden, pp. 265–289.

The Wisdom of Aḥiqar and the Wisdom of Ādurbād: A Manichaean Parallel

Nicholas Sims-Williams

The collection of maxims known as the "Wisdom of Aḥiqar", together with the accompanying story of the wise Aḥiqar, the minister and chief counsellor of the Assyrian king Sennacherib, can be traced back at least to the fifth century BCE, the date of a fragmentary Aramaic version discovered at the site of Elephantine in Egypt.[1] Thereafter both the story and the admonitions with which Aḥiqar instructs his adopted son Nadin were extremely popular and were translated or adapted into many languages, including Greek, Syriac, Ethiopic, Armenian and Arabic.[2] In a recent publication I have edited the surviving fragments of a Sogdian version of the Wisdom of Aḥiqar from the Christian monastery of Bulayïq near Turfan.[3] The Sogdian text is written in the adapted Syriac script commonly used by the Christians of this area and was certainly translated from Syriac, although the underlying Syriac text is not identical with any Syriac version so far made known and sometimes contains phrases or complete maxims which are only known from non-Syriac versions. This is in no way surprising. Since there is usually no close connection between one maxim and the next, there was nothing to prevent any editor, translator or copyist from changing their sequence, deleting those which seemed to him inappropriate or uninteresting, combining maxims of related content or structure, and inserting material of his own invention or proverbs derived from other collections.

The fact that the story and admonitions of Aḥiqar were also known in Sasanian Iran has been demonstrated by François de Blois, who listed a significant number of more or less precise correspondences between the various versions of the Wisdom of Aḥiqar and certain Pahlavi texts, in particular the *Handarz ī Ādurbād ī Mārāspandān* "Admonitions of Ādurbād son of Māraspand" *(HA)*, concluding his study with the words: "Perhaps it will be admitted that some version of the Aḥīqar story must have been at least one of the sources exploited by the compiler of Ādurbād's wisdom".[4] More recently, Yutaka Yoshida has

1 Lindenberger 1983.

2 Many of these versions are translated (and partly edited) in Conybeare *et al.* 1913. The Syriac texts published by Nau (1909, 1920) do not seem to include any additional material relevant to the maxims discussed in the present paper.

3 Sims-Williams 2014, pp. 107–124.

4 de Blois 1984, p. 50.

drawn attention to some Manichaean Sogdian passages which parallel admonitions attributed to Ādurbād, including one which also has an equivalent in the Wisdom of Aḥiqar.[5] It is worth quoting this last example to show the nature of the relationship between the various texts:[6]

> Manichaean Sogdian (L95 and other fragments)
> "The third (admonition is) that [i] [one should keep one's hand] from theft. [ii] One should be on one's guard against the wrong [way]. [iii] One should keep [oneself] from adultery".
>
> Ādurbād (*HA*, no. 108)
> "Restrain [i] (your) hand from theft, [ii] and (your) foot from going (the path of) un-dutifulness, [iii] and (your) thoughts from sinful lust".
>
> Aḥiqar (Armenian Recension B, no. 31)
> "Son, keep [i] thy hand from stealing, [ii] and thy foot from evil paths".
>
> Aḥiqar (Slavonic, no. 119)
> "My son Anadan, keep [i] thy hands from stealing, [ii] thy mouth from lying [iii] and thy body from lewdness; above all beware of a married woman".

It will be seen that all three parts of the Manichaean maxim (as restored by YOSHIDA) agree in substance with the text of Ādurbād.[7] No single text of the Wisdom of Aḥiqar has precisely the same elements, since the Slavonic differs in its second clause and the Armenian omits the third; but all three elements of the Manichaean Sogdian text are attested in one or another version of Aḥiqar.[8]

The purpose of the present article is to publish two further Manichaean Sogdian fragments containing admonitions, one of which is in part parallel to a maxim found in the *Handarz ī Ādurbād* and in part to a maxim attributed to Aḥiqar. Neither fragment can be regarded as a version of the Wisdom of Aḥiqar or the Admonitions of Ādurbād, but they have clearly borrowed from those works or from some related text. Although this subject has only a slight connection with the field of Zoroastrian literature, I hope that it may be found appropriate as a tribute to MARIA MACUCH and her pioneering work on the Pahlavi texts.

5 YOSHIDA 2001, pp. 108–111.

6 I cite the texts in the translations given by YOSHIDA 2001, p. 109 (Sogdian); DE BLOIS 1984, p. 49 (Pahlavi); CONYBEARE *et al.* 1913, pp. 11 (Slavonic), 60 (Armenian).

7 The Manichaean text, however, has a quite different form (similar to that of the Pahlavi *Mēnōy ī Xrad*), since the aphorisms are apparently spoken by a divine being as answers to questions.

8 The immediately preceding maxim in the Armenian Recension B (tr. CONYBEARE *et al.* 1913, p. 60, no. 30: "Son, keep thy mouth from lying speech, and thine eyes from immodest glances") contains a parallel to the second clause of the Slavonic version, suggesting that an editor or translator of the latter may have conflated two neighbouring aphorisms.

Texts and translations

Our two fragments are both preserved in the Berlin Turfan collection.[9] The first is M 117, whose contents were defined as “precepts” by W. B. HENNING *apud* BOYCE 1960, p. 10. One side of the page contains 16 short lines of text, while the other side is blank. Several words and phrases were cited by GERSHEVITCH in his *Grammar of Manichean Sogdian* (GERSHEVITCH 1954, henceforth: GMS) and are therefore included in the *Dictionary of Manichaean Sogdian and Bactrian* by SIMS-WILLIAMS and DURKIN-MEISTERERNST (henceforth: DMT III/2).[10]

M 117

1	qw(n•)[ ](k•••)	/1A/ …
2	ṭγw pṭβyw kw(n’[a] p)’rṭyy	you should honour …, for
3	xw nfrywncyk ’ṭyẖ	the curse and
4	rmb’ δβtyw xyδ ’’δyy	insult returns again to that person
5	s’r ’zwrṭ cn qy’	from whose
6	rwβyy nyjṭy oo δ’wn	mouth it came out. /2A/ Do not …
7	mndγrβ’kṭy pryw wy’ẖ	with fools in a
8	’nw’zky(y)[b] n’ ’’tx’z	meeting,
9	w’nw kṭfy γr’n nmy’k	lest it may cause a serious reproach
10	’ṭy pṭyδy’ nyy qwn’ṭ	and shame for you;
11	oo p’rṭyy δn γrβ’kṭyy[c]	for to quarrel with the wise
12	pryw y’r kwnyy frṭr	(is) better
13	c’nw δn mndγrβ’kṭyy	than to eat delicious food
14	[p]ryw xwcy xwrṭ xwryy	with fools.
15	[m]s n’ β’t w’nw ’ṭyy	/3A/ Moreover, let it not be so that
16	[ ](• x)ypδ γryw	[you] … yourself …

[a] Or *kw(nyy)*. [b] Could also be read as two words: *’nw’z ky(y)*. The last letter looks like *w*, but of a form which does not occur elsewhere in this text; despite DMT III/2, 13a, 106b, it is perhaps just a smudged *y* as GERSHEVITCH evidently thought (cf. GMS § 986). [c] There is apparently a double point over *r* (by anticipation of the double point over *β*).

The second fragment is M 765k, each side of which contains nine short lines of text. Although BOYCE 1960, p. 52, refers to “parts of lines”, many lines are in fact complete. The fragment comes from the bottom of a page, probably from the outer corner as the wide side margin seems to indicate. If this observation is correct, the order of Recto and Verso may be regarded as certain, but it is not known how many lines are missing from the top of the page. BOYCE gives no indication of the content of the fragment, but the fact that the Verso contains

9 Colour photos of both fragments may be found by entering the signature (with space after the initial M) on the website of the International Dunhuang Project.
10 See the concordance in DMT III/2, p. xi.

a variant to M 117, lines 11–14, was pointed out by GERSHEVITCH in his review of her *Catalogue* (GERSHEVITCH 1965, p. 159b). As in the case of M 117, several words and phrases have already been cited in print, in publications by GERSHEVITCH and HENNING (see the concordance in DMT III/2, p. xv).

M 765k

R1	[ ](wp)[	/1B/ …
R2	[p'](r)wṭyy (')'γ•[[a]](• w)[ ][b]	for [a cautionary word](?)
R3	[n]yw ''δyy nyy fškrṭyẖ	does not drive away someone else
R4	o c(')nw ṭryγn yp''q	as (does) immoderate anger;
R5	o ms n'-nγ'myẖ	morever, an untimely (and)
R6	n'-(')'γṭ-frn nyw ''δyy	unfortunate (word)
R7	nyy ''nyṭ qw(n)d(y)ẖ	cannot lead someone else
R8	c(')nw nzndy'ẖ 'ṭyy	as (do) humility and
R9	nmryẖ w'x[š]	meek words …
V1	]'[	
V2	](')[ ](k)ṭ[c] γrβ'[kṭyy]	/2B/ … that to quarrel
V3	pryw (y)'r qwnyẖ fr(ṭ)[r]	with the wise (is) better
V4	o c'nw mndγrβ'kyy (p)ryw	than to eat delicious food
V5	xwcyẖ xwrṭ xwryẖ	with a fool
V6	o qδ' r(')δδ šwyẖ	or to travel (with a fool);
V7	o [p]'r[w]ṭ(y) γrβ'k mrṭxmyy	for a wise man,
V8	y'ry[y m](y)δ'nyẖ w(')[ ]	(even) in the midst of a quarrel,
V9	[ ]•'yṭk'm[d] o kyy	will … who …

[a] *(')'γ(ṭ)[?* [b] The last word cannot be restored as *(w)['xš]*, since the lower part of the *x* should have been visible. [c] It is not clear whether the letter *k/x* immediately precedes the final *ṭ* or whether they are separated by another letter. A reading *](nyx)ṭ* seems unlikely. [d] It is difficult to interpret the trace of the first surviving letter. GERSHEVITCH (in his working notebook, now preserved at the Ancient India and Iran Trust in Cambridge) suggested *](r)'yṭk'm* "will weep", but one may also consider *](j)'yṭk'm* "will speak" or *p](š)'yṭk'm* "will cast".

Commentary

It will be seen that these two fragments only coincide for part of a single maxim: /2A/ (M 117, 11–14) ≅ /2B/ (M 765k, V2–5). It is not clear whether the two fragments represent two different collections of aphorisms, which perhaps had nothing in common apart from this one item, or two recensions of a single text. In the latter case one must assume that the sequence of the maxims is 1B {…} 1A—2A/B—3A; I shall therefore discuss them in this order.

/1B/ (M 765k, R). Although all the surviving words are reasonably well-known, this admonition is surprisingly difficult to translate as a whole. It clearly contains two sentences with parallel structure but contrasting meaning: *[n]yw ''δyy nyy fškrṭyẖ o c(')nw ṭryyn yp''q* "(it/he) does not drive away someone else as (does) immoderate anger" and *nyw ''δyy nyy ''nyṭ qw(n)d(y)ẖ c(')nw nzndy'ẖ 'tyy nmryẖ w'x[š]* "(it/he) cannot lead someone else as (do) humility and meek words".[11] The difficulty is to identify the subject(s) of the two verbs and the function of the adjectives *n'-ny'myẖ* and *n'-(')'γṭ-frn*. In GMS, § 1645, Gershevitch takes these two adjectives as qualifying *nyw ''δyy* and translates "someone else who is untimely and unlucky". To me this seems semantically awkward—the adjective "untimely" would more naturally refer to a thing than to a person—but the main problem with this interpretation is that it leaves no word in the immediate vicinity of the verb *nyy ''nyṭ qw(n)d(y)ẖ* "(it/he) cannot lead" which could be its subject. The subject could of course have been expressed earlier in the text, in or before line 2; but in that case the verb in line 3 should have the same subject, and it is hard to imagine a single subject which would suit both verbs. I have therefore adopted a different construction, assuming that the two adjectives qualify the subject of *nyy ''nyṭ qw(n)d(y)ẖ* and that this was a neutral term (e.g. "word") which, when qualified by a different adjective, would make an equally suitable subject for the verb *nyy fškrṭyẖ*.

Gershevitch's translation of *n'-(')'γṭ-frn* as "unlucky", lit. "(to whom) fortune has not come", which is repeated in DMT III/2, p. 121b, is natural in the light of the positive equivalent *''γtprn* "(to whom) fortune has come, lucky" and its inversion *prn''γt*, both of which are used as personal names (cf. Lurje 2011, p. 67, no. 8, and p. 297, no. 897). However, since *''γt* is the past stem of *''βr* to bring" as well as of *ʿys* "to come", the compound can equally well bear the literal sense "(by which) fortune is not brought", which may be more appropriate if the adjective refers to a thing rather than a person. In this context, the adjective might imply something like "inappropriate", just as in English one can speak of an "unfortunate choice of words".

/1A/ (M 117, 1–6). Since we do not know how many lines are missing between the surviving Recto and Verso portions of M 765k, it is possible that one or more maxims may be lost at this point. On the other hand, if the two fragments do indeed belong to different recensions of a single text, it is also possible that /1B/ and /1A/ belong to the same aphorism. /1A/ includes one unknown word, *rmb'*, a noun whose meaning must be fairly close to that of the accompanying *nfrywncyk* "curse". A likely cognate is attested in the *Vessantara Jātaka*, in a passage where Mandrī contemplates the treatment which her children will receive at the hands of those to whom her husband has given them away: *rty βn*

11 The meaning of the verb *fškr-* is inconclusively discussed in DMT III/2, p. 84b. The fact that it here contrasts with *''ny* "to lead" supports the assumption that it has the same meaning as Chr. Sogd. *fšqr-* "to expel, drive away".

wβyw xw'w'nt ZY rnp'nt "they will beat and *insult you" (*VJ*, 1093–4, in BENVENISTE 1946, p. 66). The verb *rnp* here is usually taken as a variant spelling of S. *rnβ*, Man. *rnf*, which seems to mean "to fight, struggle".[12] However, though a master may beat his slaves, he does not usually fight them. It may therefore be better to regard *rnp* as a different verb, with *p* standing for [b] rather than [f]. A meaning such as "to insult, humiliate" would fit the context in the *Vessantara Jātaka*, while the noun *rmb'*, which clearly refers to some kind of evil speech, may very well be translated "insult".

/2A/ (M 117, 6–14) and /2B/ (M 765k, V). This is the aphorism with parallels in the *Handarz ī Ādurbād* and the Wisdom of Aḥiqar. It is also the only passage where the two Manichaean fragments overlap. As a preliminary I set out the two versions in interlinear fashion, with the text of M 765k in italics:

M 117 δ'wn mndγrβ'kṭy pryw wy'ẖ 'nw'zky(y) n' ''tx'z
M 117 w'nw kṭfy γr'n nmy'k 'ṭy pṭyδy' nyy qwn'ṭ oo
M 117 p'rṭyy δn γrβ'kṭyy pryw y'r kwnyy frṭr
M 765k](k)ṭ γrβ'[kṭyy] pryw (y)'r qwnyẖ fr(ṭ)[r] o
M 117 c'nw δn mndγrβ'kṭyy [p]ryw xwcy xwrṭ xwryy
M 765k c'nw mndγrβ'kyy (p)ryw xwcyẖ xwrṭ xwryẖ o
M 765k qδ' r(')δδ šwyẖ o [p]'r[w]ṭ(y) γrβ'k mrṭxmyy
M 765k y'ry[y m](y)δ'nyẖ w(')[…]•'yṭk'm o kyy …

The first part of this admonition, which is attested only in M 117, contains two difficult words, *'nw'zky(y)* and *''tx'z*.

In GMS § 986 *'nw'zky(y)* is interpreted as the obl. form of the *-*aka*-stem *'nw'zy* "crowd, assembly", but no other instance of the reappearance of the original **k* before the obl. case ending can be cited. Several alternative explanations could be envisaged,[13] but the simplest is to assume that *'nw'zky(y)* is the obl. of an abstract noun **'nw'zky'*, cf. C. *γwbty* as obl. of *γwbty'* "glory" etc., SIMS-WILLIAMS 1982, pp. 15–16. For the redundant use of the abstract suffix *-y'* see GMS § 1111 and SIMS-WILLIAMS 2014, p. 35.

More seriously problematic is the word *''tx'z*, which seems to be an otherwise unknown verb in the 2 sg. imperative. In view of its strange shape—the "routine etymology" **ā-(a)ti-xāza-* is scarcely credible—it seems worth considering the possibility that it is a mistake, perhaps for **''x'z*. Such a verb is possibly attested by *''x'zyyẖ* in M 900, A5 (cited by GERSHEVITCH 1952, p. 490), although it must

12 Thus BENVENISTE 1940, p. 197; YOSHIDA 1994, pp. 24–25; MORANO 2009, p. 187; DMT III/2, p. 167b. SCHWARTZ 1970, p. 302, suggested that *rnβ* may mean "to mate with", but the relevant paragraph is deleted in the offprint which he kindly sent me.

13 For instance, that the final *-kyy* is a distributive suffix (GERSHEVITCH 1949, pp. 63–65), giving the translation "in one assembly after another"; or that *'nw'zk* is a variant form of the noun, whose final *-k* may have diminutive force (see GMS § 988, and cf. the case of M. *pṭqrkṭyy*, pl. of **pṭqrk* "picture", which must be distinguished from S. *ptkr'y* "image, idol" as stated in DMT III/2, p. 153b, contra GMS § 987).

be admitted that this word has no context and could equally well be a nominal form. A verb *ʾʾxʾz*, if it existed, might be cognate with Pth. *ʾxʾz-*, interpreted by some as "to rise up (*ʾbr* = against)",[14] by others as "to fight, do battle",[15] or with Pth. *xʾz-* "to devour", Khot. *khāś-* "to eat, drink". The Admonitions of Ādurbād, nos. 87 and 97 (cited below), which refer to a "gathering" or "assembly" (MP *hanjaman*) and thus provide the only close parallel to this part of the maxim, have *ma nišīn* "do not sit", but several other meanings such as "stand", "associate" or "drink" could be thought to fit the context and to receive some support from one or another of the versions of Aḥiqar cited below.

The next part of the text is attested in both M 117, 11–14, and M 765k, V2–5. Apart from one unclear word at the beginning of this passage, where the two texts seem to have different conjunctions, *pʾrṭyy* "for, because" in M 117, perhaps *](k)ṭ* "that, (in) that, in as much as" in M 765k, the differences between the two copies are very slight: "with" expressed by *δn … pryw* or by *pryw* alone; sg. *mndγrβʾkyy* "a fool" versus pl. *mndγrβʾkṭyy* "fools". The antithetical construction which we see here—"it is better to quarrel with the wise than to eat delicious food with a fool"—is identical to that of the Aḥiqar texts, of which a typical example is Arm. B, no. 6: "Son, it is better with the wise man to hew stones than with a foolish man to drink wine". In place of the reference to some kind of heavy labour, such as carrying or splitting stones, the Manichaean text introduces the idea of a quarrel, which may derive from another maxim (Arm. B, no. 40): "Son, better is hatred and a quarrel with a righteous man than sweetness and compassion at the hands of a lawless man". The replacement of "drinking wine" by "eating delicious food" is less significant, since it may have arisen merely as the result of the ambiguity of the verb *xwr-* "to eat" or "to drink";[16] alternatively, the wording may have been influenced by that of another maxim such as: "O my son! be not neighbour to the fool, and eat not bread with him …"[17] This seems all the more likely in view of the rather clumsy extension of the maxim with the words "or to travel (with a fool)" in M 765k, V6, since the two ideas of eating with a fool and travelling with a fool are also found together in Arm. A, no. 10: "… with one that is without fear go not on a journey; and with the senseless do thou not eat bread".[18] However, I have not found any parallel for the final words of M 765k, which appear to contain an explanatory gloss on what precedes: "for a wise man, (even) in the midst of a quarrel, will …"

14 ANDREAS/HENNING 1934, pp. 38 (k34), 50b; SKJÆRVØ 1983, p. 96.
15 Thus SCHWARTZ 1969, p. 446a (comparing Chor. *xʾzy-* "to battle, smite"), accepted by SUNDERMANN 1973, p. 117b; MORANO 1998, p. 135, line 17; DURKIN-MEISTERERNST 2004, p. 78a.
16 Cf. the discussion of the Sogdian maxim no. 7 in SIMS-WILLIAMS 2014, pp. 117–118.
17 Arabic, no. 19, tr. CONYBEARE *et al.* 1913, p. 134; similarly Syriac, no. 16, *ibid.*, p. 104, and other versions.
18 Tr. CONYBEARE *et al.* 1913, p. 26; similarly Slavonic, no. 13, and Turkish, no. 10, *ibid.*, pp. 3 and 88.

/3A/ (M 117, 15–16). From M 117, 15, and M 765k, V6, onwards the two texts diverge radically. While the words of M 765k, V6–9, are clearly a continuation of the preceding admonition, as discussed above, the last two lines of M 117 seem more likely to belong to a new maxim. Unfortunately the surviving words are too colourless to provide any hint of its subject.

Appendix: parallel texts

For convenient reference, I here present in translation a selection of parallels to M 117 and M 765k from the *Handarz ī Ādurbād* and various versions of Aḥiqar.

Ādurbād, *HA*
"(87) When you attend a gathering, do not sit next to a stupid man so that you may not yourself appear stupid. ... (97) When you sit in an assembly, do not sit next to a liar lest you yourself should suffer greatly thereby".[19]

Aḥiqar (Sogdian)
"(7) ... to drink(?) [wine](?) with [a fool]. (8) My son, be wise with a p[ure] man and do not stand with a wicked (man); and also do not consort with a fool, (in) that from him you will not learn wise conduct; but associate with a wise (man), that you may be(?) a good ... under(?) him".[20]

Aḥiqar (Syriac)
"(9) My son, it is better to remove stones with a wise man than to drink wine with a fool. (10) My son, pour out thy wine on the graves of the righteous, rather than drink it with evil men. (11) My son, with a wise man thou wilt not be depraved, and with a depraved man thou wilt not become wise. (12) My son, associate with the wise man, and thou wilt become wise like him; and associate not with a garrulous and talkative man, lest thou be numbered with him".[21]

Aḥiqar (Armenian Recension B)
"(6) Son, it is better with the wise man to hew stones than with a foolish man to drink wine. (7) Son, pour out thy wine on the earth, and drink it not with the lawless, lest thou be regarded even as they. ... (40) Son, better is hatred and a quarrel with a righteous man than sweetness and compassion at the hands of a lawless man".[22]

19 Tr. ZAEHNER 1956, pp. 105–106, except that his translation of *dušāgāh* as "wrong-headed" is here replaced with "stupid" in agreement with MACKENZIE 1971, p. 28, and DE BLOIS 1984, p. 49. The correctness of the latter translation is clear from *Dēnkard* VI, p. 322 (tr. SHAKED 1979, p. 129): "These are the three greatest duties of men: to turn an enemy into a friend; to turn a wicked person into a righteous one; and to turn an ignorant man *(dušāgāh)* into a sage *(dānāg)*".

20 Tr. SIMS-WILLIAMS 2014, p. 110.

21 Tr. CONYBEARE *et al.* 1913, p. 104.

22 Tr. CONYBEARE *et al.* 1913, pp. 58, 61.

References

ANDREAS, F. C./W.B. HENNING 1934: *Mitteliranische Manichaica aus Chinesisch-Turkestan*. III. Berlin (SPAW 1933, No. 27).

BENVENISTE, É. 1940: *Textes sogdiens*. Paris.

— 1946: *Vessantara Jātaka*. Paris.

DE BLOIS, F. 1984: "The admonitions of Ādurbād and their relationship to the Aḥīqar legend." In: JRAS 1984, pp. 41–53.

BOYCE, M. 1960: *A catalogue of the Iranian manuscripts in Manichean script in the German Turfan collection*. Berlin.

CONYBEARE, F.C./J. RENDEL HARRIS/A. SMITH LEWIS 1913: *The story of Aḥiḳar*. Cambridge (2nd edition).

DURKIN-MEISTERERNST, D. 2004: *Dictionary of Manichaean Middle Persian and Parthian*. Turnhout (Dictionary of Manichaean Texts III/1).

GERSHEVITCH, I. 1949: "Iranian notes." In: *Transactions of the Philological Society* 1948 [1949], pp. 61–68. [Reprinted in GERSHEVITCH 1985, pp. 25–32.]

— 1952: "Ancient survivals in Ossetic." In: *BSOAS* 14, pp. 483–495. [Reprinted in GERSHEVITCH 1985, pp. 114–126.]

— 1954: *A grammar of Manichean Sogdian*. Oxford [= GMS].

— 1965: Review of BOYCE 1960. In: *BSOAS* 28, pp. 157–160.

— 1985: *Philologia Iranica*. Wiesbaden (Beiträge zur Iranistik 12).

LINDENBERGER, J.M. 1983: *The Aramaic proverbs of Ahiqar*. Baltimore.

LURJE, P.B. 2011: *Personal Names in Sogdian texts*. Vienna 2010 [2011] (Iranisches Personennamenbuch II/8).

MACKENZIE, D.N. 1971: *A concise Pahlavi Dictionary*. London.

MORANO, E. 1998: "*My kingdom is not of this world*: revisiting the great Parthian crucifixion hymn." In: N. SIMS-WILLIAMS (ed.): *Proceedings of the Third European Conference of Iranian Studies*. Part 1: *Old and Middle Iranian Studies*. Wiesbaden, pp. 131–145 (Beiträge zur Iranistik 17).

— 2009: "Sogdian tales in Manichaean script." In: D. DURKIN-MEISTERERNST *et al.* (ed.): *Literarische Stoffe und ihre Gestaltung in mitteliranischer Zeit. Kolloquium anlässlich des 70. Geburtstags von Prof. Dr. W. Sundermann*. Wiesbaden, pp. 173–200 (Beiträge zur Iranistik 31).

NAU, F. 1909: *Histoire et sagesse d'Aḥiqar l'Assyrien*. Paris.

— 1920: *Documents relatives à Aḥiqar*. Paris.

SCHWARTZ, M. 1969: Review of H W BAILEY: *Khotanese Texts*. VI. In: *JAOS* 89, pp. 444–447.

— 1970: "On the vocabulary of the Khwarezmian *Muqaddimatu l-Adab*, as edited by J. Benzing." In: *ZDMG* 120, pp. 288–304.

SHAKED, S. 1979: *The Wisdom of the Sasanian Sages (Dēnkard VI)*. Boulder (Persian Heritage Series 34).

SIMS-WILLIAMS, N. 1982: "Some Sogdian denominal abstract suffixes." In: *Acta Orientalia* 42, 1981 [1982], pp. 11–19.

— 2014: *Biblical and other Christian Sogdian texts from the Turfan collection*. Turnhout (Berliner Turfantexte XXXII).

Sims-Williams, N./D. Durkin-Meisterernst 2012: *Dictionary of Manichaean Sogdian and Bactrian*. Turnhout (Dictionary of Manichaean Texts III/2) [= DMT III/2].

Skjærvø, P.O. 1983: *The Sassanian Inscription of Paikuli*. Part 3.2: *Commentary*. Wiesbaden.

Sundermann, W. 1973: *Mittelpersische und parthische kosmogonische und Parabeltexte der Manichäer*. Berlin (Berliner Turfantexte IV).

Yoshida, Y. 1994: "On a Manichaean Sogdian fragment expounding vanity of earthly life—text preceding Henning's 'Job story'." In: *Oriento* 37/2, pp. 16–32 [in Japanese with English abstract].

— 2001: "On the Sogdian fragments of the St. Petersburg collection." In: *Contributions to the Studies of Eurasian Languages*. Ser. 3, *Issues in Eurasian Languages* 1, pp. 105–117.

Zaehner, R.C. 1956: *The teachings of the Magi. A compendium of Zoroastrian beliefs*. London.

The Story of *Windād-Burzmihr*[1]

A Zoroastrian Entrepreneur in Early Islamic Times

DIETER WEBER

In the following article the activities of a Zoroastrian, *Windād-Burzmihr* by name, who lived in the second half of the the 7th century CE, will be outlined with the help of various documents from the so-called "Pahlavi Archive".[2] The documents mentioning the person in question are all preserved in the Bancroft Library, CA., except one that is hosted in the Iranistisches Institut der Freien Universität Berlin, Germany. They contain letters as well as ordinary economic documents and comprise a time span from year 11 PYE = 662/3 CE to year 48 PYE = 699/700 CE.[3] The following table is intended to provide a short overview about the relevant texts:

document	description	form of name	year	CE
Berk. 101, 1–2	*ō hazār-anōšayād āzarmīgtom awestād Windād-Burzmihr namāz* (see Appendix A)[4]	*Windād-Burzmihr* (addressee)	11	662/3
Berk. 127, 1[5]	*ō* x^{w}*adāyīg(?) Windād-Burzmihr namāz*	*Windād-Burzmihr* (addressee)	11	662/3

1 This article was announced in WEBER 2012, 221, note 41.—The following *sigla* will be used: **Berk.** = Pahlavi documents, Berkeley, partly published; **Berlin** = Pahlavi documents, Berlin, ed. WEBER 2008; **P.** = Pahlavi papyri and parchments, ed. WEBER 2003 (**P. 125–P. 343**); **P.Pehl.** = Pahlavi papyri and parchments of the *Papyrussammlung der Österreichischen Nationalbibliothek*, Vienna (with original inventory number, mostly unpublished).

2 Partly edited by GIGNOUX during the years 2001 through 2010 (see Bibliography) and by WEBER 2008 (the items that are preserved in Berlin).

3 For the exact dating of the documents see WEBER 2012.

4 Published here for the first time by courtesy of the authorities of the Bancroft Library, Berkeley, CA.

5 Unpublished letter.

document	description	form of name	year	CE
Berk. 217A[6]	sender of a letter	*Windād-Burzmihr*	11	662/3
Berk. 231, 2. 3. 4[7]	2 *āmār [kas] ba-tanišn ī sāl 11 abāg Windād-Burzmihr kard ud ān ī* 3 *pad kōšk az mar ī Windād-Burzmihr rāy az Windād-Burzmihr kunēd* 4 *sāl 12 az Būf xʷāstag s(atēr) 5 andar Karmār az Windād-Burzmihr* 5 *s(atēr) 20 Windād-Burzmihr*		11	662/3
Berk. 81, 1 10[8]	*Windād-Burzmihr āwišt* (see below)	*Windād-Burzmihr*	12/ 13	663/4
Berk. 203, 1[9]	*ō xʷadāyīg Windād-Burzmihr namāz*	*Windād-Burzmihr* (addressee)	13	664/5
Berk. 244, 1–2 = 8[10]	*ō hazār-anōšayād sālār Windād-Burzmihr namāz* (see below)	*Windād-Burzmihr* (addressee)	13	664/5
Berk. 257, 3[11]	fragmentary letter, no year	*Windād-Burzmihr* (addressee)		
Berk. 259, 6[12]	fragmentary, year missing, possibly patr.	*Windād-Burzmihr[*		
Berk. 172, 6[13]	*ayādgār*,[14] fragmentary, year missing	*Windād-Burzmihr*		

6 Unpublished letter to a certain *Pādōy* "from community pasturing" concerning iron for horses.
7 Now published in *BAI* 27.
8 Unpublished document of financial transactions on behalf of *Windād-Burzmihr* for year 12, payed in year 13.
9 Unpublished letter from a certain *Panāhfarrox(?)* (otherwise unknown) concerning *mijūg* 'lentils'.
10 Unpublished letter concerning wine for the *dibīr ī Amīr Abdīn* 'scribe of Amīr Abdīn'.
11 Line 2 contains the word *grāmīgtom*, also mentioned in GIGNOUX 2004, p. 46 (who says in fn. 69 that "son fils qui est partout présent et qui se nomme *Gušnwār*, n'a son doute pas exercé d'aussi importantes fonctions, car il n'a pas droit à ces qualificatifs prestigieux !"). It is impossible to trace any *Gušnwār* as a son of *Windād-Burzmihr* in the documents.
12 Unpublished.
13 Unpublished.
14 An *ayādgār*, a *memorandum*, is a document codifying that a certain person will get natural produce (which is indicated at the very beginning) from a debtor (whose name is also given) when this *ayādgār* is presented.

document	description	form of name	year	CE
Berk. 241, 10[15]	(patr.) missing context	*Windād-Burzmihrān*	30	681/2
Berlin 4, 5–6[16]	*pad gugāy-muhrīhā ī yazdān-guftār ī Windād-Burzmihr*		39	690/1
Berk. 227, 2	(patr.) (see Appendix B)[17]	*Windād-Burzmihrān*	46	697/8
Berk. 43A, 7[18] **Berk. 43B**, 3–4 **Berk. 43C**, 3 **Berk. 43D**, 2–3 **Berk. 43E**, 1–2	*[dast]gird ī Windād-burzmihr-ābād* *dastgird ī Windād-burzmihr-ābād* *[dastgird] ī Windād-burzmihr-ābād* *dastgird ī (šādīh ?) Windād-burzmihr-ābād* *dastgird ī Windād-burzmihr-ābād*	*Windād-Burzmihr-ābād*	48	699/700

In **Berk. 217A** *Windād-Burzmihr* is the sender of a letter whereas in **Berk. 101**, **Berk. 127**, **Berk. 203**, **Berk. 244** and **Berk. 257**[19] he is the addressee. Here the letters **Berk. 101** and **Berk. 244** are the most informative ones. Both are not simply addressed to *Windād-Burzmihr* but in **Berk. 101** (lines 1–2) *ō hazār-anōšnayād āzarmīgtom *awestād Windād-Burzmihr* 'to the *master of a thousand-fold ever lasting remembrance (and) most honoured *Windād-Burzmihr*' (see Appendix A) and in **Berk. 244** (lines 1–2 and 8) *ō hazār-anōšayād* ***sālār***[20] *Windād-Burzmihr namāz* 'to *Windād-Burzmihr*, the leader, of thousand-fold ever lasting remembrance'.

An indirect testimony to *Windād-Burzmihr*'s activities is revealed in **Berk. 227** (see Appendix B) where a certain amount (the surplus) of the crops of *Windād-Burzmihr*'s land had to be given (not as payment in kind but by money in cash) to the *ōstāndār*. This is a unique transaction since, in documents dealing with other persons, only direct deliverance of *gandum* or the like to the *ōstāndār* is attested. It shows that *Windād-Burzmihr* was a kind of financer, at least he was able to pay in cash.

15 Unpublished letter to *Suxrgušnasp*.
16 Ed. Weber 2008, pp. 18–23; cf. Gignoux 2010b, p. 114f.
17 Published here for the first time by courtesy of the authorities of the Bancroft Library, Berkeley, CA.
18 All five documents of this group **Berk. 43** are still unpublished.
19 The fragmentary text runs as follows: [1] *ō hamē farroxtar kard*[[2] *āzarmīgtom ud grāmīgtom* [3] *(…) Windād-Burzmihr ī* [where, at the very beginning of the third line, the text may have contained a specification of the person; cf. Appendix A (**Berk. 101**).
20 For this word the reading *sālār* is already given in Gignoux 2004, p. 46, "mais le contexte ne nous aide aucunement à préciser ce que recouvre ce terme". Cf. again Gignoux 2010a, p. 146, "Ce commandant pouvait être un ancien officier de l'aemée impériale d'un haut rang". But this is by no means certain; it may be more convincing to assume the common Pahlavi meaning of this word as 'leader, master' (CPD).

Berk. 81 and **Berk. 231** are documents that reveal intense financial activities of *Windād-Burzmihr*. The first one, sealed by *Windād-Burzmihr*, contains a list of the dividends (in cash and by trade (?) with Turkish silver and marocco leather) gained in the year 12, and the large document **Berk. 231** is a kind of accountancy for the year 11 of *Zādōy ī durgar*[21] '*Zādōy* the carpenter'. This man obviously had a cooperage and delivered vessels like *dōl* or *dōlag* to various estates. Here *Windād-Burzmihr* plays an eminent rôle as he is involved in *Zādōy*'s activities and also in the erecting of a building if we interpret the sequence in lines 2–3 correctly: *āmār [kas]*[22] *ba-tanišn ī sāl 11 abāg Windād-Burzmihr kard ud ān ī pad kōšk az mar ī Windād-Burzmihr rāy* 'someone made the reckoning together with *Windād-Burzmihr* in the course of year 11 and for the sake of what is for a pavilion from the account of *Windād-Burzmihr*'. What follows is a list of depositors from various villages or estates and their payments for year 12;[23] the total amount counts *s(atēr) 65 ud drahm 1.*

One group of documents—actually the latest one—deserves special interest where the name of *Windād-Burzmihr* functions as the basis for a village name, *Windād-Burzmihr-ābād*. This form with *-ābād* as last element is a type well known in Iranian onomastics and classified as "*fulanabad* place-names".[24] In general they are characterized by attaching the element *-ābād* to a proper name like Ahmad, Hosein or Mahmoud and the like.[25] At the time of the documents we also find, in that region, some with Iranian personal names like *Mihrǧašnasfābād*[26] (Drechsler 1999, p. 62) or *Warāzābād* (*ibid.* p. 63).

The origin of *-ābād* is not disputed but, in Bulliet's wording,

> though modern philological research must be respected as providing the last word on the subject, the folk etymology associating the word with *ab*, or 'water', should not be disregarded. If the early dictionary compilers [...] lent their authority to such a folk etymology, it may be that a simple-minded linguistic association between *abad* and 'water' has a long enough tradition in popular use to have made a significant factor in rural naming despite its being philologically in error. That is to say, 100 years ago or 1000 years ago, a qanat builder thinking about the name to give to his new village may well have had a linguistically incorrect association with water in mind. In any event, the philological debate over whether village founders felt that water was intrinsically associated with the *fulanabad*

21 When derived from *dōl* 'bucket' or *dōlakkar* when derived from *dōlag* 'pail'. The same word is also attested in **O. 39**, 3 where the earlier reading *x^{w}arakkar* 'cook' (in Weber 1992, p. 33) is obsolete now.

22 [ ] = written above the line.

23 Line 4: *andar Karmār az Windād-Burzmihr.*

24 Bulliet 2009, pp. 17–30, esp. 29–30.

25 These modern examples are depicted from Table 1.2 in Bulliet 2009, 18 for the province of Markazī where the estates mentioned in **Berk. 231** were located.

26 This name is particularly instructive as personal names ending in *-gušnasp* are well attested in the documents of the "Pahlavi Archive" as well as from Tabaristan.

> place-names they opted for has no bearing on the strong quantitative correlation between qanat irrigation and villages designated by such names.[27]

The name *Windād-Burzmihr-ābād* is the only one of this type met with in the documents from the "Pahlavi Archive". From this and from the fact, that it is only mentioned very late, we may deduce that this village is a foundation initiated by *Windād-Burzmihr* himself either on the basis of newly dug qanats or not. On the other hand this shows us a man who, after having been a lifelong manager finally earned enough money to invest it in a new village with, at that time, modern equipment.

The exact position of *Windād-Burzmihr-ābād* is not known. But as we can see in **Berk. 101** and **Berk. 231** *Windād-Burzmihr* had some relations to the estate of *Karmār* and since in this document the place *Namēwar* (mod. نیمور *Nīmwar*, southeast of Maḥallāt, Markazi province) plays an eminent rôle (see lines 5, 13, 15, and 17) *Karmār* itself should be looked for in its neighbourhood; it is noted in **Berk. 211R**, 1 as *pad Karmār dastgird* (see below Appendix A). Therefore it is very likely that *Windād-Burzmihr-ābād*, too, was situated in the same region.

As we have seen *Windād-Burzmihr*'s activities are documented from year 11 PYE = 662/3 CE through year 48 PYE = 699/700 CE when they culminate in having founded a new village called *Windād-Burzmihr-ābād*. When we follow up *Windād-Burzmihr*'s life as far as we can reconstruct it from the documents it is very unlikely that another person than *Windād-Burzmihr* himself lent his name to the village. By his very name he is characterized as a Zoroastrian who could be active as an entrepreneur in the region south of Qom in those days of early Islam.

27 Bulliet 2009, p. 22.

Appendix A

Fig. 1: **Berk. 101**
Courtesy Bancroft Library, Berkeley, CA.[29]
Parchment; H = 12cm, W = 10cm; *Verso* blank

28 I owe the informations on the documents to DAVID S. FLATTERY's "Archive Database" established for The Bancroft Library, Berkeley, CA.

Transliteration

1 ʿL hcʾlʾnwšʾb̲yýʾṭ ʾclmykṭwm
2 PKṬʾ wndʾṭbwlcmṭrʾ ***nc***
3 BBʾ hndlcpṭʾ ŠRM KBD knʾlng
4 NKSYʾ Y MRʿḤ yʾṭ-swṭʾ ʾp̄ʾryk(?)
5 BBʾ Y ŠNṬ X-I lʾd MN nlywsng(?)
6 ...-WNṭ YNSB̲WN***ty*** klmʾl W ***S***-XX-XX-X
7 ....
8 ....

Transcription

1 *ō hazār-anōšayād āzarmīgtom*
2 **awestād Windād-Burzmihr namāz*
3 *dar-handarzbed drōd was kanārang*
4 *x^{w}āstag ī x^{w}adāy ǰād-sūd abārīg(?)*
5 *dar ī sāl 11 rāy ......*
6 *...... stānēd *Karmār ud s(atēr) 50*
7 ....
8 ....

Translation

[1–2] To the master of a thousand-fold ever lasting remembrance (and) most honoured *Windād-Burzmihr*, reverence! [3] The tax collector (of) good health. *Kanārang*, [4–5] with regard (*ray*, line 5) to your money (the money of yours, Sir), of the other item of the shares in the profits (dividend) of the year 11 ...... [6] ...... he should(?) take **Karmār* and 50 Staters [7–8] *no reading and translation possible*

Commentary

In Gignoux 2004, p. 45 the first 5 lines were read: (1) ʿL ḥcʾlʾnwšbḥṭ ʾclmykṭwm (2) ʾrwnd wndʾṭbwlcmṭrʾ ***nc*** (3) BBʾ ḥndlcpṭʾ ŠRM KBD (KRʾ lwšn) (4) NKSYʾ Y MRʿH ... (5) BBʾ Y ŠNṬ 10–1 lʾd (lignes 5–10 non transcrites) – (1) *ō hazār-anōšbaxt āzarmīgtom* (2) *arwand Vindād-Burzmihr namāz* (3) *dar handarzbed drōd was (har-rōšn)* (4) *xwāstag ī xwaday ...* (5) *dar ī sāl 11 rāy* ‹ À Vindād-Burzmihr, qui a la fortune (d'être) mille fois immortel, très honoré, vaillant (?), salut! Prospérité abondante (toute lumineuse ?) De (la part du) Conseiller de la Cour, pour la propriété du seigneur ... de la Cour en l'an 11 ... ›

– Line 2: The word  cannot be read ⟨ʾrwnd⟩ (?) (Gignoux) and must not be a honorific adjective as an epitheton. It is more likely to assume a specification of the name as in **Berk. 244**, 1–2: *ō hazār-anōšayād sālār Windād-Burzmihr namāz* 'to Windād-Burzmihr', the leader, of thousand-fold immortal remembrance *Windād-Burzmihr*, reverence!' or a heterogram like ⟨'Ḥ⟩.[29] I therefore propose to read the word in question tentatively ⟨PKṬ'⟩ for general ⟨PKYṬ'⟩[30] = MP *awestād* 'master (craftsman)' (CPD 14), Man. MP 'wyst'd 'Meister' Mir.Man.II, NP *ōstāδ*, *ustāδ* 'teacher', < **abi-štāta-*.[31]

- Line 3: *dar-handarzbed* 'tax collector' acc. to S. SHAKED and E. KHURSHUDJIAN, quoted by GIGNOUX 2004, 44 and again by AZARPAY e.a. 2007, 22.—⟨kn'lng⟩ instead of *(har-rōšn)* (GIGNOUX): for *kanārang*, primarily a title (NP *kanārang* كنارنگ 'governor of a province, a grandee, margrave, landgrave' *etc.* [STEINGASS]), having become a proper name see GIGNOUX 1986, no. 488; cf. also **P. 172**, 8 (to be read *kanārang ī awešān aswārān*) and **P. 305**, 4[32].
- Lines 4–5: The interpretation of the sequence *x^wāstag ī x^wadāy ǰād-sūd abārīg(?) dar ī sāl 11 rāy* is corroborated by the comparable phrase in **Berk. 81**, 1–2: *wizārd ǰād-sūd abārīg dar ī sāl 12 rāy* 'with regard to the payment of the other item of the shares in the profits (dividend) of the year 12'.
- Line 6: ⟨klm'l⟩ must be the name of an estate, cf. **Berk. 211R**, 1: *pad *Karmār dastgird*,[33] and **Berk. 37**, 6:[34] **Karmār 190.000 drahm*, also in **Berk. 231**, 4: *andar *Karmār*, where this *dastgird* is connected with the person of *Windād-Burzmihr* (see above).

Appendix B

Transliteration

1 b'p̄k' MN Z̲K Y MN 'p̄r-'sṭ'ṭ'
2 Y d'šṭ' Y wnd'ṭbwlcmṭr'n
3 PWN b'l MN plhwṭl 'wsṭ'nd'l 'L
4 bwn' Z̲NH BYRḤ prwrṭyn' Y ŠNṬ
5 XX-XX-III-III MN 'p̄r-'sṭ'ṭ' Y pyš
6 Y mṭr' Y ŠNṬ XX-XX-III-II MN [w]h'k
7 Y ḤG PWN plhwṭl 'wsṭ'nd'l *G*-I
8 NKSY' *S*-II 'L mṭrbwhṭ'
9 YḤBWNṭ' mṭrbwhṭ' ck' ḤṬYMWNṭ

29 For example in. **P.Pehl. 566**, pp. 2–3, see WEBER 2008, p. 39.
30 JUNKER 1912, p. 122; H.S. NYBERG: *Frahang i Pahlavīk*. Wiesbaden 1988, p. 46 and comm. 81 on XII: 13c. It is true that ⟨PKṬ'⟩ seems not be attested in the *Frahang*, but cf. the duplicate forms ⟨ḤRṬ'⟩ and ⟨ḤRYṬ'⟩.
31 Acc. to I. GERSHEVITCH: *The Avestan Hymn to Mithra*. Cambridge 1959, p. 220n.
32 WEBER 2008, p. 38.
33 Unpublished.
34 Unpublished; contains a list of the names of different estates and their cash deposits (**Berk. 37**, 1: *dizīhā kē andar āsāyišn pad-iš abāyēd kardan*), given in drahms.

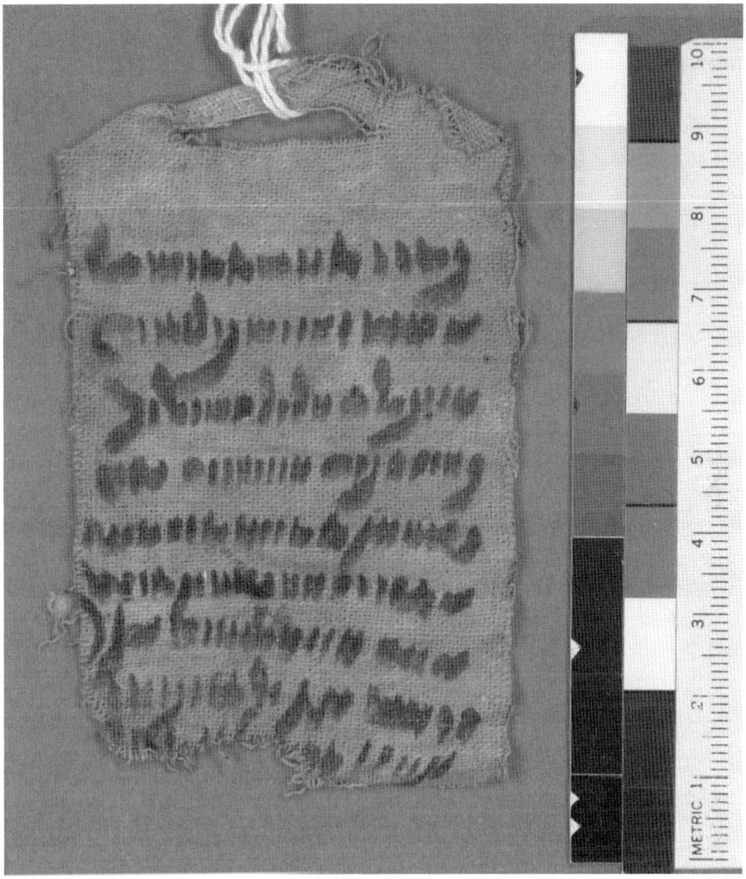

Fig. 2: Berk. 227
Courtesy Bancroft Library, Berkeley, CA.
Textile; H = 8.5 cm, W = 6 cm; Verso Marked

Transcription

1 *Bābag az an ı az abar-estad*
2 *ī dāšt ī Windād-Burzmihrān*
3 *pad bār az farroxtar ōstāndār ō*
4 *bun ēn māh Frawardīn ī sāl*
5 *46 az abar-estād ī pēš*
6 *ī Mihr ī sāl 45 az wahāg*
7 *ī gandum pad farroxtar ōstāndār g(rīw) 1*
8 *x^{w}āstag s(atēr) 2 ō Mihrbōxt*
9 *dād Mihrbōxt čak āwišt*

Translation

[1] *Bābag* gave (*dād*, line 9) **from what (belongs)** from the surplus [2] which is considered of (the lands of) *Windād-Burzmihr* [3] as duty from the most fortunate *ōstāndār* **to the** [4] ***bun***:[35] this month *Frawardīn* (1st month) of the year [5] 46 from the surplus of before (month) [6] *Mihr* (7th month) of the year 45 from the value [7] of the wheat for the most fortunate *ōstāndār* (of) 1 *grīw* [8] in cash: 2 Staters to *Mihrbōxt* [9] given. *Mihrbōxt* sealed the *čak*.

Commentary

- Line 1: For the name *Bābag* cf. Gignoux 1986, no. 171; cf. also *Bāb* **Berk. 58**, 2.—The word *abar-estād* has been unknown so far but, in this context, must denote, by its very etymology, a kind of 'surplus' of the crops.
- Lines 2–3: *pad ... dāštan* 'hold by, to; take for' (CPD).—*bār* to be understood here as 4*bār* 'load, burden; duty' (CPD).
- Line 4: *bun* seems to be the basic equipment[36] of a kind of village cooperative, the *bune* or 'work team': "Unlike landless agricultural laborers or villagers possessing cultivation rights to specific plots of land, members of *bunehs* enjoy a collective right to a share in the produce of village lands".[37] The term deserves a new discussion that will only be possible after all documents from the "Pahlavi Archive" will have been published.

[Written 2013, slightly revised 2017]

References

AZARPAY, G./K. MARTIN/M. SCHWARTZ/D. WEBER 2007: "New Information on the Date and Function of the Berkeley MP Archive." In: *BAI* 17 (2003 [2007]), pp. 17–29.

BULLIET, R.W. 2009: *Cotton, Climate, and Camels in Early Islamic Iran: A Moment in World History*. New York.

CPD = D.N. MacKenzie: *A Concise Pahlavi Dictionary*. London 1971 (reprints 1986,1990).

35 I.e. 'The contingent **from what (belongs) to the *bun*, i.e.** from the surplus which is considered of (the lands of) *Windād-Burzmihr* as duty from the most fortunate *ōstāndār*'.

36 The term *bun* was discussed by M. MACUCH in her contribution to WEBER 2008, p. 252 where she says that it "bezeichnet kurzum *alle Gegenstände eines Vermögens, die zum festen Bestandteil der Grundsubstanz rechnen, gegenüber dem Ertrag oder Zuwachs desselben.*" The interpretation drawn here from the documents of the "Pahlavi Archive" does not contradict but simply specifies the use in the given Zoroastrian community of early Islamic times.

37 BULLIET 2009, p. 25.

DRECHSLER, A. 1999: *Geschichte der Stadt Qom im Mittelalter (650–1350): politische und wirtschaftliche Aspekte*. Berlin.

GIGNOUX, PH. 1986: *Noms propres sassanides en moyen-perse épigraphique*. Wien.

— 1991: "Une nouvelle collection de documents en pehlevi cursif du début du septième siècle de notre ère." In: *Académie des Inscriptions & Belles-Lettres*, Comptes Rendus des Séances de l'année 1991, Paris, pp. 683–700.

— 1998: "Six documents pehlevis sur cuir du California Museum of Ancient Art, Los Angeles." In: *BAI* 10 (1996 [1998]) (= Studies in Honor of Vladimir A. Livshits), pp. 63–72.

— 2001: "Nouveaux documents pehlevis sur soie." In: MARIA GABRIELA SCHMIDT/ WALTER BISANG (eds.): *Philologica et Linguistica (Historia, Pluralitas, Universitas). Festschrift für Helmut Humbach zum 80. Geburtstag*. Trier 2001, pp. 281–301.

— 2003a: *Noms propres sassanides en moyen-perse épigraphique*. Supplément [1986–2001]. Wien.

— 2003b: "Sept documents économiques en pehlevi." In: A. van Tongerloo (ed.): *IRANICA SELECTA: Studies in honour of Professor Wojciech Skalmowski on the occasion of his seventieth birthday*. Turnhout 2003 (Silk Road Studies VIII), pp. 79–89 (+ pl. I–VIII, pp. 273–280).

— 2004: "Aspects de la vie administrative et sociale en Iran du 7ème siècle." In: *Contributions à l'histoire et la géographie historique de l'empire sassanide*. Bures-sur-Yvette (Res Orientales 16), pp. 37–48.

— 2008a: "Prices and Drachms in the Late Sasanian Period." In: VESTA SARKHOSH CURTIS/SARAH STEWART (eds.): *The Sasanian Era*. London (The Idea of Iran, vol. III).

— 2008b: "Lettres privées et lettres d'affaires dans l'Iran du 7ème siècle." In: *Documentary Letters from the Middle East: The Evidence in Greek, Coptic, South Arabian, Pehlevi, and Arabic (1st–15th c CE)*. Bern (Asiatische Studien/Études Asiatiques LXII, 3), pp. 827–842.

— 2009a: "Les comptes de Monsieur Friyag : Quelques documents économiques en Pehlevi." In: *Sources pour l'histoire et la géographie du monde iranien (224–710)*. Bures-sur-Yvette (Res Orientales 18), pp. 115–142.

— 2009b: "Les documents économiques de Xwarēn." In : PH. GIGNOUX/CHR. JULLIEN/FL. JULLIEN (eds.): *Trésors d'Orient – Mélanges offerts à Rika Gyselen*. Paris (Studia Iranica, Cahier 42), pp. 81–102.

— 2010a: "La société iranienne du 7e siècle AD d'après la collection de Berkeley." In: C.G. CERETI (ed.): *Iranian Identity in the Course of History. Proceedings of the Conference Held in Rome, 21–24 September 2005*. Roma (Serie Orientale Roma CV, Orientalia Romana 9), pp. 145–152.

— 2010b: "Un nouvel ouvrage de référence de la papyrologir pehlevie : Note de lecture." [review of Weber 2008] In: *Studia Iranica* 39, 1, pp. 111–120.

— 2010c: "La collection de textes attribuables à Dādēn-vindād dans l'archive pehlevie de Berkeley." In: *Sources for the History of Sasanian and Post-Sasanian Iran*. Bures-sur-Yvette (Res Orientales 19), pp. 11–134.

JUNKER, H.F.J. 1912: *The Frahang i Pahlavīk*. Ed. by H.F.J. JUNKER. Heidelberg.

STEINGASS, F. 1963: *A Comprehensive Persian-English Dictionary*. London (fifth impression).

WEBER, D. 1992: *Pahlavi Papyri, Pergamente und Ostraca. (Textband).* London (Corpus Inscriptionum Iranicarum).
— 2008: *Berliner Pahlavi-Dokumente. Zeugnisse spätsassanidischer Brief- und Rechtskultur aus frühislamischer Zeit.* Mit Beiträgen von MYRIAM KRUTZSCH und MARIA MACUCH. Wiesbaden (Iranica 15).
— 2011a: "Philippe Gignoux' Beitrag zur Interpretation der Dokumente des ‚Pahlavi Archive' in Berkeley, Ca." In: *Florilège offert à Philippe Gignoux pour son 80e anniversaire.* Textes réunis par RIKA GYSELEN et CHRISTELLE JULLIEN. Paris, pp. 283–303.
— 2011b: "An Interesting Pahlavi Letter from Early Islamic Times (Berk. 245)." In: *ZDMG* 161 (2011), pp. 91–98.
— 2012: "New Arguments for Dating the Documents from the 'Pahlavi Archive'." In *BAI* 22 (2008 [2012]), pp. 215–222.

Some New Interpretations of the Two Judeo-Persian Letters from Khotan

YUTAKA YOSHIDA

1. Introduction

One of the most remarkable recent discoveries of manuscripts from Chinese Turkestan is no doubt an almost intact sheet of a Judeo-Persian letter acquired in 2004. Prompt publication of the letter by two Chinese scholars has created a sensation among both philologists and historians.[1] Morphology, paleography, and the contents of the letter as well as the circumstances in which it has been preserved by the local people make it certain that one similar letter which A. STEIN obtained a hundred years ago from his laborers was written by the same Judeo-Persian trader; the laborers continued to excavate several sites in Dandan-Uilik even after STEIN left it.[2] It seems to me possible, if not possible to prove, that STEIN's letter is continuation of the new letter, because the latter contains a clear epistolary formula marking the beginning of a letter, which the former lacks,[3] and since the new letter is not complete as it stands in spite of the fact that the paper preserves its bottom margin.

On the archaeological grounds, the old letter has been dated towards the end of the 8th century,[4] and this dating is now confirmed by the fact that in the new letter special mention is made to the killing of Tibetans in Kashghar. On this point see below. Recently, when I read the new letter with my students, I noticed several places where one can improve the readings or translations.[5] Since Professor M. MACUCH has also contributed to the elucidation of the new letter or Letter 2, I hope that she will enjoy reading this short paper discussing it.

1 Cf. ZHANG ZHAN/SHI GUANG: "Yijian xinfaxian Youtai-Bosiyu xinzha de duandai yu shidu [A newly-discovered Judeo-Persian letter]." In: *Dunhuang Tulufan Yanjiu* 11 (2008), pp. 71–99. Its contents are discussed by V. HANSEN from the historical points of view, cf. HANSEN: *The Silk Road. A new history*. Oxford 2012, pp. 217–19.

2 On the relationship between the two letters see ZHANG/SHI 2008, pp. 75–79.

3 It seems to me that *yzyd kwdh 'y y'r b'šd* "May the Lord God be a helper" in line 1 of the old letter has been tacitly taken to constitute a part of the epistolary formula. However, now that one finds the complete formula in the new letter, this cannot be the case. For this translation see L. PAUL: *A grammar of Early Judeo-Persian*. Wiesbaden 2013, p. 122.

4 Cf. A. STEIN *apud* D. S. MARGOLIOUS: "An early Judeo-Persian document from Khotan." In: *JRAS* 1903, pp. 735–761, esp. pp. 735–746.

5 Hereafter in this article the old letter is referred to as Letter 1, while the new Letter 2.

2. *(p)nb'šy* and other Chinese elements

In Letter 2, line 31 the killing of Tibetans in Kashghar is reported: *twpyty'n r' p'q by qwštn* [tūpityān rā pāk bi kuštan(d)][6] "Tibetans were killed completely". Basing on my study of the contemporary Khotanese documents, Zhang and Shi understood that it was Uighurs who killed the Tibetans in Kashghar, and that the battle was fought in 802 CE.[7] But the next bit *w-bgdw bstn* remains obscure because the meaning of *bgdw* is not known. Then comes the following sentence, which is transliterated and transcribed as follows:

> (31) … w-sb'pwšy šwd (32)[p'] q'šgr 'b' p' sd mrnd cy sw'r w-cy py'dh
> [u-sibāpuši šud pa Kāšgar abā pā(n)-sad mrnd či savār u-či piyāda]

This sentence is translated by L. PAUL as "and the vice commander went to Kashgar with 100 men be it on horseback or on foot".[8] Following P. O. SKJÆRVØ's suggestion, ZHANG and SHI correctly take *p' sd* for [pā(n)sad] meaning "500" but do not translate the next word. Though the exact meaning of *mrnd* is not known, the context clearly indicates that it denotes a certain kind of an armed man. Obviously, an army consisting of 500 soldiers was sent to Kashghar to protect the Uighurs' march towards Khotan. Apparently, Khotan was safe this time, because, as one can see from the Karabalgasun Inscription, the Uighurs did not head toward Khotan but chased the Tibetans and their Qarluq alliance towards west into the Ferghana Valley.[9]

Let us see what follows:

> (32) … w-sbs 'y sb'pwšy {hb} (33) …nb'šy hrb r' w-sl'm w-kzym r' bysp'n prstyd
> [u-sibas i sibāpuši …nb'šy harb rā u-salām u-xazīm rā bayaspān firistīd]

6 In this paper I basically follow the transcriptions given by ZHANG and SHI.

7 Actually, it was P. O. SKJÆRVØ who drew their attention to the paper which I read in March 2006 and was subsequently published in 2009: Y. YOSHIDA: "The Karabalgasun Inscription and the Khotanese documenrs." In: D. DURKIN-MESTERERNST / CH. RECK / D. WEBER (eds.): *Literarische Stoffe und ihre Gestaltung in mitteliranischer Zeit*. Wiesbaden 2009, pp. 349–360.

8 PAUL 2013, pp. 105, 151, 161.

9 On this passage of the Karabalgasun Inscription, see YOSHIDA: "Current issues of the Bactrian studies (in Japanese)." In: *Studies on the Inner Asian Languages* XXVIII (2013), p. 56. This occasion may be taken to discuss *prw'n* found in Letter 1, line 32. It is a place name and BO UTAS compares it tentatively with Parvān located to the north of Kabul in Afghanistan, cf. idem: "The Jewish-Persian fragment from Dandān-Uiliq." In: *Orientalia Suecana* 17 (1968), pp. 123–136, esp. p. 135. However, it should rather be identified with another Parwān or what is now Aqsu in the Tarim Basin. It is located between Kucha and Kashghar and is mentioned in the *Mahrnāmag* (line 77 *prw'nc jbγw* "Yabghu of Parwan", cf. D. DURKIN-MEISTERERNST: *Dictionary of Manichaean Middle Persian and Parthian*. Turnhout 2004, p. 280a with reference to W. B. HENNING, *BSOS* 9 (1938), pp. 567–568. An itinerary from Aqsu to Khotan via Mazar Tagh is recorded in the *Xin Tangshu*, Beijing, Zhonghua shuju, 1975, p. 1150.

ZHANG and SHI render it as "After the vice commander, ...*nb'šy* sent an envoy for the battle and for the peace and victory". The last word of line 32 does look like *hb*, but the scribe tried to correct the second letter by superimposing a new letter upon it. It is difficult to figure out what the scribe had in mind, but it seems to me at least possible to read *hm* "also". The beginning of line 33 is slightly damaged and only one letter is missing, i. e. *[.]nb'šy*. In fact the lower left part of the first letter is still seen in front of a letter *n*. In my opinion it is to be restored as *p*. The word *pnb'šy* is too similar to divorce it from *peṃ'ba'ṣī* attested in IOL Khot Wood 3, which I identified with a Chinese official title *bing ma shi* 兵馬使 "commissioner for foot soldiers and horses".[10] The context of war and the dispatching of soldiers go very well with this assumption. The entire sentence ((32) ... *w-sbs 'y sb'pwšy hm* (33) *(p)nb'šy hrb r' w-sl'm w-kzym r' bysp'n prstyd*) will be translated "And after the vice commander, the commissioner for foot soldiers and horses also sent an envoy for the battle and for the peace and victory".

According to ZHANG and SHI, who again follow SKJÆRVØ's opinion, *sb'pwšy* [sibāpuši] "vice commander" is a compound consisting of New Persian *sipāh* "army" and Chinese *fu shi* 副使 "deputy, assistant". SKJÆRVØ compares the element *pwšy* with *fwšyy* of the *Mahrnāmag*, cf. DURKIN-MEISTERERNST 2004, p. 161b. Although ZHANG and SHI transcribe [puši], the spelling in Manichaean script clearly indicates that the initial consonant had been dentilabialized and that one should rather read [fuši]. Four attestations of this word in the *Mahrnāmag* are *ṭwp' fwšyy* (70), *'wlwg* (sic for *'wlwγ*) *fwšy* (94), *ṭ'ng fwšyy* (94–95), and *l' fwšyy* (95). The last two are to represent *tang fu shi* 唐副使 and *luo fu shi* 羅副使, where *fwšyy* is preceded by family names, while the remaining two seem to contain Turkish name elements. Since the Chinese component *fushi* 副使 is likely to follow either a title or a family name, one may be induced to take *sb'* to be another Chinese family name *sima* 司馬.[11] In any case, the combination of a Persian word meaning "army" and the Chinese element is least expected.

In this connection it would be of some interest to collect all the Chinese elements found in this letter. Except for *(p)nb'šy* and *sb'pwšy*, ZHANG and SHI found the following: *šg* (14, 15) < *shi* 石, *šmsy* (16) < *can si* 蚕絲, *pnkw'n* (17) < *pan guan* 判官.[12] Quite recently Bi Bo has proposed to identify *qynq'k* (28, 29) with *jin jiao* 筋脚, which appears several times in the contemporary Chinese documents discovered in Khotan and denotes a kind of swift-footed person or courier.[13]

10 Y. YOSHIDA: "On the taxation system of pre-Islamic Khotan." In: *Acta Asiatica* 94 (2007), pp. 95–126, esp. p. 112.

11 For the dialectal pronunciation [ba] for *ma* 馬 see *peṃ'ba'ṣī*. Nevertheless, one expects **syb'* rather than *sb'*.

12 *šg* and *pnkw'n* were identified by RONG XINJIANG, cf. ZHANG/SHI 2008, pp. 93–94.

13 Cf. Bi Bo, "Hetian xinfaxian hanyu huyu wenshu suojian 'jinjiao' kao [An investigation of jinjiao (lit. "tendon and foot"): based on the newly-discovered Chinese and Jewish-Persian documents from Khotan]", in: Collection of the papers circulated at "The International Symposium on Huang Wenbi and the Sino-Swedish Northwest China Scientific Expedition", Urumqi, October 2013, pp. 366–74. In view of these military titles in

Among them *šmsy* appears in the following context: (15) … *'z mr syky r' yqy* (16) *prny'n wyqy šmsy hydyh* [az mar syky rā yakē parniyān u-yakē šamsī hidya]. ZHANG and SHI's translation reads "Presents for Syky are one set of silk cloth and one set of silk yarn". However, Middle Chinese pronunciation of *can si* 蚕絲 as reconstructed by KARLGREN is **dz'ậm si*[14] and it poses considerable difficulty for this identification, in particular with regard to the initial consonant *dz'*-, which is likely to have been pronounced as [ts] in those days. Since New Persian *parniyān* means "a kind of fine painted China silk; also garments made of it",[15] it could also refer to a garment made out of special silk cloth, which was given as a bribe. Accordingly *šmsy* may also denote a product rather than material like silk yarn. In fact one Sogdian document attests *š'mtsy* "tunic" borrowed from Chinese *shan zi* 衫子.[16] Unstable nature of a foreign sound [ts] will explain the difference between *šmsy* and *š'mtsy*, and in fact *šamsï* is encountered in an Uighur document, cf. SIMS-WILLIAMS/HAMILTON 1990.

Another word ending with *-šy* in this letter is *cykšy* (12) ~ *cyk'šy* (11, 16), which is likely to denote a title ending with *shi* 使 or its homophone *shi* 史. In the *Mahrnāmag* one finds a very similar word *cygšyy*,[17] which originates from Chinese *ci shi* 刺史 "governor". However, a variant form *cyk'šy* still needs explanation and the proposed etymon must remain to be a simple guess.

3. *bgydy* and Sogdian elements

It was HENNING who first noticed a few Sogdian elements in Letter 1. They are *cmkwy* (Sogd. *cmxwy*) "harp" and *'ndryk* (Sogd. *'ntr'yk*) "eunuch".[18] In the new letter some more Sogdian elements have been discovered by the editors. One of them is the dating formula employing *sgd* (Sogd *sγt-*) "~th day": *p' dh sgd* "on the tenth day". Another element is the suffix of the ordinal number *-my* added to Persian cardinal numbers, e.g. *ššmy* "sixth", cf. ZHANG/SHI 2008, pp. 92–93. Yet another Sogdian word discovered by BI BO and SIMS-WILLIAMS is *ptkw* bor-

Chinese one may reconsider the dating of the letters; even in the course of their successful invasion into the Tarim Basin during the latter half of the 8th century, the Tibetans could have been beaten several times either by the Chinese garrisons or by the Uighurs.

14 Cited from B. KARLGREN: *Grammata Serica Recensa*. Stockholm 1957.

15 Cf. F. STEINGASS: *A comprehensive Persian-English dictionary*. London 1892 (reprint Beirut 1970), p. 244b.

16 N. SIMS-WILLIAMS/J. HAMILTON: *Documents turco-sogdien du IXe–Xe siècle de Touenhouang*. London 1990, pp. 34–35.

17 In actuality only its plural form *cygš'n* is attested in the *Mahrnāmag*. Nevertheless, the singular form *cygšyy* occurs several times in another text, cf. DURKIN-MEISTERERNST 2004, p. 132a.

18 Cf. HENNING: "Mitteliranisch." In: *HdO* 1. Abt., IV. Bd.: Iranistik, 1. Abschnitt: Linguistik. Leiden 1958, pp. 20–130, esp. pp. 79–80.

rowed from *ptkwk* meaning "string comprising thousand copper coins", which in turn is a calque of Chinese *guan* 貫.[19]

It is worth citing the context in which *cmkwy* appears, because it also contains an unknown word *bgydy*. Zhang and Shi (2008, p. 94) propose to equate *bgdw* found in Letter 2 with the word in question and read *bgydw* instead of Bo Utas's *bgydy*. However, as far as I can see from the photograph their new reading cannot be supported. Bo Utas's text and his latest translation of the passage read as follows:

24 [ ](.) r' sb'bd ydwn qw(py)d qw mr' cmkwy yqy (.)[ ]
25 [ ](c)mkwy 'ry mn qnyzq r' 'mwzwm wcnd cwst[ ]
26 [ ](.)bh byndwm n' b(yn)d'dwm by '(z) nwrbq yqy (c)[mkwy]
27 [ ](.)d dhwm t' bgydy r' by 'mwzd 'ndryq 'y sy(')[h]

"[... regarding that matter] you will say to the commander (?): [Bring] me a harp [and I have a girl! If] you bring the harp, I shall teach the girl, and look how fast [she will learn! What] I [wanted to] find, I did not find, but from *Nūrbak [I got] one ha[rp, and that one] I shall give to him, so that he shall teach *Bagīdī. The black eunuch(?) [will take care of the rest]."[20]

Although Zhang and Shi presume *bgdw* to be a noun denoting a kind of human being, its context in Letter 2 clearly shows that *bgdw* refers to what can be presented as a gift like *gnd* "sweet" and *lymcw* "?": *šb'n'n r' bgdw wgnd wlymcw hdyh* [šubānān rā bgdw u gand u-lymcw hidya] "For the herdsmen, presents are *bgdw*, sweet and *lymcw*." Therefore, it is fitting to divorce *bgdw* of Letter 2 from *bgydy* of Letter 1, which designates a human being who can be taught to play the harp. Like Bo Utas I take *bgydy* for a personal name and, in my opinion, it is to be identified with a Sogdian female name *βγγδ'y* "lit. female slave of God or Miθra" actually attested in the *Mahrnāmag*, line 134, cf. Durkin-Meisterernst 2004, p. 107b.

One may ask why the teaching of playing the harp to a Sogdian girl is mentioned in this letter. In this connection I should like to cite a rather long passage from V. Hansen's article discussing the Silk Road trade as seen from the Chinese documents discovered in Turfan.[21]

A name register from Emperor Wu's reign (690–705) lists seventy-nine people who had been omitted from earlier registers for two households. The seventy-nine names include 1 musician of inferior status (*yueshi* 樂事), 9 male and female personal retainers, also of inferior status (*buqu, kenü* 部曲，客女), and 68 female and male slaves (*nubi* 奴婢). Musicians and personal retainers belonged to the lowest legal category of the Tang Code, the inferior classes (*jianmin* 賤民), and unlike slaves, could not be bought and sold.

19 Bi Bo/N. Sims-Williams: "Sogdian documents from Khotan, I: Four economic documents." In: *JAOS* 130 (2010), pp. 497–508, esp. pp. 506–507.
20 Cf. Bo Utas: *From Old to New Persian*. Wiesbaden 2013, pp. 40–41.
21 V. Hansen: "The impact of the Silk Road trade on a local community: The Turfan Oasis, 500–800." In: E. de la Vaissière/E. Trombert (eds.): *Les Sogdiens en Chine*. Paris 2005, pp. 283–310, esp. 299–300.

> One of the two households contained 61 people, with twenty individuals under the age of fifteen. The slaves have no surnames, but the personal retainers do, and several are Central Asian; the slaves' names look as though they were translated into Chinese from another language, quite possibly Sogdian. The list is intriguing: what were all these people doing in a single household? Wu Zhen offers a daring reading: "of course the male and female slaves could have undergone training of various type—like listening and speaking basic Chinese, becoming familiar with Chinese manners and customs, and even learning some types of tasks—at the hands of the musicians and personal retainers. The goal was to increase the sale price of these slaves". It is also possible that the members of the inferior classes were also for sale (contrary to the provisions of The Tang Code) and not there simply to train the slaves. Still the large size of the household strongly supports Wu Zhen's hunch that this was a slave-producing establishment.

Thus, training of Sogdian slave girls is actually documented and it would not go too far if one assumes the same situation in this passage.

It is worth noting that one of the Sogdian elements encountered in the letters is not a noun but a suffix of the ordinal number *-my*. Borrowing of the grammatical bound morpheme is not usual and leads one to suppose an intensive language contact between the Persian and Sogdian languages. In other words, the writer of the letters is most likely to have been bilingual in the both languages. Are there any other traces of the language contact? I wonder the following three sentences beginning with *prmy* [farmāy] (2nd sg. imperative of *farmāy-* "to order") is calqued on the honorific and polite way of expressing one's request in Sogdian by means of the imperative forms of *frm'y* plus past infinitive: *prm'y 'PZYmy 'wn'kw wyδβ'γ 'krty* "Please explain that to me".[22]

Letter 1, line 4: *-yš by prmy d'dn* [-iš bi farmāy dādan] "Please give it."[23]
Letter 1, line 32: *wkwd 'z 'n swy kw'st'ry prmy qrdn* [u xod az ān sōy xwāstār-ē farmāy kardan] "Please make a request by yourself in that respect."[24]
Letter 2, line 24: *'š by prmy d'dn* [-aš bi farmāy dādan] "Please give (it) to her."[25]

If my assumption that the writer of the letters was bilingual in Persian and Sogdian is correct, then one may well ask whether he was a Sogdian who also spoke Persian or the other way round. The fact that his Persian betrays some Sogdian

22 On this construction see SIMS-WILLIAMS apud SUNDERMANN: "Probleme der Interpretation manichäisch-soghdischer Briefe." In: J. HARMATTA (ed.): *From Hecataeus to al-Ḫuwārizmī.* Budapest 1984, pp. 289–316, esp. 296, n. 20 and YOSHIDA: "Honorific and polite expressions in Sogdian (in Japanese)." In: *Philological studies on Old Central Asian manuscripts.* Kyoto 2006 (Contribution to the Studies of Eurasian Languages 10), pp. 81–94, esp. pp. 82–83.

23 PAUL (2013, p. 98) translates it as "order to give it (to him?)".

24 PAUL's translation reads "order a request to be made", cf. PAUL 2013, pp. 69, 124.

25 On *'š* in this sentence see SHAKED: "Classification of linguistic features in Early Judeo-Persian." In: W. SUNDERMANN/A. HINTZE/F. DE BLOIS (eds.): *Exegisti monumenta. Festschrift in honour of N. Sims-Williams.* Wiesbaden 2009, pp. 449–461, esp. p. 453 and Paul 2013, p. 98, where he translates it as "order to give it to her".

elements seems to support the view that Persian was a second language for him.[26] This presumption goes very well with the fact that the Khotanese *dihgān* called the writer of Letter 2 as Sogdian[27]:

> Letter 2, line 11: wmr cyk'šy r' prmwd zwd gwspnd yn swgdy by dyh [u-mar cyk'šy rā farmūd kū: zūd gōspand īn sugdī bi dih]
>
> "He ordered *cyk'šy* (and said), 'Quickly give this Sogdian the sheep!'"[28]

Assuming that the writer's mother tongue was Sogdian, one may then ask if he also wrote Sogdian. Nevertheless, it would be virtually impossible to identify the Sogdian texts written by him or by his Judeo-Persian colleagues among Sogdian texts discovered in Khotan, even if they had ever existed. However, in this connection I should like to draw attention to the Sogdian texts recently published by Sims-Williams and Bi Bo.

Our Letter 2 begins with *pnn'm yzyd kwdh yqrbqr* "In the name of God, beneficent lord". The first half of this phrase would correspond to Sogdian *pr βγy n'm*, which has been attested two times in late documents of the 10th century Dunhuang. Sims-Williams and Hamilton (1990, pp. 39–40), who first noted this formula in Sogdian, supposed that it was employed by either Christians or Muslims. It now becomes clear that Judaists could also use the phrase. It is of some interest that among the Sogdian texts discovered in Khotan and recently published by Bi Bo and Sims-Williams, one actually finds this very expression.[29] They are now preserved in the Museum of Renmin University of China and the document in question bears the signature GXW 0434. On its verso(?) side two lines are written the opposite way up to the rest of the text. My reading and translation of the two lines run as follows:

> 1 [pr]βγy n'm 'sty 1LPw ptk(w)k pny xyδ pny pr
> 2 [ ] pcγ'zδ ZY šyr'krtyh s'r zy'mt k'n
>
> "... (date?) ... In the name of God. There are 1000 strings of copper coins. You receive (2 pl. imperative) those coins for ... so that he would spend (it) for piety."[30]

26 In this connection Shaked's following statement may be cited: "None of these texts [i.e. Judeo-Persian texts, YY] can be described as a vernacular, for the writers seem to aim at presenting a literary form of Persian", cf. Shaked 2009, p. 449.

27 In Hansen's opinion, so many traders along the Silk Road were Sogdians and so few were Jewish that the *dihgān* simply mistook him for a Sogdian, cf. Hansen 2012, p. 218.

28 The translation is cited from Paul2013, pp. 162, 164.

29 As regards their provenance and dating, the authors state: "It seems likely that the newly acquired texts have a similar provenance (as the Judeo-Persian letters and other documents found in Khotan, YY) and are roughly contemporary with the Chinese and Khotanese documents; that is, they may be attributed to around the eighth to ninth centuries", cf. Bi Bo / Sims-Williams 2010, p. 498.

30 Bi Bo and Sims-Williams (2010, pp. 504–505) transliterate and translate the passage as follows:
1a](p)γyzym(?) 'sty 1LPw ptk(w)k pny s'δ(?) pny pr
2a]pc.....(?) ZY šyr'krtyh sky(?) zy'mt k'n

Can the document be written by a Judaist? Of course one cannot prove or disprove it. Nevertheless, the huge amount of coins, i.e. 1,000 strings of *pny* or 1,000,000 copper coins, does remind us of 100 strings of coins mentioned in Letter 2: (33) … *wmn hrb r' cyz* (34) *d'dwm p' m'yh 'y sd ptqw pšyz* [u-man harb rā čīz dādum pa māya i sad ptkw pašīz] "I gave something for the war with the fund of 100 strings of coins". I cannot resist the temptation to see interconnection between the Sogdian text, which could have been written by a Judaist, and the Judeo-Persian letters. Donation of considerable amount of money for the war may have seemed to the writer of the Sogdian text as *šyr'krtyh* "good deeds".

If my assumption that the writer of the letters was bilingual in Persian and Sogdian should proved to be correct, then one may also ask whether it indicates the beginning of Persianization of Sogdiana, which seems to have been completed by the tenth century.[31] However, the question goes far beyond the scope of this short article.

4. Who was the *dihgān*?

From the historical point of view Letter 2 poses several intriguing problems. One of them is the identity of a man referred to as *dyhg'n*. ZHANG and SHI translate it as *di zhu* 地主 "landlord", but it is more or less a literal meaning of the word. Designation of *dihgān/dehqān* is extensively discussed by A. TAFFAZOLĪ, who notes as follows:

> It may be inferred from various reports that in early Islamic times some *dehqāns* functioned almost as local rulers, especially in eastern Persia, and that any man of wealth or social prestige might thus be called *dehqān*.[32]

As a matter of fact, in Letter 2, he is regarded as a key person in the trade of sheep, which is one of the main concerns for the Judeo-Persian traders. From Letter 2 one understands that the *dihgān* was in the position to order *cyk'šy* to give sheep, and that bribes the trader prepared for the *dihgān* surpass by far those given to the other officials, who are likely to have been inferior in rank.[33]

> "… we are ready(?). There are 1000 strings of *pny* … *pny* for … and piety … he will spend …"

But the authors admit that they fail to make sense of this part of the document. I should like to take this opportunity to propose my reading *ctβ'r ywxth* "four rubies" for BI BO and SIMS-WILLIAMS's (2010) *ctβ'r ny'š*… in text no. 4, verso line 10.

31 On Persianization of Sogdiana see YOSHIDA: "Sogdian." In: G. WINDFUHR (ed.): *The Iranian languages*. London / New York 2009, pp. 279–335, esp. pp. 329–330.

32 Cf. *EIr* VII (1994), pp. 223–225. Remember that Dēwāštīč, who was a king of Panjkent in the early eighth century, was called *dihqan* by Ṭabarī, cf. F. GRENET / E. DE LA VAISSIÈRE: "The last days of Panjikent." In: *Silk Road Art and Archaeology* 8 (2002), pp. 178, 192.

33 Among the bribes one finds *gnd* "sugar". It now becomes clear that one of the common commodities of Sogdian traders called *shi mi* 石蜜 "*lit.* stone honey" in Chinese is to be

Among them is one *pnkw'n* in charge of sheep, and the word was identified by RONG XINJIANG with a Chinese title *pan guan* 判官. The title, which is of a considerable rank, also appears as *p'nxw'n* in the *Mahrnāmag* and *phaṃnä kvaṃnä* in the contemporary Khotanese documents. In fact in one Chinese-Khotanese bilingual document Hedin 24 dated to 798 CE, a *panguan* by the name of Fu Weiqin 富惟勤 drew up an order on behalf of the Khotanese king and the same *panguan* functioned as a supervisor of tax collection and placed his signature on Hedin 15 and 16 of 801–802 CE.[34]

The *dihgān*'s daughter is also mentioned several times in Letter 2 and in the writer's eye she must also be pleased to get support from the *dihgān* because the latter dotes on her:

(25) [twr](')[35] cyšm wrwšny'y hm yn dwktr hst dyhg'n r' wskt sb's qwn
[turā čišm u-rōšnī-ē ham īn duxtar hast dihgān rā. u-saxt sibās kun]
(26) [wg]r sb's 'y wr' qwny cyz gwm n' bwd …
[u-agar sibās i varā kunē čīz gum na buvad …]

"(Just as) your eyes and light (are) for you, this daughter is for the *dihgān*. And do show (her) gratitude, (because even) if you show her deep gratitude, nothing will be lost (i. e. it costs nothing to show gratitude)."

Judging from all these one may be induced to identify the *dihgān* with the king of Khotan, or at least a man of a comparable rank, in any case not just a landowner possessing sheep.[36] When one takes into consideration a descending order of rank in the list of the receivers of bribes in lines 14–20, one is able to partly reconstruct the social hierarchy of the contemporary society of Khotan: *dyhg'n—syky—syky cyk'šy—pnkw'n* in charge of sheep—*mrnd* in charge of sheep—*šb'n*[37]. Incidentally, in the *Mahrnāmag* rulers of the neighboring oasis

identified with what is designated by the Persian word. On *shimi* see E. SHAFER: *The golden peaches of Samarkand.* Berkeley 1963, pp. 152–154. HANSEN translates *shimi* as "muscado sugar", cf. HANSEN 2005, p. 101.

34 On the *panguan* of Hedin 15 and 16 see H. BAILEY: *Khotanese texts.* IV. Cambridge 1961, p. 108. For the dating of the Khotanese documents see ZHANG GUANDA/RONG XINJIANG: "Khotan between the second half of the 8th century and early 9th century (in Chinese)." In: *Tang studies* 3 (1997), pp. 339–361 and YOSHIDA 2009 (see above n. 7).

35 ZHANG and SHI restore *čūn tō*, i. e. *cwn tw* instead, but the gap hardly comprises as many as five letters. I also restore [wgr] for their ['gr], because one expects a new sentence to begin with a conjunction *w-*.

36 If the *dihgān* is to be identified with the king of Khotan, the dating of Letter 2 suggests that he is either Viśa' Vāhaṃ or his successor Viśa' Kīrrta. Since Viśa' Vāhaṃ should have been very old in 802 CE, the latter is more likely to be the one, for whom his young daughter could have been young and dear enough. On the two kings see P. O. SKJÆRVØ: *Khotanese manuscripts from Chinese Turkestan in the British Library.* London 2002, p. lxvii. However, the years of their reigns must be revised, cf. ZHANG GUANDA/RONG XINJIANG 1997.

37 Judging from the fact that they receive bribes, the *šb'ns* mentioned in the letter are not likely to be ordinary herdsmen but those who were in charge of looking after sheep belonging to the state or the royal house.

states bear the following titles:[38] Bešbalïq = *pnžyknδyy xwd'y* (45–46), Qočo = *cyn'nknδyy xwd'y* (55), Karashahr = *'rqcyk xwṭ'w* (88–89), Šorčuq[39] = *'wcwrcyk xwṭ'w* (110–111), Kucha = *'kwcyk syrṭwšyy* (72–73)[40], Aqsu = *prw'nc jβγw* (77), Kashghar = *k'šy xšyδ* (75).

5. Conclusion

So many places of the two Judeo-Persian letters remain obscure and I hope what I have proposed will contribute, however little, to the elucidation of such enigmatic parts.

I must admit that in this article, in particular in its latter half, I have advanced hazardous guesses, which could hardly be proved (or disproved) at least for the time being. However, one must also admit that superficial translation of what one reads from the letters will not enable us to elicit most important information embedded in the body. One must read between lines to understand the presupposed background knowledge shared by the writers and receivers of the letters, which is alluded to, if any, only vaguely.

ZHANG and SHI owe to Professor M. MACUCH the interpretation of a very crucial phrase at the end of Letter 2: *cyz b'z m' m' d'ryd* [čīz bāz mā ma dārēd] "Do not keep anything back from us".[41] The passage is preceded by *'gr 'mdh b'd p' q'šgr hr cnd kwzynh kw'hnd* [agar āmada bād pa Kāšγar har čand xuzīna xwāhand] "If he has come to Kashghar, however much expense they require". As it stands it is not particularly interesting. But if one considers the fact that the writer spent already 100 strings of coins for the war in Kashghar, this part may induce one to guess, however hazardously, about the Judeo-Persian traders' determined resolution to actively intervene the military act of the Khotanese (or possibly Tibetans, who were ruling Khotan in those days) against the Uighurs.[42]

In concluding this paper, I really hope that the recent discoveries and acquisition of new documents originating from Khotan, either in Chinese, Khotanese, Tibetan, Sogdian, or Sanskrit, will be published before long, and that we will be able to undergo in-depth studies of the interrelationship among them.

38 For this list see HENNING 1938, p. 566.

39 This is my identification. On various views on the identity of *'wcwrcyk* see N. SIMS-WILLIAMS/D. DURKIN-MEISTERERNST: *Dictionary of Manichaean Sogdian and Bactrian.* Turnhout 2012, p. 34.

40 On this title originating from *jie du shi* 節度使 "military governor", cf. YOSHIDA: "Sogdian Miscellany III." In: R.E. EMMERICK/D. WEBER (eds.): *Corolla Iranica. Papers in honour of Prof. Dr. D.N. MacKenzie on the occasion of his 65th birthday on April 8th, 1991.* Frankfurt a.M./Bern/New York/Paris, pp. 237–242, esp. p. 242, n. 19.

41 Cf. ZHANG/SHI 2008, p. 97. The English translation is cited from PAUL 2013, p. 143.

42 In any case these traders appear to be far from petty peddlers, because as many as thirty letters mentioned as sent by the writer in Letter 2, line 29 seem to imply an extensive network created by his colleagues.